Race and Ethnic Conflict

Race and Ethnic Conflict

Contending Views on Prejudice, Discrimination, and Ethnoviolence

edited by

FRED L. PINCUS
University of Maryland Baltimore County

HOWARD J. EHRLICH
Center for the Applied Study of Ethnoviolence

WESTVIEW PRESS
Boulder • San Francisco • Oxford

Copyright © 1994 by Fred L. Pincus and Howard J. Ehrlich

Published in 1994 in the United States of America by Westview Press, Inc., 5500 Central Avenue, Boulder, Colorado 80301-2877, and in the United Kingdom by Westview Press, 36 Lonsdale Road, Summertown, Oxford OX2 7EW

Library of Congress Cataloging-in-Publication Data
Race and ethnic conflict : contending views on prejudice,
    discrimination, and ethnoviolence / edited by Fred L. Pincus, Howard
    J. Ehrlich.
        p.   cm.
    ISBN 0-8133-1661-8 — ISBN 0-8133-1662-6 (pbk.)
        1. United States—Race relations.   2. United States—Ethnic
relations.   3. Prejudices—United States.   4. Discrimination—United
States.   I. Pincus, Fred L.   II. Ehrlich, Howard J.
E184.A1R23   1994
305.8'00973—dc20   94-2255
                                                                                CIP

Printed and bound in the United States of America

 The paper used in this publication meets the requirements
of the American National Standard for Permanence of Paper
for Printed Library Materials Z39.48-1984.

10   9   8   7   6   5   4   3   2   1

To our sons, Josh Pincus-Sokoloff and Andrew Webbink,
in the hope that their generation can move the world closer to a society
based on understanding rather than prejudice,
on mutual aid rather than competition,
and on participatory democracy
rather than hierarchy

Contents

Acknowledgments

Much of the preliminary work on this book was done during my 1991–1992 sabbatical from the Sociology and Anthropology Department of the University of Maryland Baltimore County. I would like to thank the staff of the department for their assistance in all of the various tasks essential in preparing this book.

I would also like to thank my parents, Sam and Leah Pincus, for sensitizing me to the problems of racial injustice when I was growing up in the 1950s. Although we had our differences, their progressive ideas have had an important influence on my thinking and writing about racial conflict in America.

Finally, I want to thank Natalie J. Sokoloff for being there.

Fred L. Pincus

My thanks to the Berkshire Forum for their generous writing fellowship. My thanks, also, to my friends and coworkers at the National Institute Against Prejudice & Violence—Bob Purvis, Adele Terrell, and Barb Larcom—for providing the intellectual engagement and personal support that has helped me maintain my own balance between theory and practice.

Howard J. Ehrlich

Credits

12. Douglas S. Massey, Testimony before the U.S. House of Representatives Sub-committee on Housing and Community Development of the Committee on Banking, Finance, and Urban Affairs, January 27, 1988.

13. Excerpted, with notes deleted, from "Employment Discrimination," U.S. Commission on Civil Rights, *Civil Rights Issues Facing Asian Americans in the 1990s* (Washington, D.C.: The Commission, 1992), pp. 130–156.

14. Excerpted from Evelyn Nakano Glenn, "Racial Ethnic Women's Labor: The Intersection of Race, Gender, and Class Oppression," in C. Bose, R. Feldberg, and N. Sokoloff, eds., *Hidden Aspects of Women's Work* (New York: Praeger, 1987), pp. 46–73, by permission of the author and the publisher.

15. Reprinted from Evelyn Torton Beck, "From 'Kike' to 'JAP': How Misogyny, Anti-Semitism, and Racism Construct the 'Jewish American Princess,'" *Sojourner: The Women's Forum* (Sept. 1988):18–20, by permission of the author and the publisher.

16. Excerpted, with notes renumbered, from Saskia Sassen, "America's Immigration 'Problem,'" *World Policy Journal* 6, no. 4 (Fall 1989):811–832.

17. Reprinted, with notes renumbered, from Milton M. Gordon, "Models of Pluralism," in *The Annals of the American Academy of Political and Social Science* 454 (1981):178–188, by permission of the author and the publisher. © 1981 by the American Academy of Political and Social Sciences.

18. Reprinted from James H. Johnson, Jr., and Melvin L. Oliver, "Interethnic Minority Conflict in Urban America: The Effects of Economic and Social Dislocations," *Urban Geography* 10, no. 5 (Sept.-Oct. 1989):449–463, by permission of the publisher.

19. Excerpted, with notes renumbered, from Heidi Tarver, "Language and Politics in the 1980s: The Story of U.S. English," *Politics and Society* 17, no. 2 (June 1989):225–245, by permission of Sage Publications, Inc. © 1989 by the Center for Social Research and Education.

20. Excerpted from Letty Cottin Pogrebin, "Different Kinds of Survival," *Deborah, Golda, and Me* (New York: Crown, 1991), pp. 292–297. © 1991 by Letty Cottin Pogrebin, reprinted by permission of Crown Publishers, Inc., Rosenstone/Wender, and the author. Excerpted from Earl Ofari Hutchinson, "My Jewish Problem or Your Black Problem?" *Ofari's Bi-Monthly* (May-June 1992), reprinted by permission of the author.

21. Excerpted from Marilynn Rashid, "Detroit: Demolished by Design," *Fifth Estate* (4632 Second Avenue, Detroit, Michigan 48201) 25, no. 2 (Winter 1990–1991):1, 15–18, 32.

22. First published as chapter 2 of *Banking on Black Enterprise: The Potential of Emerging Firms for Revitalizing Urban Economies* by Timothy Bates. Copyright 1993 by the Joint Center for Political and Economic Studies. Reprinted by permission of the Joint Center for Political and Economic Studies.

PART 1

Introduction

1

The Study of Race and
Ethnic Relations

FRED L. PINCUS AND HOWARD J. EHRLICH

Intergroup relations in the United States and throughout the world have undergone a dramatic shift since the mid-1980s. They have become more tense, more provoking, and more confusing. Major U.S. corporations are charged with not hiring or not promoting people of color. Protest activities and civil disorders follow court decisions perceived as biased in favor of police defendants who assaulted minority citizens. Persons of Latino appearance or with Hispanic names are illegally detained and sometimes deported as a result of sweeps and raids by government agents. Native Americans are coercively removed from their homelands, and their long-standing treaty rights are violated. Poor neighborhoods, especially those in which people of color are concentrated, are used as toxic-waste dump sites. Intergroup conflicts surface between blacks and Koreans, Christians and Jews, Vietnamese and whites, homosexuals and heterosexuals.

Although these conflicts are not unique to the last ten years, there are differences today as compared to other periods in American history. First, people and the news media are paying more attention to the conflicts. Second, the conflicts themselves are frequently more violent than in earlier times. Third, the presidential administrations of Ronald Reagan and George Bush fostered a more open opposition to civil rights and civil liberties than at any time since the early 1950s. This opposition, in turn, fostered the growth of the new Christian right and the resurgence of right-wing white supremacist organizations. And, fourth, American "minorities" are more empowered than in earlier times, and the acts of discrimination and violence that would have been "overlooked" in the past are now being actively opposed. Nevertheless, such conflicts can take place only in a society where prejudice, discrimination, and ethnoviolence are regarded by many as socially acceptable modes of behavior.

We are concerned here mainly with the everyday aspects of prejudice and conflict. As we proceed in our study, we will frequently shift from a historical to a sociological to a social-psychological focus. From a historical perspective, the observer examines the unique details of a specific event as it relates to the pattern of past events in which it is embedded. The sociologist focuses upon contemporary prejudice and conflicts and on those social processes (such as immigration) and institutions (such as the economy) that determine the pattern of intergroup relations in a society at a given time. The social psychologist narrows the setting to an examination of people's values, beliefs, feelings, and motivations concerning other people and how these psychological processes affect interpersonal and intergroup behavior.

We offer analyses of the state of American intergroup relations not only from various social science positions but also from different political standpoints— conservative, liberal, socialist, feminist, Marxist, anarchist, and various combinations of these. The study of intergroup relations is highly value-laden. For example, although everyone represented in this anthology is opposed to the present *extent* of inequality among Americans, some writers are willing to accept higher levels of economic inequalities than are others. Some believe it is possible to have a classless society, whereas others do not.

But all of the contributors to this book agree, more or less, on the use of social science methodology and empirical evidence to organize their arguments. It is by means of this methodology and theory that we can evaluate claims. Of course, there is never any guarantee that people will be open-minded in considering evidence contrary to their positions. However, since the evidence and claims of social scientists are public, we can reasonably expect that others will be able to evaluate competing claims with some reliability. This process of judgment is part of what you, as student and reader, will be called upon to cultivate.

INTERGROUP RELATIONS IN THE 1990s

All of us who write and teach about intergroup conflict have certain ways of understanding the current state of affairs. We begin this book by summarizing our own observations. The first is that prejudice and discrimination against ethnic groups in American society persist. The second is that there has been a change in the dominant mode of expression of prejudice and discrimination.

The ethnic-group stereotypes of an earlier day were rooted in beliefs about the biological differences among people. Today, there is no longer a widespread or strongly held sense of biological inferiority. There is, rather, a sense of "cultural" difference. So, for example, minority groups are rejected not because they are seen as innately inferior but because their lifestyle is unacceptable. Furthermore, the stereotypes of an earlier day were far more hateful and far more cruel than those of today. Today, one seldom encounters people who regard the Japanese as cruel, sly, and treacherous or who fear that Jews will kidnap their young children for ritual blood sacrifices. Fewer people today accept negative ethnic-group stereotypes than at the time of the civil rights movement.

Changes have also occurred in the motivation of people to discriminate against others in everyday settings: in public accommodations (i.e., restaurants), in schools and in the workplace, in voting practices, and in political office. To be sure, neighborhood segregation persists in almost all cities and, in many, has gotten worse. Intergroup friendships that cross ethnic and racial lines are still not as frequent as within-group friendships. Although the prevailing social norms still prescribe considerable social distance between many ethnically different people in intimate settings, much less distance is prescribed in public and casual settings. In this area, too, we see a major change relative to the period of the civil rights movement. Remember that the civil rights struggle of the 1950s was triggered by the issue of where to sit in a bus or at a lunch counter. Public transportation and restaurants are now open to all.

Why haven't the changes been greater? The contributors to this book provide various answers. Among some there is disagreement as to how those changes might be continued; others question whether such changes are even possible within the political and economic structure of this society. Historian Howard Zinn challenges us all when he writes in his essay, "Representative government, voting, and constitutional law have never proved adequate for solving critical problems of human rights."

Our third observation is that the level of violence motivated by prejudice is high and has been increasing. This form of violence, which we call "ethnoviolence," ranges from psychologically damaging slurs and name calling, to graffiti, group defamation, telephone harassment, intimidating acts, and personal threats, to property damage, arson, and physical assault. On the increase since the mid-1980s, it surged by 24 percent in one year alone (1991–1992), as reported by the National Institute Against Prejudice and Violence. This change is a substantial one. Increased ethnoviolence, however, is not so much a result of increasing prejudice as the effect of increasing violence in society. As violent behavior has increased in society, so violence as a response to intergroup contacts has increased as well.

THE CONDITIONS OF PREJUDICE AND CONFLICT

Why do prejudice and group conflict still exist in the United States in the 1990s? The contributors to this anthology present varying reasons, including the following four social conditions: (1) the history of prejudice and discrimination, (2) rapid social and economic change since World War II, (3) a culture of denial of prejudice, and (4) the differentials of power in society.

Regarding the first of these conditions—the tradition of prejudice and its current manifestations in society—we offer the following observation: Every child born into this society comes to learn its traditions and norms. Prejudice and discrimination are included among those traditions and norms. They are part of our cultural heritage. To be sure, not everyone accepts this aspect of the cultural heritage, but no one can escape dealing with it.

The second of these conditions is rapid social and economic change. Over the past forty or fifty years, amazing changes have occurred in American society. The 1950s are an appropriate starting point for assessing changes in intergroup relations. This was the decade that marked not only the onset of desegregation in schools and public accommodations but also the start of the civil rights movement. Compared to the 1990s, the United States in 1950 was a more decentralized manufacturing society, highly individualistic, strongly oriented toward a belief in small-business free enterprise. The central city was the focus of residence and business. The Cold War of the 1950s muffled dissent, Communists and political deviants were driven into the closet, and the political right wing began a new pattern of growth.

Today the country is a bureaucratized agglomeration of centralized business devoted to information processing and the provision of services. The population has shifted to the suburbs, and older cities are in a state of decline. Women left home to work in the defense industry during the war, and they never returned; thus patriarchy has been challenged. African Americans left the rural South where they had been resettled as slaves, moved to the urban centers of the North and West, and then demanded equal rights under the law; thus, too, white supremacy has been challenged. And more recently, gays and lesbians have come out of the closet, such that even heterosexuality has been challenged.

In the 1960s, television brought the world into American homes. The first televised war occurred during this decade; along with the modeling of violence on prime-time television—for the viewing pleasure of parents and children alike. The movements for social change that flourished in the late 1960s had two lasting consequences: the development of a new political consciousness with a strong commitment to egalitarianism, and the advent of democratic activism. However, the strong countercultural trends of the "new left" of that period, which extended through the early 1970s, so threatened traditional values and existing power arrangements that a serious opposition developed. The "new left" created the "new right"; and the remainder of this decade, extending through the presidential administrations of Ronald Reagan and George Bush, saw the rise of a powerful conservative movement and a new era of rightist, white supremacist organizations. By the end of the 1980s, America had become more politically polarized than at any time since the Great Depression of the 1930s.

With the end of the war in Indochina in the early 1970s, inflation and unemployment increased while the affluence, optimism, and activism of the previous decade dissipated. The 1970s witnessed what some observers termed a mean-spirited reaction to the liberal reformist programs of the 1960s—civil rights acts, Medicare, and massive programs of educational assistance. The altruism of that decade was replaced by a "me-first" orientation that carried with it a rejection of those programs designed to help African Americans and the poor.

The pace of social change increased in the 1980s. Particularly important to an understanding of intergroup relations was the rapid immigration of people of color from non-English-speaking cultures—Mexicans, Filipinos, South Koreans, Vietnamese, Indians, and Chinese. Monoculturalism and the metaphor of the melting pot was indeed being challenged. The Islamic religion became the fastest-growing religion in the United States, and conservatives and right-wing white supremacists began to redefine Christianity. As part of that redefinition, the new Christian right began to organize, overtly and covertly, in the political arena, thus adding to the polarization of society.

In the 1980s, the American occupational and income structure began to change. The growth in new jobs occurred primarily in lower-paying industries, whereas a substantial number of higher-paying jobs were made obsolete or were exported. In the opening years of the 1990s, the United States was losing an average of one million jobs annually. Although the rate of inflation slowed down, the inflation-adjusted income of the worker of 1991 was less than that of 1979. Homelessness and poverty became endemic, and by 1993 poverty was being estimated by social scientists as characteristic of one in four Americans. Meanwhile, the size of the middle class had begun to shrink, perhaps for the first time in American history, threatening the dreams and myths of earlier generations. The 1990s are now witnessing the first American generation that cannot realistically expect to do better than its families of origin.

American society has clearly undergone rapid and dramatic change. With this change has come, for many, a sense of alienation: a powerlessness and a confusion about what constitutes the new norms of behavior in such a changing world. Many others have responded by reaffirming their value orientations, which range from one end of the political spectrum to the other. It is in this social context that Americans are taking sides on the issue of ethnic-group relations.

There is a pervasive hostility to the often inadequate attempts of government to deal with continuing discrimination and the new wave of ethnoviolence. Noticeably lacking is any national resolve among religious leaders or within the business or political elites to deal with the difficulties besetting intergroup relations. Many Americans do not believe that antiminority discrimination is even a major problem. This culture of denial is the third social condition contributing to the persistence of prejudice, discrimination, and conflict. Like all cultural patterns, these are transmitted across families and friends, parents and teachers; and they are authorized and maintained by authorities in the government, the church, and the mass media. Evidence can be seen in such occasions as President Ronald Reagan's assertion that civil rights leaders exaggerate racial problems in order to keep their organizations alive (CBS News, "60 Minutes," January 15, 1989). The function of this presidential pronouncement was to tell the country that there are no racial problems of serious concern. In other cases, the issue goes unmentioned and thus does not become part of the public agenda. For example, despite four days of intergroup violence in Los Angeles (April 29 through May 2, 1992), race and ethnic-group relations were not, nor did they become, part of the political dialogue during the 1992 presidential campaign. This silence can only be regarded as a form of elite denial. Consider, too, the fact that support for programs of prejudice reduction is not on the agenda of the major philanthropic foundations in the country; indeed, one would be hard-pressed to create a substantial list of business, political, or religious elites who have been outspoken in their support of such programs.

One factor underlying this "official" denial has been the response of the American public. National polls reveal that nearly one of every two white Americans believes that blacks are as well off as whites or have the same opportunities in life. (Fewer than one out of five blacks holds the same belief.)[1] In fact, as we will show later in Part Three, on discrimination, the disadvantage of blacks has held stable throughout history and in many cases can still be described as extreme—in health, housing, income, and justice, among other comparisons.

The culture of denial has so permeated American society that it has deeply influenced the way in which many whites think about prejudice. Many white people deny that discrimination against minorities persists and thus have concluded that any interventions designed to equalize opportunities are uncalled for. In some cases, such interventions (e.g., affirmative action) are actually viewed as disadvantaging whites. This line of thought has resulted in increasing polarization of blacks and whites and growing white opposition to programs of social action. It has also become central to the appeals of the right-wing white supremacist movement, which defines the differences that do exist as "cultural" and calls for a white-only society in order to maintain a "true Christian American" culture.

The fourth social condition contributing to the development of prejudice and its manifestation as discrimination, conflict, and ethnoviolence concerns the differentials of power in society. Americans vary widely in terms of their life chances, which in turn are determined by the resources of power that people have at their disposal as individuals or as members of a group. It is our premise that the greater the differences of power in a society, the greater the discrimination against minorities. Such power differentials are maintained through social class membership and bureaucratic organization.

Bureaucracy requires that participants accept two basic principles of organization: the necessity for some people to have power and authority over others, and the requirement that participants accept an impersonal orientation (such that some people are treated as objects). Those in authority within a bureaucratic organization therefore have license to manipulate the behavior and lives of others without regard to their identity as individuals. Such depersonalization is a necessary condition of discrimination and ethnoviolence. Participation in bureaucratic organization has the effect of both validating inequality and depersonalization as acceptable modes of behavior and of subjecting people to the repeated experience of treating others in this manner.

The social class system is built on differences in wealth and power and on the lifestyles that accompany those differences. The question of why social classes persist is a central problem of sociology; and, indeed, one of the reasons for its persistence is relevant here. People are socialized to accept the basic structures and norms of their society. And most Americans believe that our class system is basically fair—that the differences in wealth and power among people have been justly brought about and that it is appropriate for families to pass along their privileges to their children.

However, although most people appear to accept the class system, the *extent* to which inequalities characterize the social classes is generally regarded as unfair. For example, many people would describe as unfair the fact that, in 1991, the average chief executive officer of a large corporation earned as much as 104 factory workers, and that, in 1992, more than twice as many black infants as white infants died before they were one year old. There is, in fact, an underlying tension about the American class system, but this tension is mediated by the belief—some would say mythological belief—that anyone can achieve wealth and power through individual efforts. It is mediated as well by a deeply rooted fear of alternatives to the political and economic design of American society, a fear fostered by those who most benefit from its present structure.

The inequalities among social classes are closely connected to those among ethnic groups. The parallels are twofold. First, "minority" Americans occupy a disproportionate number of lower-middle, working-class, and lower-class positions. Because of the considerable overlap between class and color and other ethnic identifications, accepting the class system as legitimate and fair is equivalent to accepting the system of minority stratification as legitimate and fair.

Second, the class system fosters the development of prejudice, discrimination, and conflict because it is a system of inequality. From a social-psychological perspective, treating people differently because of social class is very much like treating people differently because of ethnicity. There is a fundamental disjunction between economic inequality and the acceptance of racial and ethnic equality. This is the built-in paradox of modern society.

THE POLITICS OF INEQUALITY

As will become more apparent in the following essay, there are pivotal differences among the conservative, liberal, and radical approaches to inequality. Conservatives tend to accept the basic forms of social organization, contending that the organizational processes that have developed through time are essentially sound and self-regulating. What is needed, in the conservative view, is a change in the lifestyle and behavior of those at the lower levels of the class and organizational systems. From this standpoint, government interventions are seen as counterproductive. Liberals also tend to be accepting of the basic social forms, but they emphasize the need for government intervention in order to change the opportunity structure of society so that an equality of outcome is more closely approximated. Thus the major ameliorative programs of liberal administrations have involved affirmative action, progressive taxation, strengthening of civil rights laws, and the desegregation of schools. Conservatives and liberals agree, then, that the class and organizational systems are basically sound; they differ in their perceptions of the means to be adopted to achieve group equality.

From the radical perspective, the existing patterns of inequalities are seen as part of the social system itself. The class structure and bureaucratic forms of social organization are construed as having been built upon social inequality and as operating in such a way as to socialize people into accepting inequality both in principle and in practice. It is unrealistic, say radicals, to accept the inequities of wealth and power while realistically expecting equality in intergroup relations. Their contention is that these inequalities are mutually supportive and that all power differences need to be minimized, if not totally eradicated.

ABOUT THE BOOK

This anthology proceeded from our lack of satisfaction with the texts that were available for undergraduate courses in intergroup conflict. After many discussions, we decided to publish this supplementary compilation, which can be used with another textbook. Several principles guided us in our selection of essays.

1. We wanted to combine social-psychological analyses of attitudes with sociological analyses of social structure and policy. Part Two contains three chapters about attitudes, whereas Parts Three through Eight are more sociological in ori-

entation. When possible, we tried to select essays that combine both levels of analysis.

2. We wanted essays to be theoretically diverse. It is important for students to understand some of the important theoretical debates in the field so that they can arrive at their own decisions. Some of the essays are from conservative (right-wing) publications such as *The Public Interest, Commentary,* and *The New Republic,* whereas others are from more radical (left-wing) publications such as *Monthly Review, Fifth Estate,* and *Politics and Society.* Still others are from mainstream and professional publications not normally associated with a particular political perspective such as *The Rutgers Law Review, Urban Geography,* and *Sage Race Relations Abstracts.* Although these mainstream publications are not apolitical, they contain articles from a variety of perspectives.

The theme of theoretical diversity runs throughout this book. In Part Two, for example, one author argues that white opposition to "forced busing" and "reverse discrimination" is a manifestation of "modern prejudice"; another author strongly disagrees. Also included throughout are debates on the efficacy of black business, the success of affirmative action, the meaning of political correctness, and the viability of electoral politics.

Of course, we have our own views about these debates. But we have tried to be even-handed by presenting substantive and well-reasoned articles on both sides of each issue.

3. The essays had to be readable by the majority of college and university undergraduates. Many articles from professional journals, though important, are written with so much jargon and such complex statistics that many undergraduates cannot understand them. Although we selected essays that were substantive and based on empirical research, we eliminated many simply because of their writing style.

4. The subjects of the essays had to be relevant to undergraduates. *Relevance* is a term that was often used in the turbulent 1960s to refer to courses that spoke to the felt concerns of students at that time. On the basis of our own teaching experience, we selected essays that are important in the field and should be of general interest. Part Six, for example, includes four chapters about tensions on college campuses, and Part Seven covers the controversies surrounding the policy of affirmative action.

Our hope is that this book will stimulate thinking not only about the nature of intergroup conflict in the United States but also about policies that could help alleviate this conflict. Information is always better than ignorance, even if the proposed solutions are not always simple or straightforward.

NOTES

1. These national polls were conducted in January 1989 by Louis Harris and Associates.

2

Talking About Race, Learning About Racism

BEVERLY DANIEL TATUM

As many educational institutions struggle to become more multicultural in terms of their students, faculty, and staff, they also begin to examine issues of cultural representation within their curriculum. This examination has evoked a growing number of courses that give specific consideration to the effect of variables such as race, class, and gender on human experience—an important trend that is reflected and supported by the increasing availability of resource manuals for the modification of course content (Bronstein & Quina, 1988; Hull, Scott, & Smith, 1982; Schuster & Van Dyne, 1985).

Unfortunately, less attention has been given to the issues of process that inevitably emerge in the classroom when attention is focused on race, class, and/or gender. It is very difficult to talk about these concepts in a meaningful way without also talking and learning about racism, classism, and sexism.[1] The introduction of these issues of oppression often generates powerful emotional responses in students that range from guilt and shame to anger and despair. If not addressed, these emotional responses can result in student resistance to oppression-related content areas. Such resistance can ultimately interfere with the cognitive understanding and mastery of the material. This resistance and potential interference is particularly common when specifically addressing issues of race and racism. Yet, when students are given the opportunity to explore race-related material in a classroom where both their affective and intellectual responses are acknowledged and addressed, their level of understanding is greatly enhanced. ...

In predominantly White college classrooms, I have experienced at least three major sources of student resistance to talking and learning about race and racism. They can be readily identified as the following:

1. Race is considered a taboo topic for discussion, especially in racially mixed settings.

11

2. Many students, regardless of racial-group membership, have been socialized to think of the United States as a just society.

3. Many students, particularly White students, initially deny any personal
   prejudice, recognizing the impact of racism on other people's lives, but failing to acknowledge its impact on their own.

RACE AS TABOO TOPIC

The first source of resistance, race as a taboo topic, is an essential obstacle to overcome if class discussion is to begin at all. Although many students are interested
in the topic, they are often most interested in hearing other people talk about it,
afraid to break the taboo themselves.

One source of this self-consciousness can be seen in the early childhood experiences of many students. It is known that children as young as three notice racial
differences (see Phinney & Rotheram, 1987). Certainly preschoolers talk about
what they see. Unfortunately, they often do so in ways that make adults uncomfortable. Imagine the following scenario: A White child in a public place points to
a dark-skinned African-American child and says loudly, "Why is that boy Black?"
The embarrassed parent quickly responds, "Sh! Don't say that," The child is only
attempting to make sense of a new observation (Derman-Sparks, Higa, & Sparks,
1980), yet the parent's attempt to silence the perplexed child sends a message that
this observation is not okay to talk about. White children quickly become aware
that their questions about race raise adult anxiety, and as a result, they learn not
to ask the questions.

When asked to reflect on their earliest race-related memories and the feelings
associated with them, both White students and students of color often report feelings of confusion, anxiety, and/or fear. Students of color often have early memories of name-calling or other negative interactions with other children, and sometimes with adults. They also report having had questions that went both unasked
and unanswered. In addition, many students have had uncomfortable inter-
changes around race-related topics as adults. When asked at the beginning of the
semester, "How many of you have had difficult, perhaps heated conversations
with someone on a race-related topic? routinely almost everyone in the class
raised his or her hand. It should come as no surprise then that students often approach the topic of race and/or racism with both curiosity and trepidation.

THE MYTH OF THE MERITOCRACY

The second source of student resistance to be discussed here is rooted in students'
belief that the United States is a just society, a meritocracy where individual efforts are fairly rewarded. While some students (particularly students of color)
may already have become disillusioned with that notion of the United States, the
majority of my students who have experienced at least the personal success of college acceptance still have faith in this notion. To the extent that these students acknowledge that racism exists, they tend to view it as an individual phenomenon,

rooted in the attitudes of the "Archie Bunkers" of the world or located only in particular parts of the country.

After several class meetings, Karen, a White woman, acknowledged this attitude in her journal:

> At one point in my life—the beginning of this class—I actually perceived America to be a relatively racist free society. I thought that the people who were racist or subjected to racist stereotypes were found only in small pockets of the U.S., such as the South. As I've come to realize, racism (or at least racially orientated stereotypes) is rampant.

An understanding of racism as a system of advantage presents a serious challenge to the notion of the United States as a just society where rewards are based solely on one's merit. Such a challenge often creates discomfort in students. The old adage "ignorance is bliss" seems to hold true in this case; students are not necessarily eager to recognize the painful reality of racism.

One common response to the discomfort is to engage in denial of what they are learning. White students in particular may question the accuracy or currency of statistical information regarding the prevalence of discrimination (housing, employment, access to health care, and so on). More qualitative data, such as autobiographical accounts of experiences with racism, may be challenged on the basis of their subjectivity.

It should be pointed out that the basic assumption that the United States is a just society for all is only one of many basic assumptions that might be challenged in the learning process. Another example can be seen in an interchange between two White students following a discussion about cultural racism, in which the omission or distortion of historical information about people of color was offered as an example of the cultural transmission of racism.

"Yeah, I just found out that Cleopatra was actually a Black woman."

"What?"

The first student went on to explain her newly learned information. Finally, the second student exclaimed in disbelief, "That can't be true. Cleopatra was beautiful!" This new information and her own deeply ingrained assumptions about who is beautiful and who is not were too incongruous to allow her to assimilate the information at that moment.

If outright denial of information is not possible, then withdrawal may be. Physical withdrawal in the form of absenteeism is one possible result; it is for precisely this reason that class attendance is mandatory. The reduction in the completion of reading and/or written assignments is another form of withdrawal. I have found this response to be so common that I now alert students to this possibility at the beginning of the semester. Knowing that this response is a common one seems to help students stay engaged, even when they experience the desire to withdraw.

Following an absence in the fifth week of the semester, one White student wrote, "I think I've hit the point you talked about, the point where you don't want to hear any more about racism. I sometimes begin to get the feeling we are all hypersensitive." (Two weeks later she wrote, "Class is getting better. I think I am beginning to get over my hump.")

Perhaps not surprisingly, this response can be found in both White students and students of color. Students of color often enter a discussion of racism with some awareness of the issue, based on personal experiences. However, even these students find that they did not have a full understanding of the widespread impact of racism in our society. For students who are targeted by racism, an increased awareness of the impact in and on their lives is painful, and often generates anger.

Four weeks into the semester, Louise, an African-American woman, wrote in her journal about her own heightened sensitivity:

> Many times in class I feel uncomfortable when White students use the term Black because even if they aren't aware of it they say it with all or at least a lot of the negative connotations they've been taught goes along with Black. Sometimes it just causes a stinging feeling inside of me. Sometimes I get real tired of hearing White people talk about the conditions of Black people. I think it's an important thing for them to talk about, but still I don't always like being around when they do it. I also get tired of hearing them talk about how hard it is for them, though I understand it, and most times I am very willing to listen and be open, but sometimes I can't. Right now I can't.

For White students, advantaged by racism, a heightened awareness of if often generates painful feelings of guilt. The following responses are typical:

> After reading the article about privilege, I felt very guilty. (Rachel, a White woman)

> Questions of racism are so full of anger and pain. When I think of all the pain White people have caused people of color, I get a feeling of guilt. How could someone like myself care so much about the color of someone's skin that they would do them harm? (Terri, a White woman)

White students also sometimes express a sense of betrayal when they realize the gaps in their own education about racism. After seeing the first episode of the documentary series *Eyes on the Prize*, Chris, a White man, wrote:

> I never knew it was really that bad just 35 years ago. Why didn't I learn this in elementary or high school? Could it be that the White people of America want to forget this injustice? ... I will never forget that movie for as long as I live. It was like a big slap in the face.

Barbara, a White woman, also felt anger and embarrassment in response to her own previous lack of information about the internment of Japanese Americans during World War II. She wrote:

> I feel so stupid because I never even knew that these existed. I never knew that the Japanese were treated so poorly. I am becoming angry and upset about all of the things that I do not know. I have been so sheltered. My parents never wanted to let me know about the bad things that have happened in the world. After I saw the

movie (*Mitsuye and Nellie*), I even called them up to ask them why they never told me this. ... I am angry at them too for not teaching me and exposing me to the complete picture of my country.

Avoiding the subject matter is one way to avoid these uncomfortable feelings.

"I'M NOT RACIST, BUT ... "

A third source of student resistance (particularly among White students) is the initial denial of any personal connection to racism. When asked why they have decided to enroll in a course on racism, White students typically explain their interest in the topic with such disclaimers as, "I'm not racist myself, but I know people who are, and I want to understand them better."

Because of their position as the targets of racism, students of color do not typically focus on their own prejudices or lack of them. Instead they usually express a desire to understand why racism exists, and how they have been affected by it.

However, as all students gain a better grasp of what racism is and its many manifestations in U.S. society, they inevitably start to recognize its legacy within themselves. Beliefs, attitudes, and actions based on racial stereotypes begin to be remembered and are newly observed by White students. Students of color as well often recognize negative attitudes they may have internalized about their own racial group or that they have believed about others. Those who previously thought themselves immune to the effects of growing up in a racist society often find themselves reliving uncomfortable feelings of guilt or anger.

After taping her own responses to a questionnaire on racial attitudes, Barbara, a White woman previously quoted, wrote:

> I always want to think of myself as open to all races. Yet when I did the interview to myself, I found that I did respond differently to the same questions about different races. No one could ever have told me that I would have. I would have denied it. But I found that I did respond differently even though I didn't want to. This really upset me. I was angry with myself because I thought I was not prejudiced and yet the stereotypes that I had created had an impact on the answers that I gave even though I didn't want it to happen.

The new self-awareness, represented here by Barbara's journal entry, changes the classroom dynamic. One common result is that some White students, once perhaps active participants in class discussion, now hesitate to continue their participation for fear that their newly recognized racism will be revealed to others.

> Today I did feel guilty, and like I had to watch what I was saying (make it good enough), I guess to prove I'm really *not* prejudiced. From the conversations the first day, I guess this is a normal enough reaction, but I certainly never expected it in me. (Joanne, a White woman)

This withdrawal on the part of White students is often paralleled by an increase in participation by students of color who are seeking an outlet for what are often feelings of anger. The withdrawal of some previously vocal White students from the classroom exchange, however, is sometimes interpreted by students of color as indifference. This perceived indifference often serves to fuel the anger and frustration that many students of color experience, as awareness of their own oppression is heightened. For example, Robert, an African-American man, wrote:

> I really wish the White students would talk more. When I read these articles, it makes me so mad and I really want to know what the White kids think. Don't they care?

Sonia, a Latina, described the classroom tension from another perspective:

> I would like to comment that at many points in the discussions I have felt uncomfortable and sometimes even angry with people. I guess I am at the stage where I am tired of listening to Whites feel guilty and watch their eyes fill up with tears. I do understand that everyone is at their own stage of development and I even tell myself every Tuesday that these people have come to this class by choice. Some days I am just more tolerant than others. ... It takes courage to say things in that room with so many women of color present. It also takes courage for the women of color to say things about Whites.

What seems to be happening in the classroom at such moments is a collision of developmental processes that can be inherently useful for the racial identity development of the individuals involved. Nevertheless, the interaction may be perceived as problematic to instructors and students who are unfamiliar with the process. ...

It has become painfully clear on many college campuses across the United States that we cannot have successfully multiracial campuses without talking about race and learning about racism. Providing a forum where this discussion can take place safely over a semester, a time period that allows personal and group development to unfold in ways that day-long or weekend programs do not, may be among the most proactive learning opportunities an institution can provide.

NOTES

1. A similar point can be made about other issues of oppression, such as anti-Semitism, homophobia and heterosexism, ageism, and so on.

REFERENCES

Bronstein, P. A., & Quina, K. (Eds.). (1988). *Teaching a psychology of people: Resources for gender and sociocultural awareness.* Washington, DC: American Psychological Association.

Derman-Sparks, L., Higa, C. T., & Sparks, B. (1980). Children, race and racism: How race awareness develops. *Interracial Books for Children Bulletin,* 11(3/4), 3–15.

Hull, G. T., Scott, P. B., & Smith, B. (Eds.). (1982). *All the women are white, all the blacks are men, but some of us are brave: Black women's studies.* Old Westbury, NY: Feminist Press.

Phinney, J. (1989). Stages of ethnic identity in minority group adolescents. *Journal of Early Adolescence, 9,* 34–39.

Schuster, M. R., & Van Dyne, S. R. (Eds.). (1985). *Women's place in the academy: Transforming the liberal arts curriculum.* Totowa, NJ: Rowman & Allanheld.

3

Talking Past Each Other:
Black and White Languages of Race

BOB BLAUNER

For many African-Americans who came of age in the 1960s, the assassination of Martin Luther King, Jr. in 1968 was a defining moment in the development of their personal racial consciousness. For a slightly older group, the 1955 lynching of the fourteen-year-old Chicagoan Emmett Till in Mississippi had been a similar awakening. Now we have the protest and violence in Los Angeles and other cities in late April and early May of 1992, spurred by the jury acquittal of four policemen who beat motorist Rodney King.

The aftermath of the Rodney King verdict, unlike any other recent racial violence, will be seared into the memories of Americans of *all* colors, changing the way they see each other and their society. Spring 1992 marked the first time since the 1960s that incidents of racial injustice against an African-American—and by extension the black community—have seized the entire nation's imagination. Even highly publicized racial murders, such as those of African-American men in two New York City neighborhoods—Howard Beach (1986) and Bensonhurst (1989)—stirred the consciences of only a minority of whites. The response to the Rodney King verdict is thus a long-overdue reminder that whites still have the capacity to feel deeply about white racism—when they can see it in unambiguous terms.

The videotaped beating by four Los Angeles police officers provided this concreteness. To be sure, many whites focused their response on the subsequent black rioting, while the anger of blacks tended to remain fixed on the verdict itself. However, whites initially were almost as upset as blacks: An early poll reported that 86 percent of European-Americans disagreed with the jury's decision. The absence of any black from the jury and the trial's venue, Simi Valley, a lily-white suburban community, enabled mainstream whites to see the parallels with the Jim Crow justice of the old South. When we add to this mixture the widespread disaffection, especially of young people, with the nation's political and economic conditions, it is easier to explain the scale of white emotional involvement, unprecedented in a matter of racial protest since the 1960s.

In thirty years of teaching, I have never seen my students so overwrought, needing to talk, eager to do something. This response at the University of California at Berkeley cut across the usual fault lines of intergroup tension, as it did at high schools in Northern California. Assemblies, marches, and class discussions took place all over the nation in predominantly white as well as nonwhite and integrated high schools. Considering that there were also incidents where blacks assaulted white people, the scale of white involvement is even more impressive.

While many whites saw the precipitating events as expressions of racist conduct, they were much less likely than blacks to see them as part of some larger pattern of racism. Thus two separate polls found that only half as many whites as blacks believe that the legal system treats whites better than blacks. (In each poll, 43 percent of whites saw such a generalized double standard, in contrast to 84 percent of blacks in one survey, 89 percent in the other.)

This gap is not surprising. For twenty years European-Americans have tended to feel that systematic racial inequities marked an earlier era, not our own. Psychological denial and a kind of post-1960s exhaustion may both be factors in producing the sense among mainstream whites that civil rights laws and other changes resolved blacks' racial grievances, if not the economic basis of urban problems. But the gap in perceptions of racism also reflects a deeper difference. Whites and blacks see racial issues through different lenses and use different scales to weigh and assess injustice.

I am not saying that blacks and whites have totally disparate value systems and worldviews. I think we were more polarized in the late 1960s. It was then that I began a twenty-year interview study of racial consciousness published in 1989 as *Black Lives, White Lives*. By 1979 blacks and whites had come closer together on many issues than they had been in 1968. In the late 1970s and again in the mid-to-late 1980s, both groups were feeling quite pessimistic about the nation's direction. They agreed that America had become a more violent nation and that people were more individualistic and less bound by such traditional values as hard work, personal responsibility, and respect for age and authority. But with this and other convergences, there remained a striking gap in the way European-Americans and African-Americans evaluated *racial* change. Whites were impressed by the scale of integration, the size of the black middle class, and the extent of demonstrable progress. Blacks were disillusioned with integration, concerned about the people who had been left behind, and much more negative in their overall assessment of change.

In the 1990s this difference in general outlook led to different reactions to specific racial issues. That is what makes the shared revulsion over the Rodney King verdict a significant turning point, perhaps even an opportunity to begin bridging the gap between black and white definitions of the racial situation.

I want to advance the proposition that there are two languages of race in America. I am not talking about black English and standard English, which refer to different structures of grammar and dialect. "Language" here signifies a system of implicit understandings about social reality, and a racial language encompasses a worldview.

Blacks and whites differ on their interpretations of social change from the 1960s through the 1990s because their racial languages define the central terms, especially "racism," differently. Their racial languages incorporate different views of American society itself, especially the question of how central race and racism are to America's very existence, past and present. Blacks believe in this centrality, while most whites, except for the more race-conscious extremists, see race as a peripheral reality. Even successful, middle-class black professionals experience slights and humiliations—incidents when they are stopped by police, regarded suspiciously by clerks while shopping, or mistaken for messengers, drivers, or aides at work—that remind them they have not escaped racism's reach. For whites, race becomes central on exceptional occasions: collective public moments such as the recent events, when the veil is lifted, and private ones, such as a family's decision to escape urban problems with a move to the suburbs. But most of the time European-Americans are able to view racial issues as aberrations in American life, much as Los Angeles Police Chief Daryl Gates used the term "aberration" to explain his officers' beating of Rodney King in March 1991.

Because of these differences in language and worldview, blacks and whites often talk past one another, just as men and women sometimes do. I first noticed this in my classes, particularly during discussions of racism. Whites locate racism in color consciousness and its absence in color blindness. They regard it as a kind or racism when students of color insistently underscore their sense of difference, their affirmation of ethnic and racial membership, which minority students have increasingly asserted. Many black, and increasingly also Latino and Asian, students cannot understand this reaction. It seems to them misinformed, even ignorant. They in turn sense a kind of racism in the whites' assumption that minorities must assimilate to mainstream values and styles. Then African-Americans will posit an idea that many whites find preposterous: Black people, they argue, cannot be racist, because racism is a system of power, and black people as a group do not have power.

In this and many other arenas, a contest rages over the meaning of racism. Racism has become the central term in the language of race. From the 1940s through the 1980s new and multiple meanings of racism have been added to the social science lexicon and public discourse. The 1960s were especially critical for what the English sociologist Robert Miles has called the "inflation" of the term "racism." Blacks tended to embrace the enlarged definitions, whites to resist them. This conflict, in my view, has been at the very center of the racial struggle during the past decade.

THE WIDENING CONCEPTION OF RACISM

The term "racism" was not commonly used in social science or American public life until the 1960s. "Racism" does not appear, for example, in the Swedish economist Gunnar Myrdal's classic 1944 study of American race relations, *An American Dilemma*. But even when the term was not directly used, it is still possible to determine the prevailing understandings of racial oppression.

In the 1940s racism referred to an ideology, an explicit system of beliefs postulating the superiority of whites based on the inherent, biological inferiority of the colored races. Ideological racism was particularly associated with the belief systems of the Deep South and was originally devised as a rationale for slavery. Theories of white supremacy, particularly in their biological versions, lost much of their legitimacy after the Second World War due to their association with Nazism. In recent years cultural explanations of "inferiority" are heard more commonly than biological ones, which today are associated with such extremist "hate groups" such as the Ku Klux Klan and the White Aryan Brotherhood.

By the 1950s and early 1960s, with ideological racism discredited, the focus shifted to a more discrete approach to racially invidious attitudes and behavior, expressed in the model of prejudice and discrimination. "Prejudice" referred (and still does) to hostile feelings and beliefs about racial minorities and the web of stereotypes justifying such negative attitudes. "Discrimination" referred to actions meant to harm the members of a racial minority group. The logic of this model was that racism implied a double standard, that is, treating a person of color differently—in mind or action—than one would a member of the majority group.

By the mid-1960s the terms "prejudice" and "discrimination" and the implicit model of racial causation implied by them were seen as too weak to explain the sweep of racial conflict and change, too limited in their analytical power, and for some critics too individualistic in their assumptions. Their original meanings tended to be absorbed by a new, more encompassing idea of racism. During the 1960s the referents of racial oppression moved from individual actions and beliefs to group and institutional processes, from subjective ideas to "objective" structures or results. Instead of intent, there was now an emphasis on process: those more objective social processes of exclusion, exploitation, and discrimination that led to a racially stratified society.

The most notable of these new definitions was "institutional racism." In their 1967 book *Black Power*, Stokely Carmichael and Charles Hamilton stressed how institutional racism was different and more fundamental than individual racism. Racism, in this view, was built into society and scarcely required prejudicial attitudes to maintain racial oppression.

This understanding of racism as pervasive and institutionalized spread from relatively narrow "movement" and academic circles to the larger public with the appearance in 1968 of the report of the commission on the urban riots appointed by President Lyndon Johnson and chaired by Illinois Governor Otto Kerner. The Kerner Commission identified "white racism" as a prime reality of American society and the major underlying cause of ghetto unrest. America, in this view, was moving toward two societies, one white and one black (it is not clear where other racial minorities fit in). Although its recommendations were never acted upon politically, the report legitimated the term "white racism" among politicians and opinion leaders as a key to analyzing racial inequality in America.

Another definition of racism, which I would call "racism atmosphere," also emerged in the 1960s and 1970s. This is the idea that an organization or an environment might be racist because its implicit, unconscious structures were devised for the use and comfort of white people, with the result that people of other races will not feel at home in such settings. Acting on this understanding of racism, many schools and universities, corporations, and other institutions have changed their teaching practices or work environments to encourage a greater diversity in their clientele, students, or work force.

Perhaps the most radical definition of all was the concept of "racism as result." In this sense, an institution or an occupation is racist simply because racial mi-

norities are underrepresented in numbers or in positions of prestige and authority.

Seizing on different conceptions of racism, the blacks and whites I talked to in
the late 1970s had come to different conclusions about how far America had
moved toward racial justice. Whites tended to adhere to earlier, more limited notions of racism. Blacks for the most part saw the newer meanings as more basic.
Thus African-Americans did not think racism had been put to rest by civil rights
laws, even by the dramatic changes in the South. They felt that it still pervaded
American life, indeed, had become more insidious because the subtle forms were
harder to combat than old-fashioned exclusion and persecution.

Whites saw racism largely as a thing of the past. They defined it in terms of segregation and lynching, explicit white supremacist beliefs, or double standards in
hiring, promotion, and admissions to colleges or other institutions. Except for affirmative action, which seemed the most blatant expression of such double standards, they were positively impressed by racial change. Many saw the relaxed and
comfortable relations between whites and blacks as the heart of the matter. More
crucial to blacks, on the other hand, were the underlying structures of power and
position that continued to provide them with unequal portions of economic opportunity and other possibilities for the good life.

The newer, expanded definitions of racism just do not make much sense to
most whites. I have experienced their frustrations directly when I try to explain
the concept of institutional racism to white students and popular audiences. The
idea of racism as an "impersonal force" loses all but the most theoretically inclined. Whites are more likely than blacks to view racism as a personal issue. Both
sensitive to their own possible culpability (if only unconsciously) and angry at the
use of the concept of racism by angry minorities, they do not differentiate well between the racism of social structures and the accusation that they as participants
in that structure are personally racist.

The new meanings make sense to blacks, who live such experiences in their
bones. But by 1979 many of the African-Americans in my study, particularly the
older activists, were critical of the use of racism as a blanket explanation for all
manifestations of racial inequality. Long before similar ideas were voiced by the
black conservatives, many blacks sensed that too heavy an emphasis on racism led
to the false conclusion that blacks could only progress through a conventional
civil rights strategy of fighting prejudice and discrimination. (This strategy, while
necessary, had proved very limited.) Overemphasizing racism, they feared, was
interfering with the black community's ability to achieve greater self-determina-
tion through the politics of self-help. In addition, they told me that the prevailing
rhetoric of the 1960s had affected many young blacks. Rather than taking responsibility for their own difficulties, they were now using racism as a "cop-out."

In public life today this analysis is seen as part of the conservative discourse on
race. Yet I believe that this position originally was a progressive one, developed
out of self-critical reflections on the relative failure of 1960s movements. But perhaps because it did not seem to be "politically correct," the left-liberal community, black as well as white, academic as well as political, has been afraid of embracing such a critique. As a result, the neoconservatives had a clear field to pick
up this grass-roots sentiment and to use it to further their view that racism is no

longer significant in American life. This is the last thing that my informants and other savvy African-Americans close to the pulse of their communities believe.

By the late 1970s the main usage of racism in the mind of the white public had undoubtedly become that of "reverse racism." The primacy of "reverse racism" as "the really important racism" suggests that the conservatives and the liberal-center have, in effect, won the battle over the meaning of racism.

Perhaps this was inevitable because of the long period of backlash against all the progressive movements of the 1960s. But part of the problem may have been the inflation of the idea of racism. While institutional racism exists, such a concept loses practical utility if every thing and every place is racist. In that case, there is effectively nothing to be done about it. And without conceptual tools to distinguish what is important from what is not, we are lost in the confusion of multiple meanings.

BACK TO BASICS

While public discourse was discounting white racism as exaggerated or a thing of the past, the more traditional forms of bigotry, harassment, and violence were unfortunately making a comeback. (This upsurge actually began in the early 1980s but was not well noticed, due to some combination of media inattention and national mood.) What was striking about the Bernhard Goetz subway shootings in New York, the white-on-black racial violence in Howard Beach, the rise of organized hate groups, campus racism, and skinhead violence is that these are all examples of old-fashioned racism. They illustrate the power and persistence of racial prejudices and hate crimes in the tradition of classical lynchings. They are precisely the kind of phenomena that many social analysts expected to diminish, as I did.

If there was one positive effect of this upsurge, it was to alert many whites to the destructive power of racial hatred and division in American life. At the same time, these events also repolarized racial attitudes in America. They have contributed to the anger and alienation of the black middle class and the rapid rise of Afrocentrism, particularly among college students.

As the gap in understanding has widened, several social scientists have proposed restricting the concept of racism to its original, more narrow meaning. However, the efforts of African-Americans to enlarge the meaning of racism is part of that group's project to make its view of the world and of American society competitive with the dominant white perspective. In addition, the "inflated" meanings of racism are already too rooted in common speech to be overturned by the advice of experts. And certainly some way is needed to convey the pervasive and systematic character of racial oppression. No other term does this as well as racism.

The question then becomes what to do about these multiple and confusing meanings of racism and their extraordinary personal and political charge. I would begin by honoring both the black and white readings of the term. Such an attitude might help facilitate the interracial dialogue so badly needed and yet so rare today.

Communication can only start from the understandings that people have. While the black understanding of racism is, in some sense, the deeper one, the white views of racism (ideology, double standard) refer to more specific and recognizable beliefs and practices. Since there is also a cross-racial consensus on the immorality of racist ideology and racial discrimination, it makes sense whenever possible to use such a concrete referent as discrimination, rather than the more global concept of racism. And reemphasizing discrimination may help remind the public that racial discrimination is not just a legacy of the past.

The intellectual power of the African-American understanding lies in its more critical and encompassing perspective. In the Rodney King events, we have an unparalleled opportunity to bridge the racial gap by pointing out that racism and racial division remain essential features of American life and that incidents such as police beatings of minority people and stacked juries are not aberrations but part of a larger pattern of racial abuse and harassment. Without resorting to the overheated rhetoric that proved counterproductive in the 1960s, it now may be possible to persuade white Americans that the most important patterns of discrimination and disadvantage are not to be found in the "reverse racism" of affirmative action but sadly still in the white racism of the dominant social system. And, when feasible, we need to try to bridge the gap by shifting from the language of race to that of ethnicity and class.

RACE OR ETHNICITY?

In the American consciousness the imagery of race—especially along the black-white dimension—tends to be more powerful than that of class or ethnicity. As a result, legitimate ethnic affiliations are often misunderstood to be racial and illegitimate.

Race itself is a confusing concept because of the variance between scientific and common sense definitions of the term. Physical anthropologists who study the distribution of those characteristics we use to classify "races" teach us that race is a fiction because all peoples are mixed to various degrees. Sociologists counter that this biological fiction unfortunately remains a sociological reality. People define one another racially, and thus divide society into racial groups. The "fiction" of race affects every aspect of peoples' lives, from living standards to landing in jail.

The consciousness of color differences, and the invidious distinctions based on them, have existed since antiquity and are not limited to any one corner of the world. And yet the peculiarly modern division of the world into a discrete number of hierarchically ranked races is a historic product of Western colonialism. In precolonial Africa the relevant group identities were national, tribal, or linguistic. There was no concept of an African or black people until this category was created by the combined effects of slavery, imperialism, and the anticolonial and Pan-African movements. The legal definitions of blackness and whiteness, which varied from one society to another in the Western hemisphere, were also crucial for the construction of modern-day races. Thus race is an essentially political construct, one that translates our tendency to see people in terms of their color or other physical attributes into structures that make it likely that people will act for or against them on such a basis.

The dynamic of ethnicity is different, even though the results at times may be similar. An ethnic group is a group that shares a belief in its common past. Members of an ethnic group hold a set of common memories that make them feel that their customs, culture, and outlook are distinctive. In short, they have a sense of peoplehood. Sharing critical experiences and sometimes a belief in their common fate, they feel an affinity for one another, a "comfort zone" that leads to congregating together, even when this is not forced by exclusionary barriers. Thus if race is associated with biology and nature, ethnicity is associated with culture. Like races, ethnic groups arise historically, transform themselves, and sometimes die out.

Much of the popular discourse about race in America today goes awry because ethnic realities get lost under the racial umbrella. The positive meanings and potential of ethnicity are overlooked, even overrun, by the more inflammatory meanings of race. Thus white students, disturbed when blacks associate with each other, justify their objections through their commitment to *racial* integration. They do not appreciate the ethnic affinities that bring this about or see the parallels to Jewish students meeting at the campus Hillel Foundation or Italian-Americans eating lunch at the Italian house on the Berkeley campus.

When blacks are "being ethnic," whites see them as being "racial." Thus they view the identity politics of students who want to celebrate their blackness, their *chicano-ismo,* their Asian heritages, and their American Indian roots as racially offensive. Part of this reaction comes from a sincere desire, almost a yearning, of white students for a color-blind society. But because the ethnicity of darker people so often gets lost in our overracialized perceptions, the white students misread the situation. When I point out to my class that whites are talking about race and its dynamics and the students of color are talking about ethnicity and its differing meaning, they can begin to appreciate each other's agendas.

Confounding race and ethnicity is not just limited to the young. The general public, including journalists and other opinion makers, does this regularly, with serious consequences for the clarity of public dialogue and sociological analysis. A clear example comes from the Chicago mayoral election of 1983. The establishment press, including leading liberal columnists, regularly chastised the black electorate for giving virtually all its votes to Harold Washington. Such racial voting was as "racist" as whites voting for the other candidate because they did not want a black mayor. Yet African-Americans were voting for ethnic representation just as Irish-Americans, Jews, and Italians have always done. Such ethnic politics is considered the American way. What is discriminatory is the double standard that does not confer the same rights on blacks, who were not voting primarily out of fear or hatred as were many whites.

Such confusions between race and ethnicity are exacerbated by the ambiguous sociological status of African-Americans. Black Americans are *both* a race and an ethnic group. Unfortunately, part of our heritage of racism has been to deny the ethnicity, the cultural heritage of black Americans. Liberal-minded whites have wanted to see blacks as essentially white people with black skins. Until the 1960s few believed that black culture was a real ethnic culture.

Because our racial language is so deep-seated, the terminology of black and white just seems more "natural" and commonsensical than more ethnic labels like African-American or European-American. But the shift to the term African-American has been a conscious attempt to move the discourse from a language of race to a language of ethnicity. "African-American," as Jesse Jackson and others have pointed out, connects the group to its history and culture in a way that the racial designation, black, does not. The new usage parallels terms for other ethnic groups. Many whites tend to dismiss this concern about language as mere sloganeering. But "African-American" fits better into the emerging multicultural view of American ethnic and racial arrangements, one more appropriate to our growing diversity. The old race relations model was essentially a view that generalized (often inappropriately) from black-white relations. It can no longer capture—if it ever could—the complexity of a multiracial and multicultural society.

The issue is further complicated by the fact that African-Americans are not a homogeneous group. They comprise a variety of distinct ethnicities. There are the West Indians with their long histories in the U.S., the darker Puerto Ricans (some of whom identify themselves as black), the more recently arrived Dominicans, Haitians, and immigrants from various African countries, as well as the native-born African-Americans, among whom regional distinctions can also take on a quasi-ethnic flavor.

Blacks from the Caribbean are especially likely to identify with their homeland rather than taking on a generic black or even African-American identity. While they may resist the dynamic of "racialization" and even feel superior to native blacks, the dynamic is relentless. Their children are likely to see themselves as part of the larger African-American population. And yet many native-born Americans of African dissent also resist the term "African-American," feeling very little connection to the original homeland. Given the diversity in origin and outlook of America's largest minority, it is inevitable that no single concept can capture its full complexity or satisfy all who fall within its bounds.

For white Americans, race does not overwhelm ethnicity. Whites see the ethnicity of other whites; it is their own whiteness they tend to overlook. But even when race is recognized, it is not conflated with ethnicity. Jews, for example, clearly distinguish their Jewishness from their whiteness. Yet the long-term dynamic still favors the development of a dominant white racial identity. Except for recent immigrants, the various European ethnic identities have been rapidly weakening. Vital ethnic communities persist in some cities, particularly on the East Coast. But many whites, especially the young, have such diverse ethnic heritages that they have no meaningful ethnic affiliation. In my classes only the Jews among European-Americans retain a strong sense of communal origin.

Instead of dampening the ethnic enthusiasms of the racial minorities, perhaps it would be better to encourage the revitalization of whites' European heritages. But a problem with this approach is that the relationship between race and ethnicity is more ambiguous for whites than for people of color. Although for many white groups ethnicity has been a stigma, it also has been used to gain advantages that have marginalized blacks and other racial minorities. Particularly for working-class whites today, ethnic community loyalties are often the prism through which they view their whiteness, their superiority.

Thus the line between ethnocentrism and racism is a thin one, easily crossed—as it was by Irish-Americans who resisted the integration of South Boston's schools in the 1970s and by many of the Jews and Italians that sociologist Jonathan Rieder describes in his 1985 book *Canarsie*.

White students today complain of a double standard. Many feel that their college administrations sanction organization and identification for people of color, but not for them. If there can be Asian business organization and a black student union, why can't there be a white business club or a white student alliance? I'd like to explain to them that students of color are organized ethnically, not racially, that whites have Hillel and the Italian theme house. But this makes little practical sense when such loyalties are just not that salient for the vast majority.

Out of this vacuum the emerging identity of "European-American" has come into vogue. I interpret the European-American idea as part of a yearning for a usable past. Europe is associated with history and culture. "America" and "American" can no longer be used to connote white people. "White" itself is a racial term and thereby inevitably associated with our nation's legacy of social injustice.

At various California colleges and high schools, European-American clubs have begun to form, provoking debate about whether it is inherently racist for whites to organize as whites—or as European-Americans. Opponents invoke the racial analogy and see such organizations as akin to exclusive white supremacist groups. Their defenders argue from an ethnic model, saying that they are simply looking for a place where they can feel at home and discuss their distinctive personal and career problems. The jury is still out on this new and, I suspect, burgeoning phenomenon. It will take time to discover its actual social impact.

If the European-Americans forming their clubs are truly organizing on an ethnic or panethnic rather than a racial model, I would have to support these efforts. Despite all the ambiguities, it seems to me a gain in social awareness when a specific group comes to be seen in ethnic rather than racial terms. During the period of the mass immigration of the late nineteenth century and continuing through the 1920s, Jews, Italians, and other white ethnics were viewed racially. We no longer hear of the "Hebrew race," and it is rare for Jewish distinctiveness to be attributed to biological rather than cultural roots. Of course, the shift from racial to ethnic thinking did not put an end to anti-Semitism in the United States—or to genocide in Germany, where racial imagery was obviously intensified.

It is unrealistic to expect that the racial groupings of American society can be totally "deconstructed," as a number of scholars are now advocating. After all, African-Americans and native Americans, who were not immigrants, can never be exactly like other ethnic groups. Yet a shift in this direction would begin to move our society from a divisive biracialism to a more inclusive multiculturalism.

To return to the events of spring 1992, I ask what was different about these civil disturbances. Considering the malign neglect of twelve Reagan-Bush years, the almost two decades of economic stagnation, and the retreat of the public from issues of race and poverty, the violent intensity should hardly be astonishing.

More striking was the multiracial character of the response. In the San Francisco Bay area, rioters were as likely to be white as nonwhite. In Los Angeles, Latinos were prominent among both the protesters and the victims. South Central Los Angeles is now more Hispanic than black, and this group suffered perhaps 60 percent of the property damage. The media have focused on the specific grievances of African-Americans toward Koreans. But I would guess that those who trashed Korean stores were protesting something larger than even the murder of a fifteen-year-old black girl. Koreans, along with other immigrants, continue to enter the country and in a relatively short time surpass the economic and social position of the black poor. The immigrant advantage is real and deeply resented by African-Americans, who see that the two most downtrodden minorities are those that did not enter the country voluntarily.

During the 1960s the police were able to contain riots within the African-American community. This time Los Angeles police were unable to do so. Even though the South Central district suffered most, there was also much destruction in other areas including Hollywood, downtown, and the San Fernando Valley. In the San Francisco Bay area the violence occurred primarily in the white business sections, not the black neighborhoods of Oakland, San Francisco, or Berkeley. The violence that has spilled out of the inner city is a distillation of all the human misery that a white middle-class society has been trying to contain—albeit unsuccessfully (consider the homeless). As in the case of an untreated infection, the toxic substances finally break out, threatening to contaminate the entire organism.

Will this widened conflict finally lead Americans toward a recognition of our common stake in the health of the inner cities and their citizens, or toward increased fear and division? The Emmett Till lynching in 1955 set the stage for the first mass mobilization of the civil rights movement, the Montgomery bus boycott later that year. Martin Luther King's assassination provided the impetus for the institution of affirmative action and other social programs. The Rodney King verdict and its aftermath must also become not just a psychologically defining moment but an impetus to a new mobilization of political resolve.

4

Theoretical Perspectives in Race and Ethnic Relations

JOE R. FEAGIN AND CLAIRECE BOOHER FEAGIN

In the United States, explanatory theories of racial and ethnic relations have been concerned with migration, adaptation, exploitation, stratification, and conflict. Most such theories can be roughly classified as either *order* theories or *power-conflict* theories, depending on their principal concerns. *Order theories* tend to accent patterns of inclusion, of the orderly integration and assimilation of particular racial and ethnic groups to a core culture and society, as in the third and fourth of the outcomes just described. The central focus is on progressive adaptation to the dominant culture and on stability in intergroup relations. *Power-conflict* theories give more attention to the first and fifth outcomes—to genocide and continuing hierarchy—and to the persisting inequality of the power and resource distribution associated with racial or ethnic subordination. In the United States most assimilation theories are examples of order theories. Internal colonialism theories and class-oriented neo-Marxist viewpoints are examples of power-conflict theories. There is considerable variation within these broad categories, but they do provide a starting point for our analysis.

ASSIMILATION AND OTHER ORDER PERSPECTIVES

In the United States much social theorizing has emphasized assimilation, the more or less orderly adaptation of a migrating group to the ways and institutions of an established group. Hirschman has noted that "the assimilation perspective, broadly defined, continues to be the primary theoretical framework for sociological research on racial and ethnic inequality." The reason for this dominance, he suggests, is the "lack of convincing alternatives."[1] The English word *assimilate* comes from the Latin *assimulare*, to make similar."

Robert E. Park

Robert E. Park, a major sociological theorist, argued that European out-migration was a major catalyst for societal reorganization around the globe. In his view intergroup contacts regularly go through stages of a *race relations cycle*. Fundamental social forces such as out-migration lead to recurring cycles in intergroup history: "The race relations cycle which takes the form, to state it abstractly, of *contacts, competition, accommodation* and eventual *assimilation,* is apparently progressive and irreversible."[2] In the contact stage migration and exploration bring people together, which in turn leads to economic competition and thus to new social organization. Competition and conflict flow from the contacts between host peoples and the migrating groups. Accommodation, an unstable condition in the race relations cycle, often takes place rapidly. It involves a forced adjustment by a migrating group to a new social situation. ... Nonetheless, Park and most scholars working in this tradition have argued that there is a long-term trend toward assimilation of racial and ethnic minorities in modern societies. "Assimilation is a process of interpenetration and fusion in which persons and groups acquire the memories, sentiments, and attitudes of other persons or groups, and, by sharing their experience and history, are incorporated with them in a common cultural life."[3] Even racially subordinate groups are expected to assimilate.[4]

Stages of Assimilation: Milton Gordon

Since Park's pioneering analysis in the 1920s, many U.S. theorists of racial and ethnic relations and numerous textbook writers have adopted an assimlationist perspective, although most have departed from Park's framework in a number of important ways. Milton Gordon author of the influential *Assimilation in American Life,* distinguishes a variety of initial encounters between race and ethnic groups and an array of possible assimilation outcomes. While Gordon presents three competing images of assimilation—the melting pot, cultural pluralism, and Anglo-conformity—he focuses on Anglo-conformity as the descriptive reality. That is, immigrant groups in the United States, in Gordon's view, have typically tended to give up much of their heritage for the dominant, preexisting Anglo-Saxon core culture and society. The touchstone of adjustment is viewed thus: "If there is anything in American life which can be described as an overall American culture which serves as a reference point for immigrants and their children, it can best be described, it seems to us, as the middle-class cultural patterns of, largely, white Protestant, Anglo-Saxon origins, leaving aside for the moment the question of minor reciprocal influences on this culture exercised by the cultures of later entry into the United States."[5]

Gordon notes that Anglo-conformity has been substantially achieved for most immigrant groups in the United States, especially in regard to cultural assimilation. Most groups following the English have adapted to the Anglo core culture. Gordon distinguishes seven dimensions of adaptation:

1. *cultural assimilation:* change of cultural patterns to those of the core society;
2. *structural assimilation:* penetration of cliques and associations of the core society at the primary-group level;
3. *marital assimilation:* significant intermarriage;

4. *identification assimilation:* development of a sense of identity linked to the core society;
5. *attitude-receptional assimilation:* absence of prejudice and stereotyping;
6. *behavior-receptional assimilation:* absence of intentional discrimination;
7. *civic assimilation:* absence of value and power conflict.[6]

Whereas Park believed structural assimilation, including primary-group ties such as intergroup friendships, flowed from cultural assimilation, Gordon stresses that these are separate stages of assimilation and may take place at different rates.

Gordon conceptualizes structural assimilation as relating to primary-group cliques and relations. Significantly, he does not highlight as a separate type of structural assimilation the movement of a new immigrant group into the *secondary groups* of the host society—that is, into the employing organizations, such as corporations or public bureaucracies, and the critical educational and political institutions. The omission of secondary-structural assimilation is a major flaw in Gordon's theory. Looking at U.S. history, one would conclude that assimilating into the core society's secondary groups does *not necessarily* mean entering the dominant group's friendship cliques. In addition, the dimension Gordon calls *civic assimilation* is confusing since he includes in it "values," which are really part of cultural assimilation, and "power," which is a central aspect of structural assimilation at the secondary-group level.

Gordon's assimilation theory has influenced a generation of researchers. ... In a recent examination of Gordon's seven dimensions of assimilation, J. Allen Williams and Suzanne Ortega drew on interviews with a midwestern sample to substantiate that cultural assimilation was not necessarily the first type of assimilation to occur. For example, the Mexican Americans in the sample were found to be less culturally assimilated than African Americans, yet were more assimilated structurally. Those of Swiss and Swedish backgrounds ranked about the same on the study's measure of cultural assimilation, but the Swedish Americans were less assimilated structurally. Williams and Ortega conclude that assimilation varies considerably from one group to another and that Gordon's seven types can be grouped into three more general categories of structural, cultural, and receptional assimilation.[7]

In a later book, *Human Nature, Class, and Ethnicity* (1978), Gordon has recognized that his assimilation theory neglects power issues and proposed bringing these into his model, but so far he has provided only a brief and inadequate analysis. Gordon mentions in passing the different resources available to competing racial groups and refers briefly to black-white conflict, but gives little attention to the impact of economic power, inequalities in material resources, or capitalistic economic history on U.S. racial and ethnic relations.[8]

Focused on the millions of white European immigrants and their adjustments, Gordon's model emphasizes *generational* changes within immigrant groups over time. Substantial acculturation to the Anglo-Protestant core culture has often been completed by the second or third generation for many European immigrant groups. The partially acculturated first generation formed protective communities and associations, but the children of those immigrants were considerably more exposed to Anglo-conformity pressures in the mass media and in schools.[9]

Gordon also suggests that substantial assimilation along certain other dimensions, such as the civic, behavior-receptional, and attitude-receptional ones, has occurred for numerous European groups. Most white groups have also made considerable progress toward equality at the secondary-structural levels of employment and politics, although the dimensions of this assimilation are neither named nor discussed in any detail by Gordon.

For many white groups, particularly non-Protestant ones, structural assimilation at the primary-group level is underway, yet far from complete. Gordon suggests that substantially complete cultural assimilation (for example, adoption of the English language) along with structural (primary-group) pluralism form a characteristic pattern of adaptation for many white ethnic groups. Even these relatively acculturated groups tend to limit their informal friendships and marriage ties either to their immediate ethnic groups or to *similar* groups that are part of their general religious community. Following Will Herberg, who argued that there are three great community "melting pots" in the United States—Jews, Protestant, and Catholics—Gordon suggests that primary-group ties beyond one's own group are often developed with one's broad socioreligious community, whether that be Protestant, Catholic, or Jewish.[10]

In his influential books and articles Gordon recognizes that structural assimilation has been retarded by racial prejudice and discrimination, but he seems to suggest that non-European Americans, including African Americans, will eventually be absorbed into the core culture and society. He gives the most attention to the gradual assimilation of middle-class non-Europeans. In regard to blacks he argues, optimistically, that the United States has "moved decisively down the road toward implementing the implications of the American credo of [equality and justice] for race relations"—as in employment and housing. This perceived tremendous progress for black Americans has created a policy dilemma for the government: should it adopt a traditional political liberalism that ignores race, or a "corporate liberalism" that recognizes group rights along racial lines? Gordon includes under corporate liberalism government programs of affirmative action, which he rejects.[11] ...

Some assimilation-oriented analysts such as Gordon and Alba have argued that the once prominent ethnic identities, especially of European American groups, are fading over time. Alba suggests that there is still an ethnic identity of consequence for non-Latino whites, but declares that "a new ethnic group is forming—one based on a vague *ancestry* from anywhere on the European continent."[12] In other words, such distinct ethnic identities as English American and Irish American are gradually becoming only a vague identification as "European American," although Alba emphasizes this as a trend, not a fact. Interestingly, research on intermarriages between members of different white ethnic groups has revealed that large proportions of the children of such marriages see themselves as having multiple ethnic identities, while others choose one of their heritages, or simply "American," as their ethnic identity.[13]

Ethnogenesis and Ethnic Pluralism

Some theorists working in the assimilation tradition reject the argument that most European American groups have become substantially assimilated to a generic Anglo-Protestant or Euro-American identity and way of life. A few have explored models of adjustment that depart from Anglo-conformity in the direction of ethnic or cultural pluralism. Most analysts of pluralism accept some Anglo-conformity as inevitable, if not desirable. In *Beyond the Melting Pot,* Glazer and Moynihan agree that the original customs and home-country ways of European immigrants were mostly lost by the third generation. But this did not mean the decline of ethnicity. The European immigrant groups usually remained distinct in terms of name, identity, and, for the most part, primary-group ties.[14]

Andrew Greeley has developed the interesting concept of *ethnogenesis* and applied it to white immigrant groups, those set off by nationality and religion. Greeley is critical of the traditional assimilation perspective because it assumes "that the strain toward homogenization in a modern industrial society is so great as to be virtually irresistible."[15] Traditionally, the direction of this assimilation in the United States is assumed to be toward the Anglo-Protestant core culture. But from the ethnogenesis perspective, adaptation has meant more than this one-way conformity. The traditional assimilation model does not explain the persistence of ethnicity in the United States—the emphasis among immigrants on ethnicity as a way of becoming American and, in recent decades, the self-conscious attempts to create ethnic identity and manipulate ethnic symbols.[16]

... Greeley suggests that in many cases host and immigrant groups had a somewhat similar *cultural* inheritance. For example, some later European immigrant groups had a cultural background initially similar to that of earlier English settlers. As a result of interaction in schools and the influence of the media over several generations the number of cultural traits common to the host and immigrant groups often grew. Yet late in the adaptive process certain aspects of the heritage of the home country remained very important to the character of the immigrant-ethnic group. From this perspective, ethnic groups share traits with the host group *and* retain major nationality characteristics as well. A modern ethnic group is one part home-country heritage and one part common culture, mixed together in a distinctive way because of a unique history of development within the North American crucible.[17]

A number of research studies have documented the persistence of distinctive white ethnic groups such as Italian Americans and Jewish Americans in U.S. cities, not just in New York and Chicago but in San Francisco, New Orleans, and Tucson as well. Yancey and his associates have suggested that ethnicity is an "emergent phenomenon"—that its importance varies in cities and that its character and strength depend on the specific historical conditions in which it emerges and grows.[18]

Some Problems with Assimilation Theories

Most assimilation theorists take as their examples of ethnic adaptation white European groups migrating more or less voluntarily to the United States. But what of the adaptation and assimilation of non-European groups beyond the stage of initial contact? Some analysts of assimilation include nonwhite groups in their theories, despite the problems that arise from such an inclusion. Some analysts have argued that assimilation, cultural and structural, is the necessary, if long-term, answer to the racial problem in the United States. ...

More optimistic analysts have emphasized progressive inclusion, which will eventually provide black Americans and other minority groups with full citizenship, in fact as well as principle. For that reason, they expect ethnic and racial conflict to disappear as various groups become fully assimilated into the core culture and society. Nathan Glazer, Milton Gordon, and Talcott Parsons have stressed the egalitarianism of U.S. institutions and what they view as the progressive emancipation of non-European groups. Gordon and others have underscored the gradual assimilation of middle-class black Americans over the last several decades. Full membership for black Americans seems inevitable, notes Parsons, for "the only tolerable solution to the enormous [racial] tensions lies in constituting a single societal community with full membership for all."[19] The importance of racial, as well as ethnic, stratification is expected to decline as powerful, universalistic societal forces wipe out the vestiges of earlier ethnocentric value systems. White immigrants have desired substantial assimilation, and most have been absorbed. The same is expected to happen eventually for non-European groups.

Assimilation theories have been criticized as having an "establishment" bias, as not distinguishing carefully enough between what *has* happened to a given group and what the establishment at some point felt *should have* happened. For example, a number of Asian American scholars and leaders have reacted vigorously to the application of the concept of assimilation to Asian Americans, arguing that the very concept originated in a period (1870–1925) of intense attacks by white Americans on Asian Americans. The term was thus tainted from the beginning by its association with the dominant European American group's ideology that the only "good groups" were those that assimilated (or could assimilate) in Anglo-conformity fashion.

Unlike Park, who paid substantial attention to the historical and world-economy context of migration, many of today's assimilation theorists do not analyze sufficiently the historical background and development of a particular racial or ethnic group within a national or world context. In addition, assimilation analysts such as Gordon tend to neglect the power imbalance and inequality in racial and ethnic relations, which are seen most clearly in the cases of non-European Americans. As Geschwender has noted, "they seem to have forgotten that exploitation is the driving force that gives meaning to the study of racial and ethnic relations."[20]

Biosocial Perspectives

Some U.S. theorists, including assimilationists, now accent a biosocial perspective on racial and ethnic relations. The idea of race and ethnicity being deeply rooted in the biological makeup of human beings is an old European and American notion that has received renewed attention from a few social scientists and biologists in the United States since the 1970s. In *Human Nature, Class, and Ethnicity,* for example, Gordon suggests that ethnic ties are rooted in the "biological organism of man." Ethnicity is a fundamental part of the physiological as well as the psychological self. Ethnicity "cannot be shed by social mobility, as for instance social class background can, since society insists on its inalienable ascription from cradle to grave." What Gordon seems to a have in mind is not the old racist notion of the unchanging biological character and separateness of racial groups, but rather the rootedness of intergroup relation, including racial and ethnic relations, in the everyday realities of kinship and other socially constructed group boundaries. Gordon goes further, however, emphasizing that human beings tend to be "selfish, narcissistic and perpetually poised on the edge of aggression." And it is these selfish tendencies that lie behind racial and ethnic tensions.[21] Gordon is here adopting a Hobbesian (dog-eat-dog) view of human nature. ...

Although decidedly different from the earlier biological theories, the modern biosocial analysis remains problematical. The exact linkages between the deep genetic underpinnings of human nature and concrete racial or ethnic behavior are not spelled out beyond some vague analysis of kin selection and selfish behavior. ...

Another difficulty with the biosocial approach is that in the everyday world, racial and ethnic relations are *immediately social* rather than biological. As Edna Bonacich has pointed out, many racial and ethnic groups have mixed biological ancestry. Jewish Americans, for example, have a very mixed ancestry: as a group, they share no distinct biological characteristics. Biologically diverse Italian immigrants from different regions of Italy gained a sense of being Italian American (even Italian) in the United States. The bonds holding Jewish Americans together and Italian Americans together were not genetically based or biologically primordial, but rather the result of real *historical* experiences as these groups settled into the Untied States. Moreover, if ethnicity is primordial in a biological sense, it should always be a prominent force in human affairs. Sometimes ethnicity leads to recurring conflict, as in the case of Jews and Gentiles in the United States; in other cases, as with Scottish and English Americans, it quietly disappears in the assimilation process. Sentiments based on common ancestry are important, but they are activated primarily in the concrete experiences and histories of specific migrating and host groups.[22]

Emphasizing Migration: Competition Theory

... The *human ecology* tradition in sociological thought draws on the ideas of Park and other ecologists and emphasizes the "struggle of human groups for survival" within their physical environments. This tradition, which highlights demographic trends such as the migration of groups and population concentration in cities, has been adopted by competition analysts researching racial and ethnic groups.[23]

Competition theorists such as Susan Olzak and Joane Nagel view ethnicity as a social phenomenon distinguished by boundaries of language, skin color, and culture. They consider the tradition of human ecology valuable because it emphasizes the stability of ethnic population boundaries over time, as well as the impact of shifts in these boundaries resulting from migration; ethnic group membership often coincides with the creation of a distinctive group niche in the labor force. Competition occurs when two or more ethnic groups attempt to secure the same resources, such as jobs or housing. Competition theorists have accented the ways in which ethnic group competition and the accompanying ethnic solidarity lead to collective action, mobilization, and protest.[24]

According to competition theorists, collective action is fostered by immigration across borders and by the expansion of once-segregated minorities into the same labor and housing markets to which other ethnic groups have access. A central argument of these theorists is that collective attacks on a subordinate ethnic group—immigrant and black workers, for instance—increase at the local city level when the group moves up and out of segregated jobs and challenges other groups and not, as one might expect, in cities where ethnic groups are locked into residential segregation and poverty. ...

Competition theorists explicitly contrast their analyses with the power-conflict views we will discuss in the next section, perspectives that emphasize the role of capitalism, economic subordination, and institutionalized discrimination. Competition theorists write about urban ethnic worlds as though institutionalized racism and capitalism-generated exploitation of workers are not major forces in recurring ethnic and racial competition in cities. As we have seen, they emphasize migration and population concentration, as well as other demographic factors. ...

POWER-CONFLICT THEORIES

The last few decades have witnessed the development of power-conflict frameworks explaining U.S. racial and ethnic relations, perspectives that place much greater emphasis on economic stratification and power issues than one finds in assimilation and competition theories. Within this broad category of power-conflict theories are a number of subcategories, including the internal colonialism viewpoint, and a variety of class-based and neo-Marxist theories. ...

Internal Colonialism

Analysts of internal colonialism prefer to see the racial stratification and the class stratification of U.S. capitalism as *separate but related* systems of oppression. Neither should be reduced in social science theories to the other. An emphasis on power and resource inequalities, particularly white-minority inequalities, is at the heart of the internal colonialism model.

The framework of internal colonialism is built in part upon the work of analysts of *external colonialism*—the worldwide imperialism of certain capitalist nations, including the United States and European nations.[25] For example, Balandier has noted that capitalist expansion has affected non-European peoples since the fifteenth century: "Until very recently the greater part of the world population, not belonging to the white race (if we exclude China and Japan), knew only a status of dependency on one or another of the European colonial powers."[26] External colonialism involves the running of a country's economy and politics by an outside colonial power. Many colonies eventually became independent of their colonizers, such as Britain or France, but continued to have their economies directed by the capitalists and corporations of the colonial powers. This system of continuing dependency has been called *neocolonialism*. Neocolonialism is common today where there are few white settlers in the colonized country. Colonies experiencing a large in-migration of white settlers often show a different pattern. In such cases external colonialism becomes *internal colonialism* when the control and exploitation of non-Euopean groups in the colonized country passes from whites in the home country to white immigrant groups within the newly independent country.[27]

Non-European groups entering later, such as African slaves and Mexican farm workers in the United States, can also be viewed in terms of internal colonialism. Internal colonialism here emerged out of classical European colonialism and imperialism and took on a life of its own. The origin and initial stabilization of internal colonialism in North America predate the Revolutionary War. The systematic subordination of non-Europeans began with "genocidal attempts by colonizing settlers to uproot native populations and force them into other regions."[28] Native Americans were killed or driven off desirable lands. Slaves from Africa were a cheap source of labor for capital accumulation before and after the Revolution. Later, Asians and Pacific peoples were imported as contract workers or annexed in an expansionist period of U.S. development. Robert Blauner, a colonialism theorist, notes that agriculture in the South depended on black labor; in the Southwest, Mexican agricultural development was forcibly taken over by European settlers, and later agricultural development was based substantially on cheap Mexican labor coming into what was once northern Mexico.[29]

In exploiting the labor of non-European peoples, who were made slaves or were paid low wages, white agricultural and industrial capitalists reaped enormous profits. From the internal colonialism perspective, contemporary racial and ethnic inequality is grounded in the economic *interests* of whites in low-wage labor—the underpinning of capitalistic economic exploitation. Non-European groups were subordinated to European American desires for *labor* and *land*. Internal colonialism theorists have recognized the central role of *government* support of the exploitation of minorities. The colonial and U.S. governments played an important role in legitimating slavery in the sixteenth through the nineteenth centuries and in providing the government soldiers who subordinated Native Americans across the nation and Mexicans in the Southwest.

Most internal colonialism theorists are not concerned primarily with white immigrant groups, many of which entered the United States after non-European groups were subordinated. Instead, they wish to analyze the establishment of racial stratification and the control processes that maintain persisting white dominance and ideological racism. Stokely Carmichael and Charles Hamilton, who in their writings in the 1960s were among the first to use the term *internal colonialism*, accented institutional racism—discrimination by the white community against blacks as a group.[30] From this perspective African Americans are still a "colony" in the United States in regard to education, economics, and politics. ...

A Neo-Marxist Emphasis on Class

Analysts of racial and ethnic relations have combined an internal colonialism perspective with an emphasis on class stratification that draws on the Marxist research pioneered by [black sociologists W.E.B.] Du Bois and [Oliver] Cox. Mario Barrera, for example, has suggested that the heart of current internal colonialism is an interactive structure of class *and* race stratification that divides our society. Class, in the economic-exploitation sense of that term, needs to be central to a colonialism perspective. Basic to the U.S. system of internal colonialism are four classes that have developed in U.S. capitalism:

1. *capitalists:* that small group of people who control capital investments and the means of production and who buy the labor of many others;
2. *managers:* that modest-sized group of people who work as administrators for the capitalists and have been granted control over the work of others;
3. *petit bourgeoisie:* that small group of merchants who control their own businesses and do most of their work themselves, buying little labor power from others;
4. *working class:* that huge group of blue-collar and white-collar workers who sell their labor to employers in return for wages and salaries.

The dominant class in the U.S. political-economic system is the capitalist class, which in the workplace subordinates working people, both nonwhite and white, to its profit and investment needs. And it is the capitalists who decide whether and where to create jobs. They are responsible for the flight of capital and jobs from many central cities to the suburbs and overseas.

Barrera argues that each of these classes contains important segments that are set off in terms of race and ethnicity. Figure [4.1] suggests how this works. Each of the major classes is crosscut by a line of racial segmentation that separates those suffering institutionalized discrimination, such as black Americans and Mexican Americans, from those who do not. Take the example of the working class. Although black, Latino, and other minority workers share a similar *class* position with white workers, in that they are struggling against capitalist employers for better wages and working conditions, they are *also* in a subordinate position because of structural discrimination along racial lines within that working class. Barrera notes that the dimensions of this discrimination often include lower wages for many minority workers, as well as their concentration in lower-status occupations. Many Americans suffer from both class exploitation (as wage workers) and racial exploitation (as workers of color).

Ideology and Oppositional Culture

Internal colonialism theorists have studied the role of cultural stereotyping and ideology in limiting the opportunities of subordinate groups of color. A racist ideology dominates an internal colonialist society, intellectually dehumanizing the colonized. Stereotyping and prejudice, seen in many traditional assimilation theories as more or less temporary problems, are viewed by colonialism analysts as a way of rationalizing exploitation over a very long period, if not permanently. Discrimination is a question not of individual bigots but rather of a system of racial exploitation rationalized by prejudice.[31]

In his book on the English colonization of Ireland, Michael Hechter has developed a theory of internal colonialism that emphasizes how the subordinate group utilizes its own culture to *resist* subordination. Hechter argues that in a system of internal colonialism, cultural as well as racial markers are used to set off subordinate groups such as African Americans in the United States and the Irish in the

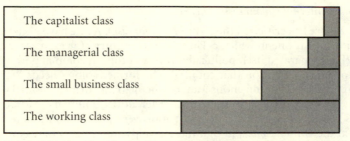

FIGURE [4.1]   The Class and Race Structure of Internal Colonialism
Note: Shaded area represents nonwhite segment.

United Kingdom. Resistance to the dominant group by the subordinate group often takes the form of cultural solidarity in opposition to the dominant culture. This solidarity can become the basis for protest movements by the subordinated group.[32]

Beginning in the 1960s, a number of power-conflict scholars and activists have further developed this idea of *oppositional culture* as a basis for understanding the resistance of non-European groups to the Euro-American core culture. Bonnie Mitchell and Joe Feagin have built on the idea of oppositional culture suggested in the work of Hechter and Blauner.[33] They note that in the centuries of contact before the creation of the Untied States, Mexico, and Canada, North America was populated by a diverse mixture of European, African, and Native American cultures. The U.S. nation created in the late 1700s encompassed African enslavement and the genocide of native Americans. Faced with oppression, these and other victims of internal colonialism have long drawn on their own cultural resources, as well as their distinctive knowledge of Euro-American culture and society, to resist oppression in every way possible.

The cultures of those oppressed by European Americans have not only provided a source of individual, family, and community resistance to racial oppression and colonialism but have also infused, albeit often in unheralded ways, some significant elements into the evolving cultural mix that constitutes the core culture of the United States. The oppositional cultures of colonized groups such as African Americans, Latino Americans, and Native Americans have helped preserve several key elements of U.S. society, including its tradition of civil rights and social justice. Another key element, ironically enough given the usual white image of minority families, is the value of extended kinship relations. The tendency toward extended kin networks is both culturally encouraged and economically beneficial for oppressed minority groups. For example, research on black and Latino communities has found extensive kinship networks to be the basis of social and economic support in difficult times. Native American groups have also been known for their communalism and extended family networks.[34]

... This reality contrasts with the exaggerated stereotypes of endemic family pathology in these groups. Internal colonialism theories accent both the oppression of minority Americans and the oppositional cultures that enable minority groups not only to survive but also to resist oppression, passively and actively.

Criticism of Internal Colonialism Theories

... Joan Moore has criticized the term *neocolonialism*. As we have noted, a neocolonial situation is one in which a Third World country (for example, an African
country) has separated itself politically from a European colonial power but continues to be dependent on that country. The former colony needs "foreign experts." It has a class of indigenous leaders who help the former colonial power exploit the local population. It has a distinct territorial boundary. Moore suggests
that this neocolonialism model does not apply very well to subordinate nonwhite
groups in the United States, in that these groups are not generally confined to a
specific bounded territory, nor do they contain the exploitative intermediary elite
of Third World neocolonialism. This space-centered critique has been repeated
by Omi and Winant, who argue that the social and spatial intermixing of white
and nonwhite groups in the United States casts serious doubt on the internal colonialism argument about territorially bounded colonization.[35]

However, most internal colonialism researchers have recognized the differences between internal colonial and neocolonial oppression. These theorists note
that the situations of minority groups in the United States are different from
those of, for instance, Africans in a newly independent nation still dependent on a
European country. In response to Moore's critique, internal colonialism analysts
might argue that there are many aspects of colonialism evident in U.S. racial and
ethnic relations; they might emphasize that non-European groups in the United
States (1) are usually residentially segregated, (2) are typically "superexploited" in
employment and deficient in other material conditions when compared with
white immigrants. (3) are culturally stigmatized, and (4) have had some of their
leaders co-opted by whites. While these conditions in the United States are not
defined as precisely as they are in the case of Third World neocolonialism, they
are similar enough to allow the use of the idea of colonialism to assess racial and
ethnic relations in the United States.

The Split Labor Market View: Another Class-Based Theory

Colonialism analysts such as Blauner are sometimes unclear about whether all
classes of whites benefit from the colonization of nonwhites, or just the dominant
class of capitalist employers. A power-conflict perspective that helps in assessing
this question is the *split labor market* view, which treats class in the sense of position in the "means of production." This viewpoint has been defended by Edna
Bonacich. She argues that in U.S. society the majority-group (white) workers do
not share the interests of the dominant political and economic class, the capitalists. Yet both the dominant employer class and the white part of the working class
discriminate against the nonwhite part of the working class.[36]

... Bonacich emphasizes that discrimination against minority workers by ordi-
nary white workers seeking to protect their own privileges, however limited these
may be, is important. Capitalists bring in nonwhite laborers to decrease labor
costs, but white workers resist because they fear job displacement or lower wages.
For example, over the last century white workers' unions have restricted the access
of black workers to many job ladders, thus splitting the labor market and reducing black incomes. ... White workers gain and lose from this structural racism.

They gain in the short run, because there is less competition for privileged job categories from the nonwhites they have excluded. But they lose in the long run because employers can use this cordoned-off sector of nonwhites to undercut them.[37]

"Middleman" Minorities and Ethnic Enclaves

Drawing on insights of earlier scholars, Bonacich has explored the in-between position, in terms of power and resources, that certain racial and ethnic groups have occupied in stratified societies. These groups find their economic niche serving elites and workers as small-business people positioned between producers and consumers. Some ethnic and racial groups become small-scale traders and merchants doing jobs that dominant groups are not eager to do. For example, many first-generation Jewish and Japanese Americans, excluded from mainstream employment by white Protestants, became small-scale merchants, tailors, restaurant operators, or gardeners. These groups have held "a distinctive class position that is of special use to the ruling class." They "act as a go-between to this society's more subordinate groups."[38]

Bonacich and Modell have found that Japanese Americans fit the middleman minority model. Before World War II Japanese Americans resided in highly organized communities. Their local economies were based on self-employment, including gardening and truck farming, and on other nonindustrial family businesses. The group solidarity of the first generation of Japanese Americans helped them establish successful small businesses. However, they faced hostility from the surrounding society, and in fact were driven into the businesses they developed because they were denied other employment opportunities. By the second generation there was some breakdown in the middleman position of Japanese Americans, for many of that generation moved into professional occupations outside the niche economy.[39]

Some middleman minorities, such as Jewish and Korean American merchants in central cities, have become targets of hostility from less well off groups, such as poor African Americans. In addition, strong ethnic bonds can make the middleman group an effective competitor, and even Anglo-Protestant capitalists may become hostile toward an immigrant middleman minority that competes too effectively. Thus Jewish Americans have been viewed negatively by better-off Anglo-Protestant merchants, who have the power to discriminate against them, as well as by poor black renters and customers with whom Jews deal as middleman landlords and merchants. ...

A somewhat similar perspective, *enclave theory*, examines secondary-structural incorporation into the economy, especially the ways in which certain non-European immigrant groups have created social and economic enclaves in cities. Both the middleman and the enclave perspectives give more emphasis to economic inequality and discrimination than assimilation perspectives, and they stress the incorporation of certain groups, such as Asians and Cubans, into the United States through the means of small businesses and specialized ethnic economies. The major differences between the two viewpoints seem to stem from the examples emphasized. Groups accented by enclave theorists, such as Cuban Americans, have created ethnic enclaves that are more than merchant or trading economies—they often include manufacturing enterprises, for example. In addition, ethnic enclaves usually compete with established Anglo-Protestant business elites. In contrast, the middleman minorities and those described as enclave minorities develop trading economies and are likely to fill an economic niche that *complements* that of established white elites. However, the aforementioned research of Bonacich on Jewish Americans suggests that there is little difference between the real-world experiences of those described as middleman minorities. ...

Women and Gendered Racism: New Perspectives

Most theories of racial and ethnic relations have neglected gender stratification, the hierarchy in which men as a group dominate women as a group in terms of power and resources. In recent years a number of scholars have researched the situations of women within racial and ethnic groups in the United States. Their analyses assess the ways in which male supremacy, or a patriarchal system, interacts with and operates within a system of racial and ethnic stratification. Discussing racial and ethnic cultures around the globe, Adrienne Rich has defined a *patriarchal system* as "a familial-social, ideological, political system in which men—by force, direct pressure, or through ritual, tradition, law and language, customs etiquette, education, and the division of labor—determine what part women shall or shall not play, and in which the female is everywhere subsumed under the male."[40]

Asking whether racism or patriarchy has been the primary source of oppression, social psychologist Philomena Essed examined black women in the United States and the Netherlands.[41] She found racism and sexism interacting regularly. The oppression of black women can be seen as *gendered racism*. For example, under slavery African American women were exploited not only for labor but also as sex objects for white men. And after slavery they were excluded from most job categories available to white men and white women; major employment changes came only with the civil rights movement of the 1960s. Today racism has many gendered forms. In the U.S. mass media the white female is the standard for female beauty. Minority women are often stereotyped as matriarchs in female-headed families and are found disproportionately in lower-status "female jobs," such as typists. Some women of color are closely bound in their social relations with those who oppress them in such areas as domestic employment ("maids") and other low-paid service work.[42]

In her book *Black Feminist Thought* Patricia Hill Collins argues that a black feminist theoretical framework can help highlight and analyze the negative stereotypes of black women in white society—the stereotypes of the docile mammy, the domineering matriarch, the promiscuous whore, and the irresponsible welfare mother. These severely negative images persist among many whites because they undergird white discrimination against black women in the United States.[43]

Scholars assessing the situations of other women of color, including Native American, Asian, and Latino women, have similarly emphasized the cumulative and interactive character of racial and gender oppression and the necessity of liberating these women from white stereotypes and discrimination. For example,

Denise Segura has examined labor-force data on Mexican American women and developed the concept of "triple oppression," the mutually reinforcing and inter-active set of race, class, and gender forces whose cumulative effects "place women of color in a subordinate social and economic position relative to men of color and the majority white population."[44]

Class, the State, and Racial Formation

Looking at the important role of governments in creating racial and ethnic desig-nations and institutionalizing discrimination, Michael Omi and Howard Winant have developed a theory of *racial formation*. Racial tensions and oppression, in their view, cannot be explained solely in terms of class or nationalism. Racial and ethnic relations are substantially defined by the actions of governments, ranging from the passing of legislation, such as restrictive immigration laws, to the im-prisonment of groups defined as a threat (for example, Japanese Americans in World War II). Although the internal colonialism viewpoint gives some emphasis to the state's role in the exploitation of nonwhite minorities, it has not developed this argument sufficiently.

Omi and Winant note that the U.S. government has shaped the politics of race: the U.S. Constitution and a lengthy series of laws openly defined racial groups and interracial relationships (for example, slavery) in racist terms. The U.S. Con-stitution counted each African American slave as three-fifths of a person, and the Naturalization Law of 1790 explicitly declared that only *white* immigrants could qualify for naturalization. Many non-Europeans, including Africans and Asians, were prevented from becoming citizens. Japanese and other Asian immigrants, for example, were until the 1950s banned by law from becoming citizens. In 1854 the California Supreme Court ruled that Chinese immigrants should be classified as "Indians"(!), therefore denying them the political rights available to white Americans.[45]

For centuries, the U.S. government officially favored northern European im-migrant groups over non-European and southern European groups such as Ital-ians. For example, the Immigration Act of 1924 was used to exclude Asian immi-grants and most immigrants from southern and eastern Europe, whom political leaders in Congress saw as racially inferior and as a threat to their control of the society. North European Americans working through the government thereby shaped the subsequent racial and ethnic mix that is the United States.

Another idea accented by Omi and Winant is that of *social rearticulation,* the recurring historical process of rupturing and reconstructing the understandings of race in this country. The social protest movements of various racial and ethnic groups periodically challenge the government's definition of racial realities, as well as individual definitions of those realities. The 1960s civil rights movement, for instance, rearticulated traditional cultural and political ideas about race in the United States, and in the process changed the U.S. government and broadened the involvement of minority Americans in the politics of that government. New social movements regularly emerge, sometimes bringing new identities and political norms.[46]

Resistance to the Dominant Group

Recent research has highlighted the many ways in which powerless groups fight back against the powerful. One power-conflict theorist who has made an important contribution to our understanding of how the oppressed react to oppression is James Scott. Influenced by the work of scholars such as John Gaventa on the many "faces of power" Scott has shown that at the heart of much interaction between the powerless and the powerful is intentional deception.[47] For example, the African American slaves were not free to speak their minds to their white masters, but they did create a crucial discourse among themselves that was critical of their white oppressors. Scott cites a proverb of African slaves on the Caribbean island of Jamaica: "Play fool, to catch wise." Looking closely at the lives of slaves and the poor everywhere, Scott has developed the idea of a backstage discourse by the oppressed that includes views that cannot be discussed in public for fear of retaliation. In addition to secret ideological resistance on the part of slaves and other poor people, a variety of other resistance tactics are used, including foot-dragging, pilfering, dissimulation, and flight. Scott cites Afro-Christianity as an example of how African American slaves resisted the "ideological hegemony" (attempts to brainwash) of white slavemasters. In public religious services African American slaves controlled their gestures and facial expressions and pretended to accept Christian preaching about meekness and obedience. Backstage, where no whites were present, Afro-Christianity emphasized "themes of deliverance and redemption, Moses and the Promised Land, the Egyptian captivity, and emancipation."[48] For slaves the Promised Land meant the North and freedom, and the afterlife was often viewed as a place where the slaves' enemies would be severely punished.

Historian Sterling Stuckey has noted that slave spirituals, although obviously affected by Christianity, "take on an altogether new coloration when one looks at slave religion on the plantations where most slaves were found and where African religion, contrary to the accepted scholarly wisdom, was practiced." The religion of African Americans mixed African and European elements from the beginning. Yet at its core the expressive, often protest-inclined African values prevailed over the European values.[49] Stuckey has shown that African culture and religion were major sources of the slaves' inclination to rebellion. The work of Scott and Stuckey can be linked to the analyses of Hechter and Mitchell and Feagin that we cited previously, for they too have accented the role of an oppositional culture in providing the foundation of resistance to racial oppression.

We can conclude this discussion of the most important critical power-conflict theories by underscoring certain recurring themes:

1. a central concern for racial and ethnic inequalities in economic position, power, and resources;
2. an emphasis on the links of racial inequalities to the economic institutions of capitalism and to the subordination of women under patriarchal systems;
3. an emphasis on the role of the government in legalizing exploitation and segregation and in defining racial and ethnic relations;

4. an emphasis on resistance to domination and oppression by those oppressed.

NOTES

1. Charles Hirschman, "America's Melting Pot Reconsidered," *Annual Review of Sociol-ogy* 9 (1983): 397–423.

2. Robert E. Park, *Race and Culture* (Glencoe, Ill.: Free Press, 1950), p. 150 (italics added).

3. Robert E. Park and Ernest W. Burgess, *Introduction to the Science of Society* (Chicago: University of Chicago Press, 1924), p. 735.

4. Janice R. Hullum, "Robert E. Park's Theory of Race Relations" (M.A. thesis, University of Texas. 1973), pp. 81–88; Park and Burgess, *Introduction to the Science of Society*, p. 760.

5. Milton M. Gordon, *Assimilation in American Life* (New York: Oxford University Press, 1964), pp. 72–73.

6. Ibid., p. 71.

7. Silvia Pedraza, *Political and Economic Migrants in America: Cubans and Mexicans* (Austin: University of Texas Press, 1985), pp. 5–7; Richard Alba, *Ethnic Identity: The Trans-formation of White America* (New Haven: Yale University Press, 1990), p. 311; J. Allen Williams and Suzanne T. Ortega, "Dimensions of Assimilation," *Social Science Quarterly* 71 (1990): 697–709.

8. Milton M. Gordon, *Human Nature, Class, and Ethnicity* (New York: Oxford University Press, 1978), pp. 67–89.

9. Gordon, *Assimilation in American Life*, pp. 78–108.

10. See Will Herberg, *Protestant—Catholic—Jew*. rev. ed. (Garden City, N.Y.: Doubleday, Anchor Books, 1960).

11. Milton M. Gordon, "Models of Pluralism: The New American Dilemma," *Annals of the American Academy of Political and Social Science* 454 (1981): 178–88.

12. Alba, *Ethnic Identity*, p. 3.

13. Stanley Lieberson and Mary Waters, "Ethnic Mixtures in the United States," *Sociol-ogy and Social Research* 70 (1985): 43–53; Cookie White Stephan and Walter Stephan, "After Intermarriage," *Journal of Marriage and the Family* 51 (May 1989): 507–19.

14. Nathan Glazer and Daniel P. Moynihan, *Beyond the Melting Pot* (Cambridge: M.I.T. Press and Harvard University Press, 1963).

15. Andrew M. Greeley, *Ethnicity in the United States* (New York: John Wiley, 1974), p. 293.

16. Ibid., pp. 295–301.

17. Ibid., p. 309.

18. William L. Yancey, D. P. Ericksen, and R. N. Juliani, "Emergent Ethnicity: A Review and Reformulation," *American Sociological Review* 41 (June 1976): 391–93. See also Greeley, *Ethnicity in the United States*, pp. 290–317.

19. Talcott Parsons, "Full Citizenship for the Negro American? A Sociological Problem," in *The Negro American*, ed. Talcott Parsons and Kenneth B. Clark (Boston: Houghton Mifflin, 1965–66), p. 740.

20. James Geschwender, *Racial Stratification in America* (Dubuque, Iowa: Wm. C. Brown, 1978), p. 58.

21. Gordon, *Human Nature, Class, and Ethnicity*, pp. 73–78. See also Clifford Geertz, "The Integrative Revolution," in *Old Societies and New States*, ed. Clifford Geertz (New York: Free Press, 1963), p. 109.

22. Edna Bonacich, "Class Approaches to Ethnicity and Race," *Insurgent Sociologist* 10 (Fall 1980): 11.

23. Frederik Barth, "Introduction," in *Ethnic Groups and Boundaries: The Social Organization of Culture Difference* (Oslo: Universitets Forlaget, 1969), pp. 10–17.

24. Susan Olzak, "A Competition Model of Collective Action in American Cities," in *Competitive Ethnic Relations,* ed. Susan Olzak and Joane Nagel (Orlando, Fla.: Academic Press, 1986), pp. 17–46.

25. Ronald Bailey and Guillermo Flores, "Internal Colonialism and Racial Minorities in the U.S.: An Overview," in *Structures of Dependency,* ed. Frank Bonilla and Robert Girling (Stanford, Calif.: privately published by a Stanford faculty–student seminar, 1973), pp. 151–53.

26. G. Balandier, "The Colonial Situation: A Theoretical Approach," in *Social Change,* ed. Immanuel Wallerstein (New York: John Wiley, 1966), p. 35.

27. Pablo Gonzalez-Cassanova, "Internal Colonialism and National Development," in *Latin American Radicalism,* ed. Irving L. Horowitz et al. (New York: Random House, 1969), p. 130; Bailey and Flores, "Internal Colonialism," p. 156.

28. Bailey and Flores, "Internal Colonialism," p. 156.

29. Blauner, *Racial Oppression in America,* p. 55. Our analysis of internal colonialism draws throughout on Blauner's provocative discussion.

30. Stokely Carmichael and Charles Hamilton, *Black Power* (New York: Random House, Vintage Books, 1967), pp. 2–7.

31. Guillermo B. Flores, "Race and Culture in the Internal Colony: Keeping the Chicano in His Place," in *Structures of Dependency,* ed. Bonilla and Girling, p. 192.

32. Michael Hechter, *Internal Colonialism* (Berkeley: University of California Press, 1975), pp. 9–12; Michael Hechter, "Group Formation and the Cultural Division of Labor," *American Journal of Sociology* 84 (1978): 293–318; Michael Hechter, Debra Friedman, and Malka Applebaum, "A Theory of Ethnic Collective Action," *International Migration Review* 16 (1982): 412–34. See also Geschwender, *Racial Stratification in America,* p. 87.

33. Joe Feagin and Bonnie Mitchell, "America's Non-European Cultures: The Myth of the Melting Pot," in *The Inclusive University: Multicultural Perspectives in Higher Education,* ed. Benjamin Bowser, Gale Auletta, and Terry Jones (forthcoming).

34. Carol B. Stack, "Sex Roles and Survival Strategies in an Urban Black Community," in *Women, Culture and Society,* ed. Michelle Zimbalist Rosaldo and Louise Lamphere (Stanford, Calif.: Stanford University Press, 1974), p. 128; Ronald Angel and Marta Tienda, "Determinants of Extended Household Structure: Cultural Pattern or Economic Need? *American Journal of Sociology* 87 (1981–82): 1360–83.

35. Joan W. Moore, "American Minorities and 'New Nation' Perspectives," *Pacific Sociological Review* 19 (October 1976): 448–55; Michael Omi and Howard Winant, *Racial Formation in the United States* (New York: Routlege & Kegan Paul, 1986), pp. 47–49.

36. Bonacich, "Class Approaches to Ethnicity and Race," p. 14.

37. Barrera, *Race and Class in the Southwest,* pp. 201–3; Bonacich, "Class Approaches to Ethnicity and Race," p. 14

38. Bonacich, "Class Approaches to Ethnicity and Race," pp. 14–15.

39. Edna Bonacich and John Modell, *The Economic Basis of Ethnic Solidarity* (Berkeley: University of California Press, 1980), pp. 1–37. For a critique, see Eugene Wong, "Asian American Middleman Minority Theory: The Framework of an American Myth," *Journal of Ethnic Studies* 13 (Spring 1985): 51–87.

40. Quoted in Michael Albert et al., *Liberating Theory* (Boston: South End Press, 1986), p. 35.

41. Philomena Essed, *Understanding Everyday Racism* (Newbury Park, Calif.: Sage Publications, Inc., 1991), pp. 30–32.

42. Ibid., p. 32.

43. Patricia Hill Collins, *Black Feminist Thought: Knowledge, Consciousness, and the Politics of Empowerment* (Boston: Unwin Hyman, 1990), pp. 40–48.

44. Denise A. Segura, "Chicanas and Triple Oppression in the Labor Force," in *Chicana Voices: Intersections of Class, Race and Gender,* ed. Teresa Cordova et al. (Austin, Tex.: Center for Mexican American Studies, 1986). p. 48.

45. Omi and Winant, *Racial Formation in the United States,* pp. 75–76.

46. Howard Winant, "Racial Formation Theory and Contemporary U.S. Politics," in *Exploitation and Exclusion,* ed. Abebe Zegeye, Leonard Harris, and Julia Maxted (London: Hans Zell, 1991), pp. 130–40.

47. James C. Scott, *Domination and the Arts of Resistance* (New Haven: Yale University Press, 1990); John Gaventa, *Power and Powerlessness* (Urbana, Ill.: University of Illinois Press, 1980).

48. Scott, *Domination and the Arts of Resistance,* p. 116.

49. Sterling Stuckey, *Slave Culture* (New York: Oxford University Press, 1987), pp. 27, 42–46.

PART 2

Prejudice

One common problem for students is that words used by social scientists often take on meanings different from those of the same words in our everyday language. There are numerous reasons for such discrepancies, including the need of sociologists and psychologists to share precisely the critical definitions of their theory. Consider, for instance, those social scientists whose goal is to construct a theory of prejudice and to devise techniques of measuring it. For them a high degree of specificity is required, whereas such precision is seldom necessary in informal discussion.

Students are sometimes further confused by the fact that different social scientists use different definitions of the same term. Again, there are numerous reasons; but the central explanation is that theorists want a concept to take on a meaning specific to their particular theory. Our goal here is the same. Accordingly, we shall specify a definition of *prejudice* that is in common usage. (For a review of definitions of this term, see Ehrlich, 1973.) As will become clear, the way in which *prejudice* is defined has important implications for understanding the articles that follow.

We define *prejudice* as "an attitude toward a category of people." Note that we are not talking here about an attitude toward a particular person. Just as there is an obvious difference between hating your boss and hating all bosses, there is a difference between hating Salim because he is an obnoxious person and hating him because he is an Asian Indian.

Attitudes can be favorable or unfavorable, positive or negative. In the context of prejudice, however, we are most often talking about unfavorable attitudes. Thus we will specify the direction of prejudice only when it is positive.

The key to understanding the concept of prejudice is to comprehend the meaning of *attitude*. An attitude is an interrelated set of beliefs, feelings, and motivations about some object or class of objects. Beliefs, feelings, and motivations—all three of these components are involved in an attitude, and all three are interrelated. To say that a person is prejudiced against some group means that this person holds a set of beliefs about that group, has an emotional reaction to that group, and is motivated to behave in a certain way toward that group. Each of these components is learned. We learn what people around us believe about a group. We learn how to respond emotionally to a group. And we learn how to organize our behavior toward that group.

Prejudice, then, is not something people are born with. Yet beliefs about groups (often referred to as *stereotypes*) are learned very early. Children as young as three and four years of age often begin to learn the prevailing stereotypes of a group long before they can identify the group or, for that matter, comprehend the full meaning of what they have learned. In those early years, parents are the major teachers of prejudice. Consider the white parent who tells a boy that he cannot play with the children of color across the street because they are dirty. The parent is communicating a behavioral norm (cannot play with) and a stereotype (dirty). All too soon, repetition of similar messages will have motivated the boy to respond aversely to his neighbors and, hence, to avoid playing with them. Think of all the messages you received in your family about others who were of a different background.

In order for a group to be a target of prejudice in society, a consensus has to have been reached that the group is an "acceptable" target. Thus, for example, Episcopalians are not a socially acceptable target; but Jews are. The reasons are both social and historical. It is the state of relations between groups in society that determines the dimensions of prejudice toward a specific group. By the same token, people's attitudes can be changed if both the nature of intergroup relations and the individual's beliefs, feelings, or motivations are changed. Of course, the latter is more easily changed than the former. But both must be accomplished in the long run.

These three components of attitude have elements in common; yet, paradoxically, they function differently. Consider, for example, the element of direction. Every belief, feeling, and motivation has a particular direction—that is, positive or negative, warm or cold, attractive or repulsive. An attitude is balanced if all its components are pointed in the same direction. Thus a person with very negative beliefs, a strong emotional response, and the motivation to avoid contact with or be openly hostile toward other persons because of their ethnicity could be described as highly prejudiced. But these elements do not always line up in the same direction. Take the case of a white woman with favorable beliefs about blacks who intends to deal openly and without discrimination except that she feels uncomfortable in personal encounters with blacks. This person's attitudes are unbalanced. Unbalanced attitudes are less stable and less predictive of behavior than are balanced attitudes. In this last example, furthermore, the woman may not even be fully aware of how her emotions influence her behavior. In various studies, social psychologists have observed whites who knowingly maintain greater physical distance, exhibit less eye contact, and even smile less in personal encounters with dark-skinned individuals.

There are two other elements associated with each of the three attitude components. Not only is the structure of an attitude complex, but people hold an extraordinary number of discrete attitudes; hence many social scientists tend to classify attitudes by their content. A person's attitudes toward whites, blacks, children, bisexuals, atheists, animals, authorities, and so on can be gathered together under the rubric of *equality*. And, generally, these larger categories of attitudes are referred to as *values*. A value, like an attitude, tends toward equilibrium; that is, the attitudes that make it up are all pointed in more or less the same direction.

In fact, one of the confirmed findings in the field of prejudice derives from this observation of balance and equilibrium: Prejudice is highly generalized. People who are prejudiced against one group tend to be prejudiced against others. This generality of prejudice extends even to attitudes toward oneself. People with negative self-attitudes tend to have negative attitudes toward others. These findings have great implications for attitude change: If attitudes toward one group (or oneself) can be changed, attitudes toward others can likely be changed as well.

There is a myth about attitudes in general and prejudice in particular. That myth is the proposition that "attitudes are difficult to change." Granted, some individuals are closed-minded and their belief systems are highly resistant to change; but among most people, attitudes are relatively easy to change. The work of the advertising industry is a case in point. Advertising entails an application of attitude theory whereby people are taught new beliefs, have their emotions manipulated, and are motivated to purchase the advertiser's product. With regard to prejudice, a substantial body of research indicates that such attitudes are relatively easy to manipulate.

We need to keep in mind that attitudes are not overt behaviors. The behavioral parallel to prejudice is what we generally refer to as *discrimination*. Discrimination refers to actions that deny equal treatment to persons perceived to be members of some social category (such as a particular ethnicity). The result is the restriction of opportunities and rewards available to others while maintaining those opportunities and rewards for one's own social group.

Attitudes are generally consistent with behavior. People do tend to behave in keeping with what they think, feel, and intend to do. However, the relation between prejudice and discrimination, between attitudes and behavior, is not a mechanical one. The expression of attitudes in behavior is a learned response, as is the ability to recognize behaviors that are incongruent with attitudes. Of course, any given situation or role may evoke contradictory expectations for behavior or multiple attitudes that are not consistent. This complex relationship is still under study, but the important point here is that if attitude changes are to be maintained, the new attitudes have to be clearly expressible in behavior. Moreover, if changes in behavior are to be lasting, the underlying attitudes must be changed as well.

Another concept frequently referred to is that of *racism*. In Chapter 3, Robert Blauner provided a brief history of the changes in the meaning of this term. As his overview makes clear, even ostensibly neutral scientific concepts can become political. Given the history of this usage, we as editors usually reserve *racism* for more informal discourse, in order to avoid, as Blauner put it, becoming "lost in the confusion of multiple meanings." It is important that we try to maintain a distance between the *process* of social inquiry and the political implications that often coexist with such inquiry. When the language of research becomes mired in multiple meanings and political ideology, then the stage is set for bias.

Part Two focuses on some of the behavioral consequences of prejudice. In the process of examining the societal implications of discrimination, the contributing authors discuss people's attitudes and the relation of those attitudes to the social context in which they behave. The essays themselves are examples of how differing perspectives on prejudice lead to differing conceptions of social problems and behaviors. All of the contributors to this section are social psychologists, but they represent different perspectives.

There are two basic themes in the chapters that follow. One deals with the ways in which the *content* of prejudice has changed. This theme is central to the discussion of differences among traditional, modern, and symbolic forms of prejudice (generally referred to in these essays as *racism*). And inasmuch as changes in prejudice reflect changes in intergroup relations, the discussion focuses on changes that have occurred over the past twenty-five years.

The second theme, one that arises in many debates these days, deals with the *consequences* of prejudice. Within this context, two main questions are raised. First, has white prejudice toward blacks essentially changed? Second, are the social policies that have been developed to eliminate discrimination and inequality operating fairly? Although these themes are introduced here, they will recur throughout many sections of this anthology.

REFERENCES

Howard J. Ehrlich. 1973. *The Social Psychology of Prejudice.* New York: Wiley.

5

New Patterns of Prejudice: The Different Worlds of 1984 and 1964

THOMAS F. PETTIGREW

Race relations in the United States have changed over the past two decades. While there is consensus on this generalization, there is little agreement over the nature and significance of these changes.

Two political extremes have emerged from this debate. One, associated with political left, regards the changes as largely cosmetic with little erosion of the bases of the nation's legacy of racism. This position is often held by the generation who are inexperienced with the deep South of the 1930's, 40's, and 50's; it uses absolute justice rather than the recent past as a referent. The other extreme is held by the political right which considers the changes to be so sweeping that the basic civil rights problems of the past have been resolved. This latter position is usually associated with those who previously resisted alterations in race relations and now wish to rationalize either the "benign neglect" or the retrogression of current governmental civil rights policy.

As usual, reality is not so neat. The political left overlooks fundamental structural changes that have occurred in American society over the past generation and that have altered the racial context significantly. The political right overlooks persistent racial problems which have yet to be resolved—indeed, in some cases these problems have festered and grown worse.

The thesis of this paper is that although much has changed since 1964, severe and difficult manifestations of both individual and institutional racism remain a prominent part of American life. ... Racism is typically far more subtle, indirect, and ostensibly nonracial now than it was in 1964, during the full swing of the Civil Rights Movement. Consequently, detection and remedy have become more difficult. Even the definitions of, as well as the methods of measuring, "prejudice" and "discrimination," have been brought into question. ...

An extensive body of social psychological research has developed over the past decade which details how prejudice typically operates today. This work gains credibility because of the growing convergence of results attained through a variety of different methods: probability public opinion surveys, laboratory experiments, quasi-experiments in the field, and intensive interviewing. There is no question that the traditional forms of "dominative racism" (Kovel 1970, 32) remain and coexist with the new forms uncovered by this recent research, but the old forms are less prevalent and influential than they were twenty years ago.

Modern antiblack prejudice is characterized by the following six features: (1) rejection of gross stereotypes and blatant discrimination; (2) normative compliance without internalization of new behavioral norms of racial acceptance; (3) emotional ambivalence toward black people that stems from early childhood socialization and a sense that blacks are currently violating traditional American values; (4) indirect "micro-aggressions" against blacks which is expressed in avoidances of face-to-face interaction with blacks and opposition to racial change for ostensibly nonracial reasons; (5) a sense of subjective threat from racial change, and (6) individualistic conceptions of how opportunity and social stratification operate in American society.

1. Rejection of Gross Stereotypes and Blatant Discrimination: The Civil Rights Movement of the 1960's brought the stark images of "Sheriff Clark" and "Bull Connor" forms of traditional antiblack prejudice into America's living rooms, giving traditional overt prejudice a disreputable image. Modern prejudice typically rejects the gross and global stereotypes (e.g., blacks as superstitious) and blatant forms of indisputable racial discrimination (e.g., refusal to hire qualified blacks on racial grounds alone). Evidence of this rejection comes from many sources, and there are strong reasons for believing that it is genuine within its carefully circumscribed scope.

In 1942, only 42% of whites surveyed believed that blacks had the same intelligence as whites, but by 1956 the percentage had risen to 78%, where it has remained. Likewise, only 42% of whites surveyed in 1942 thought blacks "should have as good a chance as white people to get any kind of job," but 95% thought so by 1972 (Pettigrew 1979, 118–19). Since 1964, similar changes in the attitudes of whites have occurred. Thus, in 1964, a fourth of adult whites favored "strict racial segregation" compared to only 5% by 1978. Similarly, in 1964 only 53% of whites thought "blacks have a right to live wherever they can afford," but by 1976, 84% thought so (Converse et al. 1980, 61, 66). Note, however, that these questions are on broad, global items and are of a hypothetical quality that averts personal involvement and threat.

2. Normative Compliance Without Internalization: New behavioral norms of racial interaction were established by the Civil Rights Movement during the 1960's, especially among young and better educated Americans. Just as gross stereotypes and blatant discrimination came to be seen as disreputable in many quarters, open hostility and rejection of face-to-face racial interaction also came to be disapproved.

Nevertheless, the emergence of new norms does not signify their full acceptance. Kelman (1961, 62–71) makes a useful distinction between compliance and internalization. Compliance in the racial context means that whites follow the new norms only when they are under the surveillance of significant others who can reward and punish. Internalization means that whites have adopted the new norms as their own personal standard of behavior and will follow them without surveillance. This clarifying distinction helps to explain several aspects of today's racial scene. The distinction emphasizes the importance of clearly defined organizational norms of nondiscrimination backed by enforced sanctions. It also suggests that some whites who at first simply comply with the new norms of racial equality will in time internalize them.

Black Americans, too, must learn the new norms. Often this process entails unlearning past lessons and overcoming suspicions that whites will inevitably discriminate. Nondiscriminatory organizational norms provide the opportunity for racial interaction. If whites repeatedly violate the new norms, blacks will not adopt the new norms either. Similarly, distrusting behavior by blacks can evoke white rejection. Until internalization is widespread, the process will obviously be delicate, with both races testing the limits of the unfamiliar situation. How could it be otherwise after three-and-a-half centuries of unequal racial interaction? What is clear, however, is that internalization of the new norms cannot occur without new interracial environments in schools, neighborhoods, athletic teams, work places, that reinforce the new behavioral expectations.

So where are we in 1984? Although there are no precise methods for gauging the population as a whole, a number of laboratory and field experiments in social psychology suggest tentative answers.

In a wide variety of situations, most whites and blacks seem to comply to the new norms without full internalization. This conclusion emerges from such studies as Wispe and Freshey's (1971; Gaertner 1976, 198) field study at a Kansas supermarket. Black and white women, matched for social class, appearance, and age, dropped their groceries as they left the store in the path of oncoming pedestrians. The dependent variable was the amount of help each woman received from passersby. Old-style racist norms would dictate that whites help the white woman but ignore the black woman. This did not happen. In compliance with the new norms, approximately the same proportion of whites stopped to help the two women. However, "the new pattern" of racism is revealed by the unequal amount of help they provided. On 63% of the occasions with the white woman, the white passerby gave complete help by picking up all of the dropped groceries. But in 70% of the encounters with the black woman, the passersby gave perfunctory help by picking up only a few packages. This suggests a general failure to internalize the new norms.

3. *Racial Ambivalence:* Social psychological experiments also support Kovel's (1970, 249–89) psychoanalytic contentions that modern antiblack prejudice involves considerable ambivalence created by earlier racist socialization and the new norms of nondiscrimination (Jones 1972, 118–27). Adding to this early socialization are the attitudes of many whites that affirmative action "violate[s] such traditional American values as individualism and self-reliance ..." (Kinder & Sears 1981, 416).

Experiments that measure differential behavior toward members of another race often explore parameters of assistance provision, nonverbal behavior, and aggression. Forty-three "assistance" studies, such as the supermarket experiment, reveal varying degrees of discrimination (Crosby, Bromley & Saxe 1980). Nineteen (44%) noted that subjects gave more aid to their own race than to the opposite race. Black subjects were as likely to demonstrate this tendency as were white subjects. Consistent with compliance but not internalization, white were less likely to discriminate in face-to-face than in noncontact situations (e.g., over the phone).

Research on nonverbal behavior shows that white college students often sit further away, use a less friendly voice tone, make less eye contact and more speech errors, and terminate the interview faster when interacting with a black rather than a white (Hendricks & Bootlin 1976; Weitz 1972; Word, Zanna & Cooper 1974, 111–19).

Aggression research indicates the prejudice is inhibited when negative sanctions are a possible consequence. Donnerstein and Donnerstein (1973, 1976) developed an experimental procedure that socially sanctions aggression. The subject applies bogus shocks to "a learner," a confederate of the experimenter, each time an error is made in a learning task. The intensity of the shock applied is considered an index of direct aggression; the duration of the shock an index of indirect aggression. The possibility of later retaliation, censure, or loss of anonymity all affected the behavior of white subjects toward the black, but not the white, targets. The possibility of negative consequences led white subjects to employ less direct aggression against blacks. One study found more complex but similar effects for black subjects (Wilson & Rogers 1975).

Katz, Glass and Cohen (1973, 431–32) show how these results relate to ambivalence. Using the Donnerstein procedure, these investigators had white subjects administer either "mild" or "strong" shocks to either black or white "learners." As expected, guilt-reducing denigration of the victim was greatest in the "strong shock to the black learner" condition. Furthermore, this denigration was expressed most by the highly ambivalent subjects—those who revealed both anti-black attitudes and "sympathy with the racial underdog."

4. The Indirect Expression of Modern Prejudice: Ambivalence, denial, even guilt all act to cause modern antiblack prejudice to be expressed in increasingly indirect and subtle forms. Three such forms are: indirect micro-aggressions against blacks, avoidance of face-to-face interaction with blacks, and opposition to racial change for ostensibly nonracial reasons. The experiments just reviewed demonstrate how modern prejudice is acted out in micro-aggressions, such as less help and longer shocks. From a psychoanalytic perspective, Kovel (1970, 263) stressed the avoidance mechanism as a means of keeping race out of mind. Thus, avoidance operates nonverbally in interracial interaction in such ways as greater distance, a less friendly voice, less eye contact and shorter interviews.

Survey evidence suggests that opposition to racial change for apparently nonracial reasons is a widespread expression of modern prejudice. As noted, white Americans overwhelmingly reject blatant forms of discrimination. About 90% believe black and white children should attend "the same schools," and recall that 95% favor equal job opportunity. Yet in 1978 only 24% believed the federal government should "see to it that white and black children go to the same school," and this percentage declined from 43% in 1966. Likewise, in 1975 only 34% agreed that the federal government should "see to it that the blacks get fair treatment in jobs," a percentage that remained constant from 1964 (Converse et al. 1980, 87, 91).

Using the older model of direct racial bigotry, one could dismiss such contradictions by arguing that the large majorities who oppose abstract discrimination are simply giving lip service to the new norms but do not really mean what they say. This interpretation, however, cannot explain why the same white respondents do not pay lip service to these norms on a variety of other items, including such concrete remedies as busing and affirmative action. Indeed, this old-style interpretation misses the essence of modern prejudice. There is considerable evidence for accepting these survey data largely at face value: whites do oppose both blatant discrimination and concrete remedies to correct them. This apparent contradiction is fueled by subjective threat and shaped by a particular conception of opportunity in America.

5. *Subjective Threat:* Many commentators on American race relations, both in the mass media and the social sciences, adopt a rational, self-interest model. They argue that it is the objective threat of racial change that understandably motivates much white opposition. This view postulates that "realistic" white resistance is caused by the fear of having black families as neighbors, having one's children transported to interracial schools, and having affirmative action programs at work. As reasonable as this argument may seem, repeated studies using a wide variety of measures and samples show objective threat of racial change to be a weak predictor of white racial attitudes and behavior (Bobo 1983; Caditz 1975; Kelley 1974; Kinder & Rhodebeck 1982, 203–13; Kinder & Sears 1981; Jacobson 1978; McConahay 1982, 714–17; McClendon & Pestello 1982; Sears, Hensler & Speer 1979, 380; Sears & Kinder 1971, 66–8; Sears, Lau, Tyler & Allen 1980, 670; Weidman 1975). Whites directly involved in racial change are generally not more resistant; in fact, they are often less resistant (even after controlling for possible self-selection biases).

Much of the same research, however, shows that subjective threat—perceived dangers from racial alterations rather than objective involvement—does motivate white opposition. Just as imagined dangers are generally far worse than real threats, the vague feeling that most black demands threaten one's life-style can easily generate more defensiveness than can the actual programs of change. Thus, the perception of fraternal deprivation—the sense that one's own group is being unfairly surpassed and ignored—is a consistent predictor of white votes against black mayoralty candidates in Gary, Cleveland, Newark, and Los Angeles (Vanneman & Pettigrew 1972). These feelings are further heightened by political and media use of such emotionally charged labels as "reverse discrimination." In addition, those whites who already harbor antiblack attitudes are more likely to perceive such a threat; in other words, racial prejudice and subjective threat are interrelated.

6. *Individualistic Conceptions of Opportunity in America:* The various aspects of modern prejudice become more understandable when placed within a broader context of the prevalent beliefs white Americans have about the nation's social structure. ...

A 1980 national telephone survey reported by Kluegel and Smith (1982; 1983) shows that 92% of whites regard their chance of "getting ahead" as equal to or better than average. Moreover, 78% think they have achieved a standard of living beyond that of their family of origin. Their own experience, therefore, tells them that America is a land of opportunity; they worked hard and "made it." This success, consistent with their work ethic values, leads most whites to adopt "the dominant ideology" (Huber & Form 1973, 1–14): Opportunity is available for the talented and ambitious and achievement is individually determined. Therefore, the unequal distribution of rewards in society is just, for wealth reflects effort and ability. This ideology leads a majority of Americans to explain poverty with individualistic reasons (lack of effort, thrift, morals, and ability of the poor) rather than structural reasons (tax structure and failure of government and industry to provide good training, sufficient jobs, and decent wages) (Feagin 1975, 91–102; Huber & Form 1973, 100–17).

Within this context, it is not surprising that for whites racial discrimination is not a particularly salient phenomenon. White 49% of whites surveyed thought that "some" discrimination exists, blacks are thought to have as good a chance to get ahead as "the average person in America," and to be the beneficiaries of "some" or "a lot" of positive "preferential treatment" and of "great" improvements in their chances to succeed. If blacks are doing that well in current American society, it follows that such remedies as school desegregation and affirmative action are not necessary. With this presumed "declining significance of race," the explanation for continued black poverty is simply the same ostensibly nonracial reason that accounts for white poverty—sloth. Every black "success case" in the new middle class can be seen as "proof" that skin color is no longer a barrier to achievement. Given the inordinate attention devoted to them by such institutions as the mass media and the administration, these "success cases" are the most visible to the white world. Consequently, this racial subcase of the dominant ideology of individualism is further enhanced.

Modern prejudice is subtle and indirect. It is a part of widely and deeply held values, and it is reinforced institutionally. Old-fashioned bigotry can still be found throughout the nation, but confusion between it and modern prejudice obscures the current phenomenon. In fact, it is its careful separation from the older, cruder types of bigotry that helps to distinguish these new patterns of racism. ...

REFERENCES

Bobo, L. 1983. Whites' opposition to busing: Symbolic racism or realistic group conflict? *J. Person. Soc. Psych.* 45:1196–1210.

Caditz, J. 1975. Dilemmas over racial integration: Status consciousness vs. direct threat. *Sociol. Inquiry* 45(4):51–8.

Converse, P. E. et al. 1980. *American social attitudes data sourcebook: 1947–1978.* Cambridge: Harvard Univ. Press.

Crosby, F., S. Bromely, and L. Saxe. 1980. Recent unobtrusive studies of black and white discrimination and prejudice: A literature review. *Psych. Bull.* 87:546–63.

Donnerstein, E., and M. Donnerstein. 1973. Variables in interracial aggression: Potential ingroup censure. *J. Person. Soc. Psych.* 27:143–50. 1976. Variables in interracial aggression. *J. Soc. Psych.* 100:111–21.

Feagin, J. R. 1975. *Subordinating the poor.* Englewood Cliffs, N.J.: Prentice-Hall.

Gaertner, S. 1976. Nonreactive measures in racial attitude research: A focus on "liberals." In *Towards the elimination of racism,* ed. P. A. Katz, 183–211. New York: Pergamon.

Hendricks, M., and R. Bootzin. 1976. Race and sex as stimuli for negative affect and physical avoidance. *J. Soc. Psychol.* 98:111–20.

Huber, J., and W. H. Form. 1973. *Income and ideology.* New York: Free Press.

jacobson, C. K. 1978. Desegregation rulings and public attitude changes: White resistance or resignation? *Am. J. Sociol.* 84:698–705.

Jones, J. M. 1972. *Prejudice and racism.* Reading, MA: Addison-Wesley.

Katz, I., D. C. Glass, and S. Cohen. 1973. Ambivalence, guilt, and the scapegoating of minority group victims. *J. Exp. Soc. Psych.* 9:423–36.

Kelley, J. 1974. The politics of school busing. *Pub. Opinion Quart.* 38:23–39.

Kelman, H. C. 1961. Processes of opinion change. *Pub. Opinion Quart.* 25:57–78.

Kinder, D. R., and L. A. Rhodebeck. 1982. Continuities in support for racial equality, 1972 to 1976. *Pub. Opinion Quart.* 46:195–215.

Kinder, D. R., and D. O. Sears. 1981. Symbolic racism versus racial threats to the good life. *J. Person. Soc. Psych.* 40:414–31.

Kluegel, J. R., and E. R. Smith. 1982. Whites' beliefs about blacks' opportunity. *Am. Sociol. Rev.* 47:518-32. 1983. Affirmative action attitudes: Effects of self-interest, racial affect, and stratification beliefs on whites' views. *Soc. Forces* 61:797–824.

Kovel, J. 1970. *White racism: A psychohistory.* New York: Pantheon.

McClendon, M. J. and F. P. Pestello, 1982. White opposition: To busing or to desegregation? *Soc. Sci. Quart.* 63:70–82.

McConahay, J. B. 1982. Self-interest versus racial attitudes as correlates of anti-busing attitudes in Louisville: Is it the busses or the blacks? *J. of Politics* 44:692–720.

Pettigrew, T. F. 1979. Racial change and social policy. *Annals Am. Acad. Political and Soc. Sci.* 441:114–31. 1980. The changing—not declining—significance of race. *Contemp. Sociol.* 9:19–21. 1981. The case for metropolitan approaches to public school desegregation. In *Race and schooling in the city,* eds. A. Yarmolinsky, L. Liebman, and C. S. Schelling, 163–81. Cambridge: Harvard Univ. Press.

Sears, D. C., C. P. Hensler, and L. Speer. 1979. Whites' opposition to "busing": Self-interest or symbolic politics? *Am. Pol. Sci. Rev.* 73:369–84.

Sears, D. C., and D. R. Kinder. 1971. Racial tensions and voting in Los Angeles. In *Los Angeles: Viability and prospects for metropolitan leadership,* ed. W. Z. Hirsch, 51–88. New York: Praeger.

Sears, D. C., R. R. Lau, T. R. Tyler, and H. M. Allen. 1980. Self-interest or symbolic politics in policy attitudes and presidential voting. *Am. Pol. Sci. Rev.* 74:670–84.

Ward, C. O., M. P. Zanna, and J. Cooper. 1974. The nonverbal mediation of self-fulfilling prophecies in interracial interaction. *J. Exp. Soc. Psychol.* 10:109–20.

Wispe, L. G., and H. G. Freshley. 1971. Race, sex, and the sympathetic helping behavior: The broken bag caper. *J. Person. Soc. Psychol.* 17:59–65.

6

Social Psychology's "Racism"

BYRON M. ROTH

Most readers of [*The Public Interest*] and similar journals are familiar with the critique of the civil-rights agenda—especially the policies of forced busing and admissions or hiring quotas—that Thomas Sowell, Nathan Glazer, Charles Murray, and others have advanced. Such readers know that most Americans have opposed these polices all along; they think that this opposition testifies to the good sense of the American electorate.

But the reaction of most social scientists, in particular social psychologists, is quite different. Social psychologists generally support such policies, and they have difficulty understanding why others do not. In fact, their attempts to explain the opposition are almost invariably demeaning to the American people. The "problem" that they think requires an explanation is well stated by Donald Kinder:

> Denial of equal rights and opportunities to blacks no longer enjoys majority support. On voting rights, public accommodations, housing, and employment practices, racist sentiment has drastically diminished; in some cases it has virtually disappeared. ... This is a striking change and a momentous achievement. Nevertheless, political conflict over racial matters has not exactly disappeared. Indeed, affirmative action, racial quotas, "forced busing," and the "welfare mess" are among the most contentious public issues of our time. Forty years after Myrdal, in the wake of dramatic changes in public opinion and social custom, *why do so many white Americans continue to resist efforts designed to bring about racial equality?* [Emphasis added.]

Instead of taking the opposition to affirmative action at face value, understanding it as the product of honest disagreement over how best to achieve racial equality, many social scientists see it as an attempt to "resist" equality. In trying to explain that resistance, their theories caricature affirmative action's opponents as hopelessly naive, secretly prejudiced, or venal and uncaring. Studiously avoiding the many well-known and well-received critiques of affirmative-action policies, the theories reveal a singular insularity among social scientists.

THE NAIVETÉ EXPLANATION

The least ingenious explanation of the public's disagreement with the civil-rights agenda is that the electorate is naive. According to this view, Americans do not understand how severely our society is stratified, and how many difficulties blacks and other minorities face in their efforts to achieve "equity." Americans who believe in the Protestant ethic are said to possess a childlike faith in individualism. In their book *Race and Equality,* Paul Sniderman of Stanford and Michael Hagen of Berkeley comment as follows on Americans' belief in this "folk ideology":

> Individualism, then, is an ethic: It is a bedrock belief in the ethic of self-reliance. Individuals must take care of themselves. They must not pretend to be victims of circumstance, or ask for specific favors, in an effort to get others to do for them what they should do for themselves. ...
>
> Individualism, so conceived, is an ungenerous idea. It is not ungenerous in the sense of being misanthropic. But it refuses to acknowledge that some are in fact handicapped and must overcome obstacles that are not of their making and that others do not face. In this sense the individualist lacks empathy for those disadvantaged by race or by poverty or by gender. ...

According to the authors, the naive popular culture spreads such views. "[f]or it deals directly with ideas about success and failure—about the importance of individual effort, for example, as expressed in the conviction that anyone with talent and a willingness to work can get ahead in America.

If you agree with the following statements, the authors contend, you adhere to the ethic of "ungenerous individualism":

> It's a lack of skill and abilities that keep many black people from getting a job. It's not just because they are black. When a black person is trained to do something, he is able to get a job.
>
> Black people may not have the same opportunities as whites, but many blacks haven't prepared themselves enough to make use of the opportunities that come their way.

On the other hand, if you agree with the following, you exhibit a more sophisticated and generous understanding: "Even with the new programs, minorities still face the same old job discrimination once the program is over." In other words, if one rejects the view that coercive government action is necessary to counter discrimination, one ungenerously resists racial equality. There is not the slightest indication that Sniderman and Hagen have considered that the "wrong" responses to their statements may be more correct than their preferred alternatives. Conceivably, the public has learned something in the last twenty-five years that many social scientists have yet to understand: that if anything, the faith of poor blacks in the liberal agenda—their reliance on government support—has worsened their plight. Nor do Sniderman and Hagen seem aware that minorities may be harmed by accepting the thesis that American society is hopelessly discriminatory.

Other researchers also attribute hostility toward quotas to American naiveté. In a 1983 *Social Forces* article on attitudes toward affirmative action, James Kluegal and Eliot Smith argue that while whites—recognizing that blacks suffered from discrimination in the past—support programs to "assist blacks to acquire skills," they nevertheless oppose preferential hiring quotas "because they are thought to violate dominant equity norms." This opposition, the authors contend, is based on ignorance:

> The premise that affirmative action programs are necessary to equalize opportunity requires that whites believe that the stratification system currently does not provide equal opportunity for all persons and groups. In this regard the seeming insensitivity of whites to the socioeconomic disadvantage of blacks may stem more from racial segregation, and the resulting limited and naive perspective whites have on blacks' circumstances, than from prejudice and racism.

In fact, however, most Americans are not naive about how people get ahead in America: Kluegal and Smith are. As shown by Thomas Sowell, William Julius Wilson, and Ben Wattenberg, or simply by a fair reading of the census data, most of the evidence indicates that those who adopt the work ethic do quite well in America. Kluegal and Smith certainly offer no evidence to the contrary.

SYMBOLIC RACISM

By far the most influential explanation for opposition to busing and quotas is offered by John M. McConahay, David O. Sears, and Donald Kinder. They and various coworkers have generated a sizable collection of works that blame this opposition on what they call "symbolic racism." All objective measures of white Americans' attitudes reveal a steady decline in racism. But since opposition to busing and quotas remains high, these researchers hypothesize that some more elusive form of racism may explain it. Kinder and Sears argue that Americans rationalize this new racism in terms of a commitment to traditional values.

> In years gone by, it was easy to specify the content of this early-learned prejudice: it centered on intentional and legitimate discrimination and segregation. However, over the past thirty years, white opposition to equal opportunity has sharply declined. On voting rights, schools, public accommodations, housing, and employment practices, segregationist sentiment has all but disappeared. White America has become, in principle at least, racially egalitarian—a momentous and undeniably significant change. Since the explicitly segregationist, white supremacist view has all but disappeared, it can no longer be a major political force.
>
> What has replaced it, we suggest, is a new variant that might be called symbolic racism. This we define as a blend of antiblack affect and the kind of traditional American moral values embedded in the Protestant ethic[,] ... a form of resistance to change in the racial status quo based on moral feelings that blacks violate self-reliance, the work ethic, obedience, and discipline. Whites may feel that individuals should be rewarded on their merits, which in turn should be based on hard work and diligent service. Hence symbolic racism should find its most vociferous expression on political issues that involve "unfair" government assistance to blacks ... ; welfare ... ; "reverse discrimination" and racial quotas ... ; "forced" busing ... ; or "free" abortions for the poor. ...

Thus agreement with traditional American values provides a cover for the expression of deeply felt prejudice, and hence is evidence of racial hostility.

But how do Kinder and Sears know whether people who hold such views are racists and not simply upholders of traditional values? To distinguish opposition based on racial animosity from opposition based on political belief would require independently validated measures of each, which Kinder and Sears do not provide. Instead they measure "symbolic racism" by means of a questionnaire that hopelessly confuses the two types of opposition. They based their 1981 paper on the attitudes of voters in Los Angeles mayoral elections, for instance, on responses to the following questions:

1. Do you think that most Negroes/blacks who receive money from welfare programs could get along without it if they tried, or do they really need the help?

2. [Agree or disagree:] Because of past discrimination it is sometimes necessary to set up quotas for admission to college of minority group students.

3. Do you think Los Angeles city officials pay more, less, or the same attention to a request or complaint from a black person?

4. Of the groups on the card, are there any which you think have gained more than they are entitled to?

5. [Agree or disagree:] It is wrong to set up quotas to admit black students to college who don't meet the usual requirements.

6. [Agree or disagree:] Over the past two years blacks have got more than they deserve.

7. In Los Angeles, would you say many, some, or only a few blacks miss out on jobs or promotions because of racial discrimination?

8. [Agree or disagree:] Negroes/blacks shouldn't push where they're not wanted.

9. [Agree or disagree:] Busing elementary school children to schools in other parts of the city only harms their education.

10. [Agree or disagree:] In some cases it is best for children to attend elementary schools outside their neighborhood.

11. Are you in favor or opposed to the busing of children to achieve racial desegregation?

12. If the Supreme Court ordered busing to achieve racial desegregation of public schools would you be opposed to it?

13. [Agree or disagree:] If necessary, children should be bused to achieve racial desegregation.

One's symbolic-racism "score" is determined by how many questions one answers in the "wrong" way. Those who oppose busing and quotas are therefore guaranteed to score high on symbolic racism, even if they get credit for all the other items. If they also disapprove of welfare policies and the political activism of black militants, they would be considered hopeless symbolic racists. Item 8, "Blacks shouldn't push where they're not wanted," does seem to suggest segregationist attitudes. But even this is not clear, for while 64 percent of respondents agreed with that statement, 70 percent of the people who responded to a questionnaire distributed at the same time and reported in the same article said that they would not mind if a black moved next door to them.

The authors advance no evidence to show that this new "symbolic" racism (which seems simply to mirror the attitudes held by many reputable public figures at the time) was related to real racism. In fact, Sears's coworker John B. McConahay stressed in an earlier paper that there was no relation. McConahay found that symbolic racism was most highly correlated with such things as identifying with the Republican party and believing that children should be taught patriotism in schools. This finding is hardly surprising, since the symbolic-racism scale really measures political conservatism. The only independent validation of Kinder and Sears's symbolic-racism scale was the voting behavior of the respondents. Those who scored high on symbolic racism (i.e., expressed prevailing conservative views) were found to be more likely to vote for a white Republican (Yorty) in the mayoral election than a black Democrat (Bradley). This perfectly rational voting pattern was characterized by Kinder and Sears as "antiblack voting behavior."

Yet despite these weaknesses, Kinder and Sears's research won "the 1978 Gordon Allport Intergroup Relations Prize from the Society for the Psychological Study of Social Issues." Carried out "under the direction of Thomas Pettigrew" (a highly respected social psychologist), the research is widely reported in most introductory texts in social psychology as solid scientific evidence of the racism of American society.

It is true that the Sears, Kinder, and McConahay position has met some criticism. Paul Sniderman (creator of the "naiveté" explanation) and Philip E. Tetlock have attacked as "scandalous" the confusion of racism and political conservatism. But Sniderman and Tetlock have also insisted that it is an error to claim that old-fashioned racism has "all but disappeared." Kinder's reply is revealing. He agrees that he and Sears overstated the case, but then points to much research that shows a very weak connection between traditional racial prejudice and attitudes on such matter as busing:

> McConahay (1982) found a small effect of traditional racial prejudice on opposition to busing in Louisville; Bobo (1983) found no effect in 1972 and a tiny effect in 1976 using national samples; Sears and Kinder (1971) and Kinder and Sears (1981) put the question aside since racial prejudice, measured in traditional ways, had virtually vanished from the Los Angeles suburbs; only McClendon (1985) found a sizable effect due to old fashioned racism. By these results, the political impact of traditional forms of racial prejudice pale against those due to symbolic racism.

"Symbolic racism," then, is a phantom conjured up to substitute for a racism that has declined in significance.

Missing in the exchange between Kinder and his critics, and in this literature in general, is any hint of the possibility that people oppose preferential hiring out of a *well-reasoned* attachment to traditional American values. There is not the slightest indication that America's prosperity and the wealth of opportunities that have traditionally been open to new immigrants are in part accounted for by those very values. The assumption that America is an ungenerous and racist society is simply too deeply ingrained in the liberal orthodoxy to be challenged by evidence to the contrary, even the evidence that the researchers gather themselves. No one questions, furthermore, how a prejudice that is so hard to detect can also do enough harm to require the coercive abandonment of widely shared and important values.

"REALISTIC" GROUP-CONFLICT THEORY

Many researchers have attempted to determine whether white opposition to affirmative-action policies is the result of symbolic racism or of the "real" racial threat that those policies purportedly pose to whites. Lawrence Bobo, the leading spokesman for the view that real racial threat is involved, puts it this way:

> The central thesis underlying the present discussion is that racial attitudes reflect the existing economic, social and political relationships between black and white Americans; in other words, the real features of group relations and conflict. Specifically, American social organization allows and fosters in whites the belief that blacks, in so far as they demand changes in the racial status quo, are a threat to their lifestyles, as well as to other valued resources and practices. ... Further progress in the struggle for racial equality and integration such as affirmative action goals or quotas will likely ... upset some aspect of the social experience of most whites (e.g. eliminate segregated schools and housing). Therefore whites come to view a policy like busing as threatening to states of affairs with which they are quite comfortable—threatening to a social world and position in society they accept and value.

Bobo thinks that whites have a group interest in maintaining the racial status quo; he believes that improvements for blacks are "challenges to [whites'] group status or position." For Bobo "the contemporary features of inequality and group conflict are ... focused on the pace of change and matters of resource distribution (like access to quality schools)."

But what is the empirical basis for this group-conflict view? Sears and his coworkers had argued that actual self-interest was *not* important in determining opposition to such policies as busing. They found, for instance, that people who had children in school did not have different attitudes toward busing than those without children, or with children beyond school age. Bobo reanalyzed their data and reached similar conclusions. He thinks, however, that this finding is not critical, since "[p]eople can form an opinion about an ongoing and controversial issue like busing simply by thinking in terms of the interests of 'myself and people like me.'" Bobo identified the factors most highly associated with anti-busing sentiment and concluded:

> Perhaps the most significant result of the present research is the discovery that perceived threat and applied policy predispositions are the strongest predictor of whites' opposition to busing. ... Indeed, an apparent anomaly in the results points out the value of particular perceived threat variables. Questions about the *character* or methods of the civil rights movement ("Actions Hurtful" and "Actions Violent") *did not* influence opposition to busing, but questions concerned with the *pace* and *implications* of change did ("Civil Rights Push" and "Dislike Black Militants"). Taken together, these results go far in explaining the discrepancy between whites' tendency to endorse principles of integration and equality ... and the simultaneous tendency to reject specific integrationist policies like busing.

Yet why should opposition to busing be correlated with attitudes toward the pace of civil-rights change, but not with attitudes toward civil-rights methods? "Civil Rights Push" was measured by responses to this question: "Some say the civil rights people have been trying to push too fast. Others feel they haven't pushed fast enough. How about you? ... " "Actions Hurtful," on the other hand, was measured by responses to the following: "Do you think the actions black people have taken have, on the whole, helped their cause, or, on the whole, hurt their cause?" But given all the political heat that busing has generated, most people who oppose busing probably think that it decreases sympathy for blacks and thus hurts their cause. Bobo never quite resolves this "apparent anomaly." His confusing and seemingly contradictory findings simply do not justify his conclusion that whites think that blacks threaten their social status.

This is not to deny that some whites oppose affirmative action out of a real conflict of interest. After all, if a black applicant is given preferential admission to a prestigious university, a nonblack applicant must be denied a place. The same is true of minority set-asides and other affirmative-action programs. But Bobo's research does not directly address such issues. The survey does not ask respondents whether they believe that busing will harm their children's education, or whether their children will be endangered by being bused to an integrated school—even though such questions might clarify things. Nor does Bobo acknowledge that people may oppose busing and quotas because they believe them to endanger society by fostering group resentment and promoting intergroup hostility. Raising these questions, of course, would highlight the rational bases for opposition to affirmative action and busing. Like those whom he criticizes, Bobo ignores the possibility that people might honestly consider quotas and busing unwise and counterproductive.

WHERE IS THE UNDERCLASS?

One of the literature's most glaring weaknesses is its failure to consider class as an important determinant of perceptions about race. The "American public" whose responses to various questionnaires are analyzed is generally a middle-class population, whose attachment to the Protestant ethic is well-known. Middle-class Americans tend to place great value on home ownership, neighborhood respectability, and education. The questionnaires ask such people to take positions on "blacks." But to what blacks do the questions refer? All of them are surprisingly vague on this point, especially in light of the widely acknowledged chasm that has developed between middle-class blacks and "underclass" blacks. The incomes, educations, and lifestyles of the former are increasingly indistinguishable from those of their white counterparts. Underclass blacks, however, are marked by social pathologies—illegitimacy, crime, school failure, drug abuse, unemployment, and so on—that are alien to most members of the middle class, whether black or white. This dichotomy within the black population is ignored in the debates about the meaning of white attitudes toward busing and quotas.

Among the obvious reasons for whites' rejection of quotas, and for their refusal to see discrimination as the bugbear described by civil-rights advocates, is the fact that blacks—even very poor blacks—who hew to "middle-class" mores by postponing parenthood, finishing school, and avoiding drugs and crime are doing quite well; by contrast, those in the underclass, whose behavior violates those mores, fare badly. Given this undeniable reality, how is one supposed to choose between the following statements from Sniderman and Hagen's questionnaire?

> A. Many blacks have only themselves to blame for not doing better in life. If they tried harder, they'd do better.

> B. When two qualified people, one black and one white, are considered for the same job, the black won't get the job no matter how hard he tries.

To choose "A" is to be labeled "ungenerous" toward the plight of blacks, even though the statement is obviously correct. By contrast, the second statement is patently absurd. The contradictory responses that people give to such questionnaires does not point to their ambivalence about racial equality. Instead it suggests that the questionnaires were designed and interpreted by social scientists who are insulated from reality.

The researchers' obliviousness to the black underclass also calls into question their easy assertions about the extent of "old-fashioned redneck" racism. For instance, all researchers agree that support for segregation is a mark of real racism. It is typically measured by responses to questions like the following ones, asked by Gallup pollsters during 1978 and 1980:

1. Would you, yourself, have any objection to sending your children to school where a few of the children were black? [95 percent of the respondents said "no."]
2. Would you, yourself, have any objection to sending your children to school where half the children were black? [76 percent said "no."]
3. Would you, yourself, have any objection to sending your children to school where more than half the children were black? [42 percent said "no."]
4. If a black person came to live next door would you move? [86 percent said "no," 10 percent said that they might, and 4 percent said "yes."]
5. Would you move if black people came to live in great numbers in your neighborhood? [46 percent said "no," 33 percent said that they might, and 21 percent said "yes."]

Do the objections of a majority of white parents to their children's attending a largely black school indicate lingering racial hostility? Might they instead point to the *fact* (not merely the perception) that many such schools are dangerous places with inadequate educational standards? Do the 33 percent who said that they might move (and the 21 percent who said they would move) if large numbers of blacks moved into their neighborhoods reject integration "in practice"? Or do these figures reflect a concern that the "large numbers of blacks" might include many members of the underclass? Few members of the middle-class—whether white or black—see underclass blacks are desirable neighbors.

In truth, the hard data that supposedly buttress the analyses of whites' racial attitudes are susceptible to a wide variety of interpretations. By no means do the data justify social scientists in their competing and demeaning explanations of Americans' "resistance to racial equality."

Most Americans know—and are prepared to admit—that the lot of blacks in this country is often hard. These same Americans oppose paternalistic government policies that run counter to traditional American values; they consider such policies unsound, unwise, and unlikely to help blacks in the long run. All surveys indicate that Americans support efforts to assure blacks a fair shake. They also reveal a broad consensus that, given a fair shake, blacks can and should make it on their own. If the American people hold such beliefs, as this research suggests, perhaps they are correct and the social scientists who denounce them are wrong.

In 1975 Nathan Glazer, in his *Affirmative Discrimination,* said that America's use of racial quotas signals that

> we have abandoned the first principle of a liberal society, that the individual and the individual's interests and good and welfare are the test of a good society, for we now attach benefits and penalties to individuals simply on the basis of their race, color and national origin. The implications of this new course are an increasing consciousness of the significance of group membership, an increasing divisiveness on the basis of race, color and national origin, and a spreading resentment among disfavored groups against favored groups.

Glazer was right to deplore this shift. Most Americans agreed with him all along. It appears at long last that the Supreme Court may have begun to see the wisdom of the public's good sense on these issues. Perhaps even the social scientists will ultimately get the message.

7

Does Modern Prejudice Exist?
A Comment on Pettigrew and Roth

FRED L. PINCUS

Although Thomas Pettigrew (Chapter 5) and Byron Roth (Chapter 6) have dramatically different views on prejudice and race relations in the 1990s, they agree that the following contentions hold true:

- Traditional white prejudice toward blacks has declined; that is, most whites agree with abstract principles of integration and racial equality.
- Most whites *believe* that discrimination against blacks has declined and that blacks who hold traditional American values can be economically successful.
- Most whites *believe* that the lack of success among blacks is attributable to a defective culture, especially to lack of motivation and pathological family structure.
- Most whites *believe* that many policies intended to implement racial equality, such as court-ordered busing and affirmative action, are unnecessary and unfair.

This level of agreement is quite remarkable, given the different perspectives of the two authors.

The authors' disagreements are even greater. On the one hand, Pettigrew argues that whites are *mistaken* in their beliefs. Racial discrimination, he maintains, still exists in a variety of forms and is the *main cause* of black poverty. Motivational and family problems among blacks, to the extent that they exist, are the *result* of discrimination and poverty, not the cause. Finally, Pettigrew, a political liberal, argues that government programs such as court-ordered school busing and affirmative action are essential if racial equality is to be achieved.

According to Pettigrew, a new cluster of antiblack beliefs and feelings has replaced traditional antiblack attitudes. He refers to these beliefs as "modern prejudice." One of the major components of modern prejudice, Pettigrew notes, is its *indirect* expression. Traditional pejorative terms such as *nigger* have been replaced by more "respectable" terms like *welfare cheat*. Traditional opposition to school integration has been replaced by opposition to "forced busing," one method of implementing integration. The traditional belief in the biological inferiority of blacks has been replaced by criticisms of their cultural "pathology." Blacks who do not accept traditional American values, say some whites, can expect to be poor—or may even *deserve* to be poor.

Although Pettigrew does not offer an empirical measure of modern prejudice, several other social scientists have developed a measure of "symbolic racism," a closely related concept. According to John McConahay, David Sears, and Donald Kinder (whom Pettigrew cites in Chapter 5), most whites develop deep antiblack feelings during childhood but can no longer express these feelings directly because of the social norms against prejudice. Instead, whites express their antiblack feelings by criticizing blacks for violating traditional values and by opposing policies that promote integration and equality.

Roth, a political conservative, agrees that many whites dislike black *underclass behavior* and oppose many liberal government policies. He disagrees with Pettigrew and other liberal social scientists that these attitudes constitute modern prejudice or symbolic racism. According to Roth, whites are *correct* in their assessment that the pathology of black culture is the major cause of black poverty. Whites are accepting of blacks who work hard and hold traditional values, says Roth, but they object to the behavior patterns associated with the black underclass. Many blacks on welfare really could get along without it, continues Roth, and busing white children to predominantly black schools in poor neighborhoods is dangerous and unnecessarily intrusive to white children and their families. These attitudes, says Roth, are expressions of political conservatism and the belief in traditional American values. To say that they constitute some new form of racial prejudice, he continues, is an intellectual hoax.

How can we make any sense out of these conflicting views? Although the scholars who study race relations do not always agree on important issues, it is possible to clarify some of the major questions facing them. Roth is certainly on solid ground when he argues that not all conservatives are necessarily prejudiced and that mere opposition to liberal programs should not be equated with prejudice. Liberals and radicals are far too quick to assume that white opponents of hiring quotas would refuse to employ minority workers or that white opponents of court-ordered busing would refuse to send their children to a desegregated neighborhood school.

On the other hand, Pettigrew also has a strong argument when he says that much of the opposition to liberal programs and underclass pathology is more than just political ideology. This opposition is often expressed in political behavior. For example, we have seen numerous examples of how some conservative politicians have used racial symbols associated with modern prejudice to appeal to antiblack feelings among white voters. In the 1991 election for governor of Louisiana, for instance, David Duke, a former grand dragon of the Ku Klux Klan, won more than half the white vote by making "welfare cheats" and "reverse discrimination" central components of his campaign. Although Duke insisted that he was not being antiblack, his use of the symbols of modern prejudice was evident.

An incident from the 1988 presidential election can also be used as an example of modern prejudice. Willie Horton, a black convicted murderer who was a prisoner in Massachusetts, murdered and raped a white woman while on a weekend leave from prison. Former President George Bush's campaign committee publicized this incident, ostensibly to portray the soft-on-crime policies of Massachusetts Governor Michael Dukakis, Bush's Democratic opponent. In addition to the law-and-order message, all of the ads feature pictures of Horton, looking dangerous and dark-skinned. According to Bush's critics, no words were necessary to convey the stereotype of black males as criminals lusting after white women. Is this an example of modern prejudice, of traditional prejudice, or of a nonprejudiced ad that is simply in bad taste?

A half-century ago, Gunnar Myrdal (1944) described "the American dilemma" as a conflict between antiblack prejudice and the American belief in equal opportunity. He hoped that white Americans would become increasingly disturbed about this contradiction and voluntarily move toward more support for equality.

It took the civil rights movement of the 1950s and the black power movement of the 1960s to force whites to dismantle the more blatant aspects of legal discrimination. Only then did it become socially unacceptable to express traditional prejudice in public. Yet, although most whites do not see themselves as prejudiced, many continue to be fearful and resentful of blacks and other people of color. These feelings, often expressed indirectly through symbols, are intertwined with the perception that blacks reject traditional American values such as hard work, respect for authority, and the sanctity of the nuclear family.

Modern prejudice is expressed toward other people of color as well. Cultural criticisms are a major component of anti-Latino attitudes. Mexicans and Puerto Ricans, for example, are criticized for relying too much on Spanish and not learning English fast enough. Bilingual classrooms and street signs are seen as threats to the integrity of American culture.

The Japanese, too, are still viewed as threatening, but the nature of the threat has changed. They are no longer seen as the cunning "yellow peril" who care nothing for human life, as depicted in old World War II movies. (Recall that these movies emphasized suicide missions by Japanese pilots that threatened American sailors and human waves of Japanese soldiers that threatened to overrun American soldiers and Marines.) Rather, Japan now threatens to overrun our economy. Japanese-owned companies, and their owners and workers, are disliked for "stealing American jobs" through "unfair competition." Japanese capitalism is also seen as a threat to American culture. Many Americans of all races were outraged upon learning that the Nintendo corporation planned to buy a major-league baseball team and another Japanese company wanted to run the concessions in Yosemite National Park.

Japan has, indeed, challenged American capitalism; but so has Germany. Yet one hears few stories about Germans stealing American jobs, engaging in unfair trade practices, or threatening American culture. This double standard toward economic competitors mirrors the greater prejudice toward the Japanese than toward the Germans during World War II, when the two countries were political enemies of the United States. (Only the Japanese were put into American concentration camps.) Now, during the 1990s, the traditional prejudice toward Japan is simply being redefined to make it more socially acceptable.

Getting back to Chapters 5 and 6, note that Roth makes some important empirical criticisms of the Pettigrew-Kinder-Sears approach to modern prejudice. In the scale used to measure modern prejudice/symbolic racism, for example, Roth correctly argues that a negative answer to the question "Are you in favor of or opposed to the busing of children to achieve racial desegregation?" should not be used to indicate the existence of prejudice; rather it may simply indicate the presence of conservatism.

On the other hand, empirical data strongly suggest that opposition to busing is more than simply an indication of conservative objection to government intervention. For example, Howard Schuman, Charlotte Steeh, and Lawrence Bobo (1985) studied American attitudes toward government intervention between the middle 1960s and middle 1970s. Although white support for government intervention in school desegregation declined during this period, white support for government intervention into the desegregation of public accommodations increased. Whites also exhibited increased support for federal involvement in universalistic health care. Presumably, white conservatives should have opposed all of these policies.

Pettigrew has argued that much of the opposition to court-ordered busing is caused by modern prejudice. How would Roth respond to these apparently contradictory findings?

Note that some of the statements included in the questionnaire formulated by D. R. Kinder and D. C. Sears (see Chapter 6) go beyond conservative ideology. For example, "Over the past two years, blacks have got more than they deserve" and "Negroes/blacks shouldn't push where they're not wanted" come closer to measuring modern prejudice.

Roth offers other empirical criticisms. If modern (symbolic) prejudice were a valid concept, he says, someone who scores high on tests of modern prejudice would also score high on tests of traditional prejudice. Since empirical studies have shown that there is no relationship between modern and traditional prejudice, he concludes, the concept of modern prejudice has no validity.

In fact, the research shows *low* but *positive* correlations between traditional and modern prejudice. Whether or not these correlations are meaningful is a matter of interpretation, on which experts can differ. Roth may be correct when he argues that the correlations should be higher if modern prejudice were a valid concept. However, the low correlations may be due to poor measurement.

Roth also makes the following statements: "Most of the evidence indicates that those who adopt the work ethic do quite well in America" and "Blacks ... who hew to 'middle-class' mores by postponing parenthood, finishing school, and avoiding drugs and crime are doing quite well." The implicit assumption here is that members of the black underclass do not take advantage of available opportunities because they lack middle-class culture.

This is only one side of a larger controversy: Are blacks poor because of their attitudes and culture, or are they poor because they lack economic opportunity? In evaluating the aforementioned statements made by Roth, readers should consider the following points:

- We can assume that members of the so-called underclass would be excluded from the category of year-round full-time workers. Yet income data collected by the federal government show that white year-round full-time workers earn considerably more than comparable blacks and Hispanics, even after job category has been controlled for.
- It is true that black and Hispanic year-round full-time workers who have more education tend to have higher incomes, more skilled jobs, and lower unemployment rates than less educated blacks and Hispanics. But it is also true that whites, at the same level of education, tend to have higher incomes, better jobs, and lower unemployment rates than comparable blacks and Hispanics.

Which factor best explains these data: racial differences in middle-class values, or the continued existence of racial discrimination in employment, supported in part by modern prejudice?

Clearly, further research—especially more empirical documentation—is needed before we can decide whether modern prejudice is a valid concept. Thus far, critics of modern prejudice have not refuted the argument that some conservative beliefs can be indirect expressions of antiblack attitudes, nor have they convincingly argued that black inequality is caused by black culture rather than continuing white prejudice and discrimination.

REFERENCES

Myrdal, Gunnar. 1944. *An American Dilemma: The Negro Problem and Modern Democracy.* New York: Harper.

Schuman, Howard, Charlotte Steeh, and Lawrence Bobo. 1985. *Racial Attitudes in America: Trends and Interpretations.* Cambridge: Harvard University Press.

PART 3

Discrimination

Racial discrimination has been a prominent and ugly reality in the United States for more than four centuries. People of color have been treated differently than whites and have suffered physically, economically, culturally, psychologically, and politically.

Blacks were forcibly brought over from Africa in the sixteenth and seventeenth centuries as indentured servants and slaves. After the abolition of slavery in the mid-nineteenth century, southern states imposed an all-encompassing system of legal segregation that continued unabated until the 1960s. Even after the passage of the Civil Rights Act (1964), the Voting Rights Act (1965), and numerous other pieces of legislation and administrative guidelines, discrimination continues to be a widespread problem throughout the country.

Though never the victims of slavery, Hispanics were certainly the victims of white discrimination. The United States conquered Mexico during the nineteenth century and took over what is now the southwestern part of the United States. Puerto Rico has been an American colony since 1898. During the twentieth century, Hispanic immigrants, both documented and undocumented, have been disproportionately employed as migrant workers, low-paid restaurant and hotel workers, and workers in garment factory sweatshops.

Native Americans, of course, were the first targets of new American colonists. Their subjugation continued throughout subsequent generations as the country expanded westward. The military conquest and attempted extermination of Native Americans are infamous examples. The resettlement of conquered tribes on reservations was detrimental not only to their economies and their cultures but also to the developing culture of the United States.

Asians, too, have been the victims of white discrimination. Imported as low-paid contract railroad workers in the mid-nineteenth century, they were barely tolerated. A number of states passed laws prohibiting Chinese people from owning property. After these imported railroad workers were no longer needed, Congress in 1882 passed the Chinese Exclusion Act, which prevented further Chinese immigration. American immigration legislation in the first half of the twentieth century gave small quotas to potential immigrants from Asia, as well as to immigrants from Africa and Latin America. During World War II, Japanese residents on the West Coast, both citizens and noncitizens, were forced into concentration camps as potential "enemies of the state."

Yet people of color have not been the only victims of discrimination. White immigrants (especially non-Protestants from southern and eastern Europe) also have a history of mistreatment. Irish, Italian, and Polish immigrants have been denied employment and housing. And Catholics and Jews have suffered because of their religious beliefs. Indeed, anti-Jewish attitudes persist to this day. However, the discrimination against most of these white groups has been neither as persistent nor as intense as that toward people of color.

STATISTICAL DISPARITIES

Statistics collected by the federal government show the results of past and present discrimination against people of color. With the exception of Asians, people of color lag behind whites on all indicators of economic well-being.

The 1990 U.S. census provides the following data on median household income:

Asians	$36,784
Whites	$31,435
Hispanics	$24,156
Native Americans	$20,025
Blacks	$19,758

According to these figures, black household income is only 63 percent of white income and Hispanic household income is only 77 percent of white income (Barringer, 1992). Great disparities also characterize the median incomes of Asian households, such that Vietnamese and Cambodian incomes are similar to those of blacks.

Significant racial/ethnic differences can be found among individual workers as well. The following statistics, taken from the Current Population Reports (U.S. Bureau of the Census, 1992), apply to year-round full-time workers; part-time and intermittent full-time workers are excluded. In 1990, the median incomes for male year-round full-time workers were as follows: $30,598 for whites; $22,176 for blacks; and $20,556 for Hispanics. (Unfortunately, corresponding data for Asians and Native Americans were not reported.) Black males earned 72 percent of the income of white males, and Hispanic males earned only 67 percent of the income of white males.

Although female year-round full-time workers made less than comparable males, the racial/ethnic pattern for women is similar: $20,759 for whites; $18,838 for blacks; and $16,480 for Hispanics. The racial/ethnic gap among women is less than that among men. Black women earned 91 percent of the income of white women, and Hispanic women earned 79 percent of the income of white women.

Disparities in wealth are even greater than those in income. Whereas income refers to the money that comes in each year (wages, salary, dividends, interest, transfer payments, etc.), wealth refers to the value of what a person or household owns (from clothing and cars to corporate stocks and bonds). In 1988, median household net-worth (what is owned minus what is owed) was distributed as follows: $43,279 for whites; $4,169 for blacks; and $5,548 for Hispanics. White households possessed more than ten times the wealth of black households and almost eight times the wealth of Hispanic households (Eargle, 1990).

Unemployment differences between whites and people of color are also pronounced. The official unemployment rates for 1992, according to the Bureau of Labor Statistics, were as follows: 6.5 percent for whites; 14.1 percent for blacks; and 11.4 percent for Hispanics. Blacks were more than twice as likely to be unemployed than whites, whereas Hispanics were 1.8 times more likely to be unemployed than whites.

As troubling as these statistical disparities may be, the lack of progress in eliminating them is even more discouraging. For many years, the government has kept statistics on family income, which is slightly different than household income. In 1992, the most recent year reported, black families earned only 54 percent of the income made by white families—a figure identical to the 54 percent reported in 1959. Hispanic families in 1992 were *worse* off relative to whites than they had been in 1971, when the government first started keeping separate figures for Hispanics. In 1992, Hispanic families earned only 61 percent of the income made by white families, compared to 71 percent in 1971.

The unemployment gap has also held stable. Since 1959, black unemployment has been double that of whites. And more recently, since 1981, black unemployment has reached as high as 2.5 times that of whites. In fact, the 1991 figure—black unemployment 2.1 times higher than white unemployment—is the lowest gap recorded in a number of years.

Yet in spite of such negative figures overall, several positive statistical trends can be noted. For instance, the educational gap between blacks and whites has declined (as discussed in Part Six of this volume). In addition, the income gap between black two-parent families and comparable white families has been getting smaller. In 1992, black two-parent families earned 80 percent of the income made by white two-parent families; in 1970, the comparable figure was 70 percent. The implication of these findings will be discussed in the following sections.

EXPLANATIONS OF STATISTICAL DISPARITIES

Social scientists of all political persuasions acknowledge these statistical disparities. Most would agree that they can largely be explained by past and present discrimination. The majority of essays in Part Three support this argument. However, some social scientists maintain that discrimination plays only a minor role.

Conservatives, for example, often argue that cultural choices account for most of the differences noted. The underclass culture, which is said to be passed on from generation to generation, emphasizes living in the present rather than planning for the future, remaining dependent on welfare rather than trying to find employment, and feeling powerless about the chances of becoming upwardly mobile. This culture of poverty, say conservatives, prevents people from taking advantage of opportunities that might be available to them.

Using this analysis, conservatives argue that the difference between black and white family incomes can be attributed to the expectation and/or desire of poor women to bear and raise children without the help of a husband. More than 40 percent of black families are headed by women. If black women have chosen to bear children out of wedlock, especially as teenagers, they can expect to have low incomes, say conservatives.

The problem with comparing the incomes of *all* black and white families, according to conservatives, is that a large proportion of black female-headed families are being compared with predominantly two-parent white families (Murray, 1984). It is for this reason black families are reported to be making only 54 percent of the income earned by white families. If, on the other hand, one looks at the incomes of two-parent families only, the figure is 80 percent. The conclusion is that blacks who choose middle-class family structures are more economically successful than those who do not.

Rather than emphasizing cultural variables, some conservatives and a few liberals argue that differences in "human capital" (i.e., skills and credentials) can explain most of the statistical disparities. Black/white differences in unemployment and income, they argue, can be explained by differences in education. Blacks have lower levels of education and, therefore, can be expected to have fewer as well as lower-paying jobs. Conservatives often use the culture argument to explain the black/white differences in human capital. For example, black female-headed families are less able than white families to motivate their children to get an education and to help them while they are in school.

Unfortunately, neither the culture argument nor the human capital argument is supported by statistical evidence. Note, for instance, that the income of two-parent black families is about 80 percent of that of comparable white families. Although this gap is smaller than the 54 percent figure for all families, it is still substantial. In addition, although both partners in black two-parent families are much more likely to be working full time than white two-parent families, they still have lower incomes. Finally, looking at the data for female-headed families only, we find that black families make only 58 percent of the income earned by white families. At best, cultural differences in family structure explain only part of the statistical disparity between black and white family incomes.

Similarly, differences in human capital, as measured by years of education, cannot explain differences in individual income and unemployment. Even at the same level of education, blacks and Hispanics exhibit higher unemployment rates than whites. For example, among college graduates in 1991 who were 24 years of age and younger and no longer enrolled in school, black unemployment was 1.8 times higher and Hispanic unemployment 1.4 times higher than that for whites.

People of color have lower incomes than whites, even at the same level of education. For example, consider the median incomes of year-round full-time workers who were 25 years of age and older in 1990 and had five or more years of college. Black males earned only 77 percent of the income made by white males. Hispanic males earned only 89 percent of the white male income. And even for Asian male college graduates, the figure was only 90 percent (Barringer, 1992). The race/ethnic gap for females was much smaller—97 percent for blacks and 94 percent for Hispanics. Asian women college graduates were the only group to have earned incomes identical to those of comparable whites. Like the cultural argument, the human capital argument can, at best, explain only part of the statistical disparities discussed earlier.

In addition, there are conceptual problems with the two arguments. First, both assume that one can separate culture and human capital from discrimination. Second, the causal relationship between variables is questionable.

Conservatives tend to argue that both family structure and years of education are *independent* of discrimination. They also assume that female-headed families and low levels of education among blacks are cultural choices rather than results of discrimination. The correlation between female-headed families/low education and low income then becomes a causal relationship: *Culture* causes *female-headed families,* which in turn result in *low income.*

However, culture itself is in part the result of socioeconomic conditions. One might also argue that the large number of black female-headed families is a *result* of discrimination, not a cause. Unemployed and low-paid black men, for example, do not have enough money to support a family and, therefore, cannot fulfill one of the major social responsibilities associated with traditional definitions of masculinity. Fathering in the absence of responsibility for the children may be an alternative source of masculinity for such men.

Low levels of educational achievement are another result of discrimination. Schools in poor black neighborhoods are notoriously bad, in part because of teachers' low expectations, tracked curricula, and a lack of financial resources. A good argument can be made that the schools themselves, whether intentionally or not, are a major contributing factor to the low educational levels among poor blacks.

In addition, poor parents, who face both educational and employment discrimination themselves, are often unable to provide the same help to their children that middle-class parents can. Again, this factor is not just cultural in nature; it is also the result of prior discrimination.

A third explanation of statistical disparities that minimizes discrimination is associated with social scientists on the left rather than with conservatives. According to this "structural explanation," changes in the U.S. economy during the late twentieth century have disproportionately hurt poor people of color (Wilson, 1987). In order to maintain profits in the face of foreign competition, many U.S. manufacturers have tried to reduce labor costs by moving their operations outside of the country, where labor costs and taxes are cheaper and environmental regulations are more lax. The result has been a dramatic reduction in the number of available well-paying blue-collar jobs.

Since a high proportion of these jobs have been un-unionized, membership in labor unions has declined. This trend, combined with the attacks against unions by the Reagan administration, has resulted in a weakened labor movement.Finally, the new jobs in the growing service sector of the economy are disproportionately un-unionized and low paying, whereas the better-paying, more skilled positions require job experience and/or educational credentials.

All workers have been hurt by the loss of jobs and the decline in unionization—but black and Hispanic workers have been hurt the most. A greater proportion of minority families than white families have been dependent on unionized blue-collar jobs. Moreover, white displaced workers have fared better than minorities in their efforts to find new jobs. The concentration of poor blacks in the inner city and the movement of jobs to the suburbs have only exacerbated the situation (Wilson, 1987). Although these trends have little to do with discrimination, they tend to widen statistical disparities that may have been the result of previous discrimination.

We are sympathetic with the argument that "structural" changes have a disproportionately negative impact on people of color. However, as the chapters in Part Three will show, discrimination is still a significant and independent problem. Both discrimination and the larger socioeconomic trends operate concurrently and must be confronted together if racial/ethnic equality is to become a reality.

Fred L. Pincus ("From Individual to Structural Discrimination") begins this section of the book with a discussion of different types of discrimination. In addition to analyzing intentional discrimination at both the individual and structural levels, he argues that some social policies that appear to be race-neutral in intent have discriminatory *effects.*

William Julius Wilson ("The Limited Vision of Race: Discrimination Is Not the Sole Problem") argues that large-scale economic and political trends have a disproportionately negative impact on poor blacks. Wilson's proposed solution is a "holistic approach" that goes beyond the issue of race discrimination.

The remaining essays in Part Three document the continuing problem of race discrimination. Joe R. Feagin ("The Continuing Significance of Race: Antiblack Discrimination in Public Places") shows that even well-educated blacks are victims of discrimination. And Joleen Kirschenman and Kathryn M. Neckerman ("'We'd Love to Hire Them, But ...': The Meaning of Race for Employers") explain that employers discriminate against poor blacks and Hispanics because of behavior that is associated with poverty.

Douglas S. Massey ("Residential Segregation in American Cities") points out that people of color face housing discrimination in most major American cities. And the U.S. Commission on Civil Rights ("Employment Discrimination Against Asian Americans") discloses that even this culturally and economically diverse group faces discrimination in the workplace.

Evelyn Nakano Glenn ("Racial Ethnic Women's Labor: The Intersection of Race, Gender, and Class Oppression") discusses the triple oppression of black, Chinese, and Mexican women on the basis of race, gender, and class. Finally, Evelyn Torton Beck ("From 'Kike' to 'JAP': How Misogyny, Anti-Semitism, and Racism Construct the 'Jewish American Princess'") discusses the stereotypes of Jewish women and the discriminatory functions served by this stereotyping.

REFERENCES

Barringer, Felicity. 1992. "A Census Disparity for Asians in the U.S." *New York Times,* September 29.

Eargle, Judith. 1990. *Household Wealth and Asset Ownership: 1988.* Washington, D.C.: U.S. Bureau of the Census, Current Population Reports, Series P-70, No. 22.

Murray, Charles. 1984. *Losing Ground.* New York: Basic Books.

U.S. Bureau of the Census. 1992. Current Population Reports, Series P-60, No. 180, *Money Income of Households, Families and Persons in the U.S. 1991*. Washington, D.C.: Government Printing Office.

Wilson, William Julius. 1987. *The Truly Disadvantaged: The Inner City, the Underclass, and Public Policy*. Chicago: University of Chicago Press.

8

From Individual to Structural Discrimination

FRED L. PINCUS

People often think of racial discrimination in terms of the actions of individual prejudiced white people against individual people of color. However, as we have already shown, prejudice (an attitude) does not necessarily lead to discrimination (an overt behavior), and discrimination is not always caused by prejudice.

Group discrimination can exist at many different levels. An individual teacher who mistreats a Hispanic student is different from a school system that refuses to admit Hispanics. An individual personnel officer who decides not to hire a qualified black applicant is different from an entire state police department that refuses to hire black officers.

In their influential book *Black Power,* which was published more than a quarter of a century ago, Stokely Carmichael and Charles Hamilton differentiated "individual racism" from "institutional racism." The former involved the behavior of white individuals toward blacks and other minorities, and the latter involved the behavior of the entire white society and its institutions toward people of color.

Since *racism* is a pejorative word often used imprecisely, I shall modify the Carmichael/Hamilton typology and apply it to the concept of discrimination. My discussion here deals with three different types of race/ethnic discrimination: individual, institutional, and structural.

1. *Individual discrimination* refers to the behavior of individual members of one race/ethnic group that is intended to have a differential and/or harmful effect on the members of another race/ethnic group. This category includes a wide range of behavior by majority-group individuals or small groups—from anti-Asian graffiti and name calling, to an employer's refusal to hire blacks or a landlord's refusal to rent to Hispanics, to physical attacks against Native Americans.

According to this definition, actions by individual minority-group members against the majority group can also be characterized as "individual discrimination." Examples might include antiwhite graffiti by blacks, physical attacks against whites by Hispanics, or employment discrimination by Asians against whites. Each of these actions entails intentional antiwhite treatment that has a differential and/or harmful impact.

2. *Institutional discrimination* is quite different in that it refers to the policies of majority institutions, and the behavior of individuals who implement these policies and control these institutions, that are intended to have a differential and/or harmful effect on minority groups. A major goal of institutional discrimination is to keep minority groups in a subordinate position within society. Hence this concept is much broader than that of individual discrimination.

Sometimes, institutional discrimination is embodied in laws and government policy. From the 1890s until the 1950s, for example, most southern states had laws that *legally* discriminated between blacks and whites in all areas of life—from voting, education, and employment to religion, public accommodations, and restaurants. These laws had broad support among the white population and were even given the stamp of approval by the U.S. Supreme Court in 1896. Legal segregation, which has been referred to as the "Jim Crow System," is a clear example of institutional discrimination, and it goes far beyond the level of individual actions.

Blacks are not the only victims of institutional discrimination in the United States. Whites seized the land of Native Americans by brutally defeating them on the battlefield and then confining them to reservations. Treaties with Indian Nations were routinely broken by the government, and entire tribes were forcibly moved from one reservation to another, often with fatal results.

Asians have also been victims. After Japan attacked Pearl Harbor in 1941, all Japanese people on the West Coast were taken from their homes and placed in internment camps for the duration of the war. Both citizens and noncitizens were forced to sell their property at a great loss.

Although most discrimination by federal, state, and local governments is now illegal, examples of institutional discrimination can still be found. One such example is "gerrymandering," the illegal drawing of electoral districts in such a way as to intentionally minimize the electoral power of minority groups. Police and fire departments in many cities across the country have illegally refused to hire and promote *qualified* blacks and Hispanics at the same rate as comparably qualified whites. (This practice has resulted in a series of lawsuits and controversial affirmative action programs that we will discuss later in the book.) And even the prestigious Federal Bureau of Investigation illegally discriminated against black and Hispanic agents until 1992, when the FBI entered into a consent decree to end a lawsuit by black agents.

Institutional discrimination can be detected in the private sector as well. Real estate associations often "steer" blacks away from white neighborhoods and show them houses and apartments in predominantly minority neighborhoods. Banks in various cities have "redlined" certain minority areas (that is, they have refused to grant mortgages to people who live in these areas regardless of whether they meet the financial qualifications specified), and they have granted smaller mortgages at higher interest rates. Moreover, large corporations have been convicted of racial discrimination in hiring and promotion, and private social clubs often refuse to admit minority members.

Since the majority group generally controls the major institutions, institutional discrimination is almost always carried out by the majority group against the minority group—not the other way around. For the most part, minority groups lack the power with which to practice institutional discrimination. Nevertheless, the refusal by a black-controlled city government to hire whites would be an example of institutional discrimination.

3. Finally, there is a third type of discrimination that some would say is not really discrimination at all. *Structural discrimination* refers to the policies of majority institutions, and the behavior of the individuals who implement these policies and control these institutions, that are race-neutral in intent but have a differential and/or harmful effect on minority groups. The key element in structural discrimination is not the intent but the effect of keeping minority groups in a subordinate position.

Although it is sometimes difficult to determine whether a particular phenomenon is an example of institutional or structural discrimination, the differences between the two are important both conceptually and in terms of social policy. Both types have the *effect* of keeping minority groups subordinate, but only institutional discrimination is *intended* to keep minority groups subordinate. Some examples of structural discrimination follow.

It is well known that blacks and Hispanics are underrepresented on the nation's college campuses. Most colleges, however, have what appear to be race-neutral meritocratic entrance requirements: Anyone who meets the requirements will be admitted regardless of race, ethnicity, gender, and so on. Requirements usually include high school grades, scores on SAT or ACT tests, teacher recommendations, and the like. And most educators sincerely believe that schools with the most rigorous entrance requirements offer the highest-quality educations.

It is also well known that, for a variety of reasons, blacks and Hispanics on the average tend to get lower high school grades and to score lower on the SAT than do whites. Accordingly, a smaller proportion of blacks and Hispanics than whites are admitted to college, especially to the more prestigious schools. In this case, we can say that college entrance requirements constitute an example of structural discrimination because they have a negative effect on blacks and Hispanics.

The criteria that educators believe to be important are less accessible to black and Hispanic students than to whites. As a rule, college managers and faculty members do not intend to be racially discriminatory, and many even feel quite badly about the harm done to black and Hispanic students as a result of these requirements. However, most also do not want to change the requirements.

It is possible, of course, that the underrepresentation of blacks and Hispanics on college campuses is being caused by institutional discrimination. A few colleges may still refuse to admit any black students. Others may purposely inflate entrance requirements as a way of screening out most minority students. Individual discrimination may also be taking place, as when a recruiting officer chooses to avoid black high schools when looking for potential students.

Another example of structural discrimination can be found in the context of job qualifications. Many employers require new employees to have earned a bachelor's degree even though there may be no direct connection between a college education and the skills required for the job in question. The employer, of course, may *believe* that college-educated people will be better workers. Since a smaller percentage of blacks and Hispanics get bachelor's degrees than do whites, blacks will be underrepresented among those who qualify for the job. This is a case of structural discrimination because blacks and Hispanics are negatively affected by the educational requirement for the job, even though there may be no intent to subordinate them.

On the other hand, an employer who used the bachelor's degree requirement intentionally to screen out blacks and Hispanics would be committing a form of institutional discrimination. And an individual personnel manager who refused to hire a qualified black applicant would be guilty of individual discrimination.

Consider yet another example: Insurance rates for homes, businesses, and cars are generally higher in black communities than in white communities, in part because of the higher rates of street crime in lower-income black communities. Insurance companies argue that it is good business to charge higher rates in areas where they will have to pay out more in claims, and they insist that they charge high rates in high-crime white areas as well. Yet in spite of the apparently race-neutral determination of insurance rates, the average black ends up paying more than the average white. So this, too, is an example of structural discrimination.

The "good business" argument can also be seen in the banking practice of granting loans and mortgages. The lower an individual's income, the less likely that individual is to be able to pay back the loan. Banks, therefore, are reluctant to give loans to lower-income people; and if they grant any at all, the loans are likely to be small. Since blacks tend to earn lower incomes than whites, they find it more difficult to get loans. Consequently, they have a harder time buying homes and starting businesses. Accordingly, the lending practices of banks are examples of structural discrimination, even though the banks themselves may be following standard business procedures.

Although banks and insurance companies routinely use the "good business" argument to justify structural discrimination, they sometimes practice institutional discrimination as well. Banks often "redline" black communities, and insurance companies have been known to charge higher rates in black communities than in white ones, even after controlling for crime rates.

Many social scientists and much of the general public would be reluctant to apply the term *structural discrimination* to the examples listed here, given the absence in these examples of any intent to harm minority groups or keep them subordinate. I assert, however, that the negative *effects* constitute discrimination. Thus even policies that are intended to be race-neutral and are carried out by well-intentioned people can perpetuate racial inequality.

Like institutional discrimination, structural discrimination is almost always a matter of majority group against minority group, not the other way around. Again, since most social institutions work to the advantage of the majority group, few if any institutional policies favor the minority group. Groups with little power are generally unable to implement policies that are structurally discriminatory.

Although it is sometimes difficult to know whether a given policy that negatively affects minority-group members is a case of individual, institutional, or structural discrimination, an understanding of the conceptual differences among these three categories is important. Since the different types of discrimination have different origins, different policies are required for their elimination. In trying to eliminate individual and institutional discrimination, for example, activists can appeal to the moral and legal principles of equal opportunity and racial fairness. In particular, they might argue that race-neutral meritocratic policies that promote equal opportunity should be the rule in education, employment, housing, and so on.

Where structural discrimination is concerned, however, policies that are race-neutral in intent are not race-neutral in effect. Since policymakers involved with structural discrimination have not tried to harm or subordinate minorities, it makes no sense for activists to appeal to their sense of racial fairness. The policymakers already believe that they are being racially fair. Instead, activists must convince these policymakers to reevaluate some of the fundamental policies upon which their institutions are based.

If banks are practicing institutional discrimination by "redlining" minority areas, for example, activists can demand that the banks treat each person in that area as a distinct individual. All individuals, inside or outside the redlined area, who meet the banks' universal credit requirements should receive a mortgage. Race or neighborhood should not be a factor.

Confronting the profit-oriented business practices of banks, which I have included in the category of structural discrimination, is more problematic. Even without redlining, banks grant fewer mortgages to blacks than to whites because of racial differences in income and wealth. Bankers can argue that they are simply being good race-neutral capitalists and may even express sincere regret that more blacks do not qualify for loans and mortgages. To deal with this problem, activists must confront the profit-oriented business practices themselves, not the racial views of the bank officials. Perhaps banks have to forgo some of their profits in order to help poor black communities. Perhaps the federal government must subsidize more loans to low-income blacks and create not-for-profit banks in low-income areas.

Alternative arguments are also needed to confront racial inequality in higher education. Colleges that refuse to admit Hispanics who meet their admissions standards are practicing institutional discrimination. If activists can successfully show that qualified Hispanics are not being admitted, they can try to bring public pressure on the colleges to get them to stop discriminating. If this effort failed, the activists could probably sue the colleges in a court of law.

Combatting structurally discriminatory admissions standards in higher education requires a different approach. Educators can justify admissions standards by saying that certain grade-point averages and SAT scores are essential to the mission of academic excellence in their institutions, even though a relatively small percentage of Hispanics are able to qualify.

Activists must call on educators to modify their standards, not their racial views. (Certainly Hispanics do not benefit from the standards currently in place.) Indeed, colleges should devote more resources to remedial and support programs for Hispanics who do not meet the entrance requirements. Also needed are new pedagogical techniques, including a more multicultural curriculum, that would be more suited to Hispanic students. And perhaps colleges could shoulder some of the responsibility for improving the quality of high schools attended by Hispanic students.

All three types of discrimination coexist as major problems in American society. And all three must be confronted if racial equality is to be achieved. Individual and institutional discrimination are the most visible. Yet even if they were completely eliminated, the prospect of racial equality would be jeopardized by continuing structural discrimination.

9

The Limited Visions of Race: Discrimination Is Not the Sole Problem

WILLIAM JULIUS WILSON

In the mid-1960s a series of insightful articles were written by black and white intellectuals that raised questions about the direction and goals of the black protest movement.[1] Basically, the authors of these articles made it clear that from 1955 to 1965 the chief objectives of the civil rights movement were to integrate public accommodations and to eliminate black disenfranchisement. These were matters of constitutional rights and basic human dignity, matters that affected blacks and other minorities exclusively and therefore could be defined and addressed simply as problems of civil rights. However, these authors noted that despite the spectacular victories in the area of civil rights, by the latter half of the 1960s a more complex and fundamental set of problems had yet to be attacked—problems of jobs, education, and housing that affected not only blacks but other minorities and whites as well.

A consistent theme running throughout these articles is that in the period from 1955 to 1963, all blacks, regardless of their station in life, were concerned about the banning of discrimination in public accommodations and in voting. As Bayard Rustin observed, "Ralph Bunch was as likely to be refused service in a restaurant or a hotel as any illiterate sharecropper. This common bond prevented the latent class differences and resentments from being openly expressed."[2] However, it did not take long to realize that the group that had profited the most from the civil rights legislation up to 1965 was middle-class blacks—blacks who had competitive resources such as steady incomes, education, and special talents. As Kenneth Clark argued in 1967, "The masses of Negroes are now starkly aware of the fact that recent civil rights victories benefited a very small percentage of middle-class Negroes while their predicament remained the same or worsened."[3]

What these observers were telling us in the mid-1960s is that a close examination of ghetto black discontent, most dramatically seen in the riots of that period, reveals issues that transcend the creation and implementation of civil rights laws.

"To the segregation by race," Bayard Rustin observed, "was now added segregation by class, and all the problems created by segregation and poverty—inadequate schooling, substandard and overcrowded housing, lack of access to jobs and job training, narcotics and crime—were greatly aggravated."[4] In short, for ghetto blacks the problems move beyond the issue of civil rights. The late Martin Luther King, Jr., recognized this point in 1968 when shortly before his death he asked, "What good is it to be allowed to eat in a restaurant if you can't afford a hamburger?"[5] It would not be unfair to suggest that he was probably influenced by the thoughts of Bayard Rustin, who, four years earlier in his now-classic article "From Protest to Politics," phrased the matter in much the same way: "What is the value of winning access to public accommodations for those who lack money to use them?"[6]

Thus, these perceptive civil rights advocates recognized in the 1960s that removing artificial racial barriers would not enable poor blacks to compete equally with other groups in society for valued resources because of an accumulation of disadvantages flowing from previous periods of prejudice and discrimination, disadvantages that have been passed on from generation to generation. Basic structural changes in our modern industrial economy have compounded the problems of poor blacks because education and training have become more important for entry into the more desirable and higher-paying jobs and because increased reliance on labor-saving devices has contributed to a surplus of untrained black workers. In short, once the movement faced these more fundamental issues, argued Rustin in 1965, "it was compelled to expand its vision beyond race relations to economic relations, including the role of education in society."[7]

THE PROBLEM OF THE RACE RELATIONS VISION

During the same period in which problems of structural inequality were being raised, scholars such as Kenneth Clark, Lee Rainwater, and Elliot Liebow were also raising important issues about the experiences of inequality.[8] ... What was both unique and important about these studies in the 1960s was that discussions of the experiences of inequality were inextricably tied to discussions of the structure of inequality. Thus, in reading these works one received a clear understanding of how the economic and social situations into which so many poor blacks are born produce modes of adaptation and create subcultural patterns that take the form of a "self-perpetuating pathology."[9] In other words, and in sharp contrast to approaches that simply "blame the victim" or that use a "culture-of-poverty" thesis to explain group disadvantages, the works of scholars such as Clark, Rainwater, and Liebow not only presented a sensitive portrayal of the destructive features of ghetto life, they also provided a comprehensive analysis of the deleterious structural conditions that produce these features.

However, arguments stressing economic relations in determining the structure of inequality and in significantly influencing the experiences of inequality began to compete with a new definition, description, and explanation of the black condition. This new approach, proclaimed as the "black perspective," revealed an ideological shift from interracialism to racial solidarity. It first gained currency among militant black spokespersons in the late 1960s and became a theme in the writings of young black academics and intellectuals by the early 1970s. ... Although the "black perspective" represented a variety of views and arguments on issues of race, the trumpeting of racial pride and self-affirmation was common to all the writings and speeches on the subject. Thus interracial cooperation and integration were being challenged by the ideology of racial solidarity, and the rhetoric of black militancy, symbolized by the cry of Black Power, gradually moved from expressions of selective to generalized hostility toward whites.

The complex factors associated with this shift in emphasis cannot be reviewed in full detail here, but I should like to point out that the declining support for interracialism and the rising emphasis on black solidarity in the late 1960s was typical of a pattern that has been repeated throughout the history of dominant-subordinate group relations in multiethnic societies.

More specifically, in a multiracial society such as the United States where racial groups share the same social order (i.e., where an interdependent relationship exists between the racial groups), sentiments for integration and interracialism tend to emerge when the struggle against racial inequality appears hopeful. Such periods have included the three decades following the emancipation of slaves in the North in the early nineteenth century, the Reconstruction era, the New Deal era, and the era of successful nonviolent resistance movements during the late 1950s and early 1960s. On the other hand, sentiments for racial separation and racial solidarity tend to emerge when minority race members perceive the struggle against racial inequality as hopeless or when they experience intense disillusionment and frustration immediately following a period of optimism or heightened expectations.[10] Such periods have included the disheartening decades of the 1850s in the United States when nationalistic sentiment among free blacks in the North reached its peak before the Civil War; the violent period of Jim Crow segregation and biological racism in the late nineteenth and early twentieth centuries when the movements of Booker T. Washington, Bishop Turner, Marcus Garvey, and the Harlem Renaissance emerged; and the "law and order" period of the late 1960s and early 1970s, when the Black Power movement crystallized and black cultural nationalism flourished.

Consistent with the dominant focus on racial solidarity in the late sixties was an emphasis on we versus they and black versus white. Since the accent was on race, little attention was paid to the social-economic differences within the black community and the implications they had for different public policy options, and little discussion was devoted to problems with the economy and the need for economic reform. Thus, the promising move in the early and mid-1960s to pursue programs of economic reform by defining the problems of American economic organization and outlining their effect on the minority community was offset by slogans calling for "reparations," or "black control of institutions serving the black community." This is why Orlando Patterson was led to proclaim in a later analysis that black ethnicity had become "a form of mystification, diverting attention from the correct kinds of solutions to the terrible economic conditions of the group," thereby making it difficult for blacks to see the inextricable connection between their own fate and the structure of the modern American economy.[11]

Meanwhile, during this period of racial solidarity, significant events ... were unfolding in inner-city communities across the nation that profoundly affected the lives of millions of blacks and dramatically revealed that the problems earlier described by observers such as Clark and Rustin had reached catastrophic proportions.

However, because the government not only adopted and resolutely implemented antidiscrimination legislation to enhance minority individual rights but also mandated and purposefully enforced affirmation and related programs to promote minority group rights, it was clear that by 1980 many thoughtful American citizens, including civil rights supporters, were puzzled by recent developments in the black community. Despite the passage of antidiscrimination legislation and the creation of affirmative action programs, they sensed that conditions were getting worse, not better, for a significant segment of black Americans. This perception had emerged because of the constant flow of pessimistic reports concerning the sharp rise in black unemployment, the substantial decline of blacks in the labor force, the steady drop in the black-white family income ratio, the consistent increase in the percentage of blacks on the welfare rolls, the remarkable growth of single-parent households, and the persistent problems of black crime and black victims of crime. The perception was reinforced by the almost uniform cry among black leaders that conditions were deteriorating and white Americans had abandoned the cause of blacks as well. In the face of these developments, there were noticeable signs (even before Ronald Reagan was elected president and well before his administration adopted a conspicuously laissez-faire attitude toward civil rights) that demoralization had set in among many blacks who had come to believe that "nothing really works" and among many whites who were otherwise committed to social reform.

These recent developments in the black community will remain puzzling, and the feeling that "nothing really works" will likely become more widespread if advocates of minority rights fail in significant numbers to understand that many contemporary problems of race cannot be satisfactorily addressed ... solely by race-specific programs to eliminate racial discrimination and eradicate racial prejudices. ...

A HOLISTIC APPROACH: RACIAL PROBLEMS
AND SOCIETAL ORGANIZATION

The development of a holistic approach involves an attempt to relate problems associated with race to the broader issues of societal organization. By the term *societal organization* I refer to the working arrangements of society, including those that have emanated from previous arrangements, that specifically involve processes of ordering relations and actions with respect to given social ends, and that represent the material outcomes of those processes. These working arrangements can be best described in terms of their institutional and technological dimensions. The institutional dimensions of societal organization (such as the economic, political, and educational) embody modes of social interaction that are structured by a constellation of statuses and roles and guided by norms and values. They therefore represent the social, normative, and cultural orders of society. The technological dimensions of societal organization (e.g., stages of industrialization and the degree of urbanization) represent the material outcomes of systematic and goal-directed social relations and action.

At any given time, groups can be stratified in terms of the benefits and privileges they receive from existing working arrangements and in terms of the influence they yield because of these arrangements. And group variation in behavior, norms, and values will reflect variation in access to organizational channels of privilege and influence. Support of existing societal working arrangements will therefore vary depending upon the degree to which groups are stratified in relation to them. And these arrangements may be quite satisfactory for one group and exceedingly problematic for another. Accordingly, to speak of problems of societal organization is to speak of the way that existing working arrangements (ranging from the way relations and actions are ordered to levels of technology, rates of economic growth, and rates of unemployment) adversely affect certain groups in society, even though other groups may be unaffected or may even benefit from these arrangements. And the number and size of groups adversely affected are indications of the problems of societal organization.

To study problems of race in terms of societal organization, therefore, entails a detailed investigation of not only the political, economic, and other institutional dimensions of societal organization that affect intra- and intergroup experiences, but also the technological dimensions. The basic theoretical argument I am proposing is that the dimensions of societal organization impose constraints on intergroup interaction whereby intergroup relations are structured, racial antagonisms are channeled, and racial group access to rewards and privileges is differentiated. And the changes in the institutional dimensions of societal organization or in the technological dimensions often bring about changes in the patterns of intergroup interaction. Moreover, significant changes in *intragroup* experiences accompany changes in societal organization. Let me demonstrate how the principal ideas in this brief theoretical discussion can illuminate recent problems associated with race in America and suggest new approaches to public policy.

PROBLEMS OF RACE, SOCIETAL ORGANIZATION, AND PUBLIC POLICY

Since World War II, both political changes of the state and structural changes in the economy have contributed to a gradual and continuous process of deracialization in the economic sector; in other words, a process in which racial distinctions gradually lose their importance in determining individual mobility in the United States. The expansion of the economy, on the one hand, facilitated the movement of blacks from southern rural areas to the industrial centers of the nation and created job opportunities leading to greater occupational differentiation within the black community. On the other hand, the state, instead of reinforcing the racial barriers that were created during the previous periods, has, in recent years, promoted racial equality. Partly in response to the pressure of increased black political resources (resulting from the growing concentration of blacks in large industrial cities) and partly in response to the pressures of black protest movements (in many ways, a manifestation of greater black political strength), the government has consistently intervened on behalf of blacks with the enactment and enforcement of antidiscrimination legislation. In short, a combination of changes in political and economic dimensions of societal organization created greater economic mobility opportunities for a substantial segment of the black population.[12]

The curious paradox, however, is that whereas economic growth since World War II enabled many blacks to experience occupational mobility, recent structural shifts in the economy have diminished mobility opportunities for others. And whereas antidiscrimination legislation has removed many racial barriers, not all blacks are in a position to benefit from it. Indeed, as I have attempted to show in previous chapters, the position of the black underclass has actually deteriorated during the very period in which the most sweeping antidiscrimination legislation and programs have been enacted and implemented. The net effect is a growing economic schism between poor and higher-income blacks.

Accordingly, people who argue that *current* racial bias is the major cause of the deteriorating economic plight of the black poor fail to recognize how the fate of poor blacks is inextricably connected with the structure and functioning of the modern American economy. The net effect is that policy programs are recommended that do not confront the fundamental cause of poverty—underemployment and unemployment. In other words, policies that do not take into account the changing nature of the national economy will not effectively handle the economic dislocation of low-income blacks. Factors that must be considered are the economy's rate of growth and the nature of its variable demand for labor; matters that affect industrial employment, such as profit rates, technology, and unionization; and patterns of institutional and individual migration that are a result of industrial transformation and shifts.

For example, a recent study by the Illinois Advisory Committee to the United States Commission on Civil Rights reported that among the 2,380 firms in their statewide sample that had left the central cities and relocated in the suburbs between 1975 and 1978, black employment decreased by 24.3 percent compared to a white employment drop of only 9.8 percent. This study also found that although minorities were 14.1 percent of the statewide work force between 1975 and 1978, they were 20 percent of the formerly employed workers in the firms that shut down.[13] Furthermore, a recent study on the effects of deindustrialization on the national labor force found that blacks are disproportionately concentrated in industries that have "borne the brunt of recent" plant closings, such as the automobile, rubber, and steel industries.[14] Moreover, industries that were most adversely affected (lowered job opportunities) by the impact of foreign trade from 1964 to 1975 had an average minority work force of 11.5 percent compared to one of 7.4 percent in industries that were favorably affected. And, finally, the detrimental effects of the decline in central-city industries that employ a substantial number of young workers were concentrated among the black males.[15]

Thus minorities, particularly poor and working-class minorities, are not only adversely affected by periodic recessions, they are also vulnerable to the structural economic changes of the past two decades because of their disproportionate concentration in industries with the largest number of layoffs due to economic cutbacks, plant closings, and the relocation of firms to cheaper labor sites and to the suburbs.

Other problems that have been defined in race-specific terms (such as the quality of inner-city schools, school desegregation, and residential segregation) have also been partly created and exacerbated by nonracial factors such as demographic changes responding to industrial shifts or transformations. Just as the changes in the economy have fundamentally altered the job market situation for inner-city blacks, so too has the class and racial composition of urban public schools and residential neighborhoods been affected by population movements responding to economic changes. The technological and economic shifts of the post–World War II period precipitated the movement toward decentralization and residential development in the suburbs. Once these processes were under way, they became part of a vicious cycle of metropolitan change and relocation. The flight of the more affluent families to the suburbs has meant that the central cities are becoming increasingly the domain of the poor and the stable working class. Thus, in major cities, such as New York, Chicago, Atlanta, Washington, D.C., Philadelphia, St. Louis, and Detroit, not only have public schools become overwhelmingly populated with minority students, but the background of both minority and white students is primarily working or lower class. And in certain underclass neighborhoods in the inner city, neither children from middle-class families nor those from working-class families are represented in the public schools. The more affluent white and minority families are increasingly opting to send their children to parochial or private schools if they remain in the central city or to suburban schools if they move to the metropolitan fringe.

Moreover, changes in societal organization have created situations that enhance racial antagonisms between those groups that are trapped in central cities and are victimized by deteriorating services and institutions that serve the city. In addition to problems experienced by poor minorities, inner-city white ethnics have encountered mounting difficulties in maintaining their quality of life. Many of these people originally bought relatively inexpensive homes near their industrial jobs. Because of the deconcentration of industry, the racially changing neighborhood bordering their communities, the problems of neighborhood crime, and the surplus of inner-city housing created by the population shift to the suburbs, housing values in their neighborhoods have failed to keep pace with those in the suburbs. As the industries in which they are employed become suburbanized, a growing number of inner-city white ethnics find that not only are they trapped in the inner city because of the high costs of suburban housing, but they are physically removed from job opportunities.[16] This situation increases the potential for racial tensions as white European ethnics compete with blacks and the rapidly growing Hispanic population for access to and control of the remaining decent schools, housing, and neighborhoods. And explanations that their negative response to minority encroachment is due to racial prejudice hardly capture the dynamic factors of societal organization that channel racial antagonisms.

Finally, policymakers must understand how some aspects of American societal organization have direct consequences for group cultural behavior. The more unequal the distribution of scarce resources among groups in a society, the more differentiation there is in group social participation in the institutions of society and in group culture. Group variation in behavior, norms, and values reflects variation in group access to organizational channels of privilege and influence. Since class background and race are two major factors in determining group access to such channels, the opportunities available to the ghetto underclass, a group that represents the combination of both race and class subordination, are therefore more limited and the structural constraints are greater. Ghetto-specific culture is a response to these structural constraints and limited opportunities.

However, the notion of a ghetto subculture is not to be equated with the popular conception of *culture of poverty*. [Elsewhere,] I distinguished the concept *culture of poverty* from the concept *social isolation* to highlight the association between the ghetto subculture and structural constraints and opportunities. Nonetheless, some readers may still have difficulty distinguishing the two concepts because the very meaning of *social isolation* implies that ghetto-specific cultural traits are not irrelevant in understanding the behavior of inner-city residents. But, what distinguishes the two concepts is that although they both emphasize the association between the emergence of certain cultural traits and the structure of social constraints and opportunities, *culture of poverty*, unlike *social isolation*, places strong emphasis on the autonomous character of the cultural traits once they come into existence. In other words, these traits assume a "life of their own" and continue to influence behavior even if opportunities for social mobility improve. As Oscar Lewis puts it, "By the time slum children are age six or seven, they have usually absorbed the basic values and attitudes of their subculture and are not psychologically geared to take full advantage of changing conditions or increased opportunities which may occur in their lifetime."[17] Although Lewis later modified his position by placing more weight on external societal forces than on self-perpetuating cultural traits to explain the behavior of the poor, conservative social scientists have embellished the idea that poverty is a product of "deeply ingrained habits" that are unlikely to change following improvements in external conditions.[18] On the other hand *social isolation* is one of several concepts included in my discussion of the social transformation of the inner city ... that link ghetto-specific behavior with the problems of societal organization. More specifically, concepts such as *social buffer, concentration effects,* and *social isolation* are used to describe the social and institutional mechanisms that enhance patterns of social dislocations originally caused by racial subjugation but that have been strengthened in more recent years by such developments as the class transformation of the inner city and changes in the urban economy. As I have tried to emphasize, the significance of increasing social isolation is not that ghetto culture went unchecked following the removal of higher income families from many inner-city neighborhoods, but that the increasing exodus of these families made it more difficult to sustain the basic institutions in these neighborhoods (including churches, stores, schools, recreational facilities, etc.) in the face of increased joblessness caused by the frequent recessions during the 1970s and early 1980s and changes in the urban job structure. As the basic institutions declined, the social organization of inner-city neighborhoods (sense of community, positive neighborhood identification, and explicit norms and sanctions against aberrant behavior) likewise declined. This process magnified the effects of living in highly concentrated urban poverty areas—effects that are manifested in ghetto-specific culture and behavior.

If my concept of *social isolation* does not imply self-perpetuating cultural traits, am I completely ruling out the possibility that some cultural traits may in fact take on a life of their own for a period of time and thereby become a constraining or liberating factor in the life of certain individuals and groups in the inner city? It would be dogmatic to rule out this possibility, however, ... as economic and social situations change, cultural traits, created by previous situations, likewise *eventually* change even though it is possible that some will linger on and influence behavior for a period of time.[19] Accordingly, the key conclusion from a public policy perspective is that programs created to alleviate poverty, joblessness, and related forms of social dislocation should place primary focus on changing the social and economic situations, not the cultural traits, of the ghetto underclass.

CONCLUSION

To hold, as I do, that changes in social and economic situations will bring about changes in behavior and norms raises the issue of what public policy can deal effectively with the social dislocations that have recently plagued the ghetto underclass. In this chapter I have outlined a holistic approach emphasizing the problems of societal organization. My purpose is to show not only the complexities of the issue currently associated with race and to explain why they cannot be firmly grasped by focusing solely or even mainly on racial discrimination but also to reinforce the argument underlined [elsewhere,] namely, that it is necessary to move beyond race-specific public policy to address the problems of the truly disadvantaged. For example, I argued in this chapter that (1) the vulnerability of poor urban minorities to changes in the economy since 1970 has resulted in sharp increases in joblessness, poverty, female-headed families, and welfare dependency despite the creation of Great Society programs, and despite antidiscrimination and affirmative action programs; (2) the War on Poverty and race relations visions failed to relate the fate of the poor minorities to the functionings of the modern American economy and therefore could not explain the worsening conditions of inner-city minorities in the post–Great Society and post–civil rights periods; (3) liberals whose views embody these visions have not only been puzzled by the recent increase of inner-city social dislocations, they have also lacked a convincing rebuttal to the forceful arguments by conservative scholars that erroneously attribute these problems to the social values of the ghetto underclass; and (4) the growing emphasis on social values deflects attention from the major source of the rise of inner-city social dislocations since 1970—changes in the nation's economy.

Any significant reduction of the problems of black joblessness and the related problems of crime, out-of-wedlock births, single-parent homes, and welfare dependency will call for a far more comprehensive program of economic and social reform than what Americans have usually regarded as appropriate or desirable. In short, it will require a radicalism that neither Democratic nor Republican parties have as yet been realistic enough to propose. ...

NOTES

1. Bayard Rustin, "From Protest to Politics: The Future of the Civil Rights Movement," *Commentary* 39 (February 1964): 25–31; idem, "A Way Out of the Exploding Ghetto," *New York Times Magazine*, August 13, 1967; idem, "The Long Hot Summer," *Commentary* (October 1967): 39–45; Tom Kahn, "Problems of the Negro Movement," *Dissent* 11 (Winter 1964): 108–38; and Kenneth B. Clark, "The Present Dilemma of the Negro," paper presented at the Annual Meeting of the Southern Regional Council, Atlanta, Ga., November 2, 1967.

2. Rustin, "Lessons of the Long Hot Summer," p. 43.

3. Clark, "Present Dilemma of the Negro," p. 8.

4. Bayard Rustin, "The Blacks and the Unions," *Harper Magazine*, May 1971, p. 74.

5. Martin Luther King, Jr., "Showdown for Non-Violence," *Look*, April 16, 1968, p. 24.

6. Rustin, "From Protest to Politics," p. 25.

7. Ibid., p. 25.

8. Kenneth B. Clark, *Dark Ghetto: Dilemmas of Social Power* (New York: Harper and Row, 1965); Lee Rainwater, "Crucible of Identity: The Negro Lower-Class Family," *Dædelus* 95 (Winter 1966): 172–216; and Elliot Liebow, *Tally's Corner: A Study of Negro Streetcorner Men* (Boston: Little, Brown, 1967).

9. Clark, *Dark Ghetto*, p. 27.

10. See William Julius Wilson, *Power, Racism, and Privilege: Race Relations in Theoretical and Sociohistorical Perspectives* (New York: Free Press, 1976).

11. Orlando Patterson, *Ethnic Chauvinism: The Reactionary Impulse* (New York: Stein and Day, 1977), p. 155.

12. See William Julius Wilson, *The Declining Significance of Race: Blacks and Changing American Institutions*, 2d ed. (Chicago: University of Chicago Press, 1980).

13. Illinois Advisory Committee, *Shutdown: Economic Dislocation and Equal Opportunity*, report to the United States Commission on Civil Rights, June 1981.

14. Barry Bluestone and Bennett Harrison, *The Deindustrialization of America* (New York: Basic Books, *1982*).

15. Richard McGahey and John Jeffries, "Employment, Training, and Industrial Policy: Implications for Minorities," paper prepared for a conference on Industrial Policy and Minority Economic Opportunity, sponsored by the Joint Center for Political Studies and the A. Philip Randolph Educational Fund, New York, N.Y., October 14, 1983.

16. John D. Kasarda, "Urbanization, Community, and the Metropolitan Problem," in *Handbook of Contemporary Urban Life*, ed. David Street et al. (San Francisco: Jossey-Bass, 1978).

17. Oscar Lewis, "Culture of Poverty," in *On Understanding Poverty: Perspectives from the Social Sciences*, Daniel Patrick Moynihan, ed. (New York: Basic Books, 1968), p. 188.

18. For a good discussion of this point see Stephen Steinberg, *The Ethnic Myth: Race, Ethnicity, and Class in America* (New York: Atheneum, 1981).

19. Herbert Gans, "Culture and Class in the Study of Poverty: An Approach to Anti-Poverty Research," in *On Understanding Poverty: Perspectives from the Social Sciences*, ed. Daniel Patrick Moynihan (New York: Basic Books, 1968), pp. 201–8.

10

The Continuing Significance of Race: Antiblack Discrimination in Public Places

JOE R. FEAGIN

Title II of the 1964 Civil Rights Act stipulates that "all persons shall be entitled to the full and equal enjoyment of the goods, services, facilities, privileges, advantages, and accommodations of any place of public accommodation ... without discrimination or segregation on the ground of race, color, religion, or national origin." The public places emphasized in the act are restaurants, hotels, and motels, although racial discrimination occurs in many other public places. Those black Americans who would make the greatest use of these public accommodations and certain other public places would be middle-class, i.e., those with the requisite resources.

White public opinion and many scholars have accented the great progress against traditional discrimination recently made by the black middle class. ... Racial discrimination as a continuing and major problem for middle-class blacks has been downplayed as analysts have turned to the various problems of the "underclass." For example, Wilson (1978, pp. 110–1) has argued that the growth of the black middle class since the 1960s is the result of improving economic conditions and of government civil rights laws, which virtually eliminated overt discrimination in the workplace and public accommodations. According to Wilson, the major problem of the 1964 Civil Rights Act is its failure to meet the problems of the black underclass (Wilson 1987, pp. 146–7).

Here I treat these assertions as problematic. Do middle-class black Americans still face hostile treatment in public accommodations and other public places? If so, what form does this discrimination take? Who are the perpetrators of this discrimination? What is the impact of the discrimination on its middle-class victims? How do middle-class blacks cope with such discrimination?

ASPECTS OF DISCRIMINATION

Discrimination can be defined in social-contextual terms as "actions or practices carried out by members of dominant racial or ethnic groups that have a differential and negative impact on members subordinate racial and ethnic groups" (Feagin and Eckberg 1980, pp. 1–2). This differential treatment ranges from the blatant to the subtle (Feagin and Feagin 1986). Here I focus primarily on blatant discrimination by white Americans targeting middle-class blacks. Historically, discrimination against blacks has been one of the most serious forms of racial/ethnic discrimination in the United States and one of the most difficult to overcome, in part because of the institutionalized character of color coding. I focus on three important aspects of discrimination: (1) the variation in sites of discrimination; (2) the range of discriminatory actions; and (3) the range of responses by blacks to discrimination.

Sites of Discrimination

There is a spatial dimension to discrimination. The probability of experiencing racial hostility varies from the most private to the most public sites. If a black person is in a relatively protected site, such as with friends at home, the probability of experiencing hostility and discrimination is low. The probability increases as one moves from friendship settings to such outside sites as the workplace, where a black person typically has contacts with both acquaintances and strangers, providing an interactive context with greater potential for discrimination.

In most workplaces, middle-class status and its organizational resources provide some protection against certain categories of discrimination. This protection probably weakens as a black person moves from those work and school settings where he or she is well-known into public accommodations such as large stores and city restaurants where contacts are mainly with white strangers. On public streets blacks have the greatest public exposure to strangers and the least protection against overt discriminatory behavior, including violence. A key feature of these more public settings is that they often involve contacts with white strangers who react primarily on the basis of one ascribed characteristic. The study of the micro-life of interaction between strangers in public was pioneered by Goffman (1963; 1971) and his students, but few of their analyses have treated hostile discriminatory interaction in public places. A rare exception is the research by Gardner (1980; see also Gardner 1988), who documented the character and danger of passing remarks by men directed against women in unprotected public places. Gardner writes of women (and blacks) as "open persons," i.e., particularly vulnerable targets for harassment that violates the rules of public courtesy.

The Range of Discriminatory Actions

In his classic study, *The Nature of Prejudice*, Allport (1958, pp. 14–5) noted that prejudice can be expressed in a series of progressively more serious actions, ranging from antilocution to avoidance, exclusion, physical attack, and extermination. Allport's work suggests a continuum of actions from avoidance, to exclusion or rejection, to attack. In his travels in the South in the 1950s a white journalist who changed his skin color to black encountered discrimination in each of these categories (Griffin 1961). In my data, discrimination against middle-class blacks still ranges across this continuum: (1) avoidance actions, such as a white couple crossing the street when a black male approaches; (2) rejection actions, such as poor service in public accommodations; (3) verbal attacks, such as shouting racial epithets in the street; (4) physical threats and harassment by white police officers; and (5) physical threats and attacks by other whites, such as attacks by white supremacists in the street. Changing relations between blacks and whites in recent decades have expanded the repertoire of discrimination to include more subtle forms and to encompass discrimination in arenas from which blacks were formerly excluded, such as formerly all-white public accommodations.

Black Responses to Discrimination

Prior to societal desegregation in the 1960s much traditional discrimination, especially in the South, took the form of an asymmetrical "deference ritual" in which blacks were typically expected to respond to discriminating whites with great deference. According to Goffman (1956, p. 477) a deference ritual "functions as a symbolic means by which appreciation is regularly conveyed to a recipient." Such rituals can be seen in the obsequious words and gestures—the etiquette of race relations—that many blacks, including middle-class blacks, were forced to utilize to survive the rigors of segregation. ...

Deference rituals can still be found today between some lower-income blacks and their white employers. In her northeastern study Rollins (1985, p. 157) found black maids regularly deferring to white employers. Today, most discriminatory interaction no longer involves much asymmetrical deference, at least for middle-class blacks. Even where whites expect substantial deference, most middle-class blacks do not oblige. For middle-class blacks contemporary discrimination has evolved beyond the asymmetrical deference rituals and "No Negroes served" type of exclusion to patterns of black-contested discrimination. Discussing race and gender discrimination in Great Britain, Brittan and Maynard (1984) have suggested that today "the terms of oppression are not only dictated by history, culture, and the sexual and social division of labor. They are also profoundly shaped at the site of the oppression, and by the way in which oppressors and oppressed continuously have to renegotiate, reconstruct, and re-establish their relative positions in respect to benefits and power" (p. 7). Similarly, white mistreatment of black Americans today frequently encounters new coping strategies by blacks in the ongoing process of reconstructing patterns of racial interaction.

Middle-class strategies for coping with discrimination range from careful assessment to withdrawal, resigned acceptance, verbal confrontation, or physical confrontation. Later action might include a court suit. Assessing the situation is a first step. Some white observers have suggested that many middle-class blacks are paranoid about white discrimination and rush too quickly to charges of racism (Wieseltier 1989, June 5; for male views of female "paranoia" see Gardner 1988). But the daily reality may be just the opposite, as middle-class black Americans often evaluate a situation carefully before judging it discriminatory and taking additional action. This careful evaluation, based on past experiences (real or vicarious), not only prevents jumping to conclusions, but also reflects the hope that white behavior is not based on race, because an act not based on race is easier to endure. After evaluation one strategy is to leave the site of discrimination rather than to create a disturbance. Another is to ignore the discrimination and continue with the interaction, a "blocking" strategy similar to that Gardner (1980, p. 345) reported for women dealing with street remarks. In many situations resigned acceptance is the only realistic response. More confrontational responses to white actions include verbal reprimands and sarcasm, physical counterattacks, and filing lawsuits. Several strategies may be tried in any given discriminatory situation. In crafting these strategies middle-class blacks, in comparison with less-privileged blacks, may draw on middle-class resources to fight discrimination.

THE RESEARCH STUDY

To examine discrimination, I draw primarily on 37 in-depth interviews from a larger study of 135 middle-class black Americans in Boston, Buffalo, Baltimore, Washington, D.C., Detroit, Houston, Dallas, Austin, San Antonio, Marshall, Las Vegas, and Los Angeles. The interviewing was done in 1988–1990; black interviewers were used. I began with respondents known as members of the black middle class to knowledgeable consultants in key cities. Snowball sampling from these multiple starting points was used to maximize diversity.

... While I report below mainly on the responses of the 37 respondents who detailed specific incidents of public discrimination, in interpreting the character and meaning of modern discrimination I also draw on some discussions in the larger sample of 135 interviews and in five supplementary and follow-up interviews of middle-class blacks conducted by the author and two black consultants.

"Middle class" was defined broadly as those holding a white-collar job (including those in professional, managerial, and clerical jobs), college students preparing for white-collar jobs, and owners of successful businesses. ...

DESCRIPTIVE PATTERNS

Among the 37 people in the subsample reporting specific instances of public-place discrimination, 24 reported 25 incidents involving public accommodations discrimination, and 15 reported 27 incidents involving street discrimination. Some incidents included more than one important discriminatory action; the 52 incidents consisted of 62 distinguishable actions.

Although all types of mistreatment are reported, there is a strong relationship between type of discrimination and site, with rejection/poor-service discrimination being most common in public accommodations and verbal or physical threat discrimination by white citizens or police officers most likely in the street.

The reactions of these middle-class blacks reflect the site and type of discrimination. ... The most common black responses to racial hostility in the street are withdrawal or a verbal reply. In many avoidance situations (e.g., a white couple crossing a street to avoid walking past a black college student) or attack situations (e.g., whites throwing beer cans from a passing car), a verbal response is difficult because of the danger or the fleeting character of the hostility. A black victim often withdraws, endures this treatment with resigned acceptance, or replies with a quick verbal retort. In the case of police harassment, the response is limited by the danger, and resigned acceptance or mild verbal protests are likely responses. Rejection (poor service) in public accommodations provides an opportunity to fight back verbally—the most common responses to public accommodations discrimination are verbal counterattacks or resigned acceptance. Some black victims correct whites quietly, while others respond aggressively and lecture the assailant about the discrimination or threaten court action. A few retaliate physically. ...

RESPONSES TO DISCRIMINATION: PUBLIC ACCOMMODATIONS

Two Fundamental Strategies: Verbal Confrontation and Withdrawal

In the following account, a black news director at a major television station shows the interwoven character of discriminatory action and black response. The discrimination took the form of poor restaurant service, and the responses included both suggested withdrawal and verbal counterattack.

> He [her boyfriend] was waiting to be seated. ... He said, 'You go to the bathroom and I'll get the table. ...' He was standing there when I came back; he continued to stand there. The restaurant was almost empty. There were waiters, waitresses, and no one seated. And when I got back to him, he was ready to leave, and said, "Let's go." I said, "What happened to our table?" He wasn't seated. So I said, "No, we're not leaving, please." And he said, "No, I'm leaving." So we went outside, and we talked about it. And what I said to him was, you have to be aware of the possibilities that this is not the first time that this has happened at this restaurant or at other restaurants, but this is the first time it has happened to a black news director here or someone who could make an issue of it, or someone who is prepared to make an issue of it.
>
> So we went back inside after I talked him into it and, to make a long story short, I had the manager come. I made most of the people who were there (while conducting myself professionally the whole time) aware that I was incensed at being treated this way. ... I said, "Why do you think we weren't seated?" And the manager said, "Well, I don't really know." And I said, "Guess." He said, "Well I don't know, because you're black?" I said, "Bingo. Now isn't it funny that you didn't guess that I didn't have any money (and I opened up my purse) and I said, "because I certainly have money. And isn't it odd that you didn't guess that it's because I couldn't pay for it because I've got two American Express cards and a Master Card right here. I think it's just funny that you would have assumed that it's because I'm black." ... And then I took out my card and gave it to him and said, "If this happens again, or if I hear of this happening again, I will bring the full wrath of an entire news department down on this restaurant." And he just kind of looked at me. "Not [just] because I am personally offended. I am. But because you have no right to do what you did, and as a people we have lived a long time with having our rights abridged. ..." There were probably three or four sets of diners in the restaurant and maybe five waiters/waitresses. They watched him standing there waiting to be seated. His reaction

to it was that he wanted to leave. I understood why he would have reacted that way, because he felt that he was in no condition to be civil. He was ready to take the place apart and ... sometimes it's appropriate to behave that way. We hadn't gone the first step before going on to the next step. He didn't feel that he could comfortably and calmly take the first step, and I did. So I just asked him to please get back in the restaurant with me, and then you don't have to say a word, and let me handle it from there. It took some convincing, but I had to appeal to his sense of, this is not just you, this is not just for you. We are finally in a position as black people where there are some of us who can genuinely get their attention. And if they don't want to do this because it's right for them to do it, then they'd better do it because they're afraid to do otherwise. If it's fear, then fine, instill the fear.

This example provides insight into the character of modern discrimination. The discrimination was not the "No Negroes" exclusion of the recent past, but rejection in the form of poor service by restaurant personnel. The black response indicates the change in black-white interaction since the 1950s and 1960s, for discrimination is handled with vigorous confrontation rather than deference. The aggressive black response and the white backtracking underscore Brittan and Maynard's (1984, p. 7) point that black-white interaction today is being renegotiated. It is possible that the white personnel defined the couple as "poor blacks" because of their jeans, although the jeans were fashionable and white patrons wear jeans. In comments not quoted here the news directors rejects such an explanation. She forcefully articulates a theory of rights—a response that signals the critical impact of civil rights laws on the thinking of middle-class blacks. The news director articulates the American dream: she has worked hard, earned the money and credit cards, developed the appropriate middle-class behavior, and thus has under the law a *right* to be served. There is defensiveness in her actions too, for she feels a need to legitimate her status by showing her purse and credit cards. One important factor that enabled her to take such assertive action was her power to bring a TV news team to the restaurant. This power marks a change from a few decades ago when very few black Americans had the social or economic resources to fight back successfully.

This example underscores the complexity of the interaction in such situations, with two levels of negotiation evident. The negotiation between the respondent and her boyfriend on withdrawal vs. confrontation highlights the process of negotiating responses to discrimination and the difficulty in crafting such responses. Not only is there a process of dickering with whites within the discriminatory scene but also a negotiation between the blacks involved. ...

The confrontation response is generally so costly in terms of time and energy that acquiescence or withdrawal are common options. An example of the exit response was provided by a utility company executive in an east coast city:

I can remember one time my husband had picked up our son ... from camp; and he'd stopped at a little store in the neighborhood near the camp. It was hot, and he was going to buy him a snowball. And the proprietor of the store—this was a very old, white neighborhood, and it was just a little sundry store. But the proprietor said he had the little window where people could come up and order things. Well, my husband and son had gone into the store. And he told them, "Well, I can't give it to you here, but if you go outside to the window, I'll give it to you." And there were other [white] people in the store who'd been served [inside]. So, they just left and didn't buy anything.

Here the act seems a throwback to the South of the 1950s, where blacks were required to use the back or side of a store. This differential treatment in an older white neighborhood is also suggestive of the territorial character of racial relations in many cities. The black response to degradation here was not to confront the white person or to acquiesce abjectly, but rather to reject the poor service and leave. Unlike the previous example, the impact on the white proprietor was negligible because there was no forced negotiation. This site differed from the previous example in that the service was probably not of long-term importance to the black family passing through the area. In the previous site the possibility of returning to the restaurant, for business or pleasure, may have contributed to the choice of a confrontational response. The importance of the service is a likely variable affecting black responses to discrimination in public accommodations.

Discrimination in public accommodations can occur in many different settings. A school board member in a northern city commented on her experiences in retail stores.

> [I have faced] harassment in stores, being followed around, being questioned about what are you going to purchase here. ... I was in an elite department store just this part Saturday and felt that I was being observed while I was window shopping. I in fact actually ended up purchasing something, but felt the entire time I was there—I was in blue jeans and sneakers, that's how I dress on a Saturday—I felt that I was being watched in the store as I was walking through the store, what business did I have there, what was I going to purchase, that kind of thing. ... There are a few of those white people that won't put change in your hand, touch your skin—that doesn't need to go on. [Do you tell them that?] Oh, I do, I do. That is just so obvious. I usually [speak to them] if they're rude in the manner in which they deal with people. [What do they say about that?] Oh, stuff like, "Oh, excuse me." And some are really unconscious about it, say "Excuse me," and put the change in your hand, that's happened. But I've watched other people be rude, and I've been told to mind my own business. ... [But you still do it?] Oh, sure, because for the most part I think that people do have to learn to think for themselves, and demand respect for themselves. ... I find my best weapon of defense is to educate them, whether it's in the store, in a line at the bank, any situation, I teach them. And you take them by surprise because you tell them and show them what they should be doing, and what they should be saying and how they should be thinking. And they look at you because they don't know how to process you. They can't process it because you've just shown them how they should be living, and the fact that they are cheating themselves, really, because the racism is from fear. The racism is from lack of education.

This excessive surveillance of blacks' shopping was reported by several respondents in our study and in recent newspaper accounts (see Jaynes and Williams 1989, p. 140). Several white stereotypes seem to underlie the rejection discrimination in this instance—blacks are seen as shoplifters, as unclean, as disreputable poor. The excessive policing of black shoppers and the discourtesy of clerks illustrate the extra burden of being black in public places. No matter how affluent and influential, a black person cannot escape the stigma of being black, even while re-laxing or shopping. There is the recurring strain of having to craft strategies for a broad range of discriminatory situations. Tailoring her confrontation to fit the particular discrimination, this respondent interrupted the normal flow of the in-teraction to call the whites to intersubjective account and make a one-way experi-ence into a two-way experience. Forced into new situations, offending whites fre-quently do not know how "to process" such an aggressive response. Again we see how middle-class blacks can force a reconstruction of traditional responses by whites to blacks. The intensity of her discussion suggests that the attempt to "edu-cate" whites comes with a heavy personal cost, for it is stressful to "psych" oneself up for such incidents. ...

Middle-class black parents often attempt to protect their children from racial hostility in public places, but they cannot always be successful. A manager at an electronics firm in the Southwest gave an account of his daughter's first encounter with a racial epithet. After describing racist graffiti on a neighborhood fence in the elite white suburb where he lives, he described an incident at a swimming pool:

> I'm talking over two hundred kids in this pool; not one black. I don't think you can go anywhere in the world during the summertime and not find some black kids in the swimming pool. ... Now what's the worst thing that can happen to a ten-year-old girl in a swimming pool with all white kids? What's the worst thing that could happen? It happened. This little white guy called her a "nigger." Then called her a "motherfucker" and told her to "get out of the god-damn pool." ... And what initi-ated that, they had these little inner tubes, they had about fifteen of them, and the pool owns them. So you just use them if they are vacant. So there was a tube setting up on the bank, she got it, jumped in and started playing in it. ... And this little white guy decided he wanted it. But, he's supposed to get it, right? And he meant to get it, and she wouldn't give it to him, so out came all these racial slurs. So my action was first with the little boy. "You know you're not supposed to do that. Apologize right now. Okay, good. Now, Mr. Lifeguard, I want him out of this pool, and you're going to have to do better. You're going to have to do better, but he has to leave out of this pool and let his parents know, okay?"

Taking his daughter back the next day, he observed from behind a fence to make certain the lifeguard protected her. For many decades black adults and children were excluded from public pools in the South and Southwest, and many pools were closed during the early desegregation period. These accommodations have special significance for middle-class black Americans, and this may be one reason the father's reaction was so decisive. Perhaps the major reason for his swift action was because this was the first time that his daughter had been the victim of racial slurs. ...

The verbal responses of middle-class blacks to stigmatization can take more subtle forms. An 80-year-old retired schoolteacher in a southern city recounted her response to a recent experience at a drapery shop:

> The last time I had some draperies done and asked about them at the drapery shop, a young man at that shop—when they called [to him], he asked, and I heard him—

he said, "The job for that nigger woman." And I said to the person who was serving me, "Oh my goodness, I feel so sorry for that young man. I didn't know people were still using that sort of language and saying those sorts of things." And that's the way I deal with it. I don't know what you call that. Is that sarcasm? Sarcasm is pretty good. ... Well I've done that several times. This being 1989 ... I'm surprised that I find it in this day and time.

One white clerk translated the schoolteacher's color in a hostile way while the other apparently listened. Suggested here is the way many whites are content to watch overt racist behavior without intervening. The retired teacher's response contrasts with the more confrontational reactions of the previous examples, for she used what might be called "strategic indirection." With composure she directed a pointedly sarcastic remark to the clerk serving her. Mockery is a more subtle tactic blacks can use to contend with antilocution, and this tactic may be more common among older blacks. Later in her interview this angry woman characterizes such recurring racial incidents as the "little murders" that daily have made her life difficult.

Careful Situation Assessment

We have seen in the previous incidents some tendency for blacks to assess discriminatory incidents before they act. Among several respondents who discussed discrimination at retail stores, the manager of a career development organization in the Southwest indicated that a clear assessment of a situation usually precedes confrontations and is part of a repertoire of concatenated responses:

> If you're in a store—and let's say the person behind the counter is white—and you walk up to the counter, and a white person walks up to the counter, and you know you were there before the white customer, the person behind the counter knows you were there first, and it never fails, they always go, "Who's next." Ok. And what I've done, if they go ahead and serve the white person first, then I will immediately say, "Excuse me, I was here first, and we both know I was here first." ... If they get away with it once, they're going to get away with it more than once, and then it's going to become something else. And you have to, you want to make sure that folks know that you're not being naive, that you really see through what's happening. Or if it's a job opportunity or something like that, too, [we should do the] same thing. You first try to get a clear assessment of what's really going on and sift through that information, and then ... go from there.

The executive's coping process typically begins with a sifting of information before deciding on further action. She usually opts for immediate action so that whites face the reality of their actions in a decisive way. Like the account of the school board member who noted that whites would sometimes not put money directly in her hand, this account illustrates another aspect of discrimination in public accommodations: For many whites racial hostility is imbedded in everyday actions, and there is a deep, perhaps subconscious, recoil response to black color and persona.

The complex process of evaluation and response is described by a college dean, who commented generally on hotel and restaurant discrimination encountered as he travels across the United States:

> When you're in a restaurant and ... you notice that blacks get seated near the kitchen. You notice that if it's a hotel, your room is near the elevator, or your room is always way down in a corner somewhere. You find that you are getting the undesirable rooms. And you come there early in the day and you don't see very many cars on the lot and they'll tell you that this is all we've got. Or you get the room that's got a bad television set. You know that you're being discriminated against. And of course you have to act accordingly. You have to tell them, "Okay, the room is fine, [but] this television set has got to go. Bring me another television set." So in my personal experience, I simply cannot sit and let them get away with it [discrimination] and not let them know that I know that that's what they are doing. ...
>
> When I face discrimination, first I take a long look at myself and try to determine whether or not I am seeing what I think I'm seeing in 1989, and if it's something that I have an option [about]. In other words, if I'm at a store making a purchase, I'll simply walk away from it. If it's at a restaurant where I'm not getting good service, I first of all let the people know that I'm not getting good service, then I [may] walk away from it. But the thing that I have to do is to let people know that I know that I'm being singled out for a separate treatment. And then I might react in any number of ways—depending on where I am and how badly I want whatever it is that I'm there for.

This commentary adds another dimension to our understanding of public discrimination, its cumulative aspect. Blacks confront not just isolated incidents—such as a bad room in a luxury hotel once every few years—but a lifelong series of such incidents. Here again the omnipresence of careful assessments is underscored. The dean's interview highlights a major difficulty in being black—one must be constantly prepared to assess accurately and then decide on the appropriate response. ...

RESPONSES TO DISCRIMINATION: THE STREET

Reacting to White Strangers

As we move away from public accommodations settings to the usually less protected street sites, racial hostility can become more fleeting and severer, and thus black responses are often restricted. The most serious form of street discrimination is violence. Often the reasonable black response to street discrimination is withdrawal, resigned acceptance, or a quick verbal retort. The difficulty of responding to violence is seen in this report by a man working for a media surveying firm in a southern industrial city:

> I was parked in front of this guy's house. ... This guy puts his hands on the window and says, "Get out of the car, nigger." ... So, I got out, and I thought, "Oh, this is what's going to happen here." And I'm talking fast. And they're, "What are you doing here?" And I'm, "This is who I am. I work with these people. This is the man we

want to put in the survey." And I pointed to the house. And the guy said, "Well you have an out-of-state license tag, right?" "Yea." And he said, "If something happened to you, your people at home wouldn't know for a long time, would they?" ... I said, "Look, I deal with a company that deals with television. [If] something happens to me, it's going to be a national thing. ... So, they grab me by the lapel of my coat, and put me in front of my car. They put the blade on my zipper. And now I'm thinking about this guy that's in the truck [behind me], because now I'm thinking that I'm going to have to run somewhere. Where am I going to run? Go to the police? [laughs] So, after a while they bash up my headlight. And I drove [away].

Stigmatized and physically attacked solely because of his color, this man faced verbal hostility and threats of death with courage. Cautiously drawing on his middle-class resources, he told the attackers his death would bring television crews to the town. This resource utilization is similar to that of the news director in the restaurant incident. Beyond this verbal threat his response had to be one of caution. For most whites threatened on the street, the police are a sought-after source of protection, but for black men this is often not the case.

At the other end of the street continuum is nonverbal harassment such as the "hate stare" that so traumatized Griffin (1961). In her research on street remarks, Garnder (1980) considered women and blacks particularly vulnerable targets for harassment. For the segregation years Henley (1978) has documented the ways in which many blacks regularly deferred to whites in public-place communications. Today obsequious deference is no longer a common response to harassment. ...

In between the hate stare and violence are many other hostile actions. Most happen so fast that withdrawal, resigned acceptance, or an immediate verbal retort are the reasonable responses. ... [Then there is] the seldom-noted problem of "cross discrimination"—a black person may suffer from discrimination aimed at other people of color by whites unable to distinguish. The white hostility was guided by certain signals—an old car and dark skin—of minority-group status. The nighttime setting, by assuring anonymity, facilitated the hurling of racist epithets and heightened the negative impact on this woman, who found the harassment especially dangerous and repulsive because she was with her son. She drove away without replying. Later in the interview she notes angrily that in such incidents her ascribed characteristic of "blackness" takes precedence over her achieved middle-class characteristics and that the grouped thinking of racism obscures anything about her that is individual and unique.

For young middle-class blacks street harassment can generate shock and disbelief. ... This ... points up the impact of destructive racial coding on young people and hints at the difficulty black parents face in socializing children for coping with white hostility. When I discussed these street incidents involving younger blacks with two older black respondents, one a southern civil rights activist and the other an Ivy-League professor, both noted the problem created for some middle-class black children by their well-intentioned parents trying to shelter them from racism.

It seems likely that for middle-class blacks the street is the site of recurring encounters with various types of white malevolence. A vivid example of the cumulative character and impact of this discrimination was given by another black student at a white university, who recounted his experiences walking home at night from a campus job to his apartment in a predominantly white residential area:

> So, even if you wanted to, it's difficult just to live a life where you don't come into conflict with others. Because every day you walk the streets, it's not even like once a week, once a month. It's every day you walk the streets. Every day that you live as a black person you're reminded how you're perceived in society. You walk the streets at night; white people cross the streets. I've seen white couples and individuals dart in front of cars to not be on the same side of the street. Just the other day, I was walking down the street, and this white female with a child, I saw her pass a young white male about 20 yards ahead. When she saw me, she quickly dragged the child and herself across the busy street. What is so funny is that this area has had an unknown white rapist in the area for about four years. [When I pass] white men tighten their grip on their women. I've seen people turn around and seem like they're going to take blows from me. The police constantly make circles around me as I walk home, you know, for blocks. I'll walk, and they'll turn a block. And they'll come around me just to make sure, to find out where I'm going. So, every day you realize [you're black]. Even though you're not doing anything wrong; you're just existing. You're just a person. But you're a black person perceived in an unblack world. (This quote includes a clarification sentence from a follow-up interview.)

In a subsequent comment this respondent mentioned that he also endured white men hurling beer cans and epithets at him as he walked home. Again the cumulation of incidents is evident. Everyday street travel for young black middle-class males does not mean one isolated incident every few years.

... When I discussed this student's experiences with a prominent black journalist in a northeastern city, he reported that whites sometimes stop talking—and white women grab their purses—on downtown office-building elevators when he enters. These two men had somewhat different responses to such discrimination, one relatively passive and the other aggressive. In a follow-up interview the student reported that he rarely responded aggressively to the street encounters, apart from the occasional quick curse, because they happened too quickly. Echoing the black graduate student's comments about processing input and missed opportunities, he added: "I was basically analyzing and thinking too much about the incident." However, the journalist reacts more assertively; he described how he turns to whites in elevators and informs them, often with a smile, that they can continue talking or that he is not interested in their purses.

On occasion, black middle-class responses to street hostility from white strangers are even more aggressive. A woman who now runs her own successful business in a southwestern city described a car incident in front of a grocery store:

> We had a new car ... and we stopped at 7-11 [store]. We were going to go out that night, and we were taking my son to a babysitter. ... And we pulled up, and my husband was inside at the time. And this person, this Anglo couple, drove up, and they hit our car. It was a brand new car. So my husband came out. And the first thing they told us was that we got our car on *welfare*. Here we are able-bodied. He was a corporate executive. I had a decent job, it was a professional job, but it wasn't paying anything. But they looked at the car we were driving, and they made the assumption that we got it from welfare. I completely snapped; I physically abused that lady. I did.

And I was trying to keep my husband from arguing with her husband until the police could come. ... And when the police came they interrogated them; they didn't arrest us, because there was an off-duty cop who had seen the whole incident and said she provoked it.

Here we see how some whites perceive blacks, including middle-class blacks, in interracial situations. The verbal attack by the whites was laced with the stereotype about blacks as welfare chiselers. This brought forth an angry response from the black couple, which probably came as a surprise to the whites. ...

Responses to Discrimination by White Police Officers

Most middle-class blacks do not have governmental authority as their personal protection. In fact, white police officers are a major problem. Encounters with the police can be life-threatening and thus limit the range of responses. A television commentator recounted two cases of police harassment when he was working for a survey firm in the mid-1980s. In one of the incidents, which took place in a southern metropolis, he was stopped by several white officers:

"What you doing here?" I tell them what I'm doing here. ... And so [they had] me spread on top of my car. [What had you done?] Because I was in the neighborhood. I left this note on these peoples' house: "Here's who I am. You weren't here, and I will come back in thirty minutes." [Why were they searching you?] They don't know. To me, they're searching, I remember at that particular moment when this all was going down, there was a lot of reports about police crime on civilians. ... It took four cops to shake me down, two police cars, so they had me up there spread out. I had a friend of mine with me who was making the call with me, because we were going to have dinner together, and he was black, and they had me up, and they had him outside. ... They said, "Well, let's check you out." ... And I'm talking to myself, and I'm not thinking about being at attention, with my arms spread on my Ford [a company car], and I'm sitting there talking to myself. "Man, this is crazy, this is crazy."
[How are you feeling inside?] Scared, I mean real scared. [What did you think was going to happen to you?] I was going to go to jail. ... Just because they picked me. Why would they stop me? It's like, if they can stop me, why wouldn't I go to jail, and I could sit in there for ten days before the judge sees me. I'm thinking all this crazy stuff. ... Again, I'm talking to myself. And the guy takes his stick. And he doesn't whack me hard, but he does it with enough authority to let me know they mean business. "I told you stand still; now put your arms back out." And I've got this suit on, and the car's wet. And my friend's hysterical. He's outside the car. And they're checking him out. And he's like, "Man, just be cool, man." And he had tears in his eyes. And I'm like, oh, man, this is a nightmare. This is not supposed to happen to me. This is not my style! And so finally, those other cop comes up and says, "What have we got here Charlie?" "Oh, we've got a guy here. He's running through the neighborhood, and he doesn't want to do what we tell him. We might have to run him in." [You're "running through" the neighborhood?] Yeah, exactly, in a suit in the rain?! After they got through their thing and harassing me, I just said, "Man this has been a hell of a week."
And I had tears in my eyes, but it wasn't tears of upset. It was tears of anger; it was tears of wanting to lash back. ... What I thought to myself was, man, blacks have it real hard down here. I don't care if they're a broadcaster; I don't care if they're a

businessman or a banker. ... They don't have it any easier than the persons on skid row who get harassed by the police on a Friday or Saturday night.

It seems likely that most black men—including middle-class black men—see white police officers as a major source of danger and death (see "Mood of Ghetto America" 1980, June 2, pp. 32–34; Louis Harris and Associates 1989; Roddy 1990, August 26). Scattered evidence suggests that by the time they are in their twenties, most black males, regardless of socioeconomic status, have been stopped by the police because "blackness" is considered a sign of possible criminality by police officers (Moss 1990; Roddy 1990, August 26). This treatment probably marks a dramatic contrast with the experiences of young white middle-class males. In the incident above the respondent and a friend experienced severe police maltreatment—detention for a lengthy period, threat of arrest, and the reality of physical violence. The coping response of the respondent was resigned acceptance somewhat similar to the deference rituals highlighted by Goffman. The middle-class suits and obvious corporate credentials (for example, survey questionnaires and company car) did not protect the two black men. The final comment suggests a disappointment that middle-class status brought no reprieve from police stigmatization and harassment.

Black women can also be the targets of police harassment. A professor at a major white university in the Southwest describes her encounters with the police:

When the cops pull me over because my car is old and ugly, they assume I've just robbed a convenience store. Or that's the excuse they give: "This car looks like a car used to rob a 7-11 [store]." And I've been pulled over six or seven times since I've been in this city—and I've been here two years now. Then I do what most black folks do. I try not to make any sudden moves so I'm not accidentally shot. Then I give them my identification. And I show them my university I.D. so they won't think that I'm someone that constitutes a threat, however they define it, so that I don't get arrested.

She adds:

[One problem with] being black in America is that you have to spend so much time thinking about stuff that most white people just don't even have to think about. I worry when I get pulled over by a cop. I worry because the person that I live with is a black male, and I have a teen-aged son. I worry what some white cop is going to think when he walks over to our car, because he's holding on to a gun. And I'm very aware of how many black folks accidentally get shot by cops. I worry when I walk into a store, that someone's going to think I'm in there shoplifting. And I have to worry about that because I'm not free to ignore it. And so, that thing that's supposed to be guaranteed to all Americans, the freedom to just be yourself, is a fallacious idea. And I get resentful that I have to think about things that a lot of people, even my very close white friends whose politics are similar to mine, simply don't have to worry about.

This commentary about a number of encounters underscores the pyramiding character of discrimination. This prominent scholar has faced excessive surveillance by white police officers, who presumably view blacks as likely criminals. As in the previous example, there is great fear of white officers, but her response is somewhat different: She draws on her middle-class resources for protection; she cautiously interposes her middle-class status by pulling out a university I.D. card. In the verbal exchange her articulateness as a professor probably helps protect her. ...

CONCLUSION

I have examined the sites of discrimination, the types of discriminatory acts, and the responses of the victims and have found the color stigma still to be very important in the public lives of affluent black Americans. The sites of racial discrimination range from relatively protected home sites, to less protected workplace and educational sites, to the even less protected public places. The 1964 Civil Rights Act guarantees that black Americans are "entitled to the full and equal enjoyment of the goods, services, facilities, privileges, advantages, and accommodations" in public accommodations. Yet the interviews indicate that deprivation of full enjoyment of public facilities is not a relic of the past; deprivation and discrimination in public accommodations persist. Middle-class black Americans remain vulnerable targets in public places. Prejudice-generated aggression in public places is, of course, not limited to black men and women—gay men and white women are also targets of street harassment (Benokraitis and Feagin 1986). Nonetheless, black women and men face an unusually broad range of discrimination on the street and in public accommodations.

The interviews highlight two significant aspects of the additive discrimination faced by black Americans in public places and elsewhere: (1) the cumulative character of an *individual's* experiences with discrimination; and (2) the *group's* accumulated historical experiences as perceived by the individual. A retired psychology professor who has worked in the Midwest and Southwest commented on the pyramiding of incidents:

> I don't think white people, generally, understand the full meaning of racist discriminatory behaviors directed toward Americans of African descent. They seem to see each act of discrimination or any act of violence as an "isolated" event. As a result, most white Americans cannot understand the strong reaction manifested by blacks when such events occur. They feel that blacks tend to "over-react." They forget that in most cases, we live lives of quiet desperation generated by a litany of *daily* large and small events that whether or not by design, remind us of our "place" in American society.

Particular instances of discrimination may seem minor to outside white observers when considered in isolation. But when blatant acts of avoidance, verbal harassment, and physical attack combine with subtle and covert slights, and these accumulate over months, years, and lifetimes, the impact on a black person is far more than the sum of the individual instances. ...

Particular acts, even antilocution that might seem minor to white observers, are freighted not only with one's past experience of discrimination but also with centuries of racial discrimination directed at the entire group, vicarious oppression that still includes racially translated violence and denial of access to the American dream. Antiblack discrimination is a matter of racial-power inequality institutionalized in a variety of economic and social institutions over a long period of time. The microlevel events of public accommodations and public streets are not just rare and isolated encounters by individuals; they are recurring events reflecting an invasion of the microworld by the macroworld of historical racial subordination.

The cumulative impact of racial discrimination accounts for the special way that blacks have of looking at and evaluating interracial incidents. One respondent, a clerical employee at an adoption agency, described the "second eye" she uses:

> I think that it causes you to have to look at things from two different perspectives. You have to decide whether things that are done or slights that are made are made because you are black or they are made because the person is just rude, or unconcerned and uncaring. So it's kind of a situation where you're always kind of looking to see with a second eye or a second antenna just what's going on.

The language of "second eye" suggests that blacks look at white-black interaction through a lens colored by personal and group experience with cross-institutional and cross-generational discrimination. This sensitivity is not new, but is a current adaptation transcending, yet reminiscent of, the black sensitivity to the etiquette of racial relations in the old South (Doyle 1937). What many whites see as black "paranoia" (e.g., Wieseltier 1989, June 5) is simply a realistic sensitivity to white-black interaction created and constantly reinforced by the two types of cumulative discrimination cited above.

Blacks must be constantly aware of the repertoire of possible responses to chronic and burdensome discrimination. One older respondent spoke of having to put on her "shield" just before she leaves the house each morning. When quizzed, she said that for more than six decades, as she leaves her home, she has tried to be prepared for insults and discrimination in public places, even if nothing happens that day. This extraordinary burden of discrimination, evident in most of the 135 interviews in the larger sample, was eloquently described by the female professor who resented having to worry about life-threatening incidents that her "very close white friends ... simply don't have to worry about." Another respondent was articulate on this point:

> ... if you can think of the mind as having one hundred ergs of energy, and the average man uses fifty percent of his energy dealing with the everyday problems of the world—just general kinds of things—then he has fifty percent more to do creative kinds of things that he wants to do. Now that's a white person. Now a black person also has one hundred ergs; he uses fifty percent the same way a white man does, dealing with what the white man has [to deal with], so he has fifty percent left. But he uses twenty-five percent fighting being black, [with] all the problems [of] being black and what it means. Which means he really only has twenty-five percent to do what the white man has fifty percent to do, and he's expected to do just as much as the white man with that twenty-five percent. ... So, that's kind of what happens. You

just don't have as much energy left to do as much as you know you really could if you were free, [if] your mind were free.

The individual cost of coping with racial discrimination is great, and, as he says, you cannot accomplish as much as you could if you retained the energy wasted on discrimination. This is perhaps the most tragic cost of persisting discrimination in the United States. In spite of decades of civil rights legislation, black Americans have yet to attain the full promise of the American dream.

REFERENCES

Allport, Gordon. 1958. The *Nature of Prejudice*. Abridged. New York: Doubleday Anchor Books.

Benokraitis, Nijole and Joe R. Feagin. 1986. *Modern Sexism: Blatant, Subtle and Covert Discrimination*. Englewood Cliffs: Prentice-Hall.

Brittan, Arthur and Mary Maynard. 1984. *Sexism, Racism and Oppression*. Oxford: Basil Blackwell.

Feagin, Joe R. and Douglas Eckberg. 1980. "Prejudice and Discrimination." *Annual Review of Sociology* 6:1–20.

Feagin, Joe R. and Clairece Booher Feagin. 1986. *Discrimination American Style* (rev. ed.). Melbourne, FL: Krieger Publishing Co.

Gardner, Carol Brooks. 1980. "Passing By: Street Remarks, Address Rights, and the Urban Female." *Sociological Inquiry* 50:328–56.

_____. 1988. "Access Information: Public Lies and Private Peril." *Social Problems* 35:384–97.

Goffman, Erving. 1956. "The Nature of Deference and Demeanor." *American Anthropologist* 58:473–502.

Griffin, John Howard. 1961. *Black Like Me*. Boston: Houghton Mifflin.

Henley, Nancy M. 1978. *Body Politics*. Englewood Cliffs, N.J.: Prentice-Hall.

Jaynes, Gerald D. and Robin Williams, Jr. (eds.). 1989. *A Common Destiny: Blacks and American Society*. Washington, D.C.: National Academy Press.

Louis Harris and Associates. 1989. *The Unfinished Agenda on Race in America*. New York: NAACP Legal Defense and Educational Fund.

"The Mood of Ghetto America." 1980, June 2. *Newsweek*, pp. 32–4.

Moss, E. Yvonne. 1990. "African Americans and the Administration of Justice." Pp. 79–86 in *Assessment of the Status of African-Americans*, edited by Wornie L. Reed. Boston: University of Massachusetts, William Monroe Trotter Institute.

Roddy, Dennis B. 1990, August 26. "Perceptions Still Segregate Police, Black Community." *The Pittsburgh Press*, p. B1.

Rollins, Judith. 1985. *Between Women*. Philadelphia: Temple University Press.

Wieseltier, Leon. 1989, June 5. "Scar Tissue." *New Republic*, pp. 19–20.

Wilson, William J. 1978. *The Declining Significance of Race*. Chicago: University of Chicago Press.

_____. 1987. *The Truly Disadvantaged: The Inner City, the Underclass, and Public Policy*. Chicago: University of Chicago Press.

11

"We'd Love to Hire Them, But …": The Meaning of Race for Employers

JOLEEN KIRSCHENMAN AND KATHRYN M. NECKERMAN

… In this paper we explore the meaning of race and ethnicity to employers, the ways race and ethnicity are qualified by—and at times reinforce—other characteristics in the eyes of employers, and the conditions under which race seems to matter most. Our interviews at Chicago-area businesses show that employers view inner-city workers, especially black men, as unstable, uncooperative, dishonest, and uneducated. Race is an important factor in hiring decisions. But it is not race alone: rather it is race in a complex interaction with employers' perceptions of class and space, or inner-city residence. Our findings suggest that racial discrimination deserves an important place in analyses of the underclass.

RACE AND EMPLOYMENT

In research on the disadvantages blacks experience in the labor market, social scientists tend to rely on indirect measures of racial discrimination. They interpret as evidence of this discrimination the differences in wages or employment among races and ethnic groups that remain after education and experience are controlled. With a few exceptions they have neglected the processes at the level of the firm that underlie these observed differences.[1] …

The theoretical literature conventionally distinguishes two types of discrimination, "pure" and "statistical." In pure discrimination, employers, employees, or consumers have a "taste" for discrimination, that is, they will pay a premium to avoid members of another group.[2] Statistical discrimination is a more recent conception that builds on the discussions of "signaling."[3] In statistical discrimination, employers use group membership as a proxy for aspects of productivity that are relatively expensive or impossible to measure. Those who use the concept disagree about whether employers' perceptions of group differences in productivity must reflect reality.[4] In this discussion, we are concerned with statistical discrimination as a cognitive process, regardless of whether the employer is correct or mistaken in his or her views of the labor force. ...

The distinction between pure and statistical discrimination is a useful one. However, it is also useful to recognize the relationship between the two. There are several ways in which a taste for discrimination in employment practices may lead to perceived and actual productivity differences between groups, making statistical discrimination more likely. Social psychological evidence suggests that expectations about group differences in productivity may bias evaluation of job performance.[5] These expectations may also influence job placement. In particular, workers of lower expected productivity may be given less on-the-job training. Finally, and most important for our study, productivity is not an individual characteristic; rather, it is shaped by the social relations of the workplace. If these relations are strained because of tastes for discrimination on the part of the employer, supervisor, coworkers, or consumers, lower productivity may result.[6] Thus what begins as irrational practice based on prejudice or mistaken beliefs may end up being rational, profit-maximizing behavior.

DATA

This research is based on face-to-face interviews with employers in Chicago and surrounding Cook County between July 1988 and March 1989. Inner-city firms were oversampled; all results here are weighted to adjust for this oversampling. Our overall response rate was 46 percent, and the completed sample of 185 employers is representative of the distribution of Cook County's employment by industry and firm size.[7]

Interviews included both closed- and open-ended questions about employers' hiring and recruitment practices and about their perceptions of Chicago's labor force and business climate. Our initial contacts, and most of the interviews themselves, were conducted with the highest ranking official at the establishment. Because of the many open-ended questions, we taped the interviews.

Most of the structured portion of the interview focused on a sample job, defined by the interview schedule as "the most typical entry-level position" in the firm's modal occupational category—sales, clerical, skilled, semiskilled, unskilled, or service, but excluding managerial, professional, and technical. The distribution of our sample jobs approximates the occupational distribution in the 1980 census for Cook County, again excluding professional, managerial, and technical categories. In effect, what we have is a sample of the opportunities facing the Chicago job-seeker with minimal skills. ...

Although we do not present our findings as necessarily representative of the attitudes of all Chicago employers, as the rules of positivist social science would require, they are representative of those Chicago employers who spoke to a particular issue. A standard rule of discourse is that some things are acceptable to say and others are better left unsaid. Silence has the capacity to speak volumes. Thus we were overwhelmed by the degree to which Chicago employers felt comfortable talking with us—in a situation where the temptation would be to conceal rather than reveal—in a negative manner about blacks. In this paper we make an effort to understand the discursive evidence by relating it to the practice of discrimination, using quantitative data to reinforce the qualitative findings.

WE'D LOVE TO HIRE THEM, BUT ...

... Explanations for the high rates of unemployment and poverty among blacks have relied heavily on the categories of class and space.[8] We found that employers also relied on those categories, but they used them to refine the category of race, which for them is primary. Indeed, it was through the interaction of race with class and space that these categories were imbued with new meaning. It was race that made class and space important to employers.

Although some employers regarded Chicago's workers as highly skilled and having a good work ethic, far more thought that the labor force has deteriorated. When asked why they thought business had been leaving Chicago, 35 percent referred to the inferior quality of the work force. ... Several firms in our sample were relocating or seriously considering a move to the South in a search for cheap skilled labor. Employers of less skilled labor can find an ample supply of applicants, but many complained that it was becoming more difficult to find workers with basic skills and a good work ethic.

These employers coped with what they considered a less qualified work force through various strategies. Some restructured production to require either fewer workers or fewer skills. These strategies included increasing automation and deemphasizing literacy requirements—using color-coded filing systems, for example. But far more widespread were the use of recruiting and screening techniques to help select "good" workers. For instance, employers relied more heavily on referrals from employees, which tend to reproduce the traits and characteristics of the current work force: the Chicago Association of Commerce and Industry has reported a dramatic increase in the use of referral bonuses in the past few years. Or employers targeted newspaper ads to particular neighborhoods or ethnic groups. The rationale underlying these strategies was, in part, related to the productivity employers accorded different categories of workers.

For instance, whether or not the urban underclass is an objective social category, its subjective importance in the discourse of Chicago employers cannot be denied. Their characterizations of inner-city workers mirrored many descriptions of the underclass by social scientists. Common among the traits listed were that workers were unskilled, uneducated, illiterate, dishonest, lacking initiative, unmotivated, involved with drugs and gangs, did not understand work, had no personal charm, were unstable, lacked a work ethic, and had no family life or role models.

Social scientists discover pathologies; employers try to avoid them. After explaining that he hired "the best applicant," the owner of a transportation firm added, "Probably what I'm trying to say is we're not social minded. We're not worried about solving the problems of sociology. We can't afford to." But despite not being worried about the "problems of sociology," employers have become lay social theorists, creating numerous distinctions among the labor force that then serve as bases for statistical discrimination. From their own experiences and biases, those of other employers, and accounts in the mass media, employers have attributed meaning to the categories of race and ethnicity, class, and space. These have then become markers of more or less desirable workers.

These categories were often confounded with each other, as when one respondent contrasted the white youth (with opportunities) from the North Shore with the black one (without opportunities) from the South Side. Although the primary distinction that more than 70 percent of our informants made was based on race and ethnicity, it was frequently confounded with class: black and Hispanic equaled lower class; white equaled middle class. And these distinctions also overlapped with space: "inner-city" and at times "Chicago" equaled minority, especially black; "suburb" equaled white. In fact, race was important in part because it signaled class and inner-city residence, which are less easy to observe directly. But employers also needed class and space to draw distinctions within racial and ethnic groups; race was the distinguishing characteristic most often referred to, followed respectively by class and space. ...

Race and Ethnicity

When they talked about the work ethic, tensions in the workplace, or attitudes toward work, employers emphasized the color of a person's skin. Many believed that white workers were superior to minorities in their work ethic. A woman who hires for a suburban service firm said, "The Polish immigrants that I know and know of are more highly motivated than the Hispanics. The Hispanics share in some of the problems that the blacks do." These problems included "exposure to poverty and drugs" as well as "a lack of motivation" related to "their environment and background." A man from a Chicago construction company, expressing a view shared by many of our informants, said, "For all groups, the pride [in their work] of days gone by is not there, but what is left, I think probably the whites take more pride than some of the other minorities." (Interviewer: "And between blacks and Hispanics?") "Probably the same."

In the discourse of "work ethic," which looms large among the concerns of employers, whites usually came out on top. But although white workers generally looked good to employers, East European whites were repeatedly praised for really knowing how to work and caring about their work. Several informants cited positive experiences with their Polish domestic help. In the skilled occupations, East European men were sought. One company advertised for its skilled workers in Polish- and German-language newspapers, but hired all its unskilled workers, 97 percent of whom were Hispanic, through an employee network.

When asked directly whether they thought there were any differences in the work ethics of whites, blacks, and Hispanics, 37.7 percent of the employers ranked blacks last, 1.4 percent ranked Hispanics last, and no one ranked whites there. Another 7.6 percent placed blacks and Hispanics together on the lowest level; 51.4 percent either saw no difference or refused to categorize in a straightforward way. Many of the latter group qualified their response by saying they saw no differences once one controlled for education, background, or environment, and that any differences were more the result of class or space.

Although blacks were consistently evaluated less favorably than whites, employers' perceptions of Hispanics were more mixed. Some ranked them with blacks; others positioned them between whites and blacks. ...

They also believed that a homogenous work force serves to maintain good relations among workers. ... A personnel manager from a large, once all-white Chicago manufacturing concern lamented the tensions that race and ethnic diversity had created among workers: "I wish we could all be the same, but, unfortunately, we're not." An employer of an all-white work force said that "if I had one [black worker] back there it might be okay, but if I have two or more I would have trouble." But although some employers found a diverse work force more difficult to manage, few actually maintained a homogeneous labor force, at least in terms of race and ethnicity.

Employers worried about tensions not only between white and minority workers but also between Mexicans and blacks, Mexicans and Puerto Ricans, and even African and American blacks. A restaurateur with an all-white staff of waiters and a Hispanic kitchen said, "The Mexican kids that work in the kitchen, they're not, they're not kids anymore, but they don't like to work with black guys. But they don't like to work with Puerto Rican guys either." ...

Blacks are by and large thought to possess very few of the characteristics of a "good" worker. Over and over employers said, "They don't want to work." "They don't want to stay." "They've got an attitude problem." One compared blacks with Mexicans: "Most of them are not as educated as you might think. I've never seen any of these guys read anything outside of a comic book. These Mexicans are sitting here reading novels constantly, even though they are in Spanish. These guys will sit and watch cartoons while the other guys are busy reading. To me that shows basic laziness. No desire to upgrade yourself." When asked about discrimination against black workers, a Chicago manufacturer related a common view: "Oh, I would in all honestly probably say there is some among most employers. I think one of the reasons, in all honesty, is because we've had bad experience in that sector, and believe me, I've tried. And as I say, if I find—whether he's black or white, if he's good and, you know, we'll hire him. We are not shutting out any black specifically. But I will say that our experience factor has been bad. We've had more bad black employees over the years than we had good." This negative opinion of blacks sometimes cuts across class lines. For instance, a personnel officer of a professional service company in the suburbs commented that "with the professional staff, black males that we've had, some of the skill levels—they're not as orientated to details. They lack some of the leadership skills."

One must also consider the "relevant nots": what were some employers not talking about? They were not talking about how clever black workers were, they were not talking about the cultural richness of the black community, nor were they talking about rising divorces rate among whites. Furthermore, although each employer reserved the right to deny making distinctions along racial lines, fewer than 10 percent consistently refused to distinguish or generalize according to race.

These ways of talking about black workers—they have a bad work ethic, they create tensions in the workplace, they are lazy and unreliable, they have a bad attitude—reveal the meaning race has for many employers. If race were a proxy for expected productivity and the sole basis for statistical discrimination, black applicants would indeed find few job opportunities.

Class

Although some respondents spoke only in terms of race and ethnicity, or conflated class with race, others were sensitive to class distinctions. Class constituted a second, less easily detected signal for employers. Depending somewhat on the demands of the jobs, they used class markers to select among black applicants. The contrasts between their discourse about blacks and Hispanics were striking. Employers sometimes placed Hispanics with blacks in the lower class: an inner-city retailer confounded race, ethnicity, and class when he said, "I think there's a self-defeating prophecy that's maybe inherent in a lot of lower-income ethnic groups or races. Blacks, Hispanics." But although they rarely drew class distinctions among Hispanics, such distinctions were widely made for black workers. As one manufacturer said, "The black work ethic. There's no work ethic. At least at the unskilled. I'm sure with the skilled, as you go up, it's a lot different." Employers generally considered it likely that lower-class blacks would have more negative traits than blacks of other classes.

In many ways black business owners and black personnel managers were the most expressive about class divisions among blacks. A few believed poor blacks were more likely to be dishonest because of the economic pressures they face. A black jeweler said the most important quality he looked for in his help was "a person who doesn't need a job."

> (Interviewer: That's what you're looking for?)
> That's what we usually try to hire. People that don't need the job.
> (Interviewer: Why?)
> Because they will tend to be a little more honest. Most of the people that live in the neighborhoods and areas where my stores are at need the job. They are low-income, and so, consequently, they're under more pressure and there's more of a tendency to be dishonest, because of the pressure. ...

Other employers mentioned problems that occur in the workplace when there are class divisions among the workers. These are reminiscent of the tensions created by the racial and ethnic diversity described earlier. One black businesswoman told of a program wherein disadvantaged youths were sent to private schools by wealthy sponsors. She herself was a sponsor and held the program in high regard, but she hired some of these youths and they did not get along with her other young employees: "Those kids were too smart 'cause they were from a middle-class background." (Interviewer: "So these were primarily middle-class kids?") "No, they're not middle class, but they have middle-class values because they're exposed to them all the time." They made excellent employees, she said, "if you kept your store filled with just them. They're more outgoing and less afraid of the customers. But they're very intimidating to the supervisors because they know everything by the time they get to be a sophomore in high school." ...

Thus, although many employers assumed that black meant "inner-city poor," others—both black and white—were quick to see divisions within the black population. Of course, class itself is not directly observable, but markers that convey middle- or working-class status will help a black job applicant get through race-based exclusionary barriers. Class is primarily signaled to employers through speech, dress, education levels, skill levels, and place of residence. Although many respondents drew class distinctions among blacks, very few made those same distinctions among Hispanics or whites; in refining these categories, respondents referred to ethnicity and age rather than class.

Space

Although some employers spoke implicitly or explicitly in terms of class, for others "inner-city" was the more important category. For most the term immediately connoted black, poor, uneducated, unskilled, lacking in values, crime, gangs, drugs, and unstable families. "Suburb" connoted white, middle-class, educated, skilled, and stable families. Conversely, race was salient in part because it signaled space; black connoted inner city and white the suburbs. ... When asked what it would take for their firm to relocate to the inner city, respondents generally thought it an implausible notion. They were sure their skilled workers would not consider working in those neighborhoods because they feared for their safety, and the employers saw no alternative labor supply there.

The skepticism that greets the inner-city worker often arises when employers associate their race and residence with enrollment in Chicago's troubled public education system. Being educated in Chicago public schools has become a way of signaling "I'm black, I'm poor, and I'm from the inner city" to employers. Some mentioned that they passed over applicants from Chicago public schools for those with parochial or suburban educations. If employers were looking at an applicant's credentials when screening, blacks in the inner city did not do well. As one employer said, "The educational skills they come to the job with are minimal because of the schools in the areas where they generally live."

A vice president of a television station complained of the inner-city work force:

> They are frequently unable to write. They go through the Chicago public schools or they dropped out when they were in the eighth grade. They can't read. They can't write. They can hardly talk. I have another opinion which is strictly my own and that is that people who insist on beating themselves to the point where they are out of the mainstream of the world suffer the consequences. And I'm talking about the languages that are spoken in the ghetto. They are not English.

Employers were clearly disappointed, not just in the academic content and level of training students receive, but in the failure of the school system to prepare them for the work force. Because the inner city is heavily associated with a lack of family values, employers wished the schools would compensate and provide students the self-discipline needed for workers socialization. Additionally, they complained that black workers had no "ability to understand work." ... It is not only educational content per se that employers were looking for; some were concerned with the educational "experience." One talked about how it just showed "they could finish something." Thus inner city is equated with public school attendance, which in turn signifies insufficient work skills and work ethic.

... Another employer used space to refine the category of race: "We have some black women here but they're not inner city. They're from suburbs and ... I think they're a little bit more willing to give it a shot, you know, I mean they're a little bit more willing [than black men] to give a day's work for a day's pay."

Employers readily distinguished among blacks on the basis of space. They talked about Cabrini Green or the Robert Taylor Homes or referred to the South Side and West Side as a shorthand for black. But they were not likely to make these distinctions among whites and Hispanics. They made no reference to Pilsen (a largely immigrant Mexican neighborhood), Humboldt Park (largely Puerto Rican), or Uptown (a community of poor whites and new immigrants).

For black applicants, having the wrong combination of class and space markers suggested low productivity and undesirability to an employer. The important finding of this research, then, is not only that employers make hiring decisions based on the color of a person's skin, but the extent to which that act has become nuanced. Race, class, and space interact with each other. Moreover, the precise nature of that interaction is largely determined by the demands of the job. ...

CONCLUSION

Chicago's employers did not hesitate to generalize about race or ethnic differences in the quality of the labor force. Most associated negative images with inner-city workers, and particularly with black men. "Black" and "inner-city" were inextricably linked, and both were linked with "lower-class."

Regardless of the generalizations employers made, they did consider the black population particularly heterogeneous, which made it more important that they be able to distinguish "good" from "bad" workers. Whether through skills tests, credentials, personal references, folk theories, or their intuition, they used some means of screening out the inner-city applicant. The ubiquitous anecdote about the good black worker, the exception to the rule, testified to their own perceived success at doing this. So did frequent references to "our" black workers as opposed to "those guys on the street corner."

And black job applicants, unlike their white counterparts, must indicate to employers that the stereotypes do not apply to them. Inner-city and lower-class workers were seen as undesirable, and black applicants had to try to signal to employers that they did not fall into those categories, either by demonstrating their skills or by adopting a middle-class style of dress, manner, and speech or perhaps (as we were told some did) by lying about their address or work history.

By stressing employers' preconceptions about inner-city workers, we do not mean to imply that there are no problems of labor quality in the inner city: the low reading and mathematics test scores of Chicago public school students testify to these problems. But if the quality of the inner-city labor force has indeed deteriorated, then it is incumbent on employers to avoid hiring inner-city workers. This is precisely the result one would expect from William Julius Wilson's account of increased social dislocations in the inner city since the early 1970s. Because race and inner-city residence are so highly correlated, it would not be surprising if race were to become a key marker of worker productivity.

However, productivity is not an individual characteristic. Rather it is embedded in social relations. The qualities most likely to be proxied by race are not job skills but behavioral and attitudinal attributes—dependability, strong work ethic, and cooperativeness—that are closely tied to interactions among workers and between workers and employers. Our evidence suggests that more attention should be paid to social relations in the workplace. Antagonisms among workers and between workers and their employers are likely to diminish productivity. Thus employers' expectations may become self-fulfilling prophecies.

NOTES

1. One of the exceptions is Braddock and McPartland (1987).

2. Becker (1957).

3. Phelps (1972); Arrow (1973); and Spence (1973).

4. See, for example, Thurow (1975); Aigner and Cain (1977); and Bielby and Baron (1986).

5. See Bielby and Baron (1986) for a discussion.

6. Anderson (1980).

7. The sample and survey methods are described in more detail in the "Employer Survey Final Report," available from the authors.

8. Wilson (1980, 1987); and Kasarda (1985). We use the term "space" in the tradition of urban geography. We do this to draw attention to the way people categorize and attach meaning to geographic locations.

REFERENCES

Aigner, Dennis J., and Glen G. Cain. 1977. "Statistical Theories of Discrimination in Labor Markets." *Industrial and Labor Relations Review* 30 (January), pp. 175–87.

Anderson, Elijah. 1980. "Some Observations on Black Youth Employment." In *Youth Employment and Public Policy,* edited by Bernard E. Anderson and Isabel V. Sawhill. Prentice-Hall.

Arrow, Kenneth. 1973. "The Theory of Discrimination." In *Discrimination in Labor Markets,* edited by Orley Aschenfelter and Albert Rees. Princeton University Press.

Bielby, William T., and James N. Baron. 1986. "Men and Women at Work: Sex Segregation and Statistical Discrimination." *American Journal of Sociology* 91 (January), pp. 759–99.

Braddock, Jomills Henry II, and James M. McPartland. 1987. "How Minorities Continue to Be Excluded from Equal Employment Opportunities: Research on Labor Market and Institutional Barriers." *Journal of Social Issues* 43, pp. 5–39.

Kasarda, John D. 1985. "Urban Change and Minority Opportunities." In *The New Urban Reality,* edited by Paul E. Peterson. Brookings.

Phelps, Edmund S. 1972. "The Statistical Theory of Racism and Sexism." *American Economic Review* 62 (September), pp. 659–61.

Spence, Michael. 1973. "Job Market Signalling." *Quarterly Journal of Economics* 87 (August), pp. 355–74.

Thurow, Lester C. 1975. *Generating Inequality: Mechanisms of Distribution in the U.S. Economy.* Basic Books.

Wilson, William Julius. 1980. *The Declining Significance of Race: Blacks and Changing American Institutions.* 2d ed. University of Chicago Press.

———. 1987. *The Truly Disadvantaged: The Inner City, the Underclass, and Public Policy.* University of Chicago Press.

12

Residential Segregation in American Cities

DOUGLAS S. MASSEY

The results that I report reflect my best scientific judgment concerning patterns of residential segregation in 60 American metropolitan areas, which include the 50 largest urban areas in the United States plus 10 others with large concentrations of Hispanics. In my remarks, I focus on the situation of black Americans, making occasional references to Hispanics or Asians for comparative purposes. After discussing basic trends in segregation from 1970 to 1980, I discuss the uniqueness of black segregation compared to other minority groups. I then consider the process of suburbanization and its role in black segregation, and address the issue of whether black segregation might reasonably be attributed to socioeconomic factors. After considering the reasons for the persistence of high levels of black segregation, I consider its impact on black social and economic well-being. I conclude with a short statement on the importance of census data for the measurement and analysis of residential segregation.

1. TRENDS IN RESIDENTIAL SEGREGATION

In an article ... published in the American Sociological Review ... Nancy Denton and I measure trends in minority segregation using two indicators. The easiest to report is one that gives the percentage of minority members that would have to change their place of residence in order to achieve an even distribution among neighborhoods. It equals zero when every neighborhood has the same minority percentage as the urban area as a whole, and 100 when all minority and majority members live in separate neighborhoods (in the article this index is reported as a proportion ranging from 0 to 1). In general, values above 60 are considered high; those between 30 and 60 are moderate; and those under 30 are low. This index is not influenced by the relative numbers of minority and majority members, so it is possible to compare different cities and minority groups.

Our results indicate that blacks remain the most residentially segregated minority group in America. In the 60 metropolitan areas we examined, black segregation in 1980 averaged about 1.6 times that of Hispanics and twice that of Asians.

Black segregation was greatest in large metropolitan areas containing many black residents, especially in the northeast and midwest. A good example is Chicago, which contains the second largest black population in the United States, and the third largest Hispanic and Asian populations. In this metropolitan area, the black segregation score was 88, meaning that almost 90 percent of blacks would have to move to achieve an even settlement pattern; the Hispanic score was 64; and the Asian score was 44. Across metropolitan areas, Hispanic and Asian segregation generally ranged from low to moderate levels, while black indices were largely in the high range.

Although the level of black-white segregation declined in many urban areas between 1970 and 1980, significant declines occurred primarily in smaller metropolitan areas in the south and west that contain few black residents, not in large black settlements in the northeast and midwest. The largest declines were observed in places such as Albuquerque, Anaheim, Austin, and Seattle, not in Chicago, Detroit, Cleveland, or Newark. Relatively small declines also occurred in those southern metropolitan areas with large black populations, such as Atlanta, Baltimore, Memphis, New Orleans, and Miami.

In the nation's largest urban black concentrations, segregation remained very high through 1980. Among the 15 largest black settlements, the average segregation index was 84 in 1970 and 78 in 1980. In Chicago, Cleveland, Los Angeles, New York, Detroit, Newark, St. Louis, Milwaukee, Gary, and Paterson, the black segregation score remained at 80 or higher throughout the decade, indicating a very high level of segregation; and in five metropolitan areas—Newark, New York, Jersey City, Paterson, and Philadelphia—the level of black-white segregation actually increased from 1970 to 1980. Segregation indices for Hispanics and Asians never reach these high levels, even in metropolitan areas where they concentrate. In the 15 largest Hispanic settlements, for example, the average Hispanic segregation score was only 50, and in the 15 largest Asian settlements the average Asian score was only 37.

Thus, in a significant set of the nation's largest metropolitan areas, blacks experience very high levels of residential segregation from non-Hispanic whites. This high degree of segregation persisted from 1970 to 1980, especially in the northeast and midwest, and set blacks distinctly apart from other minority groups.

2. THE EXTREME NATURE OF BLACK SEGREGATION

In fact, black segregation in some metropolitan areas is even more extreme than indicated by the trends just described. In another paper ... , Nancy Denton and I compare the residential circumstances of blacks and Hispanics in terms of five separate facets, or dimensions, of segregation. These include (1) evenness, or the degree to which a minority group is distributed in equal proportions among neighborhoods; (2) exposure, the degree to which minority members come into contact with majority members within neighborhoods; (3) clustering, the extent to which minority neighborhoods combine spatially to form large agglomerations; (4) concentration, the degree to which minority populations occupy a small segment of the urban environment; and (5) centralization, the extent to which minority members are restricted primarily to neighborhoods near the city center.

Blacks are the only minority group to display high levels of segregation on all five dimensions simultaneously. In our paper, we identified a core of ten large metropolitan areas within which blacks are very highly segregated on at least four of the five dimensions. These areas contain nearly one-third metropolitan blacks, and include the metropolitan areas of Baltimore, Chicago, Cleveland, Detroit, Milwaukee, and Philadelphia—which are highly segregated on all five dimensions—and Gary, Los Angeles, New York, and St. Louis—which are segregated on four dimensions. In no metropolitan area were Hispanics or Asians highly segregated on more than three dimensions simultaneously, and in the vast majority of areas they were not highly segregated on any dimension at all.

In other words, black segregation is unique and exceptional not only because of its extreme unevenness, but also because of its multifaceted nature. Segregation on multiple dimensions is characteristic of no other minority group in the metropolitan areas we examined. Extensive residential segregation across several dimensions is important because of the social isolation it implies, and for blacks in large ghettos of the northeast and midwest, this isolation must be extreme. Not only are blacks disproportionately likely to share a neighborhood with other blacks; they are very unlikely to share a neighborhood with any whites at all. And if they go to the adjacent neighborhood, or to the neighborhood adjacent to that, they still will be unlikely to encounter a white resident. Black settlements in these metropolitan areas are large agglomerations of densely settled neighborhoods closely packed into a small area around the city center. Unless residents of these ghettos work in the mainstream economy—remember that nearly a quarter of central city black men are unemployed—they will be very unlikely to come into contact with anyone other than another black ghetto-dweller.

3. SUBURBANIZATION AND SEGREGATION

In two papers, ... Denton and I consider the process of suburbanization and the role that it plays in minority segregation. Our results indicate that black suburbanization lags far behind that of other minority groups and is generally quite limited, particularly in the northeast and midwest. In the metropolitan areas we studied, the average percentage of blacks living in suburbs was 28 percent, compared to figures of 48 percent for Hispanics and 58 percent for Asians. Black suburbanization was below that of Hispanics in 50 of 60 cases, and below that of Asians in 57. To a large degree, then, suburbs appear to be substantially closed to black settlement.

Not only are blacks much less likely than other groups to achieve suburban residence, but once within suburbs, they are subject to much higher levels of segregation. The average segregation index for blacks in suburbs in 1980 was 57, compared to figures of 38 for Hispanics and 41 for Asians. In 40 percent of the suburbs we examined, black segregation scores remained in the high range. Moderate levels of suburban segregation were again found primarily in the south and west, most often in areas with very small black populations, such as Fresno, Portland, and Seattle. For blacks in large metropolitan areas of the northeast and midwest, suburbanization held little promise for desegregation. In Chicago, New York, Cleveland, Detroit, Newark, St. Louis, Gary, and Los Angeles, black segregation indices remained well above 70 in the suburbs, and in Cincinnati, Columbus, Buffalo, Philadelphia, and Pittsburgh, they were above 60. In some places—such as Detroit, Paterson, and Gary—black segregation was actually greater in suburbs than in central cities. In contrast, Hispanics and Asians display segregation scores that are low or moderate, except for a few isolated cases.

Our results, therefore, indicate that black integration in American urban areas is blocked at three successive junctures: blacks are unable to achieve integration within central cities; they are less able than other groups to attain suburban residence; and once in suburbs, they are still highly segregated.

4. SOCIOECONOMIC EFFECTS ON SEGREGATION

An obvious question to ask is whether the persistently high levels of segregation observed for blacks in American cities, and the stark contrast between blacks and other minorities, reflect social and economic differences between the groups. Perhaps black segregation simply reflects economic segregation in the housing market.

In all of the papers mentioned so far, Denton and I examined this question using statistical models to control indirectly for levels of education, income, and occupational status. Our models all show a relatively weak and ineffective process of residential integration for blacks. Changes in the level of black education, income, or occupational status are not, in general, strongly related to the level of black segregation; even after controlling for socioeconomic status, black segregation remains high. Moreover, blacks lack a detectable process of suburbanization in response to socioeconomic advancement. The percentage of blacks in suburbs is unrelated to any of the social or economic variables we considered. As black socioeconomic status rose, the level of black suburbanization remained essentially unchanged. Increasing socioeconomic status among Hispanics and Asians, however, is strongly associated with lower segregation and higher suburbanization; and when these groups are compared with blacks in a statistical model that controls for social and economic differences between them, the contrast between blacks and the other two minority groups persists.

... We also measured the influence of socioeconomic status directly by computing segregation indices within categories of income, education, and occupation. ... We computed segregation scores for blacks making under $2,500 per year and those earning over $50,000 per year, for black laborers as well as black professionals, and for high school dropouts as well as college graduates. As shown in Figure [12.]1, we found that the level of black segregation remained high across all levels of socioeconomic status, whether measured in terms of education, income, or occupation. In contrast to Hispanics or Asians, black segregation showed a very limited tendency to fall with rising socioeconomic status. In the 60 metropolitan areas we examined, the segregation score for black laborers was 73 while

Dissimilarity: Minority Versus All Anglos, by Occupation

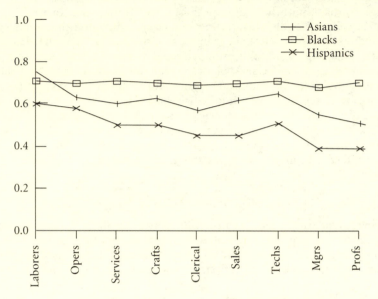

Dissimilarity: Minority Versus All Anglos, by Education (in years)

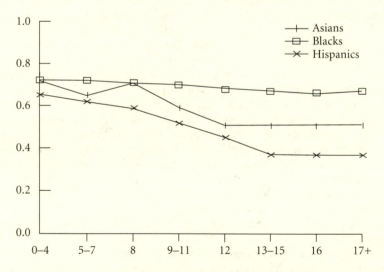

FIGURE [12.]1 Average Residential Segregation of Blacks, Hipanics, and Asians in Twenty Metropolitian Areas Where Each Group is Found in Largest Numbers: 1980.

that for black professionals was 63, both in the high range; but the Hispanic segregation score fell from 63 among laborers to 44 among professionals, and the Asian score dropped from 77 to 53.

In short, two independent lines of evidence suggest that high levels of black segregation, and the contrasting experience of blacks compared to other minority groups, cannot be attributed in any meaningful way to objective social and economic factors. Blacks are highly segregated in American urban areas for reasons apart from their disadvantaged socioeconomic status compared to whites and other minority groups.

5. THE CAUSES OF SEGREGATION

A variety of studies have tested different hypotheses to explain the persisting reality of black segregation in American urban areas. As we have seen, black segregation cannot easily be viewed as reflecting economic segregation in the housing market. Studies also cast doubt on the suggestion that blacks are not aware of housing opportunities and costs in white or suburban neighborhoods; blacks are generally quite knowledgeable about local housing markets (Farley et al., 1979). The high degree of black segregation also does not appear to reflect the voluntary desire of blacks to live near each other. In national opinion polls, a majority of black respondents consistently supports the principle of desegregation (Schuman et al., 1935); and in one local survey, 82 percent of black respondents selected an integrated 40% black neighborhood as their first or second choice (Farley et al., 1978). Another indirect statistical analysis suggested that roughly 80% of black segregation was involuntary (Lieberson and Carter, 1982).

The explanation that one returns to again and again in trying to account for the continuing reality of black segregation is the persistence of white prejudice. Although opinion polls indicate that a majority of whites reject segregation *in principle*, most whites are still unwilling to accept integration in practice. Whereas about 60% of blacks say they favor desegregation, 60% of whites indicate they prefer something "in between" complete segregation and total desegregation (Schuman et al., 1985). In concrete terms, this means that most whites are still unwilling to accept anything beyond a token black presence in their neighborhood. According to one survey, one quarter of white respondents stated they would feel uncomfortable in a hypothetical neighborhood containing one black family out 15 households; 42 percent said they would be uncomfortable with three black families, and 57 percent said they would be uncomfortable with 5 black families out of 15 (Farley et al., 1978).

These lingering fears and prejudices are translated into residential segregation through two kinds of mechanisms, which may be called active and passive discrimination. Active discrimination involves direct actions taken against blacks to prevent them from entering neighborhoods. There is ample evidence that active discrimination is a persisting problem in U.S. cities. Harassment and intimidation of black renters or homebuyers by white citizens occurs frequently (see Cass, 1986, for an example); and it is still more difficult for blacks to obtain mortgage loans in integrated areas (Pol et al., 1982; Leahy, 1985). The steering of blacks to in-

tegrated or all-black areas, and their systematically different treatment by real estate agents, have both been documented (Pearce, 1979), most recently by a Department of Housing and Urban Development audit study conducted in 40
metropolitan areas (Wienk et al., 1979).

Passive discrimination occurs when white homebuyers or renters avoid neighborhoods that contain a few black residents. In this case, no black homebuyer suffers direct discrimination and black residents experience no mistreatment at the
hands of white real estate agents or residents. White homebuyers and renters simply exercise their freedom to select their place of residence. In the local opinion
study cited earlier, 27 percent of white respondents stated that they would be unwilling to move into a neighborhood where 1 of 15 families was black; 50 percent
said they would not move into a neighborhood where 3 of 15 were black; and 73
percent said they would not enter a neighborhood where 5 of 15 families were
black (Farley et al., 1978). In contrast, 95 percent of black respondents stated they
would be willing to live in a neighborhood where two of 15 families were black.

Thus, our best evidence suggests that black segregation results from two processes of discrimination—one active, the other passive. First, whites attempt to
prevent black entry into white neighborhoods through a variety of tactics; and
second, once black entry into a neighborhood is achieved, whites avoid that area
as undesirable. As long as black demand for integrated neighborhoods remains
strong while white demand for such areas is weak and hesitant, rapid neighborhood transition from black to white is almost inevitable.

6. THE CONSEQUENCES OF SEGREGATION

If black segregation is largely involuntary, and blacks remain spatially isolated
within a relatively small set of monoracial neighborhoods for reasons outside
their control, then we can by no means consider the United States to be a race-
blind society, since neighborhoods vary on a wide range of characteristics that affect the life chances of residents. A recent study I published in collaboration with
Nancy Denton and Gretchen Condran ... explicitly examined the effect of residential segregation on black social and economic well-being using data compiled
for Philadelphia (we are currently expanding the study to cover other cities). It examined the extent to which blacks are able to take advantage of rising education,
income, and occupational status to live in neighborhoods that provide greater access to higher quality housing, better schools, safer streets, healthier surroundings, and regular contact with higher status, well-educated people.

Our analysis indicates that blacks, like whites, seek to convert socioeconomic
achievements into improved residential circumstances; as income rises, they seek
residence in integrated neighborhoods richer in amenities and resources. Because
of residential segregation, however, middle-class blacks are not free to live where
people of their means and resources usually locate. Compared to middle-income
whites, blacks of similar status face a distinctly disadvantaged residential environment, similar in quality to areas that only the poorest of whites inhabit. Given the
constraints imposed by persistent segregation and widespread segregation, middle-class blacks are subject to higher rates of crime, a less healthy environment,

and more dilapidated surroundings than their white counterparts. They must also live with people of markedly lower social class, and send their children to inferior schools attended by children from much more disadvantaged families.

Other studies indicate that, because of segregation, blacks pay higher costs than whites for housing of comparable quality (Berry, 1976; Villimez, 1980); face poorer public services and higher taxes (Schneider and Logan, 1982, 1985); and are isolated from expanding employment opportunities, which are increasingly concentrated in suburban and nonmetropolitan areas (Kasarda, 1983; Lichter, 1988).

In other words, because residential segregation continues to limit the freedom of black families to live wherever they might want, race remains a fundamental cleavage in American society, denying aspiring black families access to the full range of opportunities in our society. As long as black race remains a salient factor in allocating people to neighborhoods, blacks cannot be said to have achieved equal rights in American society. ...

The high levels of residential segregation imposed on blacks because of their race has a variety of deleterious consequences, forcing aspiring middle-class families to live in poor neighborhoods with few resources and limited opportunities, compared to middle-class white families. As long as such high levels of segregation are imposed on blacks because of their race, the United States is not a race-blind society. ...

REFERENCES

Other Works by This Author

Massey, Douglas S., and Nancy A. Denton. 1987. "Trends in the Residential Segregation of Blacks, Hispanics, and Asians: 1970–1980." *American Sociological Review* 52:802–25.

Massey, Douglas S., and Nancy A. Denton. 1988. "The Spatial Dimension of Segregation: Clustering, Centralization, and Concentration of Blacks and Hispanics in 1980." Under journal review.

Massey, Douglas S., and Nancy A. Denton. 1988. "Suburbanization and Segregation in U.S. Metropolitan Areas." *American Journal of Sociology,* forthcoming.

Denton, Nancy A., and Douglas S. Massey. 1988. "Residential Segregation of Blacks, Hispanics, and Asians by Socioeconomic Status and Generation." Under journal review.

Massey, Douglas S., Gretchen A. Condran, and Nancy A. Denton. 1987. "The Effect of Residential Segregation on Black Social and Economic Well-Being." *Social Forces* 66:29–56.

Other Works Cited

Berry, Brian J. L. 1976. "Ghetto Expansion and Single-Family Housing Prices: Chicago 1968–1972." *Journal of Urban Economics* 3:397–423.

Cass, Julia. 1986. "The Elmwood Incident." *Philadelphia Inquirer Magazine.* (May 4).

Farley, Reynolds, Suzanne Bianchi, and Diane Colasanto. 1979. "Barriers to the Racial Integration of Neighborhoods: The Detroit Case." *Annals of the American Academy of Political and Social Science* 441:97–113.

Farley, Reynolds, Howard Schuman, Suzanne Bianchi, Diane Colasanto, and Shirley Hatchett. 1978. "Chocolate City, Vanilla Suburbs: Will the Trend Toward Racially Separate Communities Continue?" *Social Science Research* 7:319–44.

Kasarda, John D. 1983. "Entry-Level Jobs, Mobility, and Urban Minority Unemployment." *Urban Affairs Quarterly* 19:21–40.

Leahy, Peter J. 1985. "Are Racial Factors Important for the Allocation of Mortgage Money?" *American Journal of Economics and Sociology* 44:183–96.

Lichter, Daniel T. 1988. "Racial Differences in Underemployment in American Cities." *American Journal of Sociology* 93:771–92.

Lieberson, Stanley, and Donna K. Carter. 1982. "A Model for Inferring the Voluntary and Involuntary Causes of Residential Segregation." *Demography* 19:511–26.

Pol, Louis G., Rebecca F. Guy, and Andrew J. Bush. 1982. "Discrimination in the Home Lending Market: A Macro Perspective." *Social Science Quarterly* 63:716–28.

Pearce, Diana M. 1979. "Gatekeepers and Homeseekers: Institutional Factors in Racial Steering." *Social Problems* 26:325–42.

Schneider, Mark, and John R. Logan. 1982. "Suburban Racial Segregation and Black Access to Local Public Resources." *Social Science Quarterly* 63:762–70.

Schneider, Mark, and John R. Logan. 1985. "Suburban Municipalities: The Changing System of Intergovernmental Relations in the Mid-1970s." *Urban Affairs Quarterly* 21:87–105.

Schuman, Howard, Charlotte Steeh, and Lawrence Bobo. 1985. *Racial Attitudes in America: Trends and Interpretations*. Cambridge, Mass.: Harvard University Press.

Villemez, Wayne J. 1980. "Race, Class, and Neighborhood: Differences in Residential Return on Individual Resources." *Social Forces* 59:414–30.

Wienk, Ron, Cliff Reid, John Simonson, and Fred Eggers. 1979. *Measuring Racial Discrimination in American Housing Markets: The Housing Market Practices Survey*. Washington, D.C.: U.S. Department of Housing and Urban Development.

13

Employment Discrimination Against Asian Americans

U.S. COMMISSION ON CIVIL RIGHTS

Asian Americans face a number of barriers to equal participation in the labor market. Many of these barriers are encountered to a greater degree by the foreign born, who often confront linguistic and cultural barriers to finding employment commensurate with their education and experience, but even third- or fourth-generation Asian Americans find their employment prospects diminished because employers have stereotypical views of Asians and prejudice against citizens of Asian ancestry. Employment discrimination, to varying degrees, is a problem facing all Asian Americans. As will be seen in the succeeding pages, employment discrimination against Asian Americans ranges from discrimination based on accent or language, to discrimination caused by our nation's immigration control laws, to artificial barriers preventing many Asian Americans from rising to management positions for which they are qualified.

This chapter details several types of employment discrimination that are frequently experienced by Asian Americans and examines the legal protections available to victims of discrimination. The chapter covers five employment discrimination issues in detail: the glass ceiling, language rights in the workplace, the certification of foreign-educated professionals, discrimination caused by the Immigration Reform and Control Act, anti-Asian discrimination in construction unions, and employment discrimination against Asian American women. ...

The perception among Asian Americans that discrimination is the root cause of their underrepresentation among higher managerial ranks is widespread. Thus, in a survey of 308 Asian American professionals and managers in the San Francisco Bay area, over two-thirds of the Chinese Americans, one-half of the Japanese Americans, and three-quarters of the Filipino Americans felt that racism was a very significant factor limiting their upward mobility.[1] Respondents also pointed to difficulties in networking, the lack of mentors, management insensitivity, and corporate culture as barriers to upper mobility.[2]

There exists some statistical evidence at the national level supporting the view that a glass ceiling exists for Asian Americans as well as for other minorities and women. A recent survey of highly successful executives in Fortune 500 companies shows that only 0.3 percent of senior executives in the United States are of Asian descent.[3] Thus, the representation of Asian Americans among senior executives is just one-tenth their representation in the population as a whole,[4] despite the high education levels of many Asian Americans. Not only are Asian Americans underrepresented at the highest levels of management, Asian Americans are underrepresented in managerial occupations in general. A recent Commission study showed that U.S.-born Asian American men were between 7 and 11 percent less likely to be in managerial occupations than non-Hispanic white men with the same measured characteristics.[5] It should be noted that since the analysis only includes U.S.-born Asian American men (and in addition adjusts for English-language proficiency), it is unlikely that English-language deficiencies or cultural barriers could be responsible for the finding of Asian underrepresentation among managers.

There also exist a number of local studies and studies of individual occupations or industries that suggest that there is indeed a glass ceiling for Asian Americans. For instance, a recent study of Asian American engineers found that they were significantly less likely to be in managerial positions or to be promoted to managerial positions than white engineers with the same measured qualifications (e.g., educational attainment, years of experience) and other characteristics (e.g., field within engineering, region of residence, other demographic factors).[6] This finding held for U.S.-born Asian Americans as well as for immigrants. A report on the city of San Francisco's civil service by Chinese for Affirmative Action, an Asian American civil rights organization, concluded that "Asian professionals are clustered in technical jobs," "there is a serious deficit of Asian administrators," and "Asian professionals face the worst promotional opportunities of all groups."[7] The report also found that Asian American professional employees were considerably overrepresented in finance and operations, while they were largely unrepresented in public safety and judicial services.[8] In addition, the ratio of administrators to professionals was lower for Asians than for any other group. Thus, 28 percent of the city's professionals but only 11 percent of the city's administrators were Asian American, whereas blacks and Hispanics had roughly the same representation among professionals as among administrators, and whites were more heavily represented among administrators than among professionals.[9]

A General Accounting Office (GAO) study of the aerospace industry also provides data suggesting that Asian Americans have difficulties moving from professional to managerial jobs in that industry.[10] An analysis of the data reported in the GAO study shows that although a higher percentage of aerospace professionals are Asian American than are either black or Hispanic, the reverse was true for managers: blacks and Hispanics both had higher percentages among managers than did Asian Americans.[11] Thus Asian Americans may be less successful in moving from professional to managerial jobs in the aerospace industry than other minority groups.[12] ...

Because the choice of whom to put in a management position is usually a highly subjective decision, Asian Americans are vulnerable to managers who subscribe to stereotypical views of Asian Americans as not having the qualities that make a good manager. In addition, the subjective nature of promotion decisions usually makes it very difficult to prove that the reason for an adverse employment decision was a discriminatory one. ...

The glass ceiling has begun to capture the national spotlight as an important barrier to equal opportunity for Asian Americans, for other minorities, and for women. ... The Department of Labor's Office of Federal Contract Compliance Programs (OFCCP) undertook a glass ceiling initiative under which "federal compliance officers will focus for the first time on examining succession plans in corporations—how individuals are selected for key high-level jobs." As a first step, the OFCCP began a thorough study of the promotion systems used at nine Fortune 500 companies. ... In 1991 the Department of Labor issued a report based on that study, finding that:

- Women and minorities do not reach the top of the corporate ladder, and minorities generally plateau at lower levels than women.
- Corporations do not have in place crucial procedures for assessing and ensuring progress towards eliminating barriers to the career advancement of women and minorities. In particular, senior-level managers were not held accountable for equal employment opportunity responsibilities.
- Corporations used word-of-mouth and employee referral to fill vacancies and did not make training and other career advancement opportunities as available to women and minorities.[13] ...

LANGUAGE RIGHTS IN THE WORKPLACE

The wave of Asian immigration beginning in 1965 and accelerating through most of the 1970s and early 1980s has brought to our shores a large number of Asian American workers with varying degrees of English-language proficiency. Some Asian American immigrants have very little command of the English language; others speak English well but are more at ease speaking in their native languages; and still others speak English fluently but retain recognizable accents. As the Asian American immigrant population has increased, language rights in the workplace have thus become a pressing civil rights issue for many Asian Americans.

Language rights in the workplace are governed by two Federal statutes that ban employment discrimination based on national origin: Title VII of the 1964 Civil Rights Act and section 1981 of the Civil Rights Act of 1866. Because of the link between national origin and language, the ban on national origin discrimination in these two statutes has been interpreted to restrict employers' ability to discriminate based on workers' English-language proficiency, accent, or desire to speak another language. ...

DISCRIMINATION BASED ON ACCENT

The Federal courts have held that not giving a person a job or a promotion because of his or her accent violates Title VII of the Civil Rights Act of 1964's prohibition of national origin discrimination except in cases where the accent significantly impairs the individual's ability to perform the job in question. The issue of whether discrimination based on accent is national origin discrimination was decided in *Carino v. University of Oklahoma Board of Regents,* a case in which a U.S. citizen of Filipino origin charged that he had been demoted from his supervisory position in a university dental laboratory because of his accent. ...

Responding to discrimination charges made by Mr. Carino in a lawsuit, his employers argued that they were justified in demoting him from his supervisorial position because his accent hampered his work as a supervisor. The district court hearing the case concluded, however, that Mr. Carino's accent did not affect his ability to perform his job. ...

A more recent case provides an example of when a person's foreign accent can be considered an acceptable justification for an adverse employment decision. In *Fragante v. City & County of Honolulu,* the Ninth Circuit held that the Honolulu Division of Motor Vehicles could legitimately deny a Filipino American with a heavy accent a job as a clerk, a position that required the incumbent to communicate with the public over the telephone and at an information counter. The court held:

> An adverse employment decision may be predicated upon an individual's accent when—but only when—it interferes materially with job performance. There is nothing improper about an employer making an *honest* assessment of the oral communications skills of a candidate for a job when such skills are reasonably related to job performance. ...

EMPLOYMENT TESTS

The potential for employer misuse of employment tests in selecting employees is an emerging civil rights issue for Asian Americans, particularly when the tests are given to those who are not native speakers of English. ...

Title VII prohibits employers from using tests in the process of employee selection if they have an adverse impact on the basis of race, color, religion, sex, or national origin and they are not justified by business necessity. If a test has an adverse impact, then the employer must demonstrate that the test is a reasonable measure of success on the job: the test must be valid (i.e., its scores are appropriate and meaningful and, usually, equally meaningful for various races, sexes, and ethnic groups) and job related. Thus, the use of any test could be judged discriminatory if it requires knowledge or understanding of English beyond the job-related skill that the test is intended to measure and it has an adverse impact. Tests of English-language proficiency may be used, however, when English is a skill necessary for success in the job.

Therefore, when English proficiency is critical to performing well on a test used in job selection, the test needs to be carefully scrutinized for job relatedness. ...

ENGLISH-ONLY RULES IN THE WORKPLACE

Employers often seek to impose rules requiring their employees to speak only English while they are on the job. Sometimes these English-only rules are blanket rules banning the use of any language other than English at any time while the employee is at work. Other times the rules are more specific, banning the use of non-English languages when the employee is performing certain duties. English-only rules are a common source of frustration and resentment for many Asian Americans and others whose primary language is not English. They feel that the rules single them out for adverse treatment based on their national origin, that they are often adopted for the purpose of discrimination, and that they repress their ability to express themselves freely.

In some instances English-only policies may be illegal discrimination based on national origin, but in other instances they may be lawful. English-only policies are unlawful when the rules are adopted for the purpose of discrimination based on national origin. Thus, the Equal Employment Opportunity Commission explicitly states that these policies are invalid when they are applied differentially to members of different national origin groups.

Even when they are not adopted for the purpose of discrimination, English-only policies may violate Title VII under an adverse impact theory if they are not justified by business necessity. The EEOC has held that blanket rules banning the use of non-English languages at all times are almost always illegal, because they will never be justified by business necessity.

> A rule requiring employees to speak only English at all times in the work place is a burdensome term and condition of employment. The primary language of an individual is often an essential national origin characteristic. Prohibiting employees at all times, in the work place, from speaking their primary language or the language they speak most comfortably, disadvantages an individual's employment opportunities on the basis of national origin. It may also create an atmosphere of inferiority, isolation and intimidation based on national origin which could result in a discriminatory working environment. Therefore the Commission will presume that such a rule violates Title VII and will closely scrutinize it.

However, EEOC regulations state that more specific English-only rules may be lawful if they can be justified by business necessity. The EEOC elaborates on what is necessary for an English-only rule to be justified by business necessity in its Compliance Manual:

> Typically, narrowly drawn rules justified by business necessity are applicable only to certain employees and only apply to those employees while they are actually performing a specific job duty or under specific circumstances. To prove an overriding business purpose sufficient to override the adverse effects of the rule, the respondent must establish that the rule is necessary to safe and efficient job performance or the safe and efficient operation of the business. In appropriate circumstances, either safety or efficiency considerations alone may justify a speak-English-only rule.
> ...

The courts have differed in their treatment of English-only rules. In a case that predated the EEOC policy on English-only rules, the Fifth Circuit held that an employer's policy requiring all employees to speak English while on duty at all times did not violate Title VII's prohibition of national origin discrimination, because the employees were all bilingual and therefore could choose to obey the rule. The court cautioned, however, that its decision applied only to English-only policies affecting *bilingual* employees:

> Our opinion does not impress a judicial imprimatur on all employment rules that require an employee to use or forbid him from using a language spoken by him at home or by his forebears. We hold only that an employer's rule forbidding a bilingual employee to speak anything but English in public areas while on the job is not discrimination based on national origin as applied to a person who is fully capable of speaking English and chooses not to do so in deliberate disregard of his employer's rule.

Despite this caveat, however, the Fifth Circuit decision is at odds with EEOC policy, which does not distinguish between English-only rules applied to bilingual persons and those applied to persons with limited English proficiency. ...

THE CERTIFICATION OF FOREIGN-EDUCATED PROFESSIONALS

Many Asian Americans and others who received their professional training outside of the United States have difficulty obtaining jobs commensurate with their education and experience in this country. Sometimes they are unable to provide documentation of their professional training and experience in their countries of origin and are forced to retrain in this country or to switch careers. Other times they find that, although they can provide diplomas and transcripts as proof of their professional education abroad, State professional certification boards often have different requirements for foreign-educated professionals than for U.S.-educated professionals. Although differential treatment of professionals educated in foreign countries has not been found to be *per se* illegal discrimination under Title VII, it can erect barriers to obtaining professional jobs that are a source of enormous frustration for Asian and other professional immigrants to this country. Furthermore, many Asian immigrant professionals suspect that the differential treatment they receive as foreign-educated professionals may in fact be a pretext for discrimination on the basis of national origin.

A case in point is the situation of graduates of foreign medical schools (FMGs), who make up roughly one-fifth of all physicians practicing in the United States. Approximately 30 percent of FMGs are U.S. citizens, and 70 percent are foreign nationals. A large proportion of foreign national FMGs come from Asian countries, especially India and the Philippines. Many FMGs came to this country in the mid-1960s when they were given preferential visa status because of a shortage of physicians in the United States. By the 1970s, however, the physician shortage had apparently become a physician surplus, generating some resentment of FMGs by graduates of U.S. medical schools (USMGs). Nevertheless, there remain many places in which America's basic health care needs are not yet being met, especially in rural and depressed areas. According to one expert, data appear to show that FMGs service these basic health care needs disproportionally:

> FMGs serve in disproportionate numbers in rural areas, often in solo and partnership practices, in public hospitals, in smaller not-for-profit hospitals, and in regions

of the country that have experienced emigration of population because of declining industry and high unemployment. Poor populations and Medicaid recipients also are often reliant on FMGs.[14]

Furthermore, foreign-born FMGs also play a critical role in providing for the health care needs of Asian immigrant communities, since recent immigrants are often prevented by language, cultural, or informational barriers from seeking treatment from American-born physicians.

To practice medicine in the United States, FMGs, like USMGs, need to be licensed by a State medical licensing board. Many FMGs have not completed residencies before coming to the Unites States and thus also need to obtain positions as residents in U.S. hospitals. Some FMGs charge that they are the victims of unfair discrimination by State licensing boards, hospitals with residency positions, and others in the medical community.[15]

In fact, State medical licensure boards throughout the country have imposed stiffer certification requirements for FMGs than for USMGs. ...

FMGs, on the other hand, point to research showing that the performance of FMGs and USMGs as physicians is indistinguishable. They stress the hardships imposed on many FMGs by requirements that they document in detail the course content, faculty resumes, facilities, etc. of their medical schools. These time-consuming requirements allegedly amount to harassment. They also argue that it is particularly unfair to base endorsement requirements for FMGs on the quality of their medical education rather than on their individual records as practicing physicians because in many instances these FMGs have been practicing medicine in the United States for many years. ...

FMGs have also charged that they are discriminated against in the allocation of residency positions and hospital privileges. ... FMGs may be in some instances protected under Title VII, which prohibits discrimination on the basis on national origin. A recent court case is pertinent here:

A physician, educated in Iran, was offered employment with an Alabama medical corporation on the condition that he was given admitting privileges at a nearby hospital. When he was initially denied hospital privileges at the hospital and later given privileges with a longer probationary period than customary, he sued the hospital, charging national origin discrimination under Title VII.

In deciding the case, the Eleventh Circuit Court ruled that a hospital that denies a doctor's application for admitting privileges can be sued for discrimination under Title VII even though it is not in any sense the doctor's employer if that denial interferes with the doctor's employment opportunities elsewhere.

DISCRIMINATION CAUSED BY THE
IMMIGRATION REFORM AND CONTROL ACT

In 1986 Congress passed the Immigration Reform and Control Act (IRCA), which authorized legal status for 3 million undocumented aliens who had entered the United States before 1982 while imposing civil and criminal penalties, "employer sanctions," on employers who hire unauthorized workers. To allay concern that employer sanctions would lead employers to discriminate against foreign-looking and foreign-sounding workers, IRCA also contained provisions aimed at preventing such discrimination. Under IRCA, employers are required to verify the work authorization of *all* workers, not just those workers employers suspect might not be authorized to work. Furthermore, IRCA makes it illegal for employers with four or more employees to discriminate in hiring, firing, or referrals against any authorized worker based on the individual's national origin or citizenship status. To enforce its antidiscrimination provisions, IRCA set up the Office of the Special Counsel for Immigration-Related Unfair Employment Practices (OSC) within the Department of Justice.

Fears that the IRCA's antidiscrimination provisions would prove to be insufficient to prevent discrimination led Congress to require the General Accounting Office (GAO) to conduct a series of three studies to determine whether IRCA's employer sanctions provision had caused discrimination. In March 1990 the third and final GAO report (hereafter, "GAO report") concluded that "a widespread pattern of discrimination has resulted against eligible workers ... [and] it is more reasonable to conclude that a substantial amount of these discriminatory practices resulted from IRCA rather than not." The GAO report confirmed the findings of numerous other reports that IRCA has resulted in widespread discrimination against foreign-looking and foreign-sounding workers.[16]

IRCA-related discrimination is likely to fall most heavily on groups that have large numbers of immigrant workers, such as Asian Americans. If employers assume that more individuals in ethnic groups with high proportions of immigrants are likely to be unauthorized workers, then they may be more suspicious of the work authorization of *all* members of the group, and they might be reluctant to hire *any* members of that group at all. For Asian Americans, this tendency is likely to be compounded by the common misperception that all Asians are foreigners. Furthermore, employers who are not thoroughly informed about all the documents that can establish an individual's work authorization may prefer familiar documents, such as social security cards, U.S. passports, or green cards, to the less familiar work authorization documents that are frequently held by new immigrants and refugees, many of whom are Asian. Other employers may mistakenly require green cards from all foreign-seeming workers, even U.S. citizens, who do not have them.

The GAO report provides confirmation that Asian Americans experience IRCA-related discrimination disproportionately. The report found that the proportion of employers adopting discriminatory practices was higher in the Western States, New York City, Chicago, and Miami, and especially high in Texas and Los Angeles. Reviewing these data, the Task Force on IRCA-Related Discrimination (Task Force) observed ... that IRCA-related discrimination is more prevalent among employers with high percentages of Hispanic or Asian employees.

Additional evidence that Asian Americans are experiencing illegal employment discrimination as a result of IRCA is provided by a study by San Francisco State University's Public Research Institute (PRI) jointly with the Coalition for Immigrant and Refugee Rights and Services (CIRRS), which analyzed data collected from a telephone survey of 416 San Francisco employers. The PRI/CIRRS report found that a large majority of San Francisco employers engage in illegal discriminatory practices:

> An overwhelming majority (97%) of sample business firms regularly engage in at least one employment practice that may be discriminatory under IRCA or other anti-discrimination laws, and 53% regularly engage in three or more.[17]

Furthermore, the report finds that San Francisco employers are particularly wary of hiring Asian Americans:

> Fifty percent of employers in the sample feel that the INS's documentation require-ments make it riskier to hire people who speak limited English. A large proportion feel it is riskier to hire Latinos (40%) and Asians (39%).[18]

There are no other studies of the effects of IRCA document discrimination specifically against Asian Americans, but many studies have found that employer confusion about IRCA has caused discrimination against foreign-looking or for-eign-sounding individuals, noncitizen, or immigrants. For instance, the New York City Commission on Human Rights (NYCCHR) conducted a hiring audit in which carefully matched individuals, one with a heavy accent and the other with-out an accent, responded to help-wanted advertisements in major New York pa-pers. NYCCHR found that the accented job applicants were often treated less fa-vorably than the job applicants without accents.

Thus, there is little doubt that many Asian Americans have been discriminated against because of IRCA's employer sanctions provisions. Aggravating this situa-tion, many Asian Americans are not aware of their rights under IRCA and do not know where or how to file IRCA-related complaints. ...

After the GAO released its finding that IRCA has caused a "widespread pattern of discrimination," the U.S. Commission on Civil Rights issued a statement call-ing for the repeal of IRCA's employer sanctions provisions. That statement said:

> The United States Commission on Civil Rights ... calls on Congress to repeal the employer sanctions provisions of the Immigration Reform and Control Act (IRCA). ... With the U.S. General Accounting Office's announcement ... that employer sanctions create a "widespread pattern of discrimination" against legal workers, there is no longer doubt that America's efforts to stem illegal immigration through sanctions have seriously harmed large numbers of Hispanic, Asian, and other "for-eign-looking" and "foreign-sounding" American workers. This discrimination is unacceptable, and its root cause—employer sanctions—should be eliminated.[19] ...

DISCRIMINATION IN
CONSTRUCTION UNIONS

Participants at the Commission's New York Roundtable Conference alleged that Asian Americans are virtually shut out of construction unions in New York City

and as a result are forced to take lower paying jobs restoring or repairing buildings. These allegations resurfaced several months later at a series of New York City
hearings on discrimination in the construction industry, and similar allegations
were made at the Commission's San Francisco Roundtable Conference. Among
the discriminatory practices allegedly engaged in by construction unions to keep
Asian Americans out are selective use of English-proficiency requirements and
unfair hiring hall practices.

Although resource constraints prevented the Commission from undertaking a
complete investigation of these allegations, available statistics confirm that Asian
Americans are underrepresented in construction unions. Nationwide, Asian
Americans constituted 0.8 percent of the membership of construction unions in
1990, although they made up 2.9 percent of the U.S. population. Asian American
representation is even lower in New York State, where Asian Americans constituted 3.9 percent of the population in 1990 but made up only 0.3 percent of the
membership of construction unions. Furthermore, among persons in New York
State with skill levels comparable to those of construction workers (i.e., the pool
of potential construction workers), Asian Americans are considerably less likely
to be employed in construction jobs than are whites: in 1980 only 2.6 percent of
the Asian Americans who reported their occupations as craftsmen, operators, or
laborers were in construction jobs, as compared to 14.5 percent of whites with
these occupations. Based on these statistics, further investigation of the allegations of construction union discrimination against Asian Americans in New York
City and of anti-Asian discrimination by unions in general is warranted.

EMPLOYMENT DISCRIMINATION AGAINST
ASIAN AMERICAN WOMEN

Although Asian Americans of both genders encounter employment discrimination based on their race, the barriers to equal employment opportunity may be
greater for Asian American women because of their gender. As women, they may
be the victims of gender discrimination and sexual harassment on the job. And as
Asian American women, especially if they are immigrants, they may be less
equipped to handle such discrimination than women of other races for two reasons. First, Asian American women, especially those who are immigrants, may
find that the small number of Asian American women in the workplace is an im-
pediment to their joining informal networks of co-workers on the job; and this in
turn may mean that when Asian American women encounter discrimination they
do not have easy access to the support and advice of their co-workers. Second, immigrant Asian American women may be less well-informed about their rights in
the workplace and culturally conditioned not to complain about mistreatment.
Their isolation from their co-workers, their ignorance of their rights, and their
reluctance to complain all make Asian American immigrant women vulnerable to
sexual harassment in the workplace and other forms of employment discrimination.

NOTES

1. Amado Cabezas, Tse Ming Tam, Brenda M. Lowe, Anna Wong, and Kathy Owyang Turner, "Empirical Study of Barriers to Upward Mobility of Asian Americans in the San Francisco Bay Area," in Gail M. Nomura, Russell Endo, Stephen H. Sumida, and Russell C. Leong, eds., *Frontiers of Asian American Studies: Writing, Research and Commentary* (Pullman, WA: Washington State University Press, 1989), p. 93.

2. Ibid.

3. Korn/Ferry International, *Korn/Ferry's International Executive Profile: A Decade of Change in Corporate Leadership* (1990), table 61, p. 23.

4. According to newly released figures from the U.S. Bureau of the Census, persons of Asian descent made up 2.9 percent of the U.S. population in 1990. Barbara Vobejda, "Asians, Hispanics Giving Nation More Diversity," *Washington Post*, June 12, 1991.

5. U.S. Commission on Civil Rights, *The Economic Status of Americans of Asian Descent: An Exploratory Investigation* (Clearinghouse Publication 95, October 1988), pp. 72–75. The characteristics controlled for in the Civil Rights Commission analysis are: education, work experience, English ability, region, location, marital status, disability, and industry of work. Ibid., table 7.7, p. 75.

6. Joyce Tang, "Asian American Engineers: Earnings, Occupational Status, and Promotions" (paper presented at the 86th annual meeting of the American Sociological Association, Cincinnati, OH, Aug. 23–27, 1991).

7. Henry Der and Colleen Lye, *The Broken Ladder '89: Asian Americans in City Government* (San Francisco: Chinese for Affirmative Action, 1989), p. 5.

8. Ibid., pp. 14–15. The occupational clustering of Asian Americans, although it does not bear directly on the issue of the glass ceiling (which applies, essentially, to promotions within occupations), may indicate the existence of other forms of employment discrimination against Asian Americans. For articles arguing that Asian Americans, especially immigrants, earn less than their white counterparts and are often forced into the "secondary labor market" (or the lower tier of the "primary labor market") or "peripheral" jobs, see Amado Cabezas and Gary Kawaguchi, "Empirical Evidence for Continuing Asian American Income Inequality: The Human Capital Model and Labor Market Segmentation," pp. 144–64 in Gary Y. Okihiro, Shirley Hume, Arthur A. Hansen, and John M. Liu, eds., *Reflections on Shattered Windows: Promises and Prospects for Asian American Studies* (Pullman, WA: Washington State University Press, 1988) and Eui Hang Shin and Kyung-Sup Chang, "Peripherization of Immigrant Professionals: Korean Physicians in the United States," *International Migration Review*, vol. 22, no. 4, pp. 609–26.

9. Ibid., p. 20.

10. U.S. General Accounting Office, *Equal Employment Opportunity: Women and Minority Aerospace Managers and Professionals, 1979–86* (Oct. 26, 1989).

11. Ibid., p. 30. The GAO study does not provide information on white professionals and managers in the aerospace industry.

12. Without further information, it remains possible that the black and Hispanic managers in the aerospace industry did not move up from professional jobs but were placed in low-level administrative/management jobs that did not require professional aerospace expertise.

13. U.S. Department of Labor, *A Report on the Glass Ceiling Initiative*, 1991, p. 5.

14. Stephen S. Mick, "Contradictory Policies for Foreign Medical Graduates," *Health Affairs*, Fall 1987, pp. 5–18.

15. Several lawsuits have been filed by Asian Americans against State licensing boards. In 1986 Dr. Kar, who had received his medical education at the University of Medical Sciences in New Delhi, and was licensed to practice medicine in two other States, filed a suit against the State of Vermont for denying his application for a license. In denying his application, the State licensing board said that his medical school had not been approved by the American Council for Graduate Medical Education of the American Medical Association (ACGME). Dr. Kar pointed out that there was no published requirement to that effect in Vermont and that the decision to adopt the requirement was made after his application was complete. (Lynn Hudson, "Doctor to Sue Vermont on License," *India Abroad,* Mar. 7, 1986.)

In 1987 two Vietnamese American doctors who had received their medical degrees from the University of Saigon filed a suit against the State of California's medical licensing boards seeking damages because they were denied medical licenses after fulfilling all the requirements. The State licensing board had decided, in a closed meeting, not to issue licenses to persons who had graduated from the University of Saigon after 1975, because it felt that it could no longer verify the quality of the education received there. (Harriet Chiang, "Foreign-Trained MDs Charge License Bias," *San Francisco Chronicle,* June 8, 1987.)

16. U.S. General Accounting Office, *Immigration Reform: Employer Sanctions and the Question of Discrimination* (Mar. 29, 1990), p. 71. GAO's conclusions are based in part on the results of a survey of employers that led GAO to project that 891,000 employers, about 19 percent of all employers, began illegal discriminatory practices as a result of IRCA. Further analysis of the GAO employer survey data reveals that roughly 499,000 employers began to discriminate on the basis of national origin, and 687,000 employers began to discriminate on the basis of citizenship. Of those starting illegal discriminatory practices, 757,000 employers began a policy of not hiring a certain category of workers, and 381,000 employers began a practice of selectively asking for work authorization papers.

17. Lina M. Avidan, *Employment and Hiring Practices Under the Immigration Reform and Control Act of 1986: A Survey of San Francisco Businesses* (Preliminary Report, Public Research Institute, San Francisco State University, and Coalition for Immigrant and Refugee Rights and Services, January 1990), p. iii.

18. Ibid., p. iv.

19. U.S. Commission on Civil Rights, "Civil Rights Commission Calls for Repeal of Employer Sanctions," News Release, Mar. 29, 1990.

14

Racial Ethnic Women's Labor: The Intersection of Race, Gender, and Class Oppression

EVELYN NAKANO GLENN

Although the "double" (race, gender) and "triple" (race, gender, class) oppressions of racial ethnic women are widely acknowledged, no satisfactory theory has been developed to analyze what happens when these systems of oppression intersect. A starting point for developing such a theory would appear to lie in those models which view race and gender stratification as part of a larger system of institutionalized inequality. During the 1970s two models that view race and gender divisions as embedded in, and helping to maintain, an overall system of class exploitation came to the fore: the patriarchy model developed by Marxist feminists to explain the subordination of women (H. Hartmann 1981; Weinbaum and Bridges 1979; C. Brown 1981; Sokoloff 1980) and the internal colonialism model developed by activists and scholars to explain the historic subordination of blacks, Hispanics, Asian Americans, and other people of color in the United States (Clark 1965; Carmichael and Hamilton 1967; Moore 1970; Barrera, Munoz, and Ornelas 1972; Blauner 1972).

At the center of the Marxist feminist analysis is the concept of patriarchy, which may be defined as a hierarchical system of power that enables men as a class to have authority and power over women (H. Hartmann 1976; Brown 1975; Sokoloff 1980). In this model the main mechanism by which control is achieved and maintained by men is the sexual division of labor, which places men in positions of authority over women and permits them to reap disproportionate benefits. Similarly, at the center of the internal colonialism model is a system of power relations by which subordinate minorities are kept politically and economically weak so they can be more easily exploited as workers. The main mechanism by which economic dependency is maintained is a colonial labor system, characterized by a segmented labor market, discriminatory barriers to desirable jobs, and separate wage scales. This system ensures that people of color are relegated to the worst jobs: insecure, low-paying, dangerous, dirty, and dead-end.

Neither model explicitly recognizes the specific situation of racial ethnic women. The patriarchy model ignores differences among women based on race. When race is discussed, it is treated as a parallel system of stratification: an analogy is often made between "women" and "minorities," an analogy that involves comparison of the subordinate status of white women and minority men. Minority women are left in limbo. Similarly, the internal colonialism model ignores gender by treating members of colonized minorities as undifferentiated with respect to gender. Analyses of racial ethnic labor have generally focused only on male workers. Yet these studies also assume that the detrimental impacts of the labor system on men are synonymous with the impacts on the group as a whole, men and women alike.

Despite the focus on only one axis of stratification, the patriarchy and internal colonialism models have some important commonalities. Each focuses on explaining the persistence of inequality and sees gender/race stratification as dynamically related to the organization of the economy. ... Each emphasizes institutional arrangements that ensure control by the dominant group over the labor of the subordinate group. There thus seems to be some common ground for developing a more integrated framework by combining insights from the two perspectives.

This chapter is a preliminary effort to identify aspects of the two models that might contribute to an integrated framework. I will start by briefly reviewing the Marxist feminist analysis of women's subordination. I will then review racial ethnic women's experience as members of colonized minorities in the United States. In light of this experience, I will examine the paid and unpaid work of Chinese, Mexican American, and black women from the mid-19th century to the present, showing how they diverge from those presumed to be typical of white women. In the concluding section, suggestions are made for revision of Marxist feminist theory to be more inclusive of the race-gender interaction.

MARXIST FEMINIST ANALYSIS

The Marxist feminist perspective views women's subordination as a product of two interacting systems: patriarchy and capitalism. ... The main mechanism by which patriarchy was established and is maintained today is the sexual division of labor. The assignment of certain tasks (usually the more onerous and/or less valued) to women, and others (usually the more highly valued) to men, is considered more or less universal.

Under capitalism the sexual division of labor takes a particular form due to the separation of production of goods, and then services, from the household. As production was industrialized, the household became increasingly privatized, and its functions reduced to consumption—that is, shopping and negotiating for services (cf. Weinbaum and Bridges 1979)—and biological and social reproduction, including child care, cleaning, preparing food, and providing emotional support for the breadwinner. As capital took over production, households became increasingly dependent on the market for goods and, therefore, on wages to purchase goods and services needed for survival. During the 19th century—in part because men could be more intensively exploited as wage laborers, while women could benefit capital as full-time consumers and reproducers—a specialization developed whereby women were assigned almost exclusive responsibility for household consumption and reproduction, and men were allocated responsibility for publicly organized production. This division became prescribed in the mid-19th century with the development of the cult of domesticity, which idealized the woman as the center of home and hearth (Welter 1966). This division of labor contributed to the subordination of women by making them economically dependent on a male wage earner. Simultaneously the domestic code controlled women's behavior by threatening those who deviated from it with the loss of their feminine identity.

The ideal of separate spheres was, of course, unattainable for many women whose fathers or husbands were unable to earn a family wage and who therefore had to engage in income-producing activities to support themselves and their families (Lerner 1969; Easton 1976). Yet the conception of women as consumers and reproducers affected them, too, depressing their position in the labor market. Women were defined as secondary workers, a status maintained by a sexual division in the labor market (occupational segregation). Jobs allocated to women were typically at the bottom of the authority hierarchy, low in wages, dead-end, and frequently insecure. The secondary position of women in the labor force meant that they had little leverage to shift the burden of household work onto husbands, so they continued to be responsible for the domestic sphere. Moreover, because of low wages and insecure jobs, women, even when employed, remained dependent on additional wages of the male earner (H. Hartmann 1976; Kessler-Harris 1982).

This analysis has much to offer. It permits us to view women's subordination as part of a larger framework of economic exploitation. It also draws connections between women's domestic work and their work in the labor force, and shows how subordination in one sphere reinforces subordination in the other. It is intended as a general analysis that encompasses all women. ...

Next, we need to examine the impacts of race stratification on racial ethnic women's work, both paid and unpaid. For this, I draw on both earlier and more recent research on the labor histories of "colonized minorities." ... I ... limit my examination to three case studies for which there is comparable information from the mid-19th century to the present: Mexican Americans in the Southwest, Chinese in California, and blacks in the South.

COLONIZED MINORITIES IN
INDUSTRIALIZING AMERICA

The United States started out as a colonial economy that offered raw resources and land to European and American capitalists. In order to develop the economic infrastructure and extract resources, capitalists needed labor, which was always in short supply. The presence of racial ethnic groups in this country is tied to this demand for labor. Most were brought to this country for the express purpose of providing cheap and malleable labor (Cheng and Bonacich 1984).

Although European immigrants were also welcomed as a source of low-wage labor, they were incorporated into the urban economies of the North. Racial ethnics were recruited primarily to fill labor needs in economically backward regions: the West, Southwest, and South (Blauner 1972). In the late 19th and early 20th centuries, Chinese men constituted from a quarter to a third of the work force (reclaiming agricultural lands, building railroads, and working in mines) and 90 percent of the domestic and laundry workers in California (Saxton 1971). During this same period, native Chicanos and Mexican immigrants (Mexicanos) were employed as miners, railroad hands, and agricultural laborers in the western states (Barrera 1979). In the years following emancipation, blacks were concentrated in agriculture, as well as in heavy construction labor and domestic service, in the South (Cheng and Bonacich 1984). All three groups helped build the agricultural and industrial base on which subsequent industrial development rested, but were excluded from the industrial jobs that resulted.

Racial ethnic labor was cheaper: ... racial ethnics were paid less (including lower benefits) and provided a reserve army to be drawn on when the economy expanded or labor was needed for a short-term project, and pushed out when the economy contracted or the particular project ended. Their cheapness was ensured by institutional barriers that undercut their ability to compete in the labor market. The labor market itself was stratified into separate tiers for whites and racial ethnics. The better-paying, more skilled, cleaner, and secure jobs in highly capitalized industries were reserved for white workers, leaving the low-paying, insecure, dangerous, seasonal, and dead-end jobs in competitive (as opposed to monopolistic) industries for people of color. A dual wage system was also characteristic of the colonial labor system; wages for racial ethnics were always lower than for whites in comparable jobs (Barrera 1979). White workers benefited because better jobs were reserved for them. The dual labor system also was a buffer for them against the effects of periodic depressions, since racial ethnics took the brunt of layoffs and unemployment.

Further, racial ethnics were prevented from competing for better work and improved conditions by legal and administrative restrictions. Restrictions on their rights and freedoms began at the time of entry or incorporation into the United States. While the exact forms of entry for the three groups differed, in all cases an element of subordination was involved. The most striking instance of forced entry was that of blacks, who were captured, torn from their homelands, transported against their will, and sold into slavery. This institution so structured their lives that even after emancipation, former slaves were held in debt bondage by the southern sharecropping system (Painter 1976). Equally involuntary was the incorporation of Mexicans residing in territories taken over by U.S. military conquest. Anglo settlers invaded what is now California, Texas, Arizona, New Mexico, and Colorado. When the United States seized the land, native Mexicans living in those areas were reduced to agricultural peons or wage laborers (Barrera 1979). An intermediate case between forced and free entry was that of the Chinese. Their immigration was the result of the economic and political chaos engendered at least in part by western colonial intrusion into China (Lyman 1974). Many Chinese men entered the United States as contract laborers so they could support destitute kin in their home villages. Under the credit ticket system, they signed away seven years of labor in exchange for their passage (Ling 1912).

These unfree conditions of entry imposed special liabilities on racial ethnics. Blacks were not citizens, and counted in the census as only three-fifths of a person; Mexicans were defined as second-class citizens; and Chinese were aliens ineligible for citizenship. All three groups were placed in separate legal categories, denied basic rights and protections, and barred from political participation. Thus, they could be coerced, intimidated, and restricted to the least desirable jobs, where they were especially vulnerable to exploitation.

The process of entry and incorporation into the labor system had profound effects on the culture and family systems of racial ethnics. Native languages, religion, and other aspects of life were constrained, destroyed, or transformed, and kin ties and family authority were undermined. As Blauner (1972, p. 66) notes, "The labor system through which people of color became Americans tended to destroy or weaken their cultures and communal ties. Regrouping and new institutional forms developed, but in situations with extremely limited possibilities."

We are most familiar with assaults on family ties of blacks under slavery due to sale of individuals regardless of kin ties, slave master control over marriage and reproduction, and the brutal conditions of life. ...

Less well known are the assaults on the culture and family lives of Chicanos and Chinese Americans. In both groups households were broken apart by the demand for male labor. Many Mexican American men were employed in mining camps and on railroad gangs, which required them to live apart from wives and children (Barrera 1979). This was also true for male migrant agricultural workers until the 1880s, when the family labor system became the preferred mode (Camarillo 1979). In the case of the Chinese, only prime-age males were recruited as workers, and wives and children had to be left behind (Coolidge 1909). The Chinese Exclusion Act of 1882 not only prohibited further entry of Chinese laborers but also barred resident laborers from bringing in wives and children (Lyman 1974; Wu 1972). This policy was aimed at preventing the Chinese from settling permanently once their labor was no longer needed.

RACIAL ETHNIC WOMEN'S WORK
IN INDUSTRIALIZING AMERICA

The specific conditions of life experienced by the three groups of women differed. However, they shared some common circumstances due to their similar positions in the colonial labor system and the similar difficulties the system created for their families. All three groups had to engage in a constant struggle for both immediate survival and the long-term continuation of the family and community. Because men of their groups were generally unable to earn a family wage, the women had to engage in subsistence and income-producing activities both in and out of the household. In addition, they had to work hard to keep their families together in the face of outside forces that threatened their integrity.

Chinese American Women

Perhaps the least is known about Chinese American women in the 19th and early 20th centuries. This may be due to the fact that very few working-class Chinese women actually resided in the United States then. For most of the period from 1860 to 1920, the ratio of men to women ranged from 13 to 20 males for every female. As late as 1930 there were only 9,742 females aged 10 or over in a population that included 53,650 males of the same age (Glenn 1983). It is estimated that over half of the men had left wives in China (Coolidge 1909). ...

In the late 19th century, aside from wives of merchants, who were still allowed entry into the United States, the only notable group of Chinese women were prostitutes (Hirata 1979; Goldman 1981). The unbalanced sex ratio created a demand for sexual services. Except for a few years when some women were able to immigrate on their own as free entrepreneurs, Chinese prostitutes were either indentured servants or outright slaves controlled by Chinese tongs or business associations. They had been sold by their parents or kidnapped and involuntarily transported. The controllers of the trade reaped huge profits from buying and selling women, and hiring out their services. Women who ran away were hunted down and returned to their captors, usually with the collusion of the police and courts. Unable to speak English and without allies, the women could not defend themselves.

Initially the Chinese were dispersed throughout the West in mining towns, railroad camps, and agricultural fields. They were subjected to special penalties, such as a foreign miner's tax in California, that rendered it difficult for them to make a living. During the economic depression of the 1870s, the Chinese were forcibly driven out of many areas (Nee and Nee 1972). They congregated in urban Chinatowns, so that by the 1880s the Chinese were a largely urban population. In place of households, the men formed clan and regional associations for mutual welfare and protection (Lyman 1977). By the early 1900s some Chinese men were able, with minimal capital, to establish laundries, restaurants, and stores, thereby qualifying as merchants eligible to bring over wives (Lyman 1968). These small businesses were a form of self-exploitation; they were profitable only because all members of the family contributed their labor and worked long hours. Living quarters were often in back of the shop or adjacent to it, so that work and family life were completely integrated. Work in the family enterprise went on simultaneously with household maintenance and child care. First up and last to bed, women had less leisure than the rest of the family. Long work hours in crowded and rundown conditions took its toll on the whole family. Chinatowns had abnormally high rates of tuberculosis and other diseases (Lee, Lim, and Wong 1969).

It is unclear what proportion of women laboring in family laundries and shops were counted as gainfully employed in the census. They undoubtedly were severely undercounted. ... In any case, some sizable proportion of women was employed as independent wage workers. As employees, Chinese women were concentrated in ethnic enterprises because of color bars in white-owned businesses. Nearly half of all gainfully employed women in 1930 worked in jobs that were typical of Chinese enterprise: ... garment operatives and seamstresses, ... sales and trade, ... laundry operatives, ... waitresses, ... and clerical workers. ... The only major form of employment outside the ethnic community was private household service. ...

Mexican American Women

The information on the work of Chicanas in the late 19th century is also sparse. Barrera (1979) suggests that prior to the 1870s, Chicano families followed the traditional division of labor, with women responsible for household work and child care. Thus, Mexican American women worked largely in the home. Under the conditions of life among working-class and agricultural families, this work was extensive and arduous (Jenson 1981). In rural areas the household work included tending gardens and caring for domestic animals. Many Chicano men were employed in extracting industries that required them to live in work camps and company towns in unsettled territories. If a wife remained with the children in the home village, she had to engage in subsistence farming and raise the children on her own. If she joined her husband in camp, she had to carry on domestic chores and child rearing under frontier conditions, forced to buy necessities in company stores that quickly used up meager wages. Even in the city the barrios often had no running water, and unsanitary conditions added to women's burdens of nursing the sick (Garcia 1980).

By the 1880s, Mexican American women were increasingly being brought into the labor force. In cities such as Los Angeles, Santa Barbara, and El Paso, Chicanas were employed as servants, cooks, and laundresses (Camarillo 1979; Garcia 1980). An economic depression in the 1880s forced more women to seek outside wage work, not only in private households but also as washerwomen in commercial laundries, and as cooks, dishwashers, maids, and waitresses in hotels and other public establishments. In this same period women entered the agricultural labor market. Prior to that time prime-age male workers were preferred for seasonal and migratory field work. In the 1880s whole families began to be used, a pattern that accelerated during World War I (Camarillo 1979, p. 91). By the 1920s family labor was common throughout the Southwest. ...

These trends are reflected in occupational patterns of Chicana women. Between 1880 and 1930, they tended to be employed in two main types of situations. A large part of the Chicana work force, 20 percent officially, was employed as farm laborers (Barrera 1979). Many of these were part of the piece rate system in which entire families worked and moved with the crops (Fisher 1953; P. Taylor 1937; McWilliams 1971). Under this system women had to bear and raise children, cook, and keep house while also working long hours in the field of packinghouse. Infants accompanied their parents to the fields, and children started working at an early age. Living conditions in migrant camps were extremely harsh. Adults rarely lived past 55, and infant and child mortality was high. Children had no regular schooling because of constant movement and the need for their labor. Schools were geared to fit agricultural schedules and provided minimal training (P. Taylor 1929). Once in the migrant pattern, it was almost impossible for families or individuals to break out.

The second type of employment for Chicanas, primarily those in cities and towns, was in unskilled and semiskilled "female" jobs. The distribution of jobs varied in different areas of the Southwest, but the most common occupations in all areas were service positions (household servants, waitresses, maids, cooks, and laundry operatives), which accounted for 44.3 percent of all employed Chicanas in 1930, and operatives in garment factories and food processing plants, which together employed 19.3 percent in 1930. ... The latter industries also employed Anglo women, but Chicanas were given the worst jobs and the lowest pay. They were victims of both occupational stratification and a dual wage system. ...

Whether engaged in subsistence farming, seasonal migratory labor, agricultural packing, laundry work, domestic service, or garment manufacturing, Chicanas had to raise their children under colonized conditions. As part of the continued legal and illegal takeover of land by Anglos in Texas and Colorado from 1848 to 1900, the Chicanos became a conquered people (McLemore 1973, 1980). Defined and treated as inferior, they saw their language and culture become badges of second-class status. Through their daily reproductive activities women played a critical role not only in maintaining the family but also in sustaining Mexican American ways of life.

Black Women

Perhaps more than any other group of women, black women were from the start exempted from the myth of female disability. They were exploited on the basis of their gender as breeders and raisers of slaves for plantation owners (Genovese 1974). Their gender also made them liable to a special form of oppression, sexual assault. Nevertheless, their gender did not spare them from hard physical labor in the fields (Jones 1984). Hooks (1981) claims plantation owners often preferred women for the hardest field work because they were more reliable workers. In addition, black women did the heavy housework and child care for white women; in that role they were subject to abuse and even physical beatings at the hands of their mistresses. As Angela Davis (1969) notes, under conditions of plantation slavery, staying alive, raising children, and maintaining some semblance of community were forms of resistance.

After emancipation, life for rural blacks remained harsh under the sharecropping system. Blacks found themselves held in debt bondage. Hooks (1981) suggests that landowners preferred sharecropping to hiring labor because black women were unwilling to be employed in the fields once slavery was abolished. With sharecropping, women's labor could be exploited intensively, since women had to work hard alongside the men in order to pay off the ever-mounting debt to the owner. One observer of black farmers noted that these women "do double duty, a man's share in the field, and a woman's part at home. They do any kind of field work, even ploughing, and at home the cooking, washing, milling, and gardening" (Lerner 1973, p. 247).

Although there were some independent black farmers, it became increasingly difficult for them to make a living. Jim Crow laws deprived blacks of legal rights and protections, and national farm policies favored large landowners. Independent black farmers were increasingly impoverished and finally were driven off the land (Painter 1976).

Aside from farming, the next largest group of black women was employed as laundresses and domestic servants. Black women constituted an exclusive servant caste in the South, since whites refused to enter a field associated with blacks since slave times (Katzman 1978). As servants, black women often worked a 14- to 16-hour day and were on call around the clock (J. Brown 1938). They were allowed little time off to meet their own domestic responsibilities, despite the fact that the majority of black domestics had children. A married domestic might see her children once every two weeks, while devoting night and day to the care of her mistress's children. Her own children were left in the care of husband or older siblings (Katzman 1978). Low wages were endemic. They had to be supplemented by children taking in laundry or doing odd jobs. Many black women testified that they could survive only through the tradition of the service pan—the term for leftover food that was at the disposal of the colored cook (Lerner 1973, p. 229).

Manufacturing and white-collar jobs were closed to black women, though some of the dirtiest jobs in industry were offered them. They were particularly conspicuous in southern tobacco factories, and to some extent in cotton mills and flour manufacturing. In the cotton mills black women were employed as common laborers in the yards, as waste gatherers, and as scrubbers of machinery. The actual manufacturing jobs were reserved for white women (Foner and Lewis 1981).
. . .

World War I saw increasing migration of blacks to the urban North and, simultaneously, the entrance of blacks into factory employment there. As late as 1910, 90.5 percent of all black women were farm laborers and servants, but between 1910 and 1920, 48,000 black women entered factory work (Lerner 1973). Most were employed in steam laundries, the rest in unmechanized jobs in industry as sweepers, cleaners, and ragpickers (Foner and Lewis 1981).

During the entire period from 1870 to 1930, black women, regardless of rural or urban residence, were notable for their high rates of labor force participation, particularly among married women. In 1900, 26.0 percent of married black women were in the labor force, compared with 3.8 percent of married white women (Pleck 1979). They thus had to contend with the double day long before this became an issue for a majority of white women. Moreover, although their wages were consistently lower than those of white women, their earnings constituted a larger share of total family income, due to the marginal and low-wage employment of black men (Byington 1974). Finally, they had to perform their double duty under poor and crowded living conditions, an educational system that provided inferior schooling for their children, uncertain income, and other trials.

RACIAL ETHNIC WOMEN'S WORK IN THE
CONTEMPORARY PERIOD

All three groups are predominantly urban today, a process that began in the late 19th century for the Chinese, during World War I for blacks, and after World War II for Chicanos. All have experienced dramatic changes in occupational distributions since 1930.

Chinese Women Since World War II

The main change in circumstances for Chinese women was that they were allowed entry into the United States in large numbers for the first time after World War II. Many separated wives were able to join their spouses under the provisions of the Walter-McCarran Act of 1953, and whole family units were able to enter after passage of the liberalized 1965 immigration law (Li 1977; U.S. Department of Justice 1977). Since World War II female immigrants have outnumbered males, and the sex ratio of the Chinese population now approaches equality, with the remaining imbalance existing only in older age categories (U.S. Census Bureau 1973). Women who have joined spouses or arrived with husbands are adapting to the postwar urban economy by entering the paid labor force. Handicapped by language, by family responsibilities, and by gender and race discrimination in the skilled trades, both husbands and wives are employed in the secondary labor market—in low-wage service and competitive manufacturing sectors. The most typical constellation among immigrant families is a husband employed as a restaurant worker, store helper, or janitor and a wife employed as an operative in a small garment shop. The shops are located in or close to Chinatowns and are typically subcontracting firms run by Chinese. They often evade minimum-wage laws by using an unofficial piece rate system (Nee and Nee 1972). ...

Postwar economic changes have undercut family enterprises such as laundries and small stores, so that working-class families today typically engage in dual wage earning. They encounter difficulties due to the long work hours of parents, and crowded and run-down housing. Working mothers are responsible for not only the lion's share of domestic chores, but often raise their children almost single-handedly. Husbands are frequently employed in the restaurant trade, which requires them to be at work from 11 in the morning until 10 in the evening or even midnight. Thus, they are rarely around while their children are awake. The women's own work hours are often prolonged because they leave work during the day to cook meals or pick up children. They make up the time by returning to the shop for evening work or by taking materials home to sew at night (Ikels and Shang 1979). Their energy is entirely absorbed by paid employment and domestic responsibilities. The one ray of light is their hope for their children's future.

Mexican American Women

The Chicano population is still characterized by continued migration back and forth between Mexico and the United States. In 1970, 16 percent of the resident population in the United States was foreign-born (Massey 1982, p. 10). Not surprisingly, Chicanos remain concentrated in the Southwest. ... Contrary to their image as rural people, four out of five (79 percent) resided in metropolitan areas. In line with the urban shift there has been a sharp reduction in the percentage of men and women engaged in agriculture. The proportion of women employed as farm workers fell from 21.2 percent in 1930 to 2.4 percent by 1979. ... As a result of mechanization of agriculture, which caused a sharp decline in the total number of farm workers, however, Chicana women constituted a higher *proportion* of women in agricultural labor in 1979 than they did in 1930. For those still involved in migrant labor, conditions remained harsh, with extensive exploitation of children despite child labor laws (Taylor 1976).

The period from 1930 to the present has seen a steady rise in the occupational status of Mexican Americans. As with other racial ethnic groups, the occupational dispersion of Chicanos is related to labor shortages during wars, especially World War II. After the war, rising numbers of Chicanas found employment in clerical and sales jobs, though they still lagged behind white women, especially in sales. The lower rates in white-collar jobs were matched by overrepresentation in blue-collar and service occupations. Mexican American women were concentrated in operative jobs, principally in garment factories, laundries, and food processing plants, which together accounted for 25.0 percent of their employment in 1979. ... These enterprises tended to be small competitive firms that paid minimum wages and often were seasonal. Another 23.4 percent of all employed Chicanas were in service jobs, including private household work.

Mexican American women have traditionally had among the lowest rates of labor force participation among racial ethnic women (Almquist and Wehrle-Einhorn 1978). However, in the 1970s they rapidly entered the labor market, so that by 1980 their rates were similar to those of whites, though lower than those for black and Asian American women (Massey 1982). The lower rates may be related to two other circumstances that usually depress employment: education and family size. Chicanas have the lowest education levels of the three groups and the largest number of children. These factors mean that when Chicanas are in the labor force, they are at a great disadvantage.

In short, though Mexican American women have achieved greater employment parity with Anglo women, they continue to have lower educational levels and heavier family burdens. In addition, they encounter racial barriers to white-collar employment.

Black Women

Black women have also experienced shifts in employment since World War II. The postwar period has seen a great decline in domestic service as a major category of women's work. Because black women were so concentrated in it, they have shown the most dramatic decline. Whereas in 1940 three out of five (59.5 percent) employed black females were in domestic service, by 1960 that proportion had dropped to a little over a third (36.2 percent), and by 1980 to one out of fourteen (7.4 percent) (U.S. Census Bureau 1943, 1973; Westcott 1982). Partially replacing service in private households has been service employment in public establishments, particularly in food service and health care, where the number of low-level jobs has proliferated. ... U.S. census data ... show that black women are also over-represented in the operatives category. ...

As in the past, there is a stratified labor market and a dual wage system. Baker and Levenson (1975a) examined the careers of black, Hispanic, and white graduates of a New York City vocational high school, and found that black and Hispanic women were disproportionately tracked into lower-paying operative jobs in the garment industry, while better-paying jobs outside the garment industry were reserved for white graduates. Years later the difference in pay and mobility was even greater as black and Hispanic women were progressively disadvantaged (Baker and Levenson 1975b).

The last barrier to fall was white-collar employment. A dramatic increase in professional-technical, clerical, and sales employment took place after 1950. ... Though black women have experienced desegregation at the level of broad occupations, they have been resegregated at the finer level of detailed job categories.

Other measures also show continued disadvantage for black women. They have a 50 percent higher unemployment rate and somewhat lower earnings (U.S. Department of Labor 1977). The largest gap is in terms of median family income, due to discrimination against black men. Even with the mother in the labor force, the median family income for black families with children under 18 was $14,461 in 1975, compared with $17,588 for similar white families (U.S. Department of Labor 1977). Even though they could not raise family income to white levels by being employed, black women's wages made a bigger difference to overall family income. The gap between blacks and whites was even greater if the mother was not employed: the median for black families without the mother in the labor force was $8,912, compared with $14,796 for whites (U.S. Department of Labor 1977). Regardless of income level, the economic fate of the black conjugal family rested on an economic partnership between men and women. Moreover, even among relatively affluent black families, the need to combat racism was a theme that infused daily life and absorbed the energy of parents in socializing their children (Willie 1981). Women's role as nurturers required them to combat the daily assaults on their children's self-esteem and to be vigilant in protecting them from psychic injury.

IMPLICATIONS FOR FEMINIST ANALYSIS

The history of racial ethnic women's work in the United States reveals their oppression not just as women but also as members of colonized minorities. As members of colonized minorities, their experiences differed fundamentally from those used to construct Marxist feminist theory. Thus, concepts within that framework require reformulation if it is to generate analyses that are inclusive of racial ethnic women. I will briefly examine three concepts in Marxist feminist theory that need to be redefined to take into account the interaction of race and gender. These are the separation of private and public spheres, the primacy of gender conflict as a feature of the family, and the gender-based assignment of reproductive labor.

The growing separation of public and private spheres with industrialization was central to early Marxist feminist analyses of women's oppression under capitalism. However, recent historical and comparative research has called into question the extent to which private and public constituted separate and bounded spheres for all classes and groups. Scholars note that in industrializing societies, working-class women engage in many income-earning activities, such as doing piecework at home, taking in boarders, or trading on the informal market, that cannot be easily categorized as private or public (Jensen 1980). Moreover, industrial wage work and family life have been found to interact in complex ways, so that, for example, women's family roles may include and overlap with their roles as workers (Hareven 1977). The examination of racial ethnic women's work adds to the critiques growing out of this research.

The nature of the split, and the extent to which women are identified with the public sphere, seem to vary by class and ethnicity; differences among groups in women's relationship to public and private spheres need to be examined. Like many other working-class women, racial ethnic women were never out of public production. They were integrated into production in varying ways. Black women were involved in agriculture and waged domestic service from the time of slavery. Chinese American women frequently engaged in unpaid labor in family enterprises, where there was little separation between public and private life. Mexican American women were initially more confined to household-based labor than were the other groups, but this labor included a great deal of actual production, since men's wages were insufficient to purchase the necessities of life. Thus, a definition of womanhood exclusively in terms of domesticity never applied to racial ethnic women, as it did not to many working-class women.

Where racial ethnic women diverge from other working-class women is that, as members of colonized minorities, their definition as laborers in production took precedence over their domestic roles. Whereas the wife-mother roles of white working-class women were recognized and accorded respect by the larger society, the maternal and reproductive roles of racial ethnic women were ignored in favor of their roles as workers. The lack of consideration for their domestic functions is poignantly revealed in the testimony of black domestics, who were expected to leave their children and home cares behind while devoting full time to the care of the white employer's home and children. Similarly, Chinese and Mexican American women and children were treated as units of labor, capable of toiling long hours without regard to their need for private life. This is not to say that racial ethnic women did not see themselves in terms of their family identities, but that they were not so defined by the larger society, which was interested in them only as workers.

Another area of divergence is in the scope of what is included in the "private" sphere. For racial ethnic women the domestic encompasses a broad range of kin and community relations beyond the nuclear family. Under conditions of economic insecurity, scarce resources, and cultural assault, the conjugal household was not self-sufficient. Racial ethnic peoples have historically relied on a larger network of extended kin, including fictive relatives and clan associations, for goods and services. This means that women's reproductive work in the "private" sphere included contributions to this larger circle, within which women took care of each other's children, loaned each other goods, and helped nurse the sick. Beyond the kin network women's work extended to the ethnic community, with much effort being expended in support of the church, political organizing, and other activities on behalf of "the race" (*la raza*). Women were often the core of community organizations, and their involvement was often spurred by a desire to defend their children, their families, and their way of life (Gilkes 1982; Yap 1983; Elasser et al. 1980). In short, race, as organized within a colonial labor system, interacted with gender (patriarchy) and class (capitalism) to determine the structure of private and public spheres, and women's relationship to these spheres. ...

In the early industrial period, racial ethnic and immigrant women were employed as household servants, thereby performing reproductive labor for white native families. The labor of black and immigrant servants made possible the woman *belle* ideal for white middle-class women. Even where white immigrant domestics were employed, the dirtiest and most arduous tasks—laundering and heavy cleaning—were often assigned to black servants. There was a three-way division of labor in the home, with white middle-class women at the top of the hierarchy, followed by white immigrants, with racial ethnics at the bottom. In the late industrial period, as capital took over more areas of life, reproductive activities were increasingly taken out of the household and turned into paid services that yielded profits (Braverman 1974). Today, such activities as caring for the elderly (old age homes), preparing food (restaurants and fast food stands), and providing emotional support (counseling services) have been brought into the cash nexus. As this has happened, women have been incorporated into the labor force to perform these tasks for wages. Within this female-typed public reproduction work, however, there is further stratification by race. Racial ethnic women perform the more menial, less desirable tasks. They prepare and serve food, clean rooms, and change bedpans, while white women, employed as semiprofessionals and white-collar workers, perform the more skilled and administrative tasks. The stratification is visible in hospitals, where whites predominate among registered nurses, while the majority of health care aides and housekeeping staff are blacks and Latinas. Just as white women in tobacco manufacturing benefited by getting cleaner and more mechanized jobs by dint of the dirty preparation work done by black women, so white women professionals enjoy more desirable working conditions because racial ethnic women perform the less desirable service tasks. The better pay white women receive allows them to purchase services and goods that ease their reproductive labor at home.

This point leads to a final consideration. It may be tempting to conclude that racial ethnic women differ from white women simply by the addition of a second axis of oppression, race. It would be a mistake, though, not to recognize the ... relation between white and racial ethnic women. Race, gender, and class interact in such a way that the histories of white and racial ethnic women are intertwined. Whether one considers the split between public and private spheres, conflict within the family and between the family and outside institutions, or productive and reproductive labor, the situation of white women has depended on the situation of women of color. White women have gained advantages from the exploitation of racial ethnic women, and the definition of white womanhood has to a large extent been cast in opposition to the definition of racial ethnic women (cf. Palmer 1983). Marxist feminist theory and the internal colonialism model both recognize white men as the dominant exploiting group; however, it is equally important to emphasize the involvement of white women in the exploitation of racial ethnic people, and the ways in which racial ethnic men have benefited from the even greater exploitation of racial ethnic women.

REFERENCES

Almquist, Elizabeth M., and Juanita Wehrle-Einhorn. 1978. "The Doubly Disadvantaged: Minority Women in the Labor Force." In *Women Working,* Ann H. Stromberg and Shirley Harkess, eds., pp. 63–88. Palo Alto, CA: Mayfield.

Baker, Sally Hillsman, and Bernard Levenson. 1975a. "Job Opportunities of Black and White Working-Class Women." *Social Problems* 22 (April):510–532.

———. 1975b. "Earnings Prospects of Black and White Working Class Women." Unpublished paper.

Barrera, Mario. 1979. *Race and Class in the Southwest.* Notre Dame, IN: University of Notre Dame Press.

Barrera, Mario, Carlos Munoz, and Charles Ornelas. 1972. "The Barrio as an Internal Colony." In *Urban Affairs Annual Review,* vol. 6, Harland Hahn, ed., pp. 465–498. Beverly Hills, CA: Sage.

Blauner, Robert. 1972. *Racial Oppression in America.* New York: Harper and Row.

Braverman, Harry. 1974. *Labor and Monopoly Capital: The Degradation of Work in the Twentieth Century.* New York: Monthly Review Press.

Brown, Carol. 1981. "Mothers, Fathers and Children: From Private to Public Patriarchy." In *Women and Revolution: A Discussion of the Unhappy Marriage of Marxism and Feminism,* Lydia Sargent, ed., pp. 239–269. Boston: South End Press.

———. 1975. "Patriarchal Capitalism and the Female-Headed Family." *Social Scientist* 40–41:28–39.

Byington, Margaret. 1974. *Homestead: The Households of a Milltown.* Pittsburgh: University of Pittsburgh Press.

Camarillo, Albert. 1979. *Chicanos in a Changing Society.* Cambridge, MA: Harvard University Press.

Carmichael, Stokely, and Charles V. Hamilton. 1967. *Black Power: The Politics of Liberation in America.* New York: Vintage.

Cheng, Lucie, and Edna Bonacich. 1984. *Labor Immigration Under Capitalism: Asian Immigrant Workers in the United States Before World War II.* Berkeley: University of California Press.

Clark, Kenneth. 1965. *Dark Ghetto.* New York: Harper and Row.

Coolidge, Mary. 1909. *Chinese Immigration.* New York: Henry Holt.

Davis, Angela Y. 1971. "Reflections on the Black Woman's Place in the Community of Slaves." *The Black Scholar* 2 (December):3–15.

Hareven, Tamara. 1977. "Family Time and Industrial Time: Family and Work in a Planned Corporation Town, 1900–1924." In *Family and Kin in Urban Communities: 1700–1920,* Tamara Hareven, ed., pp. 187–207. New York: New Viewpoints.

Hartmann, Heidi. 1976. "Capitalism, Patriarchy and Job Segregation by Sex." *Signs* 1 (Spring):137–169.

———. 1981. "The Unhappy Marriage of Marxism and Feminism: Towards a More Progressive Union." In *Women and Revolution: A Discussion of the Unhappy Marriage of Marxism and Feminism,* Lydia Sargent, ed., pp. 1–41. Boston: South End Press.

Hirata, Lucie Cheng. 1979. "Free, Indentured and Enslaved: Chinese Prostitutes in Nineteenth Century America." *Signs* 5 (Autumn):3–29.

Hooks, Bell. 1981. *Ain't I a Woman: Black Women and Feminism.* Boston: South End Press.

Ikels, Charlotte, and Julia Shang. 1979. *The Chinese in Greater Boston.* Bethesda, MD: National Institute of Aging.

Jensen, Joan M. 1981. *With These Hands: Women Working on the Land.* Old Westbury, NY: Feminist Press.

Jones, Jacqueline. 1984. *Labor of Love, Labor of Sorrow: Black Women, Work and the Family from Slavery to the Present.* New York: Basic Books.

Katzman, David H. 1978. *Seven Days a Week: Women and Domestic Service in Industrializing America.* New York: Oxford University Press.

Kessler-Harris, Alice. 1982. *Out to Work: A History of Wage-Earning Women in the United States.* New York: Oxford University Press.

Lee, L. P., A. Lim, and H. K. Wong. 1969. *Report of the San Francisco Chinese Community Citizens' Survey and Fact Finding Committee.* Abridged edition. San Francisco: Chinese Community Citizens' Survey and Fact Finding Committee.

Lerner, Gerda. 1969. "The Lady and the Mill Girl: Changes in the Status of Women in the Age of Jackson." *American Studies* 10 (Spring):5–14.

———. 1973. *Black Women in White America: A Documentary History.* New York: Vintage.

Li, Peter S. 1977. "Fictive Kinship, Conjugal Ties and Kinship Claim Among Chinese Immigrants in the United States." *Journal of Comparative Family Studies* 8, no. 1:47–64.

Ling. Pyan. 1912. "The Causes of Chinese Immigration." *Annals of the American Academy of Political and Social Science* 39 (January):74–82.

Lyman, Stanford. 1968. "Marriage and Family Among Chinese Immigrants to America, 1850–1960." *Phylon* 29, no. 4:321–330.

———. 1974. *Chinese Americans.* New York: Random House.

———. 1977. *The Asian in North America.* Santa Barbara, CA: ABC Clio.

Massey, Douglas S. 1982. *The Demographic and Economic Position of Hispanics in the United States: 1980.* Philadelphia: Population Studies Center, University of Pennsylvania.

McLemore, Dale. 1973. "The Origins of Mexican American Subordination in Texas." *Social Science Quarterly* 53 (March):656–670.

———. 1980. *Racial and Ethnic Relationships in America.* Boston: Allyn and Bacon.

McWilliams, Carey. 1971. *Factories in the Field.* Santa Barbara, CA: Peregrine.

Moore, Joan W. 1970. "Colonialism: The Case of Mexican Americans." *Social Problems* 17 (Spring):463–472.

Nee, Victor, and Brett deBary Nee. 1972. *Long Time Californ'.* New York: Pantheon.

Painter, Nell Irvin. 1976. *Exodusters: Black Migration to Kansas After the Reconstruction.* New York: Norton.

Palmer, Phyllis Marynick. 1983. "White Women/Black Women: The Dualism of Female Identity and Experience in the United States." *Feminist Studies* 9 (Spring):151–170.

Pleck, Elizabeth H. 1979. "A Mother's Wages: Income Earning Among Italian and Black Women, 1896–1911." In *A Heritage of Her Own: Toward a New Social History of American Women,* Nancy F. Cott and Elizabeth H. Pleck, eds., pp. 367–392. New York: Simon and Schuster.

Saxton, Alexander. 1971. *The Indispensable Enemy: Labor and the Anti-Chinese Movement in California.* Berkeley: University of California Press.

Sokoloff, Natalie J. 1980. *Between Money and Love: The Dialectics of Women's Home and Market Work.* New York: Praeger.

Taylor, Paul S. 1929. "Mexican Labor in the United States: Valley of the South Platte, Colorado." *University of California Publications in Economics* 6, no. 2 (June):95–235.

———. 1937. "Migratory Farm Labor in the United States." *Monthly Labor Review* 60 (March):537–549.

Taylor, Ronald. 1976. *Sweatshops in the Sun.* Boston: Beacon Press.

U.S. Census Bureau. 1943. *Sixteenth Census of the Population, 1940: Population Characteristics of the Non-White Population by Race.* Washington, D.C.: U.S. Government Printing Office.

————. 1973. *Census of the Population: 1970. Subject Reports,* Final Report PC (2) 1G, *Japanese, Chinese, and Filipinos in the United States.* Washington, D.C.: U.S. Government Printing Office.

U.S. Department of Justice. 1977. *Immigration and Naturalization Service Annual Report.* Washington, D.C.: U.S. Department of Justice.

U.S. Department of Labor, Bureau of Labor Statistics. 1977. *U.S. Working Women: A Databook.* Bulletin 1977.

Weinbaum, Batya, and Amy Bridges. 1979. "The Other Side of the Paycheck: Monopoly Capital and the Structure of Consumption." In *Capitalist Patriarchy and the Case for Socialist Feminism,* Zillah R. Eisenstein, ed., pp. 190–205. New York: Monthly Review Press.

Welter, Barbara. 1966. "The Cult of True Womanhood: 1820–1860." *American Quarterly* (Summer):151–174.

Westcott, Diane Nilsen. 1982. "Blacks in the 1970's: Did They Scale the Job Ladder?" *Monthly Labor Review* 105 (June):29–82.

Willie, Charles. 1981. *A New Look at Black Families.* Bayview, NY: General Hall.

Wolfbein, Seymour L. 1962. "Automation and Skill." *Annals of the American Academy of Political and Social Science* 340:53–59.

Wu, C. 1972. *"Chink": A Documentary History of Anti-Chinese Prejudice in America.* New York: Meridian.

Yap, Stacey G. Y. 1983. "Gather Your Strength Sisters: The Careers of Chinese American Community Workers." Ph.D. diss., Boston University.

15

From "Kike" to "JAP": How Misogyny, Anti-Semitism, and Racism Construct the "Jewish American Princess"

EVELYN TORTON BECK

The stereotyping of the Jewish American woman as the JAP, which stands for Jewish American Princess, is an insult, an injury, and violence that is done to Jewish women. The term is used widely by both men and women, by both Jews and non-Jews. When gentiles use it, it is a form of anti-Semitism. When Jews use it, it is a form of self-hating or internalized anti-Semitism. It is a way of thinking that allows some Jewish women to harm other Jewish women who are just like them except for the fact that one is okay—she's *not* a JAP. The other is not okay—she's too JAPie. The seriousness of this term becomes evident when we substitute the words "too Jewish" for "too JAPie," and feel ourselves becoming considerably less comfortable.

When I speak on college campuses, young women frequently tell me that when someone calls them a Jew they are insulted because they know it's being said with a kind of hostility, but if someone calls them a JAP they don't mind because they frequently use this term themselves. They think the "J" in JAP really doesn't mean anything—it's just there. While everyone seems to know what the characteristics of a "Jewish American Princess" are, no one ever seems to think about what they are saying when they use the term. How is it that you don't have to be Jewish to be a JAP? If this is so, why is the word "Jewish" in the acronym at all? Words are not meaningless unless we choose to close our ears and pretend not to hear.

This subject is frequently trivialized, but when it is not, when we take it seriously, it makes us extremely tense. Why is that? I think it's because it takes us into several "war zones." It brings us in touch with Jew-hating, or anti-Semitism. It brings us in touch with misogyny, or woman-hating. And it brings us in touch with class-hatred, old money vs. nouveau riche. (Jews have classically been seen as

162

intruders in the United States and have been resented for "making it.") It also puts us strongly in touch with racism. It is no accident that the acronym JAP is also the word used for our worst enemies in World War II—who were known as "the Japs." During World War II, posters and slogans saying "Kill Japs" were every-where. It was a period in which slang terms were readily used in a pejorative way to identify many different minorities: "Japs," "Kikes," "Spics," "Wops," "Chinks" were commonplace terms used unthinkingly. And women were—and, unfortu-nately, still are—easily named "bitches," "sluts," and "cunts."

In such a climate, negative stereotypes easily overlap and elide. For example, in the popular imagination, Jews, "Japs," women and homosexuals have all been viewed as devious, unreliable, and power hungry. What has happened in the de-cades following World War II is that the "Japs," whom we dehumanized when we dropped our atom bomb on them, have subliminally merged in the popular imagination with "kikes" and other foreign undesirables. (The fact that in the 1980s Japan poses a serious economic threat to the United States should not be overlooked either.) While efforts to eradicate slurs against ethnic minorities have made it not okay to use explicitly ethnic epithets, women still provide an accept-able target, especially when the misogyny is disguised as supposedly "good-natured" humor. In this insidious and circuitous way, the Jewish American woman carries the stigmas of the "kikes" and "Japs" of a previous era. And that is very serious.

The woman, the Jewish woman as JAP, has replaced the male Jew as the scape-goat, and the Jewish male has not only participated, but has, in fact, been instru-mental in creating and perpetuating that image. I want to show how some of the images of Jewish women created in American culture by Jewish men provided the roots of the "Jewish American Princess." But first I want to provide a context for understanding the development of this image. I want to look at anti-Semitism in the United States, and at misogyny, and show how the merging of anti-Semitism and misogyny creates the Jewish American Princess.

Between 1986 and 1987 there was a 17 percent rise in anti-Semitic incidents in this country. Of these incidents, 48 percent occurred in the Northeast, and the highest rates of increase were in New York State; California, particularly Los An-geles; and Florida. These are all areas where there are high concentrations of Jews. On November 9 and 10, 1987, the anniversary of *Kristalnacht*, the Night of Broken Crystal, when Goebbels staged a mass "spontaneous pogrom" in Austria and Ger-many in 1938, swastikas were painted on entrances to synagogues in a number of different cities in the United States: Chicago, Yonkers, and others dotted across the country. Windows were smashed—not simply of Jewish-owned stores, but of identifiably Jewish businesses such as kosher meat markets, a kosher fish store, a Jewish book store—in five different neighborhoods, particularly in a Chicago suburb largely populated by Holocaust survivors. Having grown up in Vienna and having lived under the Nazis, the horror of that night resonated for me in a way that it might not for those who are much younger. But that these pogrom-like episodes happened on the eve of *Kristalnacht* cannot have been an accident, and the timing of these incidents should not be lost upon us.

In response to these attacks many members of the Jewish community wanted to hide the facts, and one member of the Jewish community in Chicago actually said, "The swastikas could have meant general white supremacy; they were not necessarily aimed at Jews." They just "happened" to be placed on synagogues, right? In the same way, it just "happens" that the word "Jewish" is lodged in the very negative image of this hideous creature known as the Jewish American Princess. Anyone who is aware of Jewish history and knows about the ridicule, defamation, and violence to which Jews have been subject will not be able to write this off so easily.

The Jewish American Princess phenomenon is not new; I (as well as other Jewish feminists) have been talking about it for at least ten years now, but only recently has it been given wide public attention. One reason for this is that it is beginning to be seen in the light of increased anti-Semitism and racism, particularly on college campuses. Dr. Gary Spencer, who is a *male* professor of sociology at Syracuse University (and it is unfortunate that his being male gives him credibility over women saying the same things) closely examined the library and bathroom graffiti of his school and interviewed hundreds of students on his campus and has concluded that "JAP"-baiting is widespread, virulent, and threatening to all Jews, not "just" Jewish women (which we gather might have been okay or certainly considerably less serious).

Spencer discovered that nasty comments about "JAPS" led to more generally anti-Semitic graffiti that said among other slogans, "Hitler was right!" "Give Hitler a second chance!" and "I hate Jews." He also discovered that there were certain places in which Jewish women—JAPS—were not welcome: for example, certain cafes where Jewish women were hassled if they entered. He also found that certain areas of the university were considered "JAP-free zones" and other areas (particularly dorms) were called "Jew havens." At The American University in Washington, D.C., largely Jewish residence halls are called "Tokyo Towers," making the racial overtones of "JAP" explicit. But let the parallels to Nazi-occupied Europe not be lost upon us. Under the Nazis, movements of the Jews were sharply restricted: there were many areas which Jews could not enter, and others (like ghettos and concentration camps) that they could not leave.

What I want to do now is to show how characteristics that have historically been attributed to Jews, primarily Jewish men, have been reinterpreted in terms of women: how misogyny combined with Jew-hating creates the Jewish American Princess. And I want you to remember that Jewish men have not only participated in this trashing, but they have not protected Jewish women when other men and women have talked about "JAPs" in this way. And this fact, I think, has made this an arena into which anyone can step—an arena that becomes a minefield when Jews step into it.

Jews have been said to be materialistic, money-grabbing, greedy, and ostentatious. Women have been said to be vain, trivial and shallow; they're only interested in clothing, in show. When you put these together you get the Jewish-woman type who's only interested in designer clothes and sees her children only as extensions of herself. The Jew has been seen as manipulative, crafty, untrustworthy, unreliable, calculating, controlling, and malevolent. The Jewish Princess is seen as manipulative, particularly of the men in her life, her husband, her boyfriend, her father. And what does she want? Their *money!* In addition, she's lazy— she doesn't work inside or outside the home. She is the female version of the Jew who, according to anti-Semitic lore, is a parasite on society; contradictorily, the Jew has been viewed both as dangerous "communist" as well as non-productive "capitalist." The cartoon vision of the Jewish American Princess is someone who sucks men dry: she is an "unnatural mother" who refuses to nurture her children (the very opposite of the "Jewish mother" whose willingness to martyr herself makes *her* ludicrous). And she doesn't "put out" except in return for goods; she isn't really interested in either sexuality or lovingness. We live in a world climate and culture in which materialism is rampant, and Jewish women are taking the rap for it. The irony is they are taking the rap from non-Jews and Jewish men alike—even from some Jewish women.

Another way in which women are carrying the anti-Semitism that was directed in previous eras at Jewish men is in the arena of sexuality. Jews have been said to be sexually strange, exotic. There are many stereotypes of Jewish men as lechers. The Jewish American Princess is portrayed as both sexually frigid (withholding) and as a nymphomaniac. Here we again see the familiar anti-Semitic figure of the Jew as controlling and insatiably greedy, always wanting more, combining with the misogynist stereotype of the insatiable woman, the woman who is infinitely orgasmic, who will destroy men with her desire. Like the Jew of old, the Jewish woman will suck men dry. But she is worse than "the Jew"—she will also turn on her own kind.

There are physical stereotypes as well: the Jew with the big hook nose, thick lips, and frizzy hair. The Jewish American Princess has had a nose job and her hair has been straightened, but she too has large lips (an image we immediately recognize as racist). Jews are supposed to be loud, pushy, and speak with unrefined accents. Jewish American Princesses are said to come from Long Island and speak with funny accents: "Oh my Gawd!" The accent has changed from the lampooned immigrant speech of previous generations, but assimilation into the middle class hasn't helped the Jewish American Princess get rid of her accent. It doesn't matter how she speaks, because if it's Eastern and recognizably Jewish, it's not okay.

I also want to give you some idea of how widespread and what a money-making industry the Jewish American Princess phenomenon has become. There are greeting cards about the "JAP Olympics," with the JAP doing things like "bank-vaulting" instead of pole-vaulting. Or cross-country "*kvetching*" instead of skiing. In this card the definition of the Yiddish term *kvetch* reads: "an irritable whine made by a three-year-old child or a JAP at any age." So in addition to the all-powerful monster you also have the infantilization of the Jewish woman. And there are the Bunny Bagelman greeting cards: Bunny has frizzy hair, big lips, is wearing ostentatious jewelry—and is always marked as a Jew in some way. One of her cards reads, "May God Bless you and keep you ... rich!" Or Bunny Bagelman is a professional, dressed in a suit carrying a briefcase, but this image is undermined by the little crown she incongruously wears on her head bearing the initials "JAP." There is also a Halloween card with a grotesque female figure; the card reads, "Is it a vicious vampire? No, it's Bunny Bagelman with PM syndrome!" In analyzing these kinds of cartoons, you begin to see how sexism is absolutely intertwined with anti-Semitism.

Such attacks devalue Jewish women and keep them in line. An incident reported by Professor Spencer at Syracuse University makes this quite evident. At a basketball game, when women who were presumed to be "JAPs" stood up and walked across the floor at half-time (and it happened to Jewish and non-Jewish women), 2,000 students stood up, accusingly pointed their fingers at them, and repeatedly yelled, "JAP, JAP, JAP, JAP, JAP" in a loud chorus. This was so humiliating and frightening that women no longer got out of their seats to go to the bathroom or to get a soda. This is a form of public harassment that is guaranteed to control behavior and parallels a phenomenon called "punching" at the University of Dar El Salaam, Tanzania. Here, when women were "uppity" or otherwise stepped out of line, huge posters with their pictures on them were put all over campus, and no one was to speak to them. If you spoke to these women, you were considered to be like them. This is a very effective way of controlling people.

The threat of physical violence against Jewish women (in the form of "Slap-a-JAP" T-shirts and contests at bars) is evident on many Eastern college campuses. A disc jockey at The American University went so far as to sponsor a "fattest JAP-on-campus" contest. That this kind of unchecked verbal violence can lead to murder is demonstrated by lawyer Shirley Frondorf in a recent book entitled *Death of a "Jewish American Princess": The True Story of a Victim on Trial* (Villard Books, 1988). Frondorf shows how the murder of a Jewish woman by her husband was exonerated and the victim placed on trial because she was someone who was described by her husband as "materialistic, who shopped and spent, nagged shrilly and bothered her husband at work"—in other words, she was a "JAP" and therefore deserved what she got. This account demonstrates the dangers inherent in stereotyping and the inevitable dehumanization that follows.

One of the most aggressively sexual forms of harassment of Jewish women, which amounted to verbal rape, were signs posted at a college fair booth at Cornell University that read, "Make her prove she's not a JAP, make her swallow." Part of the mythology is that the Jewish woman will suck, but she won't swallow. So you see that as the degradation of woman *as woman* escalates, the anti-Semitism also gets increasingly louder. In a recent Cornell University student newspaper, a cartoon offered advice on how to "exterminate" JAPS by setting up a truck offering bargains, collecting the JAPS as they scurried in, and dropping them over a cliff. While the word "Jew" was not specifically mentioned, the parallels to the historical "rounding up" of Jews and herding them into trucks to be exterminated in the camps during World War II can hardly be ignored. This cartoon was created by a Jewish man.

This leads me directly to the third thing I want to discuss, namely, how and why Jewish men have participated in constructing and perpetuating the image of the Jewish American Princess as monster. How is it that the Jewish Mother (a mildly derogatory stereotype that nonetheless contained some warmth) has become the grotesque that is the Jewish American Princess, who, unlike the Jewish Mother, has absolutely no redeeming features? Exactly how the Jewish Mother (created entirely by second generation American men who had begun to mock the very nurturance they had relied upon for their success) gave birth to the Jewish American Princess is a long and complex story. This story is intertwined with the overall economic success of Jews as a class in the United States, the jealousy others have felt over this success, and the discomfort this success creates in Jews who are fearful of living out the stereotype of the "rich Jew." It is also a likely conjecture that middle-class American Jewish men view the large numbers of Jewish women who have successfully entered the work force as professionals as a serious economic and ego threat.

We find the origins of the Jewish American Princess in the fiction of American Jewish males of the last three decades. In the '50s, Herman Wouk's *Marjory Morningstar* (nee Morgenstern) leaves behind her immigrant background, takes a new name (one that is less recognizably Jewish), manipulates men, has no talent, and is only interested in expensive clothing. The postwar Jewish male, who is rapidly assimilating into American middle-class culture and leaving behind traditional Jewish values, is creating the Jewish woman—the materialistic, empty, manipulative Jewish woman, the Americanized daughter who fulfills the American Dream for her parents but is, at the same time, punished for it. It looks as if the Jewish woman was created in the image of the postwar Jewish male but viewed by her creator as grotesque. All the characteristics he cannot stand in himself are displaced onto the Jewish woman.

In the '60s, Philip Roth created the spoiled and whiny Brenda Potemkin in *Goodby, Columbus* at the same time that Shel Silverstein created his image of the perfect Jewish mother as martyr. Some of you may remember this popular story from your childhood. A synopsis goes something like this: "Once there was a tree and she loved the little boy. And he slept in her branches, and loved the tree and the tree was happy. And as the boy grew older, he needed things from her. He needed apples, so she gave him apples, and she was happy. Then she cut off her branches because the boy needed them to build a house. And she was happy. Then finally he needed her trunk because he wanted to build a big boat for himself. And she was happy. The tree gave and gave of herself, and finally the tree was alone and old when the boy returned one more time. By now, the tree had nothing to give. But the boy/man is himself old now, and he doesn't need much except a place on which to sit. And the tree said, 'An old stump is good for sitting and resting on. Come boy and sit and rest on me.' And the boy did, and the tree was happy." This "positive" entirely self-*less* mother, created as a positive wish fantasy by a Jewish man, very easily tips over into its opposite, the monstrous woman, the self-absorbed "JAP" who is negatively self-less. She has no center. She *is* only clothes, money, and show.

In concluding, I want to bring these strands together and raise some questions. Obviously Jews need to be as thoughtful about consumerism as others, but we need to ask why the Jewish woman is taking the rap for the consumerism which is rampant in our highly materialistic culture in general. We need to think about the image of the Jewish American Princess and the father she tries to manipulate. What has happened to the Jewish Mother? Why has she dropped out of the picture? If (as is likely true of all groups) some middle-class Jewish women (and men) are overly focused on material things, what is the other side of that? What about the middle-class fathers who measure their own success by what material goods they are able to provide to their wives and children and who don't know how to show love in any other way? Someone who doesn't know how to give except through material goods could easily create a child who comes to expect material goods as a proof of love and self-worth, especially if sexist gender expectations limit the options for women. We need to look more closely at the relationship between the "monster' daughter and the father who helped create her. ...

Last, I want to say that we have many false images of Jewish families. There *is* violence in Jewish families, just as there is violence in families of all groups. It is time to put the whole question of the Jewish American Princess into the context of doing away with myths of all kinds. The Jewish family is no more nor less cohesive than other families, although there is great pressure on Jewish families to pretend they are. Not all Jewish families are non-alcoholic; not all Jewish families are heterosexual; not all Jews are upper or middle class; and not all are urban or Eastern. It's important that the truth of Jewish women's (and also Jewish men's) lives be spoken. Beginning to take apart this image of the Jewish American Princess can make us look more closely at what it is that we, in all of our diversity as Jews, are; what we are striving toward; and what we hope to become.

PART 4

Immigration and Group Conflict

Several relatively distinct phases have marked the history of American immigration. These historical distinctions have involved differences in the ethnic and racial composition of the people moving, differences in the sociological factors that impelled their movement, differences in their motives for migration and where they settled, and differences in the responses made to them by the resident populations. The dominant imagery of this country as welcoming the newcomer was vital to the maintenance of egalitarian ideals and, to some extent, the myth of representative government (see the essay by Howard Zinn in Part Seven). This imagery, along with that of economic opportunity, also served to attract people. Nevertheless, the resident populations, despite their own immigrant origins, have always been ambivalent toward immigration (even if accepting of individual migrants). This ambivalence toward immigration has always been a part of American life. It is manifested today in concerns over new immigrants taking jobs from residents, thus costing taxpayers more money in the form of public assistance; in conflicts over the likelihood that newcomers will shift the balance of political power away from established interests; and in uncertainty about the value of providing political, religious, and other forms of sanctuary to those desiring to enter this country. These current concerns are the same as those expressed in the early nineteenth-century response to immigration. As a result, a given immigrant group may at times be welcomed and later rejected; at other times new restrictions might be placed on those who could enter; and at still other times specific entrants may be encouraged.

At the time of the Revolution, the white American population was mainly English and Protestant in background. Other groups, including German nationals as well as Catholics and Jews, were represented to a lesser degree. The pie chart in Figure 1 was drawn on the basis of the first census in 1790—clearly a very different time.

Note that Native Americans were not counted; indeed, they were generally treated as subhumans to be eliminated as the colonists began a westward expansion. Blacks, who were mainly slaves, made up close to 20 percent of the colonial population. Like the Indians they were neither counted nor viewed as assimilable in or even desirable to this new country's settlement.

While the post-Revolutionary phase of immigration set the stage for this new country to view itself as white, Anglo-Saxon, and Protestant, the pre–Civil War

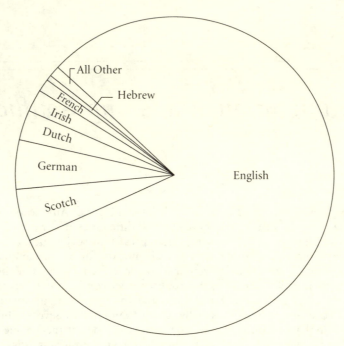

FIGURE 1 This pie chart appeared in the first U.S. census, conducted in 1790.

stage (1815–1860) saw the rise of an ethnocentric ideology that foreshadowed the development of organized bigotry in the United States. This was the period of the rise of "nativist" third parties. The Native American Party became a national third party in 1840, and it was succeeded by an even stronger organization in the 1850s.

One prominent theme of this movement was the fear that the new foreign-born voters would wrest control of the political process and, because of their ignorance of American institutions, wreck the political system if not the entire country. Labor competition also played a key role in the growth of this new bigotry. An even more prominent theme, however, was the movement's anti-Catholicism. The growth of American Catholicism and the massive wave of Irish Catholic inmigration reestablished earlier fears of a papal takeover of America. From 1790 to 1840, the number of Catholics in this country had risen from 35,000 in 1790 to 1.3 million fifty years later. These new nativists feared not only that the country would fall into the hands of the Catholic hierarchy and its allies in the European monarchies but also that convents and monasteries would proliferate as places of wickedness and vice. Although such concerns may be hard to imagine, fear of the papal menace haunted even the presidential candidacy of John F. Kennedy in 1960.

The Civil War disrupted the nativist movement. In a new phase of immigration, from 1865 to 1890, approximately 11 million people arrived, mainly from northern and western Europe—that is, from Great Britain, Germany, Scandinavia, and so on. During the next phase, from 1890 to 1930, the number of immigrants doubled, reaching 22 million. In this wave, migrants streamed from the countries of southern and eastern Europe—that is, from Austria, Bulgaria, Czechoslovakia, Finland, Greece, Hungary, Italy, Poland, Portugal, Romania, Spain, Turkey, the USSR, and Yugoslavia. These new migrants were not only different in terms of culture and language; they were also substantially poorer and, unlike the preceding wave, began to settle in ethnic enclaves in the urban centers. Concomitant with this large inmigration was the growth of a serious and powerful immigration restrictionist movement, a movement fueled by the sponsorship of political elites. Although it had started earlier with federal acts denying entry to Chinese and Japanese migrants, the turn of the century witnessed an increasing number of conditions intended to shut people out. Within two decades, Congress had ratified and established the precedent for screening people by health, social class, and political beliefs. The 1924 immigration act passed by Congress was explicitly designed to maintain the "racial preponderance [of] the basic strain on our people." A numerical limit was placed on annual immigration, and quotas were assigned to each national group in proportion to its representation in the existing population. By 1927, Congress had established the baseline of those quotas to be the U.S. population of 1890—a baseline chosen for the purpose of limiting the number of southern and eastern European migrants and favoring those from the north and west. World War II disrupted the rising bigotry, and the flow of immigrants was reduced to a trickle of refugees and displaced persons.

Until the start of World War II, these waves of semiskilled and unskilled immigrants were critical to this country's development—to the building of American cities, to westward expansion, and to providing the work force for the growth of American industry.

Figure 2 displays the number of immigrants by census period. As you can see, that number escalated following the end of World War II. A new pattern of immigration emerged in 1980–1989, a period that witnessed the second largest wave of immigration in U.S. history. This new immigration reflected greater cultural diversity than ever seen before. Mexican migrants constituted the largest group, with smaller groups arriving from the Philippines, China (the mainland, Hong Kong, and Taiwan), Korea, and Vietnam. Smaller but substantial numbers of Asian Indians and Dominicans were followed by people from Jamaica, Cuba, Iran, Cambodia, the United Kingdom, Laos, the Arab countries, Canada, and Colombia. Another distinctive character of this new phase of inmigration was the concentration of settlement: Approximately 70 percent of the newcomers settled in just six states.

After World War II, Congress enacted a series of immigration control bills that reflected myriad interests but were essentially designed to codify political restrictions on who could enter the country. The most recent of these bills were passed in 1986 and 1990. The Immigration Reform and Control Act of 1986 was intended to control the number of illegal immigrants and to rationalize immigration policy. It allowed undocumented workers to legalize their status if they could prove continuous residence in the country since January 1, 1982, or before. At the same time, the bill sought to reduce employment opportunities for undocumented workers by subjecting employers to civil and criminal penalties for hiring them.

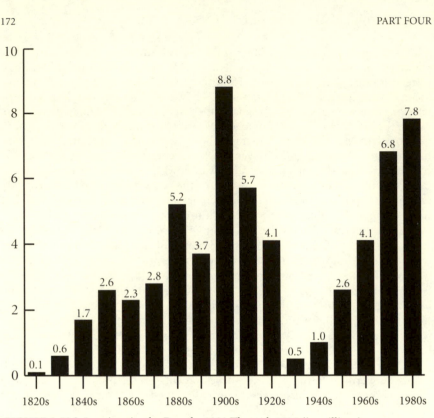

FIGURE 2 U.S. Immigration by Decade, 1821 Through 1990 (in millions)

In actuality, however, the legislation has had the effect of increasing discrimination against Hispanic workers without really reducing the flow of illegal entrants.

The Immigration Act of 1990 was designed to favor entrants on the basis of their skills and education. People with the background needed by business and industry were to be given priority. Another objective was to keep families together, so wives, husbands, children, parents, and siblings of newcomers were given priority as well. The result of this policy, however, has been to favor (and thus increase) the entry of western Europeans.

WHY DO PEOPLE MOVE, AND WHAT HAPPENS WHEN THEY DO?

There are two facets of the question as to why people move: individual motivating factors, and those larger social factors that create such motives and compel people to seek new destinations. Using a classification scheme independent of ethnicity, Alejandro Portes and Ruben Rumbaut (1990) have identified four basic types of migrants. The majority are *labor migrants*. They come to escape poverty and are attracted by the minimum wages of this country. *Professional migrants* are the well-educated elite who move to improve their socioeconomic status. Recently, this has been the case for immigrants from the Philippines, China, India, and Great Britain. *Entrepreneurial migrants* come with past experience in business, often with access to capital and labor. They are more likely to settle in the ethnic enclaves providing business services within the ethnic community. Current examples are Koreans, Cubans, and Chinese. Finally, there are the *refugees,* who are seeking asylum from the likelihood of political persecution and physical harm in their native countries. Over the past thirty years these have included significant numbers of Laotians and Cambodians, Salvadorans and Guatemalans, and Iranians. International migration is a major and often traumatic episode in people's lives. The motivations to migrate are complex, and the myriad decisions surrounding the move are highly stressful. On the whole, however, relatively few people migrate, and many who do often return to their homelands in disillusionment.

In the chapter that follows, Saskia Sassen ("America's Immigration 'Problem'") writes that most countries with a large outmigration to the United States have identifiable linkages to this country—linkages that, along with overpopulation, poverty, or unemployment, motivate migration. These linkages result from American investments in the countries in question. Among those linkages identified are the disruption of traditional work structures, especially through the recruitment of young women, and the cultural identification with Americans as a consequence of working in American- or Western-managed businesses. Of course, if a migration flow is to be practicable, the newcomers must have jobs. Sassen details how this need is filled by the rise of low-wage service-sector jobs as well as downgraded manufacturing jobs. Thus, as manufacturing jobs have been shifted to less developed countries, emigration is promoted; at the same time, the growth of these new jobs in the United States has helped to absorb the new migrants.

Milton Gordon ("Models of Pluralism: The New American Dilemma") raises the question as to how new immigrants are assimilated into American society. He proposes that there exist two basic models of assimilation: liberal pluralism and corporate pluralism. The difference between the two concerns the degree to which new immigrant groups may preserve their separate cultural practices and accommodate to the cultural practices of this society. The liberal policy requires a high degree of control over cultural expressions. Multiculturalism is politically acceptable as long as no ethnic group receives state support for establishing its own territory and language. In short, the liberal model is basically assimilationist. Separate groups may retain their own cultural practices and identity as long as they accept their cultural subordination. Although such groups are expected to struggle politically for greater independence, that struggle must be contained within the operating rules of the state.

The corporate model represents a substantial shift toward a more pluralistic conception of the nation-state. Here, some degree of multicultural separatism, including bilingualism and territorial exclusiveness, is accepted. The state is required to intervene actively in order to promote political and economic equality among the multiple ethnic groups seeking a discrete cultural—and legal—identity. An outstanding illustration of the corporate model can be seen in the political arrangements between Quebec and Canada.

Both models assume a central state government as well as an essentially strati-fied economic system. The liberal model is based on acceptance of the stratifica-tion system already in existence. It views society as a meritocracy and does not question the economic system; but it also requires equal opportunity, thus per-mitting the state to intervene so that no group may be totally oppressed. Accord-ing to this model, it is the role of state managers to ensure that all group conflicts, whether class or ethnically based, are managed such that the order of society is maintained. The corporate model adds a unique dimension whereby economic and political equality are viewed as group characteristics. In this case, the role of the state is to assist each group in achieving parity. Theoretically, then, if the dis-tribution of privilege, wealth, and power were the same in the minority society as in the majority society, corporate pluralism would have been achieved. The exis-tence of large numbers of poor people in both societies, and of great differences between the wealthy and the rest of the population, is considered irrelevant to these models.

Beyond the models themselves, economic differentials are generating consid-erable conflict. Especially among blacks, there is the general perception that im-migrants are taking their jobs as well as competing for existing public and social services in the community. The social scientific evidence seems to both support and refute these observations. Indeed, the economic effects of the new inmigration remain unclear, probably because the social and economic condi-tions of the ethnic communities of the major cities are in a state of fairly continual and rapid change. One effect of the new immigration, is, however, quite clear and consistent with sociological expectations: namely, the fact that new ethnic con-flicts have engendered a new dimension of urban, intergroup conflict. As James Johnson and Melvin Oliver point out in their essay ("Interethnic Minority Con-flict in Urban America: The Effects of Economic and Social Dislocations"), the major group conflicts of the early twentieth century in America involved white at-tacks on blacks. The sociological literature is replete with examples of these earlier "race riots." In the 1960s, this country experienced a shift toward black insurrec-tions, which typically involved attacks against white property or symbols of white control in black communities. Quite often these symbols of control were the po-lice, who in turn were sometimes involved in illegal or questionable activities. Meanwhile, additional interethnic conflicts have emerged. As Johnson and Oliver note in their observations about Los Angeles, written four years before the interethnic disorders of May 1992, blacks, Latinos, and Asians have become the major participants in these new conflicts. The common provocation among them has been the changing ethnic composition of neighborhoods brought on by the new immigration.

Central to the emergence of these more recent interethnic conflicts has been the concentration of the new immigrant groups in what were once predominantly black residential or business areas. As Sassen, Johnson, and Oliver agree, this phe-nomenon is a consequence of the changing nature of work and jobs in the central city. Another factor is the increased residential segregation in most major metro-politan areas at the same time that the housing supply has decreased and the cost of housing has risen. More and more people are thus trapped in neighborhoods that they might have left at another time. The neighborhoods themselves were depleted by the inflation that gripped society throughout the 1980s and by the governmental cutbacks in infrastructure funds as well as public assistance programs. These changes have disproportionately affected the cities inhabited by new immigrants. The result in most communities has been heightened intergroup tensions, exacerbated by the continuing victimization of people of color by overt discrimination and ethnoviolence.

CASE STUDIES

The essay by Heidi Tarver ("Language and Politics in the 1980s: The Story of U.S. English") is a case study in anti-immigrant conflict. The "official English" movement that she studies is organizationally built on a model of liberal pluralism. What Tarver does is to scrutinize the ideological statements of this movement in order to expose the implications of its program for non-English-speaking immigrants.

The dual essay by Letty Cottin Pogrebin and Earl Ofari Hutchinson ("A Dialogue on Black-Jewish Relations") can be read almost as a dialogue between two sensitive analysts, one black and one Jewish. At one level, it offers insights into the historical and sociological differences between the two groups represented by the authors and explains why these differences make intergroup cooperation and harmony so difficult. At a second level, it provides a model for analyzing the relations between other groups.

Marilynn Rashid's essay ("Detroit: Demolished by Design") is also multilayered. At face value it can be taken as a personal report of black/white relations in Detroit, Michigan. At the same time, however, it stands as an analysis of violence—violence in the form of urban changes, destruction of communities, environmental assaults on minorities, and intergroup hostility. There is an anger and pessimism here not shared by the other essayists, and with which we must deal. "Violence and rage," Rashid writes, "will continue to hold sway over our lives." The way out, she asserts, is through "a massive popular outcry condemning consumerism, industrial capitalism, patriarchy and progress while affirming community and the strength of individuals to direct their own destinies and meet their own needs." But, she adds, "this is nothing but idealistic, naive rhetoric." Perhaps.

REFERENCES

Portes, Alejandro, and Ruben Rumbaut. 1990. *Immigrant America: A Portrait*. Berkeley: University of California Press.

16

America's Immigration "Problem"

SASKIA SASSEN

Immigration has traditionally aroused strong passions in the United States. Although Americans like to profess pride in their history as "a nation of immigrants," each group of arrivals, once established, has fought to keep newcomers out. Over the past two centuries, each new wave of immigrants has encountered strenuous opposition from earlier arrivals, who have insisted that the country was already filled to capacity. (The single exception to this was the South's eagerness to import ever more slaves.) Similar efforts to shut out newcomers persist today. But those who would close the door to immigration are mistaken on two counts: not only do they underestimate the country's capacity to absorb more people, but they also fail to appreciate the political and economic forces that give rise to immigration in the first place.

U.S. policymakers and the public alike believe the causes of immigration are self-evident: people who migrate to the United States are driven to do so by poverty, economic stagnation, and overpopulation in their home countries. Since immigration is thought to result from unfavorable socioeconomic conditions in other countries, it is assumed to be unrelated to U.S. economic needs or broader international economic conditions. In this context, the decision on whether to take in immigrants comes to be seen primarily as a humanitarian matter; we admit immigrants by choice and out of generosity, not because we have any economic motive or political responsibility to do so. An effective immigration policy, by this reasoning, is one that selectively admits immigrants for such purposes as family reunification and refugee resettlement, while perhaps seeking to deter migration by promoting direct foreign investment, foreign aid, and democracy in the migrant-sending countries.

Although there are nuances of position, liberals and conservatives alike accept the prevailing wisdom on the causes of immigration and the best ways to regulate it. The only disagreement, in fact, is over how strictly we should limit immigration. Conservatives generally maintain that if immigration is not severely restricted, we will soon be overrun by impoverished masses from the Third World, although the demand for cheap agricultural labor at times tempers this position. Liberals tend to be more charitable, arguing that the United States, as the richest country in the world, can afford to be generous in offering a haven to the poor and oppressed. Advocates of a less restrictive policy also note the positive effects of immigration, such as the growth of cultural diversity and a renewed spirit of entrepreneurship.

Not surprisingly, U.S. immigration laws have reflected the dominant assumptions about the proper objectives of immigration policy. The last two major immigration reforms, passed in 1965 and 1986, have sought to control immigration through measures aimed at regulating who may enter legally and preventing illegal immigrants from crossing our borders. At the same tine, the U.S. government has attempted to promote economic growth in the migrant-sending countries by encouraging direct foreign investment and export-oriented international development assistance, in the belief that rising economic opportunities in the developing world will deter emigration. Yet U.S. policies, no matter how carefully devised, have consistently failed to limit or regulate immigration in the intended way.

The 1965 amendment to the Immigration and Naturalization Act was meant to open up the United States to more immigration, but to do so in a way that would allow the government to control entries and reduce illegal immigration. It sought to eliminate the bias against non-Europeans that was built into earlier immigration law and to regulate the influx of immigrants by setting up a series of preference categories within a rather elaborate system of general quotas.[1] Under this system, preference was given to immediate relatives of U.S. citizens and, to a lesser extent, to immigrants possessing skills in short supply in the United States, such as nurses and nannies.

The 1965 law brought about major changes in immigration patterns, but not necessarily the intended ones. The emphasis on family reunification should have ensured that the bulk of new immigrants would come from countries that had already sent large numbers of immigrants to the United States—that is, primarily from Europe. But the dramatic rise in immigration after 1965 was primarily the result of an entirely new wave of migrations from the Caribbean Basin and South and Southeast Asia. The failure of U.S. policy was particularly evident in the rapid rise in the number of undocumented immigrants entering the country. Not only did the level of Mexican undocumented immigration increase sharply, but a whole series of new undocumented flows were initiated, mostly from the same countries that provided the new legal immigration.

The outcry over rising illegal immigration led to a series of congressional proposals that culminated in the 1986 Immigration Reform and Control Act. This law was intended to rationalize immigration policy and, in particular, to address the problem of illegal immigration. It features a limited regularization program that enables undocumented aliens to legalize their status if they can prove continuous residence in the United States since before January 1, 1982, among other eligibility criteria. A second provision of the law seeks to reduce the employment opportunities of undocumented workers through sanctions against employers who knowingly hire them. The third element is an extended guest-worker program designed to ensure a continuing abundant supply of low-wage workers for agriculture.

So far, the law's overall effectiveness has been limited. While some 1.8 million immigrants applied to regularize their status[2] (a fairly significant number, though less than expected), there is growing evidence that the employer sanctions program is resulting in discrimination against minority workers who are in fact U.S. citizens, as well as various abuses against undocumented workers. Meanwhile, illegal immigration has apparently continued to rise. Congressional efforts to correct the law's shortcomings have already begun. ...

Yet even a modified version of the 1986 law has little chance of successfully regulating immigration for one simple reason: like earlier laws, it is based on a faulty understanding of the causes of immigration. By focusing narrowly on immigrants and on the immigration process itself, U.S. policymakers have ignored the broader international forces, many of them generated or at least encouraged by the United States, that have helped give rise to migration flows. ...

THE NEW IMMIGRATION

Beginning in the late 1960s, immigration patterns to the United States began to change in several important ways. First, there was a significant rise in overall annual entry levels. From 297,000 in 1965, immigration levels increased to 373,000 in 1970, rose to 531,000 in 1980, and reached 602,000 in 1986. At the same time, there was a dramatic change in the regional composition of migration flows. As recently as 1960, more than two-thirds of all immigrants entering the United States came from Europe. By 1985, Europe's share of annual entries had shrunk to one-ninth, with the actual numbers of European immigrants declining from almost 140,000 in 1960 to 63,000 in 1985. Today, the vast majority of immigrants to the United States originate in Asia, Latin America, and the Caribbean.

Asians make up the fastest growing group of legally admitted immigrants. From 25,000 entries in 1960, annual levels of Asian immigrants rose to 236,000 in 1980 and 264,700 in 1985. While these figures were elevated somewhat by the flow of Southeast Asian refugees admitted in the aftermath of the Vietnam War, refugees account for only a small proportion of the overall rise in Asian immigration. In fact, it is the Philippines, South Korea, and Taiwan, not the refugee-sending countries of Vietnam and Cambodia, that have been the largest Asian sources of immigrants. ... In the 1980s, the Asian immigration began to include new flows from nations such as Singapore, Malaysia, and Indonesia that had not previously been sources of emigration to the United States.

The increase in Hispanic and West Indian immigration, while not quite as dramatic, has nevertheless been significant. ... The top 10 immigrant-sending countries today are all in Latin America, the Caribbean Basin, or Asia. Between 1972 and 1979, Mexico, with more than half a million entries annually, was by far the largest source of legally admitted immigrants, followed by the Philippines with 290,000, South Korea with 225,000, China (defined as including both Taiwan and the People's Republic) with 160,400, India with 140,000, and Jamaica with 108,400. With the single exception of Italy, all of the countries sending more than

100,000 immigrants each year were either in the Caribbean Basin or in Asia. Other important sources of immigrants outside these regions were the United Kingdom, West Germany, and Canada, sending about 80,000 each during the 1972–1979 period. By 1987, 43 percent of the 600,000 entries were from Asia, 35 percent from Latin America and the Caribbean Basin, and only 10 percent from Europe.

It is important to note that the new Asian immigration, often thought to consist predominantly of professional and middle-class individuals, is increasingly becoming working-class migration. In several cases, what began as middle-class migrations eventually paved the way for the migration of poorer strata as well as undocumented immigrants. This has been true of South Korean migration, for example, which now includes significant numbers of undocumented immigrants and sweatshop employees, as well as of Filipino migration.

Another feature of the new immigration is the growing prominence of female immigrants. During the 1970s, women made up 60 percent of all immigrants from the Philippines, 61 percent of South Korean immigrants, 53 percent of Chinese, 52 percent of Dominicans, 52 percent of Colombians, 53 percent of Haitians, and 52 percent of immigrants from Hong Kong. Even in the well-established, traditionally male-dominated migration flow from Mexico, women now make up almost half of all legal immigrants.[3] ...

The new immigration is further characterized by the immigrants' tendency to cluster in a few key U.S. regions. ... The states of California and New York receive almost half of all immigrants, while another one-fourth go to New Jersey, Illinois, Florida, and Texas.

Moreover, the new immigrants tend to cluster in the largest metropolitan areas, such as New York, Los Angeles, San Francisco, Chicago, Houston, and Miami. ... About 40 percent of immigrants settle in the 10 largest U.S. cities. ... In these cities, immigrants make up a considerably higher proportion of the population than they do of the U.S. population as a whole. ...

THE INADEQUACY OF CLASSICAL EXPLANATIONS

The main features of the new immigration—in particular, the growing prominence of certain Asian and Caribbean Basin countries as sources of immigrants and the rapid rise in the proportion of female immigrants—cannot be adequately explained under the prevailing assumptions of why migration occurs. Even a cursory review of emigration patterns reveals that there is no systematic relationship between emigration and what conventional wisdom holds to be the principal causes of emigration—namely overpopulation, poverty, and economic stagnation.

Population pressures certainly signal the possibility of increased emigration. Yet such pressures—whether measured by population growth or population density—are not in themselves particularly helpful in predicting which countries will have major outflows of emigrants, since some countries with rapidly growing populations experience little emigration (many Central African countries fall into this category), while other countries with much lower population growth rates (such as South Korea), or relatively low density (such as the Dominican Republic), are major sources of migrants.

Nor does poverty in itself seem to be a very reliable explanatory variable. Not all countries with severe poverty experience extensive emigration, and not all migrant-sending countries are poor, as the cases of South Korea and Taiwan illustrate. The utility of poverty in explaining migration is further called into question by the fact that large-scale migration flows from most Asian and Caribbean Basin countries started only in the 1960s, despite the fact that many of these countries had long suffered from poverty.

The presumed relationship between economic stagnation and emigration is similarly problematic. It is commonly assumed that the lack of economic opportunities in less developed countries, as measured by slow growth of gross national product (GNP), plays a key role in inducing individuals to emigrate. But the overall increase in emigration levels took place at a time when most countries of origin were enjoying rather rapid economic growth. Annual GNP growth rates during the 1970s ranged from 5 to 9 percent for most of the leading migrant-sending countries. In fact, most of the key emigration countries were growing considerably faster than other countries that did not experience large-scale emigration. ...

This is not to say that overpopulation, poverty, and economic stagnation do not create pressures for migration; by their very logic, they do. ... The evidence suggests that these conditions are not sufficient by themselves to produce large new migration flows. Other intervening factors need to be taken into account—factors that work to transform these conditions into a migration-inducing situation.

Take, for example, the cases of Haiti and the Dominican Republic. At first glance, the high levels of emigration from these countries would seem to offer support for the argument that overpopulation, poverty, and economic stagnation cause migration. Yet one is struck by the fact that these conditions were present in both countries long before the massive outflow of emigrants began. What, then, accounted for the sudden upsurge?

In the case of the Dominican Republic, the answer seems to lie in the linkages with the United States that were formed during the occupation of Santo Domingo by U.S. marines in 1965 in response to the election victory of the left-wing presidential candidate Juan Bosch. The occupation not only resulted in the growth of political and economic ties with the United States but also produced a stream of middle-class political refugees who emigrated to the occupying country. The settlement of Dominican refugees in the United States in turn created personal and family linkages between the two countries. U.S.-Dominican ties were subsequently further consolidated through U.S. investment in Dominican agriculture and manufacturing for export. Migration to the United States began to increase soon thereafter, rising from a total of 4,500 for the period from 1955 to 1959 to 58,000 between 1965 and 1969. Thus, the new developments that appear to have coincided with the initiation of large-scale emigration were the establishment of close military and personal ties with the United States and the introduction of U.S. direct foreign investment.

Haiti, on the other hand, was not subjected to direct U.S. military intervention, but the establishment of linkages with the United States and the introduction of direct foreign investment seem to have played a similarly important role in producing emigration. Although Haiti has long been desperately poor, massive migration to the United States began only in the early 1970s. In this case, the key new development or intervening process appears to have been the adoption of an export-oriented economic growth policy by President Jean-Claude Duvalier in 1972. Haiti's economy was opened to foreign investment in export manufacturing and the large-scale development of commercial agriculture, with the United States serving as the key partner in this new strategy. The necessary labor supply for these new modes of production was obtained through the massive displacement of small landholders and subsistence farmers. This upheaval in Haiti's traditional occupational structure, in conjunction with growing government repression and the emergence of close political and economic links with the United States, coincided with the onset of a major migration flow to the United States.

In both cases, then, the establishment of political, military, and economic linkages with the United States seems to have been instrumental in creating conditions that allowed the emergence of large-scale emigration. Such linkages also played a key role in the migration of Southeast Asians to the United States. In the period following the Korean War, the United States actively sought to promote economic development in Southeast Asia as a way of stabilizing the region politically. In addition, U.S. troops were stationed in Korea, the Philippines, and Indochina. Together, U.S. business and military interests created a vast array of linkages with those Asian countries that were later to experience large migration flows to the United States. The massive increase in foreign investment during the same period, particularly in South Korea, Taiwan, and the Philippines, reinforced these trends.

In other words, in most of the countries experiencing large migration flows to the United States, it is possible to identify a set of conditions and linkages with the United States that, together with overpopulation, poverty, or unemployment, induce emigration. While the nature and extent of these linkages vary from country to country, a common pattern of expanding U.S. political and economic involvement with emigrant-sending countries emerges.

THE INTERNATIONALIZATION OF PRODUCTION

To understand why large-scale migrations have originated in countries with high levels of job creation due to foreign investment in production for export, it is necessary to examine the impact of such investment on the economic and labor structure of developing countries.

Perhaps the single most important effect of foreign investment in export production is the uprooting of people from traditional modes of existence. It has long been recognized that the development of commercial agriculture tends to displace subsistence farmers, creating a supply of rural wage laborers and giving rise to mass migrations to cities. In recent years, the large-scale development of export-oriented manufacturing in Southeast Asia and the Caribbean Basin has come to have a similar effect (though through different mechanisms); it has uprooted people and created an urban reserve of wage laborers. In both export agriculture and export industry, the disruption of traditional work structures as a result of the introduction of modern modes of production has played a key role in transforming people into migrant workers and, potentially, into emigrants.

In export manufacturing, the catalyst for the disruption of traditional work structures is the massive recruitment of young women into jobs in the new industrial zones. Most of the manufacturing in these zones is the sort that employs a high proportion of female workers in industrialized countries as well: electronics assembly and the manufacture of textiles, apparel, and toys. The exodus of young women to the industrial zones typically begins when factory representatives recruit young women directly in their villages and rural schools; eventually, the establishment of continuous migration streams reduces or eliminates the need for direct recruitment. The most obvious reason for the intensive recruitment of women is the firms' desire to reduce labor costs, but there are other considerations as well: young women in patriarchal societies are seen by foreign employers as obedient and disciplined workers, willing to do tedious, high-precision work and to submit themselves to work conditions that would not be tolerated in the highly developed countries.

This mobilization of large numbers of women into waged labor has a highly disruptive effect on traditional, often unwaged, work patterns. In rural areas, women fulfill important functions in the production of goods for family consumption or for sale in local markets. Village economies and rural households depend on a variety of economic activities traditionally performed by women, ranging from food preparation to cloth weaving, basket making, and various other types of crafts. All these activities are undermined by the departure of young women for the new industrial zones. ...

For men and women alike, the disruption of traditional ways of earning a living and the ascendance of export-led development make entry into wage labor increasingly a one-way proposition. With traditional economic opportunities in the rural areas shrinking, it becomes difficult, if not impossible, for workers to return home if they are laid off or unsuccessful in the job search. ... People uprooted from their traditional ways of life, then left unemployed and unemployable as export firms hire younger workers or move production to other countries, may see few options but emigration, especially if an export-led growth strategy has weakened the country's domestic market–oriented economy.

But the role played by foreign investment in allowing the emergence of large-scale emigration flows does not end there. In addition to eroding traditional work structures and creating a pool of potential migrants, foreign investment in production for export contributes to the development of economic, cultural, and ideological linkages with the industrialized countries. These linkages tend to promote the notion of emigration both directly and indirectly. Workers actually employed in the export sector—whether managers, secretaries, or assemblers—may experience the greatest degree of westernization and be most closely connected to the country supplying the foreign capital; they are, after all, using their labor power to produce goods and services for people and firms in developed countries. For these workers, already oriented toward Western practices and modes of thought in their daily experience on the job, the distance between a job in the offshore plant or office and a comparable job in the industrialized country itself is subjectively reduced. It is not hard to see how such individuals might come to re-gard emigration as a serious option.

In addition to the direct impact on workers in the export sector, the linkages created by direct foreign investment also have a generalized westernizing effect on the less developed country and its people. This "ideological" effect in promoting emigration should not be underestimated; it makes emigration an option not just for those individuals employed in the export sector but for the wider population as well. ...

While foreign investment, along with other political, military, and cultural links, helps to explain how migration becomes an option for large numbers of in-dividuals in some developing countries, it does not fully explain why the United States has been overwhelmingly the main destination for migrants. After all, Ja-pan, West Germany, the Netherlands, and Great Britain all have substantial direct foreign investment in developing countries. ...

It is in this context that the 1965 liberalization of U.S. immigration law and the unfading image of the United States as a land of opportunity acquire significance. The conviction among prospective emigrants that the United States offers unlim-ited opportunities and plentiful employment prospects, at least relative to other countries, has had the effect of making "emigration" almost identical with "emi-gration to the United States." This has tended to create a self-reinforcing migra-tion pattern to the United States. As new bridges for migrants are created by for-eign investment (in conjunction with political and military activity) and strengthened by the existence of economic opportunities in the United States, the resulting new migrations create additional bridges or linkages between the United States and migrant-sending countries. These, in turn, serve to facilitate fu-ture emigration to the United States, regardless of the origin of the foreign invest-ment that created the conditions for emigration in the first place. ...

THE NEW LABOR DEMAND IN THE UNITED STATES

At first glance, both the heavy influx of immigrants into the United States over the past two decades and their clustering in urban areas would appear to defy eco-nomic logic. Why would an increasing number of immigrants come to this coun-try at a time of high overall unemployment and sharp losses of manufacturing and goods-handling jobs? And why would they settle predominantly in the largest U.S. cities, when many of these were in severe decline as centers of light manufac-turing and other industries that traditionally employed immigrants? The liberal-ization of immigration legislation after 1965 and the prior existence of immigrant communities in major urban centers no doubt played some role in attracting im-migrants from the older, primarily European, emigration countries. But the most important reason for the continuation of large inflows among the new migrant groups has been the rapid expansion of the supply of low-wage jobs in the United States and the casualization of the labor market associated with the new growth industries, particularly in the major cities. ...

The increase in low-wage jobs in the United States is in part a result of the same international economic processes that have channeled investment and manufacturing jobs to low-wage countries. As industrial production has moved overseas, the traditional U.S. manufacturing base has eroded and been partly replaced by a downgraded manufacturing sector, which is characterized by a growing supply of poorly paid, semi-skilled or unskilled production jobs. At the same time, the rapid growth of the service sector has created vast numbers of low-wage jobs (in addition to the better-publicized increase in highly paid investment banking and management consulting jobs). Both of these new growth sectors are largely concentrated in major cities such as New York and Los Angeles. Such cities have seen their economic importance further enhanced as they have become centers for the management and servicing of the global economy; as Detroit has lost jobs to overseas factories, New York and Los Angeles have gained jobs managing and servicing the global network of factories.

These trends have brought about a growing polarization in the U.S. occupational structure since the late 1970s. Along with a sharp decline in the number of middle-income blue- and white-collar jobs, there has been a modest increase in the number of high-wage professional and managerial jobs and a vast expansion in the supply of low-wage jobs. Between 1963 and 1973, nine out of 10 new jobs created were in the middle-earnings group, while the number of high-paid jobs was shrinking. Since 1973, by contrast, only one in two new jobs has been in the middle-income category. If one takes into consideration the increase in the number of seasonal and part-time workers, then the growing inequality within the labor force becomes even more pronounced. The proportion of part-time jobs increased from 15 percent in 1955 to 22 percent in 1977. By 1986, part-time workers made up fully a third of the labor force; about 80 percent of these 50 million workers earn less than $11,000 a year. ...

TOWARD A WORKABLE IMMIGRATION POLICY

A workable U.S. immigration policy would be based on the recognition that the United States, as a major industrial power and supplier of foreign investment, bears a certain amount of responsibility for the existence of international labor migrations. The past policies of the United States toward war refugees might serve as a model for a refashioned immigration policy. Few people would argue that flows of refugees from Indochina were the result of overpopulation or economic stagnation, even though the region may in fact have suffered from these problems. Instead, it is widely recognized that U.S. military activities were to some degree responsible for creating the refugee flows. When the United States granted Indochinese refugees special rights to settle here, it was acknowledging this responsibility, at least indirectly. A similar acknowledgement is due in the case of labor migrations.

When drafting laws in most areas of foreign relations, lawmakers generally make an effort to weigh the differing degrees of responsibility of various actors and take into account such complex phenomena as the globalization of production and international flows of capital and information. Why, then, is it not possible to factor in similar considerations in the designing of immigration policy? To be sure, international migration poses special problems in this regard, since the

relationship of immigration to other international processes is not readily apparent or easily understood. But the overly simplistic approach most policymakers
have adopted until now has greatly hindered the fashioning of a fair and effective
immigration policy. The precise features of such a policy will have to be elabo-
rated through further study and debate. But one thing is clear: U.S. immigration
policy will continue to be counterproductive as long as it places the responsibility
for the formation of international migrations exclusively on the shoulders of the
immigrants themselves.

NOTES

1. Earlier agreements barred Chinese labor immigration (1882), restricted Japanese immigration (1907), and culminated in the 1924 National Origins Act. This act was the first
general immigration law in that it brought together the growing number of restrictions
and controls that had been established over a period of time: the creation of classes of inad-
missible aliens, deportation laws, literacy requirements, etc. The 1965 immigration law
ended these restrictions. In this sense it was part of a much broader legislative effort to end
various forms of discrimination in the United Sates, such as discrimination against minorities and women.

2. About 1.8 million aliens applied under the main legalization program; in addition, 1.2
million applied under special legalization programs for agriculture. While the majority applying under the main program are expected to obtain temporary resident status, it is now
becoming evident that a growing proportion may not be complying with the second requirement of the procedure, that of applying for permanent residence.

3. A similar trend is taking place in the undocumented Mexican migration. See R. Warren and J. S. Passel, *Estimates of Illegal Aliens from Mexico Counted in the 1980 U.S. Census*
(Washington, D.C.: Bureau of the Census, Population Division, 1983).

17

Models of Pluralism: The New American Dilemma

MILTON M. GORDON

Over a generation ago, Gunnar Myrdal, in his monumental study of this country's greatest and most salient issue in race relations—what was then referred to as "the Negro problem"—wrote of "an American dilemma"—the gap and implicit choice between the religious and political ideals of the American Creed which called for fair and just treatment of all people, regardless of race, creed, or color, and the overt practices of racial discrimination and prejudice directed by Whites toward Blacks which took place in the daily life of the American people. Thus this country stood at a crossroads whence it could choose to follow the existing pathway of racial discrimination and hostility or, conversely, make the decision to honor its best ideals and eliminate differential treatment of its people on the basis of race. The tension of this choice, declared Myrdal, existed not only between Americans of varying attitudes and persuasion, but also within the heart of the individual citizen.[1]

It is my contention that, at least at the level of formal governmental action, the United States of America, in the three and one half decades since Myrdal published his great study, has moved decisively down the road toward implementing the implications of the American Creed for race relations, that this is a most important step (although it obviously does not remove all aspects of racially discriminatory treatment and prejudice from the institutions and private social relations of everyday American life), and that, with respect to racial and ethnic relations, America now faces a *new dilemma*—a dilemma which is oriented toward a choice of the *kind of group pluralism* which American governmental action and the attitudes of the American people will foster and encourage. ...

A NEW DILEMMA

... In the dilemma which Myrdal presented [he] identified two divergent paths, one of them supported by the finest ideals of religious and civic morality, the

186

other buttressed not by any well-understood moral and religious conviction, but by destructive and hateful practices arising out of the worst impulses in human-kind. In the new American dilemma, however, which centers on the proper role of government in dealing with racial and ethnic relations, proponents of both sides can claim in good faith to derive their respective positions from standard moral and religious systems, one side emphasizing principles of equal treatment and in-dividual meritocracy, the other principles that call upon group compensation for undeniable past injustices. It is my conviction that this controversy and the im-portant choices involved can be discussed most expeditiously and with the opti-mum possibility for producing a useful, well-considered national debate rather than a simple emotional dismissal of one side or the other, in the larger context of types of pluralism and the choice of which type of pluralist society is most appro-priate and most beneficial for a nation composed of many ethnic groups—and specifically, for the United States of America.

THE NATURE OF PLURALISM

What, indeed, is racial and ethnic pluralism? In its most generic aspects it refers to a national society in which various groups, each with a psychological sense of its own historical peoplehood, maintain some structural separation from each other in intimate primary group relationships and in certain aspects of institutional life and thus create the possibility of maintaining, also, some cultural patterns which are different from those of the "host" society and of other racial and ethnic groups in the nation. I have referred to these two dimensions as "structural pluralism" and, in the term suggested by Horace Kallen, "cultural pluralism."[2] Note that I use the phrase "create the possibility of maintaining" in reference to variations in cul-tural patterns. I use this construction advisedly, since racial and ethnic pluralism can exist without a great deal of cultural diversity; it cannot exist at all, however, without structural separation.

As I interpret the American historical experience, using these analytical dis-tinctions, and also bringing into play the role of both the Anglo-conformity and the "melting pot" ideas, the dominant pattern with regard to our country's racial and ethnic diversity has been a composite consisting of a great deal of persistent structural pluralism, cultural pluralism in the case of the first generation of immi-grants, and the overwhelming dominance of Anglo-conformity with regard to the cultural patterns of the second and successive generations, although not to the ex-clusion of the retention of symbolic elements of the ancestral tradition[3] and, of course, with the maintenance of religious differences from the original Protestant norm, that is, Roman Catholicism and Judaism (although both in Americanized form)—and all of this spiced up with a little and flavorful bit of "melting pot."[4]

LIBERAL AND CORPORATE PLURALISM

The new element in the situation—the one which creates the dilemma of choice currently before the American people—is the role of government in racial and ethnic relations, together with ethical and philosophical issues revolving around ideas of just rewards and whether to treat persons as individuals or as members of a categorically defined group. In combination, these issues point to the delineation of two alternative theoretical patterns or models of a racially and ethnically plural society, in which the issues of cultural and structural differences figure, but are now joined by other dimensions in order to incorporate the new considerations. I have called the two patterns thus distinguished *liberal pluralism* and *corporate pluralism*.[5] I wish now to portray and analyze these alternative models of pluralism in somewhat systematic form. For that purpose, I am denoting six dimensions with which to compare and contrast the two theoretical types of racial and ethnic pluralistic societies. These are (1) legal recognition and differential treatment, (2) individual meritocracy and equality of opportunity versus group rewards and equality of condition, (3) structural separation, (4) cultural differences, (5) area exclusivism, and (6) institutional monolingualism versus institutional bilingualism or multilingualism. I shall now proceed to a consideration of these two differing types of pluralism using these dimensions.

Legal Recognition and Differential Treatment

In liberal pluralism, government gives no formal recognition to categories of people based on race or ethnicity (and, of course, religion, which may be considered a possible component of ethnicity). Furthermore, it provides no benefits to nor exerts any penalty from any individual because of his or her racial or ethnic background. It does not stipulate segregation, nor does it formally promote integration, but allows individuals of all racial and ethnic groups to work things out by themselves on the basis of freedom of choice. It may, however, intervene legally through legislation or executive orders to *prevent* discrimination in such areas as employment, education, voting, public facilities, and public accommodations. But such prevention is focused on *specific acts which can be proven to be discriminatory* and not on the promotion of integration through direct governmental action. Thus a fair employment commission's investigation and adjudication of a complaint of racial discrimination in a particular firm, agency, or educational institution would fall within the framework of liberal pluralism, while an industrywide investigation to ascertain and change particular percentages of racial and ethnic percentages of employees would not.

It is plausible to suggest that the just described pattern within the framework of "liberal pluralism" has been the general ideal and goal of the American experience, and that although, in practice, America has at times miserably failed to live up to this ideal—notably, though not exclusively, in the case of Blacks—nevertheless, recent advances in the race relations area have brought us close to full implementation of this set of desired patterns in the relationship of the American government toward its citizens.[6]

Corporate pluralism, on the other hand, envisages a nation where its racial and ethnic entities are formally recognized as such—are given formal standing as groups in the national polity—and where patterns of political power and economic reward are based on a distributive formula which postulates group rights and which defines group membership as an important factor in the outcome for individuals. In widely varying degree, nations like Belgium, the Netherlands,

Switzerland, Canada, the Soviet Union, and Lebanon contain some aspects of a corporate pluralism model. In the United States, recently introduced measures, such as government-mandated affirmative action procedures in employment, education, and stipulated public programs, and court-ordered busing of school children across neighborhood district lines to effect racial integration, constitute steps toward the corporate pluralist idea. Many proponents of these measures support them simply as transitional and compensatory devices to rectify the effects of past racial discrimination; however, it is not clear what formulas would be used to measure the designated completion of the process and whether, in fact, these procedures, if left in place for any length of time, would not simply become eventually a permanent part of the national pattern of operation.

Individual Meritocracy and Equality of Opportunity Versus Group Rewards and Equality of Condition

These are basic philosophical ideas of equality and attribution which also definitely distinguish the two types of pluralism from each other. In liberal pluralism, the unit of attribution for equity considerations is always and irrevocably the individual. The individual gets what he deserves in economic and political rewards on the basis of his merit and accomplishment. Both in theory and practice, considerations of compassion and the need for basic minimal rewards usually shore up the bottom end of the scale, but above this minimal line individual merit prevails. Equality for citizens is defined as equality of opportunity (and, of course, equality before the law), but not in terms of results or condition, a matter which is left to the myriad workings of the competitive process. Racial and ethnic factors, in this paradigm, should play no role at all in the distributive process, either positive or negative. Proponents of this model insist that it represents traditional American ideals and the principles of the Enlightenment on which the American republic was founded.

Corporate pluralism postulates a reward system, both economic and political, which gives legitimacy to the standing and stake of racial and ethnic groups in the distributive process. Political bodies, such as legislatures, judiciaries, municipal councils, and even executive offices, must reflect, to a substantial degree, the numerical weight of the various racial and ethnic groups in the total population. In the economic arena, economic justice is not achieved until the income and occupational distributions of the various groups are approximately equal, and business, professional, and government units of significant size must each, individually, show a pattern of reward of differential income, power, and status to its employees which mirrors the national population distribution of racial and ethnic groups. Presumably, *within* the required ratios, individual merit considerations will be operative. Proponents of this system argue that, at the very least, it is necessary to institute such a model of rewards for a time in order to allow a minority group which has suffered heavy discrimination in the past to catch up with the other groups with any reasonable degree of rapidity. In this system also, equality is defined as equality of condition rather than simply equality of opportunity.

Structural Separation

Liberal pluralism's formula for the resolution of structure issues—deciding what cliques, clubs, and institutions to belong to—is strictly laissez faire. Its message to the minority group member is, "If you want to form your own ethnically enclosed network of primary group relations, and your separate institutional life, go ahead. That's your business. If you don't want to, that's equally all right. If you want to marry across racial or ethnic lines, there is no legal bar. The policy in all these matters is strictly 'hands off.'"

In the American historical experience, this policy, where it was implemented (it was, of course, distinctly not implemented in the southern states for Blacks and Whites until recently), gave members of racial and ethnic minorities the maximum amount of freedom of choice in these matters. Of course, we are referring here to government policy only. In the northern states, physical intimidation and custom did what government did not attempt to do: keep people of different races apart. Second-generation immigrants (most first-generation immigrants, quite understandably, wanted to stay within their own ethnic enclaves for primary group relations) who ventured out of the ethnic social network and looked for some "neutral" social structure found that the only alternative structures were white Protestant Anglo-Saxon in nature and reluctant or unwilling to let them in, anyway. The opening up of primary group networks, after all, requires two favorable decisions, one by the aspiring entrant, the other by the gatekeeper of the social structure in which one is seeking entrance. But as far as government was concerned, except for the now defunct Jim Crow laws, the gates were legally open, and private attitudes determined the outcome.

In the case of corporate pluralism, the situation is somewhat different. Structural separation is not necessarily legally mandated, but the logic of the reward system stipulating that group membership plays a large role in educational access, occupational placement, income, political power, and similar matters places distinct pressure on members of particular racial and ethnic groups to stay within the group for marriage, close personal friendship, institutional life, and social identity. After all, if a significant portion of one's rational interests are likely to be satisfied by emphasis on one's ethnicity, then one might as well stay within ethnic boundaries and at the same time enjoy the social comforts of being among "people of one's own kind," where prejudice and discrimination toward oneself are not present. Moving across ethnic boundaries to engage in significant interethnic social relationships is likely to lead to social marginality in a society where ethnicity and ethnic identity are such salient features. Thus the logic of corporate pluralism is to emphasize structural separation.

Cultural Differences

Very much as in the case of structural issues, liberal pluralism allows members of minority groups the maximum amount of freedom to make as much or as little as they please of their ancestral cultural heritage. There are no "bonus points" for perpetuating it and no penalties for drawing away from it. Groups and individuals from within the group can make their own decisions on these matters.

There are, of course, boundaries which indicate that a certain value consensus for all groups within the national framework is expected. The attempt to introduce polygamy in the American historical experience failed because it violated this consensus. No projected set of alternative values which advocated violence, murder, or theft as desirable patterns of behavior would obviously be tolerated. But within the normal range of nondestructive behavior, much variation is allowed, and conflicts over what norms shall constitute public policy are usually settled through the usual political processes—that is, the ballot box and judicial decisions. Or if the numbers are not great and civic policy is not essentially threatened, alternative value and behavior patterns are institutionalized as allowable exceptions or variations. An American case in point would be the provisions made in national legislation for conscientious objectors to war and military service, which stem, institutionally, from the value systems of British-descended Quakers and several religious sects of German origin whose ancestors were once immigrants to America. The issue of monolingualism versus bilingualism is also, of course, a cultural one, but it is so important in itself that I am considering it separately below.

Corporate pluralism, on the other hand, places a distinct positive value on cultural diversity and encourages its perpetration. Its viewpoint is that the preservation of its own ancestral cultural patterns by each racial and ethnic group is both an institutional right and a positive virtue. From this perspective, the culture of the nation is seen as a mosaic of subcultural patterns interacting in an overall framework of integration and harmony, thus providing a richer cultural life for the nation than is possible where one standard set of cultural patterns, established by the majority, constitutes the norm. Thus members of diverse racial and ethnic groups are encouraged to lay considerable emphasis on developing and honoring their own ancestral heritage even in successive generations of the original group.

Area Exclusivism

In the liberal pluralist model, no racial or ethnic group is able to lay legal claim to a particular piece of territory within the nation and to exclude people of other identities from access or residence. This is the case both in terms of large segments of national territory and in terms of particular neighborhoods in a specific community. Thus area exclusivism is legally forbidden. Area concentration, however, which reflects the voluntary choices of members of a particular racial or ethnic group to live in the same neighborhood or to settle in a particular city, is well within the liberal framework and is likely to occur, as the American experience has shown. However, if dubiously legal or extralegal attempts (that is, the once but no longer legally permissible "restrictive covenant," real estate brokerage practices, and physical intimidation) are made to exclude members of other groups from living in a particular neighborhood or portion of the city, then the principles of liberal pluralism are flagrantly violated. It is clear that American practices in this area, although improving, still have a long way to go to achieve full implementation of these principles.

Corporate pluralism does not demand area exclusivism, but is more tolerant of it as a possible variant arrangement in the domain of racial and ethnic relations.

Its emphasis on group identity and group rights makes it less insistent on the principle of free access in travel or residence to any physical portion of the national collectivity, regardless of race, color, or creed.

Institutional Monolingualism Versus Institutional Bilingualism or Multilingualism

On the language issue, liberal pluralism and corporate pluralism stand at opposite poles. Liberal pluralism insists on institutional monolingualism—that is, that there shall be only one standard language in the nation, that this language shall be the publicly mandated language of the educational system and all legal documents and procedures, and that no other language shall have any public standing. This viewpoint does not sanction hostility to the teaching or learning of other languages as supplementary options, it does not militate against voluntary retention of other languages as taught in the home or in private supplemental schools, and in fact, may encourage bilingualism or multilingualism for cultural or pragmatic purposes. But it makes one language the standard of the nation and allows no other to assume any official status. It is a clearly delineated position which, in fact, has been basically the American position, historically and up to the very recent present, at which time it has been challenged by proponents of mandatory bilingual education in the public schools for children who are language handicapped as a result of coming from a non-English-speaking home.

Corporate pluralism, on the other hand, supports official or institutional bilingualism or multilingualism. Its position is that the various racial and ethnic groups have the right and, indeed, should be encouraged to retain their ancestral languages, that there is no reason why there must be only one official language, and that all members of the national polity should be encouraged, perhaps even compelled, to become bilingual or multilingual. The large growth in numbers and political activism of the Hispanic population in the United States and the consequent demand for bilingual education in the public schools have brought aspects of this issue to the fore in recent years in the American context. Canadian society, with its English-speaking and French-speaking populations, is an example of an institutionally bilingual nation with its attendant controversies which are still in the process of attempted resolution.

CONCLUSION

The preceding six dimensions serve to define the differences between liberal pluralism and corporate pluralism. By their conceptualization and use I have tried to make it clear that there is now an important dilemma before the American people and that this dilemma is not simply a choice between isolated and fragmented policies, but rather that there is an inherent logic in the relationship of the various positions on these public issues which makes the choice one between two patterns—two overall types of racial and ethnic pluralism each with distinctly different implications for the American way of life. Those who favor the liberal form of pluralism emphasize in their arguments the ethical and philosophical value of the idea of individual meritocracy and the notion that current generations should not be expected to pay for the sins of their fathers—or at least, those who lived here before them, whether genetically related or not. They also point to functional considerations such as the possibility that measures such as forced busing and affirmative action to ensure group quotas will create white backlash and serve as continuing major irritant in the relationships between racial and ethnic groups. Those who favor policies which fall, logically, under the rubric of corporate pluralism emphasize, in return, the moral and philosophical position which posits group rights as well as individual rights, and the need for major compensatory measures to make up for the massive dimensions of racial discrimination in the past.

And so the argument is joined. This article has been written with the distinct conviction that the argument is a momentous one and that its resolution, in whatever form, will be best served by as much intellectual clarity, thoughtfulness, and good will as we can all muster in the process. Certainly, what the American people decide about this patterned complex of issues in the last 20 years of the twentieth century will have much to do with determining the nature, shape, and destiny of racial and ethnic relations in America in the twenty-first century which will then follow.

NOTES

1. Gunnar Myrdal, with the assistance of Richard Sterner and Arnold Rose, *An American Dilemma* (New York: Harper and Brothers, 1944), particularly, chs. 1 and 45.

2. Milton M. Gordon, *Assimilation in American Life* (New York: Oxford University Press, 1964); see also my *Human Nature, Class, and Ethnicity* (New York: Oxford University Press, 1978).

3. See Herbert J. Gans, "Symbolic Ethnicity: The Future of Ethnic Groups and Cultures in America," in *On the Making of Americans: Essays in Honor of David Riesman*, eds. Herbert J. Gans, Nathan Glazer, Joseph R. Gusfield, and Christopher Jencks (Philadelphia: University of Pennsylvania Press, 1979).

4. See Milton M. Gordon, *Assimilation in American Life*, passim.

5. Milton M. Gordon, "Toward A General Theory of Racial and Ethnic Group Relations," in *Ethnicity: Theory and Experience*, eds. Nathan Glazer and Daniel P. Moynihan (Cambridge, MA: Harvard University Press, 1975). This paper is reprinted in my *Human Nature, Class, and Ethnicity*. The terms "liberal pluralism" and "corporate pluralism" were chosen because they appear to me to portray accurately and nonpejoratively the salient and historically appropriate characteristics of each type of pluralist society. It is true that many liberals today support measures which fall in the "corporate" variety of pluralism. But there has been a longer historical association of the term "liberal" with those measures and conditions which I am grouping under the term "liberal pluralism."

6. See Nathan Glazer, *Affirmative Discrimination* (New York: Basic Books, 1975), ch. 1, for a presentation of such a viewpoint.

18

Interethnic Minority Conflict in Urban America: The Effects of Economic and Social Dislocations

JAMES H. JOHNSON, JR., AND MELVIN L. OLIVER

Intergroup conflict is no stranger to the streets of urban America. From our colonial beginnings in such cities as Philadelphia (Nash, 1979) to Liberty City and Overton in Miami in 1989 (Estrada, 1989; Hackett, 1989), intergroup conflict has been expressed in violence toward both property and people. Spurred by incipient class conflict, by overt prejudice, and by the overreaction and racism of social-control agencies (e.g., the police), intergroup conflict has become an ingrained feature of urban life in American society (Blackwell, 1982; National Advisory Commission on Civil Disorders, 1968).

Racial conflict is the most well known and thoroughly studied type of intergroup conflict. It has been expressed in American society in two basic ways: (1) in overt acts of prejudice on the part of whites directed toward blacks (Chicago Commission on Race Relations, 1968; Rudwick, 1964); and (2) in acts of violence by blacks directed toward the property of whites and other signs of overt white control in black communities (Blauner, 1972; Geschwender, 1971). The former was characteristic of the race riots of the early 20th century—the Chicago race riot of 1919 is perhaps the best example (Tuttle, 1969)—and has recently resurfaced in urban America (U.S. Commission on Civil Rights, 1983)—for example, in the Howard Beach area of New York. The latter type of racial conflict is characterized by the urban rebellions of the 1960s and by the civil disorder in the Liberty City section of Miami in 1980. Provoked by a series of court cases which culminated in the questionable acquittal of four policemen in the death of a black insurance agent, blacks in Liberty City vented their frustration over what they perceived as unfair treatment in the criminal justice system in a series of violent acts against whites and local businesses which wrought 14 deaths and $200 million worth of property damage (Porter and Dunn, 1984). Underlying each of these instances of intergroup conflict have been broader changes in the social and economic fabric of urban society. Each episode was preceded by basic economic and demographic changes in urban America, including mass migrations, changing economic realities, and increasing population dislocations, which collectively created tensions and hardships for the participants (Rudwick, 1964; Wilson, 1978, pp. 75–76).

PURPOSE

The purpose of this paper is to draw attention to a new configuration of intergroup conflict in urban America. This new type of conflict is interethnic in both origin and nature. It occurs primarily among nonwhite ethnic minority groups (i.e., blacks, and Hispanics, and Asians) and is precipitated by similar types of economic and social dislocations as the former racial conflicts, albeit on a different scale and of a different magnitude. The primary objective here is to establish the interconnections among the underlying economic and sociopolitical forces and to show how they have precipitated actual instances of interethnic minority conflict in urban America.

To accomplish this objective, we will draw primarily on case-study material from Los Angeles, where instances of conflict between nonwhite ethnic minority groups are occurring with increasing frequency (Banks, 1985). Our hope is that this essay will encourage and facilitate future research on this newly emerging form of intergroup conflict.

PRECIPITANTS OF INTERETHNIC MINORITY CONFLICT

We argue here that the emergence of conflict among nonwhite ethnic minority groups and the potential for it to increase in the future in urban America is the direct consequence of: (1) increasing immigration from Mexico, other parts of Latin America, and Southeast Asia; (2) the growing penetration of the most disadvantaged members of these newly arriving immigrant groups into formerly all-black residential and business areas; and (3) major changes in the social, economic, and demographic structure of American society which place these groups in competition for scarce and valued resources. ... The discussion below therefore focuses primarily on the ways in which the latter two developments have precipitated interethnic conflict in major urban centers like Los Angeles which have served as ports of entry for large numbers of nonwhite immigrants (Anderson, 1983).

Structural Changes in the Economy and
Economic Dislocations

Over the past two decades or so, the economies of the nation's largest metropolitan areas have undergone a rather drastic restructuring both in number and kinds of jobs available to their citizens (Bluestone and Harrison, 1982; Castells, 1985; Kasarda, 1983; Scott, 1988a, 1988b). The Los Angeles economy, for example, has experienced massive employment growth since the 1950s, including the addition of more than 1 million jobs during the 1970s. This massive growth occurred primarily because Los Angeles was structurally transformed "... from being a highly specialized industrial center focused on aircraft production to a more diversified and decentralized industrial/financial metropolis" (Soja, Morales, and Wolff, 1983, p. 211). Other major cities have followed a similar pattern, losing jobs in highly specialized industries such as auto manufacturing (Detroit) and steel production (Cleveland), while gaining employment in downgraded and high-technology manufacturing as well as in advanced services (i.e., banking, real estate, etc.) (Darden, Hill, Thomas, and Thomas, 1987; Squires, Bennett, McCourt, and Nyden, 1987).

These sectoral shifts in employment growth and decline have affected various segments of the labor force in different ways. Blacks in particular have been negatively impacted by the restructuring of economic opportunities (Kasarda, 1983). Because of their disproportionate concentration in the heavy-manufacturing sector of the economy, blacks experienced massive job loss as a result of plant closings, automation and the development of flexible production systems, and the movement of industrial firms to Third World countries in search of cheap labor. In Los Angeles, an estimated 70,000 heavy manufacturing jobs were lost during the 1970s as a result of plant closings. As Soja, Morales, and Wolff (1983) have shown, the majority of the plants that closed were concentrated in low-income black and Hispanic communities. In addition, over 200 Los Angeles-based firms, including Hughes Aircraft, Northrop, and Rockwell as well as a host of smaller firms, set up production facilities in the Mexican border towns of Tijuana, Tecati, and Ensenadi during this period. In Los Angeles and other major U.S. cities such capital flight, in conjunction with the plant closings, has essentially closed off black access to what were formerly good-paying, unionized jobs (Darden, Hill, Thomas, and Thomas, 1987).

Black employment losses as a result of the decline of heavy manufacturing have not been offset by the growth of employment, either in the high-technology manufacturing, advanced services, or in the competitive or so-called downgraded manufacturing and services sectors of the economy. Employment in the high-technology and advanced-services sectors requires high levels of education and skills which most inner-city blacks do not possess, especially those who were formerly employed in heavy manufacturing. Few employment opportunities exist for blacks in the competitive sector of the economy: firms in this sector survive only to the extent that their prices remain competitive vis-à-vis national and international firms. In order to remain competitive, they offer low wages, have unattractive working conditions, and structure their workforces in illegal ways. Because their illegal status makes them less likely to complain of unfair treatment and more likely to accept economic exploitation and "dirty work," undocumented workers (particularly those of Latin origin) are preferred over blacks in such rapidly growing competitive-sector industries as garment manufacturing, subcontracting, and hospitality (e.g., hotels, motels, restaurants) (Moore, 1981). Moreover, for some blacks such jobs are unattractive when compared to public assistance or employment in the subeconomies of crime and drug-dealing.

Occurring precisely at the time when many young blacks of the baby-boom generation were about to enter the labor market, these developments, i.e., the restructuring of the economies of U.S. cities and the influx of large numbers of disadvantaged immigrants, are largely responsible for high rates of unemployment, decreasing rates of labor-force participation, and the high incidence of poverty which have plagued black urban communities since the early 1970s (Wilson, 1987). ...

Demographic Restructuring, Social Dislocations, and Spatial Isolation

In conjunction with the deleterious effects of economic restructuring, blacks also have experienced a great deal of social dislocation and become increasingly isolated spatially within U.S. cities since the early 1970s (Wilson, 1987). Dramatic changes in the demographic structure of the black population [are] partially responsible for these developments (Reid, 1982). As a consequence of high rates of joblessness among black males (Wilson, 1987), since 1960 there has been a precipitous increase in the number of black nonfamily households and and more importantly, an unprecedented increase in the number of nontraditional households, especially households headed by never-married, separated, divorced, or widowed females with young children. ...

At the same time these and related sociodemographic changes were taking place (see Reid, 1982; Wilson, 1987), black residential opportunities were becoming increasingly constrained by the rapidly escalating price of housing, especially in the nation's largest metropolitan areas. As a consequence of cutbacks in construction and increased demand, ... housing costs began to increase sharply in the early 1970s—interestingly enough, this happened roughly at the same time as the official removal of those legal and expressly exclusionary techniques formerly used to confine blacks' access to housing to selected parts of cities. In Los Angeles, for example, housing costs "escalated from an average of $30,400 for a single family detached house ... in 1970 to $124,000 in 1980, a 300% increase" (Stutz and Kartman, 1982, p. 224). By the mid-to-late 1970s, many blacks, especially those earning less than $35,000 annually, could not qualify for a loan to purchase the average-priced home in Los Angeles (Stutz and Kartman, 1982), and the situation has worsened in the 1980s as the cost of housing has continued to increase rapidly (Adams, 1988). Thus, the so-called housing affordability crisis of the post-1970 period, in combination with the deteriorating status of blacks as a consequence of the restructuring of employment opportunities, goes a long way toward explaining the increasing spatial isolation of the most disadvantaged blacks in poverty-stricken and crime-ridden inner-city ghettos, such as the south-central area in Los Angeles (Ricketts and Sawhill, 1988).

Most significant for our purposes here, the deleterious effects of economic and demographic restructuring together with the newly emerging housing market constraints have created a situation in which disadvantaged blacks and immigrant minorities are forced to compete for scarce economic and social goods (Oliver and Johnson, 1984). The poorest of the newly arriving immigrant groups, particularly those entering the U.S. illegally, have been impacted by the same forces

as blacks, but in different ways. As noted above, economic restructuring created jobs for immigrant minorities who became exploited workers in the rapidly growing competitive-sector industries (Morales, 1986; Soja, Morales, and Wolff, 1983). Working in unsafe and unregulated workplaces and making subminimum and minimum wages, these immigrants were forced into a residential niche in some of the cheapest and most deteriorating areas of U.S. cities (Garcia, 1985). In most instances, the areas in which these poor immigrants have settled were formerly all-black communities. Since the late 1960s, for example, there has been a major influx of Spanish-speaking immigrants into the formerly all-black south-central area of Los Angeles (Oliver and Johnson, 1984). Unable to find housing in the established East Los Angeles barrio, by 1970 approximately 50,000 Hispanics had settled in the city's largest black ghetto, accounting for nearly 10% of the area's total population. During the 1970s, the number of Hispanics settling in the area doubled, totaling over 100,000, or nearly 21% of the population, by decade's end.
...

At the same time that blacks have been forced to share residential space with newly arriving immigrants, they have also had to contend with the growth and spread of immigrant entrepreneurial activities in their communities (Davidson, 1987). Rather than entering the primary or secondary labor market, some members of the newly arriving immigrant groups have elected to go into business for themselves (Kim and Hurh, 1985). This so-called "ethnic economy" is dominated by the Koreans, Chinese, Cambodians, Arabs, Iranians, Cubans, and West Indians, who specialize in a range of retail and personal services (Cobas, 1987). In a number of instances, including Los Angeles, San Francisco, and Oakland, California; Harlem, New York; Washington, DC; and Miami, Florida, these immigrant merchants have proliferated in black communities (Bratcher, 1981, 1984, 1986; Davidson, 1987; Jones, 1982a, 1982b; Noel, 1981a, 1981b). ... It is the Koreans who have penetrated the small-business market in south-central Los Angeles (Light and Bonacich, 1988).

Several competing theories have been advanced to explain this phenomenon—ethnic succession (Sowell, 1980), cultural organization theory (Light, 1972, 1980), and middleman minority theory (Bonacich, 1973)—but what is of prime importance to the discussion here is the fact that their presence in black communities across the nation is an occasion for conflict (Davidson, 1987). As we show below, the emerging conflict is similar to, but in some ways distinctly different from, the kind of Black-Jewish antipathy that developed as a result of the latter's dominance of ghetto businesses in the past (Glazer and Moynihan, 1963).

DIMENSIONS OF INTERETHNIC MINORITY CONFLICT

At the most general level, the emergence of interethnic minority conflict—and the resurgence of racial conflict, for that matter—in U.S. cities is intricately related to citizens' beliefs about the impact that recent immigration has on the American society. In a recent statewide poll, for example, three fourths of the whites (75.5%) and two thirds of the blacks (66.9%) surveyed said they were worried about the changing makeup of California's population. Underlying their concerns is the belief that the immigration of people of Asian and Hispanic background "will make it hard to maintain American traditions and the American way of life" (The Field Institute, 1988). A majority of both the whites and the blacks surveyed indicated that they thought that the place of English as our common language was being endangered and the quality of education was being lowered by the recent immigration, especially the influx of Hispanics. Not surprisingly, Hispanic and Asian respondents expressed less concern about the societal impacts of the new immigration (The Field Institute, 1988).

With respect to the emergence of interethnic minority conflict, the basic bone of contention, especially between blacks and members of immigrant minority groups, is the issue of jobs. Given their deteriorating position in the American urban economy, there is a growing perception among inner-city blacks that the new immigration has hurt them economically. In a 1983 Urban Institute survey assessing attitudes toward immigration, blacks in California strongly approved (66%) the contention that "undocumented Mexicans living in the U.S. take jobs away from American citizens" (Muller and Espenshade, 1985; also see The Field Institute, 1988). While there is a divergence of opinion in the literature on the actual labor-market impacts of the new immigration (Borjas, 1987; Chiswick, Chiswick, and Miller, 1985; Muller and Espenshade, 1985), youthful blacks who feel the most deleterious effects of the economic and demographic restructuring taking place in America see the new immigrants—many of whom are gainfully employed (albeit in poor jobs)—moving into their neighborhoods as a threat to their own abilities to sustain themselves economically. In the aftermath of the uprisings in the Liberty City section of Miami in 1980, for example, one black was cited as saying that "We can't get a job because they give them to the Cubans who keep coming over here, so the only thing we can do is steal and sell dope" (Sheppard, 1980, p. 4).

The conflict is also over basic housing and social amenities. Blacks are concerned that the movement of immigrants into their residential neighborhoods represents a displacement that is motivated by racism and economic gain. In south central Los Angeles, for example, the pattern that blacks observe is very similar to the kind of blockbusting that has taken place when blacks moved into a white neighborhood. ... Once a Hispanic family moves into an apartment building, the tenement rapidly becomes all Hispanic. Landlords perceive Hispanics to be better tenants. Due to the doubling up of families and the presence of multiple wage-earners in Hispanic households, blacks charge that landlords are forcing out black tenants and replacing them with Hispanics who pay higher rents. Blacks are then forced to move out of south central Los Angeles, fleeing to other parts of Los Angeles or, in a significant number of cases, to communities outside the metropolitan area where the cost of housing is substantially lower, particularly in the expanding Riverside-San Bernadino counties area (Johnson and Roseman, 1988). The negative sentiments this process creates are never directed at the economic agents (real estate agents and landlords) but rather toward the newly arriving immigrants.

Likewise, the influx of new immigrants creates resentment on the part of long-term black residents about the sharing of social services and dominant social institutions. In Watts, blacks are concerned about the high demands that are placed upon existing public services by the new immigrants. Blacks feel a sense of exclusive entitlement to some community institutions because of the struggles that took place in the 1960s to establish them. Hispanics, particularly undocumented workers, are seen as free-riders, gaining all the benefits of such public services as the local public hospital without having paid the price to get them in the community. Nearly three of every four babies born at Martin Luther King Jr. County Hospital in Watts are Hispanic. One south central resident complained about this by saying "I don't think it's proper. When we built some of these facilities in Watts, we didn't find anyone to help us ... if they want their share of services they should get active in the community" (Hernandez and Scott, 1980, p. 22). The emotional intensity of such intolerance serves to polarize the community, making interethnic minority conflict a likely outcome of a precipitating event. This is precisely what happened in the most recent wave of civil unrest in the Overton and Liberty City sections of Miami. In January 1989 two days of violence and arson followed the killing of a black motorcyclist by a Colombian-American police officer and the death of another black youth who was a passenger on the motorcycle. Blacks immediately accused the city's Hispanic police officers of having a vendetta against black youth, but they also used this event to express their discontent about the presence of a large number of newly arriving immigrants from Nicaragua in Miami. One middle-aged black man who has lived in the Overton section of the city for nearly 40 years expressed the black community's sentiment toward the growing influx of Nicaraguan refugees by advising the media to:

> Watch what happens. They're going to give them an income, they're going to give them food stamps and a place to stay. We've been here all our lives and we can't get anything. That's the problem. That's what it's [the civil unrest] all about (Estrada, 1989, p. 1).

This event also has created a schism between American blacks and Haitians in Miami (Lamar, 1989; Schmatz, 1989).

On the other hand, recent immigrants bring with them from their host societies perceptions and prejudicial attitudes that are conducive to interethnic minority conflict. Latino attitudes toward blacks, for example, are rooted in a culture that values Anglo culture at the expense of nonwhite culture. As Henry (1980, p. 224) notes, "Mexican Americans have historically viewed blacks as 'black Anglo-Saxons' in the negative sense of their being an inferior imitation [of] and having affinity for Anglo culture." Moreover, as Oliver and Johnson (1984, p. 66) have pointed out, "Spanish culture has traditionally denigrated 'dark skin' and inferiorized its possessors." Asians, on the other hand, are continuously bombarded with American media exports which contain negative images of blacks. The impact of such exports on Asians' perceptions of blacks has been summarized in a recent paper on Korean immigrants which states that "they have learned and accepted the stereotypes of blacks as criminals, welfare recipients, drug addicts, and/or lazy through American movies, T.V. shows, and American Forces Korea Network (AFKN) Programs" (Chang, 1988, p. 20). Often the stereotyped images of blacks in the American media are translated into overtly racist remarks and behaviors by Asians who actually have had little or no direct contact with blacks. Examples of this include the widely publicized negative remarks regarding the intellectual abilities of American blacks made by two high-ranking Japanese government officials and the recent international marketing of black dolls with exaggerated physical features by a Japanese firm (*Jet*, 1988a, 1988b; *Los Angeles Sentinel*, 1988). While these and related racially offensive incidents have generated a groundswell of anti-Asian sentiment among American blacks, upon the arrival of Asians in the United States, their stereotypes of blacks are constantly reinforced through the behavior of blacks in central-city communities which are plagued by high rates of joblessness, family disorganization, and crime.

The most conspicuous form of interethnic conflict in Los Angeles has occurred between Korean businesses and their black customers (Banks, 1985; Yu, 1980). Consigned to the economically depressed south-central area of the city, disadvantaged blacks see the Korean merchants as "foreigners" who are taking advantage of their lowly plight by charging high prices, by refusing to invest any of the profits they earn by employing local black residents or otherwise aiding the community, and by being rude and discourteous in their treatment of black customers (Chang, 1988, p. 14). The relationship between members of the black community and the Korean merchants recently reached a stage of near crisis, in part because the *Los Angeles Sentinel,* the major black weekly in Los Angeles, has a kept a vigilant watch over the situation, reporting both the important and the trivial incidents of conflict (Cleaver, 1983a, 1983b, 1983c, 1983d, 1987). Asian storekeepers are derided consistently for their lack of courteousness to black customers, ranging from refusing to give a cup of water to a paying customer to trying to keep a $200.00 watch for the nonpayment of a $5.00 gas bill. Furthermore, the *Los Angeles Sentinel* consistently questions how Koreans are able to generate the capital to start or take over a business while willing black entrepreneurs are unable to raise such funds (Cleaver, 1983a, 1983b, 1983c, 1983d, 1987). Blacks, in short, see the Korean family enterprises not as an economic accomplishment in the face of strong odds, but rather as an unearned opportunity at their expense.

While the Black-Korean conflict in Los Angeles has thus far generated more smoke than fire (Aubry, 1987; Kim, 1984), the most spectacular case yet uncovered occurred in Washington, DC (Cohen, 1986; Gaines-Carter, 1986; Gilliam, 1986; Price, 1986; Williams, 1986, p. 1). In September of 1986, in the Anacostia section of the nation's capital, a Chinese merchant allegedly pulled a loaded gun on a 58-year-old black grandmother and chased her out of the store after she complained about rude treatment. The black community was outraged. The Reverend Willie Wilson, a Baptist minister in Anacostia, organized several demonstrations and called for a boycott of the carryout. At one rally, Reverend Wilson responded to the charge that he was unforgiving by saying "… but we did forgive him. If we didn't we would have cut his head off and rolled it down the street" (Greene, 1986). Such an inflammatory statement prompted outbursts from all sides. Wilson clarified his comments by indicating that they echoed some of the residents' anger toward the merchant which they initially had wanted to express in 1960s-style rioting. The event became a touchstone from which the black community debated the issue. In these debates, the issue of the lack of community economic development and the lack of sensitivity of Asian storekeepers surfaced repeatedly. After seven weeks of picketing, the issue died down only to be replayed in individual stores all over the nation (Bratcher, 1986).

CONCLUSION

In this paper we have attempted to draw attention to a newly emerging form of intergroup conflict occurring primarily among members of nonwhite ethnic minority groups in U.S. cities. Using mainly case-study material from Los Angeles, we have established the interconnections among the underlying economic and social precipitants and shown how these forces have played themselves out in specific instances of conflict over housing, jobs, and other valued resources in formerly all-black communities. Our analysis suggests that in most cities interethnic minority conflict appears to have been limited to isolated incidents involving hostile verbal exchanges and group-based protests and boycotts on the part of blacks against newly arriving immigrant entrepreneurs. In Miami, however, interethnic conflict has taken a more violent form of expression. Angered by the recent deaths of two black youths at the hands of Hispanic police officer, American blacks rebelled in two days of rioting, which were punctuated with strong statements about the negative impacts on black social and spatial well-being of the influx of successive waves of Latin American and Caribbean immigrants into the city. Our analysis suggests further that the potential is great for these types of conflict to increase in terms of both frequency and severity in the future. The economic and social situation in which blacks and immigrant minorities find themselves presently has been developing and playing itself out over a fairly substantial period of time. The most often-suggested solutions consistently refer to educational programs that may help change the stereotypical ways in which the participants in this new form of intergroup conflict look at one another. In Los Angeles these programs are well underway. Blacks and Koreans meet for "prayer breakfasts" in which common problems are emphasized and mutual understanding is pursued (Kim, 1984). It is, however, our belief that solutions to the interethnic minority conflict problem must await the resolution of the larger urban ills which are associated with the economic, social, and demographic transformations occurring in American society.

REFERENCES

Adams, John, 1988, Growth of U.S. cities and recent trends in urban real estate values. In J. H. Ausubel and R. Herman, editors, *Cities and Their Vital Systems*. Washington, DC: National Academy Press.

Anderson, Kurt, 1983 (June 13), The new Ellis Island. *Time*, Vol. 121, 18–25.

Aubry, Larry, 1987 (March 26), The state of L.A.'s Black-Korean relations. *Los Angeles Sentinel*.

Banks, Sandy, 1985 (April 15), Korean merchants, black customers—tensions grow. *Los Angeles Sentinel*.

Blackwell, James E., 1982, Persistence and change in intergroup relations: the crisis upon us. *Social Problems*, Vol. 29, 325–346.

Blauner, Robert, 1972, *Racial Oppression in America*. New York: Harper and Row.

Bluestone, Barry and Harrison, Bennett, 1982, *The Deindustrialization of America.* New York: Basic Books.

Borjas, George J., 1987, Immigrants, minorities, and labor market competition. *Industrial and Labor Relations Review,* Vol. 40, 382–392.

Bratcher, Juanita, 1981 (October 1), 47th street merchants fight Korean's store. *Chicago Defender,* 4.

———, 1984 (May 7), Discord between merchants on 47th street. *Chicago Defender,* 4.

———, 1986 (January 21), Women target Korean, immigrant shops. *Chicago Defender,* 3.

Castells, Manuel, 1985, High technology, economic restructuring, and the urban regional process in the United States. In M. Castells, editor, *High Technology, Space and Society.* Beverly Hills: Sage Publications.

Chang, Edward Taehan, 1988, Korean-black conflict in Los Angeles: perceptions and realities. Paper presented at Annual Regional Seminar on Koreans. University of California, Berkeley, April 29.

Chicago Commission on Race Relations, 1968, *The Negro in Chicago: A Study of Race Relations and a Race Riot in 1919.* New York: Arno Press.

Chiswick, B. R., Chiswick, C. U., and Miller, P. W., 1985, Are immigrants and natives perfect substitutes in production? *International Migration Review,* Vol. 19, 674–685.

Cleaver, James H., 1983a (August 18), Asian businesses in black community cause stir. *Los Angeles Sentinel.*

———, 1983b (August 18), Asian attitudes toward blacks cause raised eyebrows. *Los Angeles Sentinel.*

———, 1983c (August 25), Residents complain about alleged Asian 'problem.' *Los Angeles Sentinel.*

———, 1983d (September 1), Citizens air gripes about Asians. *Los Angeles Sentinel.*

———, 1987 (March 19), One answer to an outcry. *Los Angeles Sentinel.*

Cobas, Jose, 1987, The ethnic economy. *Sociological Perspectives,* Vol. 30, entire issue.

Cohen, Richard, 1986 (November 14), Cheung is not the problem. *Washington Post,* 1.

Darden, J. T., Hill, R. C., Thomas, J., and Thomas, R., 1987, *Detroit: Race and Uneven Development.* Philadelphia: Temple University.

Davidson, J., 1987 (July 31), Melting pot boils as influx of Asian merchants into black neighborhoods is greeted grimly. *Wall Street Journal,* 40.

Estrada, Richard, 1989 (January 20), Miami and the fire next time. *The Dallas Morning Herald,* 1.

Gaines, Carter, Patrice, 1986 (November 18), Anacostia 'could see it coming.' *Washington Post,* 1.

Garcia, Phillip, 1985, Immigration issues in urban ecology: the case of Los Angeles. In L. Maldonado and J. Moore, editors, *Urban Ethnicity in the United States: New Immigrants and Old Minorities.* Beverly Hills: Sage Publications.

Geschwender, James A., 1971, *The Black Revolt: The Civil Rights Movement, Ghetto Uprisings, Separatism.* Englewood Cliffs, NJ: Prentice-Hall.

Gilliam, Dorothy, 1986 (November 13), Seeking answers in Anacostia. *Washington Post,* 1.

Greene, Marcia, 1986 (November 17), The unquiet pastorate: Anacostia's Wilson leads store protest. *Washington Post.*

Hackett, George, 1989 (January 30), All of us are in trouble. *Newsweek,* 36–37.

Henry, Charles P., 1980, Black-Chicano coalitions: possibilities and problems. *Western Journal of Black Studies,* Vol. 4, 222–232.

Hernandez, Marita and Scott, Austin, 1980 (August 24), Latino influx: new strains emerge as Watts evolves. *Los Angeles Times,* 22.

Jet, 1988 (August 15), Black stereotypes used to market products in Japan. *Jet,* Vol. 75, 36–37.

_____, 1988b (October 31), Japanese slurs on blacks causing rift between them. *Jet,* Vol. 75, 12.

Johnson, James H., Jr. and Roseman, Curtis C., 1990, Recent Black outmigration from Los Angeles: The role of household dynamics and kinship systems. *Annals, Association of American Geographers,* forthcoming.

Jones, Angela, 1982a (February 6), Youth boycott Korean traders. *NY Amsterdam News,* 3.

_____, 1982b (February 27), Korean marts hire 4 in Flatbush boycott. *NY Amsterdam News,* 11.

Kasarda, John D., 1983, Entry-level jobs, mobility, and urban minority unemployment. *Urban Affairs Quarterly,* Vol. 19, 21–40.

Kim, C. K. and Hurh, W. M., 1985, Ethnic resource utilization of Korean immigrant entrepreneurs in the Chicago minority area. *International Migration Review,* Vol. 19, 82–111.

Kim, Sophia, 1984 (June 8), Seeking a dialogue by Koreans, Blacks. *Los Angeles Times,* Part 5, 8.

Lamar, Jacob V., 1989 (January 30), A brightly colored tinder box. *Time,* 28–29.

Light, Ivan and Bonacich, Edna, 1988, *Immigrant Entrepreneurs: Koreans in Los Angeles.* Berkeley: University of California Press.

Los Angeles Sentinel, 1988 (October 27), Maker of racist toys: Japanese firm offers sensitivity proposals. *Los Angeles Sentinel,* A1, A20.

Morales, Rebecca, 1986, The Los Angeles automobile industry in historical perspective. *Society and Space,* Vol. 4, 289–302.

Muller, T. and Espenshade, T., 1985, *The Fourth Wave.* Washington, DC: The Urban Institute Press.

Nash, Gary B., 1979, *The Urban Crucible.* Cambridge, MA: Harvard University Press.

National Advisory Commission on Civil Disorders, 1968, *Report of the National Advisory Commission on Civil Disorders.* New York: Dutton.

Noel, Peter, 1981a (July 11), Koreans vie for Harlem dollars. *NY Amsterdam News,* 3.

_____, 1981b (July 11), Will black merchants drive Koreans from Harlem? *NY Amsterdam News,* 3.

Oliver, Melvin L. and Johnson, James H., Jr., 1984, Interethnic conflict in an urban ghetto: the case of blacks and Latinos in Los Angeles. *Research in Social Movements, Conflict and Change,* Vol. 6, 57–94.

Porter, Bruce and Dunn, Marvin, 1984, *The Miami Riot of 1980.* Lexington, MA: Lexington Books.

Price, Joyce, 1986 (October 2), Carryout closed by Anacostia protesters. *Washington Times,* 1.

Reid, John, 1982, Black America in the 1980s. *Population Bulletin,* Vol. 37, 1–40.

Ricketts, Erol R. and Sawhill, Isabel V., 1988, Defining and measuring the underclass. *Journal of Policy Analysis and Management,* Vol. 7, 316–325.

Rudwick, Elliott M., 1964, *Race Riot at East St. Louis, July 2, 1917.* Carbondale, IL: Southern Illinois University Press.

Schmatz, Jeffery, 1989 (February 19), Miami's new ethnic conflict: Haitians vs. American blacks. *New York Times,* 1.

Scott, Allen J., 1988a, Flexible production systems and regional development: the rise of new industrial spaces in North America and Western Europe. *International Journal of Urban and Regional Research,* Vol. 12, 171–186.

_____, 1988b, *Metropolis: From Division of Labor to Urban Form.* Berkeley: University of California Press.

Sheppard, Nathaniel, 1980 (June 2), Miami's blacks have 'nothing to lose.' *New York Times,* 4.

Soja, Ed, Morales, Rebecca, and Wolff, Goetz, 1983, Urban restructuring: an analysis of social and spatial change in Los Angeles. *Economic Geography,* Vol. 58, 221–235.

Squires, G. D., Bennett, L., McCourt, K., and Nyden, P., 1987, *Chicago: Race, Class, and the Response to Urban Decline.* Philadelphia: Temple University Press.

Stutz, Fred and Kartman, A. E., 1982, Housing affordability, and spatial price variation in the United States. *Economic Geography,* Vol. 58, 221–235.

The Field Institute, 1988, *Statistical Tabulations from the February 1988 Survey of the Field Institute on Ethnic Minorities.* San Francisco: The Field Institute.

U.S. Commission on Civil Rights, 1983, *Intimidation and Violence: Racial and Religious Bigotry in America.* Washington, DC: U.S. Commission on Civil Rights.

Williams, Lena, 1986 (November 23), A neighborhood divided. *New York Times,* 1.

Wilson, William Julius, 1978, *The Declining Significance of Race.* Chicago: University of Chicago Press.

———, 1987, *The Truly Disadvantaged.* Chicago: University of Chicago Press.

Yu, Jin H., 1980, *The Korean merchants in the black community.* Elkins Park, PA: Phillip Jaishoh Memorial Foundation.

19

Language and Politics in the 1980s: The Story of U.S. English

HEIDI TARVER

It has become axiomatic to observe that in the era of Reaganism political discourse in the United States "has shifted to the right." The conservative movement, or New Right, has been highly successful in moving its agenda of social traditionalism, economic libertarianism, and fierce anticommunism to the center of public debate, usurping discursive terrain previously dominated by liberals.[1] ...

In the wake of successful presidential elections in 1980 and 1984, New Right leaders made broad claims about the extent of popular support for social conservatism, reinvoking the so-called silent majority and proclaiming a major realignment in U.S. politics.[2] Such claims to a conservative majority are contradicted, however, by a number of studies that seem to indicate only limited (and on some issues shrinking) support for the New Right social project. In an analysis of longitudinal national opinion data collected in the 1972–1980 General Social Surveys (GSS), for example, Carol Mueller found no evidence of a conservative trend over the 1970s on the "pro-family" issues of abortion, homosexual rights, and women's roles outside the home.[3] In extending Mueller's analysis of the GSS through 1984, Donald McQuarie found that although a stable majority continued to favor women's right to an abortion under several circumstances and the ERA, there was a clear progressive trend with respect to women's role outside the home, as well as toward sex education in public schools (over 80 percent approval), birth control for teenagers who want it (about 85 percent approval), and premarital sex.[4] And in a 1987 article analyzing social trends over the past several decades, Norval D. Glenn also found that "general change has been in a liberal direction." Using data from GSS, Gallup, and other sources, Glenn found an increase (to over 70 percent) in approval of nontraditional, nonfamily roles for women, no significant change regarding pro-choice attitudes toward abortion, and a strong progressive or egalitarian trend in attitudes on civil liberties and racial/gender equality issues.[5]

Contrary to New Right claims, then, it appears that a majority of Americans do not support the conservative social agenda that has been championed by the Reagan administration, the Moral Majority, and other sectors of the conservative movement. This conclusion is supported by the fact that on a number of key issues, the New Right has had little or no success in institutionalizing its programs, despite massive organizing efforts and widespread publicity. Prayer in public schools and the teaching of creationism, for example, are two areas where the movement has failed to achieve its goals. ...

Yet there are other areas, such as welfare reform and the dismantling of New Deal social programs, in which right-wing efforts have achieved significant results. On these issues, it appears that conservatives have been successful in establishing alliances that allow them to expand support beyond their own ranks. The 93–6 vote in the Senate in favor of Workfare, a program that will force welfare recipients to work, is an example of just such a coalition-building strategy. Without the active support of moderates and even liberals, this program (which one liberal Democrat likened to the workhouses of nineteenth-century England) would not have been enacted into law. ...

In this paper, I examine in some depth one of the more successful if lesser known movements of the Reagan era: the effort to codify English as the official national language of the United States. More specifically, I want to look at how the so-called official English movement,[6] which began in 1983 as a handful of conservative activists committed to restrictive national language policy, has been able to expand into a large, well-financed, and relatively effective national effort whose support cuts across party, class, and racial lines. The general question that I want to pose is: How has a movement that is fundamentally conservative in its political motivations and in its core elite backing succeeded in attracting widespread support that extends well beyond its natural constituency?

The current move to codify the dominance of English and promote its exclusive use in U.S. public life began in January 1983 with the formation of an organization called U.S. English. This organization was founded by Dr. John H. Tanton, former president of Zero Population Growth, and S.I. Hayakawa, the well-known semanticist and former Republican U.S. senator from California. Tanton, who a few years earlier had also founded the Federation for American Immigration Reform (FAIR) to lobby for tougher immigration laws, recruited several FAIR staffers to help lead U.S. English. Among these was Gerda Bikales, who became the organization's first executive director.

The formation of U.S. English should be viewed within the context of the more general Reagan renaissance; that is, the widespread mobilization of the right-wing during the early 1980s in an effort to reverse political and cultural trends set in motion by the U.S. defeat in Vietnam, the civil rights movement, and the feminist movement. Of special concern to Hayakawa and the other founders of U.S. English was a perceived threat to the dominance of English (and to WASP hegemony more generally) from the political and cultural mobilization of blacks and particularly of Hispanics during this period. They explain the conditions that gave rise to their efforts as follows.

The erosion of English and the rise of other languages in public life have several causes:

> Some spokesmen for ethnic groups reject the "melting pot" ideal; they label assimilation a betrayal of their own native cultures and demand government funding to maintain separate ethnic institutions.

Well-intentioned but unproven theories have led to extensive government-funded bilingual education programs, ranging from pre-school through college.

New civil rights assertions have yielded bilingual and multilingual ballots, voting instructions, election site counselors, and government-funded voter registration campaigns aimed solely at speakers of foreign languages.

Record immigration, concentrated in fewer language groups, is reinforcing language segregation and retarding language assimilation.

The availability of foreign language electronic media, with a full range of news and entertainment, is a new disincentive to the learning of English.[7]

The "official English" movement was launched, then, to "maintain the blessing of a common language" and to "reverse the spread of foreign language usage in the nation's official life." Its specific objectives, which have remained constant since the founding of U.S. English, are to (1) adopt a constitutional amendment establishing English as the official language of the United States, (2) repeal laws mandating multilingual ballots and voting materials, (3) restrict government funding of bilingual education, and (4) strengthen enforcement of English-language and civics requirements for naturalization.[8] Given that the vast majority of Americans have always been and continue to be monolingual English speakers, and that the rate of English-language assimilation has remained virtually unchanged for over a century,[9] it is clear, I think, that underlying these objectives is a deep-seated fear regarding the future of white America and its possible engulfment by other "alien" languages and cultures.

Since 1983, U.S. English has made considerable progress in achieving its goals. It has attracted several hundred thousand members and, according to its newsletter, has raised millions of dollars to finance its work in California, Florida, and elsewhere. ...

In California, where the organization has concentrated much of its efforts thus far, it has successfully passed one local (San Francisco) and two statewide ballot initiatives, the most recent being Proposition 63, which passed in November 1986 with 73 percent of the vote. What is most interesting about Proposition 63 is that it passed by substantial margins in nearly every county in the state, including those like Fresno and Los Angeles that have large Latino populations.[10] ...

On the heels of Proposition 63's success, similar ballot initiative campaigns were successfully undertaken in Florida, Colorado, and Arizona. In twelve other states, including Georgia, Illinois, and North Dakota, English has been designated the official language through legislative action.[11] ... And at the national level, an English Language Amendment bill (ELA) has been introduced in Congress; if passed, it would amend the U.S. Constitution to designate English the official national language of the United States.[12]

What are the actual practical consequences of all this legislative activity? The answer to this question is somewhat difficult to determine, insofar as the actual effects of English-language legislation will depend in large part on the political battles surrounding implementation of the new laws. ... In [most of] these cases, the intent of "official English" organizers is to use the law to eliminate bilingual education programs and multilingual voting materials and other government documents.

Opponents of the movement argue that the implications of English-language legislation go far beyond the elimination of specific programs. For Latinos in particular, the movement represents a frontal attack on the political gains that have been made in the past several decades through the official legitimization of their language and culture. Many observers see the movement as part of a resurgence of the kind of nativism that swept the country before and during World War I, when many states passed laws prohibiting public or private instruction in any language other than English. Through such laws, in combination with severely restrictive immigration legislation and a flood of "anti-alien" rhetoric, the so-called Americanization Movement attempted to implement the rapid, forced acculturation of all immigrants in the name of national unity.[13] In the 1980s we seem to be experiencing a similar swell in nationalistic sentiment combined with a thrust toward Anglo-conformity.

But although nationalism appears unquestionably as both a context and impetus for U.S. English, and as an important current within its political discourse, the movement is by no means unambiguously nativist, nor is its appeal limited to traditionally conservative sectors of the population. As noted earlier, a substantial minority of California's Latino voters, and a majority of San Francisco's overwhelmingly liberal voting population supported Proposition 63. Thus the question remains of how the "official English" movement is able to attract support from sectors of the population that fall outside what would appear to be its natural constituency. ...

U.S. ENGLISH DISCOURSE AS IDEOLOGICAL COLLAGE

When I began this project, I had certain preconceived notions about what I would find within the brochures, fact sheets, and newsletters published and distributed by U.S. English. Because I perceived their agenda to be traditionally conservative, directed toward a return to the "good old days" of a culturally and linguistically homogeneous white America, I expected that their political discourse would be constructed from familiar conservative ideological themes such as reverence of tradition, allegiance to the nation, and respect for established authority. Although these themes do indeed appear, I was surprised to discover that they do not dominate the discourse. The simple classification of U.S. English as "ideologically conservative" turned out to be highly problematic.

What I encountered instead is a hodgepodge of ideological fragments, some of which are commonly integral to a conservative worldview and others of which form part of the liberal tradition in U.S. political discourse. Sometimes the concepts and images are contradictory, often they are highly ambiguous. Many of them are popularized notions—what Gramsci called "organic" ideologies—that have been absorbed over time into the commonsense assumptions of most Americans. A closer examination of these elements provides a starting point for understanding the nature of the U.S. English phenomenon. ...

One of the most frequently repeated phrases throughout U.S. English literature is that "English is at the core" of American national identity. The idea appears to be a simple one, but it in fact encompasses a complex of concepts about the relation of English to being American. First, the language is portrayed as holding enormous intrinsic value, and although explicit disclaimers of cultural and linguistic chauvinism appear occasionally in the text ("We hold no special brief for English."), the general message is that English is king. A cursory survey of the literature turns up a multitude of laudatory references to English, calling it "sophisticated," "flexible and rich," "premier language of international communications," "eloquent," "the living carrier of our democratic ideals," "capable of subtle nuance and great precision of meaning," "a great work of art on which all mankind has spent its gifts," and so on. Although many of these commentaries on the qualities of the English language may indeed be true, their cumulative effect, in light of the fact that no other language is given the benefit of even one acclamatory adjective, is to identify English—that is, standard English[14]—as of inherently superior value.

This treasured cultural artifact is then bound in a variety of ways to American identity and, at least by implication, to American national greatness. We are told, for example, that "its eloquence shines in our Declaration of Independence and in our Constitution." More intriguing is the following quotation from an overview piece distributed by the California English Campaign: "Our English language represents our history, our values, our loyalty to our State and Country. In a fundamental sense, our language is US." ...

In the statement cited above, it is possible to identify three distinct senses in which English is defined as "at the core" of American identity. First, it represents and works as a symbol for those qualities and attributes that are contained within the phrase "American people" (more on this below). It also operates as a transmitter of cultural values across time. But English is more than simply a symbol or a means of transmission for cultural values and history; it is also essential to the state of being American. This sense of the fundamental connection between English and national identity is perhaps best communicated in the following comment by *Time* editor Henry Grunwald, reprinted in U.S. English literature: "For many immigrants, the true act of naturalization occurs when they start having dreams in English."

And there is yet a fourth sense in which the connection is drawn between English and national identity. English *makes* Americans. Consider, for example, the following statement by Theodore Roosevelt, prominently featured in a U.S. English brochure: "We have room for but one language here and that is the English language, for we intend to see that the crucible turns our people out as Americans, of American nationality, and not as dwellers in a polyglot boarding house." Here English is not only an attribute or symbol of American identity, but also a force with the power to mold human material into "American people." ...

Thus we find English portrayed as the key force of Americanization, as the symbol and carrier of American identity, and as the essence of that identity. To become American is to undergo a transformation (the image of purification by fire?) so profound that it reaches into the depths of the unconscious, into the world of dreams. To be American is to live in and through English, the language that embodies the history and values of the nation. To live in English is to live in the American tradition.

The ideas that I have outlined about the role of English in American life are closely linked to American nationalism and to the concept of national allegiance as defined within traditional conservative discourse.[15] First, both the English language and national allegiance are conceived to be essential elements of American nationalism, in that the original constitution of the nation took place in the absence of any natural community or tradition, such as existed in France or England. ...

On a secondary level, English ability becomes the verification of and symbol for allegiance to the nation. Americans are expected to be above class or ethnic interests, and loyalty must be directed toward the country and its institutions. The desire to perpetuate ethnic identification and community is portrayed as unpatriotic and essentially un-American:

> While [Horace] Kallen asked that minority cultures be given tolerance and understanding, the Ethnic Pride Movement demanded that they be accorded equivalent standing in the society. This was, in effect, a demand that the United States become a multicultural society as a matter of conscious public policy. There was no longer to be an officially sanctioned culture, loosely based on the heritage and language of the Republic's founders.[16]

Those who resist assimilation are portrayed as politically, even morally, suspect. ...

English-language ability is tied to and becomes a symbol for the "commitment to being American" and is thus portrayed as being intimately connected with both individual identity and national unity. An assimilated English speaker is by definition a patriot and a member of the body politic, both fragment and personification of the national community. And likewise, the patriot is by definition an assimilated English speaker. Uniformity here becomes the basis of national unity and security. In the words of U.S. English, "a common language is necessary to preserve the basic internal unity required for political stability and national cohesion."[17] ...

The conservative view of American identity, which emphasizes cultural homogeneity and national allegiance, is by no means the only view represented in U.S. English literature. In the same brochures, pamphlets, and newsletters, and at times sharing the page with the themes outlined above, is articulated an alternative conception of national identity that emphasizes cultural pluralism instead of homogeneity, individual freedom rather than tradition. ...

What I call the liberal conception of American national identity within U.S. English discourse emphasizes not a singular "officially sanctioned culture, loosely based on the heritage and language of the Republic's founders," but rather the cultural heterogeneity that characterizes the United States and its people. In the opening paragraph of the organization's promotional brochure, for example, it is stated that "throughout its history, the United States has been enriched by the cultural contributions of immigrants from many traditions, but blessed with one common language that has united a diverse nation and fostered harmony among its people."

The same brochure stresses that the United States is a "pluralistic society" and explicitly states as a guiding principle that "the rights of individuals and groups to use other languages and to establish privately funded institutions for the maintenance of diverse languages and cultures must be understood and respected."

In this pluralistic version of the "melting pot," English operates not as a crucible but as a necessary bridge between citizens from diverse backgrounds. S. I. Hayakawa articulated this position most clearly in a lecture at the Washington Institute for Values in Public Policy:

> What is it that made a society out of the hodgepodge of nationalities, races and colors represented in the immigrant hordes that people our nation? It is language, of course, that has made communication among all these elements possible. It is with a common language that we have dissolved distrust and fear. It is with language that we have drawn up the understanding and agreements and social contracts that made a society possible.[18]

Hayakawa's statement is interesting and revealing on several counts. First, the characterization of American nationhood is altogether different from that discussed earlier. Here the emphasis is on rational modes of thought, on "understanding," "agreements," and "social contracts" that bring people together as a society. Such a conception places the individual, rather than the social organism, at center stage. The growth and success of the society depends not on loyalty and tradition but on communication. Within this context, the value of English is represented not as transcendent or symbolic but as essentially instrumental. English is a *means* of communication, not a fundamental element of American identity or a symbol of national allegiance.

The rationalist-instrumental argument for the importance of English in American life appears repeatedly throughout U.S. English literature. In a California English campaign flier, for example, it is stated that "we must have a language of common discourse. ... We must be able to talk to each other, to understand each other and if we disagree to explore our disagreements, resolve or compromise them or agree to disagree." And such communication is portrayed as the necessary basis for a democratic system of government: "In our democratic system of government, differences are settled by argumentation, discussion, and compromise. We rely on the power and subtlety of words to find acceptable solutions. (For example, we accept 'affirmative action goals' but reject 'quotas'.)"[19]

The theme of equality or, more accurately, of equal opportunity is closely associated with the contractual notion of society, on which liberal political ideology in general and the preceding statements in particular are founded. In U.S. English discourse, it is argued that the universal usage of English in the United States is necessary in order to provide all citizens with the same tools, with a common basis from which to compete on an equal footing for the benefits the society has to offer. The logic of this argument is fundamentally different from that which equates English with American tradition. The stated concern here is not with unpatriotic minorities who reject the "officially sanctioned culture," but with "unwise governmental policies" that fail to provide non-English speakers with the necessary means and motivation for learning English. "Language ghettos" and "alien enclaves" prevent immigrants from learning English and moving into the mainstream of American society. The ELA is described as "a prudent and positive step to assure that no one in America gets locked out by permanent language barriers." ...

"AMERICAN PEOPLE" AND OTHER AMBIGUITIES

Thus far I have identified and discussed some of the major themes, concepts, and images collected together within U.S. English discourse. I have attempted to substantiate my thesis that within the discourse one encounters ideas drawn from or based in both conservative and liberal political philosophy and that some of these ideas are in fundamental contradiction. Underlying the contradictions are two distinct images of society and nationhood: one that defines the social/national bond as transcendent and one that defines it as contractual. The former gives rise to a view of English as integral to American identity and central to national unity, whereas the latter engenders an understanding of English as essentially instrumental. Given these contradictions, how are the elements that I have identified articulated into a united and effective coalition-building ideology that has proved itself able to mobilize broad-based support for the movement? ...

The key to the problem lies, I believe, in the ambiguous nature of the central symbols that operate as linchpins within the overall ideological formation. These central symbols can be characterized as (1) the nation/"melting pot," and (2) the American people/"US."

Examination of the functions performed by the concept(s) of "melting pot" in U.S. English literature provides an excellent example of the importance of ambiguity in the unification of a fragmentary discourse. The "melting pot" image is used repeatedly throughout the literature. ... As Milton Gordon has insightfully pointed out, the image of the "melting pot" holds within it the possibility of a range of interpretations.

> With regard to cultural behavior, the most characteristic implication is that the cultures of the various groups will mix and form a blend somewhat different from the cultures of any one of the groups separately. However, a neglected aspect of this model of cultural intermixture is whether all groups will make an equally influential contribution to the boiling pot. ... Indeed ... the melting pot concept may envisage the culture of the immigrants as "melting" completely into the culture of the host society without leaving any cultural trace at all.[20]

The ambiguity of the "melting pot" image is significant in that it creates the possibility of implicit linkages between concepts that have no logical relation at all. "Melting pot" can and does operate as a symbol both for the "officially sanctioned"/traditional version of American culture and for the pluralistic version. By virtue of its dual referents, it thus provides an implied connection with contradictory elements within the discourse.

The symbol of the "melting pot" is critical to the structure of U.S. English discourse in that it establishes and represents alternative images of "the nation," each of which is related to specific arguments regarding the importance of English in national life. Oscillation between the referents is produced within the text itself, but probably also takes place independently in the mind of the receiver, the result of confused and conflicting historical memory. It is as if, in the process of switching between the various nation-as-melting-pot images that are evoked by the text and that each of us carries around, what is created is a composite image, a sort of double or triple exposure, which gives the appearance of oneness despite its internal discord.

If the symbol of the "melting pot" is crucial to the logical structure and general coherence of U.S. English discourse, it is the images and concepts that become associated with the American people/"US" complex that give the discourse its power to mobilize. Once again, we are looking at a situation in which a symbol encompasses and represents multiple referents. This time, however, the nature of the symbol itself is quite different, for whereas the nation/"melting pot" complex is abstract and external to the individual, "American people" is immediate and personal. *It defines the individual—I.* How then does this process of definition and identification take place, and how does the kind of symbolic ambiguity discussed above function in relation to the mobilization of broad-based support for U.S. English initiatives? ...

What we find is that "American people" holds within it multiple subjects, each of which is bound up with a particular set of arguments about English, nationhood, democracy, and so on. There is the American qua "WASP patriot," an image of "American people" that is both patriarchal and racist and is woven into the conservative fragments of the discourse. This image can speak to and "recruit" both working-class and middle-class whites who feel culturally, politically, and economically threatened—by affirmative action, Latin American and Asian immigration, Iranian tyrants, urban crime, alien diseases, South American drug dealers, Arab terrorists, and multitudinous other "dangers." It is an image that demands the defense of an "American people" under attack and holds out hope for a return to a more comfortable America, where one can feel at home again. The following U.S. English advertisement, which was published in the 8 April 1985 issue of the *New Republic,* addresses the holders of just these fears and hopes when it says: "Already, the erosion of English has made many English-speaking citizens feel displaced and alien—strangers in their own land."

Although the "WASP patriot" holds a prominent position and is perhaps the most predictable subject residing within U.S. English discourse, it is certainly not the only one. The most salient alternative, and the image of "American people" that may be the most significant in extending the movement's base of support beyond traditional conservatives, is what I call the "good alien."

The "good alien" is the success story of immigration and the embodiment of the American dream. It is the image of the non-WASP (though not necessarily immigrant; Afro-Americans, Chicanos, and other non-WASP Americans can also be "good aliens" although they rarely achieve such status) who successfully assimilates and joins the American mainstream. The brave struggle of the "good alien" to learn English and integrate into American national life provides dramatic counterbalance to the theme of America under attack. The "good alien" is held up as an example to all would-be Americans, and is personified in such movement leaders as S. I. Hayakawa, Gerda Bikales, and Linda Chavez.

The "good alien" image is something of a crossover subject in that it provides linkage with both the tradition-oriented and communication-oriented arguments for the importance of English. Sometimes the "good alien" is portrayed as a transitional identity, a sort of stopover spot on the road to full assimilation. In this version of the "good alien" the ultimate (though in many cases unattainable) goal is to become a "WASP patriot":

> Coming to America meant entering into a covenant: the immigrant would learn English and a skill useful in the United States, and he would participate in our political system by becoming a citizen and voter. In return, he would be accepted as a political equal, *and his temporary differences from native-born Americans would be tolerated.*[21]

The other version of the "good alien" is one who is committed to and successful in American society, but still retains personal and emotional ties with the culture of origin. This image of American identity is closely linked with the liberal conception of English-as-bridge between individuals in a pluralistic society and with the idea that a common language provides the basis for equal opportunity and success. ...

The dual faces of the "good alien" are emotionally charged and ideologically powerful in that they reflect both the dearest hopes (acceptance, success, security) and the harshest disappointments (racism, powerlessness, failure) of the mythical immigrant/other experience. The images speak to and "recruit" those Americans who recognize in them some aspect of their own assimilation and bind that experience to the defense of English. ...

Although the ambiguous central symbols discussed above play the key role in joining diverse ideological fragments into an effective political discourse, there are also a few dominant themes that run through the discourse and serve to unite it in a different way. These themes appear to be universal in their appeal and operate at the unconscious and emotive level. They are woven into the text in a subtle, implicit form that creates a powerful undercurrent beneath the articulation of explicit arguments. The first of them is the theme of commonality.

Commonality appears everywhere in U.S. English discourse, beginning with the epigraph "We, the People of the United States, in Order to form a more perfect Union" inscribed in the upper left corner of the organization's letterhead. The promotional brochure is entitled "In Defense of Our Common Language." English is referred to repeatedly as "our common bond." These and similar references communicate a unity of interest and purpose that transcends ethnic and class boundaries to include all Americans. The emphasis on commonality subsumes within the discourse the identities of distinct groups, some of whom may hold antithetical interests. It represents the U.S. English program as universal, as if it were the program of the whole people.

Other themes operate at a less obvious subtextual level, through images that appear in the form of oppositions: power/weakness, order/chaos, security/fear, freedom/bondage. In all these cases, the positive image is associated with the importance and defense of English, and the negative is attached to the demise of the common language. Although a full analysis of this subtextual level is impossible here, I do wish to give a few suggestive examples.

With respect to power and weakness, immigrant resistance to assimilation is often portrayed in such a way as to suggest a direct challenge to the authority (virility, control) of "true" Americans. Quotes from Latino leaders to the effect "this country will be a bilingual, bicultural country whether it likes it or not"[22] are prominently displayed in the literature, a direct provocation of the reader. Conversely, the ability to prevail culturally over immigrants is represented as immensely positive and important: "The accommodation of migrants which the melting pot symbolized was essential to the self-image of the United States as a land of opportunity and freedom."[23] In this and numerous other examples, the "accommodation," or submission, of immigrant groups to the dominant culture is portrayed as indicative and symbolic of both national and individual power.

Vivid images of order and chaos also emerge from the texts under consideration. The cover of the U.S. English brochure, for example, is a pastiche of quotes in Chinese, Vietnamese, Samoan, Korean, and Spanish from a Seattle public school booklet. Elsewhere in the materials it is stated that "someone who does not speak your language speaks gibberish." Bilingual and multilingual nations are portrayed as unstable and disorderly ("A Belgian is a highly taxed citizen who spends his time quarrelling about language"), whereas a single language "fosters harmony" and provides stability. ...

It is through this sort of subtle emotional appeal, in combination with the use of ambiguous symbols and the interpellations of multiple subjects as discussed above, that a fragmentary and internally contradictory discourse is able to function effectively as a coalition-building ideology. ...

SOME CONCLUDING REMARKS

The 1980s have witnessed a string of significant right-wing victories in the political arena, and these successes (as well as the failures) cannot be understood without a full analysis of their ideological dimension. I have argued here that on the issue of national language policy, the right has been successful in winning support for its project because it has been able to construct a political discourse that, due to its heterogeneous nature, is able to attract broad support. An obvious implication of my argument is that a purely nativist appeal of the sort that characterized the Americanization Movement seventy years ago, one that was grounded in an explicit rejection of pluralism and a singular definition of "American people," would fail to attract significant support and would therefore remain on the fringes of American politics in the 1980s. One might go further and speculate that those sectors of the conservative movement that have remained marginal, like the efforts to institutionalize creationism and school prayer, have been unable to break out of their conservative ghetto at least in part because they have been unsuccessful in constructing effective coalition-building ideologies. If this is the case, then it points to the crucial importance of ideology in modern political life and to the need for further detailed researches into the character and operation of discourse in the construction of political movements.

NOTES

1. For a useful historical overview of the New Right, see Jerome L. Himmelstein, "The New Right," in *The New Christian Right*, ed. Robert C. Liebman and Robert Wuthnow (New York: Aldine, 1983), 13–30.

2. See, e.g., Phyllis Schlafly, "The Conservative Profamily Movement Nominated, Elected Ronald Reagan," *Conservative Digest* 7, no. 1 (1981): 20–21; Robert W. Whitaker, *The New Right Papers* (New York: St. Martin's Press, 1982).

3. Carol Mueller, "In Search of a Constituency for the New Religious Right," *Public Opinion Quarterly* 47 (1983): 217.

4. Donald McQuarie, "The New Right and the Question of Ideological Hegemony," *Psychohistory Review* 15, no. 2 (Winter 1986–87): 109.

5. Norval D. Glenn, "Social Trends in the United States: Evidence from Sample Surveys," *Public Opinion Quarterly* 51, no. 4 (Winter 1987): S109. See also John Simpson, "Moral Issues and Status Politics," in *New Christian Right*, ed. Liebman and Wuthnow; Anson Shupe and William Stacey, "The Moral Majority Constituency," in *New Christian Right*, ed. Liebman and Wuthnow; Jerome Himmelstein and James McRae, Jr., "Social Conservatism, New Republicans and the 1980 Election," *Public Opinion Quarterly* 48 (1984): 592.

6. "Official English movement" is the preferred designation of U.S. English leaders and activists. Opponents use the term "English-only movement" instead, presumably to highlight the movement's exclusionary political motives.

7. From a brochure, "In Defense of Our Common Language ... ," available from U.S. English, 1424 16th Street, N.W., Suite 201, Washington, D.C. 20036.

8. Ibid.

9. For an extensive treatment of language-assimilation patterns, see Joshua Fishman, *Language Loyalty in the United States* (New York: Arno Press, 1978).

10. Cited in Louis Freeberg, "Latinos: Building Power from the Ground Up," *California Journal*, Jan. 1987, 14.

11. The other states are Arkansas, Indiana, Kentucky, Mississippi, Nebraska, North Carolina, Tennessee, and Virginia.

12. For an extensive analysis of proposed ELAs, their legal implications and possible practical effects, see David F. Marshall, "The Language Amendment," *International Journal of the Sociology of Language* 60 (1986): 7–75.

13. See, e.g., John Higham, *Strangers in the Land: Patterns of American Nativism, 1860–1925* (New York: Atheneum, 1963).

14. Nonstandard English forms and dialects are, on the other hand, referred to as "emotional and intellectual straitjackets."

15. For an interesting discussion of conservative thought in general, particularly of the relationship of national allegiance to it, see Roger Scruton, *The Meaning of Conservatism* (New York: Penguin, 1980).

16. Gerda Bikales and Gary Imhoff, "A Kind of Discordant Harmony: Issues in Assimilation," 12; available from U.S. English.

17. From "Fact Sheet: English Language Amendment"; available from U.S. English.

18. Reprinted in *Update* 3, no. 3 (May–June 1985):1.

19. From a mailer entitled "Talking Points," distributed by U.S. English.

20. Milton Gordon, *Assimilation in American Life* (New York: Oxford University Press, 1964), 124–125.

21. Bikales and Imhoff, "A Kind of Discordant Harmony," 4.

22. Statement by Texas state Senator Hector Uribe, reprinted in *Update* 3, no. 6 (Nov.-Dec. 1985): 2.

23. Bikales and Imhoff, "A Kind of Discordant Harmony," 6.

20

A Dialogue on Black-Jewish Relations

LETTY COTTIN POGREBIN AND
EARL OFARI HUTCHINSON

I

According to a Yankelovich poll, in the last quarter-century anti-Semitism has declined among whites but increased among blacks. Today blacks are twice as likely as whites to hold significant anti-Semitic attitudes and, even more alarming, it is younger and better-educated blacks who tend to be the most bigoted. By the same token, although a 1990 poll done by the National Opinion Research Center found that Jews have more positive attitudes toward blacks and a greater commitment to equal opportunity than do other white Americans, the poll also found that a majority of Jews do not favor government help or government spending to benefit blacks. Worse still, a Harris poll found that Jews are more likely than other whites to be upset if blacks move into their neighborhood; and 20 percent of Jews said they did not want their children to attend school with blacks, as compared with only 14 percent of other whites. ... It's fair to say that black-Jewish relations are at one of their periodic flashpoints. No longer can blacks and Jews be drawn together simply because other Americans hate us both. No longer can we expect each other to agree on what constitutes racism, anti-Semitism or institutional barriers to equal opportunity. No longer can a single speech or slogan move us to march together. Now we often march in opposite directions or face each other across an abyss. Now our two communities clash regularly over issues of power, priorities, competitive oppression and conflicting self-interest. Now it takes arguing, negotiating and struggling to find common ground within our changed circumstances and new suspicions. Now I know that black-Jewish coalition building takes work and leaves scars.

I. From Letty Cottin Pogrebin, "Different Kinds of Survival," *Deborah, Golda, and Me* (New York: Crown, 1991), pp. 292–297, reprinted by permission of Alfred A. Knopf, Inc., and Rosenstone/Wender.

During the 1984 presidential campaign, when Jesse Jackson was excoriated for his "Hymietown" statement and full page ads appeared from an organization called "Jews Against Jackson," the growing enmity between our two communities reached a boiling point. In response, several black-Jewish dialogues were started. ... I helped to form a thirty-member black-Jewish women's group whose purpose was to prepare our two communities to play a constructive role at the Nairobi United Nations Conference on Women. Although it continued meeting after the conference was over, this group petered out within two years. At first, I attributed its failure to waning black interest.

"Why do you think so many black women stopped coming to our dialogue meetings even though we started out with an equal representation?" I asked a black friend who had been part of the group.

"You Jews have to stop acting like God's chosen people," she barked, her eyes hard and angry. "The world doesn't revolve around you. Relations with Jews are not a priority for most African-Americans; our main concern is *survival.*"

The differences between blacks and Jews are rarely more obvious than when each group speaks about its own "survival," a word that both use frequently but with quite dissimilar meanings. For blacks, survival means actual physical endurance, staying alive in the face of violent crime, drugs, hunger, hopelessness, and infant mortality rates that are more than triple those of whites; it means surviving as a viable community when 30 percent of the adults and 75 percent of the young live in poverty, when 44 percent of black 17-year-olds are functionally illiterate and black unemployment is twice the white rate. For Jews, survival means keeping a minority culture and a religion alive against all odds, guarding against anti-Semitism and the slippery slope that could lead from hate speech to the gas chambers, and helping to guarantee the security of Israel.

In other words, blacks worry about their actual conditions and fear for the present; Jews worry about their history and fear for the future. Black survival is threatened by poverty; Jewish survival is threatened by affluence (with its temptation of intermarriage with the more privileged minority), assimilation and moral corruption. Racism is a bacterium, potentially curable but now deadly; anti-Semitism is a virus, potentially deadly but currently contained.

"In America, though permitted to be rich, Jews are not permitted to be comfortable," asserts writer Leonard Fein. When those who make us uncomfortable are black ... we Jews somehow feel more threatened and betrayed, expecting better from our former allies. The color of the perpetrator does not determine the degree of our safety, only the degree of our surprise.

A totally assimilated Jewish friend of mine says he can never relax as long as a swastika is painted on even one wall in America. I have a recurrent dream in which my children and I are being herded into cattle cars en route to Auschwitz. Every Jew remembers that our people were powerful and well-off in the 1930s in Berlin and Prague and Warsaw, but their prosperity didn't save them. We remember how quickly Jews and Israel were scapegoated in the United States during the gas shortages of the 1970s and the farm crisis of the 1980s. ... In 1991, we heard whispers that the war in the Persian Gulf was the fault of the Jews. So, regardless of what we have accomplished in life we continue to fear the swastika and smell the smoke. ...

My cattle-car dream takes me unawares every few years, like a dormant para-site that eats away at the intestines with no apparent provocation. I have toured the Dachau concentration camp near Munich, but that was long before I had chil-dren. I lost relatives to the Nazis, but my own immediate family, spawned in the 1960s, has never been in danger. Still, I dream that dream. I tell this to my black friend with the angry eyes. I want her to remember that in her lifetime and mine, one out of every three Jews in the world was slaughtered. "Even if never personally threatened, you would need constant reassurance if one-third of your relatives had been murdered," I tell her.

My friend listens but she still doesn't get it. She grew up in a neighborhood where Jews collected the rent, ran the shops, employed black domestic workers, checked up on welfare clients and taught black children. She works now in New York City, where every Jew she sees is thriving. She points out that 30 million American blacks have only twenty-six Congressional representatives and no black senators, while 6 million American Jews have thirty-three Jewish members of the House and eight Jewish senators. Through her eyes I see how it might seem unbe-lievable that a people so affluent, powerful and *white* could possibly be quaking at the summit.

How very differently our two out-groups view the world. To blacks, America is the nation that enslaved them and continues to deny them opportunities. To Jews, it is a promised land that made good on its promises. Blacks worry that their (bad) situation will never improve—therefore their issues are fundamental issues like affordable housing, better education and affirmative action. Jews worry that our (good) situation will not last—therefore our issues are safety issues like free-dom of religion (separation of church and state), freedom of immigration (Soviet Jews, Ethiopian Jews) and a secure Israel. To summarize these complex differences in an oversimplified statement, African-Americans need relief in the form of practical economic assistance; Jews need relief in the form of normalized group and individual acceptance. ...

Dialogue has taught me that each group inaccurately perceives the negative power of the other. Blacks are not really in a position to hurt Jews, but because of their superior numbers and a few high-profile anti-Semites, Jews fear them. Jews are not really in a position to hurt blacks, but blacks believe we are determined to keep them down. African-Americans are saying, If we're supposed to be brothers and sisters, how come you're doing so well and we're in the streets? Jews are say-ing, If we're supposed to be friends, how come you keep picking on us?

Maybe Jews and blacks lock horns more than other groups because we are the only ones who take each other seriously. ... Or maybe we are encouraged to fight in public as surrogate combatants for the bigots in the dominant culture. As the media magnify every black-Jewish clash, other Americans can let off steam vicari-ously while avoiding the anger that might otherwise be directed at them. Mean-while, blacks and Jews get hooked on the oldest scam in the world: divide and conquer.

I refuse to let that happen. While I had been hurt by my friend's angry words, talking with her clarified that I was the one who had not understood. I had sug-gested that there was something wrong with African-Americans for dropping out of the dialogue, when in fact there was something wrong with the dialogue for failing to serve the needs of its black participants. Because the Jewish agenda—creating alliances—was being fulfilled, Jews kept showing up at the meetings. But the black agenda—cooperative activism—had stalled, so some black women had stopped coming. It was as simple as that. Beneath her fury, my friend was really saying, "Stop complaining. Your needs are being met and mine are not." She saw Jews getting what they craved (acceptance), while what blacks craved (assistance) wasn't forthcoming. ...

Blacks are asking Jews to go beyond tension reduction into practical nitty-gritty activism and advocacy work. They want biracial teams to organize and lobby for economic and social programs in the areas of affordable housing, child care, health, dropout prevention, education and drug treatment. They want us to mount joint press conferences, petition campaigns, conferences, demonstrations, vigils and fact-finding trips. They want public education projects, guest columns in each other's newspapers, pulpit exchanges in each other's churches and synagogues, black-Jewish pairs speaking in the schools, Jewish intellectuals promoting books by and about African-Americans, career internships for black students. They expect us to work together monitoring police prejudice, hate crimes, media distortions, vandalism, harassment. They want Jews to "interrupt" racism whenever we see or hear it. And they want financial support for black self-reliance projects—they want white resources put into programs that African-Americans control.

African-Americans may not realize it, but what they are asking Jews to do, in my opinion, is to *act Jewish*. How we each practice religious Judaism is a private matter, but the practice of moral Judaism is something I believe most Jews must express publicly through our commitments.

To be morally Jewish requires doing *tzedakah* (the Hebrew word meaning charity, caring and "right action," whose linguistic root, *tzedek,* means justice) and *gemilut hesed* (acts of lovingkindness). These are actions, not just talk. The pursuit of justice is one definition of activism. It is also, as I've said, what makes and keeps us Jews. If we lose our purpose, we lose our peoplehood and become no more than an odd collection of folks with common ancestors, unique religious laws and an uncanny potential for victimization. That's not Jewish enough for me.

II

Neither blacks nor Jews are a monolithic group. There are many differences and shades of opinions within each group.

Not ALL Jews oppose affirmative action or consider blacks criminals or welfare cheats. Many Jewish individuals and groups did oppose the anti-affirmative action Bakke and Webber Supreme Court cases. Many Jews do condemn repression, racism and economic exploitation.

II. From Earl Ofari Hutchinson, "My Jewish Problem or Your Black Problem?" *Ofari's Bi-Monthly* (May/June 1992):2–5.

And, not ALL blacks oppose Israel or consider Jews "conspirators" and exploiters. Many defend Israel's right to exist and speak out against black-on-black crime, violence, and for self-help. They do not blame poverty and racism on Jewish exploiters, but rather on corporate and government policies of neglect. Now let's look at what blacks say about Jews, and Jews say about themselves.

Slavery. City College of New York Professor Leonard Jeffries charges that Jews financed the slave trade. Is Jeffries right? A few Jewish traders and merchants built wealth through the transport, sale and trade of slaves. In states like Louisiana, some Jews owned plantations and used slave labor to work them. Judah Benjamin, a powerful Louisiana planter, served as U.S. Senator and later Secretary of War in the Confederate cabinet. He was one of the South's most articulate defenders of slavery and secession.

In some Southern cities, Jewish Temple congregations passed resolutions and issued public statements against abolition. An estimated 1,500 Jewish soldiers fought for the Confederacy.

In the North, prominent New York Rabbi Morris J. Raphall cited biblical scripture [as] "proof" that "slaveholding is no sin." Southern newspapers quoted his speeches approvingly. In 1853, the American Anti-Slavery Society was perplexed "that Jews had not taken steps with regard to the slavery question."

BUT, does this means that Jews were pro-slavery? No. Jewish traders and planters were only a small proportion of those involved in the slave business. Slavery was highly profitable and many merchants, bankers, shipowners, North and South, engaged in the trade. Even some Africans and a few black Americans bought and sold slaves.

Many Jews backed the abolition movement. Jews rode with John Brown in Kansas. The *Jewish Messenger* repeatedly editorialized against slavery. Also, several Jewish leaders rebutted Rabbi Raphall. When war came, Rabbis in Cincinnati, Chicago, New York and Philadelphia championed the Union cause. And more than 6,000 Jewish soldiers served in the Union army, some in all-Jewish regiments.

Economic Exploitation. "In every black ghetto, Jews own the major businesses. Every night they go home with the black community's money." Is Malcolm X right? Early Jewish immigrants found the doors of corporations and banks shut tight. They had to work the economic margins to survive. In poor black neighborhoods, wages and rents were low, and needy customers plentiful. So many became merchants and property owners in these areas.

And there were abuses. David Caplovitz in his study, "The Merchant and the Low Income Consumer," documented the questionable credit, lending and retail practices of some of these merchants.

Worse, many Jewish merchants refused to employ or train blacks. In the 1930s, blacks in Harlem, Chicago and Los Angeles launched massive boycotts and demonstrations against their racist hiring practices. During the black uprisings of the 1960s many Jewish-owned stores were burned.

BUT, does this mean that Jews were the major exploiters of blacks? No. Other first generation immigrants—Greeks, Armenians, Italians also opened stores, and bought property in black neighborhoods. Some also sold shoddy goods at high prices and charged excessive rents.

As small mom and pop owners, most operated under a handicap. They lacked credit and capital to buy in volume and make needed repairs on their property. The high prices in the ghetto often reflected more the cost of business necessity than malice.

As for racism, many of those who boycotted and demonstrated against job discrimination were Jews. Most were either Socialists, Communists or radical trade unionists. Also, during a time when much of private industry and labor unions consigned blacks to menial and dirty jobs, the stores—many Jewish-owned—that did eventually hire blacks were often the only places they could find meaningful employment.

The small merchants and landlords got the blame for the ghetto exploitation. Yet the banks that refused to lend, the corporations that refused to hire and promote, the schools that refused to educate, and the public officials who refused to respond to black needs waltzed away unscathed.

Racial Stereotypes. "The motion picture industry was largely a Jewish invention." Charles Silberman is right. In the early years of this century, filmmaking was considered a marginal industry. Jewish businessmen saw the opportunities. They bought into the fledgling studios and made the movies that entertained Americans.

Hollywood, however, did more than entertain, it also reinforced negative images. Blacks on screen played an endless procession of "Tom," "coon," and "Mammy" roles and the public believed the stereotypes. The servile image of blacks changed with the upsurge of the civil rights and black power movements of the 1960s.

BUT, does this mean that Jews are to blame for creating the myth of black inferiority? No. The vicious caricatures and stereotypes of blacks were deeply embedded in much of American thought long before Jews bought into the movie industry.

From the end of Reconstruction to World War I, Northern and Southern newspapers routinely depicted blacks as lazy, moronic and criminal. These myths were heavily propagated by academics and public officials. Black scholars such as W.E.B. DuBois, Carter G. Woodson and J. A. Rogers challenged these stereotypes in books, magazines and newspapers. They were aided by Jewish scholars such as Franz Boas, Melville Herskovitts and Herbert Aptheker. In time, black and Jewish writers managed to at least make racial stereotyping less respectable.

The Grand Alliance. In Phillip Roth's *Goodbye, Columbus,* a character continually asks: "Is it good for the Jews or bad for the Jews." The question is: Did Jewish leaders support civil rights because of self-interest rather than conscience? Some did. Speaking of the aid Julius Rosenwald gave to black education and social causes, nearly a century ago, *The American Hebrew* noted: "by helping the colored people in this country, doubtless he also serves Judaism." Jewish historians pointed to the threat of Klan violence, and the lynching of Leo Frank in 1915, as the catalyst that sparked Jewish organizations to take action on racial violence.

Even the financial, organizational and leadership support many Jews gave the NAACP and Urban League did not silence the critics. They charged that Jews "used" black organizations for their own ends.

During the 1960s, when black activists demanded greater control of SNCC and CORE, major Jewish organizations quickly withdrew their money and support. Jewish leaders denounced both organizations for calling for black power, Pan Africanism, and support of the Palestinians. In the 1970s, blacks and Jews repeatedly clashed over education, busing, affirmative action. Some of the clashes were violent.

The *volte face* by some Jews on civil rights was accompanied by a political shift to the right. From the Roosevelt years, Jews, like blacks, were the bedrock of Democratic Party liberalism. By 1972, Jews had grown more conservative. In that year's presidential election, Nixon received 35 percent of the Jewish vote. A decade later, Jews divided their votes nearly equally between Reagan and Carter. Today, many Jewish middle and upper income voters are staunch Republican Party supporters.

BUT, does this mean that the historic "grand alliance" was borne of Jewish self-interest? No. From the early 1900s through the Great Depression, Jews in the Socialist, Communist, and labor organizations were in the forefront of the battle against lynching, the poll tax, job and housing discrimination, and trade union segregation.

Four years before the Supreme Court's Brown school desegregation ruling, the American Jewish Congress, Anti-Defamation League, and numerous Jewish Community Councils filed briefs against school segregation. Jewish legislators, attorneys, agencies, and voters played a strong activist role in challenging the legal barriers of discrimination. In the 1960s, thousands of Jewish students marched, sat-in and demonstrated for civil rights.

The civil rights victories improved the quality of life for African-Americans. This is why black leaders such as Adam Clayton Powell, A. Phillip Randolph, Paul Robeson, and Martin Luther King, Jr. praised the heroic efforts of Jewish organizations in the struggle for equality.

Can the "Grand Alliance" of the Past Be Rebuilt? Not in the old way. On issues such as affirmative action or Israel, blacks and Jews must call a truce and cooperate on the issues and problems of mutual concern.

They can fight for more private and public spending on jobs, social services, national health care, small business development, professional training and education to expand the pool of opportunities for African-Americans and Jews.

They can march and demonstrate against Klan, Nazi, and Aryan nation violence, and for tougher laws against race-religious hate crimes. They can challenge anti-Semitism among blacks and racism among Jews. They can serve only to inflame both communities.

Progressive Jewish organizations such as the New Jewish Agenda and the National Black Political Agenda can form coalitions to support: full employment, police reform, demilitarization, democracy in South Africa, independent political organizing, labor and environmental protections and economic democracy.

The grand alliance between blacks and Jews may be history, the issues and problems that brought it into being are not. Neither blacks nor Jews can afford to forget that.

REFERENCES

David Caplovitz, "The Merchant and the Low-Income Consumer," *Negro-Jewish Relations in the United States.*
Leonard Dinerstein, ed., *Anti-Semitism in the United States.*
Stanley Feldstein, *The Land That I Show You: Three Centuries of Jewish Life in America.*
Roberta Feuerlicht, *The Fate of the Jews.*
Nat Hentoff, ed., *Black Anti-Semitism and Jewish Racism.*
Irving Howe, *World of Our Fathers: The Journey of the East Europeans to America and the Life They Found and Made.*
Bertram Korn, *American Jewry and the Civil War.*
Charles Silberman, *A Certain People.*
Robert Weisbord and Arthur Stein, *Bittersweet Encounter: The Afro-American and the American Jew.*

21

Detroit: Demolished by Design

MARILYNN RASHID

It's Thursday afternoon, and I'm jogging my two or three miles on the track at the downtown Detroit YMCA overlooking the gym where a group of about sixteen mostly black men are playing basketball. The man and woman who were running when I started have finished, so I'm alone and keeping an eye on the game to fight the boredom of running on an indoor track.

Some months ago, I noticed the heightened level of intensity and rage in these pick-up basketball games, and today, thinking about the numerous incidents of urban violence I've observed and heard about recently, I am mesmerized by the quick and constant shifting back and forth between play and anger, hilarity and loud hostility. There are no referees in these games, so the disagreements over points and fouls are worked out through indignant shouting, screaming accusations, insults and occasional shoving and fighting.

When these blow-ups occur, the few white players almost always step back and wait silently for the resolution, while a number of the black players not involved in the confrontation yell at the others to stop fighting and play ball. The din of their voices is deafening but they always resume play eventually. Today, one such outburst ends with one man shoving another and shouting, "Suck it, you fucking bitch!"

I've been going to the downtown "Y" for several years now, and I've come to appreciate this place as one of the few centers of racially integrated activity in my daily life. I've lived in this city, which is now 80% black, all my life, but except for alienated activities like grocery shopping and riding the bus, I do few social every-day things with blacks. The "Y" is one of the welcome exceptions. People are generally friendly and tolerant. I've had some thought-provoking encounters and discussions with women of various ages and races in the locker room and the sauna.

The men, too, are usually kind and open. Numerous times on my way to and from the track, I've heard black men complaining to each other about the constant hostility on the basketball court; they wish the others could get it together, put aside their differences and not waste so much time fighting.

Today, as I run above the blaring voices watching as these strong angry men shove, shout at and curse each other with sexist, anti-female epithets, I remember that I am a small white female alone on the track, and with paranoid abandon, I imagine their rage overflowing the court, their incensed eyes filling up the gym, rising until they see me there to become a target for all their frustration and resentment and disillusionment. But as always, I finish my run. The men temporarily resolve their altercation. The game goes on.

*   *   *

This past summer, my sister was riding her bike down an inner-city street on her way home from work. Three black youths, dressed fashionably and with in-vogue flat-top hair styles, walked out and stood in the middle of the street facing her, smiling as she approached. It happened too quickly for her to stop or turn around. Staring at her and still smiling, they shoved her into the path of an on-coming car. Fortunately, the car slammed on its brakes and she wasn't seriously injured, although her arm and leg were badly cut and her hand was sprained.

The old deaf black man who was driving the car ran out to help her, screaming at the young men. My sister screamed and cursed at them too. One of them picked up a piece of concrete and threw it at her. When they started walking back toward her, she got on her bike and rode away.

The other night, a friend of mine who works at a neighborhood bar waited on an extremely distraught young black woman. She told my friend that she was "trying to deal with something," and when encouraged to talk, explained that she'd just visited a woman friend of hers in intensive care in the hospital. The woman had been beaten unconscious at her own birthday party by men who were supposedly guests at the celebration. She was beaten so badly that her friend could not even recognize her, and days after the attack she was still in a coma. Why were these things happening, my friend asked her. The woman shook her head slowly and replied, "It's a fashion, a fad, a sick fad." ...

The tales of violence go on and on. Here are some that appeared in the papers: Two black men are severely beaten by whites outside a rock concert hall on the city's east side. Some days later, several young black men beat up a white man in the same area. Rival gangs of blacks and whites attack each other at a street festival in nearby Hamtramck. Seven youths are injured. Two black vagrants are seriously beaten by as many as 20 black youths in downtown Detroit. A white man drives his car into a group of blacks, mostly children, killing three people and seriously injuring others. A 19-year-old black man from Detroit is beaten to death in Rose-ville, a predominantly white Detroit suburb. Three white teenagers are charged with his murder.

NO CENTER, NO HEART

Detroit is not the murder capital of the country any more, but it has been experiencing an alarming upsurge in violence, much of which you won't read about in the papers. The feeling of paranoia and fear that even long-time Detroit residents are now experiencing recalls the tense climate of the city in the mid-sixties, before the '67 riot, and in the early seventies, when whites were fleeing en masse to the suburbs. But there are many differences in the political atmosphere now, and there are multi-faceted aspects of the violence we're seeing, rooted in racism, class oppression, sexism, the destruction of community, and the vapid values promoted by a pervasive consumer society. Most everyone would agree that very little, if anything, has changed for the better in the city of Detroit since the '67 riots.

The population of Detroit has plummeted in the last two decades as not only whites, but middle-class blacks, continue the migration out of the city. The edges of the metropolitan area have expanded voraciously with astounding speed into the few remaining rural stretches until they have linked up with the expanding metropolitan areas of other cities. There is nothing but urban sprawl between them, and the entire area is chopped up by a huge expressway complex that also grows and grows, tentacling out into one neighborhood after another, destroying natural connections between people and places, keeping working people off the streets and in their cars, addicted to a frenetic sense of speed, and plagued by a never satisfied need to "escape."

In Detroit itself now, there is no center, no heart. The old downtown is full of virtually empty office buildings, vacated in moves to new shiny complexes on the river or in the suburbs. The neighborhoods that have managed to survive are like threatened islands of life with large expanses of devastation in between.

Except for the poor and working class neighborhoods of the southwest side, made up of Latinos, blacks, Poles and Arabs, the one or two integrated neighborhoods in the city are middle-class. Many of those families pay for their children to attend private or area Catholic schools which are more likely to be somewhat racially mixed. But the vast majority of Detroit youth are consigned to the public school system which continues to be a breeding ground for violence and desperation, reflecting the harsh reality of daily life for blacks in all large urban American areas.

INJUSTICE AT EVERY TURN

In a country in which 71.1% of privately-owned wealth is in the hands of 10% of American families, in a country in which the rich are consistently getting richer and the poor and working class are getting robbed, prospects are exceedingly grim for inner city youth. ...

People who get off the freeways and into the fractured heart of this city will see evidence of immiseration at every turn, where the insidious, business-as-usual operation of capitalism has created a highly visible, exceedingly desperate, and primarily black underclass.

The ranks of the homeless—at least 10,000 in Detroit—have swelled to the point where working people are constantly barraged on the streets with requests for money or pleas to pump their gas or wash their car windows. There's increasing competition among garbage pickers in my neighborhood and in numerous others throughout the city. These are the abandoned ones whose misery is built into the system. If this class did not exist here, it would of necessity come into being somewhere else.

Not only for the impoverished and oppressed, but for the vast majority of inner-city dwellers, life under U.S. capitalism is ugly, brutish and often short. According to federal researchers, the homicide rate for young men in the U.S. is from 4–73 times the rate in other industrialized nations. Research for the National Center for Health Statistics shows that for the year 1987, 21.9 men per 100,000 were killed, between the ages 16–24; for black men that rate was 85 per 100,000, an increase of 40% since a low in 1984. Nationally, homicide is the leading cause of death among black men, as well as for young black women in specific urban areas.

According to the research cited above, Michigan was the most treacherous state for young black men, with a homicide rate of 232 per 100,000, largely concentrated in the Detroit area.

By far, the two most available "apparent" paths out of the cycle of poverty and despair for young blacks are also professions rooted in authoritarianism and violence—one legitimate by this society's standards, the other illegitimate. The U.S. armed forces have been able to fill their ranks with the nation's poor by taking full advantage of their bleak future, claiming to teach skills that will be "marketable" in civilian society and offering educational benefits beyond the time of service. For a huge portion of service-men and -women, joining the armed forces is overwhelmingly an act of economic desperation. Needless to say, the environment of military training and service is infused with male dominance, power and coercive discipline. Here violence is institutionalized and controlled by a hierarchy based on the "virtues" of authoritarianism.

If the army doesn't attract poor urban youth, often the world of petty and not so petty crime does; here again, force and violence reign. Drug running, dealing and thievery often begin as acts of economic survival, but in crime-dominated neighborhoods where a large percentage of the population is armed and where the police are corrupt and trigger happy, the risks are high and the chances of living past the age of thirty are very slim.

FEEDING RACIST ATTITUDES

If young offenders are not cynical, violent and angry at the outset of their careers, reform schools and the prison system will likely mold them into ruthless criminals schooled in injustice, weary of being victimized, and ready to prey on others weaker than they. The victims of social victims are usually those closest to them, often women and children, usually people in their own families and communities. Studies show that 95% of all violence against blacks is committed by blacks.

Instead of pointing to the dire conditions in which blacks live in this country, such statistics have fed racist attitudes. The racist perception that is reinforced is that blacks are more prone to violence than whites, and even that domestic violence is more acceptable in Black-American culture. The result is a double standard in which blacks are targeted by the police and the "justice" system in ways that whites are not. According to the National Youth Survey, when white and black teenagers commit the same offense, police are seven times more likely to charge the blacks with a felony, and the courts are more likely to imprison the black offenders. As prisons are the institutional indoctrinators of criminal lifestyles, it is not surprising that youths of all races leave prisons more skilled in crime than when they entered, and the cycle continues.

Nowhere is the legitimation of racist practices more blatant than in the Reagan/Bush domestic drug war. According to recent studies on FBI arrests, blacks are being arrested a rate highly disproportionate to their drug use. Blacks make up about 12% of regular drug users and 16% of regular cocaine users, and yet last year they made up more than 48% of those arrested on charges involving cocaine and heroin.

Though black drug users in impoverished cities are likely to be more visible, the vast majority of drug use and drug dealing goes on in middle and upper middle class white suburban neighborhoods. The highly publicized, get-tough, police crackdown on low-level drug users has been devastating for inner-city neighborhoods; it has done nothing but increase the misery of daily life.

Despite these and other government-sponsored attempts to "clean up" the neighborhoods, urban school drop-out rates, gang activity and violent crime all continue to climb. Racism and class oppression rear their massive heads in other connected arenas. White, middle- and upper-class first-time offenders are more likely to be admitted to drug rehabilitation programs, to be paroled or pardoned, to receive counseling and community support. Poor and working class blacks are more likely to go to jail.

CULTURAL DISINTEGRATION

Remembering the statistic that shows blacks as the primary victims of black crime, and then thinking of the numerous recent incidents involving both blacks and whites, one is tempted to conclude that crime in poor black communities is increasing to the point where it's breaking through its borders and affecting us all. But that is obviously only part of the picture. And again, such a partial conclusion focuses on black violence and fails to address the larger context; the seeds of the violence lie elsewhere.

The cultural disintegration so rapidly taking place in black urban communities is reflective of mass industrial society where family and community ties have been whittled away by the social and political forces of the corporate market. The voids in these fractured communities are being filled at breakneck speed with rage and cynicism or colonized by the empty promise of consumerism. ...

The black pride messages of the civil rights movement were extremely powerful and significant for black Detroit communities in the sixties. Slogans like "Freedom Now" and "Black Is Beautiful" were charged with a revolutionary fervor and potential that is difficult to imagine today. The black urban youth of the nineties has had no similar experience; their sense of this period of promise is formed, not by continuity or direct involvement, but by media images and a few textbook accounts that flatten, distort and historicize. It has little relevance to their present daily battles for survival.

And, too, in the face of the glaring injustice that continues to block their paths, one must admit that these ideals, for all their intensity, did not bring blacks the freedom they demanded; and it is likely that today's black youth are sorely aware of this.

Martin Luther King's dream, after so much struggle, is still a dream, and acknowledging that reality brings bitterness, cynicism and further alienation. While significant black voices (Malcolm X, King, the Panthers) were systematically silenced and destroyed, the movement was insidiously co-opted by politicians like Detroit's mayor Coleman Young who, after getting a strong political foothold through his identification with civil rights and trade unions, was quickly bought out by the corporations to become a classic puppet of the system, giving the illusion of black power while ignoring the continued demise of poor and working class communities in the city.

Clearly, the corporations run the cities, and nowhere is this more apparent than in Detroit, where time and time again viable neighborhoods were destroyed to build factories that promised jobs but delivered further cultural disintegration and misery.

THE SUPERFICIAL PROMISE OF STYLE

After the rich contexts of community, class solidarity and shared experience are obliterated, only the market remains to fill the vacuum. The images of (primarily male) power, wealth and prestige that have always driven mainstream (i.e. commodity) culture are now disseminated more pervasively than ever. The slick, techno-messages of sophisticated films, music videos, television and advertising appear as the key to all that is missing in one's life. As the powerlessness increases, so the bizarreness of the mimicry of power is magnified. Thus 1920s style shootouts between armed, expensively dressed teenage gangs has become a not uncommon occurrence at high school dances and house parties.

In the sixties and early seventies, a profound social consciousness led many people, young and old, to seek freedom, solidarity, love and peace. But today, while yuppies look for the most state-of-the-art compact disc player or the least touristy vacation spot, impoverished urban youth are looking for the right hightops or the perfect hairstyle. Almost everyone is after the fastest, slickest or classiest car. Television and other mass media promise to satisfy every need. They offer it all, and often in the terms of a violent elitist society, with sometimes blatant and other times thinly veiled metaphors of sexism and domination.

We are sadly quite accustomed to hearing of acts of violence rooted in poverty, racism, sexism and drugs, but what is most confounding of late is that street violence has also become a fashion, a style, a macho peer-pressure game removed from the visceral reality of its consequences, void of genuine emotion and tragedy, saturated instead with superficial intensity and a distanced, mediatized sense of adventure. It often seems that the perpetrators of such crimes are watching themselves on a tv or video screen, while they act out scenes of violence and domination, scenes in which they come out on top, they subdue, overpower, destroy and win. One suspects they are watching themselves through their mind's camera eye, with little or no human attention to their victims, because no one else is truly watching or acknowledging their existence in any significant way. ...

We should not be surprised at the increasing level of violence in a nation-state engendered and maintained through the conquest and subjugation of tribal and community-based people and through the exploitation and despoliation of the earth. Competition, confrontation and hierarchical control are valued and encouraged on many levels in this society—in schools, in sports, in the workplace, in the State Department. It is not only in urban areas that violence is on the rise, but in countless rural and small-town communities as well which are not immune to the social disaffection and alienation typical of most cities. And certainly, the ubiquitous, captivating media messages influencing inner-city dwellers penetrate small-town and rural consciousness as well.

But violence is truly in vogue on the streets of U.S. cities. It is advertised on sale on every tv channel, in every video game, in every competitive sport, and American youths have been brought up to be good consumers who realize that if they can't be free or loved, at least they can be tough and have style.

What is most tragic, perhaps, is that this violence, bereft of social consciousness, is so clearly misdirected; it rarely, if ever, confronts those institutions of society responsible for the oppression, those forces that maintain themselves through continued exploitation. Instead, as it impulsively and compulsively mirrors the media spectacle and targets one's own family or community, it becomes self-directed, self-defeating, self-destructive.

NO SYMPATHY, NO COMPASSION

Though I live in the inner city, I have a part-time teaching job in a wealthy Detroit suburb. ... Lately, I have come to look at those wealthy suburban streets as flaunting a more insidious, more entrenched and more powerful kind of violence than the kind I've been discussing in this article. For, clearly, this prosperous suburb exists on the backs of those impoverished inner-city neighborhoods. There is a bold arrogance that comes with class privilege and economic security and comfort. Certainly, there are exceptions, but for the most part there is little or no sympathy in these affluent communities for the plight of the poor, the homeless, the unemployed.

"Te compadeces de los destechados?" I asked one of my students, after explaining the Spanish verbal phrase "to sympathize with" and the noun for the homeless, "los destechados." No, he answered, in slow perfect Spanish, I don't sympathize with the homeless. And when asked why not, he confidently explained that there were plenty of jobs for people if they really wanted to work, and then went on to complain about welfare fraud. A middle-class black student of mine whose family recently moved to the suburbs from the city denounced AIDS victims, telling me they got what they deserved, they made their choices, opted to take drugs, chose to be gay or not to use condoms. He also denigrated the city, saying he now has no reason to go "down there."

All the counter-arguments put forth by a few other more sensitive students and myself are refuted with a moralistic self-assurance that astounds me in people so young. Only when accused of being cold and uncaring are they temporarily taken aback, because these characteristics obviously do not fit into their self-conceptions. All in all, it is virtually impossible to confront with words such profound ignorance in people who are ostensibly so "intelligent," so secure with their place in the world.

Most educated middle-class whites in the 1960s and 1970s could not get away with voicing such attitudes. Their position brought with it a certain humility and compassion and a responsibility, at least in words, if not in action, to acknowledge the injustice of a system that granted them privilege and denied others, on the basis of class or race, the basic necessities of survival. But in the last ten years or so, the white and now the black middle-class as well have succumbed to a pervasive social rationalization for their material affluence—a lifestyle which frenetically attempts to mask the spiritual emptiness and social alienation of their own existence.

Not only do they fail to see the connections between their prosperity and the economic misery of the black underclass, but many blame the poor for their poverty and misfortune. ...

ENVIRONMENTAL RACISM

There is yet another kind of violence visited upon poor minority communities everywhere, but particularly in large industrial cities. This violence comes in the form of environmental pollution, and its effects on poor urban residents have been deadly. With calculated, institutional racism, corporate decisions are made to locate polluting industry, hazardous waste facilities, landfills and incinerators in poor minority neighborhoods where residents are uninformed, uneducated or too overwhelmed with basic daily survival to organize themselves in protest.

Recent studies on demographics and the locations of hazardous waste sites found that the one variable which best explains the existence of hazardous waste facilities in a community was its racial composition. Communities with a single hazardous waste facility were found to have twice the percentage of people of color as communities with no such facility. Communities with the largest levels of waste activity (two or more hazardous waste facilities or one of the nation's largest landfills) had three times the minority representation of those communities without any such activity. Three of the nation's five largest landfills are sited in predominantly black or Latino neighborhoods. The chemical industry has prospered through deliberate neglect, through its attack on the environment and its willingness to jeopardize the health of the poor. Though environmentalists are now acknowledging the existence of these "sacrifice communities" and beginning to link issues of social justice and pollution, there is little hope of substantive change in the policy of a corporate capitalist system fired by uncontained growth and production, profit and greed.

In the Detroit area, such policies have been the rule for a long time. The southwest side, made up of poor minority communities, is one of the most polluted areas in the country. It is heavily occupied by steel plants, refineries, incinerators, hazardous waste treatment plants and contaminated waste sites. Needless to say, the incidence of cancer, respiratory disease and birth defects in this area is extremely high and continues to climb.

The Detroit trash incinerator, at this point the world's largest, was sited on the city's near east side in an area inhabited mostly by poor blacks and elderly whites. Though not yet burning to its 4,000 ton-per-day capacity, it continues to fail mercury emissions tests and to pour out dangerous levels of numerous other contaminants, including cancer-inducing dioxins.

Other more recently proposed incinerators in outlying areas appear to have a much better chance of being defeated for two reasons—these communities have benefited educationally from the protests surrounding the Detroit incinerator, and they are not poor minority communities. They have managed to organize themselves quickly. Because of their better economic and educational standing, they have access to resources and political inroads to force local bureaucrats to listen to them. Such conditions do not exist in the impoverished community around Detroit's incinerator, and it is feared that, ironically, these outlying areas, in defeating their incinerators, will insure the continued operation of the Detroit facility as it may likely be fueled with the refuse from these and other surrounding communities. ...

Studies often prove the obvious. We all know that chemical pollution makes people physically sick and adds substantially to the generalized feelings of depression and powerlessness that already exist due to the oppressive conditions of their daily lives. ...

Back at the "Y," I now notice that the basketball games are a little more subdued due to the presence of a big white YMCA official (possibly the minister who works here) in a suit and tie, standing on the foul line with his arms folded authoritatively over his chest. He rocks a bit forward onto his toes, then back to center. His expression is serious as he "oversees" the game. I'm quite sure that the players themselves complained to the office about the constant fighting, and that the office responded in this way.

Such official acknowledgment brings with it the false message that government, church and social organizations will take care of things, while the apathy, complacency and powerlessness of individuals and communities grow. City and church officials busy themselves trying to allay people's fears and attempting to foster a more positive image of Detroit so that potential investors won't look elsewhere. But of course the corporate structure remains intact and corporate decisions continue to diminish the quality of our lives.

I am not surprised by the official response, that it affirms male dominance and hierarchy, that it works through the church and the military, that it seeks to quell present and potential rage by offering "marketable" skills and the promise of employment. I am not surprised that it aims to bolster the broken self-image of the black male while making no mention of the self-image of the black female. It must be assumed that though she is equally and often more at risk, though incidents of rape and other forms of sexual and domestic violence continue to soar, her self-conception is not threatened and that she endures in spite of it all.

Of course, I don't think for a moment that any of these programs or tactics will be effective on any significant scale even on their own terms. As long as we seek authority outside ourselves—as long as we demand to be policed even during our hours of play and leisure—violence and rage, repressed or manifest, will continue to hold sway over our lives.

What I would like to see and hear in response to this crisis is a massive popular outcry condemning consumerism, industrial capitalism, patriarchy and progress, while affirming community and the strength of individuals to direct their own destinies and meet their own needs. And here the self divides. For this is nothing but naive, idealistic rhetoric, words that mean little or nothing from within the monster; there are no whole communities here capable of voicing such demands and acting on their needs and desires. We're talking Detroit reality here. People are struggling to feed their families, to keep them from killing each other, to survive the week, not to change the world.

Within this context, there is little hope of any radical transformation. Sorting through the layered complexities of violence and racism in our city brings no solace. We are the targets of black underclass rage just as much as white suburban, self-righteous racists, and we're more available. Like everyone else, we too are hooked into a system that destroys us, we too are struggling to hang on to the dissolving threads of a fragmented community.

We're left wringing our hands and driving our cars down freeways that we know have irreparably fractured our connections with each other. We're left running around and around on an indoor track while "the man" looks on, and while the neighborhood kids run down to the corner store to turn in the bottles they've ripped off from the homeless man in the alley. And now they're off to play the "Contra War" video game, while their big brothers and sisters are on their way to the Persian Gulf.

PART 5

Ethnic Business

The issue of minority ownership of businesses has been widely discussed in the 1980s and 1990s. The public perception is that whereas Asians are doing quite well as entrepreneurs (i.e., as business owners), other people of color are lagging behind. Most social scientists and policymakers believe that in order for a racial/ethnic group to be economically successful, its members must own a substantial number of businesses. In an ideal nondiscriminatory marketplace, many contend, minorities would own businesses in proportion to their distribution in the population; for example, Hispanics, who make up 9 percent of the population, would own 9 percent of the businesses.

This is far from reality. The most recent comprehensive data can be obtained from the Census Bureau's 1987 Survey of Minority-Owned Businesses, which is discussed by William O'Hare (1992) and *Wall Street Journal Reports* (1992). The businesses surveyed include partnerships, individual proprietorships, and Subchapter S corporations. We have summarized some of their major findings in Table 1. Most important, people of color are underrepresented among business owners. Although they make up almost 25 percent of the population, people of color own only 9 percent of all businesses. Blacks, Native Americans, and Hispanics are severely underrepresented, whereas Asians are slightly underrepresented.

It is instructive to look at the dramatic differences within each group. The easiest way to see these differences is by examining rates of business ownership for every 1,000 members of a group. Among Asians and Pacific Islanders, for example, Koreans have the highest ownership rate (102/1,000). That is, for every 1,000 Koreans, there are 102 who own their own business. This figure is quite high when compared with the 67/1,000 ownership rate among all business owners. Asian Indians are a distant second (76/1,000). The remaining groups, in descending order, are Japanese (66), Chinese (63), Vietnamese (50), Filipino (33), and Hawaiian (22).

Differences in business ownership rates also exist among Hispanics. Cubans have the highest rate of ownership at 63 per 1,000. "Other Hispanics" come in at a distant second (21), followed by Mexicans (19) and Puerto Ricans (11).

The fourth column of Table 1 indicates that minority-owned firms also experience a disproportionately low percentage of sales. Although people of color own 9 percent of all firms, their businesses account for only 3.9 percent of all sales. Asian-owned firms account for 1.7 percent of sales, followed by Hispanics, blacks,

TABLE 1   Minority Business Ownership in 1987

Race/Ethnicity of Firm Owner	% of 1990 U.S. Population[a]	% of All Firms[b]	% of All Sales[c]	% Growth Between 1982 and 1987	
				Firms[d]	Sales[e]
White	80.3	91.0	96.1	(n.a.)	(n.a.)
Black	12.1	3.1	1.0	37.6	105.5
Hispanic	9.0	3.1	1.2	80.5	110.3
Asian/Pacific	2.9	2.6	1.7	89.3	161.8
Native American	0.8	0.2	0.04	57.5	84.0
Total				14.2	106.2

[a]This is the percent distribution of the entire U.S. population. For example, 80.3 percent of the population is white. The total does not add to 100 percent because Hispanics can be of any race and a small percentage of people are classified as being in "other races."

[b]This is the percent distribution of all firms. For example, 91.0 percent of all firms are owned by whites.

[c]This is the percent distribution of all sales. For example, 1 percent of all the sales of all firms were made by black-owned firms.

[d]This is the percentage of growth in the number of firms between 1982 and 1987. The total figure is the figure for *all* firms, 91 percent of which are white-owned. For example, the number of Asian/Pacific islander–owned firms increased by 89.3 percent during that period.

[e]This is the percentage of growth of sales between 1982 and 1987. Again, the total figure is the figure for the sales of *all* firms. For example, the sales of Hispanic-owned firms increased by 110 percent during that period.

SOURCE: Adapted from *Wall Street Journal Reports* (1992), p. R4.

and Native Americans. Although there are fewer Asian-owned firms than either black- or Hispanic-owned firms, the Asian firms account for a higher percentage of total sales because the average Asian-owned firm experiences higher sales and is more likely to have at least one paid employee than its black and Hispanic counterparts.

Minority ownership rates have been increasing faster than those of whites. Between 1982, the year of the previous census of minority-owned firms, and 1987, the ownership rate of *all* firms (white and minority) grew by 14.2 percent. The ownership rate for Asians grew by 89.3 percent, six times faster than the growth rate for all firms. Hispanics were not far behind at 80.5 percent. The growth rates for business ownership among blacks (37.6 percent) and Native Americans (57.5 percent) were all larger than those for all businesses. Hence the race/ethnic ownership gap, though still large, declined somewhat.

Changes in the total sales of all firms and minority firms are more mixed. The sales of *all* firms grew by 106.2 percent between 1982 and 1987. Asian sales skyrocketed by 161.8 percent. Hispanic and black sales grew at a rate close to that of all businesses. Native American sales grew at a substantially lower rate. Aside from Asian firms, minority-owned businesses are not catching up to their white counterparts in sales.

The data from the 1987 survey show that with the exception of Asians, there is little hope that minorities will achieve a proportionate rate of business ownership or sales in the near future. At the current rate, for example, Hispanics would achieve parity in 125 years. Whites will continue to own a disproportionate share of all firms and, hence, will continue to dominate the economy.

These findings lead to an obvious question: Why is the non-Asian minority business community so weak? Most observers would agree that the history of discrimination against people of color, especially blacks, has made it more difficult for them to gain access to the capital and credit that are essential to beginning a business. We should also note the *current* discriminatory practices that hurt minority-owned businesses: banks refusing to extend credit, insurance companies charging high rates, white businesses and consumers preferring to patronize other whites.

Alternative explanations for the lack of further minority business development do not attribute it to discrimination. Some social scientists argue that minority *culture* fails to emphasize characteristics essential to success in business, such as discipline, hard work, planning for the future, and family stability. The reason that some Asian/Pacific groups do succeed, the argument continues, is that their culture emphasizes these characteristics.

There is also the issue of the *human capital* necessary for business success. The relatively low level of education and lack of previous business experience among blacks, Hispanics, and Native Americans make it difficult for them to be successful entrepreneurs. In addition, many minorities are said to have made the "wrong" choice in opening businesses in less-profitable nongrowth fields, such as personal services, rather than in the more profitable growth field of, say, computers. And, again, Asians are said to be more successful because they have more human capital. This argument can also be used to explain why, among Hispanics, Cubans are more successful than Mexicans and Puerto Ricans.

Many social scientists and policymakers would agree that a stronger minority business community is essential if minorities are to take their rightful places in pluralist America. A stronger minority business class, they argue, would result in more jobs and greater economic and political clout for minority communities. Successful businesspeople would also provide positive role models for minority youth.

In order to accomplish these goals, the argument continues, schools and colleges would have to do a better job developing the human capital in minority communities. Educators would have to be more rigorous in the teaching of both values and cognitive skills, and minority students would have to take the responsibility to apply themselves in school. All levels of government would have to provide counseling for minority entrepreneurs and programs intended to ensure that minorities get their fair share of government contracts and bank credit. Ironically, it was the conservative administration of former president Richard Nixon that took the initial steps in the federal government's attempt to promote "minority capitalism." Finally, white corporations would have to increase their purchases from and subcontracts to minority-owned businesses.

A few social scientists, mostly on the left, raise questions about the priority placed on minority capitalism. First, they argue, even if people of color achieved proportional representation in the world of business, the economy would still be dominated by large multinational corporations owned by a small group of wealthy whites. This powerful business class is reluctant to share its wealth and power with anyone, white or minority. Small businesses, regardless of the race of their owners, have trouble competing with giant corporations.

And, indeed, most minority businesses are relatively small. Only one black-owned corporation, TLC Beatrice International Holdings, is large enough to be listed in the Fortune 500. Whereas TLC Beatrice had 5,000 employees and sales of more than $1.5 billion in 1991, the second largest black-owned corporation had 2,710 employees and sales of only $261 million. Only two other black-owned corporations had sales in excess of $100 million (*Black Enterprise*, 1992).

In fact, the 100 largest black-owned industrial and service corporations, called the "Black Enterprise 100," had combined sales of $5 billion and a total of 32,590 employees. One single company, the Scott Paper Corporation, ranking 102 on the Fortune 500 (*Fortune*, 1992), had sales of $5 billion. Bristol-Myers Squibb, the fiftieth largest corporation in terms of employees, had 53,500 people on the payroll, almost 20,000 more than all the Black Enterprise 100 combined. The thirty-eight black-owned banks and savings and loans (S&Ls) had combined deposits of $1.8 billion in 1991. This total was less than that of the fiftieth largest bank in the country.

Given the reality of late twentieth-century capitalism, it is doubtful that many minority-owned companies will grow big enough to compete with the multinational corporations that dominate the economy. Hence the ability of minority-owned businesses to provide a significant number of jobs for their communities is limited. A small number of *individual* minority-group members will benefit from starting their own businesses, but the minority *community* will not.

Left-wing critics have also argued that politicians and the business class have tried (though not always successfully) to control the growth of minority businesses so as to meet their own needs. For instance, the Nixon administration hoped that minority businesspeople could help stem the growing urban rebellions of the late 1960s. And white corporations have used minority businesses as "middleman minorities" to help sell their products and services in minority communities.

Not surprisingly, minority business owners have often taken a conservative political stance, with negative effects on their communities (Marable, 1983; Ofari, 1970). They may, for example, protect their profits by opposing new taxes that could be used to fund important social programs. They may look to white business executives, who generally exhibit a limited sense of responsibility toward minority communities, as role models. Finally, they may oppose large-scale political mobilization of their communities, as it might hurt their short-term business interests.

Left-wing critics of the minority business strategy have suggested alternative development strategies. Not-for-profit ventures, the proceeds of which would help the entire community rather than individual stockholders, is one possibility. Worker-owned businesses and farms would be another. Of course, a dramatic expansion of government-funded programs to promote community development is still essential. Economic coalitions with other minority groups and with working-class whites are also important.

The three chapters in Part Five present different viewpoints on minority businesses. Timothy Bates ("Traditional and Emerging Lines of Black Business Enterprise") argues that the development of black businesses is good for the black community. Despite the discriminatory barriers faced by black businesses in the past, he is optimistic that newly emerging black businesses can grow and prosper. Pyong Gap Min ("Problems of Korean Immigrant Entrepreneurs") explains how Korean immigrants, despite their continuing dependency on white landlords and business executives, are able to successfully run small businesses. Finally, Earl Ofari Hutchinson ("Black Capitalism: Self-Help or Self-Delusion?") raises serious questions about the role of black businesses. He also demonstrates that even successful black businesses cannot replace either the political mobilization of the black community or the expansion of government programs to help the disadvantaged.

REFERENCES

Black Enterprise. 1992. "BE 100s: Overview." *Black Enterprise* 22, no. 1 (June):99–113.

Fortune. 1992. "The Fortune 500." *Fortune* 125, no. 8 (April 20):216–316.

Marable, Manning. 1983. *How Capitalism Underdeveloped Black America.* Boston: South End Press.

Ofari, Earl. 1970. *The Myth of Black Capitalism.* New York: Monthly Review Press.

O'Hare, William. 1992. "Reaching for the Dream." *American Demographics* (January):32–36.

Wall Street Journal Reports. 1992. "Black Entrepreneurship." *Wall Street Journal* (April 3): R1–R20.

22

Traditional and Emerging Lines of Black Business Enterprise

TIMOTHY BATES

Traditionally, the typical firm in the black business community has been the mom and pop food store, the beauty parlor, the barbershop. These tiny firms have been concentrated in black neighborhoods and have served local clienteles. Breaking into larger-scale lines of business has always been difficult for self-employed blacks due to barriers and constraints deeply rooted in American society. Although many of these constraints still linger, over the last few decades the black community has begun to enter the business mainstream.

Critics of minority business development programs have often assumed that black business startups would simply mirror, with all their limitations, the traditional fields of black entrepreneurship (Brimmer and Terrell, 1971; Markwalder, 1981). A recurring theme is the notion that black-owned businesses are heavily concentrated in several lines of small-scale service and retailing activity that hold minimal potential for growth. In fact, the lines of black enterprise that are growing today are not the small neighborhood establishments. Rather, they are the larger firms operating in industries where, historically, minority presence has been minimal. Many of the black entrepreneurs who run them have college degrees. Their mode of operation also sets them apart from traditional minority businesses—their mean annual sales volumes are far higher than sales among traditional firms, and they often have paid employees, serve as racially diverse clientele, and sell to other businesses, including large corporations and the government.

Because minority ownership within these growth industries has in the past been minimal, such lines of minority business are commonly (and throughout this chapter) referred to as "emerging" businesses. Emerging minority firms whose growth has been particularly rapid include the skill-intensive service industries: finance, business services, and various professional services. Even the construction industry, certainly not a new line of black enterprise, is nevertheless evolving into an emerging line of black business: growth in construction receipts has accrued to large-scale firms that do not rely primarily upon a minority clientele (Bates and Grown, 1992). The growth of this and other emerging lines of black business has been heavily aided by corporate and government minority set-aside programs.

Recent studies of small business dynamics indicate that all minority groups—Asians and Hispanics as well as blacks—tend to prosper in self-employment in direct proportion to the degree that they are moving away from traditional fields like personal services (Bates, 1989; Bates and Dunham, 1992). Traditional black firms tend to be small in scale, have high failure rates, and generate few jobs; this is because their owners tend to have low levels of education and skill and to invest little financial capital in their ventures. By contrast, emerging black firms, started by better-educated owners who invest more money in them than do traditional owners, are larger, fail less often, and generate more jobs.

The findings of Bates (1992) clearly show that hiring practices among white owners of small businesses continue to exclude minorities; black owners, in contrast, consistently hire minority workers. Even those white-owned small business employers whose firms are physically located in inner-city minority communities employ a work force that is predominantly white. Many of these employer firms operating in minority communities employ no minorities whatsoever. Black-owned firms operating in urban minority communities, in contrast, utilize a labor force made up overwhelmingly of minority workers; only 3.2 percent of these firms employ a work force that is 50 percent or more white (Bates, 1992). Black firms located outside of minority neighborhoods similarly rely upon minority workers; most white-owned businesses in these same areas have no minority employees.

In sum, success within today's black business community may be largely explained by the dual trends of traditional versus emerging firms. By increasing their investments of financial capital, education, and professional skill, black entrepreneurs over the past three decades have begun to move into emerging fields, where the chances for success are highest. In light of the aversion that nonminority small business owners have towards employing blacks, an alternative strategy for opening up job opportunities is to promote creation and expansion of the group—black employers—that has already demonstrated its commitment to minority hiring.

TRADITIONAL LINES OF BLACK ENTERPRISE
IN HISTORICAL PERSPECTIVE

A long-term perspective on the development of black enterprise is vital for understanding why the trends in the traditional and emerging sectors have moved in such different directions. From its origins, the black community has been shaped by limited access to credit, limited opportunities for education and training, and white stereotypes about the roles of minorities in society. In his landmark 1944 book, *An American Dilemma,* economist Gunner Mydral observed,

> The Negro businessman encounters greater difficulties than whites in securing credit. This is partially due to the marginal position of Negro business. It is also partly due to prejudicial opinions among whites concerning business ability and personal reliability of Negroes. In either case a vicious circle is in operation keeping Negro business down.

The role played by discrimination in shaping black business has been all-encompassing. Labor market discrimination has made it difficult for blacks to accumulate the minimal wealth required for initial investment in a new business. The dearth of black-owned construction companies in unionized urban areas was partially caused by the traditional practice of barring blacks from entering apprentice programs in the building trades.

Limited educational opportunities have, historically, handicapped black entrepreneurs in many lines of business. Until recently, even those who attended college were hemmed in by social attitudes about which occupations were appropriate for blacks. Between 1912 and 1938, 73 percent of black college graduates became either preachers or teachers (Holsey, 1938). A fortunate few were allowed into medicine, dentistry, and law, areas where they could serve an all-black clientele, but graduates were exceedingly rare in fields such as engineering, accounting, and general business. Such constraints produced a black business community consisting largely of very small firms concentrated in a few lines of business—beauty parlors, barber shops, restaurants, cleaning and pressing, shoe shine, mom and pop food stores.

More fundamentally, the traditional black business community was shaped by a specific time period—the 19th century—and a specific region: the South. The case of the skilled black artisan illustrates how profoundly discrimination has undermined and distorted the emergence of black entrepreneurship. At one time blacks dominated many of the South's skilled trades; as of the end of the Civil War, they accounted for an estimated 100,000 out of a total of 120,000 artisans in the Southern states (Kelsey, 1903). Rather than depending upon white labor, slavemasters typically relied upon their enslaved black workers who were trained in carpentry, blacksmithing, and other skilled trades. Mechanics working in bondage were often allowed to hire out on their own in return for a fixed sum of money or a percentage of their own earnings. Skilled white workers appealed to their government, demanding that blacks be restricted by law to menial jobs. The white workers' efforts largely failed, however, because the planter-dominated legislatures saw limitations on slave labor as a threat to the value of their property.

The circumstances of emancipation undermined the black artisan class. Their jobs no longer shielded by the slave-owners, these artisans now had to compete in a free, unprotected market while whites were protected by craft unions and Jim Crow institutions. South Carolina, for example, required after 1865 that blacks seeking work as artisans, mechanics, or shopkeepers purchase licenses—priced at 10 dollars annually—which whites were not required to buy (Ransom and Sutch, 1977). Meanwhile, the craft unions effectively diminished the ranks of black artisans through the union's system of apprenticeship. This last tactic was most effective in the heavily unionized Northern cities (Bates and Fusfeld, 1984).

Since white entrepreneurs avoided trades that connoted servility, in certain fields blacks had virtually no competition. Personal service occupations were freely open to those of them who could obtain enough capital. In the antebellum South, blacks had a near monopoly as cooks, as well as on barber shops, beauty parlors, and cleaning and pressing establishments (Bates, 1973). While low social status was in this sense an asset to most black entrepreneurs, it was a distinct handicap to the few who ventured into merchandising. By the mid-19th century, most Southern states had passed laws forbidding blacks from running firms in fields that required a knowledge of reading and writing, relegating them to occupations that society deemed appropriate with freed-slave status.

Little changed over the next century. In 1944, the first large-scale quantitative study of the black business community was undertaken. Joseph Pierce's survey of 3,866 black firms in 12 cities revealed an industry concentration reminiscent of the antebellum South (Pierce, 1947). Six lines of personal services and retailing dominated his sample of black firms; beauty parlors and barber shops, 1,055; eating places, 741; food stores, 293; cleaning and pressing, 288; shoe shine and repair, 183; funeral parlors, 126. When Pierce asked black businessmen to rank the most significant obstacles to entrepreneurship, they most frequently cited lack of capital.

Similar findings were arrived at by less comprehensive studies undertaken over the next 25 years: the black business community was consistently found to consist of small-scale operations concentrated in a few lines of activity that offered little potential for growth (Bates, 1973). As late as the 1960s, the most common lines of business mirrored the black business community before the Civil War.

EASING THE HISTORIC CONSTRAINTS

The barriers to black business progress described above—limited education, training, access to capital, and the rest—have eased substantially over the last 25 years. In the 1960s, government loans became widely available to actual and prospective black entrepreneurs (Bates and Bradford, 1979). The commercial banks' tradition of minimal contact between lending departments and black customers eroded as the government introduced new guarantees against default. These guarantees induced thousands of banks to extend business loans to minorities. At the same time, college enrollment among black students grew dramatically in the 1960s and 1970s, especially in business-related fields (Watkins, 1985).

While increased loan availability typified minority business promotion in the 1960s, corporate and government targeting of procurement dollars and "set-asides" for minority firms did not become a major force until the late 1970s. Since then, large consumer products corporations have routinely earmarked procurement dollars to minority firms, advertised in minority-owned publications, and deposited funds in minority-owned banks.

Local governments have been widely using minority set-asides and preferential procurement throughout the 1980s, a trend that reflects the growing political power of blacks (and Hispanics) in many central cities. Atlanta, Chicago, Los Angeles, Philadelphia, Detroit, New Orleans, Dallas, and Minneapolis are among the large cities that have shown major support for minority business development activities. Indeed, Bates and Williams (1993) document one important manifestation of this local political power: the performance of black business in cities with presiding black mayors turns out to be noticeably better than that in other cities.

One consequence of widened access to capital and education has been entry into previously unexplored new markets. While the traditional black business community was dominated by very small firms serving a ghetto clientele, the lure of market opportunity in recent years has induced entrepreneurs to create larger firms oriented toward corporate and government clienteles.

OWNER ARCHETYPES: SUCCESSFUL AND UNSUCCESSFUL

In the universe of all self-employed individuals, the incidence of college attendance has risen steadily through time. This increase in educational attainment has been even more rapid among blacks than among nonminorities: between 1970 and 1980, census data show, college attendance rose among self-employed blacks by 120 percent, versus a 91.7 percent increase for their nonminority cohorts. The entrepreneurial importance of education is underlined by the fact that whereas among all self-employed blacks only 28 percent had attended college, in the emerging minority field of finance, insurance and real estate, 66 percent attended college, the majority completing four-year degrees (Bates, 1987).

That advanced levels of education and professional skill are pivotal to black entrepreneurial growth has been confirmed by other studies as well. In explaining the rising number of black-owned firms between 1972 and 1977, Handy and Swinton (1984) found that for a given metropolitan area (SMSA) growth could be most accurately predicted by three closely interrelated variables: (1) growth in the available pool of black professional and managerial manpower; (2) the initial level of black professional and managerial manpower; (3) the general level of education among blacks living in the metropolitan area.

Building on what is known not only about educational attainment but about other traits and resources entrepreneurs enter business with, it is possible to sketch two composite portraits from the 1980s: one of the archetypal black business owner who succeeded, and one of the archetypal owner who failed.

The archetypal success: a college graduate, over age 35 but under 60, with an above average income, who enters business outside of such traditional areas as personal services, increasingly in such emerging fields as finance, insurance, and real estate. In terms of firm size (sales volume, total assets), the business is above average. Cash flow is strong relative to debt obligations. And the owner's initial investment of funds is relatively large; according to one recent study the size of this investment is the strongest predictor of success (Bates, 1989).

The archetypal failure: a low-income individual who has not graduated from high school and enters business in a small-scale retail operation or in a service line of business that is not skill intensive. Financial investment is low and the firm size is small. The firm is often unable to achieve a scale sufficient to provide the entrepreneur with a decent income. With or without a loan, discontinuance is likely.

Entrepreneurial success is highly correlated with both education and income levels: promising business operators tend to be above average in both categories. The question that invariably arises when government assistance accrues to higher income, well educated black entrepreneurs is—"Why help those who are already successful?" This objection can be addressed at two levels. First, programs that target assistance to lower income, less educated entrepreneurs simply produce mass business failure (Bates, 1983). Second, the capable entrepreneurs are the ones who are likely to achieve the economic development goal, provided, of course, that the other ingredients of business success (capital and markets) are present. It is the viable firms, after all, that permit further business expansion and job creation. The presence of business success stories lure younger, better educated blacks into self-employment, and this further promotes the economic development thrust of black entrepreneurship.

TRENDS IN INDUSTRY COMPOSITION: 1960–1980

Although black firms today remain most heavily overrepresented in personal services, the least profitable and least capital-intensive industry, the diversification that began in earnest during the 1960s has continued, bringing a gradual but pervasive change to the black business landscape. Areas of rapid growth have become concentrated in such nontraditional fields as wholesaling and business services.

Although diversification had been well under way by 1972, national statistics at that time portrayed a black business community whose industry base was still quite narrow. In that year 63.7 percent of all black firms as measured by the *1972 Survey of Minority-Owned Business Enterprises* (1975) were concentrated in eight industry groups:

1.	Personal services	34,693 firms
2.	Miscellaneous retail	16,005
3.	Special trade contractors	15,616
4.	Eating & drinking places	14,346
5.	Food stores	11,887
6.	Business services	10,472
7.	Trucking & warehousing	9,938
8.	Gas stations	6,597

This 1972 ranking was unpromising, since few of these dominant industry groups would be growth areas in the 1970s. Retailing and personal services exhibited little growth in sales, while several retail lines, particularly gas stations and food stores, actually shrank both in number of firms and in aggregate sales and employment. Indeed, overall employment among black-owned firms declined in four of those eight industry groups between 1972 and 1977: only in business services did employment during this period enjoy rapid growth. Looking at the scene 10 years later, we find that black firms were still most heavily overrepresented, relative to white-owned firms, in personal services, and most underrepresented in manufacturing. Table [22.1] shows how these disparate industry patterns in 1982 distinguished black-owned firms from firms owned by white males, which make up 72 percent of the small business universe and therefore represent

TABLE [22.1]   Industry Distribution by Race of Owners:
Nationwide Random Samples of Firms, 1982

Industry Group	Black Firms	White Male Firms
Agriculture, forestry, mining	2.1	5.4
Construction	6.7	13.0
Manufacturing	2.1	9.0
Transportation, communication	11.3	8.3
Wholesale	1.7	2.9
Retail	27.3	21.8
Finance, insurance, real estate (FIRE)	3.7	7.2
Business services	5.5	5.6
Professional services	15.9	14.4
Personal services	13.2	3.3
All other services	10.6	9.0
Total[a]	100.0	100.0
(N=)	4,524	7,341

[a]Firms that did not report their industry affiliation (5.9 percent of the white male sample and 7.0 percent of the black sample) are excluded from this table.

SOURCE: CBO survey data (unpublished), 1982

the "norm" for standard comparisons. (These distributions were generated from the Census Bureau's 1982 CBO survey, described in Bates, 1990.) It is worth noting that personal services, which is the least capital-intensive industry group, offers both black and white owners the lowest remuneration (Bates, 1987). Manufacturing, on the other hand, is the most capital-intensive, and has therefore been an area where self-employment has been difficult for blacks.

Fifty-six percent of the black firms sampled by the CBO reported 1982 annual sales below $25,000, as compared with 37.9 percent of white firms. Furthermore, 75.4 percent of these black firms had no paid employees. By contrast, white firms were more than three times as likely to be represented in the highest-sales category—$200,000 plus—as were black firms, only 4.8 percent of whom achieved that ranking.

In sum, despite nearly 20 years of convergence in industry concentration, blacks remain overrepresented in very-small-scale lines of business—in personal services and retailing—while white male firms are found disproportionately in the largest-scale and highest-earning lines (Bates, 1987).

THE SHIFT TOWARD SKILL-INTENSIVE FIRMS

It is not valid to generalize about the nature of black enterprise solely on the basis of cross-sectional data. Since cross-sectional industry figures focus on one point in time, they invariably highlight the laggard position of self-employed blacks, even though most personal service and small-scale retail firms owned by nonminorities are marginal operations too. The firms that typify much of the nation's small business sector are frequently struggling enterprises that bring their owners paltry returns; failure rates are quite high irrespective of the owners' race. More insight may be gained into the changing nature of the black entrepreneurial world by examining comparable data on black firms from *different* points in time.

Such a review shows that although marginal operations are undoubtedly numerous within the black entrepreneurial community, a clear trend has emerged toward more skill-intensive lines of business. In 1960, owners of personal services accounted for nearly 30 percent of self-employed minority entrepreneurs, while fewer than 10 percent ran skill-intensive enterprises such as those in professional services, business services, and finance, insurance, and real estate. By contrast, among the more recently established black-owned firms (in the CBO survey), namely those that began operations in the 1976–1982 period, only 10.3 percent were in personal services while 25 percent were in skill-intensive industries.

Even in certain broad industrial categories that are not generally labeled skill-intensive, such as construction, the distribution of sub-industries show that minority firms have changed markedly. While special trade contractors in areas such as painting and carpentry have decreased in incidence, minority-owned general contracting and heavy construction firms have substantially increased. The stagnation of retailing, including the steady decline of food stores, masks the fact that drug stores have been steadily expanding in incidence. These shifts reflect the movement toward more skill-intensive and capital-intensive lines of business within each of the broad industrial groupings (shown in Table [22.1]). The overall industry shift between 1960 and 1980 is telling. In 1960, two lines of business—personal services and retailing—accounted for well over half of all minority enterprises, while smaller concentrations were working in construction and "other services." Collectively, these four most common fields—personal services, retail, construction, and "other services"—accounted at that time for 81.3 percent of self-employed minorities. Nevertheless, over the next two decades, *all* of the growth—as measured by the proportions of minority entrepreneurs in various lines of business—took place *outside* these four lines of minority enterprise. The most rapid growth took place in four other fields which, collectively, more than doubled their relative share of the minority entrepreneur pool: business services; wholesale; transportation and communication; and finance, insurance, and real estate. Table [22.2] data are skewed somewhat by the behavior of Asian entrepreneurs, who clung much more tightly to retailing self-employment than blacks. Thus, the shift away from retailing among self-employed blacks is more pronounced that the Table [22.2] numbers suggest.

The shift toward skill-intensive industries is reflected in figures on owners' earnings and education. Census data from public use samples indicate that in 1960, minority entrepreneurs (under age 65) had, on average, 7.6 years of education and mean self-employment earnings of $1,812; their earnings lagged behind those of minorities who worked as employees. By 1980, minority entrepreneurs under age 65 reported 11.5 years of education and mean earnings (from all sources) that *exceeded* those of minority employees by a wide margin—specifically, $16,105 for male entrepreneurs versus $11,235 for male employees. (These

TABLE [22.2]   Time Trends in Self-Employment: Percent in Various Industry Groups[a] of All Minority Self-Employed, 1960 to 1980

	1960	2980	Percent Change Since 1960	Industry Growth Rate
Construction	16.7	16.5	−1.2	Stagnant
Manufacturing	4.1	6.0	46.3	Moderate
Transportation, communications, and utilities	3.9	6.0	53.8	Rapid
Wholesale	1.7	3.6	111.8	Rapid
Retail	25.4	25.4	0.0	Stagnant
Finance, insurance, and real estate	1.4	4.0	185.7	Rapid
Business services	2.4	6.6	175.0	Rapid
Repair services	5.2	6.9	32.7	Moderate
Personal services	28.9	14.7	−49.1	Declining
Other services	10.3	10.3	0.0	Stagnant
Total	100.0	100.0		

[a] Excludes agriculture, doctors, and lawyers.

SOURCE: Decennial Census of Population, public-use samples for 1960 and 1980.

findings emerged from earlier studies by the author based on 1960, 1970, and 1980 census data; see Bates, 1987 and 1988.) All of this suggests that the status of entrepreneurs within the black community as a whole has undergone profound changes.

Even within the skill-intensive industries, the specialties blacks have moved into have changed considerably. Thirty years ago, blacks were concentrated in the fields of medicine, law, and insurance. Today, common lines of business include these fields as well as consulting firms, ad agencies, engineering services, accounting, employment agencies, computer software, and so forth. These findings reflect the trends toward diversity that are vitally important for comprehending the trajectory of black entrepreneurship.

CONCLUSION

Critics of minority business development programs have often assumed that emerging firms would be replicas of such common traditional lines of business as personal service and small-scale retail firms. Evidence presented in this chapter largely refutes the notion that new and expanding black businesses conform to the stereotype of the tiny firms of the past. The growing lines of black enterprise today are dominated by larger-scale firms that are likely to serve a racially diverse clientele; increasingly, these enterprises sell to other businesses, including large corporations, and to units of government. Particularly rapid growth areas include wholesaling and skill-intensive service industries, particularly finance and busi-

ness services. The construction industry—certainly not a new line of black enterprise—is evolving into an emerging line of business; growth in construction has
been most rapid among the large-scale firms that do not rely primarily upon a
minority clientele.

Policies that successfully assist the more capable, viable black-owned businesses produce a derivative benefit—job creation—for minority communities.
Even when firms locate in nonminority areas, geographic separation has not sev-
ered the employment link between black job seekers and black-owned businesses.
In the vitally important sense, black enterprise promotes minority community
economic development.

REFERENCES

Bates, Timothy, *Black Capitalism: A Quantitative Analysis* (New York: Praeger, 1973).

Bates, Timothy, "Small Business Administration Loan Programs," in *Sources of Financing
for Small Business,* eds. Paul Horvitz and R. Richardson Pettit (Greenwich, Connecticut:
JAI Press, 1983).

Bates, Timothy, "Self-Employed Minorities: Traits and Trends," *Soeial Science Quarterly* 68
(1987).

Bates, Timothy, *An Analysis of the Earnings Levels of Self-Employed Minorities* (Los Angeles:
UCLA Center for Afro-American Studies, 1988).

Bates, Timothy, "Small Business Viability in the Urban Ghetto," *Journal of Regional Science*
29 (1989).

Bates, Timothy, "The Characteristics of Business Owners Data Base," *Journal of Human Resources* (1990).

Bates, Timothy, *Banking on Black Business* (Washington, D.C.: Joint Center for Political
and Economic Studies, 1992).

Bates, Timothy, and William Bradford, *Financing Black Economic Development* (New York:
Academic Press, 1979).

Bates, Timothy, and Constance Dunham, "Facilitating Upward Mobility Through Small
Business Ownership," in *Urban Labor Markets and Individual Opportunity,* eds. George
Peterson and Wayne Vroman (Washington, D.C.: Urban Institute, 1992).

Bates, Timothy, and Caren Grown, "Commercial Bank Lending Practices and the Development of Black-Owned Construction Companies," *Journal of Urban Affairs* (1992).

Bates, Timothy, and Daniel Fusfeld, *Political Economy of the Urban Ghetto* (Carbondale:
Southern Illinois University Press, 1984).

Bates, Timothy, and Darrell Williams, "Racial Politics: Does It Pay?" *Social Science Quarterly* (forthcoming).

Brimmer, Andrew, and Henry Terrell, "The Economic Potential of Black Capitalism," *Public Policy* 19 (1971).

Handy, John, and David Swinton, "The Determinants of the Rate of Growth of Black-
Owned Businesses," *Review of Black Political Economy* 12 (1984).

Holsey, Albion, "Seventy-Five Years of Negro Business," *The Crisis* 45 (1938).

Kelsey, Carl, "The Evolution of Negro Labor," *Annals of the American Academy of Political
and Social Science* 21 (1903).

Markwalder, Donald, "The Potential for Black Business," *Review of Black Political Economy*
12 (1983).

Mydral, Gunner, *The American Dilemma* (New York: Harper and Bros., 1944).

Pierce, Joseph, *Negro Business and Business Education* (New York: Harper and Bros., 1947).

Ransom, Richard, and Richard Sutch, *One Kind of Freedom* (New York: Cambridge University Press, 1977).

U.S. Bureau of the Census, *Survey of Minority-Owned Business Enterprises, 1972* (Washington, D.C.: U.S. Department of Commerce, 1975).

Watkins, Linda, "Minorities' Enrollment in College Retreats After Its Surge in '70s," *Wall Street Journal* (May 29, 1975).

23

Problems of Korean Immigrant Entrepreneurs

PYONG GAP MIN

Historically, immigrants have shown a higher self-employment rate than native born Americans (Light, 1979; Light and Sanchez, 1987; Newcomer, 1961). Some recent immigrant groups from Third World countries, like white immigrants at the turn of the century, concentrate in small business. One such recent immigrant group that shows an unusually high self-employment rate is the Korean. A recent study (Min, 1989) indicates that 53 percent of Korean male workers and 45 percent of all Korean workers in Los Angeles are self-employed. The 1980 census (1984:12) showed that Korean immigrants had the highest self-employment rate among 17 recent immigrant groups, although the census underestimated the self-employment rate (Light and Bonacich, 1988). ...

Korean entrepreneurs, like other immigrant entrepreneurs are successful in labor intensive small businesses mainly because they work long hours. Many Korean entrepreneurs have health and psychological problems caused by long hours of work. Moreover, the majority of Korean businesses seem to be located in crime-ridden, low income residential and downtown commercial areas where business operation involves the risk of physical danger. In addition, a significant proportion of Korean owned businesses are located in minority areas, distributing corporate products to minority customers. Because of this middleman minority role, Korean immigrant entrepreneurs have received a high level of hostility and rejection from minority customers.

The economic success of Korean immigrant entrepreneurship, no matter how significant it may be, should not prevent us from paying attention to these and other problems Korean entrepreneurs face. Yet, there seems to be no study that has examined in detail various problems any group of minority/immigrant entrepreneurs face. This article bridges the gap in research on ethnic/immigrant entrepreneurship by analyzing problems of Korean immigrant entrepreneurship. It focuses on Korean entrepreneurs' problems in seven major areas: 1) overwork, 2) physical danger, 3) rejection and hostility by minority clients, 4) exploitation by suppliers, 5) exploitation by landlords, 6) status inconsistency, and 7) a slowing of assimilation.

THE MIDDLEMAN MINORITY PERSPECTIVE

One theoretical perspective widely used to explain the phenomenon of an immigrant group's concentration in small business is the middleman minority. Various social scientists seem to define the middleman minority differently. However, an underlying assumption reflected in the middleman minority literature (Blalock, 1967; Bonacich, 1973, 1980; Bonacich and Jung, 1982; Cobas, 1987; Hamilton, 1978; Light, 1979; Portes and Manning, 1986; Rinder, 1959; Waldinger, 1989; Zenner, 1978, 1980, 1982) is that middleman minorities concentrate in trade, distributing merchandise produced by the dominant group to minority customers. Two major implications of this assumption, which are important for understanding problems of middleman minority groups, seem to be that middleman minorities are politically dependent upon the majority group serving its economic interests, and that they encounter hostilities and rejection from minority customers. Several researchers (Bonacich, 1980; Bonacich et al., 1976; Bonacich and Jung, 1982; I. Kim, 1981; Light and Bonacich, 1988; Portes and Manning, 1986; Waldinger, 1989) have indicated that Korean immigrant entrepreneurs in the United States take the role similar to the traditional middleman minority role. Bonacich (Bonacich, 1980; Bonacich and Jung, 1982; Light and Bonacich, 1988) in particular has related Korean immigrants' commercial activities to the middleman minority role in corporate capitalism. That is, in her view, recent Korean immigrants serve the interests of U.S. corporations by distributing corporate products to low income and minority areas.

As pointed out elsewhere (Min, 1988a), Korean entrepreneurs are not middlemen in the sense that either the U.S. government or U.S. corporations have encouraged Korean immigrants to enter small business. However, I believe that the middleman minority perspective is useful in understanding Korean immigrant entrepreneurship in the sense that Korean entrepreneurs serve a much larger proportion of low income, minority customers than the chance factor allows, and that much of the merchandise Korean merchants distribute to minority customers is produced by corporations. Korean entrepreneurs' problems have much to do with their dependence upon minority customers and non-Korean, white wholesalers and manufacturers. Thus, the middleman minority seems to be the most useful theoretical perspective in analyzing problems of Korean immigrant entrepreneurs.

DATA SOURCES

Three major data sources were utilized for this study. First, data were collected in the Los Angeles Korean community, Five hundred and fifty-seven Korean employed adult immigrants in Los Angeles and Orange counties were personally interviewed in the fall of 1986 to investigate the economic and other positive effects of Korean businesses on the Korean community (Min, 1989). ...

Second, ethnic newspapers and this investigator's personal observations of the Korean community were also important data sources, particularly for Korean entrepreneurs' conflicts with minority customers, white wholesalers and landlords.

Third, previous studies on Korean immigrants in general and Korean immigrant entrepreneurship in particular provide valuable insights and information. While a large number of previous studies substantiate the findings presented here, three books in particular (I. Kim, 1981; Light and Bonacich, 1988; Min, 1988a) have been most useful in this study.

OVERWORKING

The American mass media have depicted Korean immigrant businesses as very successful. If we define business success as becoming a millionaire, few Korean immigrants can be considered to be successful businessmen. However, the vast majority of Korean entrepreneurs are successful as depicted by the American mass media if we define business success as "survival and modest growth to the point where many people can make a decent living by American standards" (Bonacich et al., 1976). The Los Angeles survey (Min, 1989), for example, shows that 43 percent of Korean business owners reported that their annual income in 1986 would be $50,000 or more in comparison to only 20 percent of non-business respondents. Only 16.8 percent of U.S. households reached the income level of $50,000 in 1986. ...

Korean immigrants concentrate in labor intensive small businesses such as the grocery, laundry and fast food service (I. Kim, 1981; Kim and Hurh, 1985; Min, 1988a, 1989). One of the main reasons Korean immigrants are successful in these labor intensive small businesses is that they work extremely long hours. ...

Although long hours of work help Korean immigrants survive in labor intensive small businesses, it deprives them of leisure activities and, in many cases, causes health problems. ... In fact, many Koreans complain about the lack of sleep. Most Korean business owners stay in a little store most of the day, every day, which makes their work very tedious. The lack of recreation and leisure activities makes Korean business owners vulnerable to depression and other psychological problems. Kuo's study (1984) reveals that Koreans scored highest among four Asian groups on a depression scale. This high depression level may be due to their high self-employment in labor intensive small businesses, as well as to the language barrier.

PHYSICAL DANGER

In addition to the problem of overwork, many Korean entrepreneurs face the problem of physical danger when their business is located in low income, crime-ridden areas. ... Korean entrepreneurs operating businesses in minority areas take the middleman minority role, distributing corporate products to lower income minority members. This role makes Korean merchants vulnerable to crime, vandalism and other problems associated with lower income, minority areas. When asked what the major problems are in operating businesses in lower income, minority areas, the vast majority of Korean business owners in Atlanta indicated robberies and shoplifting (Min, 1988a). Many Korean stores become easy targets of robbery because they stay open 24 hours or until late at night.

REJECTION BY MINORITY CUSTOMERS

In addition to physical danger, Korean merchants in minority areas are subject to strikes, boycott and other forms of rejection by minority customers (I. Kim, 1981; Light and Bonacich, 1988; Min, 1988b). The boycott of Korean merchants by New York Harlem residents in 1984–1985 typifies the interracial conflicts between Korean ghetto merchants and black customers (*Choong Ang Daily of New York,* February 16, 1985; W. Kim, 1986). The boycott started after a black customer, who had an argument with a Korean store owner, was arrested by the police. The boycott, which spread to the entire Harlem area, lasted six months until the F.B.I. intervened. Korean merchants have been targets of editorial attacks by black newspapers in New York, Los Angeles, Baltimore and Philadelphia (*Amsterdam News,* September 17, 1988; *Creed,* 1989; *Good News,* February 8, 1978; *The Tribune,* July 12, 16, 27, 1977). ...

Another large-scale boycott movement against Korean merchants [occurred] in a Brooklyn black area. The boycott started in July, 1988 after a scuffle between a Korean grocery owner and a black woman customer who allegedly tried to steal merchandise (*The Korean Central Daily,* August 31, 1988; *The Sae Gae Times,* September 9, October 6, November 3, 1988). At first, black residents asked the Korean store owner to apologize for beating the customer. Later, the leaders of the December 12th Movement, a radical black nationalist organization, took advantage of the situation for a massive movement against Korean ghetto merchants. They asked for a return of the Korean owned store to the black community and organized a boycott of all Korean owned stores located in the Fulton Street area of Brooklyn. Black boycott and Korean community leaders have met several times to resolve the interracial conflict, but have been unable to reach a reasonable compromise. ...

DEPENDENCE UPON WHITE SUPPLIERS

Whereas Korean entrepreneurs serve a proportionally larger number of black and other minority members as customers, they depend upon white suppliers for merchandise (I. Kim, 1981; Min, 1988b). While this dependence does not involve physical danger or boycott, it involves some (while not systematic) exploitation of, and discrimination against, Koreans by outgroup members. Korean business owners who sell Korean imported merchandise such as wigs, handbags, jewelry and toys depend upon co-ethnic suppliers. They receive preferential treatment from co-ethnic suppliers in prices, item selections, the speed of delivery and other aspects of transaction (I. Kim, 1981; Min, 1984a). However, Koreans in other business specialty areas such as the grocery/liquor, the green grocery, the fish retail, and the dry cleaning service largely depend upon white suppliers (Kim and Hurh, 1985; Min, 1988a). They may experience discrimination from white suppliers in terms of the quality of merchandise, price, speed of delivery and parking allocations. I. Kim (1981:118–119) wrote about discrimination Korean produce retailers in New York received from wholesalers at the Hunts Market. A white fish wholesaler's discrimination against Korean fish retailers in price and quality of merchandise led to a massive demonstration by Koreans in New York (*Sae Gae Times,* July 16, November 16, 1988).

Many Korean grocers very often buy soft drinks and other grocery items from white owned chain grocery stores at prices lower than those some big corporations charge to Korean owned stores. Bonacich (Bonacich, 1979a, 1979b; Bonacich et al., 1976; Light and Bonacich, 1988) argues that Korean small businesses mainly serve the interests of big U.S. corporations, and her argument seems to have some dimension of truth. Many Korean entrepreneurs claim that they have difficulty starting less labor intensive and more lucrative businesses such as houseware retail stores because white suppliers discourage them from moving into new areas.

DEPENDENCE UPON LANDLORDS

Korean entrepreneurs can generally change suppliers if they do not like their prices and/or services, although it is not always possible. However, Korean entrepreneurs cannot change landlords as easily as they change suppliers. Thus, the dependence upon landlords has the potential to involve a higher level of exploitation. Many Korean immigrants buy a failing business or open a new one and then turn it into a thriving business within a few years (Min, 1988a). As Korean owned businesses become more successful, some landlords raise rents by a significant margin over a short period. Korean immigrants' strong competition to acquire business premises is partly responsible for this rent hike. It is not uncommon that when a Korean immigrant leases a building for business operation, another Korean offers a higher rent to the landlord. This escalating rent problem is most serious in New York. A large number of Korean immigrants operate general merchandise stores, produce retail shops and restaurants along Broadway in Manhattan. ... Korean business owners generally agree that "the money earned by our hard work goes more to white landlords than to ourselves." They also agree that Korean immigrants greatly contributed to the development of the Broadway area as an active commercial area, but that it is landlords who most benefit from the development (*Sae Gae Times,* July 8, 1988). The point here is not that landlords discriminate particularly against Korean merchants, but that Koreans' dependence upon landlords is a great structural barrier to their entrepreneurial activities. ...

STATUS INCONSISTENCY

The vast majority of Korean immigrants held white collar and professional occupations in Korea (Hurh and Kim, 1984:58; Min, 1984b; I. Kim, 1981; Yu, 1983). However, most of these immigrants cannot find similar occupations in the United States. Instead, they find low paying, menial jobs in the so-called secondary sector. Korean immigrants turn to self-employment in small business as an alternative to a dead-end, blue collar job (Min, 1984b). Self-employment in a small business gives Korean immigrants two major advantages over employment in the American labor market (Min, 1984b). First, self-employment helps them to

TABLE [23.1]   Comparison of Three Groups in Occupational Status

Occupational Status	Number of Cases	Mean	SD	Significance at the 0.05 Level
Pre-Immigrant Occupation				
(1) Self-Employed Professionals	21	70.71	15.32	(1) and (2) = Yes
(2) Entrepreneurs	155	50.74	16.16	(2) and (3) = No
(3) Employees	189	52.22	17.56	(1) and (3) = Yes
Total	365	52.66	17.41	
First Occupation in the U.S.				
(1) Self-Employed Professionals	31	46.42	33.23	(1) and (2) = Yes
(2) Entrepreneurs	202	28.34	14.42	(2) and (3) = No
(3) Employees	308	26.80	16.76	(1) and (3) = Yes
Total	541	28.50	17.84	
Current Occupation				
(1) Self-Employed Professional	32	69.46	20.10	(1) and (2) = Yes
(2) Entrepreneurs	207	38.74	11.22	(2) and (3) = No
(3) Employees	314	35.61	17.67	(1) and (3) = Yes
Total	553	38.75	17.53	

Note: Duncan's Occupational Socioeconomic Index updated for application to the 1980 census occupational classification by Stevens and Cho, 1985.

achieve economic mobility faster. Second, it gives Korean immigrants a sense of autonomy which may not be found in employment in the general labor market.

In spite of these two advantages, small business proprietorship does not help Korean immigrants to solve one major problem—the problem of status inconsistency. Status inconsistency refers to the situation in which any two of the three major status dimensions—education, occupation and income—are unbalanced (Lenski, 1954; Geschwender, 1968). Most Korean immigrants face three kinds of status inconsistency, one between education and income, another between education and the post-immigrant occupation and the third between pre-immigrant and post-immigrant occupations (Hurh et al., 1979:46, 47; Min, 1984b, 1988a).

Many Korean immigrants achieve economic mobility through self-employment and thus solve the problem of the education-income imbalance. However, since most Korean entrepreneurs are engaged in labor intensive, blue collar businesses, entry into business does not significantly enhance their social status (Min, 1984b, 1988a). Thus, most Korean entrepreneurs suffer from the other two kinds of status inconsistency. Immigrants seem to evaluate their occupational status by comparing it to the pre-immigrant occupational status. The discrepancy between pre-immigrant and current occupations may therefore be more important for understanding Korean immigrants' subjective definition of status inconsistency than that between education and the current occupation. Table [23.1] presents Los Angeles Korean immigrants' occupational status by the type of employment for 1) the major occupation in Korea, 2) the first occupation in the United States and 3) the current occupation. Occupational status is measured using Duncan's Occupational Socioeconomic Index, updated for application to the 1980 census occupational classification by Stevens and Cho (1985). As expected, the immigration of Koreans to the United States led to significant downward mobility. The average pre-immigrant occupational status for the total sample was 52.7, but it dropped to 28.5 with immigration. All three groups—self-employed professionals, entrepreneurs and employees—underwent similarly high levels of downward mobility with immigration.

The third part of Table [23.1] indicates occupational status at the time of the interview. The average occupational prestige score rose to 38.8 over the seven year period (the average length of residence). Although the respondents improved their occupational levels by approximately 10, their current occupational levels are far below the levels of occupations they held in Korea. Self-employed professionals enjoy occupational levels close to pre-immigrant occupational levels. But the other two groups experience high levels of status inconsistency between pre-immigrant and post-immigrant occupations. Although Korean entrepreneurs on the average have a higher occupational level than employed Koreans, the difference is not statistically significant. Thus, Korean immigrants cannot enhance their social status through self-employment in small businesses, although they achieve economic mobility. ...

A SLOWING OF ASSIMILATION

A number of studies have shown that ethnic business enhances ethnic solidarity (Bonacich 1973, 1975; Bonacich and Modell, 1980; Chan and Cheung, 1982; Gold, 1987; Light, 1984; Reitz, 1980; Sengstock, 1974; Zenner, 1982). It has also been shown how Korean immigrants' concentration in small businesses buttresses their ethnic attachment and group solidarity (Min, 1988b). However, strong ethnic attachment very often hinders assimilation, although the two are not necessarily mutually exclusive (Hurh and Kim: 1984:Chapter 4). Thus, Korean immigrants' concentration in small business, while helpful to the development of ethnicity, has a negative influence on assimilation.

Korean entrepreneurs are slower in assimilation than Korean workers employed in the general labor market because the operation of blue collar businesses does not require a high level of English. Although the majority of Korean entrepreneurs serve American customers, their style of service does not involve much spoken interaction, but rather is limited to basic conversations and names of merchandise items. Korean business owners depend mainly upon family members and other Korean immigrants for the operation of their businesses. Both entrepreneurs and employees have social interactions with fellow Koreans during most work hours, speaking the Korean language. ... Less than half of the Los Angeles Korean entrepreneurs always speak English at work, in comparison to 75 percent of Korean workers in the American labor market. Although Korean entrepreneurs speak English at work more frequently than Korean workers employed in Korean firms, they use it much less frequently than those employed in American firms.

Moreover, Korean entrepreneurs extend frequent social interactions with fellow Koreans to off-duty hours, thus limiting their social interactions with Americans. ... As expected, Korean entrepreneurs meet Americans for dinner or a picnic more frequently than Koreans employed in ethnic firms, but less frequently than those employed in American firms. Among self-employed Koreans, professionals maintain more frequent social interactions with Americans than nonprofessional proprietors. ...

Less frequent social interactions with Americans at the formal (work) and informal bases suggest that Korean immigrant entrepreneurs are slower to culturally assimilate than Koreans employed in non-Korean firms. The frequency of speaking English at home is probably the most accurate indicator of cultural assimilation. ... A larger proportion of Korean workers employed in American firms than either those self-employed or those employed in Korean firms reported that they always speak English at home.

Koreans in the ethnic market, either as business owners or as employees, are structurally disadvantaged in assimilation, and the vast majority of Korean immigrant workers (75% in the case of the Los Angeles Korean community) are in the ethnic subeconomy. Since a higher proportion of Korean immigrant workers are segregated in the ethnic subeconomy than other Asian immigrant groups, Korean immigrants as a group are likely to be slower than other Asian immigrant groups to assimilate into American society.

SUMMARY

This study, using the middleman minority perspective, has analyzed major problems of Korean immigrant entrepreneurs. To summarize the foregoing analysis, overwork is a major problem most Korean immigrant proprietors face. Korean entrepreneurs' extremely long hours of work do not allow them time for leisure activities and recreations, which has detrimental effects on their health. Many Korean small business owners have achieved economic mobility through self-employment in small business only to have their health deteriorate.

A significant proportion of Korean businesses are located in low income, inner city, minority and transitional areas where robberies, shoplifting and other crimes are more frequent. A number of Korean ghetto merchants have been victims of murder or injury during armed robberies. Thus, physical danger should be considered to be one of the major problems Korean immigrant entrepreneurs face.

A larger proportion of Korean businesses than the chance factor allows are located in low income, minority areas, and the location of Korean owned businesses in minority areas has led to interracial conflict with minority customers, especially with black customers. Korean entrepreneurs in New York and other major Korean centers have encountered strikes, boycotts and other forms of rejection by black customers.

Korean entrepreneurs are vulnerable to exploitation because they are dependent upon outgroup members for supplies of merchandise and on landlords for leasing store buildings. They may experience discrimination from white suppliers in prices, item selection, speed of delivery and parking allocations. However, Korean merchants' dependence upon landlords may involve a higher level of exploitation in that as their businesses become more successful, some landlords have raised rents by a significant margin within a short period. Thus, dependence upon landlords is another structural barrier to Korean immigrant entrepreneurship.

Korean immigrants are engaged in low level, blue collar businesses, and thus Korean entrepreneurs face the problem of status inconsistency. Although most Korean entrepreneurs enjoy a higher standard of living in the United States than in Korea, they generally experience downward occupational mobility. Almost all Korean adult immigrants face downward mobility, but Korean immigrant entrepreneurs are more preoccupied with the status problem probably because they are relieved from economic pressure.

Finally, Korean immigrant entrepreneurs are slower to assimilate into American society than those Korean workers in the general labor market. Korean business owners, depending largely upon family members and other co-ethnic employees for business operation, generally speak the Korean language and maintain Korean customs in the store. They also maintain more frequent social interactions with fellow Koreans even during off-duty hours, reducing their social interactions with Americans. Thus, self-employment, although effective for achieving economic mobility and maintaining ethnic ties, has a negative influence on cultural and social assimilation.

REFERENCES

Blalock, H. M. 1967. *Toward a Theory of Minority Group Relations*. New York: John Wiley,

Bonacich, E. 1980. "Middleman Minorities and Advanced Capitalism," *Ethnic Groups*, 2:211–219.

———. 1979a. "The Present, Past, and Future of Split Labor Market Theory," *Research in Race and Ethnic Relations*, 1:16–64.

———. 1979b. "U.S. Capitalism and Korean Immigrant Small Business: A Study in the Relationship between Class and Ethnicity." Unpublished Manuscript. Department of Sociology, University of California, Riverside.

———. 1975. "Small Business and Japanese/American Ethnic Solidarity," *Amerasia Journal*, 3:96–112.

———. 1973. "A Theory of Middleman Minorities," *American Sociological Review*, 37:547–559.

Bonacich, E., and T. H. Jung. 1982. "A Portrait of Korean Small Business in Los Angeles: 1977." In *Koreans in Los Angeles*. Edited by E.Y. Yu, E. Phillips and E.S. Yang. Los Angeles: Center for Korean-American and Korean Studies, California State University. Pp. 75–98.

Bonacich, E., I. Light, and C. C. Wong. 1976. "Small Business among Koreans in Los Angeles." In *Counterpoint: Perspective on Asian Americans*. Edited by E. Gee. Los Angeles: University of California Press. Pp. 437–449.

Bonacich, E., and J. Modell. 1980. *The Economic Basis of Ethnic Solidarity: Small Business in the Japanese American Community*. Berkeley: University of California Press.

Chan, J., and Y. W. Cheung. 1982. "Ethnic Resources and Business Enterprise: A Study of Chinese Businesses in Toronto." Paper Presented at the Annual Meeting of the American Sociological Association, San Francisco.

Cobas, J. A. 1987. "Ethnic Enclaves and Middleman Minorities: Alternative Strategies of Immigrant Adaptation," *Sociological Perspectives*, 30:143–161.

Geschwender, J. 1968."Status Inconsistency and Individual Unrest," *Social Forces*, 46:477–483.

Gold, S. 1988. "Patterns of Interaction and Adjustment among Soviet Refugees," *Contemporary Jewry*, 9:87–103.

Hamilton, G. 1978. "Pariah Capitalism: Paradox of Power and Dependence," *Ethnic Groups*, 1:1–15.

Hurh, W. M., and K. C. Kim. 1984. *Korean Immigrants in America: A Structural Analysis of Ethnic Confinement and Adhesive Adaptation*. Madison: Fairleigh Dickinsen University Press.

Hurh, W. M., K. C. Kim and H.C. Kim. 1979. *Assimilation Patterns of Immigrants in the U.S.: A Case Study of Korean Immigrants in the Chicago Area*. Washington, DC: University Press of America.

Kim,W.D. 1986. "Korean Merchants and Blacks." In *The Korean Community in America*. Edited by I. Kim, C. Kim and D. S. Ha. New York: The Korean Association of New York. Pp. 226–230.

Kim, I. 1981. *New Urban Immigrants: The Korean Community in New York*. Princeton: Princeton University Press.

Kim, K. C., and W. M. Hurh. 1985. "Ethnic Resources Utilization of Korean Immigrant Entrepreneurs in the Chicago Minority Area," *International Migration Review*, 19:82–111. Spring.

Kuo, W. H. 1984. "Prevalence of Depression among Asian-Americans," *The Journal of Nervous and Mental Disease*, 172.

Lenski, G. 1954. "Status Crystallization: A Non-Vertical Dimension of Social Process," *American Sociological Review*, 19:405–413.

Light, I. 1984. "Immigrant and Ethnic Enterprise in North America," *Ethnic and Racial Studies*, 7:195–216.

———. 1980. "Asian Enterprise in America: Chinese, Japanese, and Koreans in Small Business," In *Self-Help in Urban America: Patterns of Minority Business Enterprise*. Edited by S. Cummings. New York: Kenikart Press. Pp. 33–57.

———. 1979. "Disadvantaged Minorities in Self-Employment," *International Journal of Comparative Sociology*, 20:31–45.

———. 1972. *Ethnic Enterprise in America: Business and Welfare among Chinese, Japanese, and Blacks*. Berkeley: University of California Press.

Light, I., and E. Bonacich. 1988. *Immigrant Entrepreneurs: Koreans in Los Angeles, 1965–1982*. Berkeley: University of California Press.

Light, I., and A. Sanchez. 1987. "Immigrant Entrepreneurs in 272 SMSAs," *Sociological Perspectives*, 30:467–486.

Min, P. G. 1989. "Some Positive Functions of Ethnic Business for an Immigrant Community: Korean Immigrants in Los Angeles." Final Report Submitted to the National Science Foundation.

———. 1988a. *Minority Business Enterprise: Korean Small Business in Atlanta*. Staten Island, NY: The Center for Migration Studies.

———. 1988b."Korean Immigrant Entrepreneurship; A Multivariate Analysis," *Journal of Urban Affairs*, 10:197–212.

———. 1984a. "A Structural Analysis of Korean Business in the United States," *Ethnic Groups*, 6:1–25.

———. 1984b. "From White-Collar Occupations to Small Business: Korean Immigrants' Occupational Adjustment," *The Sociological Quarterly*, 25:333–352.

Min, P. G., and C. Jaret. 1985. "Ethnic Business Success: The Case of Korean Small Business in Atlanta," *Sociology and Social Research*, 69:412–435.

Model, S. 1985. "Comparative Perspectives in the Ethnic Enclave: Blacks, Italians, and Jews in New York City," *International Migration Review,* 19:64–81. Spring.

Newcomer, M. 1961. "The Little Businessman: A Business Proprietor in Poughkeepsie, N.Y.," *Business History Review,* 35:477–531.

Portes, A., and R. Manning. 1986. "The Immigrant Enclaves: Theory and Empirical Examples." In *Competitive Ethnic Relations.* Edited by J. Nagel and S. Olzak. New York: Academic Press.

Reitz, J. 1980. *The Survival of Ethnic Groups.* Toronto: McGraw-Hill.

Rinder, I. D. 1959. "Strangers in the Land: Social Relations in the Status Gap," *Social Problems,* 8:253–261.

Sengstock, M. 1974. "Iraqi Christians in Detroit: An Analysis of an Ethnic Occupation." In *Arabic-Speaking Communities in American Cities.* Edited by B. Aswad. Staten Island, NY: Center for Migration Studies.

U.S. Bureau of the Census. 1984. *1980 Census of Population, Vol. 1.: Characteristics of Population.* Chapter D: "Detailed Population Characteristics," Part 1: "United States Summary."

Waldinger, R. 1989. "Structural Opportunity or Ethnic Advantage? Immigrant Business Development in New York," *International Migration Review,* 23(1):48–72. Spring.

Zenner, W. 1982. "Arabic-Speaking Immigrants in North America as Middleman Minorities," *Ethnic and Racial Studies,* 5:457–477.

———. 1980. "Theory of Middleman Minorities: A Critical Review." In *Sourcebook on the New Immigration.* Edited by S. Bryce-Laporte. New Brunswick, NJ: Transaction Books. Pp. 419–425.

24

Black Capitalism: Self-Help or Self-Delusion?

EARL OFARI HUTCHINSON

Nearly a century ago Booker T. Washington argued that political rights and social legislation should take a back seat to building black wealth and economic self-sufficiency. Washington's backers, mainly black businesspeople, farmers, ministers, and Republican politicians, agreed with his view that "brains, property and character for the Negro will solve the question of civil rights." Washington founded the National Negro Business League in 1900 with the express goal of organizing support for a business-oriented approach to black advancement.

Militant black leaders led by the NAACP's W.E.B. DuBois roundly condemned Washington's philosophy. His critics—largely upwardly mobile, Northern, college-educated professionals—believed that his approach amounted to little more than a shameful accommodation to segregation and exploitation. DuBois put it bluntly: "Washington's program practically accepts the alleged inferiority of the Negro races."[1]

As the NAACP grew in strength and the civil rights movement gathered steam during the 1960s, Washington's program was discredited as outdated and reactionary. During the 1960s, Washington's name became an epithet that young black militants flung at anyone they considered an "Uncle Tom."[2]

But times have changed, and the pendulum has swung back. At the NAACP's national conference in 1988, executive director Benjamin Hooks gave the first hint that the political winds had shifted. Hooks noted, "We know that black America must do much of the work itself for it is our future we must save." Since then, the NAACP has consistently sounded the theme of self-help and "economic empowerment" at its conferences. Dozens of local and national black organizations have followed the NAACP's lead and made black business development and economic self-help the centerpiece of the black agenda.[3]

There are three reasons why. First, during the Reagan era, massive cuts in job programs and social services, coupled with the assault on affirmative action and civil rights, left black leaders frustrated and dismayed with government. The conviction grew among black leaders that government had become an enemy rather than an ally of the black poor.

A second reason is the spectacular growth of the black middle class since 1980. According to Census Bureau figures, by 1987, 40 percent of black high school graduates were attending college, 64 percent of blacks owned homes, and 27 percent of black families were earning more than $25,000 yearly.[4]

The middle-class advance has also brought a sharp rise in black purchasing power. Black leaders estimate that black consumers spend an estimated $150 billion dollars yearly on goods and services—dollars that can be "recycled" into thriving businesses and community programs that can provide jobs and social services for the black poor. Black economic strength, black leaders say, will ultimately translate into greater political power for blacks in general.[5]

Third, black leaders point to the phenomenal economic success of Korean, Chinese, Vietnamese, and Cuban immigrants. These groups have prospered in business, finance, real estate, manufacturing, and retail trade. They have built powerful business and trade associations that provide capital, credit, and technical training for their members. Equally important, their political influence—particularly in Miami, New York, Los Angeles, and San Francisco—has grown along with their economic clout.[6]

At first glance, these are powerful reasons for which economic self-help appears to be a vibrant and attractive goal. But let's probe deeper. Asian and Hispanic immigrants did not start at the bottom. A study of Korean small businesses in Atlanta in 1984 found that 79 percent were able to secure loans or credit from banks. Many of the merchants had operated successful businesses in Korea, were highly trained in management and retailing, and had strong family and business ties.

These immigrants got an added boost from the Korean government when it permitted them to take up to $100,000 from the country to start new businesses. The immigrants also made skillful use of the "kye" system, which operates as a kind of rotating credit association in which Korean entrepreneurs receive loans, subsidies, business training, and investment information.[7]

The pattern was repeated with the first wave of Vietnamese immigrants who came to America immediately after the fall to the Communists of the U.S.-backed South Vietnamese government in 1974. Many held college degrees and had either owned businesses or were employed in the professions or skilled trades in South Vietnam. In addition, the federal government poured millions into a comprehensive and costly resettlement program for these refugees of the "Communist terror."[8]

Far from being a model of "bootstrap" uplift, the Cuban refugees who fled Castro in the early 1960s also benefited from the largesse of the American government. They received substantial sums for resettlement, welfare and income subsidies, as well as business loans and grants. Like the Vietnamese, many of the Cubans were college educated and had been technicians, managers, and business or land owners in Cuba.[9]

How important to their business success was the political and economic help the immigrants received? One has only to compare the figures for economic growth among African Americans, Latinos, and Asians. In 1987, black firms averaged $46,592 in sales. The average of Asian-American companies was $93,221. And the $2.4 billion in total assets of Republic National and Capital, the two largest

Cuban-owned banks in Miami, exceeded the combined assets of all thirty-six black-owned banks in America.

Even if blacks have not enjoyed the instant entrée into business and government that immigrants have experienced, black self-help advocates argue that they can still fashion into a formidable power base the billions of consumer dollars spent by blacks. The problem, however, is that black consumer dollars are just that—consumer dollars, not investment dollars.

And despite the increased numbers of blacks in managerial, technical, and professional positions in corporations, more than 70 percent of the nearly 12 million black workers in America are still concentrated in clerical, service, and trade jobs. A sizable portion of blacks are employed as unskilled laborers. The median income for blacks of $19,758 is slightly more than half that for whites and Asians, and considerably less than the income of Latino households ($24,156).

With respect to net wealth, the gap between blacks and whites is even more glaring. The average for white households is $39,135; for blacks, $3,397. Moreover, African Americans own less than 1 percent of the nation's stock holdings.[10]

The Reagan budget cuts pushed even more blacks into the ranks of the unemployed. By 1987, more than 30 percent of blacks fell below the poverty line. Lacking competitive technical and labor skills, the black underclass became even more marginalized and unemployable. Welfare, minimum-wage labor, and crime became their only means of survival.

The growing poverty and disparity in wealth means that blacks have very little discretionary income or savings. They spend their paychecks almost exclusively on basic household goods and services. The major corporations exercise near-monopoly domination over this consumer market, controlling production, supply, and transport of all basic food and household items.

This is no accident. The economic infrastructure of African American communities historically has never been designed for capital retention or inflow. The iron-clad control of domestic markets by major corporations is akin to a kind of domestic colonialism. Black consumers buy goods from white producers, for whom black workers serve as a low-wage pool of labor. This near-permanent "capital flight" from black communities virtually ensures that black business will stay at the outer fringes of the corporate economy.[11]

A look at the economy of the ghetto today shows little change in the traditional business patterns. The small mom and pop stores, catering businesses, beauty and barber shops, video and record shops, service enterprises, and small grocery stores still make up the bulk of old or start-up businesses in African American communities. Largely sole proprietorships capable of providing employment only to the owner or family members, they are plagued by the problems of small business—higher prices, limited stocks, and a narrow consumer base. More than 80 percent fail within two years.

The expansion in the mid-1980s by black entrepreneurs into petroleum and energy, manufacturing, automotive sales, investment, equity trading, and communications did not provide large-scale employment for blacks. Indeed, these largely finance and capital-intensive industries tend to create few jobs. The top 100 black industrial and service companies that constituted the 1991 Black Enterprise 100, for instance, provided employment for only 32,590 blacks—less than 1 percent of the general black work force.[12]

The top black firms are subject to the same market fluctuations as white corporations. If inflation-conscious consumers buy fewer cars, new clothes, radios, or tapes, auto dealers, clothing manufacturers, and electronic assembly firms are hurt—no matter what the color of the owner.

Black savings and loans (S&Ls) and auto dealers are a good case in point. They directly felt the shock waves from the S&L shakeout. In 1989, twelve out of the thirty-three black S&Ls could not meet the minimum tangible capital requirements established by government regulators. Seven were declared insolvent and placed under direct government supervision.

Since June 1990, more than 20 percent of all minority auto dealers have failed. To halt this slide, the Minority Automobile Dealers Association demanded that the government provide more low-interest loans, training programs, and greater access to foreign car sales.[13]

Although some black firms have prospered, most prospective black entrepreneurs still find the door shut when they seek credit and capital from lending agencies or managerial and technical training from corporations. The result is that black capitalism is still largely a myth. The $5 billion in sales by the Black Enterprise 100 in 1991 pales beside the $2.2 trillion in sales racked up by Fortune 500 companies during the same year.[14]

Overall, the gross revenues for black business hover at about 3 percent of the corporate total. The relative strength of black business vis-à-vis the American economy did not change even during the mid-1980s, the so-called go-go years for black business growth.

The immediate prospects for change are hardly much better. The high cost of oil and raw materials, continuing strong market competition from Western Europe and Japan, inflationary pressures, corporate mergers, and leveraged buyouts have sent American business into a deep tailspin. And it can get worse. A Department of Commerce report notes that if the present economic trends continue, by the year 2000 Japanese and European firms could surpass U.S. companies in all areas of advanced research and technologies. This outcome would launch another round of belt-tightening by the major corporations, rendering them even less able or willing to assist minority business.

Given the problems of national economic decline and the continuing impoverishment of African Americans, black leaders will have to do some deep soul-searching and ask themselves, What are the limits of race loyalty? They expect black consumers to loyally support black businesses because they are black, too. Yet they do not say what black businesses are willing to give in return. Indeed, they have presented no visible blueprint that shows how the black dollars in their hands will be used to provide tangible economic and social benefits.[15]

Black leaders constantly point to the example of the Jews. They say that Jews support Jews and that's why they have advanced. But the Jewish experience is totally different from that of African Americans. Jewish consumers know that many Jewish merchants have a deeply ingrained sense of responsibility and duty to their communities.

This economic bonding is the product of centuries of religious and social persecution suffered in the ghettos of Russia and Eastern Europe. Jewish consumers
expect that a portion of the dollars they spend in transactions with Jewish merchants will be "recycled" into a wide array of social, cultural, and educational programs and services that benefit Jewish communities. If anything, this is the lesson
that African Americans must learn in the context of ethnic success.[16]

But in the bigger context of changing American capitalism and the global
economy, if black businesses are to have any prospect of becoming competitive,
they must adopt the following strategies:

- Pool capital into a development fund to provide loans, credit, resources,
  training, and a contact network for new business development.
- Become more efficient and continue to diversify. Black firms must concentrate more capital in research and development to upgrade products and
  services. Mergers, joint ventures, stock trading, and expansion into international markets are critical mechanisms for growth.
- Expand their consumer base. Black firms must provide efficient service and
  sell quality goods at competitive prices in order to generate patronage by all
  segments of the consumer market—not just by blacks.

The growth of efficient black business and socially responsible black entrepreneurs is desirable, of course; but black leaders must be realistic. Black business
and self-help programs cannot magically cure the ills of African Americans.
There is also the danger that black business, given its inherent capitalist nature,
will create greater wealth for a small black elite. The resultant deepening of class
divisions among African Americans would simply perpetuate the exploitation of
African American workers and the poor.

Despite the massive assault on government programs and services during the
Reagan years, the hard truth is that only the federal government can provide the
mass resources needed to revitalize African American communities. Since the
New Deal, the World War II military build-up, and the postwar recovery, government spending, not private industry, has fueled economic growth and job development in America. The federal entitlement program, civil rights legislation,
equal opportunity statutes, and affirmative action goals enacted during the
Lyndon Johnson administration broke down the barriers for blacks to universities
and corporations.[17]

It was hardly coincidental that black business experienced its single biggest
period of growth from 1977 to 1980. Sales for the Black Enterprise 100 nearly doubled, from $886 million to $1.53 billion. This increase was due largely to the initiatives advanced during President Jimmy Carter's administration in an effort to
strengthen federal programs that provided grants, loans, and technical training to
minority businesses.

The centerpiece of the federal action toward minority business during the
Carter term was the "8A set-aside" program. This plan mandated that national,
state, and local agencies allocate a fixed percentage of their contracts exclusively
to minority firms. By the time Carter left the White House in 1980, the govern-

ment had nearly tripled the amount of business it did with black firms—from $1 billion to $2.7 billion.[18]

Under Reagan, the federal government rapidly backpedaled away from its commitment to minority business. Cuts in Small Business Administration (SBA) funds and programs, along with adverse Supreme Court rulings on minority contracting and affirmative action, knocked many black firms out of the economic box. The economic plans offered by the Bush administration, as well as by the Democrats in the wake of the Los Angeles uprising in 1992, indicate a continuation of the policy of federal withdrawal from direct aid to urban areas.

Both Congress and the White House have touted "enterprise zones" as the answer to the urban economic crisis. In his 1992 State of the Union address, Bush told Congress that these zones "will empower the poor." Both Bush and Congress proposed the use of federal and state tax incentives to induce businesses to locate in designated "enterprise zones."

There is nothing new here. The "enterprise zone" concept was first approved by Congress in 1980. The idea was to create special business zones in or near economically depressed, low-income neighborhoods. The businesses themselves would then provide skills training and jobs for local residents. Supposedly, they would also stimulate the growth of minority business.

Do enterprise zones work? Evidence of their success is at best spotty. A 1991 study by the National Center for Enterprise Zone Research found that the 155 zones in twenty-eight states created minimal employment for local residents and few business opportunities for minority firms. From 1987 to 1990, the Watts enterprise zone in Los Angeles generated a meager 159 jobs and almost no new black business growth. Eleanor Holmes Norton, District of Columbia congressional representative, bluntly dismissed enterprise zones as a conservative scheme to evade expenditure of money on the poor and development of "a comprehensive urban policy."[19]

The failed economic policies of the Reagan-Bush years are precisely the reason African Americans have no choice but to put government back on their agenda. They must mount a massive black prodemocracy-style campaign to pressure the White House and Congress to commit resources, and they must initiate new programs toward the economic rebuilding of African American communities. Black leaders and organizations must spearhead that effort by organizing community task forces, political action groups, and mass protest drives.

The funds are certainly there. The Bush administration had no difficulty digging up the estimated $2.5 billion a month required to support American troops in Saudi Arabia during the Gulf War. So African Americans need not be ashamed to demand more federal dollars and programs to meet their needs. After all, they pay billions yearly to the government in taxes and fees. When they insist that the government create jobs, supply skill training and business development programs, and provide income support as well as quality health care, they are not asking for charity. On the contrary, they are asking only for a "fair share" return on their own money.

Nor will these demands encourage dependency, as claimed by many Republican and Democratic conservatives and some blacks. Despite the rhetoric of many

business leaders, corporations are not antigovernment. Savvy corporate heads regard government as a necessary arbiter to protect their economic interests.

Certainly Chrysler, Lockheed, and the savings and loans did not consider
themselves wards of Uncle Sam when they asked for government bail-out funds.
Defense contractors do not regard the billions they receive in weapons manufacturing contracts as encroachments on their economic sovereignty and decisionmaking ability. And agribusiness does not complain that price supports and crop
subsidies are stunting its growth.

This "corporate welfarism" costs the taxpayer billions annually. If corporations
can look to the federal government for help keeping their bootstraps up, then why
should African Americans (who have much less) not do the same?[20]

Black leaders must continue to demand that the multibillion-dollar "peace
dividend" from the Cold War's end be used to tackle the massive problems of the
black underlcass. These funds could provide low-interest home loans, stimulate
small-business expansion, fund a national health insurance plan, rebuild the
crumbling infrastructure of the inner cities, and support art and cultural projects.
Such measures alone would create thousands of private- and public-sector jobs
for African Americans.

Self-help and "black capitalism" must not be regarded as the sole plans for economic rescue of African Americans. The problems of crime, drugs, poverty, and
institutional racism that confront African American communities demand both
economic *and* political solutions. African Americans cannot afford to forget that.

NOTES

1. See W.E.B. Dubois, *The Souls of Black Folks* (New York: Fawcett), p. 48. See also Emma
L. Thornbrough, ed., *Booker T. Washington* (Englewood Cliffs, N.J.: Prentice-Hall, 1969), p.
59; Louis R. Harlan, *Booker T. Washington: The Wizard of Tuskeegee, 1901–1915* (New York:
Oxford University Press, 1983), pp. 359–378; and Arnold Rampersad, *The Art and Imagination of W.E.B. DuBois* (New York: Schocken, 1990), pp. 81–84.

2. For a fuller discussion of why Booker T. Washington became a pariah in the eyes of
1960s Black Power advocates, see Robert L. Allen, *Black Awakening in Capitalist America*
(Garden City, N.Y.: Doubleday, 1969), pp. 79–85; Harold Cruse, *Rebellion or Revolution?*
(New York: William Morrow, 1968), pp. 156–166; and Nathan Hare "How White Power
Whitewashes Black Power," in Floyd B. Barbour, ed., *The Black Power Revolt* (Boston: Por-
ter Sargeant, 1968), pp. 182–188.

3. *Los Angeles Times*, July 13, 1988; July 10, 1990; July 8, 1991.

4. U.S. Department of Commerce, Bureau of the Census, *We, The Black Americans*
(Washington, D.C.: Government Printing Office, 1986), pp. 3, 8, 11, 12.

5. See Dorothy J. Gaiter, "Short-Term Despair, Long-Term Promise," *Wall Street Journal*, April 4, 1992, p. 1; and Guy Halverson, "Minorities Have Purchasing Clout," *Christian
Science Monitor*, November, 24, 1991, p. 8. See also the magazine *Black Enterprise*, which
regularly features how-to articles detailing methods by which black entrepreneurs can better tap the black consumer market.

6. For background on and analysis of the success that recent Asian immigrants have enjoyed in business and politics, see Ronald Takaki, *Strangers from a Different Shore* (New
York: Penguin, 1989).

7. Pyong Gap Min, "Filipino and Korean Immigrants in Small Business: A Comparative Analysis," *Amerasia* 13, no. 1 (1986–1987):54–60; Takaki, *Stranger from a Different Shore,* pp. 436–445.

8. Barry N. Stein, "Occupational Adjustment of Refugees: The Vietnamese in the United States," *International Migration Review* 13, no. 1 (Spring, 1979):29–40; Takaki, *Strangers from a Different Shore,* pp. 458–459.

9. Frank D. Bean and Marta Tienda, *The Hispanic Population of the United States* (New York: Russell Sage Foundation, 1987), pp. 30–40; Alejandro Portes and Robert Bach, "Immigrant Earnings: Cuban and Mexican Immigrants in the United States," *International Migration Review* 14 (1980):315–341; David Treadwell, "Hard Road for Black Businesses," *Los Angeles Times,* September 20, 1991, p. 20.

10. *Los Angeles Times,* July 25, 1992, p. A19; "The Black Middle Class," *Business Week,* March 14, 1988, p. 64; U.S. Census Bureau, *The Black Population in the United States, March 1990 and 1989* (Washington, D.C.: Government Printing Office, 1991), pp. 15–16.

11. Daniel Fusfield, *The Political Economy of the Urban Ghetto* (Carbondale, Ill.: Southern Illinois University Press, 1982), pp. 12–36, 136–170; Manning Marable, *How Capitalism Underdeveloped Black America* (Boston: South End Press, 1983), pp. 133–167; Earl Ofari Hutchinson, *The Myth of Black Capitalism* (New York: Monthly Review Press, 1970), pp. 66–87.

12. "The BE Top 100" *Black Enterprise* (June 1992), pp. 100, 110; U.S. Census Bureau, *The Black Population in the United States,* p. 8.

13. Dawn M. Baskersville, "One Step Forward, Two Steps Back," *Black Enterprise* (November 1991), p. 49; Frank McCoy, "Weathering a Weak Economy," *Black Enterprise* (January 1991), p. 46.

14. "The Fortune 500," *Fortune Magazine,* April 20, 1992, p. 224; *Los Angeles Times,* September 20, 1991, p. A20.

15. Karen Tumulty, "Global Competition: Can the U.S. Still Play by Its Rules?" *Los Angeles Times,* June 8, 1992, pp. A1, A8; Joel Kurtzman, *The Decline and Crash of the American Economy* (New York: W. W. Norton, 1988), pp. 99–119; Donald Barlett and James B. Steele, *America: What Went Wrong?* (Kansas City, Mo.: Andrews and McNeel, 1992), pp. 89–104.

16. Gerald Krefetz, *Jews and Money: Myths and Reality* (New Haven, Conn.: Ticknor & Fields, 1982), pp. 207–231; Nathan Glazer, "The American Jew and the Attainment of Middle-Class Rank: Some Trends and Explanations" (pp. 138–146), and Fred L. Strodtbeck, "Family Interaction, Values and Achievement" (pp. 147–168), both in Marshall Sklare, ed., *The Jews: Social Patterns of an American Group* (Glencoe, Ill.: Free Press, 1968).

17. William Appleman Williams, *The Great Evasion* (Chicago: Quadrangle Books, 1964), pp. 84–85; Forest Chrisman and Alan Pifer, *Government for the People* (New York: W. W. Norton, 1987), pp. 59–115.

18. Derek T. Dingle, "Whatever Happened to Black Capitalism?" *Black Enterprise* (August 1990), pp. 164, 162.

19. Eleanor Holmes Norton, "Whatever Happened to Enterprise Zones?" *Black Enterprise* (April 1992), p. 20; John Schwada, "L.A.'s Zone Program Is Unproven," *Los Angeles Times,* June 14, 1992, p. A39.

20. Bartlett and Steele detail the high cost of domestic and foreign bailouts, defense industry waste, and their impact on the economy in *America: What Went Wrong?* pp. 40–65, 105–124, 143–161, and 189–211.

PART 6

Education

Education has been seen both as part of the solution to race and ethnic conflict and as part of the problem. On the one hand, education yields opportunities for upward mobility. Getting more minorities through the increasingly meritocratic educational institutions should bring them more economic equality, so the argument goes.

On the other hand, a variety of racial barriers in education are said to keep minorities from getting through the educational system. In addition to the barriers of prejudice and discrimination, critics contend, the educational system is structured in a way that works to the disadvantage of most minority students.

THE STATISTICS

The available data can be used to support both views. The level of educational inequality between whites and minorities has dramatically declined. Yet whites and Asians continue to receive more years of schooling than other minorities.

The Department of Education (Snyder, 1992) publishes data on the percentage of the population 25–29 years old that has completed high school. In 1990, for example, 83 percent of the nonwhite population and 86 percent of the white population had completed high school. The rate at which nonwhites completed high school was 97 percent of that among whites (83/86 = .97). If the white and non-white rates were equal, the nonwhite rate would be 100 percent of the white rate.

Similar data have been collected since 1920, when the nonwhite rate of high school completion was only 29 percent of the white rate. In other words, over the past seventy years, the racial gap in high school completion has been almost eliminated.

Although the majority of "nonwhites" are black, the number of well-educated Asians has increased dramatically in the past two decades. A more accurate measure would be the comparison between white and black rates of high school completion. Fortunately, the American Council on Education (ACE) provides this information on 18- to 24-year-olds for the years from 1970 to 1990 (Carter and Wilson, 1992): In 1970 the high school completion rate among blacks was only 73 percent of the white rate, whereas by 1990 the black rate was 93 percent of the white rate.

The ACE also provides data comparing white and Hispanic high school completion rates, but with even more discouraging results. In 1972, the Hispanic completion rate was 64 percent of the white rate. By 1990, the Hispanic/white gap had closed only slightly, to 66 percent.

The ACE data can be used to examine college attendance rates as well. In 1990, 32.5 percent of white 18- to 24-year-olds were enrolled in college, compared with 25.4 percent of blacks and 15.8 percent of Hispanics. The black rate was 78 percent of the white rate in 1990, a dramatic increase from the 1970 figure of 57 percent. The Hispanic rate was 49 percent of the white rate in 1990, a slight decline from the 1972 figure of 51 percent. Although the black/white gap in college enrollment has decreased somewhat since the 1970s, the Hispanic/white rate has not.

Data collected by the Department of Education, on the rates at which four years of college are completed, also reveal a decline in educational inequality. In 1920, the nonwhite rate of college completion was only 27 percent of the white rate. By 1990, the nonwhite rate had reached 75 percent of the white rate. The historical trend, then, is toward greater equality.

These data, however, *understate* the racial gap in college completion rates, since highly educated Asians are included in the nonwhite category. Fortunately, the Department of Education provides separate 1990 data for the college-completion rates of 25- to 29-year-old blacks and whites. The *black* college-completion rate of 13.4 percent was lower than the *nonwhite* rate of 18.2 percent. In other words, although nonwhites completed college at 75 percent the rate of whites, blacks completed college at slightly more than half (55 percent) the rate of whites, and Hispanics completed college at one-third (34 percent) the rate of whites. In spite of a genuine decrease in educational inequality for blacks in terms of years of school completed, the racial gap is still quite substantial.

Finally, we would like to point out the huge *class* differences in educational inequality. In 1991, for example, only 5 percent of the population from families in the lowest income quartile (earning below $21,539 annually) had a bachelor's degree by the time they were 24 years old. The comparable figure for people in the richest income quartile (earning above $61,636 annually) was 64 percent (*Postsecondary Education Opportunity*, 1993).

Even more significant is the fact that the bachelor's degree gap between the top and bottom income quartiles is getting *larger*. In 1991, people in the top income quartile were almost thirteen times more likely to have a bachelor's degree than those from the bottom quartile. In 1970, those in the top quartile were "only" seven times more likely to have a bachelor's degree.

THE EXPLANATION

Although all sides acknowledge the preceding data, there are dramatically different explanations as to why these racial differences in education exist. There are at least three major explanations of racial differences in education: skills and culture, discrimination, and structure. We shall briefly consider each of these below.

Skills and Culture. Most conservatives, and some liberals, argue that the reason whites and Asians do better in school than blacks, Hispanics, and Native Americans is that they are more skilled. Overwhelming evidence does show that, in any given year during elementary and secondary school, whites and Asians are better than blacks and Hispanics at reading, writing, and math. The racial differences in academic skills can be seen in grades, scores on achievement tests, and virtually any other measure of academic achievement.

The important question, of course, is *why* whites and Asians tend to exhibit academic skills superior to those of other minorities. Many social scientists attribute these skill differences to cultural variables such as more stable homes, higher levels of encouragement from parents and significant others, a stronger emphasis on personal discipline, norms rejecting academic achievement, and the development of a linear intellectual process that emphasizes rationality and logic. White and Asian families are also said to be more active in their children's schools than are black and Hispanic families.

The lower level of achievement of non-Asian minorities, on the other hand, is believed to be due to cultural factors that are less conducive to educational achievement, including family disorganization, lower levels of parental encouragement and involvement in education, a lack of emphasis on personal discipline, norms rejecting academic achievement, and a nonlinear intellectual style. Language problems are also said to be impediments, especially for Hispanics.

The solution to educational inequality, according to the skills/culture explanation, is to help minority students cope more effectively with existing schools. In addition to providing minority students with tutoring and help with study habits, theorists in this area would emphasize the need for changes in the minority culture, including more parental involvement and greater family stability. Among the school changes recommended would be an increase in the academic demands on minority students.

Discrimination. Most analysts would agree that racial discrimination in education has existed in the past—especially prior to the 1954 *Brown* v. *Board of Education* decision of the U.S. Supreme Court, which outlawed legal segregation in the public schools. Many would also argue that segregation is a continuing problem in schools and colleges, even though it may not be as obvious as in the past.

The overwhelming majority of black and Hispanic students still attend predominantly minority public schools. In the 1988–1989 school year, 63 percent of black students and almost three-quarters of Hispanic students attended schools at which the student population was at least half minority. Since 1970, the segregation rate of black students has declined somewhat, but the segregation rate of Hispanics has increased (Schmidt, 1992).

Predominantly minority schools tend to be older and less well funded relative to schools in white communities. Some white teachers are still prejudiced toward minority students and treat them unfairly. The schools themselves often hold minority students to low expectations and offer less rigorous curricula. Indeed, the students often conform to those expectations by performing poorly. Ethnoviolence, which includes everything from prejudicial name calling to physical attacks, also poisons the atmosphere of schools and colleges.

The solutions to educational inequality, according to discrimination theorists, include more thorough racial integration of public schools and colleges, the elimination of funding differentials between white and minority schools, and the removal of prejudiced teachers and staff members. Finally, ethnoviolence is not to be tolerated, regardless of whether it originates from other students or from teachers.

Structure. According to this explanation, the structure of education has evolved in such a way that it perpetuates educational inequality. So-called meritocratic schools sort out the winners from the losers, and minority students are disproportionately found among the losers.

Because of their relatively low grades and test scores, minority students tend to be disproportionately placed in lower tracks in public schools and are not prepared to attend college. In a national study of eighth-grade math classes in 1988, for example, more than one-third of blacks and Native Americans and one-quarter of Hispanics were in "low-ability" classes, compared to 15 percent of whites and 17 percent of Asians. On the other hand, only 10 percent of Native Americans, 15 percent of blacks, and 18 percent of Hispanics were in the "high-ability" classes, compared to 35 percent of whites and 47 percent of Asians ("Education Life," 1992).

The curriculum in schools and colleges tends to be "Eurocentric" in that it focuses on the white historical and cultural traditions that can be traced back to Western Europe. The cultural and historical traditions of Africa, Asia, and Latin America tend to be ignored or downplayed. Similarly, the problems faced by minorities in the United States tend to be ignored or minimized.

Both white and minority students are finding it more and more difficult to finance college educations due to increases in the cost of tuition, housing, books, and supplies. And economic recession along with political decisions made by conservative administrations in Washington have resulted in declining amounts of financial aid for students, creating additional barriers for minority students who try to complete four years of college.

In order to turn things around, say structural theorists, the meritocratic structure of education, which emphasizes "sorting" over learning, must be transformed. Tracking in public schools must be eliminated. The transition from two-year to four-year colleges must be made easier. Adequate financial aid, in the form of grants rather than loans, must be made available to all who need it. Finally, the curriculum of schools and colleges must reflect the history, culture, and present experience of students from all races and ethnic groups.

EDUCATION AND PREJUDICE

What is the relationship of education to prejudice and group conflict? There is a widespread belief that increased education decreases prejudice (and presumably such related factors as discrimination and conflict). Most Americans have faith in education—and central to that faith is the belief that formal education will make one a more tolerant person. There is a kernel of truth to that stereotype of education, as evidenced by the correlation between years of schooling and lower prejudice: As years of schooling go up, prejudice goes down. That correlation, however, is so small as to make clear that other, more important factors are involved.

The most important of these other factors, not surprisingly, is the *content* of what gets taught. Obviously people can and do attend many years of school with little or no positive intergroup contacts and little or no formal education in intergroup relations and cultural differences. During the 1960s, curricular reform was a major social issue as the prevailing movements for change sought to correct for the absence of minority concerns both in curriculum materials and in the telling of history. These reform issues are again before us; but the struggles are now directed more toward the universities, where the issue has come to be identified as "multiculturalism" in higher education.

The five chapters in this section deal with the issues mentioned above—ethnoviolence, multiculturalism, and discrimination. Howard Ehrlich ("Campus Ethnoviolence") reviews research showing that ethnoviolence by whites against people of color is a major problem at colleges and universities. He then discusses some of the causes underlying this problem as well as some potential solutions.

Edward Alexander ("Race Fever"), on the other hand, argues that the charges of racism against white educators and educational institutions have been exaggerated. The real perpetrators of racial intolerance, he says, are minorities and their white radical supporters who promote self-serving ethnic studies programs and affirmative action policies.

The two essays on multiculturalism also have different perspectives. Diane Ravitch ("Multiculturalism: E Pluribus Plures") argues that most schools and colleges already discuss the contributions of different racial and ethnic groups within the context of American pluralism. The problem, she says, is with those "particularistic multiculturalists" who distort American history, culture, and education by using the schools to raise the self-esteem of specific minority groups.

Molefi Kete Asante ("Multiculturalism: An Exchange") argues that the curricula of most schools and colleges can still best be described as "Eurocentric" because racial and ethnic minorities are not thoroughly integrated into the curriculum. Afrocentric educators want the black experience to be incorporated into the curriculum at every level.

Finally, Deborah Woo ("The 'Overrepresentation' of Asian Americans: Red Herrings and Yellow Perils") argues that Asians are discriminated against by colleges and universities because they are too successful. She compares the present discrimination against Asians with past discrimination against Jews.

REFERENCES

Carter, Deborah J., and Reginald Wilson. 1992. *Minorities in Higher Education, 1991: Tenth Annual Status Report.* Washington, D.C.: American Council on Education.

"Education Life." 1992. *New York Times* (November 1), Section 4a.

Postsecondary Education Opportunity. 1993. "Disparities in Higher Education Opportunity Across Family Income Levels Were Huge and Growing in 1991," no. 11, pp. 1–6.

Schmidt, Peter. 1992. "Study Shows a Rise in the Segregation of Hispanic Students." *Education Week* (January 15): 1, 19.

Snyder, Thomas D. 1992. *Digest of Education Statistics, 1992.* Washington, D.C.: Government Printing Office.

25

Campus Ethnoviolence

HOWARD J. EHRLICH

The front page headline of the weekly *Chronicle of Higher Education* read: "New Outbreak of Cross-Burnings and Racial Slurs Worries Colleges." The dateline was January 12, 1981. The story reported ethnoviolent incidents at Harvard, Purdue, Williams, Wesleyan, Cornell, Iowa State, University of Wisconsin, and University of Massachusetts. You could easily mistake this story—in terms of the incidents described and the rhetoric of the college administrators quoted—for one written today.

As the major news media were not ready to put campus ethnoviolence on their agenda, this story did not break in the major news media until the last half of the 1985–1986 academic year. Three dramatic incidents received slight national coverage: the destruction of anti-apartheid shanties at Dartmouth, an attempt by white University of Texas students (wearing Ronald Reagan masks) to throw a black student out of a dormitory window, and a cross-burning in the yard of a black sorority house at the University of Alabama in Tuscaloosa. But it wasn't until the start of the following school year, 1986–1987, that an incident at the Citadel in Charleston, South Carolina, became the starting point for the news media's expanded coverage of campus ethnoviolence. The incident was a perfect scenario for a media morality play: harassment of a black student and a cross-burning at a southern military school, replete with Civil War regalia and a history of intergroup conflict. The student ultimately dropped out, presumably in reaction to the harassment.

Today, on college campuses across the United States—regardless of size, prestige, type of school, or region of the country—intergroup hostilities are being played out in traditional as well as newer patterns. Racist posters, signs and fliers, spray-painted graffiti, and even T-shirts bearing group slurs are common. Minority students, as well as staff and faculty, have received intimidating and threatening mail and telephone calls. Physical assaults and property damage, though less common, have also done serious harm.

This essay addresses the multifaceted dimensions of ethnoviolence on campus. In the process of reviewing the systematic studies of campuses since the National Institute Against Prejudice and Violence initiated this research in 1986, I discuss the following issues: the extent of ethnoviolent behaviors on campuses and differ-ences on the basis of ethnicity, race, religion, gender, and sexual orientation; the extent of revictimization (i.e., how frequently the same students are targeted for attack); the prevalence of covictimization (i.e., how an incident of ethnoviolence affects those who see or hear about it); the uniquely traumatic effects of being a victim of prejudice-motivated acts; what we know about the perpetrators of these acts; and why victimized students do not always report such incidents. Finally, I close with a discussion of the conservative undercurrents of intergroup conflicts on campus and an analysis of the new targets of campus bigotry.

SURVEYS OF CAMPUS ETHNOVIOLENCE

In the spring of 1987, I undertook a systematic study of ethnoviolence on the cam-pus of the University of Maryland Baltimore County (UMBC). This school, part of the state system, is a primarily undergraduate institution of approximately 9,000 students, located in a predominantly white suburb of Baltimore. Several highly publicized incidents have occurred on the campus, including a sit-in pro-testing administrative inaction that overlapped with the period of study (Ehrlich, Pincus, and Morton, 1987).

Two close replications of this original study as well as three comparable studies have since been conducted (see Peterson, 1990; Taylor 1990). All five studies used variants of the same survey questionnaire, providing highly reliable data. Also re-cently completed have been more specialized studies concerned with prejudice-motivated violence directed at people because of their gender or sexual orienta-tion (Berrill, 1992; Koss, Gidycz, and Wisniewski, 1987).

"Ethnoviolence," our primary concern here, is defined as an act motivated by prejudice and intended to do psychological or physical harm to people because of their ethnic-group membership. (I use the term *ethnic group* in its modern, inclu-sive sociological sense, which encompasses, among others, groups identified by their sexual orientation as well as the more traditional groups of race, religion, nationality, and national origin.) In general, the campus ethnoviolence rates re-ported here have been determined by sampling students and asking them to re-port on their experiences.

THE BASIC FINDINGS

I now turn to what I think are some of the more reliable and replicated findings. As might be expected, there are substantial differences across campuses in the percentage of students reporting victimization based on prejudice, ranging over-all from 10 to 22 percent. These differences may be attributable, in part, to cam-pus size, the diversity of the campus population, and whether or not the school has a residential or commuter campus. Certainly each school has its own history of intergroup relations as well as unique cultural dimensions. Across all campuses, forms of verbal aggression—name calling, insults, and harassing be-havior—are the most common expressions of campus ethnoviolence, accounting for approximately three out of five incidents. Threats and actual physical assaults constituted 16 percent of all incidents. Harassment occurred in 12 percent of the cases and property damage in another 7 percent.

The groups who are victimized also vary by campus. Past research indicates that the size and visibility of a minority group are the best predictors of whether its members will be victimized (Ehrlich, 1973). Five to 15 percent of white students report being victimized. The corresponding figures for ethnic minority students are 12 to 60 percent. My estimate based on current research is that the overall minority student median is 25 percent. That is, in any given year, *one out of every four minority students* is victimized for reasons of prejudice. What happened to these students? Here are some examples:

- A Chinese-American student sat down at the end of a library table. At the other end, a group of students who had been sitting there began telling ethnic jokes and directing anti-Asian slurs at her. She left. She was angry, hurt, and badly upset, and afraid to return to the library alone.
- A gay male student, during an intimate conversation with his two roommates, told them of his affectional orientation. They became verbally abusive and physically assaulted him.
- A fraternity sent its pledges out on a "scavenger hunt" in which they were to return with photos of themselves with "Oriental girls."
- A black columnist at a student newspaper depicted white people as "irredeemable racists" and called for blacks to "unite, organize and execute" whites who pose a threat.
- Two students were attacked on campus by a group of skinheads. The two students, who were white, believed that they were attacked because of their "punk" hairstyles and clothes. The skinheads yelled derogatory remarks at them, kicked and struck one of them, and pushed the other into a cement wall. The attack was broken up by five male student bystanders.
- Swastikas were painted on two cars and a walkway outside of a predominantly Jewish fraternity. One student whose car was vandalized complained that the police did not take his case seriously. He said that an officer told him, "Go to the federal government. I deal with criminals." Another officer told him that this was not a racial incident because "Jews aren't another race."
- Two organizations representing minority students, United Coalition Against Racism and Latin American Solidarity Committee, received fliers that read, "Faggots, Niggers and Spic Lovers—BEWARE! You have gone beyond acceptable criticism. Never again will you go unpunished." The fliers were slipped under their office doors.
- One campus newspaper ran a racist editorial cartoon; another published a letter praising Hitler's eugenics programs; a campus radio program conducted a call-in ethnic joke fest; a computer bulletin board was used for displaying various epithets and slogans of bigotry.
- Native American students were subjected to racial taunts during the annual Indian Days Pow Wow. The American Indian Club filed a formal complaint, charging that participants were subjected to abusive comments and racial slurs, including war whoops.

- Two white male students were attacked inside a doughnut store about 2 A.M. The attackers, who were black, shouted, "You can't look at me like that," and "You white cheesecakes are going to pay." One student was struck and received a cut under his eye.
- Members of a fraternity painted "KKK" and "We hate niggers" on the chests of two white pledges and then dumped them on the grounds of a predominantly black college nearby. On being observed, the two naked white students were chased across campus until they found sanctuary in the college security office.
- On the second day of an exhibit by a gay artist at a campus art gallery, about thirty students entered the gallery and made hostile, homophobic comments. One woman said, "I think [the artist] is a fucking psycho and I hope he dies." That night, vandals broke into an adjoining theater and unsuccessfully attempted to break into the gallery. They used shaving cream to spray antigay slurs inside the theater and on windows outside the gallery.
- Anonymous fliers that proclaimed April as "White Pride Month" were found around campus. The fliers charged that "affirmative action ... makes it tough to be white." Fliers were pinned to shanties that had been built to protest racism in South Africa. Several of the shanties were torn down.
- Racial epithets were written on the walls and mirror of a residence-hall room assigned to a Latino student.
- A sign in front of a black fraternity was defaced with the message "KKK—Go back to Africa."
- Leaflets proclaiming that the Holocaust was a hoax were passed out in front of the Hillel Foundation, a Jewish student organization.
- A music professor told his class that black music is dirty and that blacks were better off as slaves because they ate regularly and had roofs over their heads.
- A fraternity held a "border party" where, in order to gain entrance, guests had to crawl under a barbed-wire barrier.
- About a dozen members of a White Student Union, wielding clubs and chains, attacked three white antiracist protestors who were picketing outside the campus radio station.

Some students can go through an entire school year and never experience a single act of ethnoviolence, but others are *revictimized;* that is, they become victims more than once. Such incidents are typically unrelated, but some students are the continuing targets of one or more perpetrators.

Revictimization may be especially significant on a campus where size and closeness render a victim easily accessible to perpetrators. In this essay, I can provide an estimate of revictimization involving only one campus. On that campus, one of every four student victims of ethnoviolence was revictimized at least one time during the academic year.

Covictimization

One need not be directly attacked in order to experience the distress of victimization. I use the term *covictim* to describe the status of persons who are aware of attacks on others who share their ethnic identity. Covictims may have directly *witnessed* an ethnoviolent attack on another person, or they may have *heard* about it from the victim or from others. For the covictim, attacks on peers are seen as threats not only to the entire group but also to their own personal well-being. Covictims, then, are all of those persons who have seen or heard about an ethnoviolent incident and are emotionally affected as a result.

Looking across campuses and at all students—black, white, Latino, Asian, and so on—studies in ethnoviolence suggest that potential covictimization rates range from 35 to 61 percent. Yet these overall figures mask the fact that groups vary in terms of both their awareness of themselves *as* groups and their means of communication.

In the UMBC study under discussion here, 64 percent of the black students were covictims, as were 60 percent of the Jewish students. Studies of antigay violence at Yale, Rutgers, and Penn State reveal covictimization rates among gay and lesbian students of 76 percent, 57 percent, and 66 percent, respectively (Berrill, 1992). These figures reflect a substructure of group tensions. As incidents are related, details become magnified and distorted; listeners and tellers alike become anxious, angry, and maybe even frightened. As the campus atmosphere changes, the perceptions of students are altered as well.

The inclusion of incidents of gender-based violence (ranging from rape and physical assault to sexual harassment) would escalate most of the figures I have cited here. Studies completed in the 1980s indicate that 30 to 92 percent of female undergraduates reported experiencing some form of unwanted sexual attention. For example, from a national sample of 3,187 female college students, 11 percent reported being raped and 10 percent reported rape attempts during the academic year (Koss, Gidycz, and Wisniewski, 1987). Women graduate students appear more likely than undergraduates to be harassed, and more than half of women medical students report sexual harassment (Baldwin, Daugherty, and Eckenfels, 1991). Finally, one study reports that 48 percent of women faculty have been harassed by male students (McKinney and Maroules, 1991). The overall rate of gender-based violence I estimate to be in the 25 to 30 percent range.

Studies focusing exclusively on violence against gay, lesbian, and bisexual students have been conducted at Penn State, Yale, Rutgers, the University of Illinois, Oberlin College, and the University of Massachusetts at Amherst. According to these studies, rates of verbal harassment range from 45 to 76 percent, threats of physical violence range from 15 to 26 percent, and actual assaults range from 5 to 6 percent (Berrill, 1992). The frequency and intensity of homophobic violence, especially violence against gay men, appear to be even more pronounced than in gender-based or other ethnoviolent attacks.

One reason for the increasing ethnoviolence on college campuses is that current students are more prejudiced than their earlier cohorts. Leonard Gordon's tracking of student stereotyping reveals an increase not only in the assignment of negative stereotypes but also in the intensity of endorsement of such stereotypes (Gordon, 1991). The actual number of students displaying prejudice is low: Gordon estimates the figure at 10 percent of the total. However, given the numerical increase in college populations, 10 percent may now constitute a critical mass. Indeed, Gordon's estimate reflects a considerable base of group intolerance. Certainly the national-values survey of Milton Rokeach and Sandra Ball-Rokeach (1989) indicates that "equality" as a value has declined in importance among Americans.

Additional evidence indicates changes in still other values among young adults. For example, in their comparisons of national samples of high school seniors, Eileen Crimmins and her associates (1991) noted that, in the ten years between 1976 and 1986, fewer seniors reported "finding purpose and meaning in life" as an important life goal whereas considerably more wanted to "make a lot of money." Specifically, fewer than half of all high school seniors in 1976 considered having a lot of money to be "extremely important"; in 1986, almost two-thirds did so. On the basis of their questionnaire, which encompassed fourteen life goals, the researchers observed that "the evidence suggests a shift from public to private concerns" (Crimmins, Easterlin, and Saito, 1991). This shift from altruistic to egoistic concerns is consistent with the findings of Gordon (1991) and Rokeach and Ball-Rokeach (1989).

EFFECTS OF ETHNOVIOLENCE

Two important facets of ethnoviolent victimization need to be pointed out. First, persons victimized for reasons of prejudice often suffer more than those victimized for other reasons. Second, an observer cannot predict the level of victim trauma simply by noting the nature of the act itself. Interwoven with the effects of the act are the past experiences and personality of the victim, the status of the perpetrator, and even the historical context of the act. Furthermore, in the context of increased group tensions, what at one time might have been construed as an awkward or insensitive act may now be construed as a blatant violation of civil or social relations. Thus, one student may become traumatized by a single instance of name calling, while another confidently battles her way through an entire semester of harassment, threats, and property damage.

Research on victimization by the National Institute Against Prejudice and Violence indicates that people who are physically or psychologically attacked for reasons of prejudice are often more traumatized than people who are victims of other sorts of crimes (*FORUM*, 1990; Weiss, Ehrlich, and Larcom, 1991–1992). Black and white victims of ethnoviolence, for example, report more symptoms of psychophysiological stress than do black and white victims of other crimes.

Campus studies show similar results. In the UMBC study, one out of three student victims reported that an ethnoviolent incident had seriously affected their interpersonal relations on campus. At a similarly sized state university in New York, almost 15 percent of victim responses reflected a withdrawal from social relationships while another 11 percent indicated difficulties in relations with family, friends, and significant others as a result of the ethnoviolent incident.

The politics of victimization on campus is not much different from that of other settings (Elias, 1986). Student victims tend to be ignored; their fright, anger, and suffering are trivialized. Moreover, they sometimes become a spectacle, often subtly revictimized in the political struggle to affirm or reconstruct the moral order of the campus. In this struggle, the issue of victim rights and services is often underplayed.

The Perpetrators

Two other dimensions of campus ethnoviolence merit discussion: Who did it, and did the victims report it?

Regarding the perpetrators, very little is known. At least half of the incidents under study here were committed covertly; among those committed publicly, the victims were unfamiliar with their assailants. However, there are strong indications that perpetrators are most likely to be white and that members of fraternities are overrepresented among known perpetrators. Fraternity houses as well as dormitories seem to be key sites at which incidents occur. And, indeed, the sexist, elitist, and anti-intellectual socialization of fraternity members has been well documented (Martin and Hummer, 1989; Moffat, 1989; Sanday, 1991).

These data are consistent with the findings of the survey taken by the Campus Violence Prevention Center in 1991. According to this survey, perpetrators of campus crimes (assault, rape, robbery, vandalism, theft, etc.) were more likely to be male athletes or fraternity/sorority members and to have lower grade-point averages (Bausell, Bausell, and Siegel, 1991). The survey also revealed that 7 percent of campus crimes involved elements of group prejudice.

Reporting the Incidents

Who reports their victimization to campus police, student affairs offices, residence hall advisers—or any other school official? The answer is practically no one: Eighty to 94 percent of the student victims under study said that they had made no report to any college official or to campus security.

These rates of nonreporting are substantially higher than those determined by the National Crime Survey, which attributes nonreporting to approximately two-thirds of the victims of personal crimes (Bureau of Justice Statistics, 1990). But the rates are consistent with other evidence involving gender-based violence or ethnoviolence. For example, a *New York Times*/CBS poll (October 11, 1991) revealed that 87 percent of women harassed at work did not report it.

Students specify four main reasons for not reporting what happened to them. The first (and the most frequent reason stated) is that the incident was not serious or important. This response can be seen as a form of denial or detachment. Second, the formal authorities would do nothing; and, third, there was nothing the authorities could do. Although these reasons suggest denial on the part of the victims, they may also reflect students' assumptions about the sincerity or competence of campus authorities. The fourth reason is based on fear. People fear retaliation by the perpetrator, or they fear that reporting the incident will only create more trouble for them.

SOME POLICY IMPLICATIONS

Every social problem brings out the "social mechanics." Campus ethnoviolence has not escaped their tinkering. Their perspective is to view the university (or any institution) as a mechanical system, and their role as mechanics is to find the broken or malfunctioning parts and fix or redesign them. This mechanistic model is common to much of the policymaking in intergroup relations. The news media, as well, tend to view conflict in this simple fashion.

The signal instance of the application of this mechanical model to ethnoviolence on campus has been the "speech code." Are students uttering ethnic or sexist insults? If so, then there's something wrong with the system that controls students. So the mechanic "fixes" the campus regulations on student conduct such that offensive speech is outlawed. This mechanical tinkering not only fails to comprehend the basis for the system failure, but its "quick fix" orientation frequently leaves behind a new set of problems. In the context of speech codes, these new problems are almost as formidable as those the codes are supposed to solve. The varying opinions reflected in the U.S. Supreme Court decision of June 1992 for *R.A.V. v. City of St. Paul, Minnesota*, highlight many of these problems. At the same time, this decision has rendered most of the existing speech codes inoperable.

We will find it helpful to contrast the mechanical model with a holistic model. The latter recognizes the systemic character of social institutions. A college, as an institution, is something more than the sum of its parts. It is also part of the larger system. Accordingly, what happens on a college campus is partly determined by what happens in the larger society. Campus ethnoviolence can be resolved, but not without dealing with intergroup conflict in the society.

For the most part, students arrive at college with little in the way of multicultural experiences. Their backgrounds have generally been confined to segregated neighborhoods and schools. Their friendship circles tend to be racially homogeneous. And the vicarious intergroup experiences they might have gained through the media of mass education or mass entertainment provide little compensation or correction.

The incoming students thus enter a world of greater diversity. But it is an age-segregated world of essentially equally naive actors, all now removed from the observability and constraints of their families and significant others. On most campuses whites are not likely to encounter many black, or Hispanic, or other minority students, and they have even less exposure to minority faculty. Even so, intergroup contacts will be more frequent and likely more intimate than was previously the case in their home situations.

The research does indicate that students who experienced multiethnic friendships in high school tend to have such friendships in college as well (Taylor, 1990). A key factor in both high school and college friendships is the ethnic composition of the schools themselves. That is, the opportunities for friendships were a pivotal determinant of actual friendships. The motivations for friendship are also significant. The Diversity Project at the University of California (Berkeley) suggests "that while *both African American and white freshman students want more interracial experiences and contacts, they want them on different terms.* African Americans want more classes and programs and institutional commitments and responses. Whites want more individual, personal contacts developed at their own time and leisure" (Institute for the Study of Social Change, 1991, p. 14; italics in original).

Certainly college educators can influence the attitudes and values of their students. For instance, they can increase the opportunities for interaction among white and minority students as well as the opportunities for working together on educationally meaningful projects. Both measures require changes in the traditional approach to education. But past attempts to institute such changes have often caused the change agents themselves—the faculty and staff involved in the intergroup and multicultural education of students—to become the targets of conservative efforts to maintain the status quo.

THE CONSERVATIVE UNDERCURRENTS OF CAMPUS ETHNOVIOLENCE

The role of right-wing and highly conservative organizations has been a somewhat understated dimension of campus ethnoviolence. It is not that these organizations are necessarily or directly implicated in ethnoviolent events. Rather, they function (sociologically) to provide the intellectual and moral justification for social inequalities. They promote values of individualism, meritocracy, and hierarchy that are essentially elitist. These organizations sometimes have actual "chapters" on campus; one example is the White Student Union. (Actually, although the activities of this group have been widely publicized, there are only three campus-based White Student Unions in existence. Many more have started and failed.) More typically, though, they operate by providing financial support, by maintaining a base for networking across campuses, and by supplying stock propaganda.

Probably the most significant networks are the National Association of Scholars (NAS) and the Madison Center for Educational Affairs, formerly the Institute for Educational Affairs (Diamond, 1991). The NAS represents a directed effort at organizing right-wing faculty. It has official chapters on local campuses and members across the United States. It has also established its own research center and employment service and has formed caucuses in several academic societies.

The Madison Center, funded by conservative corporate foundations such as Coors, Mobil, Olin, Scaife, and Smith-Richardson, supports conservative graduate students and junior faculty. It has also supported an estimated sixty-four conservative campus newspapers (Seligman and Simpson, 1991). While most of these newspapers have not survived, their purpose has been to promote authoritarian values. Many are continuing as a disruptive force on various campuses. As Diamond's (1991) research indicates, NAS and the Madison Center have developed a systematic strategy for right-wing organizing and activism on campus.

Other right-of-center organizations active on college campuses include Accuracy in Academia, Intercollegiate Studies Institute, Students for America, Young America's Foundation, The Way International, Tony and Susan Alamo Foundation, Unification Campus Ministry, CAUSA, and the New Alliance Party.

THE NEW TARGETS

Responses to ethnoviolence have included the reconsideration of university methods for recruiting and retaining minority faculty and students, the redesigning of freshman orientation programs, the revision of student codes of conduct, and the introduction of changes in course content and curricula. These reformist responses came under strong attack at the beginning of the decade, at a time when the reform movement was being dubbed by the news media as a movement for "political correctness" (PC).

The reforms proposed for course and curricular changes have been oriented toward reducing ethnocentrism both in course content and in methods of instruction. In the jargon of college educators, these reforms have sought to replace the "monocultural" approach with a "multicultural" approach. But this movement for multicultural educational reform faces two serious obstacles. (1) Internally, the movement has not achieved a consensus on its goals, with the result that a wide range of proposals have been put forth in the name of "multiculturalism." Although this lack of consensus is to be expected in the beginning stages of a reform movement, it makes the movement more vulnerable to attack. (2) Externally, multiculturalism has been viewed as corrupting both "traditional" values and existing educational practices. As *Newsweek* editorialized, multiculturalism "is an attack on the primacy of the Western intellectual tradition" (December 24, 1990). By implication, it is also an attack on the conservative faculty who control not only the university departments and divisions at many schools but also numerous academic professional associations. Related to this circumstance is another, sometimes explicit, dimension to the movement for multiculturalism. Many of its proponents see it as an integral part of a movement for the democratization of education. Although colleges and academic societies have strong democratic elements, they are essentially hierarchical and somewhat authoritarian institutions. Even though reformists' ideas about institutional democracy seem even less well developed than those about curriculum reforms, the mere suggestion of democracy has threatened not only the conservative faculty but also other institutions with increasing influence on college curricula (Dickson, 1984; Ehrlich, 1985).

On May 4, 1991, President George Bush, in a commencement address at the University of Michigan, told the nation that this movement for political correctness had led to political intolerance. "Political extremists," he said, "roam the land, abusing the privilege of free speech, setting citizens against one another on the basis of their class or race."

This extraordinary act of political doublethink by the president—during which the victims and their advocates were essentially labeled as victimizers—did not originate in the White House. The president had simply given his seal to the "anti-PC" movement defined by a year of mass media coverage—including cover stories in *Newsweek, The Atlantic Monthly,* and *The New Republic;* extensive accounts in the *New York Times, Time, Fortune,* and the *Wall Street Journal;* and substantial coverage by conservative columnists and periodicals. A word search of *political/politically* along with *correct/correctness* was conducted by D. Charles Whitney and Ellen Wartella (1992) in 33 U.S. metropolitan newspapers as well as 435 general-interest U.S. and Canadian magazines. From 1990 to 1991, the terms' appearance increased by 600 percent in newspapers and by more than 700 percent in magazines. Three years earlier there were 97 percent fewer references in newspapers and almost none at all in magazines.

On December 24, 1990, *Newsweek* ended the year with a vitriolic, eight-page cover story on the "tyranny of PC." The story concluded that political correctness was a plot of Marxist origin and essentially amounted to "a totalitarian philoso-phy." Its grip on U.S. campuses was so great, *Newsweek* reported, that "one defies it at one's peril." The PC threat, however, seemed far less apparent in the annual survey of senior campus administrators conducted by the American Council on Education, or ACE (El-Khawas, 1991). After adding questions about political cor-rectness to its 1990–1991 questionnaire, the ACE found that conflicts involving political correctness were not especially commonplace. Administrators were asked: "In the past year, this institution has experienced significant controversy over the political or cultural content of _____." This was followed by a checklist referring to "course texts," "information presented in the classroom," and "in-vited speakers or lecturers." The percentages of respondents checking these con-flicts were 3 percent, 4 percent, and 10 percent, respectively. In addition, the ques-tionnaire asked whether the administration had "received complaints from faculty of pressure to alter the political or cultural content of their courses." Only 5 percent of respondents answered "yes."

In an earlier day, many of those who opposed school desegregation argued that their opposition was based not on prejudice but on their concern with the behav-ioral effects of riding on a bus. In an analogous and similarly specious fashion, the opponents of "political correctness" argue for their own freedom from big-otry and state their concern with academic freedom. They see campus programs for the reduction of ethnoviolence as unnecessary, and they redefine as bigots the advocates of ethnic and feminist studies and multiculturalism in curricula. As conservatives manipulate the campus political process, the activists in the move-ments for equality and multiculturalism are becoming the new targets of ethno-violence.

REFERENCES

Baldwin, DeWitt C., Steven R. Daugherty, and Edward J. Eckenfels. 1991. "Student Percep-tions of Mistreatment and Harassment During Medical School—A Survey of Ten United States Schools." *Western Journal of Medicine* 155(2):140–145.

Bausell, R. Barker, Carole R. Bausell, and Dorothy G. Siegel. 1991. *The Links Among Alcohol, Drugs and Crime on American College Campuses: A National Followup Study.* Towson, Md.: Campus Violence Prevention Center, Towson State University.

Berrill, Kevin T. 1992. "Anti-Gay Violence and Victimization in the United States: An Overview." In Gregory M. Herek and Kevin T. Berrill, eds., *Hate Crimes: Confronting Violence Against Lesbians and Gay Men.* Newbury Park, Calif.: Sage Publications.

Bureau of Justice Statistics. 1990. *Criminal Victimization in the United States, 1988.* Wash-ington, D.C.: U.S. Department of Justice.

Crimmins, Eileen M., Richard A. Easterlin, and Yasuhiko Saito. 1991. "What Young Adults Want." *American Demographics* (July):24–33.

Diamond, Sara. 1991. "Readin', Writin', and Repressin'."*Z Magazine* (February):45–48.

Dickson, David. 1984. *The New Politics of Science.* New York: Pantheon Books.

Ehrlich, Howard J. 1973. *The Social Psychology of Prejudice.* New York: John Wiley & Sons.

———. 1985. *The University-Military Connection* (Research Group One Report No. 30). Baltimore: Vacant Lots Press.

———. 1990. *Campus Ethnoviolence and the Policy Options* (Institute Report No. 4). Balti-more: National Institute Against Prejudice and Violence.

Ehrlich, Howard J., Fred L. Pincus, and Cornel Morton. 1987. *Ethnoviolence on Campus: The UMBC Study* (Institute Report No. 2). Baltimore: National Institute Against Prejudice and Violence.

Elias, Robert. 1986. *The Politics of Victimization.* New York: Oxford University Press.

El-Khawas, Elaine. 1991. *Campus Trends, 1991.* Washington, D.C.: American Council on Education.

FORUM. 1990. "Group Violence in the U.S.A." *FORUM* 5, no. 1 (January/February). (*FORUM* is the newsletter of the National Institute Against Prejudice and Violence.)

Gordon, Leonard. 1991. "Racism on College Campuses: Reflections on Causes and Policies to Address the Problem." Paper presented to the National Conference on Racial and Ethnic Relations in American Higher Education, San Antonio, Texas (June).

Institute for the Study of Social Change. 1991. *The Diversity Project: Final Report.* Berkeley: University of California Press.

Koss, Mary P., C. A. Gidycz, and N. Wisniewski. 1987. "The Scope of Rape: Incidence and Prevalence in the National Sample of Higher Education Students." *Journal of Consulting and Clinical Psychology* 55:162–170.

McKinney, Kathleen, and Nick Maroules. 1991. "Sexual Harassment." In E. Grauerholz and M. Koralewski, eds., *Sexual Coercion.* New York: Lexington Books.

Martin, Patricia Yancey, and Robert A. Hummer. 1989. "Fraternities and Rape on Campus." *Gender and Society* 3:457–473.

Moffat, Michael. 1989. *Coming of Age in New Jersey: College and American Culture.* New Brunswick, N.J.: Rutgers University Press.

Peterson, Donald R. 1990. *Students Speak on Prejudice.* New Brunswick, N.J.: Rutgers University, Committee to Advance Our Common Purposes.

Rokeach, Milton, and Sandra J. Ball-Rokeach. 1989. "Stability and Change in American Value Priorities, 1968–1981." *American Psychologist* 44:775–784.

Sanday, Peggy Reeves. 1991. *Sex, Brotherhood, and Privilege on Campus.* New York: New York University Press.

Seligman, Miles, and Cymbre Simpson. 1991. "Behind Right-Wing Campus Newspapers." *Extra* (September/October):9.

Taylor, Anthony. 1990. *Campus Discrimination and Prejudice.* New York: SUNY College at Cortland.

Weiss, Joan C., Howard J. Ehrlich, and Barbara E. K. Larcom. 1991–1992. "Ethnoviolence at Work" (Institute Report No. 6). *Journal of Intergroup Relations* 18(4):21–33.

Whitney, D. Charles, and Ellen Wartella. 1992. "Media Coverage of the 'Political Correctness' Debate." *Journal of Communication* 42(2):83–94.

26

Race Fever

EDWARD ALEXANDER

American universities are aflame with race fever. Official committees on "racism and cultural diversity," departmental commissioners of moral sanitation, and freelance vigilantes are in a state of high alert for signs (real or alleged) of "racism." Their Argus-eyes maintain unrelaxing surveillance of statistical charts documenting failure to meet racial quotas in hiring and enrollment, of verbal insults by "white" students against "people of color," and of classroom remarks by professors imprudent enough either to risk generalization about a group *or* to declare that generalizations about groups tell us nothing about individuals.

Such diligence rarely goes unrewarded. Since many American campuses have "populations" larger than hundreds of American cities, it is hardly remarkable that incidents of behavior less than saintly, including racial harassment, should occur. What is remarkable is the way in which such incidents are now regularly exploited by political opportunists, people Joseph Epstein has labeled "the intellectual equivalent of ambulance-chasers." A few instances should suffice to illustrate the general pattern.

At Southern Methodist University (SMU) in Dallas earlier this year, a freshman was "reported to university officials" for singing "We Shall Overcome" in a "sarcastic manner" during a late-night dormitory discussion. The campus was still vibrating from this shocking violation of the school's "racial-harassment rules" when it learned of a still more flagrant one, in which a white graduate student "was reported for calling a Hispanic classmate a Mexican in a derogatory manner after an intramural football game." Although the student whom the New York *Times* dubbed "the victim" of the slur received an immediate apology from the culprit, apology was also demanded, and received, by the university's judicial board and then by its "intercultural affairs office." But since Big Brother (very much like his omnipresent Big Sister, ever watchful for sexism) is not easily placated, this triune apology had to be supplemented by penance in the form of thirty hours of community service to minority organizations in Dallas.

In 1986 SMU had established a course called "Black and White." Its purpose was, as one satisfied student enrolled in it declared, to teach that "whites must be sensitive to the African-American community rather than the other way around."

Sensitivity traffic is heavy, but it flows in only one direction. Any suggestion that members of a formerly despised and mistreated group may be capable of wrong-doing is punished with utmost severity. "The spirit of improvement," wrote John Stuart Mill in a famous understatement, "is not always a spirit of liberty."

There is only one sense in which these courses in sensitivity training conform to old-fashioned ideas about liberal education: their main purpose seems to be to ventilate the moral sensibilities or, if I may change my metaphor, to flex the moral muscles in an imaginary gymnasium rather than to put one in touch with the truth about the actual world. At Emory University in Atlanta, a black student gained national attention in March when she reported several incidents of racial harassment, including the ransacking of her dormitory room, the scrawling of racial slurs on its walls, and the receipt of death threats in the mail. These threats, so Sabrina Collins alleged, caused her to curl into a fetal ball and to lose the power of speech. But by June, local prosecutors reviewing the case concluded that it was all a hoax, and that the only Emory student who participated in the harassment of Sabrina Collins was Sabrina Collins herself. Her imagination, it seems, had been fueled by an eagerness to impede an inquiry into suspicions that she had cheated in a chemistry class. This fiasco, however, did nothing to dampen the zeal of those who had been lashing the university authorities for their failure to combat the racism that had victimized Collins. "It doesn't matter ... whether she did it or not," said the president of the Atlanta chapter of the NAACP, "because of all the pressure these black students are under at these predominantly white schools. If this will highlight it, if it will bring it to the attention of the public, I have no problem with that." No problem, that is, with falsehood, with fraud, or with the doctrine that members of an oppressed group are incapable of doing wrong.

Innocents who wander into these modern Salems will quickly discover the profound truth of Abigail M. Thernstrom's description of the universities and colleges as "islands of repression in a sea of freedom." In the 1970 revised edition of Beyond the Melting Pot, a study of race and ethnicity in New York City, Daniel P. Moynihan and Nathan Glazer wrote that "Race has exploded to swallow up all other distinctions, or so it would appear at the moment." Yet even Senator Moynihan must have been surprised by the incendiary effect of his saying to the students of Vassar College, in a February lecture, that "the United States of America provides a model of a reasonably successful multiethnic society." The blundering ear of the Vassar thought police heard Moynihan say that the U.S. was "a model of ethnic cooperation," and construed this alleged remark to be racist. For good measure they alleged (and Moynihan denied) that he had told a Dutchess County (N.Y.) official who is from Jamaica to go back to that country if he didn't like the U.S.

As is often the case in such incidents, what actually happened was far less important than the keen desire of the race-obsessed witchhunters to exploit what was *alleged* to have happened. Leaders of the Black Student Union at Vassar demanded an apology from the college administration for the remarks they themselves had foisted on Moynihan and his removal from the Eleanor Roosevelt professorship, under which rubric he had given his lecture. As the handbook of student activism clearly states that bullying, however satisfying to the militant spirit, must never be its own reward, small wonder that demands soon were also made for the establishment of a task force on racism, for the creation of a black student center, for the opening of an intercultural center, and for bountiful provision of the other desiderata of progressive race-thinking. Students who declined to join the demonstration, even if they supported its demands, were denounced by its leaders as—surprise!—racists too. One of these leaders announced, with touching candor, that he and his fellow tribunes had for some time been seeking a way to bend the college administration to their will: "This was the perfect catalyst."

To witness an outbreak of race fever at first hand is to have an experience, not soon forgotten, of just how lethal is the mixture of aspirants to victim status with pretenders to guilt, who compound for sins they are inclined to by damning those they have no mind to.

The University of Washington in Seattle, with 34,000 students and over 2,500 faculty, is one of the largest on the West Coast. It has had considerable experience of spectacular confrontations over the issue of race. In March 1970 the Black Student Union and the Seattle Liberation Front (led by the future editor of *Tikkun*, Michael Lerner, and described by then Washington State Attorney General—now U.S. Senator—Slade Gorton as an organization "totally indistinguishable from fascism and Nazism") accused the university of complicity in racism because it refused to cancel an athletic competition with Brigham Young University, a Mormon school. A mob composed of members of these two organizations and their followers invaded six university buildings, brutally beating over a dozen instructors and students who disobeyed the order to strike. Nowadays far greater results can be achieved with less arduous methods.

Like any university that cherishes its credentials as a progressive institution, Washington encourages its administrators to search out manifestations of racism and use them as occasions for reeducation of staff and faculty. In my own department (English), in March 1989, the chairman, after diplomatically settling an altercation between a white secretary and a black one, urged us all to attend a program on "Exploring Diversity," in which the campus Office of Human Rights would enlighten us respecting the "new consciousness about diversity, about the changing demography of our institution and our society." His memo was positive in tone, and avoided all denunciation. This, it turned out, was a colossal error. He was immediately "reprimanded" by unnamed "colleagues" for the "indirect, insensitive" language of his memo—the insensitivity consisting, of course, in his failure to brandish the talisman of "racism." Instead of throwing said colleagues out of his office with a warning never to return again, my chairman at once sent out a much longer memo, which thanked the censorious colleagues for revealing to him his own "insensitivity," mentioned "racism" repeatedly, and apologized profusely for the use of "language that encourages just the kind of action that resulted in the need for this meeting." Again, even more insistently than before, he urged everyone to attend the scheduled "workshop." (Wasn't it Kingsley Amis who said that "If there's one word that sums up everything that's gone wrong since the war, it's Workshop"?)

It soon turned out, however, that this departmental unpleasantness was but a local skirmish in a larger struggle. On May 3, 1989, William P. Gerberding, president of the university, stepped on a mine while addressing an awards dinner for

minority students. He made a very small "ethnic" joke while conferring the Hispanic American Recognition Award on a student in civil engineering. Perhaps,
jested Gerberding, the student had acquired his interest in the highway system
while "driving down the highway at 70 mph in the middle of the night to keep
ahead of immigration authorities."

The honoree "didn't know if I should take it as a joke or not." But he soon received guidance from higher authority. The organization of Chicano students
(Movimiento Estudiantil Chicano de Aztlan, or MECHA), when it learned of the
joke, informed the student that he certainly *ought* to have been offended. Ernesto
Sandoval, the "Commissioner" of MECHA, summoning the indignation worthy
of his title, complained that the university "had done nothing about this" and declared that an offense of such enormity could not be committed with impunity.
He also stoked the fire of his wrath by remembering, now, that a year earlier
Gerberding had publicly urged university students to work hard to keep pace with
the Japanese—an obviously racist use of "the yellow peril."

Within a few hours, Sandoval had received a letter of apology from President
Gerberding. But the letter was deemed "unsatisfactory" because it was insuffi-
ciently contrite and self-abasing. Gerberding said he would "try again." But again
he failed: apology number two, though it amplified number one by heaping
praise on the whole Hispanic population, still failed to utter the magical term
"racism." Besides, it was not a *public* apology: "If he offended our community in
public," said the Commissioner, "then he can apologize to us in public."

Ever willing to try harder, Gerberding agreed to apologize, now for the third
time, at a public forum to be held in the aptly named Red Square in the center of
the campus. He also consented to participate in a seminar especially designed for
administrators found to be inadequately endowed with "ethnic and racial sensitivity." But if Gerberding thought that confessing to racism and agreeing to reeducation had opened the way to absolution, he was soon to be disillusioned. The
200 students (out of 34,000) who assembled to pass judgment on him were in no
mood to be merciful.

Gerberding recited nearly all the banalities his tormentors wanted to hear. He
announced that the university's true purpose is "the celebration of diversity,"
which he defined (just as his audience does) entirely in racial terms: "Diversity includes all of you folks out in front of me, white, black, all in betweens." Like them,
he took it as self-evident truth that mind is a function of physiology, that the apparent fruits of intellect actually originate in genetics, and that all people belonging to a particular ethnic group either are, or should be, of one mind and will.
Therefore, if you want intellectual diversity, you need a racial recipe that mixes
"white, black, [and] all in betweens" in exact proportion to their presence in the
general population.

Meanwhile, the assembled embodiments and celebrants of diversity were alter-
nately heckling and chanting, in metronomically monotonous unison, the inspir-
ing verses: "Hey, hey! Ho, ho! Racism has got to go!" Their collective toothbaring,
their will to offend, to bully, to humiliate, comported oddly with the image of victim they so passionately claimed for themselves. Furthermore, however pleased
the demonstrators might have been by Gerberding's instinctive compliance with
the psychology of abdication, they wanted something tangible. As one smarmy,

self-righteous lout at the front of the mob put it: "Since you can publicly admit your insensitivities and shortcomings toward people of color and racial issues, we expect your support of the Ethnic Studies Requirement as a sign of your new awareness and of our needs." Campus bullies, like Middle Eastern terrorists, hold to the conviction that no bad deed of theirs should go unrewarded.

For a year, a faculty-student Task Force on Ethnicity had been assessing a proposal that would compel every student at the University of Washington to devote one-quarter of the Humanities and Social Science credits required for a bachelor's degree to Ethnic Studies courses. The ideal (if not the actual) purpose of such courses would be to "sensitize" the American majority toward this country's minority groups and to build a curricular bulwark against the omnipresent evil of racism. But since Gerberding did not have the authority to force the hand of the committee, the anti-racism struggle now shifted to the final deliberations of the group, which the demonstrators were urged to attend (and to influence).

Whether it was by accident or by the intervention of invisible powers, I entered the spectators' gallery of the crucial meeting just as the committee, which had already been in session for an hour, began to consider the Jewish question. Other "white" groups, such as Italian and Irish Americans, had, I learned, been denied most-favored-minority status at an earlier stage of the committee's deliberations. Now it was the turn of the Jews to be measured. Are the Jews a minority in this country? Is anti-Semitism a form of racism? Hardly abstruse questions, one might suppose; and yet they roused intense debate. The students, representing African Americans, Native Americans, Asian Americans, and Chicano/Latino Americans—otherwise known as the "major" minorities—unanimously opposed the inclusion of Jews and anti-Semitism in the Ethnic Studies curriculum. They seemed genuinely bemused by the idea that people not in their political party should have the temerity to invade their turf and poach on the (very considerable) spoils of their anticipated victory. Their recommended solution—eventually approved by the committee—was to substitute "people of color" for the term "minorities" wherever it appeared in committee documents.

The prize for semantic juggling was won not by the students, however, but by the two professorial representatives of the Ethnic Studies program itself, both of whom have also presided over Afro-American Studies. Professor Joseph Scott could not assent to the inclusion of Jews and anti-Semitism in the proposed scheme of courses unless other "Semitic" peoples, most particularly the Palestinian Arabs, were also included. Professor Johnella Butler also opposed inclusion of Jews because Jewish persons are not necessarily of "Semitic descent" and "anti-Semitism is not institutionalized in the country."

These remarks brought a raising of the collective eyebrow and even some tittering. For it appeared that of the 37,000 who teach and learn at the University of Washington, the only ones ignorant of the fact that anti-Semites hate Jews and not "Semites" were the professors of Ethnic Studies, the officially designated historians and exorcists of racism. Some uncharitable observers, to be sure, suspected that if you touched the delicate, exotic fruit of this professorial ignorance, it would quickly lose its bloom and turn out to be not so much ignorance of the history as guilt of the sin of racism. Could the spiteful introduction of Palestinian Arabs into a discussion of American minorities be innocent? Could the assertion by a grown-up and heavily degreed woman that institutional anti-Semitism (as if that were the only kind) is absent from this country be indicative less perhaps of a susceptibility to balderdash than of a desire to make up for that absence? The more closely one observes the actions and the moral temper of the leaders of the campus campaign against racism all across this country, the more urgently does the old adage "Physician, heal thyself" rise to one's lips.

It is hardly a secret that a majority of the more assiduous practitioners of progressive race-thinking at the universities define themselves as Marxists. At first glance this might seem surprising, because Marxism traditionally sought to explain everything by the material motives of class and property, not biology. But Marxism, as Jacques Barzun and Gertrude Himmelfarb have pointed out, is itself essentially racist in form and effect, depending as it does on a depiction of the bourgeois as, in Barzun's words, "not a human being with individual traits, but a social abstraction, a creature devoid of virtue or free will and without the right to live."

The collapse of the Marxist regimes of Central and Eastern Europe, the embarrassing fact that the first truly working-class revolution in history has been made (by Solidarity) against a *socialist* government, may have dulled the luster of economic determinism; but they have not extinguished the deep-seated modern desire to reduce human spirit and culture to matter. "Drive out nature with a fork," says Horace, "nevertheless she will continually return." With a little job retraining, yesterday's economic determinist becomes today's race (and "gender") determinist, seeking in physical origin and genes the key to mind, and excoriating colleagues who, in the already immortal words of Harvard's Derrick Bell, "look black and think white."

It is a sorry irony that "celebration of diversity" has become the slogan of self-proclaimed reformers of an institution called the university, a word whose origin and ideal meaning suggest that many parts have been "turned into one"— *universum*. If, as we still have good reason to believe, humanity is an infinitely varied repetition, then people of many groups, of diverse backgrounds, of a thousand dispositions can, if they practice tolerance and self-restraint, communicate with each other through the vehicle of mind. The university, in its ideal character, is predicated on the assumption that values which originate in the self or the group or the nation can be extradited and made available to those who share with the originators nothing except the human status. It aspires to Matthew Arnold's ideal of disinterestedness, the free play of the mind, unhampered by sect or party, over "the best that has been thought and said in the world."

That our universities have failed to achieve the perfection of this nobly inclusive ideal, no one should deny. But will turning it on its head in favor of the superstition that members of particular groups have one mind and live solely for a political purpose really extend cultural choice and individual rights? Do we really want our universities to become training schools for prigs and Pecksniffs who pride themselves on the ability to spot racism at a distance of twenty miles, who choose their professional "role models" according to race, and who scan their reading lists for proportional representation by race, "gender," and class, but who can no longer fathom the meaning and implication of Wordsworth's definition of the poet as "a man speaking to men"?

27

Multiculturalism: E Pluribus Plures

DIANE RAVITCH

Questions of race, ethnicity, and religion have been a perennial source of conflict in American education. The schools have often attracted the zealous attention of those who wish to influence the future, as well as those who wish to change the way we view the past. In our history, the schools have been not only an institution in which to teach young people skills and knowledge, but an arena where interest groups fight to preserve their values, or to revise the judgments of history, or to bring about fundamental social change. In the nineteenth century, Protestants and Catholics battled over which version of the Bible should be used in school, or whether the Bible should be used at all. In recent decades, bitter racial disputes— provoked by policies of racial segregation and discrimination—have generated turmoil in the streets and in the schools. The secularization of the schools during the past century has prompted attacks on the curricula and textbooks and library books by fundamentalist Christians, who object to whatever challenges their faith-based views of history, literature, and science.

Given the diversity of American society, it has been impossible to insulate the schools from pressures that result from differences and tensions among groups. When people differ about basic values, sooner or later those disagreements turn up in battles about how schools are organized or what the schools should teach. Sometimes these battles remove a terrible injustice, like racial segregation. Some-times, however, interest groups politicize the curriculum and attempt to impose their views on teachers, school officials, and textbook publishers. Across the country, even now, interest groups are pressuring local school boards to remove myths and fables and other imaginative literature from children's readers and to inject the teaching of creationism in biology. When groups cross the line into ex-tremism, advancing their own agenda without regard to reason or others, they threaten public education itself, making it difficult to teach any issues honestly and making the entire curriculum vulnerable to political campaigns.

For many years, the public schools attempted to neutralize controversies over race, religion, and ethnicity by ignoring them. Educators believed, or hoped, that the schools could remain outside politics; this was, of course, a vain hope since the schools were pursuing policies based on race, religion, and ethnicity. Nonetheless, such divisive questions were usually excluded from the curriculum. The textbooks minimized problems among groups and taught a sanitized version of history. Race, religion, and ethnicity were presented as minor elements in the American saga; slavery was treated as an episode, immigration as a sidebar, and women were largely absent. The textbooks concentrated on presidents, wars, national politics, and issues of state. An occasional "great black" or "great woman" received mention, but the main narrative paid little attention to minority groups and women.

With the ethnic revival of the 1960s, this approach to the teaching of history came under fire, because the history of national leaders—virtually all of whom were white, Anglo-Saxon, and male—ignored the place in American history of those who were none of the above. The traditional history of elites had been complemented by an assimilationist view of American society, which presumed that everyone in the American melting pot would eventually lose or abandon those ethnic characteristics that distinguished them from mainstream Americans. The ethnic revival demonstrated that many groups did not want to be assimilated or melted. Ethnic studies programs popped up on campuses to teach not only that "black is beautiful," but also that every other variety of ethnicity is "beautiful" as well; everyone who had "roots" began to look for them so that they too could recover that ancestral part of themselves that had not been homogenized.

As ethnicity became an accepted subject for study in the late 1960s, textbooks were assailed for their failure to portray blacks accurately; within a few years, the textbooks in wide use were carefully screened to eliminate bias against minority groups and women. At the same time, new scholarship about the history of women, blacks, and various ethnic minorities found its way into the textbooks. At first, the multicultural content was awkwardly incorporated as little boxes on the side of the main narrative. Then some of the new social historians (like Stephan Thernstrom, Mary Beth Norton, Gary Nash, Winthrop Jordan, and Leon Litwack) themselves wrote textbooks, and the main narrative itself began to reflect a broadened historical understanding of race, ethnicity, and class in the American past. Consequently, today's history textbooks routinely incorporate the experiences of women, blacks, American Indians, and various immigrant groups.

Although most high school textbooks are deeply unsatisfactory (they still largely neglect religion, they are too long, too encyclopedic, too superficial, and lacking in narrative flow), they are far more sensitive to pluralism than their predecessors. ... The latest generation of textbooks bluntly acknowledges the racism of the past, describing the struggle for equality by racial minorities while identifying individuals who have achieved success as political leaders, doctors, lawyers, scholars, entrepreneurs, teachers, and scientists.

As a result of the political and social changes of recent decades, cultural pluralism is now generally recognized as an organizing principle of this society. In contrast to the idea of the melting pot, which promised to erase ethnic and group differences, children now learn that variety is the spice of life. They learn that America has provided a haven for many different groups and has allowed them to maintain their cultural heritage or to assimilate, or—as is often the case—to do both; the choice is theirs, not the state's. They learn that cultural pluralism is one of the norms of a free society; that differences among groups are a national resource rather than a problem to be solved. Indeed, the unique feature of the United States is that its common culture has been formed by the interaction of its subsidiary cultures. It is a culture that has been influenced over time by immigrants, American Indians, Africans (slave and free) and by their descendants. American music, art, literature, language, food, clothing, sports, holidays, and customs all show the effects of the commingling of diverse cultures in one nation. Paradoxical though it may seem, the United States has a common culture that is multicultural.

Our schools and our institutions of higher learning have in recent years begun to embrace what Catherine R. Stimpson of Rutgers University has called "cultural democracy," a recognition that we must listen to a "diversity of voices" in order to understand our culture, past and present. This understanding of the pluralistic nature of American culture has taken a long time to forge. It is based on sound scholarship and has led to major revisions in what children are taught and what they read in school. The new history is—indeed, must be—a warts-and-all history; it demands an unflinching examination of racism and discrimination in our history. Making these changes is difficult, raises tempers, and ignites controversies, but gives a more interesting and accurate account of American history. Accomplishing these changes is valuable, because there is also a useful lesson for the rest of the world in America's relatively successful experience as a pluralistic society. ...

Alas, these painstaking efforts to expand the understanding of American culture into a richer and more varied tapestry have taken a new turn, and not for the better. Almost any idea, carried to its extreme, can be made pernicious, and this is what is happening now to multiculturalism. Today, pluralistic multiculturalism must contend with a new, particularistic multiculturalism. The pluralists seek a richer common culture; the particularists insist that no common culture is possible or desirable. The new particularism is entering the curriculum in a number of school systems across the country. Advocates of particularism propose an ethnocentric curriculum to raise the self-esteem and academic achievement of children from racial and ethnic minority backgrounds. Without any evidence, they claim that children from minority backgrounds will do well in school *only* if they are immersed in a positive, prideful version of their ancestral culture. If children are of, for example, Fredonian ancestry, they must hear that Fredonians were important in mathematics, science, history, and literature. If they learn about great Fredonians and if their studies use Fredonian examples and Fredonian concepts, they will do well in school. If they do not, they will have low self-esteem and will do badly.

At first glance, this appears akin to the celebratory activities associated with Black History Month or Women's History Month, when schoolchildren learn about the achievements of blacks and women. But the point of those celebrations is to demonstrate that neither race nor gender is an obstacle to high achievement. They teach all children that everyone, regardless of their race, religion, gender, ethnicity, or family origin, can achieve self-fulfillment, honor, and dignity in society if they aim high and work hard.

By contrast, the particularistic version of multiculturalism is unabashedly fil-
iopietistic and deterministic. It teaches children that their identity is determined
by their "cultural genes." That something in their blood or their race memory or
their cultural DNA defines who they are and what they may achieve. That the culture in which they live is not their own culture, even though they were born here.
That American culture is "Eurocentric," and therefore hostile to anyone whose
ancestors are not European. Perhaps the most invidious implication of particularism is that racial and ethnic minorities are not and should not try to be part of
American culture; it implies that American culture belongs only to those who are
white and European; it implies that those who are neither white nor European are
alienated from American culture by virtue of their race or ethnicity; it implies
that the only culture they do belong to or can ever belong to is the culture of their
ancestors, even if their families have lived in this country for generations. ...

The pluralist approach to multiculturalism promotes a broader interpretation
of the common American culture and seeks due recognition for the ways that the
nation's many racial, ethnic, and cultural groups have transformed the national
culture. The pluralists say, in effect, "American culture belongs to us, all of us; the
U.S. is us, and we remake it in every generation." But particularists have no interest in extending or revising American culture; indeed, they deny that a common
culture exists. Particularists reject any accommodation among groups, any interactions that blur the distinct lines between them. The brand of history that they
espouse is one in which everyone is either a descendant of victims or oppressors.
By doing so, ancient hatreds are fanned and recreated in each new generation.
Particularism has its intellectual roots in the ideology of ethnic separatism and in
the black nationalist movement. In the particularist analysis, the nation has five
cultures: African American, Asian American, European American, Latino/His-
panic, and Native American. The huge cultural, historical, religious, and linguistic differences within these categories are ignored, as is the considerable intermarriage among these groups, as are the linkages (like gender, class, sexual
orientation, and religion) that cut across these five groups. No serious scholar
would claim that all Europeans and white Americans are part of the same culture,
or that all Asians are part of the same culture, or that all people of Latin-Ameri-
can descent are of the same culture, or that all people of African descent are of the
same culture. Any categorization this broad is essentially meaningless and useless.

Several districts—including Detroit, Atlanta, and Washington, D.C.—are developing an Afrocentric curriculum. *Afrocentricity* has been described in a book
of the same name by Molefi Kete Asante of Temple University. The Afrocentric
curriculum puts Africa at the center of the student's universe. African Americans
must "move away from an [*sic*] Eurocentric framework" because "it is difficult to
create freely when you use someone else's motifs, styles, images, and perspectives." Because they are not Africans, "white teachers cannot inspire in our children the visions necessary for them to overcome limitations." Asante recom-
mends that African Americans choose an African name (as he did), reject
European dress, embrace African religion (not Islam or Christianity) and love
"their own" culture. He scorns the idea of universality as a form of Eurocentric arrogance. The Eurocentrist, he says, thinks of Beethoven or Bach as classical, but
the Afrocentrist thinks of Ellington or Coltrane as classical; the Eurocentrist lauds

Shakespeare or Twain, while the Afrocentrist prefers Baraka, Shange, or Abiola. Asante is critical of black artists like Arthur Mitchell and Alvin Ailey who ignore Afrocentricity. Likewise, he speaks contemptuously of a group of black university students who spurned the Afrocentrism of the local Black Student Union and formed an organization called Inter-race: "Such madness is the direct consequence of self-hatred, obligatory attitudes, false assumptions about society, and stupidity."

The conflict between pluralism and particularism turns on the issue of universalism. Professor Asante warns his readers against the lure of universalism: "Do not be captured by a sense of universality given to you by the Eurocentric viewpoint; such a viewpoint is contradictory to your own ultimate reality." He insists that there is no alternative to Eurocentrism, Afrocentrism, and other ethnocentrisms. In contrast, the pluralist says, with the Roman playwright Terence, "I am a man: nothing human is alien to me." A contemporary Terence would say "I am a person" or might be a woman, but the point remains the same: You don't have to be black to love Zora Neale Hurston's fiction or Langston Hughes's poetry or Duke Ellington's music. In a pluralist curriculum, we expect children to learn a broad and humane culture, to learn about the ideas and art and animating spirit of many cultures. We expect that children, whatever their color, will be inspired by the courage of people like Helen Keller, Vaclav Havel, Harriet Tubman, and Feng Lizhe. We expect that their response to literature will be determined by the ideas and images it evokes, not by the skin color of the writer. But particularists insist that children can learn only from the experiences of people from the same race.

Particularism is a bad idea whose time has come. It is also a fashion spreading like wildfire through the education system, actively promoted by organizations and individuals with a political and professional interest in strengthening ethnic power bases in the university, in the education profession, and in society itself. One can scarcely pick up an educational journal without learning about a school district that is converting to an ethnocentric curriculum in an attempt to give "self-esteem" to children from racial minorities. ...

Pluralism can easily be transformed into particularism, as may be seen in the potential uses in the classroom of the Mayan contribution to mathematics. The Mayan example was popularized in a movie called *Stand and Deliver,* about a charismatic Bolivian-born mathematics teacher in Los Angeles who inspired his students (who are Hispanic) to learn calculus. He told them that their ancestors invented the concept of zero; but that wasn't all he did. He used imagination to put across mathematical concepts. He required them to do homework and to go to school on Saturdays and during the Christmas holidays, so that they might pass the Advanced Placement mathematics examination for college entry. The teacher's reference to the Mayans' mathematical genius was a valid instructional device: It was an attention-getter and would have interested even students who were not Hispanic. But the Mayan example would have had little effect without the teacher's insistence that the class study hard for a difficult examination.

Ethnic educators have seized upon the Mayan contribution to mathematics as the key to simultaneously boosting the ethnic pride of Hispanic children and attacking Eurocentrism. One proposal claims that Mexican-American children will be attracted to science and mathematics if they study Mayan mathematics, the Mayan calendar, and Mayan astronomy. Children in primary grades are to be taught that the Mayans were first to discover the zero and that Europeans learned it long afterwards from the Arabs, who had learned it in India. This will help them see that Europeans were latecomers in the discovery of great ideas. ...

This proposal suggests some questions: Is there any evidence that the teaching of "culturally relevant" science and mathematics will draw Mexican-American children to the study of these subjects? Will Mexican-American children lose interest or self-esteem if they discover that their ancestors were Aztecs or Spaniards, rather than Mayans? Are children who learn in this way prepared to study the science and mathematics that are taught in American colleges and universities and that are needed for advanced study in these fields? Are they even prepared to study the science and mathematics taught in *Mexican* universities? If the class is half Mexican-American and half something else, will only the Mexican-American children study in a Mayan and Aztec mode or will all the children? But shouldn't all children study what is culturally relevant for them? How will we train teachers who have command of so many different systems of mathematics and science?

The efficacy of particularist proposals seems to be less important to their sponsors than their value as ideological weapons with which to criticize existing disciplines for their alleged Eurocentric bias. In a recent article titled "The Ethnocentric Basis of Social Science Knowledge Production" in the *Review of Research in Education,* John Stanfield at Yale University argues that neither social science nor science are objective studies, that both instead are "Euro-American" knowledge systems which reproduce "hegemonic racial domination." The claim that science and reason are somehow superior to magic and witchcraft, he writes, is the product of Euro-American ethnocentrism. According to Stanfield, current fears about the misuse of science (for instance, "the nuclear arms race, global pollution") and "the power-plays of Third World nations (the Arab oil boycott and the American-Iranian hostage crisis) have made Western people more aware of nonscientific cognitive styles. These last events are beginning to demonstrate politically that which has begun to be understood in intellectual circles: namely, that modes of social knowledge such as theology, science, and magic are different, not inferior or superior. They represent different ways of perceiving, defining, and organizing knowledge of life experiences." One wonders: If Professor Stanfield broke his leg, would he go to a theologian, a doctor, or a magician?

Every field of study, it seems, has been tainted by Eurocentrism, which was defined by a professor at Manchester University, George Ghevarughese Joseph, in *Race and Class* in 1987, as "intellectual racism." Professor Joseph argues that the history of science and technology—and in particular, of mathematics—in non-European societies was distorted by racist Europeans who wanted to establish the dominance of European forms of knowledge. The racists, he writes, traditionally traced mathematics to the Greeks, then claimed that it reached its full development in Europe. These are simply Eurocentric myths to sustain an "imperialist/racist ideology," says Professor Joseph, since mathematics was found in Egypt, Babylonia, Mesopotamia, and India long before the Greeks were supposed to have developed it. Professor Joseph points out too that Arab scientists should be credited with major discoveries traditionally attributed to William Harvey, Isaac Newton, Charles Darwin, and Sir Francis Bacon. But he is not concerned only to argue historical issues; his purpose is to bring all of these different mathematical traditions into the school classroom so that children might study, for example, "traditional African designs, Indian *rangoli* patterns and Islamic art" and "the language and counting systems found across the world."

This interesting proposal to teach ethnomathematics comes at a time when American mathematics educators are trying to overhaul present practices, because of the poor performance of American children on national and international assessments. Mathematics educators are attempting to change the teaching of their subject so that children can see its uses in everyday life. There would seem to be an incipient conflict between those who want to introduce real-life applications of mathematics and those who want to teach the mathematical systems used by ancient cultures. I suspect that most mathematics teachers would enjoy doing a bit of both, if there were time or student interest. But any widespread movement to replace modern mathematics with ancient ethnic mathematics runs the risk of disaster in a field that is struggling to update existing curricula. If, as seems likely, ancient mathematics is taught mainly to minority children, the gap between them and middle-class white children is apt to grow. It is worth noting that children in Korea, who score highest in mathematics on international assessments, do not study ancient Korean mathematics.

Filiopietism and ethnic boosterism lead to all sorts of odd practices. In New York State, for example, the curriculum guide for eleventh grade American history lists three "foundations" for the United States Constitution, as follows:

A. Foundations
    1. 17th and 18th century Enlightenment thought
    2. Haudenosaunee political system
       a. Influence upon colonial leadership and European intellectuals (Locke, Montesquieu, Voltaire, Rousseau)
       b. Impact on Albany Plan of Union, Articles of Confederation, and U.S. Constitution
    3. Colonial experience

Those who are unfamiliar with the Haudenosaunee political system might wonder what it is, particularly since educational authorities in New York State rank it as equal in importance to the European Enlightenment and suggest that it strongly influenced not only colonial leaders but the leading intellectuals of Europe. The Haudenosaunee political system was the Iroquois confederation of five (later six) Indian tribes in upper New York State, which conducted war and civil affairs through a council of chiefs, each with one vote. In 1754, Benjamin Franklin proposed a colonial union at a conference in Albany; his plan, said to be inspired by the Iroquois Confederation, was rejected by the other colonies. Today, Indian activists believe that the Iroquois Confederation was the model for the American Constitution, and the New York State Department of Education has decided that they are right. That no other state sees fit to give the American Indians equal billing with the European Enlightenment may be owing to the fact that the Indians in New York State (numbering less than forty thousand) have been more politically effective than elsewhere or that other states have not yet learned about this method of reducing "Eurocentrism" in their American history classes. ...

Today, there are a number of books and articles advancing controversial theories about the origins of civilization. An important work, *The African Origin of Civilization: Myth or Reality,* by Senegalese scholar Cheikh Anta Diop, argues that ancient Egypt was a black civilization, that all races are descended from the black race, and that the achievements of "western" civilization originated in Egypt. The views of Diop and other Africanists have been condensed into an everyman's paperback titled *What They Never Told You in History Class* by Indus Khamit Kush. This latter book claims that Moses, Jesus, Buddha, Mohammed, and Vishnu were Africans; that the first Indians, Chinese, Hebrews, Greeks, Romans, Britains, and Americans were Africans; and that the first mathematicians, scientists, astronomers, and physicians were Africans. A debate currently raging among some classicists is whether the Greeks "stole" the philosophy, art, and religion of the ancient Egyptians and whether the ancient Egyptians were black Africans. George G. M. James's *Stolen Legacy* insists that the Greeks "stole the Legacy of the African Continent and called it their own." James argues that the civilization of Greece, the vaunted foundation of European culture, owed everything it knew and did to its African predecessors. Thus, the roots of western civilization lie not in Greece and Rome, but in Egypt and, ultimately, in black Africa.

Similar speculation was fueled by the publication in 1987 of Martin Bernal's *Black Athena: The Afroasiatic Roots of Classical Civilization,* Volume 1, *The Fabrication of Ancient Greece, 1785–1985,* although the controversy predates Bernal's book. In a fascinating foray into the politics of knowledge, Bernal attributes the preference of Western European scholars for Greece over Egypt as the fount of knowledge to nearly two centuries of racism and "Europocentrism," but he is uncertain about the color of the ancient Egyptians. ... The debate reached the pages of the *Biblical Archeology Review* last year in an article titled "Were the Ancient Egyptians Black or White?" The author, classicist Frank J. Yurco, argues that some Egyptian rulers were black, others were not, and that "the ancient Egyptians did not think in these terms." The issue, wrote Yurco, "is a chimera, cultural baggage from our own society that can only be imposed artificially on ancient Egyptian society."

Most educationists are not even aware of the debate about whether the ancient Egyptians were black or white, but they are very sensitive to charges that the schools' curricula are Eurocentric, and they are eager to rid the schools of the taint of Eurocentrism. It is hardly surprising that America's schools would recognize strong cultural ties with Europe since our nation's political, religious, educational, and economic institutions were created chiefly by people of European descent, our government was shaped by European ideas, and nearly 80 percent of the people who live here are of European descent. The particularists treat all of this history as a racist bias toward Europe, rather than as the matter-of-fact consequences of European immigration. Even so, American education is not centered on Europe. American education, if it is centered on anything, is centered on itself. It is "Americentric." Most American students today have never studied any world history; they know very little about Europe, and even less about the rest of the world. Their minds are rooted solidly in the here and now. When the Berlin Wall was opened in the fall of 1989, journalists discovered that most American teenagers had no idea what it was, nor why its opening was such a big deal. Nonetheless, Eurocentrism provides a better target than Americentrism.

In school districts where most children are black and Hispanic, there has been a growing tendency to embrace particularism rather than pluralism. Many of the children in these districts perform poorly in academic classes and leave school without graduating. They would fare better in school if they had well-educated and well-paid teachers, small classes, good materials, encouragement at home and school, summer academic programs, protection from the drugs and crime that ravage their neighborhoods, and higher expectations of satisfying careers upon graduation. These are expensive and time-consuming remedies that must also engage the larger society beyond the school. The lure of particularism is that it offers a less complicated anodyne, one in which the children's academic deficiencies may be addressed—or set aside—by inflating their racial pride. The danger of this remedy is that it will detract attention from the real needs of schools and the real interests of children, while simultaneously arousing distorted race pride in children of all races, increasing racial antagonism and producing fresh recruits for white and black racist groups. ...

The rising tide of particularism encourages the politicization of all curricula in the schools. If education bureaucrats bend to the political and ideological winds, as is their wont, we can anticipate a generation of struggle over the content of the curriculum in mathematics, science, literature, and history. Demands for "culturally relevant" studies, for ethnostudies of all kinds, will open the classroom to unending battles over whose version is taught, who gets credit for what, and which ethno-interpretation is appropriate. Only recently have districts begun to resist the demands of fundamentalist groups to censor textbooks and library books (and some have not yet begun to do so).

The spread of particularism throws into question the very idea of American public education. Public schools exist to teach children the general skills and knowledge that they need to succeed in American society, and the specific skills and knowledge that they need in order to function as American citizens. They receive public support because they have a public function. Historically, the public schools were known as "common schools" because they were schools for all, even if the children of all the people did not attend them. Over the years, the courts have found that it was unconstitutional to teach religion in the common schools, or to separate children on the basis of their race in the common schools. In their curriculum, their hiring practices, and their general philosophy, the public schools must not discriminate against or give preference to any racial or ethnic group. Yet they are permitted to accommodate cultural diversity by, for example, serving food that is culturally appropriate or providing library collections that emphasize the interests of the local community. However, they should not be expected to teach children to view the world through an ethnocentric perspective that rejects or ignores the common culture. For generations, those groups that wanted to inculcate their religion or their ethnic heritage have instituted private schools—after school, on weekends, or on a full-time basis. There, children learn with others of the same group—Greeks, Poles, Germans, Japanese, Chinese, Jews, Lutherans, Catholics, and so on—and are taught by people from the same group.

Valuable as this exclusive experience has been for those who choose it, this has not been the role of public education. One of the primary purposes of public education has been to create a national community, a definition of citizenship and culture that is both expensive and *inclusive*.

The curriculum in public schools must be based on whatever knowledge and practices have been determined to be best by professionals—experienced teachers and scholars—who are competent to make these judgments. Professional societies must be prepared to defend the integrity of their disciplines. When called upon, they should establish review committees to examine disputes over curriculum and to render judgment, in order to help school officials fend off improper political pressure. Where genuine controversies exist, they should be taught and debated in the classroom. Was Egypt a black civilization? Why not raise the question, read the arguments of the different sides in the debate, show slides of Egyptian pharaohs and queens, read books about life in ancient Egypt, invite guest scholars from the local university, and visit museums with Egyptian collections? If scholars disagree, students should know it. One great advantage of this approach is that students will see that history is a lively study, that textbooks are fallible, that historians disagree, that the writing of history is influenced by the historian's politics and ideology, that history is written by people who make choices among alternative facts and interpretations, and that history changes as new facts are uncovered and new interpretations win adherents. They will also learn that cultures and civilizations constantly interact, exchange ideas, and influence one another, and that the idea of racial or ethnic purity is a myth. ...

The question of self-esteem is extraordinarily complex, and it goes well beyond the content of the curriculum. Most of what we call self-esteem is formed in the home and in a variety of life experiences, not only in school. Nonetheless, it has been important for blacks—and for other racial groups—to learn about the history of slavery and of the civil rights movement; it has been important for blacks to know that their ancestors actively resisted enslavement and actively pursued equality; and it has been important for blacks and others to learn about black men and women who fought courageously against racism and who provide models of courage, persistence, and intellect. These are instances where the content of the curriculum reflects sound scholarship, and at the same time probably lessens racial prejudice and provides inspiration for those who are descendants of slaves. But knowing about the travails and triumphs of one's forebears does not necessarily translate into either self-esteem or personal accomplishment. For most children, self-esteem—the self-confidence that grows out of having reached a goal—comes not from hearing about the monuments of their ancestors but as a consequence of what they are able to do and accomplish through their own efforts.

As I reflected on these issues, I recalled reading an interview a few years ago with a talented black runner. She said that her model is Mikhail Baryshnikov. She admires him because he is a magnificent athlete. He is not black; he is not female; he is not American-born; he is not even a runner. But he inspires her because of the way he trained and used his body. When I read this, I thought how narrowminded it is to believe that people can be inspired *only* by those who are exactly like them in race and ethnicity.

28

Multiculturalism: An Exchange

MOLEFI KETE ASANTE

We are all implicated in the positions we hold about society, culture, and education. Although the implications may take quite different forms in some fields and with some scholars, such as the consequences and our methods and inquiry on our systems of values, we are nevertheless captives of the positions we take, that is, if we take those positions honestly.

In a recent article in *The American Scholar* (Summer 1990), Diane Ravitch reveals the tensions between scholarship and ideological perspectives in an exceedingly clear manner. The position taken in her article "Multiculturalism: E Pluribus Plures" accurately demonstrates the thesis that those of us who write are implicated in what we choose to write. This is not a profound announcement since most fields of inquiry recognize that a researcher's presence must be accounted for in research or a historian's relationship to data must be examined in seeking to establish the validity of conclusions. This is not to say that the judgment will be invalid because of the intimacy of the scholar with the information but rather that in accounting for the scholar's or researcher's presence we are likely to know better how to assess the information presented. Just as a researcher may be considered an intrusive presence in an experiment, the biases of a scholar may be just as intrusive in interpreting data or making analysis. The fact that a writer seeks to establish a persona of a non-interested observer means that such a writer wants the reader to assume that an unbiased position is being taken on a subject. However, we know that as soon as a writer states a proposition, the writer is implicated and such implication holds minor or extreme consequences.

The remarkable advantage of stating aims and objectives prior to delivering an argument is that the reader knows precisely to what the author is driving. Unfortunately, too many writers on education either do not know the point they are making or lose sight of their point in the making. Such regrettably is the case with Diane Ravitch's article on multicultural education.

Among writers who have written on educational matters in the last few years, Professor Ravitch of Columbia University's Teacher's College is considered highly quotable and therefore, in the context of American educational policy, influential. This is precisely why her views on multiculturalism must not remain unchallenged. Many of the positions taken by Professor Ravitch are similar to the positions taken against the Freedmen's Bureau's establishment of black schools in the South in the 1860s. Then, the white conservative education policymakers felt that it was necessary to control the content of education so that the recently freed Africans would not become self-assured. An analysis of Ravitch's arguments will reveal what Martin Bernal calls in *Black Athena* "the neo-Aryan" model of history. Her version of multiculturalism is not multiculturalism at all, but rather a new form of Eurocentric hegemonism.

People tend to do the best they can with the information at their disposal. The problem in most cases where intellectual distortions arise is ignorance rather than malice. Unlike in the political arena where oratory goes a long way, in education, sooner or later the truth must come out. The proof of the theory is in the practice. What we have seen in the past twenty-five years is the gradual dismantling of the educational kingdom built to accompany the era of white supremacy. What is being contested is the speed of its dismantling. In many ways, the South African regime is a good parallel to what is going on in American education. No longer can the structure of knowledge which supported white hegemony be defended; whites must take their place, not above or below, but alongside the rest of humanity. This is a significantly different reality than we have experienced in American education and there are several reasons for this turn of events.

The first reason is the accelerating explosion in the world of knowledge about cultures, histories, and events seldom mentioned in American education. Names of individuals and their achievements, views of historiography and alternatives to European perspectives have proliferated due to international interaction, trade, and computer technology. People from other cultures, particularly non-Western people, have added new elements into the educational equation. A second reason is the rather recent intellectual liberation of large numbers of African-descended scholars. While there have always been African scholars in every era, the European hegemony, since the 1480s, in knowledge about the world, including Africa, was fairly complete. The domination of information, the naming of things, the propagation of concepts, and the dissemination of interpretations were, and still are in most cases in the West, a Eurocentric hegemony. During the twentieth century, African scholars led by W.E.B. DuBois began to break from the intellectual shackles of Europe and make independent inquiries into history, science, origins, and Europe itself. For the first time in five hundred years, a cadre of scholars, trained in the West, but largely liberated from the hegemonic European thinking began to expose numerous distortions, often elevated to "truth" in the works of Eurocentric authors. A third reason for the current assault on the misinformation spread by white hegemonic thinkers is the conceptual inadequacy of simply valorizing Europe. Few whites have ever examined their culture critically. Those who have done so have often been severely criticized by their peers: the cases of Sidney Willhelm, Joe Feagin, Michael Bradley, and Basil Davidson are well known.

As part of the Eurocentric tradition, there seems to be silence on questions of hegemony, that is, the inability to admit the mutual conspiracy between race doctrine and educational doctrine in America. Professor Ravitch and others would maintain the facade of reasonableness even in the face of arguments demonstrating the irrationality of both white supremacist ideas on race and white hegemonic ideas in education. They are corollary and both are untenable on genetic and intellectual grounds.

EUROCENTRIC HEGEMONISM

Let us examine the argument of the defenders of the Eurocentric hegemony in education more closely. The status quo always finds its best defense in territoriality. Thus, it is one of the first weapons used by the defenders of the white hegemonic education. Soon after my book *The Afrocentric Idea* was published, I was interviewed on "The Today Show" along with Herb London, the New York University professor/politician who is one of the founders of the National Association of Professors. When I suggested the possibility of schools weaving information about other cultures into the fabric of the teaching-learning process, Professor London interrupted that "there is not enough *time* in the school year for what Asante wants." Of course there is, if there is enough for the Eurocentric information, there is enough time for cultural information from other groups. Professor Ravitch uses the same argument. Her strategy is to cast serious examinations of the curriculum as pressure groups, much like creationists in biology. Of course, the issue is neither irrational nor sensational; it is pre-eminently a question of racial dominance, the maintenance of which, in any form, I oppose. On the contrary, the status quo defenders, like the South African Boers, believe that it is possible to defend what is fundamentally anti-intellectual and immoral: the dominance and hegemony of the Eurocentric view of reality on a multicultural society. There is space for Eurocentrism in a multicultural enterprise so long as it does not parade as universal. No one wants to banish the Eurocentric view. It is a valid view of reality where it does not force its way. Afrocentricity does not seek to replace Eurocentricity in its arrogant disregard for other cultures.

THE PRINCIPAL CONTRADICTIONS

A considerable number of white educators and some blacks have paraded in single file and sometimes in concert to take aim at multiculturalism. In her article Professor Ravitch attempts to defend the indefensible. Believing, I suspect, that the best defense of the status quo is to attack, she attacks diversity, and those that support it, with gusto, painting straw fellows along the way. Her claim to support multiculturalism is revealed to be nothing more than an attempt to apologize for white cultural supremacy in the curriculum by using the same logic as white racial supremacists used in trying to defend white racism in previous years. She assumes falsely that there is little to say about the rest of the world, particularly about Africa and African Americans. Indeed, she is willing to assert, as Herbert London has claimed, that the school systems do not have enough time to teach all that Afrocentrists believe ought to be taught. Nevertheless, she assumes that all that is not taught about the European experience is valid and necessary. There are some serious flaws in her line of reasoning. I shall attempt to locate the major flaws and ferret them out.

Lip service is paid to the evolution of American education from the days of racial segregation to the present when "new social historians" routinely incorporate the experiences of other than white males. Nowhere does Professor Ravitch demonstrate an appreciation for the role played by the African American community in overcoming the harshest elements of racial segregation in the educational system. Consequently, she is unable to understand that more fundamental than eliminating racial segregation has to be the removal of racist thinking, assumptions, symbols, and materials in the curriculum.

However, there is no indication that Professor Ravitch is willing to grant an audience to this reasoning because she plods deeper into the same quagmire by attempting to conceptualize multiculturalism, a simple concept in educational jargon. She posits a *pluralist* multiculturalism—a redundancy—then suggests a particularistic multiculturalism—an oxymoron—in order to beat a dead horse. The ideas are non-starters because they have no reality in fact. I wrote the first book in this country on trans-racial communication and edited the first handbook on intercultural communication, and I am unaware of the categories Professor Ravitch seeks to forge. She claims that the pluralist multiculturalist believes in pluralism and the particularistic multiculturalist believes in particularism. Well, multiculturalism in education is almost self-defining. It is simply the idea that the educational experience should reflect the diverse cultural heritage of our system of knowledge. I have contended that such is not the case and cannot be the case until teachers know more about the African American, Native American, Latino, and Asian experiences. This position obviously excites Professor Ravitch to the point that she feels obliged to make a case for "mainstream Americans."

THE MYTH OF MAINSTREAM

The idea of "mainstream American" is nothing more than an additional myth meant to maintain Eurocentric hegemony. When Professor Ravitch speaks of mainstream, she does not have Spike Lee, Aretha Franklin, or John Coltrane in mind. Bluntly put, "mainstream" is a code word for "white." When a dean of a college says to a faculty member, as one recently said, "You ought to publish in mainstream journals," the dean is not meaning *Journal of Black Studies* or *Black Scholar*. As a participant in the racist system of education, the dean is merely carrying out the traditional function of enlarging the white hegemony over scholarship. Thus, when the status quo defenders use terms like "mainstream," they normally mean "white." In fact, one merely has to substitute the words "white controlled" to get at the real meaning behind the code.

MISUNDERSTANDING MULTICULTURALISM

Misunderstanding the African American struggle for education in the United States, Professor Ravitch thinks that the call to multiculturalism is a matter of anecdotal references to outstanding individuals or descriptions of civil rights. But neither acknowledgment of achievements per se, nor descriptive accounts of the African experience adequately conveys the aims of the Afrocentric restructuring, as we shall see. From the establishment of widespread public education to the current emphasis on massaging the curriculum toward an organic and systemic recognition of cultural pluralism, the African American concept of nationhood has been always central. In terms of Afrocentricity, it is the same. We do not seek segments or modules in the classroom but rather the infusion of African American studies in every segment and in every module. The difference is between "incorporating the experiences" and "infusing the curriculum with an entirely new life." The real unity of the curriculum comes from infusion, not from including African Americans in what Ravitch would like to remain a white contextual hegemony she calls mainstream. No true mainstream can ever exist until there is knowledge, understanding, and acceptance of the role Africans have played in American history. One reason the issue is debated by white scholars such as Ravitch is because they do not believe there is substantial or significant African information to infuse. Thus, ignorance becomes the reason for the strenuous denials of space for the cultural infusion. If she knew or believed that it was possible to have missed something, she would not argue against it. What is at issue is her own educational background. Does she know classical Africa? Did she take courses in African American studies from qualified professors? Those who know do not question the importance of Afrocentric or Latino infusion into the educational process.

THE MISUSE OF SELF-ESTEEM

Professor Ravitch's main critique of the Afrocentric, Latinocentric, or Americentric (Native American) project is that it seeks to raise "self-esteem and self-respect" among Africans, Latinos, and Native Americans. It is important to understand that this is not only a self-serving argument, but a false argument. In the first place, I know of no Afrocentric curriculum planner—Asa Hilliard, Wade Nobles, Leonard Jeffries, Don McNeely being the principal ones—who insists that the primary aim is to raise self-esteem. The argument is a false lead to nowhere because the curriculum planners I am familiar with insist that the fundamental objective is to provide accurate information. A secondary effect of accuracy and truth might be the adjustment of attitudes by both black and white students. In several surveys of college students, research has demonstrated that new information changes attitudes in both African American and white students. Whites are not so apt to take a superior attitude when they are aware of the achievements of other cultures. They do not lose their self-esteem, they adjust their views. On the other hand, African Americans who are often as ignorant as whites about African achievements adjust their attitudes about themselves once they are exposed to new information. There is no great secret in this type of transformation. Ravitch, writing from the point of view of those whose cultural knowledge is reinforced every hour, not just in the curriculum, but in every media, smugly contends that she cannot see the value of self-esteem. Since truth and accuracy will yield byproducts of attitude adjustments, the Afrocentrists have always argued for the accurate representation of information.

Afrocentricity does not seek an ethnocentric curriculum. Unfortunately, Diane Ravitch chose to ignore two books that explain my views on this subject,

The Afrocentric Idea (1987) and *Kemet, Afrocentricity and Knowledge* (1990) and instead quotes from *Afrocenricity* (1980), which was not about education but about personal and social transformation. Had she read the later works she would have understood that Afrocentricity is not an ethnocentric view in two senses. In the first place, it does not valorize the African view while downgrading others. In this sense, it is unlike the Eurocentric view, which is an ethnocentric view because it valorizes itself and parades as universal. It becomes racist when the rules, customs, and/or authority of law or force dictate it as the proper view. This is what often happens in school curricula. In the second place, as to method, Afrocentricity is not a naive racial theory. It is a systematic approach to presenting the African as subject rather than object. Even Ravitch might be taught the Afrocentric Method!

AMERICAN CULTURE

There is no common American culture as is claimed by the defenders of the status quo. There is a hegemonic culture to be sure, pushed as if it were a common culture. Perhaps Ravitch is confusing concepts here. There is a common American *society,* which is quite different from a common American culture. Certain cultural characteristics are shared by those within the society but the meaning of *multicultural* is "many cultures." To believe in multicultural education is to assume that there are many cultures. The reason Ravitch finds confusion is because the only way she can reconcile the "many cultures" is to insist on many "little" cultures under the hegemony of the "big" white culture. Thus, what she means by multiculturalism is precisely what I criticized in *The Afrocentric Idea,* the acceptance of other cultures within a Eurocentric framework.

In the end, the neat separation of pluralist multiculturalists and particularistic multiculturalists breaks down because it is a false, straw separation developed primarily for the sake of argument and not for clarity. The real division on the question of multiculturalism is between those who truly seek to maintain a Eurocentric hegemony over the curriculum and those who truly believe in cultural pluralism without hierarchy. Ravitch defends the former position.

Professor Ravitch's ideological position is implicated in her mis-reading of several scholars' works. When Professor John Stanfield writes that modes of social knowledge such as theology, science, and magic are different, not inferior or superior, Ravitch asks, "If Professor Stanfield broke his leg, would he go to a theologian, a doctor, or a magician?" Clearly she does not understand the simple statement Stanfield is making. He is not writing about *uses* of knowledge, but about *ranking* of knowledge. To confuse the point by providing an answer for a question never raised is the key rhetorical strategy in Ravitch's case. Thus, she implies that because Professor George Ghevarughese Joseph argues that mathematics was developed in Egypt, Babylonia, Mesopotamia, and India long before it came to Europe, he seeks to replace modern math with "ancient ethnic mathematics." This is a deliberate misunderstanding of the professor's point: mathematics in its modern form owes debts to Africans and Asians.

Another attempt to befuddle issues is Ravitch's gratuitous comment that Koreans "do not study ancient mathematics" and yet they have high scores. There are probably several variables for the Koreans making the highest scores "in mathematics on international assessments." Surely one element would have to be the linkage of Korean traditions in mathematics to present mathematical problems. Koreans do not study European theorists prior to their own; indeed they are taught to honor and respect the ancestral mathematicians. This is true for Indians, Chinese, and Japanese. In African traditions, the *European* slave trade broke the linkage, and the work of scholars such as Ahmed Baba and Hypathia remains unknown to the African American and thus does not take its place in the family of world mathematics.

Before Professor Ravitch ends her assault on ethnic cultures, she fires a volley against the Haudenosaunee political system of Native Americans. As a New Yorker, she does not like the fact that the state's curriculum guide lists the Haudenosaunee Confederation as an inspiration for the United States Constitution alongside the Enlightenment. She says readers "might wonder what it is." Bluntly put, a proper education would acquaint students with the Haudenosaunee Confederation, and in that case Professor Ravitch's readers would know the Haudenosaunee as a part of the conceptual discussion that went into the development of the American political systems. Only a commitment to white hegemony would lead a writer to assume that whites could not obtain political ideas from others.

Finally, she raises a "controversy" that is no longer a controversy among reputable scholars: Who were the Egyptians? Most scholars accept a simple answer: They were Africans. The question of whether or not they were black was initially raised by Eurocentric scholars in the nineteenth century seeking to explain the testimony of the ancient Greeks, particularly Herodotus and Diodorus Siculus, who said that Egyptians were "Black with wooly hair." White hegemonic studies that sought to maintain the false notion of white racial supremacy during the nineteenth century fabricated the idea of a European or an Asian Egyptian to deny Africa its classical past and to continue the Aryan myth. It is shocking to see Professor Ravitch raise this issue in the 1990s. It is neither a controversial issue nor should it be to those familiar with the evidence.

The debate over the curriculum is really over a vision of the future of the United States. Keepers of the status quo, such as Professor Ravitch, want to maintain a "white framework" for multiculturalism because they have no faith in cultural pluralism without hierarchy. A common culture does not exist, but this nation is on the path toward it. Granting all the difficulties we face in attaining this common culture, we are more likely to reach it when we allow the full participation of all ethnic groups in a quest for a usable curriculum. In the end, we will find that such a curriculum, like inspiration, will not come from this or that individual model but from integrity and accuracy.

29

The "Overrepresentation" of Asian Americans: Red Herrings and Yellow Perils

DEBORAH WOO

> The flesh of a herring that has been cured in salt has a strong reddish color. These fish, though tasty, have a powerful odor before being cooked, and at one time were used to train hunting dogs to follow a scent. Moreover, if a red herring was dragged across the trail of an animal the dogs were pursuing, they'd chase the herring rather than the game. A "red herring across the trail" has therefore long had the sense of a deliberate distraction, as in an argument. (Claiborne, 1988: 193–4)

To refer to something as a "red herring" is to suggest that it is a deliberate distraction from pursuit of the "real" issue.This paper is concerned with how the major discourse on admissions policies at American universities has frequently masked a defence of entrenched privilege.

The language of "inclusion," for example, can be deceptive, serving covertly as the grounds for exclusion. Thus, in the 1920s, President A. Lawrence Lowell of Harvard sought to limit the growing number of Jews by changing admissions policies. His rationale was to invoke regional diversity, to include a wider band of the American landscape "by letting in boys from schools in other parts of the country which did not hitherto fit our requirements" (Synnott, 1979:7). Since Jews were concentrated in the northeast, regional quotas constituted a thinly veiled attempt to limit their numbers. "Diversity" thus surfaced conveniently as a red herring to protect university officials from the charge that they were discriminating on the basis of race, ethnicity, or religion. The language of diversity has re-emerged in the 1980s, but this time it is Asian Americans who have come to be viewed as an overrepresented minority, whose numbers must be controlled for the sake of "diversity." In talking about the need for "cultural diversity" on the various University of California campuses, President Gardner has expressly denied that quotas are a viable way of achieving this diversity. He nevertheless grants that such quotas may become "inevitable" if Asian American enrollment continues to grow.

> It seems to me that if we continue on the present path [of admitting highly qualified Asian American students], it inevitably will lead to quotas, so I don't wish to continue on this path. ... I want to build into our admissions process criteria that take account of ethnicity for purposes of assuring a pluralistic student body responsive to the changing demographics of California, but only as part of a number of criteria that we apply for the purpose of assuring that an entering freshman class is possessed of the kind of experience, potential, ethnic differences, social differences, rural and urban differences and so forth to enrich the whole learning environment and experience that these young people have. ... We will apply some of the criteria the private institutions routinely apply in making judgments about who to admit so that the freshmen class is diverse. (Wang, 1988: 14)

While the specific focus of this paper is on certain parallels between the Jewish and Asian American experience, the implications are much broader: namely, that *whenever* ethnic minorities begin seriously to threaten the status of dominant groups, admissions criteria are strategically redefined. While intellectual achievement has remained a central academic value, the "lowering of standards" has been acceptable, tolerated without much controversy, and even celebrated *when made on behalf of underachieving males who are white Anglo-Saxon Protestants.* When blacks, Latinos and other minorities, on the other hand, have sought "affirmative" measures to redress long-standing historical exclusion against them as a group, there has been strong and unprecedented resistance and backlash. ...

It is a given that academic history has been punctuated by divergences from meritocratic ideals. In the present historical moment, the tendency is to associate such deviations with affirmative action programmes for minorities. A main argument of this paper, however, is that admissions policies have been historically, systematically and routinely weighted heavily in favour of white majority males. Indeed, it is not unreasonable to speak of such policies as equivalent to "affirmative action" programmes. Their aim, however, has not been to redress historical injustice by opening the doors to previously disadvantaged groups but to perpetuate and buttress the interests of groups which have already benefited directly from favourable treatment. Moreover, practices amounting to "affirmative action" for white Gentile males have been pursued not only through outright discrimination but through surreptitious means, informal quotas, and the manipulation of admissions criteria. It is this context of unfair advantage that opponents of present-day affirmative action policies frequently ignore when they equate such policies with "reverse discrimination" or argue for "colour-blind" practices.

The following section looks at how increasing university enrollments among Asian Americans have revived an old image of them as "yellow perils". Within this new context, however, they have been viewed in a dual light—as an overrepresented group whose numbers need to be controlled and, on the other hand, as the grounds for attacking affirmative action students, largely black and Latino. This latter position is argued by John Bunzel, a long-time critic of affirmative action. The second major section of this paper looks at how exclusionary policies in university admissions were historically directed against Jews, while the final section takes up the issue of exclusion against Asian Americans. While the parallels between the Jewish and Asian experience are noteworthy, the issue of cultural diversity in the 1990s nevertheless differs from that in the early part of this century. The conclusion suggests that new criteria might by incorporated to truly reflect cultural diversity while simultaneously addressing issues of equity.

THE "OVERREPRESENTATION" OF ASIAN AMERICANS: THE NEW "YELLOW PERIL"

Although Asians resided in California before it became the thirty-first state in 1850, restrictive immigration laws suppressed their numbers until after the Second World War. With the passage of the 1965 Immigration Act, they became the fastest-growing minority in the country. Like the Jews who immigrated to New York between 1880 and 1920, they would have a major impact on the school systems in which they enrolled in substantial numbers.

Despite attempts to link Asian interests with those of white students in a backlash against other minorities, increasing Asian American college enrollment poses a more direct threat to white students. It is a much publicized fact that Asian Americans have high school and college completion levels exceeding those of all other ethnic groups, including whites. According to a 1980 national survey, 78 percent of Asian/Pacific high school seniors expected to earn a four-year college degree, compared to only 46 percent of white seniors. As the state with the largest Asian American population (1,247,000), California enrolled 43 percent (or 193,000) of the nation's 448,000 Asian American high school graduates in 1980. In 1986, 33 percent of the state's Asian American high school graduates were "academically eligible" for admission to the University of California, Berkeley, whereas only 16 percent of white high school graduates qualified. By the autumn of 1987, Asian Americans made up 28 percent of all applicants; whites made up 54.9 percent. According to Wang (1988:6), "This 2:1 ratio is impressive when one considers the fact that white high school graduates in California outnumbered Asian Americans by 6:1." ...

This general trend of increasing Asian American enrollment has not only become apparent at other major colleges in the country as well, but has been lauded by the news media. ... The majority of these reports cite cultural factors to explain this educational success. As early as the mid-1960s, such cultural explanations surfaced to fuel public discussions and prompted invidious comparisons with other minorities, who were pressed to emulate the Asian American model.

This global and uncritical portrayal of Asian American success has since been criticized and countered with more refined statistical data. More revealing, however, as to the politics behind positive (or negative) evaluations of a group is the way in which images of Asian Americans have been manipulated to serve dominant white interests. As noted, Asians were dubbed a "model minority" to justify undercutting programmes for other American minorities. But when increasing Asian American admissions have been paired with declining white enrollment, positive portrayals are remarkable absent. They are not a "model" for whites. Increasingly, former praise is replaced by concerns about Asian American "overrepresentation," recalling earlier characterizations of them as "yellow perils," "heathens" and unassimilables." ...

In short, now that Asian American educational successes appear to challenge the relative status of white students, the response has ranged from explicit hostility to exclusionary policies.

A significant portion of the *zeitgeist* of the present period is captured in the public discourse around higher education. Within this context, a new and curious dialogue has begun to take place around the old and familiar issues of "meritrocratic achievement" versus "affirmative action." In the past, affirmative action programmes to assist members of underrepresented groups (namely, blacks, Latinos, and American Indians) have been criticized for their corrosive effect on a system of meritocracy. Conservatives were quick to point to the fact that Asian Americans somehow managed to succeed without special attention given to them as a group. While many commentators have taken this position to the public stage, John Bunzel, currently a Research Fellow at Standford's Hoover Institute, has broadened this debate to incorporate an attack on admissions policies that recruit underrepresented minorities, such as Latinos and blacks. ...

THE EXCLUSION OF JEWS: RACIAL, SOCIAL, HISTORICAL, OR INDIVIDUAL DISCRIMINATION?

In the early 1900s, most urban Americans were white. Blacks were located mainly in the rural south, Latinos and Hispanics in the southwestern part of the United States, and Asians were primarily in the west, although they were few in number. The only major ethnic minorities were the growing numbers of Italians, Greeks, Lithuanians, Poles, Russians and Jews, who were part of the great wave of immigration that issued mainly from South, Central, and Eastern Europe between the years 1880 and 1920.

The average American citizen at this time did not view higher education as necessary or essential for mobility. A young person could look forward to a livelihood on the family farm, or take up a trade in one of the outlying towns. Venturing into nascent urban life opened up the possibility of employment in a factory or emerging small business enterprise. Regardless of one's particular life prospect, it was unusual for a job to require a college education, and the low rate of college attendance reflected this fact:

> As late as the first decade of this century, only about two of every hundred young people between the ages of eighteen and twenty-four went to college. At that time, only a handful of universities enrolled as many as two thousand undergraduate and graduate students combined; only five medical schools required any college preparation for admission. (Levine, 1986: 13) ...

Colleges were so desperate for students that "even the most prestigious institutions were scrambling to fill their classes ... admitting many with academic credentials below their stated admissions requirements" (Levine, 1986: 16–17). ...

The best colleges at this time were basically finishing schools where the sons of the corporate elite or business professionals came, not to compete as individuals for top grades, but rather to meet prospective associates and otherwise acquire the informal trappings and polish of "gentlemen" (Karabel, 1984). Academic learning was not only unfashionable but less than genteel given the purpose of mingling and forming social relationships that would extend beyond graduation. More important than grades was developing "character" (e.g. through sport and other extracurricular activities) and otherwise acquiring social skills by socializing with those of like status (Oren, 1985: 19). A "Gentleman's C" was considered respectable, a sign that one was above the tasteless, outward striving. In this context, it is not surprising that the report cards of the most successful corporate leaders and politicians would be mediocre by today's standards. Insofar as colleges such as the "Big Three" (Harvard, Yale and Princeton) were rivals, they were rivals not so much for the "best and the brightest" but for those students with the proper family background and social standing.

Colleges were exclusive and elitist and, for many years, almost all white and almost all male. In terms of social class composition, there was almost no social diversity to speak of. Ethnic and racial minorities were a highly unusual sight on the college campuses. However, the one major exception—aspiring immigrant Jews—would begin to test the gates of the universities by the early 1900s. ...

Columbia would feel the first strong swells of this new wave of students most keenly. Dean Frederick Keppel predicted that the "Jewish problem" would have to be confronted "by every college of the first class" since "they will go to no other" (Wechsler, 1977: 135). Even though Jews made up only 1.19 percent of the nation's total number of college students, they were concentrated within commuting distance of some of the northeast's most prestigious schools (Levine, 1986: 148). As a consequence, they soon became a noticeable presence not only at Columbia but at other nearby college campuses. Within the space of a few years, their percentages doubled or tripled at Harvard, Yale and Princeton. Yet, put into perspective, the Jewish proportion of the total student body was still relatively small. ...

Insofar as private colleges depended on the economic backing of their wealthy WASP constituency, it was against the objective interests of the institutions to encourage the presence of needy Jews, who were more likely to require rather than contribute financial resources. The other factor that negatively affected their reception was their social distance from WASP culture. Jews from Northwestern Europe had entered the country prior to the 1840s, but it was the less refined and aggressive nature of their Russian and East European counterparts that gave rise to serious concerns about their assimilation and growing influence. By 1910, immigrants from Southern and Eastern Europe made up 10 percent of the US population. Attempts to halt this flow at the national level took the form of literacy tests in 1917 and, ultimately, of quotas in 1924 based on each European country's figures from the 1890 census, a strategy biased in favour of Northwestern Europeans. Yet before the 1924 immigration law capped the tide, Jews from South, Central and Eastern Europe were already a noticeable presence not only in the high schools but the colleges.

The reasons given to justify ethnic exclusion or closure are revealing. Taken singly, each claim is logically or factually problematic. Taken together, their coherence as a set of rationalizations lies in preserving WASP privilege. Thus, it did not matter that, individually, certain propositions were weakly grounded. Their common aim was the exclusion of Jews. ...

Most reasons given to justify anti-Jewish feelings tended to focus on perceived cultural traits rather than low academic performance: Jews were criticized for their "clannishness," poor manners, lower standard of ethics and interest only in studies (Oren, 1985: 76). Parochialism and clannishness were said to have a damaging effect on the collegial atmosphere of the campus. Whatever the status of such accusations, these same attitudes would seem to apply equally to WASPs, insofar as snobbery led to social avoidance of those who were not of the same class, breeding, or cultural background. Indeed, there are more clear incidents of native-born sons engaging in such behaviour than there were of immigrants doing the same. ...

Complaints about Jews, in fact, frequently centered on their single-minded commitment to study and intellectual pursuits. Jews were the "grade-grubbers." They were the "'grinds,' 'fruits,' 'meatballs,' and 'black men' of minority ethnic origins and a public school education" (Oren, 1985: 20). Criticized for upsetting the academically noncompetitive atmosphere that had prevailed thus far, they were also held accountable for undermining the competitive atmosphere. A dean at Yale University expressed his dismay over the fact that competition from Jews dampened the competitive spirit of Gentiles: "Dean Frederick S. Jones of Yale blamed the declining interest in scholarship among Gentiles on the academic success of the Jewish student, who was seen as the 'greasy grind.' Undergraduates would no longer compete for 'first honors,' because they did 'not care to be a minority in a group of men of higher scholarship record, most of whom are Jews'" (Synnott, 1979: 15). ...

Once an exclusionary orientation was adopted, campus administrators had only to come up with workable or feasible measures for exclusion. Many selective admissions procedures which we are familiar with today originated as a direct outgrowth of attempts to keep out the undesirable Jewish element. From the 1920s to the late 1940s, administrators and admissions personnel armed themselves with an array of artillery aimed at this purpose: college board examinations, psychological or intelligence tests, emphasis on a geographically diverse student population, the allocation of scholarships and financial aid, alumni preference, photographs, questionnaires and personal interviews.

Although it is not clear which college provided the main impetus or leadership behind such exclusion, each tried to keep abreast of what the other was doing while developing its own specific restrictive methods. Columbia, for example, claimed to have successfully lowered Jewish enrollment from 40 to 20 percent through psychological testing (Oren, 1985: 52). Yale's Board of Admissions became the first to institute a policy of alumni preference that proved more reliable and effective. By 1930 Jews were only 8.2 percent of the Yale class (Oren, 1985: 55).

Many colleges in the northeast found it strategic to adopt a policy of recruiting from a broader geographical constituency since Jews were likely to be residents from local metropolitan areas. To facilitate this objective, Columbia considered reorganizing its scholarship programmes by establishing competitive awards in each state and each Canadian province (Wechsler, 1977: 152). While this particular plan was eventually rejected for being to costly, scholarships and financial aid were in other ways increasingly awarded to non-Jews, so that at Columbia Protestants eventually received two-thirds of all awards and, by 1937, 88 percent of them. In 1937, Dean of Students Nicholas McKnight was obliged to acknowledge that moves to promote geographical diversity and subsidize non-Jews undermined Columbia's meritocratic goals by facilitating the recruitment of those "less well-prepared for the Columbia College program of study than the students from New York and its environs" (Wechsler, 1977: 164–5).

Harvard's top-seventh plan initially failed to reduce the number of Jews. By waiving the college examination for students in the highest seventh of their graduating class, the Committee on Methods of Sifting for Admissions claimed this would "facilitate access to College by capable boys from schools which do not ordinarily prepare their pupils for college examination" (Karabel, 1984: 13). The plan, however, did not alter the trend toward increasing Jewish enrollment: " ... the highest-seventh plan failed to stem the flow of Jewish students to Harvard. Indeed, of the 276 top-seventh plan students who entered Harvard in 1925, 115 (44.7 percent) were Jewish. Overall, the proportion of Jews in the freshman class had actually increased—despite Lowell's best efforts—between 1922 and 1925 from 21.5 to 27.6 percent" (Karabel, 1984: 14). ...

Insofar as objective tests failed to screen out a sufficient proportion of undesirable applicants, the colleges moved increasingly towards controlling admissions through *supplementing* academic criteria with new, non-academic considerations such as "character" or "leadership." During Harvard's faculty deliberations on restriction, Professor Hockings had motioned, "that a special committee be appointed by the President to consider principles and methods for more effectively sifting candidates for admission in respect to character," the goal being to systematically incorporate character requirements as objective criteria rather than leaving them to the "subjective caprice" of committee members (Synnott, 1979: 62). Columbia's faculty went to task defining those social characteristics for which information was to be requested of applicants. Leadership, for example, was "measured not only by academic excellence, but also by participation in activities such as school publications, musical and other organizations, athletics, patriotic activities, debating, student government, and by the receipt of honors and prizes" (Wechsler, 1977: 156). While it became apparent that the resulting list included the very criteria which the high schools were to have already sifted for, such evaluative criteria nevertheless gave colleges additional flexibility in selecting candidates of their choice. Application forms were revised to ensure proper ethnic identification. Harvard, for example, collected face-sheet data on "race and color," "religious preference," personal name changes, "maiden name of mother," and "birthplace of father" (Synnott, 1979: 258, footnote 24). Yale omitted questions about race and religion (fearing charges of anti-Semitism), but felt that father's full name and birthplace and mother's maiden name could accomplish the same objectives when combined with the comments of high school principals and headmasters (Synnott, 1979: 155). Photos of the candidate or the candidate's father served the same purpose, as did personal interviews which permitted an even better opportunity to make judgements about ethnicity.

In sum, the historical evidence overwhelmingly points to exclusionary policies against Jews that were never formally explicated as "racial" quotas per se. Rather, the rationales that quietly circulated regarding the undesirability of Jews eventually led to formal admissions procedures that were continually *shifting* so as to achieve the right "proportion" of student diversity. The effect of such policies on Jewish numbers would be significant at the Big Three:

> Beginning with the class of 1928, Yale aimed at stabilizing its proportion of Jewish students at around 10–12 percent. During the same year, 1924, Princeton almost halved its number of successful Jewish candidates in order to admit more, and usually less, than the percentage of Jews in the national population—about 3 percent. Two years later, with the class of 1930, Harvard began to reduce its Jewish enrollment from about 25–27 percent to about 10–16 percent. (Synnott, 1979: 20)

Restrictive admissions were apparent as late as the late 1940s even though the Second World War reduced anti-Semitic sentiments, democratized education, and led to a general concern for increasing academic standards (Synnott, 1979: 205–6, 212, 222).

ADMISSIONS CRITERIA IN THE 1980s:
SHIFTING SANDS

The latter half of this century has seen dramatic changes both in the economic landscape and in the demographic make-up of college-oriented students. With the onset of the First World War a college education began to be viewed as vital to the aspirations of many. The casual, informal atmosphere that originally surrounded admissions when the universities were socially and culturally homogeneous gave way to more formal admissions. In these last two decades of the century, admission into the nation's leading colleges and universities has become fiercely competitive. In the University of California, Berkeley, for example, applicants admitted on academic grounds alone frequently have scores which exceed the minimum requirements. There is a keen competition for first-year places that did not exist in the nation's colleges even thirty years ago. At UC Berkeley, "This competition has resulted in thousands of students with perfect grades to be denied admission—2150 students with at least 4.0 GPAs in fall 1987, for instance" (*Asian Week*, 1987: 3).

The year 1984 marked the beginning of a controversy that would develop around Asian American admissions. Asians, whom Vice Chancellor Park had predicted would constitute one-third of the undergraduate body on the Berkeley campus by 1990, began instead to *decline* in numbers. In 1983, Asian American student enrolment at the University of California, Berkeley, was 27.3 percent. In 1984, Asian American enrolment dropped to 24.1 percent, an abrupt shift given an otherwise steady increase over the previous three years. A similar pattern was found at other college campuses. Between 1980 and 1984, "... there was a dramatic and disproportional decrease in the percentage of applicants who were admitted to UCLA. In 1980, 82 percent of Asian American applicants were admitted. But in 1984, it decreased to 40.7 percent" (*East-West*, 12/6/85). Were Asian Americans suddenly performing poorly? Or were there attempts to exclude them? In May of 1985 the *New York Times* reported that,

> Although Asian Americans apply at a higher rate than members of most groups, they are admitted at a lower rate, even though they are as well qualified academically as, if not better than, other applicants.

> At Brown, Asian-American students admitted to the classes of 1984–1987 averaged 1 point higher on the verbal portion of the Scholastic Aptitude Test than whites who were admitted, and 18 points higher on the math portion, 4 points higher on college-entrance achievement tests, and 2 percentiles higher in class rank.

> During that same period, 21 percent of the whites who applied were accepted at Brown, and 18 percent of the Asian-Americans who applied were accepted. (Winerip, 1985: 19)

An Asian American Task Force formed in 1984 to investigate the matter at Berkeley. Among their findings were two major changes in admissions policy that directly affected Asian American applicants: (1) a covert revision of admissions criteria for that year, which *raised* the minimum verbal SAT score to 400, and (2) the dropping of low-income Asian applicants from the EOP programme, one in which Asians participated at a higher rate than Caucasians (*Asian Week,* 1987).

The State Auditor General later issued a 350-page report, which further confirmed discrepancies in admissions policy. A major finding was that whites gained admission to UC Berkeley's five colleges at rates higher than Asians, despite the fact that in most instances Asians had higher grades and test scores. One reason offered to counter the charge of discrimination was the "existence of 'protected' categories of students, mostly Caucasian, who are admitted outside of the normal admissions process." These students are evaluated not only on the basis of scholastic criteria but non-academic, supplemental criteria that include disabilities, rural residence, athletic ability and participation in special academic programmes, factors which "as they are currently evaluated ... give an advantage to Caucasians" (*Asian Week,* 1987: 11). Subjective criteria also entered into admissions evaluations in three of UCB's five colleges, yet there was no written policy that would allow one to document how they were implemented. ...

Up to and including 1984, an applicant's grade point average (GPA) *or* test scores—*depending on which was higher*—was the major factor determining admissibility at the highly competitive level. As noted earlier, Asian Americans generally perform better than white students where GPA is concerned while doing more poorly on verbal tests. This fact, among others, was implicitly used to discriminate among candidates, adversely affecting Asian Americans.

[There were] sixteen available options for sifting candidates, [and] the Office of Admissions and Records ... [had] adopted precisely those options that adversely affected Asian American applicants. The minimum GPA score was raised from 3.75 to 3.95; ... a minimum SAT-verbal score for whites and Asians ... was implemented; Asian Americans who were among the less competitive [Equal Opportunity Program] applicants were redirected to other campuses; ... and fewer Asian American applicants were referred to the Special Action Committee [which dealt with "protected categories"].

Although Asian Americans were the one group which these policy changes had the most adverse impact upon, the Shack committee felt that the consequences did not warrant the attribution of racial bias.

CONCLUSION:
THE NATION'S UNIVERSITIES AT THE CROSSROADS

Since the controversy over Asian admissions began, events have set in motion proposals for new admissions standards. At the University of California, mention has been made of the need to take greater consideration of criteria "besides academic performance" (*Notice*, 1988). At the national level, the American College Testing Program recently announced plans to alter its exams radically to include "a wider range of mathematical knowledge and more abstract reading skills." This move constitutes the first major overhaul since ACT was created in 1959. The College Board, in turn, has begun a three-year review that could similarly lead to "a new essay examination and open-ended rather than multiple-choice mathematics questions" (Fiske, 1989).

The pursuit of such radical measures places the nation at a fork in the road. If one takes the cynical view, one cannot help but raise questions as to why such measures are being conceived at a time when Asian American enrolment has become a controversial issue. It raises legitimate suspicion that the justification for these changes is only ostensibly "to increase standards" at a time when Asian achievement along these standards has led others to view them as "models" of excellence. Indeed, some of the proposed changes coincide with stereotypes of Asian American students as academically successful but narrow and not well-rounded.
...

Since non-academic factors are often mentioned to account for the lower admission rates of "more academically qualified" Asian American students, one would expect that when these factors are controlled for, the disparity would decrease, were it not for some other bias. A review of admissions data for Stanford, however, revealed that even when whites and Asians were comparable along these non-academic lines, Asian Americans were admitted at lower rates. ...

If, then, we take the skeptical attitude of interest group conflict, college admission is headed in a direction aimed at institutionalizing biases so as to keep the number of Asian admissions down. To the extent, however, that Asian Americans are able to meet these additional criteria as well, particularly as they overcome many of the language barriers that now face them, the temptation for university officials to impose informal quotas and restrictions is likely to be greater than ever. ...

In the early part of this century, Jewish enrolment was curbed by continually adjusting admissions criteria so that their numbers were controlled without formalizing racial quotas. Thus, army intelligence tests were adopted at Columbia in 1919 as a screening device that would, according to Dean Hawkes, "limit the number or proportion of foreign students without adopting a policy of exclusion" (Wechsler, 1977: 159). When Gentiles seemed to do better on these tests than Jews, the belief was that such tests selected for natural or native intelligence that presumably predominated more in "Nordic" racial stocks than in other groups. As Wechsler (1977: 160), however, points out, the discrepancy in test scores could as easily have been explained by the fact that "these tests were written in English, which might not have been the soldier's first language." As note earlier, Harvard eliminated college entrance examinations, in which Gentiles fared relatively poorly, in favour of the top-seventh plan. When Jews continued to show up in larger numbers than desired, from certain localities, the policy was to "cut out the whole locality." When the demands of the First World War drew on the youth from older American stock, Columbia's President Nicholas Murray Butler bemoaned the fact that the college was "largely made up of foreign born and children of those but recently arrived in this country." He went so far as to argue that special admissions policies were necessary "in order to fortify and to hold the position that the University should itself, by an affirmative process of selection and not merely by a negative process of exclusion, choose those upon whom it wishes to expend its funds and its energies" (Wechsler, 1977: 155).

Affirmative action, therefore, truly began decades ago on behalf of white Gentile males, long before programmes were initiated on behalf of disadvantaged minorities. Affirmative action programmes have stigmatized minorities, as if notions of merit were colour-blind. It should be clear, given this history as a backdrop, that standards were modified to conform with "special interests" and needs. Particularistic criteria thereby became universalistic ones. There are a number of ways in which standards of "merit" can be constructed. A more visionary future would involve serious consideration and effort towards incorporating the strengths of diverse cultural groupings as part of standard admissions criteria. There would, under these circumstances, be less need for "affirmative action" programmes, which have served to stigmatize minorities with the mistaken belief that they are "less qualified" overall.

... Present concern about the "overrepresentation" of Asian Americans, when combined with attacks on affirmative action policies affecting other minorities, raises serious questions about what "cultural diversity" will mean. Nationwide testing seems headed in·a direction bent on creating new requirements that have not been fully deliberated with this cultural diversity as a goal. Whether or not this is the case, a deep and abiding consideration is whether or not new admissions procedures will be used to further the interests of entrenched privilege or whether they will be creatively adjusted, adapted and shaped to increase access for those diverse and historically excluded segments of this society.

REFERENCES

Asian Week (1987) "Special Report," October.

Ames Asian Americans and Pacific Islanders Advisory Group (1988) *Strategic Plan*. Ames Research Center, Moffett Field, CA.

Burnham, Paul S. and Hewitt, Benjamin A. (1967) *Thirty-year Follow-up of Male College Students*. Washington, DC: Department of Health, Education, and Welfare, May.

Claiborne, Robert (1988) *Loose Cannons and Red Herrings: A Book of Lost Metaphors*. New York and London: W. W. Norton.

Fiske, Edward B. (1989) "More Sophisticated Skills Stressed in Changed College Entrance Test," *New York Times National* (3 Jan.).

Karabel, Jerome (1984) "Status-group Struggle, Organizational Interests, and the Limits of Institutional Autonomy: The Transformation of Harvard, Yale, and Princeton, 1918–1940," *Theory and Society* 13(1): 1–40.

Levine, David O. (1986) *The American College and the Culture of Aspiration, 1915–1940.* Ithaca and London: Cornell University Press.

Notice (1988) "UC Regents Adopt First-ever Admissions Policy; Criteria Besides Academic Performance Included," 11(8).

Oren, Dan A. (1985) *Joining the Club: A History of Jews at Yale.* New Haven: Yale University Press.

Synnott, Marcia Graham (1979) *The Half-opened Door: Discrimination and Admissions at Harvard, Yale, and Princeton, 1900–1970.* Westport Conn. and London: Greenwood Press.

Tsuang, Grace (1989) "Assuring Equal Access of Asian Americans to Highly Selective Universities," *The Yale Law Journal* 98 (3): 659–87.

Wang, L. Ling-Chi (1988) "Meritocracy and Diversity in Higher Education: Discrimination against Asian Americans in the Post-Bakke Era", *The Urban Review* 20 (3): 1–21.

Wang, L. Ling-Chi (1989a) "Report on Anti-Asian Bias in UC Admissions Process 'Seriously Flawed,'" *East-West News* (9 March).

Wang, L. Ling-Chi (1989b) "Asian Admission Report Fails to Address the Issue of Bias," unpublished paper (6 March).

Wechsler, Harold Stuart (1977) *The Qualified Student: A History of Selective College Admissions in America.* New York: John Wiley.

Winerip, Michael (1985) "Asian-Americans Question the Admissions Policies at Ivy League Colleges," *The New York Times* (30 May).

PART 7

Policy and Politics

Part Seven deals with politics and change. When most people think of "politics," what likely comes to mind is the process of working within the traditional structure of government to achieve some end. The main political action, in this context, is selection of representatives for office at the local, state, and federal levels by means of elections.

Racial and ethnic minorities, according to this view, can achieve more power in society by participating in the political process. Thus, minority candidates should run for office, and minority communities should organize voter registration campaigns to support candidates who are sympathetic to their interests. The underlying assumption here is that the electoral system will be responsive to the needs of minority communities once those communities get mobilized.

When politics is defined more broadly, however, the traditional conception becomes far too restrictive. In this anthology, we define politics as any collective action that is intended to support, influence, or change social policy or social structures. This definition goes beyond simply working within the existing system of government.

Consider the following list of political actions:

- Predominantly black and Latino hospital workers go out on strike against a national chain of private nursing homes to force their employer to recognize their union. After two weeks, the employer agrees to collective bargaining.
- Asian students at a large West Coast university refuse to leave the president's office until he agrees to provide funds for an Asian Studies Program. After several days of negotiation, the students are arrested by police and charged with trespassing.
- A multiracial group decides to establish an alternative school for adults who want to learn more about how left-wing perspectives and political activities can lead to racial equality. Classes are held in teachers' homes, and the small tuition is divided between the teachers and the school organizers.
- Armed Native Americans patrol the roads leading into their northeastern reservation in an effort to prevent state police from entering in search of a

Native American activist. They claim that the reservation is a sovereign nation and that the state police have no jurisdiction. After several days, the police leave.

- Thousands of blacks and Hispanics in Los Angeles burn and loot stores and attack motorists after the acquittal of four white police officers who were videotaped brutally beating a black motorist suspected of drunk driving. In three days, an estimated fifty-one people are killed and the property damage is estimated at $800 million.

All of these actions, we assert, are deeply political, even though they do not involve the electoral process. (1) The hospital workers used traditional collective bargaining channels to redress their grievances. The underlying assumption was that through the union, they could get better wages and fringe benefits and have more control over their own labor. (2) The Asian sit-in employed nonviolent but civil disobedient tactics to force decisionmakers to listen to the wishes of minority groups. Here the assumption was that the system would not be responsive if they went through legitimate channels; extralegal tactics had to be used. (3) The organizers of the multiracial alternative school believed in the importance of creating alternative institutions under the direct control of those who participate in them. The assumption was that the existing educational structure would not be responsive to the desires of multiracial progressive people who wish to fundamentally change it. (4) The armed action by Native Americans to protect the sovereignty of the reservation provoked a direct confrontation with the armed representatives of the state. The assumption here was that force is the only way to oppose an illegitimate political system. And (5) the urban disorders in Los Angeles represented, in part, a spontaneous outpouring of anger against a political system that is perceived as illegitimate. These acts of rage, which are usually illegal and violent, often force political leaders to take notice of minority problems that might otherwise be ignored.

The question of what kind of political participation is most effective in representing and protecting minority interests is a critical one; but, not surprisingly, there is no consensus on the answer. Two of the chapters that follow are optimistic about minority participation in electoral politics. Nathan Glazer ("The Emergence of an American Ethnic Pattern") argues that, since the end of the Civil War, the trend in politics has been toward the inclusion of racial, ethnic, and immigrant groups. And Arch Puddington ("The Question of Black Leadership") argues that the action of militant and radical black leaders who work outside of the electoral process have hurt the ability of more moderate and responsible blacks to operate within the traditional electoral system.

Two other chapters raise questions about the limits of electoral politics. Howard Zinn ("Representative Government: The Black Experience") argues that blacks have gained concessions from the federal government only after fighting for them, most often outside the electoral process. He expects that blacks will have to continue this struggle of nonviolent civil disobedience in the coming years. Manning Marable ("Black Politics and the Challenges for the Left") argues that the only effective way to use electoral politics is for activist politicians to see their electoral campaigns as part of a larger multiracial protest movement.

A wide variety of policies have been suggested to combat racial inequality. Liberal and conservative policies suggest different ways of reducing racial and ethnic inequality within the existing capitalist economic system and the two-party political system. Radical policy, on the other hand, suggests that both capitalism and the two-party system must be eliminated in order to achieve racial and ethnic equality.

Liberals have traditionally called for more government involvement in the prevention of discrimination, especially at the federal level, in the form of civil rights legislation and administrative regulations. They have also called for increased government spending so as to provide more services in the areas of education, job training, health care, and housing for poor and minority communities. The War on Poverty that took place during the 1960s is a good example of liberal policy in action.

Conservatives, on the other hand, are wary of social programs funded by the federal government and call for policies that will provide incentives for expansion of the business community. In particular, they call for enterprise zones, where businesses would receive tax incentives to locate in poor inner-city neighborhoods and to hire neighborhood workers. Rather than advocating aid to public schools in poverty areas, conservatives suggest that educational vouchers be provided so as to enable more poor parents to send their children to better public schools and to private and parochial schools.

Radicals differ from both liberals and conservatives in that they view the capitalist system as the root cause of poverty and racial inequality. Their policies are intended to mobilize people of all races and ethnic groups to take control of their own lives. According to this view, the power of the capitalist class and government bureaucrats should be replaced by a more democratically controlled economy and political system.

The specific policy of the following essays is affirmative action, one of the most controversial policies to evolve since the late 1960s. Affirmative action requires that government contractors achieve statistical parity in their work forces and that employers meet hiring quotas that give preferential treatment to minorities. Supporters have argued that affirmative action is necessary because the current economic and political structure inhibits both equal opportunity and equal results. Opponents say that meritocratic decisionmaking is sufficient and that any other criterion is both socially unjust and unconstitutional.

Political labels are not always good predictors as to how people line up on the affirmative action issue. Although political conservatives, as a group, tend to oppose affirmative action, both liberals and radicals are split on the issue. Some liberal and many radical analysts believe that affirmative action programs are merely patches in an otherwise faulty system that needs total replacement. And many observers—conservatives, liberals, and radicals alike—are concerned that the occasional inequities of such programs, coupled with confused or inept administration, have increased group tensions and ethnoviolence at the workplace.

On the one hand, then, Fred L. Pincus ("The Case for Affirmative Action") describes federal affirmative action procedures and guidelines and reviews the empirical evidence of the effectiveness of these programs. He concludes that affirmative action is one of many important tools needed in the struggle for racial equality. On the other hand, William R. Beer ("Resolute Ignorance: Social Science and Affirmative Action") argues that affirmative action is neither effective nor fair but, rather, is politically divisive. He concludes that it should be eliminated as soon as possible.

30

The Emergence of
an American Ethnic Pattern

NATHAN GLAZER

In the middle of the last decade, we in the United States seemed to have reached a national consensus as to how we should respond to the reality of racial and ethnic-group prejudice and racial and ethnic-group difference. Almost simultaneously, we began to move away from that consensus into new divisions and a new period of conflict and controversy. The consensus was marked by three major pieces of legislation: the Civil Rights Act of 1964, the Voting Rights Act of 1965, and the Immigration Act of 1965. Following the passage of the Civil Rights and Voting Rights acts, the Federal government intervened firmly in the South to end the one hundred-year resistance of the white South to full political, civil, and social equality for blacks, insofar as this resistance was embodied in law and public practice. The passage of the Immigration Act of 1965 marked the disappearance from Federal law of crucial distinctions on the basis of race and national origin. The nation agreed with this act that there would be no effort to control the future ethnic and racial character of the American population and rejected the claim that some racial and ethnic groups were more suited to be Americans than others.
...

The consensus of the middle 1960s ... is not to be understood as an historically new response to the unprecedented events of those years—the vicious resistance in great parts of the South to the efforts of blacks to practice their political rights, the South's resistance to school desegregation, the shocking assassination of a President identified with the hopes of suppressed minority groups. It is to be understood rather as the culmination of the development of a distinctive American orientation to ethnic difference and diversity with a history of almost 200 years. The orientation was shaped by three decisions. They were not taken all at once, or absolutely, or in full consciousness of their implications, but the major tendencies of American thought and political action have regularly given their assent to them.

The three decisions were:

First, the entire world would be allowed to enter the United States. The claim that some nations or races were to be favored in entry over others was, for a while, accepted, but it was eventually rejected. And once having entered into the United States—and whether that entry was by means of forced enslavement, free immigration, or conquest—all citizens would have equal rights. No group would be considered subordinate to another.

Second, no separate ethnic group was to be allowed to establish an independent polity in the United States. This was to be a union of states and a nation of free individuals, not a national of politically defined ethnic groups.

Third, no group, however, would be required to give up its group character and distinctiveness as the price of full entry into the American society and polity.

There is of course an inevitable breathtaking arrogance in asserting that *this* has been *the* course of American history. It would be almost equally breathtaking to assert that *any* distinctive course can be discerned in the history of the shaping of the American people out of many different stocks. It is in part an act of faith to find any *one* course that the development of American society has in some way been reaching toward: It smacks of the unfashionable effort to give a "purpose," a direction, to history. Certainly this direction is not to be thought of as some unconscious immanent tendency continuing to reveal itself in American history. Direction in history is taken only in the concrete actions of men and of groups of men. Those actions in the United States have included—in direct conflict with the large direction I have described—the enslavement of the Negro, anti-immigrant and anti-Catholic movements that have arisen again and again in American life, the near extermination of the American Indian, the maintenance of blacks in a subordinated and degraded position for a hundred years after the Civil War, the lynching of Chinese, the exclusion of Oriental immigrants, the restriction of immigration from Southern and Eastern Europe, the relocation of the Japanese and the near confiscation of their property, the resistance to school desegregation, and so forth. If we are to seek a "direction" in American history that defines a distinctive approach to the relationship of the various ethnic groups that make up American society, the sequence of events just listed might well be made the central tendency of American history. Many current writers and scholars would have it so: They argue that racism defines our history—racism directed against blacks, Indians, Mexican Americans, Puerto Ricans, Filipinos, Chinese, Japanese, and some European ethnic groups. Many would have it that even the last ten years should be interpreted as a losing battle against this racism, now evident in the fact that colleges and universities resist goals and targets for minority hiring, that preferential admissions to professional schools are fought in the courts, that the attempt to desegregate the schools in the North and West has now met a resistance extremely difficult to overcome, that housing for poor and minority groups is excluded from many suburbs.

I think this is a selective misreading of American history: that the American polity has instead been defined by a steady expansion of the definition of those who may be included in it to the point where it now includes all humanity; that the United States has become the first great nation that defines itself not in terms of ethnic origin but in terms of adherence to common rules of citizenship; that no one is now excluded from the broadest access to what the society makes possible; and that this access is combined with a considerable concern for whatever is necessary to maintain group identity and loyalty. This has not been an easy course to shape or maintain, or to understand. There have been many threats to this complex and distinctive pattern for the accommodation of group difference that has developed in American society. The chief threats in the past were, on the one hand, the danger of a permanent subordination of certain racial and ethnic groups to others, of the establishment of a caste system in the United States; and on the other hand, the demand that those accepted into American society become Americanized or assimilated, and lose any distinctive group identity. The threat of the last ten years to this distinctive American pattern, however, has been of quite another sort. The new threat that followed the most decisive public actions ever taken to overcome subordination and caste status was that the nation would, under the pressure of those recently subordinated to inferior status, be permanently sectioned on the basis of group membership and identification, and that an experiment in a new way of reconciling a national polity with group distinctiveness would have to be abandoned. Many did not and do not see this latter possibility as any threat at all, but consider it only the guarantee and fulfillment of the commitment of American society to admit all peoples into full citizenship. They see the threat to a decent multigroup society rising from quite another direction: the arrogance and anger of the American people, specifically those who are descended from colonists and earlier immigrants, aroused by the effort to achieve full equality for all individuals and all groups. The prevailing understanding of the present mood is that those who have their share—and more—want to turn their backs on the process that is necessary to dismantle a caste society in which some groups are held in permanent subordination. I think this is a radical misreading of the past few years. ...

I have suggested there were three major decisions—decisions not taken at any single point of time, but taken again and again throughout our history—which defined this American distinctiveness. The first was that all should be welcome and that the definition of America should be a political one, defined by commitment to ideals, and by adherence to a newly created or freshly joined community defined by its ideals, rather than by ethnicity. Inevitably, "American" did come to denote an "ethnicity," a "culture," something akin to other nations. A common life did create a common culture, habits, language, a commonness which parallels the commonness of other nations with their more primordial sense of commonness. But whereas all European and many Asian nations have grown out of a primordial group of long history, bound together by culture, religion, language, in the American case there was a continual struggle between the nation understood in these terms—terms akin to those in which the French, or English, or Germans understood themselves—and the nation understood in very different terms.

Yehoshua Arieli describes a number of ways in which a pattern of national identification has been achieved. In some cases, national identification is imposed by force; in others, it has grown gradually, and "... resulted from a long-established community of life, traditions, and institutions. ..." But "... in the United States, national consciousness was shaped by social and political values which claimed universal validity and which were nevertheless the American way of life. Unlike other Western nations, America claimed to possess a 'social system' fundamentally opposed to and a real alternative to ..."—and here I edit Arieli, but not against his meaning—"... [other social systems], with which it competed by claiming to represent the way to ultimate progress and a true social happiness." These different terms in which American nationality defined itself consisted not only of the decisive revolutionary act of separation from England and self-definition as a separate nation. They also included for many of those who founded and helped define the nation the rejection of ethnic exclusivity.

Three writers to my mind have, in recent years, given the best definition of what it meant to found a nation in this way: Seymour Martin Lipset in *The First New Nation;* Hans Kohn in his book *American Nationalism: An Interpretive Essay;* and Yehoshua Arieli in *Individualism and Nationalism in American Ideology.* ...

Lipset argues that the American nation from the beginning established and defined its national identity on the basis of its decisive break, through revolution, with England, and, by extension, with the entire old world. This weakened the ethnic identification with England. Further, two values became dominant in American society and the shaping of American character, equality and achievement, and these values can be seen sharply marked in American society from the beginning of its independent political existence. One point about these two values that I would emphasize is that, by their nature, they cannot remain ethnically exclusive. And the most far-sighted of the early leaders understood this. Thus, to quote Hans Kohn:

> Thomas Jefferson, who as a young man had opposed immigration, wished in 1817 to keep the doors of American open, "to consecrate a sanctuary for those whom the misrule of Europe may compel to seek happiness in other climes." ... This proclamation of an open port for immigrants was in keeping with Jefferson's faith in America's national mission as mankind's vanguard in the fight for individual liberty, the embodiment of the rational and humanitarian ideals of eighteenth century man. ...

Hans Kohn continues, summarizing Jefferson's point of view, ...

> To facilitate the process of integration, Jefferson strongly opposed the settlement of immigrants in compact groups, and advocated their wide distribution among the older settlers for the purpose of "quicker amalgamation."

Of course, to one tradition we can oppose another. If Jefferson was positive about the immigration of other groups, Benjamin Franklin was suspicious. "For many years," Arieli writes, "he strenuously argued against the wisdom of permitting the immigration of non-English settlers, who 'will never adopt our language or customs anymore than they can acquire our complexion.'" ...

There were two traditions from the beginning, traditions exemplified by different men and social groups, and carried in tension within the same men. Yet even to say there were two traditions makes the issue somewhat sharper than it could have been during the early history of the United States. After all, the very men who spoke about the equal rights of all men accepted slavery. If they spoke of the United States as a sanctuary for all, they clearly thought of men very like themselves who might be seeking it and were not confronted with the hard realities of men of very different culture, religion, and race taking up their offer. In addition, we must take account of the expansive rhetoric of a moment in which a nation was being founded. Yet stipulating all of these cautions, there was a development implied in the founding documents and ideas which steadily encouraged the more inclusive definitions of who was eligible to become a full participant in American life. In the Revolution and its aftermath, limitations on participation in public life by the propertyless, Catholics, and Jews were lifted. Waiting in the wings, so to speak, were other categories, implied in the founding principles. That some others waited for almost two centuries, and that their equality came not only because of founding principles but because of complex social and political developments, is true; but the principles were there, exerting their steady pressure, and indeed even in 1975 much of the argument over how to define full equality for different groups revolves around a Constitution that dates to 1787. ...

In certain periods, it seems clear, one voice or another was dominant. The uprising of the white South in the Civil War marked the most determined effort to change the pattern into one in which other races and groups, labeled inferior, were to be held in permanent subjection and subordination. A new justification was to be established for the "heresy," as Arieli dubs it—and in the American context, heresy it was. Justification was to be found in religion, in pragmatic necessity, in political theory, even surprisingly enough in Auguste Comte's new-founded science of sociology, which was drawn upon to show the superiority of slave labor to Northern, immigrant, free labor, and of a society founded on slavery to one founded on free immigration.

> It is revealing that one great effort to avoid the conflict consisted of the rapid upsurge of the "American" party [the "Know-Nothings"] which labored to unite discordant political factions by making ethnic and religious loyalties the basis of national identification. It sought to substitute for traditional American values a nationalism of the Old World type based on common descent and religion, and thus to divert against the "foreigners" the antagonisms that existed among the native-born. Similarly, the theory of race which justified Negro slavery also aimed to create an identity between North and South on the basis of a common belief in white superiority and through territorial expansion. ...

After early remarkable successes, the Know-Nothings disintegrated before the rise of the new Republican party, thus setting a pattern that other nativist movements were to follow again and again, such as the American Protective Association of the 1890s and the Ku Klux Klan of the 1920s—first a sudden upsurge that seemed to carry all before it, and then, equally suddenly, disintegration. The challenges to the central American pattern, brief and intense, were rapidly overtaken by the major tendency to a greater inclusiveness. The Know-Nothings disintegrated, and the South lost the war. The heresy was, for a while, extirpated.

In the wake of the Civil War, the great Southern heresy that had threatened the idea of American nationality as broadly inclusive seemed crushed. As John Higham writes of those postwar years:

> America had developed a fluid, variegated culture by incorporating alien peoples into its midst, and the experience had fixed in American thought a faith in the nation's capacity for assimilation. This faith, carrying with it a sense of the foreigner's

essential identification with American life, expressed itself in a type of nationalism that had long offset and outweighed the defensive spirit of nativism. A cosmopolitan and democratic ideal of nationality made assimilation plausible to Americans. ...

The twin ideals of a common humanity and of equal rights continued in the 1870's and 1880's to foster faith in assimilation. Temporarily the tasks of post-war reconstruction even widened assimilationist ideals; for the Radical Republicans' effort to redeem the southern Negro, to draw him within the pale of the state, and to weld the two races into a homogeneous nationality discouraged emphasis on human differences. To James Russell Lowell, for example, just and equal treatment of black men meant simply an enlargement of the Christian mission which the United States had long performed in bringing together the peoples of all nations in a common manhood. And Elisha Mulford, philosopher of Reconstruction, argued that the nation "is inclusive of the whole people. ... There is no difference of wealth, or race, or physical condition, that can be made the ground of exclusion from it."

But of course, new threats and new heresies were rising, and the United States was soon to enter a dark age in which the promise of an all-embracing citizenship and nationality, already a hundred years old, was, for a while, quite submerged. ...

For fifty years, between the 1890s and the 1930s, exclusivism was dominant. It affected many groups—blacks and Orientals, Jews and Catholics, Indians and Mexican Americans—in many ways. Once can at least explain some of the reasons for the reaction against admitting all people into the country and to full citizenship. People of position felt threatened by the incoming flood of immigrants. Workers and shopkeepers without stable positions also felt threatened, by the Chinese, the blacks, the Catholics, the immigrants, with the same fears that Franklin had expressed 150 years before over the Germans "under-living, under-selling, and under-working" the English. Those not in direct competition with the immigrant and the black felt the fears just as strongly, as we see in the case of the farmers, who tried to understand the sudden falls in price which threatened to destroy them by resorting to a belief in dark plots by international financial forces. Fears do not justify prejudice, discrimination, and racism, but they help explain it. And the expansion of American society to include strangers from all over the world was not without its real losses as well as its imaginary fears. ...

In the North, exclusivism expressed itself in resistance to immigration from Eastern and Southern Europe and suspicion of immigrant settlements in the cities—of their habits, their culture, their impact on political life and on urban amenities. The Negroes were present—they always had been—but they were so few and so far down the social scale that they were scarcely seen as a threat to anything. In the South, exclusivism was directed primarily against the Negroes, though Catholics and Jews came in for their share of prejudice and, on occasion, violence. In the West, the Chinese and the Japanese were the main targets of a pervasive racism which included the Mexicans and the Indians.

The dismantling of this system of prejudice and discrimination in law and custom began in the 1930s. In the North, the ethnic groups created by the new immigration began to play a significant role in politics; and blacks, after the disenfranchisement of the 1890s, began again to appear in politics. The last mass anti-Catholic movement was the Klan's in the 1920s. It had a short life, and was in eclipse by the time Al Smith ran for president in 1928. Anti-Semitism had a longer

life, but the war against Hitler ended with the surprising discovery that anti-Semitism, so strong in the thirties, was undergoing a rapid and unexpected deflation.
And similarly with anti-Chinese and Japanese prejudice. The immigration restriction law of 1924 was modified to accept at least token numbers of people from
all nations and races in 1952, and all elements of national or racial preference were
expunged in 1965.

Of course, the major bastion of race discrimination was the South, and the legal subordination of the Negro there remained firm throughout the 1930s and
1940s. But twenty years of liberal domination of national politics, by a coalition in
which in Northern cities blacks played an important role, finally made its effects
felt in the administration of President Truman. The Armed Forces were
desegregated, national demands for the enfranchisement of Southern blacks became stronger and began to receive the support of court decisions, and a major
stage in the elimination of discriminatory legislation was reached with the Supreme Court decision of 1954 barring segregation in the public schools. With the
Civil Rights Act of 1964 and the Voting Rights Act of 1965, the caste system of the
South was dismantled. The thrust for equality now shifted from the legal position
of the group to the achievement of concrete advances in economic and political
strength.

Thus for the past forty years, the pattern of American political development
has been to ever widen the circle of those eligible for inclusion in the American
polity with full access to political rights. The circle now embraces—as premature
hyperbolic statements made as long as 200 years ago suggested it would—all humanity, without tests of race, color, national origin, religion, or language. ...

31

Representative Government:
The Black Experience

HOWARD ZINN

Amid the enthusiastic celebrations in 1987 surrounding the Bicentennial of the Constitution, novelist James Michener wrote,

> The writing of the Constitution of the United States is an act of such genius that philosophers still wonder at its accomplishment and envy its results. Fifty five typical American citizens ... fashioned a nearly perfect instrument of government. ... Their decision to divide the power of the government into three parts—Legislative, Executive, Judicial—was a master stroke.[1]

In the abolitionist movement of the early nineteenth century, there was no such enthusiasm. William Lloyd Garrison, editor of *The Liberator,* held up a copy of the Constitution before several thousand people at a picnic of the New England Anti-Slavery Society and burned it, calling it "a covenant with death and an agreement with hell," and the crowd shouted "Amen!"

Ex-slave Frederick Douglass, invited to deliver a Fourth of July speech in 1852, told his white audience,

> The rich inheritance of justice, liberty, prosperity and independence, bequeathed by your fathers, is shared by you, not by me. The sunlight that brought light and healing to you, has brought stripes and death to me. This Fourth of July is yours, not mine. You may rejoice, I must mourn.

During our 1987 celebrations, former Chief Justice Warren Burger, chairman of the Bicentennial Commission, delivered the usual superlatives to the Founding Fathers and the Constitution. But the sole black Supreme Court Justice Thurgood Marshall spoke this way:

> In this bicentennial year, we may not all participate in the festivities with flag-waving fervor. Some may more quietly commemorate the suffering, struggle, and sacri-

fice that has triumphed over much of what was wrong with the original document, and observe the anniversary with hopes not realized and promises not fulfilled.[2] ...

Today, Americans still celebrate the Constitution; they learn in school about checks and balances and what Michener called "the master stroke" of dividing the government into Executive, Legislative, and Judicial branches. We hold elections, vote for president and representatives in Congress, and think *that* is democracy. Yet for black people in this country, none of those institutions—not the Constitution, not the three branches of government, not voting for representatives—has been the source of whatever progress has been made toward racial equality. ...

The history of blacks in the United States exposes dramatically the American political system. What that history makes clear is that our traditional, much-praised democratic institutions—representative government, voting, and constitutional law—have never proved adequate for solving critical problems of human rights. ...

The American revolutionists ... were moved by ... the necessity to overthrow monarchical rule, to put forth a rhetoric that would win popular support, and then to set up a government that would be more democratic than a monarchy. It would be a representative government (a revolutionary idea at the time), but one that would represent the interests of the wealthy classes most of all. And so, the Declaration of Independence, a masterpiece of rhetorical idealism, was followed by the Constitution, a masterpiece of ambiguous practicality.

That combination of rhetoric and ambiguity appeared in the Bill of Rights itself, in the Fifth Amendment, which says no person shall be deprived of "life, liberty, or property" without due process of law. The white person might be thankful that "liberty" was safe, but the black slave, knowing he or she was "property," might well be unimpressed. Indeed, when the Supreme Court in 1857 had to decide between Dred Scott's liberty and his former master's property, it decided for property and declared Dred Scott a nonperson, to be returned to slavery.

Those were not "fifty-five typical American citizens" (James Michener's phrase) who drew up the Constitution. At that convention, there was no representation of black people, who at that time numbered about one-fifth of the population of the states. There was no representation of women, who were about half the population, and certainly no representation of Indians, whose land all of the colonists were occupying. ...

The Constitution was blatant in its representation of the interests of the slaveholders. It included the provision (Article IV, Section 2) that escaped slaves must be delivered back to their masters. Roger Sherman pointed out to the Convention that the return of runaway horses was not demanded with such specific concern, but he was ignored.

In eighty-five newspaper articles *(The Federalist Papers),* arguing for the ratification of the Constitution among New York State voters (blacks, women, Indians, and whites without property were excluded), James Madison, Alexander Hamilton, and John Jay were quite frank. Madison wrote ... that representative government was a good way of calming the demand of people "for an equal division of property, or for any other improper or wicked object." It would accomplish this by creating too big a nation for a revolt to spread easily and by filtering the anger of rebels through their more reasonable representatives. ...

[While modern representative government is indeed] an improvement over monarchy, and may be used to bring about some reforms, it is chiefly used by those holding power in society as a democratic facade for a controlled society and a barrier against demands that threaten their interests.

The experience of black people reveals this most clearly, but there is instruction in it for every citizen. The Constitution did not do away with slavery; it legalized it. Congress and the president (including later the antislavery but politically cautious Abraham Lincoln) had other priorities that came ahead of abolishing slavery. Billions of dollars were invested in southern slaves, and northern political leaders, wanting to keep what power they had, did not want to rock the national boat.

It became clear to those who wanted to abolish slavery that they could not depend on the regular structures of government. So they began to agitate public opinion. This was dangerous not just in the South, where blacks were enslaved, but in the North, where they were segregated and denied the right to vote, their children excluded from public schools, and they were treated as inferiors in every way.[3]

A free black man in Boston, David Walker, wrote the pamphlet *Walker's Appeal*, a stirring call for resistance, in 1829:

> Let our enemies go on with their butcheries. ... Never make an attempt to gain our freedom ... until you see your way clear—when that hour arrives and you move, be not afraid or dismayed. ... They have no more right to hold us in slavery than we have to hold them. ... Our sufferings will come to an end, in spite of all the Americans this side of eternity. ... 'Every dog must have its day,' the American's is coming to an end.

Georgia offered $1,000 to anyone who would kill David Walker. One summer day in 1830, David Walker was found dead near the doorway of the shop where he sold old clothes. The cause of death was not clear.

From the 1830s to the Civil War, antislavery people built a movement. It took ferocious dedication and courage. White abolitionist William Lloyd Garrison, writing in *The Liberator*, breathed fire: "I accuse the land of my nativity of insulting the majesty of Heaven with the greatest mockery that was ever exhibited to man." A white mob dragged him through the streets of Boston in chains, and he barely escaped with his life.

The Liberator started with twenty-five subscribers, most of them black. By the 1850s, it was read by more than 100,000. The movement had become a force.

Black abolitionists were central to the antislavery movement. Even before Garrison published *The Liberator*, a black periodical, *Freedom's Journal*, had appeared. Later, Frederick Douglass, ex-slave and abolitionist orator, started his own newspaper, *North Star*. A conference of blacks in 1854 declared "it is emphatically our battle; no one else can fight it for us."

The Underground Railroad brought tens of thousands of slaves to freedom in the United States and Canada. Harriet Tubman, born into slavery, had escaped alone as a young woman. She then made nineteen dangerous trips back into the South, bringing over 300 slaves to freedom. She carried a pistol and told the fugitives, "You'll be free or die." ...

No more shameful record of the moral failure of representative government exists than the fact that Congress passed the Fugitive Slave Act, the president signed it, and the Supreme Court approved it.

The act forced captured blacks to prove they were not someone's slave; an owner claiming him or her needed only an affidavit from friendly whites. For instance, a black man in southern Indiana was taken by federal agents from his wife and children and returned to an owner who claimed he had run away nineteen years ago. Under the act more than 300 people were returned to slavery in the 1850s.

The response to it was civil disobedience. "Vigilance committees" sprang up in various cities to protect blacks endangered by the law. In 1851 a black waiter named Shadrach, who had escaped from Virginia, was serving coffee to federal agents in a Boston coffeehouse. They seized him and rushed him to the federal courthouse. A group of black men broke into the courtroom, took Shadrach from the federal marshals, and saw to it that he escaped to Canada. Senator Webster denounced the rescue as treason, and the president ordered prosecution of those who had helped Shadrach escape. Four blacks and four whites were indicted and put on trial, but juries refused to convict them.[4] ...

In Christiana, Pennsylvania, in September 1851, a slaveowner arrived from Maryland with federal agents to capture two of his slaves. There was a shoot-out with two dozen armed black men determined to protect the fugitives, and the slaveowner was shot dead. President Fillmore called out the marines and assembled federal marshals to make arrests. Thirty-six blacks and five whites were put on trial. A jury acquitted the first defendant, a white Quaker, and the government decided to drop the charges against the others.

Rescues took place and juries refused to convict. In Oberlin, Ohio, a group of students and one of their professors organized the rescue of an escaped slave; they were not prosecuted.

A white man in Springfield, Massachusetts, had organized blacks into a defense group in 1850. His name was John Brown. In 1858, John Brown and his band of white and black men made a wild, daring effort to capture the federal arsenal at Harper's Ferry, Virginia, and set off a slave revolt throughout the South. Brown and his men were hanged by the collaboration of the state of Virginia and the national government. He became a symbol of moral outrage against slavery. The great writer Ralph Waldo Emerson, not an activist himself, said of John Brown's execution: "He will make the gallows holy as the cross."

What Garrison had said was necessary—"a most tremendous excitement" was shaking the country. The abolitionist movement, once a despised few, began to be listened to by millions of Americans, indignant over the enslavement of 4 million men, women, and children.

Nevertheless when the Civil War began, Congress made its position clear, in a resolution passed with only a few dissenting votes: "This war is not waged ... for any purpose of ... overthrowing or interfering with the rights of established institutions of those states, but ... to preserve the Union."

As for President Lincoln, his caution, his politicking around the issue of slavery (despite his personal indignation at its cruelty) had been made clear when he campaigned for the Senate in 1858. At that time he told voters in Chicago: "Let us discard all this quibbling about ... this race and that race and the other race being inferior, and therefore they must be placed in an inferior position."

But two months later, in southern Illinois, he assured his listeners: "I will say, then, that I am not, nor ever have been, in favor of bringing about in any way the social and political equality of the white and black races. ... I as much as any other man am in favor of having the superior position assigned to the white race."[5]

The abolitionists went to work. To their acts of civil disobedience and of armed resistance, they added more orthodox methods of agitation and education. Petitions for emancipation poured into Congress in 1861 and 1862. Congress, responding, passed a Confiscation Act, providing for the freeing of slaves of anyone who fought with the Confederacy. But it was not enforced.

When the Emancipation Proclamation was issued at the start of 1863, it had little practical effect. It only declared slaves free in states still rebelling against the Union. Lincoln used it as a threat to Confederate states: if you keep fighting, I will declare your slaves free; if you stop fighting, your slaves will remain. So, slavery in the border states, on the Union side, [was] left untouched by the proclamation.
...

By the summer of 1864 approximately 400,000 signatures asking legislation to end slavery had been gathered and sent to Congress. The First Amendment's right "to petition the government for a redress of grievances" had never been used so powerfully. In January 1865 the House of Representatives, following the lead of the Senate, passed the Thirteenth Amendment, declaring slavery unconstitutional.

The representative system of government, the constitutional structure of the modern democratic state, unresponsive for eighty years to the moral issue of mass enslavement, had now finally responded. It had taken thirty years of antislavery agitation and four years of bloody war. It had required a long struggle—in the streets, in the countryside, and on the battlefield. Frederick Douglass made the point in a speech in 1857:

> Let me give you a word of the philosophy of reforms. The whole history of the progress of human liberty shows that all concessions yet made to her august claims have been born of struggle. ... If there is no struggle there is no progress. Those who profess to favor freedom and yet deprecate agitation, are men who want crops without plowing up the ground. They want rain without thunder and lightning. They want the ocean without the awful roar of its many waters. The struggle may be a moral one; or it may be a physical one; or it may be both moral and physical, but it must be a struggle. Power concedes nothing without a demand. It never did and it never will.[6]

A hundred years after the Civil War, Frederick Douglass's statement was still true. Blacks were being beaten, murdered, abused, humiliated, and segregated from the cradle to the grave and the regular organs of democratic representative government were silent collaborators.

The Fourteenth Amendment, born in 1868 of the Civil War struggles, declared "equal protection of the laws." But this was soon dead—interpreted into nothingness by the Supreme Court, unenforced by presidents for a century.

Even the most liberal of presidents, Franklin D. Roosevelt, would not ask Congress to pass a law making lynching a crime. Roosevelt, through World War II, maintained racial segregation in the armed forces and was only induced to set up a commission on fair employment for blacks when black union leader A. Philip Randolph threatened a march on Washington. President Harry Truman ended segregation in the armed forces only after he was faced with the prospect—again it was by the determined A. Philip Randolph—of black resistance to the draft.

The Fifteenth Amendment, granting the right to vote, was nullified by the southern states, using discriminatory literacy tests, economic intimidation, and violence to keep blacks from even registering to vote. From the time it was passed in 1870 until 1965, no president, no Congress, and no Supreme Court did anything serious to enforce the Fifteenth Amendment, although the Constitution says that the president "shall take care that the laws be faithfully executed" and also that the Constitution "shall be the Supreme Law of the land."

If racial segregation was going to come to an end, if the century of humiliation that followed two centuries of slavery was going to come to an end, black people would have to do it themselves, in the face of the silence of the federal government. And so they did, in that great campaign called the civil rights movement, which can roughly be dated from the Montgomery Bus Boycott of 1955 to the riot in Watts, Los Angeles, in 1965, but its roots go back to the turn of the century and it has branches extending forward to the great urban riots of 1967 and 1968.

I speak of roots and branches, because the movement did not suddenly come out of nowhere in the 1950s and 1960s. It was prepared by many decades of action, risk, and sacrifice; by many defeats; and by a few victories. The roots go back at least to the turn of the century, to the protests of William Monroe Trotter; to the writings of W.E.B. DuBois; to the founding of the National Association for the Advancement of Colored People (NAACP); to the streetcar boycotts before World War I; to the seeds sown in black churches, in black colleges, and in the Highlander Folk School of Tennessee; and to the pioneering work of radicals, pacifists, and labor leaders.[7]

It is a comfort to the liberal system of representative government to say the civil rights movement started with the Supreme Court decision of 1954 in *Brown v. Board of Education of Topeka*. That was when the Supreme Court finally concluded that the Fourteenth Amendment provision of "equal protection of the laws" meant that public schools had to admit anyone, regardless of color. But to see the origins of the movement in that decision gives the Supreme Court too much credit, as if it suddenly had a moral insight or a spiritual conversion and then read the Fourteenth Amendment afresh.

The amendment was no different in 1954 than it had been in 1896, when the Court made racial segregation legal. There was just a new context now, a new world. And there were new pressures. The Supreme Court did not by itself reintroduce the question of segregation in the public schools. The question came before it because black people in the South went through years of struggle, risking their lives to bring the issue into the courts.

Local chapters in the South of the NAACP had much to do with the suits for school desegregation. The NAACP itself can be traced back to an angry protest in Boston in 1904 of the black journalist William Monroe Trotter against Booker T. Washington. Washington, a black educator, founder of Tuskegee Institute, favored peaceful accommodation to segregation. Trotter's arrest and his sentence of thirty days in prison aroused that extraordinary black intellectual W.E.B. DuBois, who wrote later, "when Trotter went to jail, my indignation overflowed. ... I sent out from Atlanta ... a call to a few selected persons for organized determination and aggressive action on the part of men who believe in Negro freedom and growth." That "call to a few persons" started the Niagara Movement—a meeting in Niagara, New York, in 1905 that led to the founding of the NAACP in 1911. ...

It seems a common occurrence that a hostile system is made to give ground by a combination of popular struggle and practicality. It had happened with emancipation in the Civil War. In the case of school desegregation, the persistence of blacks and the risks they took became joined to a practical need of the government. The *Brown* decision was made at the height of the cold war, when the United States was vying with the Soviet Union for influence and control in the Third World, which was mostly nonwhite.

Attorney General Herbert Brownell, arguing before the Supreme Court, asked that the "separate but equal" doctrine, which allowed segregation in the public schools, "be stricken down," because "it furnishes grist for the communist propaganda mills, and it raises doubt, even among friendly nations, as to the intensity of our devotion to the democratic faith."[8] ...

By the provision of the Fourteenth Amendment for equal protection, there should have been no segregation of the buses in Montgomery, Alabama, in 1955. If the amendment had meaning, Rosa Parks should not have been ordered out of her seat to give it to a white person; she should not have been arrested when she refused. But the federal government was not enforcing the Constitution. The checks and balances were check-mated and out of equilibrium, and the black population of Montgomery had to get rid of bus segregation by their own efforts.

They organized a citywide boycott of the buses. Black people, old and young, men and women, walked miles to work. One of those people, an elderly lady who walked several miles to and from her job, was asked if she was tired. She replied, "My feets is tired, but my soul is rested." ...

Finally, the government responded. In November 1956, a year after the boycott began, the Supreme Court outlawed segregation on local bus lines.[9] ...

Why did four black college students have to sit at a "whites only" lunch counter in Greensboro, North Carolina, on February 1, 1960, and be arrested? Why did there have to be a "sit-in movement" to end discrimination in restaurants, hotels, and other public places throughout the South? Was it not the intent of the Thirteenth Amendment, as Justice John Harlan said back in 1883, to remove not only slavery but the "badges" of slavery? Was it not the intent of the Fourteenth Amendment to make all blacks citizens, and did not the Constitution (Article IV, Section 2) say that "the citizens of each State shall be entitled to all privileges and immunities of citizens in the several States"?[10] ...

So it would take a struggle to relieve black parents of the problem of telling their little children that they could not sit at *this* lunch counter, use *this* water fountain, enter *this* building, or go to *this* movie theater. It would take sit-ins in city after southern city. There would be beatings and arrests. There would be in the year 1960 sit-ins and demonstrations in a hundred cities involving more than 50,000 people, and over 3,600 demonstrators would spend time in jail. ...

There was an electric effect of all this on black people around the country. Bob Moses, who would later become an organizer of the movement in Mississippi, told how, sitting in his Harlem apartment, he saw on television the pictures of the Greensboro sit-in:

> The students in that picture had a certain look on their faces, sort of sullen, angry, determined. Before, the Negro in the South had always looked on the defensive, cringing. This time they were taking the initiative. They were kids my age, and I knew this had something to do with my own life.[11]

The young black veterans of the sit-ins from the Deep South, along with some blacks from the North and a few whites, formed a new organization, the Student Nonviolent Coordinating Committee (SNCC). They became the "point" people (to use a military term: those who go ahead into enemy territory) for the civil rights movement in the Deep South.

In the spring of 1961 the Congress of Racial Equality (CORE) organized the "Freedom Rides": whites and blacks rode together on buses throughout the South to try to break the segregation pattern in interstate travel. The two buses that left Washington, D.C., on May 4, 1961, headed for New Orleans, never got there. In South Carolina, riders were beaten. In Alabama, a bus was set afire. Freedom Riders were attacked with fists and iron bars. The southern police did not interfere with any of this violence, nor did the federal government. FBI agents watched, took notes, did nothing.

CORE decided to call off the rides. SNCC, younger, more daring (more rash, some thought) decided to continue them. Before they started out, they called the Department of Justice in Washington to ask for protection. A SNCC staff member, Ruby Doris Smith (one of my students at Spelman College), told me about the phone call: "The Justice Department said no, they couldn't protect anyone, but if something happened, they would investigate. You know how they do." ...

The law was clear. Presumably, representative government had done its work by enacting the Fourteenth Amendment, which called for equal protection of the law. In 1887 Congress had enacted the Interstate Commerce Act, which barred discrimination in interstate travel, and the courts had reinforced this in the 1940s and 1950s. But it took the Freedom Rides and the embarrassing publicity surrounding them that went around the world to get the federal government to do something. In November 1961, through the Interstate Commerce Commission, it issued specific regulations, asking that posters be put on all interstate terminals and establishing the right of travel without segregation.

Even that was not seriously enforced. Two years later, in Winona, Mississippi, a group of blacks who used the white waiting room were arrested and brutally beaten. Constitutional government did not exist for them. ...

I had another opportunity to see if the federal government would enforce its own laws in November 1963 when I traveled to Selma, Alabama, to participate in

Freedom Day. It was a day when black people in Dallas County were being organized to come to Selma, the county seat, and register to vote. It was a dangerous
thing for a black person to do in Dallas County, and so a mass meeting was held
the evening before in a black church, with speeches designed to build people's
courage for the next day. Novelist James Baldwin came and so did comedian Dick
Gregory, who tried to diminish fear with laughter. And there were the thrilling
voices of the Selma Freedom Singers.

The next day, black men and women, elderly people, and mothers carrying babies lined up in front of the county courthouse where the voting registrar had his
office. The street was lined with police cars. Colonel Al Lingo's state troopers were
out in force, carrying guns, clubs, gas masks, and electrified cattle prods. Sheriff
Jim Clark had deputized a large group of the county's white citizens, who were
there, also armed. It looked like a war.

The federal building in Selma was across the street from the county courthouse. When two SNCC workers climbed up on the steps of the building and held
up signs facing the courthouse that read Register to Vote, Sheriff Jim Clark and
his deputies mounted the steps and dragged them off into police cars.

That federal building also housed the local FBI. Two FBI agents were out on
the street taking notes. Two representatives of the Justice Department's Civil
Rights Division were also there. We were all watching the arrest of two men for
standing on federal property urging people to register to vote; I turned to one of
the Justice Department lawyers. "Don't you think federal law has just been violated?" I asked.

The Justice man said, "Yes, I suppose so."

"Are you going to do something about that?"

"Washington is not interested." ...

The FBI has the power to make arrests when federal law is violated before its
eyes. Would its agents let a bank robber do his work and just watch and take
notes? They would apprehend a bank robber, but not a local southern policeman
violating a black man's constitutional rights. When I wrote an article for the *New
Republic* on what happened in Selma, pointing to the failure of the U.S. government to enforce its own laws, Burke Marshall of the Justice Department replied.
He defended the federal government's inaction, speaking mystically of "federal-
ism," which refers to the division of power between states and federal government. But the Fourteenth Amendment had made a clear statement about that division of power and gave the federal government the right to forbid the states
from doing certain things to its citizens. And a number of laws were on the books
to buttress the Fourteenth Amendment. ...

[President] Kennedy had not planned to introduce new civil rights legislation.
But in the late spring of 1963 he put his force behind a new, sweeping civil rights
law, designed to outlaw segregation in public accommodations, eliminate segregation in state and local facilities, provide for fair employment regardless of race,
and also put a bit more teeth into the federal government's actions against discrimination in schools and in voting.

What had changed Kennedy's mind was the mass demonstrations in Birmingham, Alabama, in the spring of 1963. These were organized by Martin Luther King
and the Southern Christian Leadership Conference, along with local black leaders

like Fred Shuttlesworth. Thousands of children marched in the streets, against firehoses and billy clubs and police dogs. The photos of police brutality, of children being smashed against the wall by high-power hoses, of a boy being attacked by a police dog, went around the world.

The demonstrations spread beyond Birmingham. In the ten weeks following the children's march, over 3,000 people were arrested in 758 demonstrations in 75 southern cities. By the end of 1963, protests had taken place in 800 cities across the country. Congress debated furiously the provisions of the new civil rights law, which it finally passed, after a year of debate and filibuster—the longest debate on any bill in history. That became the Civil Rights Act of 1964.

The same summer that the new law was being debated, events in Mississippi revealed the limits of the federal government's commitment to racial equality, how little meaning there was to that end product of representative government, the federal statute.

The civil rights groups working together in Mississippi—SNCC, CORE, and SCLC—decided that they needed help and that they should call on young people from all over the country to come to Mississippi in the summer of 1964. The plan was to engage in an all-out effort to end segregation, to register black Mississippians to vote, to encourage local black people by showing how much national support they had.

Everyone connected with the plan knew it would be dangerous. Black people in Mississippi faced that danger every day, all their lives. ...

Three young people with the summer project—a black Mississippian named James Chaney and two whites from the North, Michael Schwerner and Andrew Goodman—disappeared while on a trip to Neshoba County, Mississippi, to investigate the burning of a black church. Chaney and Schwerner were staff members of CORE. Goodman was a summer volunteer and had just arrived in Mississippi hours before.

Two days later their burned station wagon was found, but no trace of the three men. On August 4, forty-four days after their disappearance, their bodies were found buried on a farm. James Chaney had been brutally beaten, so badly that a pathologist examining him said he had "never witnessed bones so severely shattered, except in tremendously high speed accidents such as aeroplane crashes." All three had been shot to death.[12]

In 1988 a film called *Mississippi Burning* was seen throughout the country. It was the story of the FBI search for the murderers of Chaney, Goodman, and Schwerner. It portrayed the FBI as the heroes of the investigation that led to the discovery of the bodies and the prosecution of a number of Neshoba County men. One of those prosecuted was Deputy Sheriff Cecil Price, who had arrested them for speeding and then released them from jail in a prearranged plan to have them murdered. Price and several others were found guilty, spent a few years in prison.[13]

Those of us who were involved in the Mississippi Summer were angered by the movie. We knew how the FBI, again and again, had failed to do its duty to enforce federal law where the rights of black people in the South were at stake, how many times they had watched bloody beatings and done nothing, how the law had been violated before their eyes and they made no move. And we knew how outrageously they had behaved, along with the entire federal government, when the three young men disappeared. ...

It may well be that there was no way of saving the lives of the three young men after their disappearance. But there had certainly been a way of *preventing* what happened, if the government had only met the movement's request that it station federal marshals in Mississippi, to be on the spot, to accompany people into dangerous situations like Neshoba County. Don't they send police to guard the payrolls of banks?

Most of all, the behavior of the FBI and the Justice Department in that situation tells something about the moral and emotional remoteness of liberal constitutional government from the deepest grievances of its citizens. It tells us how important is Frederick Douglass's admonition that those who want the rain of freedom must themselves supply the thunder and lightning.

Later that same summer the Democratic party refused to seat a black delegation from Mississippi that claimed 40 percent of the seats (the percentage of blacks in the state). Instead the Credentials Committee voted to give 100 percent of the Mississippi seats to the official white delegates. It was representative government for whites, exclusion for blacks.

By 1965 it was clear that despite the Fifteenth Amendment, which said that citizens could not be denied the right to vote on grounds of race, and despite the civil rights acts of 1957, 1960, and 1964, all concerned with voting in some way, blacks in the Deep South were still not being allowed to vote.

A little-noticed clause of the Fourteenth Amendment, Section 2, says that if citizens are unfairly denied the right to vote, the representation in Congress of that state can be reduced. This would be the job of the president, who officially gets the census and decides on the number of representatives from each state. But no president, liberal or conservative, Republican or Democrat, had ever invoked this part of the Constitution—although it would have been a powerful weapon against racial discrimination in voting.

In the spring of 1965 the Southern Christian Leadership Conference began a campaign for voting rights in Selma, Alabama, around the same time that President Lyndon Johnson was discussing with Congress a new voting rights bill. Martin Luther King, Jr., went to Selma to join the action.

On March 7, later called "Bloody Sunday," a column of civil rights activists, beginning the long walk from Selma to the state capital in Montgomery, was confronted by state troopers demanding they turn back. They continued to walk, and the troopers set on them with clubs, beating them viciously, until they were dispersed and the bridge was splattered with blood.

During that campaign in Selma, Jimmie Lee Jackson, a black man, was shot in the stomach by a state trooper and died hours later. James Reeb, a white minister from the North, was clubbed to death by angry whites as he walked down the street. ...

The Voting Rights Act of 1965, for the first time, took the registration of blacks out of the hands of racist registrars in areas with a record of discrimination and put the force of the federal government behind the right to vote. David Garrow, in his book *Protest at Selma,* calls the new law "a legislative enactment that was to stimulate as great a change in American politics as any one law ever has."[14] It resulted in a dramatic increase in black voters and the election of black officials all through the Deep South.

What is clear from Garrow's careful study is how the protest movement in Selma was crucial in bringing about the Voting Rights Act. He gives some credit to the federal courts, but he says, "black southerners were unable to experience truly substantial gains in voting rights until, through their own actions, they were able to activate the federal executive and Congress." Furthermore, "the national consensus in favor of that bill ... was primarily the result of the very skillful actions of the SCLC in Selma."[15]

Voting brought some black Americans into political office. It gave many more the feeling that they now had political rights equal to that of whites. They were now *represented* in local government and in Congress, at least more than before.

But there were limits to what such representation could bring. It could not change the facts of black poverty or destroy the black ghetto. After all, black people in Harlem or the South Side of Chicago had the right to vote long ago; they still lived in Harlem or the South Side, in broken-down tenements, amid rats and garbage. Thirty to 40 percent of young blacks were unemployed. Crime and drugs are inevitable in that atmosphere.

So it is not surprising that almost exactly at the time the Voting Rights Act was being enacted in 1965, the black ghetto of Watts, Los Angeles, erupted in a great riot. Or that in 1967 there were disorders, outbreaks, and uprisings in over a hundred cities, leaving eighty-three people dead, almost all blacks. And in 1968, after Martin Luther King was assassinated, there were more outbreaks in cities all over the country, with thirty-nine people killed, thirty-five of them black.[16]

But riots are not the same as revolution. The *New York Times* reported in early 1978: "The places that experienced urban riots in the 1960s have, with a few exceptions, changed little, and the conditions of poverty have spread in most cities."

The constitutional system set up by the Founding Fathers, a system of representation and checks and balances, was a defense in depth of the existing distribution of wealth and power. By arduous struggle and sacrifice, blacks might compel it to take down its "whites only" signs here and there. But poverty remained as the most powerful barrier to equality.

That is the barrier Madison spoke of when he said the system being set up in the new United States of America would prevent "an equal division of property or any other improper or wicked object." It is the fact of *class*, however disguised it is by the procedures of modern liberal societies. ...

No representative can adequately represent another's needs; the representative tends to become a member of a special elite; he has privileges that weaken his sense of concern over his constituents' grievances. The anger of the aggrieved loses force as it is filtered through the representative system (something Madison saw as an advantage in *Federalist #10*). The elected official develops an expertise that tends toward its own perpetuation. Representatives spend more time with one another than with their constituents, become an exclusive club, and develop what Robert Michels called "a mutual insurance contract" against the rest of society.[17]

We can see the difficulties in the United States, which has one of the most praised systems of representative government in the world. People have the right to vote, but the choices before them are so limited, they see so little difference between the candidates, they so despair of their vote having any meaning, or they are so alienated from society in general because of their own misery that roughly 50 percent of those eligible to vote do not vote in presidential elections and over 60 percent do not vote in local elections.

Money dominates the election process. The candidate for national office either has to have millions of dollars or have access to millions of dollars. (In 1982 a senator from Minnesota spent $7 million on his campaign.) Money buys advertising, prime time on television, a public image. The candidates then have a certain obligation to those with money who supported them. They must *look* good to the people who voted for them, but *be* good to those who financed them.[18]

Voting is most certainly overrated as a guarantee of democracy. The anarchist thinkers always understood this. As with Rousseau, we might not be sure of their solutions, but their critique is to the point. Emma Goldman, talking to women about their campaign for women's suffrage, was not *opposed* to the vote for women, but did want to warn against excessive expectations:

> Our modern fetish is universal suffrage. ... I see neither physical, psychological, nor mental reasons why woman should not have the equal right to vote with man. But that can not possibly blind me to the absurd notion that woman will accomplish that wherein man has failed. ... The history of the political activities of men proves that they have given him absolutely nothing that he could not have achieved in a more direct, less costly, and more lasting manner. As a matter of fact, every inch of ground he has gained has been through a constant fight, a ceaseless struggle for self-assertion, and not through suffrage.[19]

Helen Keller, who achieved fame for overcoming her blindness and deafness and displaying extraordinary talents, was also a socialist, and wrote the following in a letter to a woman suffragist in England:

> Are not the dominant parties managed by the ruling classes, that is, the propertied classes, solely for the profit and privilege of the few? They use us millions to help them into power. They tell us, like so many children, that our safety lies in voting for them. They toss us crumbs of concessions to make us believe that they are working in our interest. Then they exploit the resources of the nation not for us, but for the interests which they represent and uphold. ... We vote? What does that mean? It means that we choose between two bodies of real, though not avowed, autocrats. We choose between Tweedledum and Tweedledee.[20]

[Elsewhere] I noted how the vote for president means so little in matters of foreign policy; after the president is elected he does as he likes. We should also note that voting for members of Congress is meaningless for the most important issues of life and death. That is not just because it is impossible to tell at election time how your representative will vote in a future foreign policy crisis. It is also because Congress is a feeble, often nonexistent factor in decisions on war and peace, usually following helplessly along with whatever the president decides. That fact makes a shambles of "representative" government. ...

Direct democracy is possible in small groups, and a wonderful idea for town meetings and neighborhood meetings. There could be discussions in offices and factories, a workplace democracy that neither the commissars of the Soviet Union nor the corporate executives of the United States and often not even the trade union leaders in these countries allow today.

To make national decisions directly is not workable, but it is conceivable that a network of direct democracy groups could register their opinions in a way that would result in some national consensus. Lively participation and discussion of the issues by the citizenry would be a better, more democratic, more reliable way of representing the population than the present stiff, controlled system of electoral politics.

There is already experience with special democratic procedures. Many states have provisions for initiatives and referenda. Citizens, by petition, can initiate legislation, call for general referenda, change the laws and the Constitution. That leads to a lively discussion among the public and something close to a real democratic decision. Except that so long as there are wealthy corporations dominating the media with their money, they can virtually buy a referendum the way they now buy elections.

There is also the idea of proportional representation, so that instead of the two-party system of Democrats and Republicans monopolizing power (after all, a two-party system is only one party more than a one-party system), Socialists and Prohibitionists and Environmentalists and Anarchists and Libertarians and others would have seats in proportion to their following. National television debates would show six points of view instead of two.

The people who control wealth and power today do not want any real changes in the system. (For instance, when proportional representation was tried in New York City after World War II and one or two Communists were elected to the City Council, the system was ended.) Also, when one radical congressman, Vito Marcantonio, kept voting against military budgets at the start of the cold war era, but kept getting elected by his district time after time, the rules were changed so that his opponent could run on three different tickets and finally beat him.

Someone once put a sign on a bridge over the Charles River in Boston: If Voting Could Change Things, It Would Be Illegal. That suggests a reality. Tinkering with voting procedures—proportional representation, initiatives, etc.—may be a bit helpful. But still, in a society so unequal in wealth, the rich will dominate any procedure. It will take fundamental changes in the economic system and in the distribution of wealth to create an atmosphere in which councils of people in workplaces and neighborhoods can meet and talk and make something approximating democratic decisions.

No changes in procedures, in structures, can make a society democratic. This is a hard thing for us to accept, because we grow up in a technological culture where we think: If we can only find the right mechanism, everything will be okay, then we can relax. But we can't relax. The experience of black people in America (also Indians, women, Hispanics, and the poor) instructs us all. No Constitution, no Bill of Rights, no voting procedures, no piece of legislation can assure us of peace or justice or equality. *That* requires a constant struggle, a continuous discussion among citizens, an endless series of organizations and movements, creating a pressure on whatever procedures there are.

The black movement, like the labor movement, the women's movement, and the antiwar movement, has taught us a simple truth: The official channels, the formal procedures of representative government, have been sometimes useful, but never sufficient, and have often been obstacles, to the achievement of crucial human rights. What has worked in history has been *direct action* by people engaged together, sacrificing, risking together, in a worthwhile cause.

Those who have had the experience know that, unlike the puny act of voting, being with others in a great movement for social justice not only makes democracy come alive—it makes the people engaged in it come alive. It is satisfying, it is pleasurable. Change is difficult, but if it comes, that will most likely be the way.

NOTES

1. James Michener, "The Secret of America," *Parade*, Sept. 15, 1985.

2. "Remarks of Thurgood Marshall at the Annual Seminar of the San Francisco Patent and Trademark Law Association in Maui, Hawaii," May 6, 1987.

3. See Leon Litwack, *North of Slavery* (University of Chicago Press, 1961).

4. For excellent accounts of the resistance to the Fugitive Slave Act, see James McPherson, *Battle Cry of Freedom* (Oxford University Press, 1988), 82–83.

5. Quoted by Richard Hofstadter, *The American Political Tradition* (Vintage, 1974), 148.

6. Ibid., 169–170.

7. Alden Morris, *The Origins of the Civil Rights Movement* (The Free Press, 1985), traces the complex and fascinating roots of the civil rights movement.

8. Quoted by John Hope Franklin, *From Slavery to Freedom* (Knopf, 1967), 556. Also in William Strickland, "The Road Since Brown," [*The Black Scholar* (Sept.-Oct. 1979)].

9. *Browder v. Gayle* 352 U.S. 903 (1956).

10. *Civil Rights Cases* 109 U.S. 3 (1883).

11. See the chapter "Out of the Sit-ins" in Howard Zinn, *SNCC: The New Abolitionists* (Greenwood Press, 1985).

12. *Post Mortem Examination Report of the Body of James Chaney*, by David Spain, M.D. (in my personal files).

13. See Seth Cagin and Philip Dray, *We Are Not Afraid: The Story of Goodman, Schwerner, and Chaney and the Civil Rights Campaign for Mississippi* (Macmillan, 1988).

14. Quoted by David Garrow, *Protest at Selma: Martin Luther King, Jr. and the Voting Rights Act of 1965* (Yale University Press, 1978), 236.

15. Ibid., 235.

16. On the Watts riots, see Robert Conot, *Rivers of Blood, Years of Darkness* (William Morrow, 1968). On the 1967 and 1968 uprisings, see the report of the National Advisory Committee on Civil Disorders. (Bantam, 1968).

17. Robert Michels, *Political Parties* (Free Press, 1966).

18. See Philip M. Stern, *The Best Congress Money Can Buy* (Pantheon, 1988).

19. Emma Goldman, "Woman Suffrage," in *Anarchism and Other Essays* (Dover, 1969), 195–211.

20. Philip Foner, ed., *Helen Keller: Her Socialist Years* (International Publishers, 1967).

32

The Question of Black Leadership

ARCH PUDDINGTON

The question of black leadership has been placed in sharp focus by a recent series of unsettling and sometimes ugly incidents.

First, there were the highly publicized travails of Washington, D.C., Mayor Marion Barry. Having scoffed at repeated reports of drug use, and indeed having enlisted, with considerable fanfare, in a "Down With Dope" campaign aimed at the Washington schools, Barry sat down without obvious embarrassment in a courtroom while witness after witness attested to his prodigious appetite for crack cocaine and a videotape showed him sharing the drug with a female acquaintance in a hotel room just prior to his arrest by federal authorities.

Although hardly the first American politician to be brought down by addiction to drugs or alcohol, Barry can certainly claim some distinction in his attitude of arrogant unrepentance, a stance which was modified only at the time of his sentencing for conviction of cocaine possession. And just as disturbing as the mayor's behavior was the generally tolerant, and in some cases supportive, response of the Washington black political establishment. While a few voices called for Barry's retirement from public affairs, most either maintained a studied silence or actually endorsed the theory that Barry was the victim of a white conspiracy to deprive black America of strong leaders. Barry himself gave credence to the idea of a white master plan to persecute black political leadership in denouncing the American "injustice system" after drawing a six-months jail sentence.

In New York, meanwhile, the trial of three black youths accused of participating in the beating and rape of the Central Park jogger took on a particularly nasty edge when supporters of the defendants began harassing the victim as she arrived at and left the courthouse. Egged on by a motley crew of "community activists" and radical attorneys, the crowd yelled obscenities, accused the jogger of deliberately lying, and chanted, "The boyfriend did it!"—meaning that the woman's lover had committed the rape and she, to conceal the fact, had falsely accused the young black men.

New York was also the scene of a prolonged boycott by blacks of two Korean-American grocery stores in the Flatbush section of Brooklyn. The action was launched after accusations that store personnel had struck a black female customer. Unfortunately, the facts remain murky, largely due to a policy of noncooperation with law-enforcement officials and the press adopted by the alleged victim and her attorney (a policy that has become an almost automatic tactic in any racial incidents in New York in which radical black attorneys like C. Vernon Mason and Alton Maddox and "advisers" like the Reverend Al Sharpton become involved). People attempting to enter the stores were forced to run a gauntlet of jeers and curses, the most obnoxious of which were reserved for those blacks who rejected the notion that a self-appointed "boycott committee" had the right to decide where they did their shopping. Attempts at conciliation (themselves half-hearted) by New York's black mayor, David Dinkins, were unavailing; it appeared that nothing short of driving the stores out of business would satisfy the boycott leaders.

Then there was the case of Gus Savage, a black Chicago Congressman notorious for his erratic behavior and racialist views. Accused of sexually harassing a Peace Corps worker while in Africa on congressional business, Savage dismissed the charges as a "white media plot." Savage's tactics in dealing subsequently with a primary challenge by a strong black opponent were just as tawdry. Indeed, Savage ran a one-issue campaign which obsessively concentrated on his opponent's having received campaign funds from outside the congressional district—to be precise, money from Jewish sources. Again and again, Savage spoke of "Jewish money," "the Jewish lobby," "pro-Israel money." At one rally he read from a selective list of his opponent's contributors: selective, that is, insofar as all the names mentioned by Savage were obviously Jewish. Far from leading to defeat, this strategy carried Savage to victory.

Then, although it qualifies more as phenomenon than incident, there is the re-emergence of Louis Farrakhan as a major and increasingly accepted presence in black American affairs. Some would argue against defining the head of the Nation of Islam as a black leader, but Farrakhan simply can no longer be written off as a marginal figure. Wherever he speaks, he draws large and enthusiastic audiences, and this includes the many college campuses he visits. Black civil-rights and elected officials, who in the past were willing to distance themselves in public from Farrakhan's race-supremacist philosophy, now allow his far-fetched pronouncements to pass in silence, or even go out of their way to lend credibility to his views. For instance, Farrakhan recently spoke at no less a forum than the annual conference of the Congressional Black Caucus, where he demanded "reparations" for American blacks and accused whites of complicity in black-on-black violence. Another striking piece of evidence pointing to Farrakhan's elevated stature is the attention lavished on him by the "white" press. This past year both the Washington *Post* and the Washington *Times* took the unusual step of publishing lengthy verbatim excerpts from interviews with Farrakhan, thus treating him with a seriousness hardly merited by the ludicrousness of his ideas.

The press, however, is less concerned about Farrakhan's ideas than it is fascinated by the rise to a position of influence of a man who openly espouses a philosophy of black racial superiority. Farrakhan, to be sure, has lately avoided the kind of extreme inflammatory declarations he used to make. But while no longer openly praising Hitler or describing Judaism as a "gutter religion," Farrakhan continues to concentrate his appeal on a combination of black chauvinism and anti-Semitism, both of which go over quite well with his largely middle-class audiences. ...

Although differing in some respects, the cases listed here contain a number of important common features. First, while the incidents and individuals are routinely described as controversial, there is very little controversy as to the basic facts. By his own, grudging, admission, we know that Marion Barry had a drug problem during his tenure as mayor. And based on overwhelming evidence, we can conclude that the jogger defendants were guilty, that the Korean store boycott is unjustified and racist, that the presence of Gus Savage in Congress dishonors that institution, and that Louis Farrakhan is a black racist.

Second, no matter how damning the evidence, many blacks cling to the notion that Barry, Savage, Farrakhan, the jogger defendants, and others are the victims of white racist persecution, whether exercised through the media, the courts, the federal government, or a mythical world Jewish conspiracy.

Finally, except in rare instances, neither the misbehavior of prominent blacks nor the extreme or paranoid views of their supporters have drawn rebukes from mainstream figures in the black community. On the contrary, such figures have sometimes lent credibility to white-conspiracy fantasies. Thus, in the middle of the Barry affair, Benjamin Hooks, the executive director of the NAACP, warned that organization's national convention of "the vicious assault on black leaders." Thus, too, among Chicago's black political establishment, Gus Savage's strategy was regarded with approval, and the city's leading black journalist, Vernon Jarrett, referred to Savage as "one of the country's most dependable black elected officials" and condemned his opponent's reliance on "outsider" money (a position which might interest the black Democrat Harvey Gantt, whose recent campaign against Senator Jesse Helms was heavily funded by liberal sources outside North Carolina).

In the case of Savage, at least, his anti-Jewish diatribes did provoke the sharp censure of Ron Brown, the black chairman of the Democratic party, and more muted criticism from two black Congressmen, Charles Rangel and William Gray, who had attended a Savage victory rally at which he crowed about his triumph over the Jews. But in general, black leaders inclined to challenge militant elements have learned that there are risks involved in such an undertaking, as evidenced by David Dinkins's experience in attempting to deal with the boycott of the Korean-owned stores.

Elected largely because of his promise to restore harmony to New York's troubled racial environment, Dinkins initially dealt with the boycott, his first major racial controversy, by adopting a position of studied neutrality. Eventually, after it became clear that, given the boycotters' adamant position, "quiet diplomacy" was getting nowhere, Dinkins issued a statement condemning the action: "I oppose all bigotry against anyone everywhere," he said. "I abhor it. I denounce it." While Dinkins's actions did not match the toughness of his words (his administration actually opposed enforcing a court order requiring the picketers to stand at least 50 feet from the targeted stores), his statement was important in identifying the boycott as an act of racial bias.

The response of the boycott supporters was not long in coming. The day after Dinkins's statement, C. Vernon Mason derided the mayor as a "lover of white people," who "ain't got no African left in him." Predictably, Mason tossed in a bit of anti-Semitism for good measure: Dinkins, he sneered, "got too many yarmulkes on his head." Yet despite Mason's unsavory reputation (he was, among other things, one of the leading perpetrators of the Tawana Brawley fraud), few black voices were raised in Dinkins's defense—or, for that matter, in condemnation of Mason's slanders. On the contrary, public support for the boycott was announced by a cross-section of the black-community leadership, including journalists, elected officials, and clergymen. Congressman Major Owens, who represents a Brooklyn district, spoke of "these outsiders, be they Koreans or Asians or whites, [who] come into the main streets of our neighborhoods to make money." The city's black newspapers endorsed the boycott, as, in most emphatic terms, did callers to black radio stations. One of the sharpest polemics was written by the Reverend Lawrence Lucas, a prominent black Catholic priest. Lucas accused the mayor of having caved into "pressure from the white media, the white economic/political structure, the white federal government, and the white City Council and their Negro stooges."

It is true that David Dinkins, the first black mayor of New York, remains highly popular among his black constituents, while Mason, Maddox, and Sharpton are looked on by many blacks as a source of embarrassment. Nonetheless, Dinkins is clearly off the mark when he tries to dismiss his militant critics as deriving their credibility solely from the media's appetite for sensationalism. Al Sharpton has gained prominence because he understands that there is in the inner city a constituency for a politics based on resentment, anger, and race hatred. When issues can be framed as pitting blacks against Asian merchants, the "criminal-justice system," the white (sometimes "Zionist") media, or white politicians, then an irresponsible position built on innuendo, conspiracy theories, character assassination, or lies will often find support among large segments of the black population.

The potential constituency for such a politics of race demagoguery was most vividly, and disturbingly, illustrated by a New York *Times*-WCBS poll which found that fully 32 percent of blacks believed that black politicians were being singled out for investigation, and another 45 percent thought that this might be true. In the same poll, fully 25 percent of blacks answered in the affirmative when asked if they believed that "the government deliberately makes sure that drugs are easily available in poor black neighborhoods in order to harm black people," and another 35 percent responded that the charge might be true, leaving only one-third of the black respondents to dismiss the notion outright. More astonishing yet, 10 percent of blacks polled agreed with the incredible suggestion that AIDS was "deliberately created in a laboratory in order to infect black people."

These bizarre and self-destructive fantasies are by no means prevalent only among the black poor. There are numerous reports of middle-class professionals coming to embrace what Jim Sleeper, in his recent book, *The Close of Strangers,* has called "ever-more baroque theories of white genocidal conspiracy." Even more appalling, however, is the role of those prominent blacks who, instead of providing a much needed dose of truth-telling, are actually feeding the notion of a genocidal white master plan against blacks.

Nowhere is this tendency more pronounced than on the question of drugs. According to Farrakhan, "the epidemic of drugs and violence in the black community stems from a calculated attempt [by whites] to foster black self-destruction." The much acclaimed black film-maker Spike Lee believes "it is no mistake that the majority of drugs in this country is being deposited in black and Hispanic lower-income neighborhoods." As evidence, Lee cites a scene from the movie *The Godfather* in which Mafia chieftains decide that the drug trade will be concentrated in black neighborhoods. Andrew Cooper, publisher of the *City Sun*, a black weekly based in Brooklyn, contends, "There's just too much money in narcotics. People really believe they are being victimized by The Man. If the government wanted to stop it, it could stop it." And for Father Lawrence Lucas, drugs are just one element in a massive white scheme to destroy young black males:

> There is an element that finds this a beautiful aspect of the genocidal attitude toward African-American youth. You're killing them with drugs. You're killing them with the crime connected with drugs. You send them to jail and eliminate African-American males as fathers. White middle-class Americans are the ones who make the money on the billions spent on law enforcement necessary to keep feeding black and Hispanic youths through the jail mill. It's a little bit too coincidental not to believe this was orchestrated by a group of people for other purposes.

Most black leaders do not share the opinions expressed by Father Lucas, but they are loath to challenge those who disseminate the clichés, falsehoods, and fantasies which are increasingly becoming normal fare in black discourse. A case in point is the NAACP's Benjamin Hooks who, while rejecting "white-devil" theories, felt compelled to sympathize with those preaching such ideas by speaking of the "anguished cry of people who really don't understand how [the drug problem] got started in the first place and why it's out of control."

For Hooks, the main problem seemed to be white society's "absolute indifference bordering on the criminal" toward the drug problem in the inner cities. On this score, Hooks's complaint that the drug problem became a drug crisis only when it spread from black neighborhoods to the white suburbs has merit. There is also some justice in David Dinkins's assertion that real outrage over violent crime in New York was elicited only after a young white Utah tourist was killed while defending his family from thugs on a Manhattan subway platform. But the problem here is that blacks themselves, to the extent that they react defensively or with hostility toward attempts to diagnose the black community's ills, are partly responsible for the larger society's indifference toward the inner city's plight. The shabby treatment of Daniel P. Moynihan, James P. Coleman, and other white scholars stands as a cautionary example to those tempted to conduct research on racial themes, especially if there is a danger that the conclusions might clash with the prevailing black position on litmus-test issues like affirmative action.

Furthermore, those who contend that the debate over sensitive racial issues can only be carried out by blacks must confront the disgraceful attempts to silence any black who questions the orthodoxy of the day. Glenn Loury of Harvard has been called a "traitor" to his race for talking too much about the internal pathologies of the black community, while Thomas Sowell of the Hoover Institution is routinely described as a front man for white domination because of his attacks on affirmative action and his insistence that blacks adhere to high academic standards. More recently, Shelby Steele, a black critic of affirmative action who, on other issues, tends toward a liberal stance, has been denounced by Hooks as a "lowdown dirty rascal"; indeed, Hooks has labeled all blacks who dissent from the orthodox position on affirmative action as "some of the biggest liars the world ever saw," and a "new breed of Uncle Toms." ...

Ironically, the notion that a qualification for leadership in the black community is a measure of antagonism toward whites and toward the American system in general emerged only after the basic goals of the civil-rights movement had been won. Martin Luther King, Jr. and the other leaders of that movement were not bitter critics of "white America," and repeatedly emphasized their respect for America's democratic institutions and economic prosperity. A degree of black alienation was perhaps inevitable during the angry last few years of the 1960s, particularly when it became clear that the disappearance of segregation would not automatically lead to dramatic changes in black economic conditions. Nonetheless, it would have been reasonable to expect that separatist and nationalist ideas—and postures—would fade away as the external barriers to black social and economic progress continued to fall.

Why, then, did this not happen? Of the many reasons, one of the most important is the influence of the white Left. To direct attention to this factor is not to resurrect the old canard about undue Communist influence on the civil-rights movement or on Dr. King. But the fact remains that Marxist ideas and political movements, including Communism, have found a receptivity among black intellectuals and politicians which is unusually high by historical American standards and unprecedented at the present time. This has been particularly true for politically motivated blacks in Northern cities like New York, Detroit, and Chicago, where the Communist party made inroads in the trade unions, among writers and intellectuals, and in other spheres in which blacks began to participate during the '30s and '40s. Ultimately an impressive number of blacks who had been members of the party or had reached political maturity in a party-influenced milieu rose to various positions of leadership, ranging from community organizer to city councilman to mayor to member of Congress.

Again, the point is not that the civil-rights movement was "dominated" by Communists or left-wingers, but rather that the course of black political development was strongly tinged by a Marxist perspective which seeks not the reform of American institutions but their outright rejection. One manifestation has been a marked preference among blacks concerned about foreign affairs for revolutionary Third World regimes over more moderate, pro-U.S., or democratic ones. Thus Gus Savage, a supporter of Henry Wallace's 1948 presidential campaign, could still speak more than thirty years later of "the charismatic and brilliant Marxist-Leninist, Fidel Castro, heroic leader of Cuba's socialist revolution." Similarly, a well-known New York figure, Jitu Weusi (formerly Leslie Campbell), referring to a 1987 march protesting the killing of a black man in the Howard Beach neighborhood of Queens, said he was particularly pleased to see so many "young people out in the streets with posters of Malcolm X and Mao Zedong." Another New York figure, the Reverend Herbert Daughtry, believes that nationalism and socialism "can walk together more comfortably than nationalism and capitalism."

In fact, it is difficult to think of a more insidious combination of ideologies than state socialism and black nationalism. By teaching that poverty and inequality derive from the class nature of capitalist society, Marxism provides a ready-made rationalization for the plight of the inner city that is at heart subversive of the idea of personal responsibility and hence demoralizing to the individuals. And despite its superficial message of bootstrap enterprise, black nationalism likewise preaches a message of resignation by drumming home the theme that white racism and the subjugation of "persons of color" undergird the entire structure of American capitalism.

But as Jim Sleeper among others has pointed out, Marxism is not the only unfortunate legacy bequeathed to black America by the white Left. From civil libertarians came the idea that expelling disruptive students from the public schools was racist, as was the practice of screening applicants for public housing; the consequence was to weaken two institutions of crucial importance to the lives of poor blacks. From radical social scientists like Frances Fox Piven and Richard Cloward emerged the idea that blacks should eschew normal politics while attempting to disrupt the system through massive enrollment in the welfare system; the result was to make blacks more dependent on the state while eroding white support for the welfare safety net. From respected liberal social analysts like David Danzig came the notion that it was absurd to "hold the Negro to an extreme and outmoded doctrine of individual merit." And from radicals and liberals of all stripes came the most devastating idea of all: that society was to regard the black criminal, even the violent criminal, as a victim—of racism, poverty, bigoted police—instead of as predatory menace to individual citizens and to the health of black neighborhoods.

Although there is general agreement that crime is a common factor in the deterioration of inner-city institutions—from schools to housing to public transportation to stores—there is more evasiveness and outright dishonesty among black leaders on this issue than on any other. Even those who reject the corrosive theories of white conspiracy find it difficult to accept the premise that black criminals are responsible for their actions. In response to the rape-assault of the Central Park jogger, the Reverend Daughtry could think of nothing better to do than insist that "All of us must share the blame," since "This is a violent society. We are all guilty for creating it and we all must work to eliminate it." With the exception of Mayor Dinkins, it was hard to find any black politicians, or educators, or editors, or, for that matter, clergymen willing to denounce the assailants in forthright terms. Instead, New York's leading black newspaper, the *Amsterdam News,* published account after account comparing the defendants with the Scottsboro boys (the classic case of young blacks being falsely accused of raping a white woman)—a view with which most of New York's politically active black clergy seemed to agree.

Other black leaders tend to share Daughtry's view that the society, and not the individual criminal, is responsible for inner-city crime. For Congressman John Conyers of Detroit, "The root of the problem is a society that economically has no use for these kids." His fellow member of the Congressional Black Caucus, Charles Rangel of New York, told a Harlem rally honoring Nelson Mandela that blacks here, like blacks in South Africa, understand what it means to be a political prisoner, citing as evidence the large percentage of young black men who have had encounters with the criminal-justice system.

There are, fortunately, other black voices, which straightforwardly identify the criminal as the chief threat to the stability of minority neighborhoods, and who dismiss the excuses for minority criminal behavior whether these emanate from white liberals, black politicians, or the criminals themselves, who often demonstrate familiarity with the latest elegant sociological rationalization for their actions. ...

Another, and thoroughly depressing, aspect of the debate over the predicament of black America is the wholesale resurrection of some of the most sterile ideas and discredited movements and individuals of the past. Demands that universities establish black-studies programs have been expanded to embrace proposals for "Afrocentric" curricula in the public schools. A crude anti-Semitism, reminiscent of the anti-Jewish outbursts of the '60s, has reemerged. There is even a Black Panther militia in Milwaukee; its leader sits on the Board of Aldermen, which he uses as a forum to issue threats of violent uprisings unless massive investments are made in black neighborhoods. Meanwhile, ex-Panther notable Bobby Seale was a featured speaker at a recent Washington seminar on racism; Seale told the student audience that he was available to help plan strategy, provide bail money, or "when you need some guns." And in New York, militant demagogues who gained notoriety during racial clashes two decades ago have reappeared after years of quiescence; prominent among them is Sonny Carson, who having served a prison term for kidnapping, has returned as a Brooklyn "community organizer," and is now a leading force in the Korean store boycott.

If this recrudescent black nationalism is less overtly menacing than when H. Rap Brown and Huey Newton were leading chants of "Burn, Baby, Burn," it still stands as deeply subversive of normal black participation in American society. ...

There is also a tendency to treat black anti-Semitism less seriously than in the past. This is certainly not due to any decrease in public expressions of anti-Jewish sentiments. From Louis Farrakhan's ravings about Jewish plots to destroy black leaders to obnoxious clichés about Jewish domination of the media and entertainment industry (voiced by Spike Lee, among others), black obsession with Jewish achievements remains undiminished, even though the Jewish economic role in the inner city, previously said to be the major cause of resentment, hardly exists anymore. While not entirely ignored, the latest anti-Semitic outbursts have not triggered the kind of agonized debates which followed on the heels of previous incidents.

Yet another irony in this situation is that the confusion and disarray which plague the black community's racial leadership coincide with the emergence of a growing number of impressive black leaders throughout the key institutions of American society: sports, the military, journalism, education, law enforcement, politics. Of particular interest is the steady increase of black elected officials who represent majority white constituencies, a group which includes congressmen, mayors, and Governor Douglas Wilder of Virginia. That blacks now serve as mayors of such predominantly white cities as Seattle, Washington and Augusta, Maine, is a tribute both to the talent and energy of the individual politicians and to the decline of prejudice among white voters, a trend that has held steady even as urban racial tensions have worsened.

Almost universally, however, the most successful black politicians do not aspire to the mantle of race leadership, as that concept is traditionally understood. "I'm a governor who happens to be black, not a black who happens to be governor," Wilder has declared, in pointed contradistinction to Jesse Jackson's description of himself as "a black who happens to be an American." Clearly, future success in the political world requires a further broadening of the horizons of individual black politicians. At the same time, this suggests that elected officials will play a distinctly less visible role in narrowly defined racial issues than will clergymen, civil-rights officials, journalists, or academics.

Historically, of course, it was precisely the ministers, writers, teachers, and civil-rights workers who both defended blacks against racial persecution and served as the black community's authoritative voice of morality. Indeed, in the decades prior to the civil-rights revolution, preachers and editors were unapologetic in their strictures against crime, liquor, and "loose living," and the great black scholars did not shrink from subjecting Negro society to rigorous examination. By contrast, today's race leadership has largely abandoned the role of moral arbiter for a single-minded focus on the politics of racial resentment.

This is nothing less than a tragedy. For black neighborhoods will not be revived by attacking white society or through affirmative action or ten-point political programs, of either the liberal or conservative variety. The beginning of a solution will come about only when black leaders insist that the lying be stopped: about American society; about whites; about crime, work, family responsibility, and the treatment of women. Of course, moral exhortation will not by itself lift the black poor into the middle class. But unless and until the issue of values is firmly addressed within the black community itself, there is simply no possibility of beginning to grapple with the inner city's economic predicament, the source of so much righteous but misplaced rage.

33

Black Politics and
the Challenges for the Left

MANNING MARABLE

In the 1980s, there were two fundamental responses by African-Americans to the economic and social crisis generated by Reaganism. The first was represented at the local level by the mayoral campaigns of Harold Washington in Chicago and Mel King in Boston, and at the national level by the Rainbow presidential campaigns of Jesse Jackson in 1984 and 1988. These electoral campaigns were the products of democratic social protest movements, the consequence of thousands of protests against plant closings, cutbacks in housing, healthcare, and jobs, racial discrimination in the courts, and political process at the local level. The Jackson campaigns were a revolt against both Reaganism in the Republican Party and the capitulation of the Democratic Party to the repressive policies of the Reagan administration. In capitalist societies with parliamentary governments, the Rainbow campaign would have been expressed as a multiracial, left social democratic party, a political formation calling for the state to eliminate racial discrimination and disparities of income between people of color and whites and to expand federal expenditures for human needs, employment, and education. Jackson's discourse was grounded in a tradition of resistance and the previous struggles against Jim Crow, a heritage which defined politics not simply as an electoral phenomena, but as the struggle for power on a variety of fronts. In effect, the Rainbow campaign called for a progressive social contract, a positive relationship between the people and the state which would guarantee full employment, universal health care, and housing; safeguard civil rights, and create the material and social conditions for a more democratic and egalitarian order.

The black petty bourgeoisie supported Jackson's effort along with the African-American working class and the unemployed, but for different reasons. The poor and working class had been hit with a severe deterioration of wages, the expansion of drug traffic in their neighborhoods, and the collapse in public transportation systems, health care, and social infrastructure. Voting for Jackson was a protest against Reaganism, racism, and the political domination of the two-party system. The black middle strata mobilized for different reasons. In the period

1979–87, African-American managers and professionals actually had larger income increases than whites with identical educational backgrounds and vocations. (Conversely, the rate of income growth for blacks in all other vocational categories was much lower than that of whites.) Much of the gain to this new professional/managerial stratum had come from affirmative action policies of the federal government. More than half of all black college graduates have jobs tied directly to public-sector spending. Reaganism represented a very real threat to the fragile gains of the middle class elite. The Democratic Party's failure to vigorously contest cutbacks in economic set-asides for nonwhite entrepreneurs, the nonenforcement of affirmative action and equal opportunity legislation, and the destruction of the Civil Rights commission also alienated and outraged most middle class blacks. They saw Jackson as a symbolic advocate of their own interests.

In the quarter century since the passage of the historic Voting Rights Act of 1965, the number black elected officials has soared from 100 to 6,700. The overwhelming majority of these are elected from majority black constituencies. The principal reason for this is that most whites simply will not vote for a black candidate, regardless of his/her political program, party affiliation, or personality. This means that in virtually all cases, African-Americans never consider running for statewide offices or in Congressional or mayoral races in which whites constitute more than sixty percent of the electorates. Consequently, since middle class black politicians look to black workers and the unemployed for votes, they are usually forced to articulate a social democratic-style agenda to win popular support. Their own immediate class interests are not fully served because the weight of the black petty bourgeoisie is very small compared to that of other classes within the black community.

The second response to the economic and social crisis is a form of electoral accommodationism. "Accommodationism" is historically a gradualistic response within African-American politics, which seeks reforms by cooperation with the white corporate establishment, collaboration with the more conservative elements of the major parties, and an advocacy or private self-help and the development of a minority entrepreneurial strata. Booker T. Washington was the architect of accommodation during the era of Jim Crow, the first prominent advocate of "black capitalism." Nearly a century later, in a period of expanding racial segregation and manifestations of racist violence, in a political context of pessimism and defeat for the black left, and in the social chaos spawned by drugs and the decay of social institutions, the political space for a new type of accommodationism has developed. The new accommodationists seek to articulate the interests of sections of the white middle class and corporate interests, rather than the black community. The accommodationist reformers still use the discourse of the civil rights movement, but lack any political commitment to civil disobedience or disruptive activities to achieve more equal rights and economic justice for the black working class. Unlike Booker T. Washington, this new leadership of the black middle class does not have to embrace legal racial segregation to win white support, but it does have to espouse a compromising approach to black political and economic development and to do nothing to challenge the brutal class oppression and social deterioration in the urban ghetto. This neo-accommodationist approach can be described as "post black politics."

The November 1989 elections of David Dinkins as New York City's mayor and Douglas Wilder as Governor of Virginia symbolize this second approach, despite the fact that both victories have been widely applauded as triumphs over American racism. To be sure, Dinkins is a progressive Democrat on many issues, and no doubt he is preferable to both former mayor Ed Koch and the Republican candidate in the general election, Rudolph Giuliani. The more moderate Wilder was clearly superior to the anti-reproductive rights, conservative demagogue he opposed in Virginia's gubernatorial election. However, neither election represented a fundamental advance for the masses of black working class and poor people, nor advanced a progressive or left social-democratic strategy which might push the boundaries of bourgeois politics to the left.

Both candidates, and especially Wilder, ran essentially mainstream-oriented campaigns, rather than constructing broad-based coalitions of black, Latino, and white workers, liberals, and leftists, on the model of Harold Washington's campaign. Both had recognized years ago that their own electoral constituencies of African-Americans were too small to provide the necessary core for successful bids to high office. Over a decade, they cultivated political records which would place them well within the moderate mainstreams of their respective political cultures in order to appeal to white liberal-to-centrist constituencies.

This was especially the case with Wilder. After the mid-1970s he effectively remade himself in the image of the classical Southern patriarch—conservative, procorporate, anti-crime, and abundantly safe. He couldn't cross the color line personally, but he would do so in terms of his political image. So Wilder sought to become a Southern version of Los Angeles mayor Thomas Bradley, a moderately conservative politician who was "post black"—beyond identification with race. Wilder reversed his opposition to the death penalty. He backed away from his earlier advocacy of granting the District of Columbia full statehood rights, which in effect would place two African-Americans into the U.S. Senate. Moving away from liberal Keynesianism in economic policy, Wilder opposed any changes in Virginia's rigid "right to work" laws, which prohibit compulsory membership in unions within individual businesses.

After four terms in Virginia's Senate, Wilder was successfully elected Lieutenant Governor, the state's second highest office, in 1985. Almost immediately speculation began concerning his chances for governor, since Virginia prohibits incumbent governors from seeking reelection. One of Wilder's chief difficulties was maintaining his natural base among the African-American electorate, which had strongly supported the insurgent presidential campaigns of Jesse Jackson in both 1984 and 1988, while reassuring white voters that he was just as conservative and pro-business as any Southern white politician. Wilder placed one foot in each of two dramatically divergent political cultures, recognizing that both were necessary for him to achieve his goal. He praised Jackson personally, but took pains to distinguish the charismatic campaigner's liberal-left agenda from his own. He defused the critics by suggesting, somewhat falsely, that Jackson's electoral mobilization represented symbolism without substance. "Jesse runs to inspire," Wilder observed, "I run to win."[1]

The political terrain of New York permitted Dinkins to assume a more liberal ideological posture than Wilder's. Nevertheless, he made several strategic political compromises to secure the support of the white upper middle class, and especially Jewish voters who had supported neoconservative mayor Ed Koch in the Democratic primaries. Dinkins distanced himself from Jackson politically, and reminded white voters that he had denounced black nationalist leader Louis Farrakhan. Dinkins's lieutenants shunned efforts by Brooklyn's Arab-American Democratic Club to hold a fund-raising event, for fear of alienating the Jewish electorate. Campaign manager Bill Lynch told Arab-American leaders "not to seek to be visibly associated with the candidate," but Dinkins staffers added that they would still accept their financial contributions. In effect, New York City's Arab-American community of 100,000 was disavowed by a "liberal" who had worked closely with them in the past.[2] After his election, Dinkins and his associates refused to honor promises of appointments to several black progressives and nationalists who had been pivotal in mobilizing African-American voters.

Rather than denying the reality of race, Wilder and Dinkins sought to "transcend" the color line, offering generous platitudes of how racism had supposedly declined in significance during the 1980s. The problem with this perspective is that all the evidence suggests that white voters still remain highly race conscious, far more so than African-Americans or Latinos. Since black democrats can never hope to escape the burden of racial prejudice entirely, they must address the issue squarely and without rhetorical subterfuge. The strategy of declaring victory against racial prejudice may produce some short-term victories, but it will only reinforce white supremacy within the electoral process in the long run.

A second, and paradoxical, problem challenges black political activists, community leaders, and civil rights advocates. They must now ask themselves, "What has the African-American electorate actually won?" Once safely in office, will Doug Wilder's administration actually produce more government jobs for Virginia's blacks, or a more aggressive affirmative action policy than that of the previous white Democratic governor? Will Wilder's conservative support of right to work laws advance the interests of African-American blue collar, semiskilled, and unemployed workers? How will a Wilder administration provide better health services, public welfare, and quality education to the most dispossessed classes when he campaigned specifically on a "no tax increase" platform?[3] Can Dinkins really empower the African-American and Hispanic neighborhoods at the expense of the corporations, real estate developers, and banks? How can Dinkins's economic and social policies really be significantly to the left of those of former mayor Ed Koch, when before the election, the black Democrat named Koch's former deputy mayor Nathan Leventhal to lead his transition team? With the exception of Dinkins's educational policy group, most of the transition planning team were clearly more conservative than the new mayor's electoral constituency.

The Dinkins-Wilder victories represent unique problems for both Jesse Jackson and more generally for the American left. Jackson's strategy in 1984 was essentially to build a broad-based coalition of forces representing roughly 80 percent of black America, combined with small fractions of the Latino, progressive white, and labor constituencies. Jackson stood for a liberal/black revolt against the failure of the Democratic Party to mount a strong opposition to the social devastation of Reaganism.

The 1988 Jackson campaign was different in many ways from the 1984 experience. First, it was much more an electoral effort than a social protest movement in electoral form. In 1984, the vast majority of black elected officials had opposed Jackson, or only belatedly embraced the Rainbow; in 1988, they were generally out front, and used their influence to steer the movement toward the safe boundaries of acceptable bourgeois politics. Consequently, the black nationalists, Marxists, gay and lesbian activists, left environmentalists, and others exercised less leverage in setting the Rainbow's agenda than they had previously. There was also a subtle change in Jackson, particularly in the wake of his stunning defeat of Dukakis in the March 1988 Michigan caucuses. The best evidence indicates that Jackson actually believed that he could be the Democratic Party's presidential nominee, or failing this, that he might achieve the Vice Presidential nomination. Even people on the left argued that Jackson might pull off the electoral upset. Ron Daniels, the head of the Rainbow, was transferred to the electoral campaign. The Rainbow itself as a national independent political force was not developed, and today it remains a political shell rather than a viable formation.

When the inevitable occurred, and Dukakis got the nomination and shifted to the right, Jackson and the Rainbow were not prepared to advance a coherent program of critical support for the Democratic nominee, while developing their own apparatus to the left of the party. After the election, Ron Brown's promotion as head of the Democratic National Committee and the year-long speculation about Jackson's potential challenge to Marion Barry in Washington's mayoral race indicate that even the more progressive elements of the black leadership placed their individual upward mobility ahead of the empowerment of the Black masses as a whole.

Both the Democratic Socialists of America and the Communist Party, in different ways, have pursued a strategy of moving American politics to the left by working with Democratic Party liberals. The hope has been to polarize the Democrats in such a manner that either the conservatives (e.g., Sam Nunn, Charles Robb, Lloyd Bentsen) purge the left, or the liberals force out the right. We have to recognize that neither of these options exhaust the possibilities. Most of us have not anticipated an ideological shift among many African-American or Latino politicians, using racial solidarity rhetoric to ensure minority voter loyalty, but gradually embracing more moderate to conservative public policy positions, especially on economic issues. The real model for this nationally isn't Wilder, but Philadelphia Representative William Gray, who has been groomed for the Vice Presidency for six years.

But the left must establish an independent identity, organizationally and programmatically. An inside-outside strategy which supports progressive Democrats must also be prepared to run candidates for public office against both Democrats and Republicans, especially in municipal and congressional races. The left must establish a network bringing together progressive local constituencies around projects which define politics as a struggle for empowerment, not just in electoral terms. It must recruit the thousands of young people who were politically developed through the anti-apartheid mobilizations of the mid-1980s and involved in the Jackson campaign. At a minimum, such a network would require a statement of principles for operational unity, a national publication, and the local autonomy necessary for groups to engage in independent nonelectoral, community-based struggles.

Along with the development of institutions, the left and the black movement must reassess the potential weaknesses and strengths of mounting yet another national presidential campaign behind Jackson. We need to be clear that Jackson will never be awarded the Democratic Party's presidential nomination, even if he wins every primary and caucus. The rules will be changed to deny him victory— or even more drastic measures will be taken. Moreover, the Democratic Party will never be transformed into a left social democratic, much less socialist, formation. There is too much history, ideological baggage, and domination by sectors of the ruling class for progressives to achieve a transformation from within. More than channelling our meager resources into a costly, labor-intensive national campaign, we desperately need to reinforce our organizational capacity for non-electoral as well as electoral struggles at grassroots levels. Socialism and black liberation cannot be achieved merely by electing a socialist president. It requires the careful and difficult construction of a thousand black, Latino, and progressive formations and local movements in cities, towns, and rural areas.

A socialist labor party in the traditional sense would be premature, at least at this point, but an effective network or loose progressive confederation could accomplish much. But we cannot build consensus for social justice and fundamental, structural changes within the political economy simply by continuing to tail liberals, even those like Jackson. We must demand a greater political price from such politicians for our critical support; and if it is not forthcoming, we must be prepared to employ our resources elsewhere. The selection of the "lesser evil" election after election is in the long run self-defeating. We should engage in a "war of position," the building of the political culture and structures of radical democracy, not advocating traditional Keynesian liberalism. There will never be a distant "war of maneuver" against capital so long as American Marxists act like liberals, because liberals will inevitably act like Republicans in order to get elected. A radical, democratic vision of social change, socialism-from-below, but in a popular discourse which the majority of blacks, Latinos, feminists, and the American working people readily understand, must inform our political practice and strategic decisions for the 1990s.

NOTES

1. Michael Oreskes, "Black Candidate in Virginia: Campaign Is Not a Crusade," *New York Times,* 3 November 1989. Also see B. Drummond Ayres, Jr., "Black Virginia Politician Takes Run at History," *New York Times,* 16 April 1989; and Tom Wicker, "Drama in Virginia," *New York Times,* 3 November 1989.

2. James Zogby, "Dinkins Has Locked Arab Americans Out of His Campaign" *City Sun,* 18–24 October, 1989; Celestine Bohlen, "Arab Group Says Dinkins Shunned Their Bid to Help," *New York Times,* 19 October 1989; and Howard Kurtz, "Arab Americans in New York Say Mayoral Nominees Spurn Support," *Washington Post,* 16 October 1989.

3. Immediately following his election, Wilder urged Democrats to move to the right ideologically and programmatically. Democratic presidential campaigns must support the "values of the overwhelming majority of the people in this country," including the "free enterprise system" and "holding the line on taxes." See Robin Toner, "Enter the Mainstream, Wilder Tells Democrats," *New York Times,* 14 November 1989.

34

The Case for Affirmative Action

FRED L. PINCUS

Affirmative action programs are at the center of an intense controversy in the 1990s. Proponents argue that programs that take race and gender into account are necessary to promote genuinely equal opportunity and more equal outcomes. Opponents, on the other hand, argue that programs utilizing quotas and "reverse discrimination" are unfair to white males.

This twenty-five-year-old debate raises a number of complex legal, political, and philosophical issues concerning the role that government should play to promote equal opportunity. Most citizens in the 1990s would agree that government, especially the federal government, should protect individual citizens from being discriminated against on the basis of their race, ethnicity, or gender.

There is a widespread belief that employment and educational decisions should be based on meritocratic criteria—that is, on "objective" assessments of an individual's skills, abilities, and motivation. A person's race, ethnicity, gender, or religion should not matter: Fair decisions are "color-blind" or "gender-blind."

There is less agreement, however, about how to ensure that employers, educators, and public officials act in a meritocratic manner. And there is still less agreement about what action should be taken when meritocratic policies do not result in equal outcomes. Should the government provide equal opportunity, or should it ensure equal outcomes? Finally, some scholars question even the notion that meritocratic standards are objective and neutral to begin with.

In this chapter, I define *affirmative action* as those policies intended to achieve race and gender equality that go beyond meritocratic decisionmaking by taking race and gender into account. In this context, I will describe and analyze the goals and timetables administered by the Office of Federal Contract Compliance Programs (OFCCP), court-ordered hiring and promotion quotas, and scholarships intended for minority students. Due to limitations of space, I will not discuss such issues as testing, college admissions, and minority-owned business set-asides. I will, however, emphasize the racial aspects of affirmative action, with a somewhat less detailed focus on the gender aspects.

After describing each program, I will present the available empirical evidence about the effectiveness of that program. In the end, I will argue that affirmative action programs constitute an essential tool to be used in the struggle for racial and gender equality. Attempts to limit or roll back affirmative action should be strongly resisted.

AFFIRMATIVE ACTION PROCEDURES

The only federal program legally called "affirmative action" is based on Executive Order 11246 issued by President Lyndon B. Johnson in 1965. Guidelines to implement this program were first issued in 1968 and revised in 1971.[1] The Office of Federal Contract Compliance Programs is the agency that administers affirmative action guidelines.

Federal contractors and subcontractors (excluding those in construction) who have fifty or more employees *and* federal contracts worth $50,000 or more are required to develop an affirmative action plan within 120 days of receiving a contract. Failure to develop and implement an affirmative action plan could result in the debarring of a contractor; in this event, the contractor would lose the current contract and be declared ineligible to receive additional contracts.

Contractors must first conduct a *utilization study* of their employees. Basically, they must count the number of employees in each department and in each occupational category and identify women and minority employees. The employer must be able to make the following types of statements: "In the maintenance department, X percent of skilled blue-collar workers are black" or "In the sales department, Y percent of the managers are Hispanic."

Next, the employer must determine the percentage of minority and female employees who are in the "availability pool"—that is, those who are *qualified* and potentially available for the job. This issue is complex and requires some explanation.

For most clerical, sales, blue-collar, and service jobs, the availability pool is the labor force in the immediate geographical area of the employer. For less-skilled jobs, the availability is calculated as the percentage of minorities or women in the surrounding labor force. If the labor force is 10 percent Asian, for example, the availability of Asian clerical workers would be 10 percent. In more-skilled jobs such as carpentry, on the other hand, the availability would be the percentage of minority workers employed in that job. The surrounding labor force might be 15 percent black, but the availability of black carpenters may be only 5 percent.

For professional and managerial jobs, however, the availability may well be statewide or even national. Among social workers, for example, the Hispanic availability might be defined as the percentage of Hispanics getting social work degrees throughout a particular state within the last five years. Among college faculty, on the other hand, the availability of female sociologists might be the percentage of Ph.D.'s in sociology granted to women within the past five years throughout the entire country.

There are many pages of regulations specifying how these figures are calculated. The important point here is that the availability pool is an estimate of the percentage of *qualified* minority and female workers in a particular job category.

Employers must then compare the distribution of minority or female employees in a specific job category in a specific department to the distribution of minority or female employees in the availability pool. If the actual employment is equal to or greater than the availability (e.g., the availability of women accountants is 20 percent, and 20 percent of the accountants actually employed are female), the employer is "in compliance." If, however, the actual employment distribution is below the availability figure (e.g., only 10 percent of the accountants are female), the employer is "underutilized." The employer must follow the same procedure for each job category in each department.

If a contractor is underutilized, a set of goals and timetables must be included in the affirmative action plan. The goal is to hire enough qualified female or minority employees to reach the percentage distribution stated in the availability pool. In the above example, the contractor tries to hire enough qualified female accountants so that 20 percent of all accountants are female. The timetable must reasonably take into account the conditions of that contractor. Employers with big turnovers might be able to reach the goal in a few months, whereas those with little turnover might take a few years.

Next, the contractor must specify the procedures necessary to achieve the goal. For the most part, these procedures will entail an effort to "expand the availability pool." The contractor might, for instance, design an advertisement reading "Equal Opportunity Employer; Women and Minorities Encouraged to Apply," take out an advertisement targeted at qualified women and minorities, send letters to well-known qualified women and minorities asking for referrals, send letters to schools that train large numbers of qualified women and minorities, and make recruiting trips to conferences that might be attended by qualified women and minorities.

After the contractor designates an employee as the affirmative action representative who oversees this process, the affirmative action plan is complete. The contractor does *not* have to submit the plan to the Office of Federal Contract Compliance Programs for approval; the plan must simply be kept on file in the contractor's office. However, the contractor is expected to make a "good-faith effort" to implement the plan.

What happens if the contractor fails to meet the goal specified in the plan? Suppose the contractor had a goal to hire one black administrator but actually hired one white male. Does the contractor face the loss of the federal contract?

Probably not. First of all, no one but the employer is likely to know that the goal was not met. More important, the contractor is required only to make a good-faith effort to achieve the goal, not to actually succeed. In the unlikely event that the employer is ever investigated by the OFCCP, he or she would simply have to show that the proper procedures were followed—in other words, that women and minorities were encouraged to apply for the position. If the contractor can demonstrate that the white male who applied for the administrative position was more qualified than the black and female applicants, there is no problem. Affirmative action guidelines *require* meritocratic hiring.

These affirmative action regulations involve a certain amount of effort and cost on the part of federal contractors. But they do not force contractors to hire unqualified people, nor do they permit reverse discrimination. All that is required of the contractors is that they be able to justify why their employment levels are below the percentages in the availability pool.

Construction contractors, too, are required to establish goals and timetables. But they are not required to have full affirmative action plans on file because they do not have the same kind of stable labor force as a manufacturer might have. Many construction contractors hire different people from one job to the next.

Some contractors have pressured personnel officers to illegally hire unqualified underutilized minorities, so as to avoid problems with OFCCP officials. It is difficult to determine how extensive this practice is. The OFCCP does, however, conduct "compliance reviews" of certain contractors who are suspected of not fully complying with guidelines. A compliance officer spends about three weeks conducting one of these reviews. In 1991, the OFCCP completed 5,379 compliance reviews, a 14 percent decline from the 6,232 reviews conducted in 1989. In three-quarters of these reviews, the contractor agreed to change some aspect of the affirmative action plan to bring it into compliance (Pincus, 1993).

Although this may seem a large number of reviews, it is important to remember that there may be as many as 250,000 contractors (no one knows for sure) and an even larger number of subcontractors in the United States. At the rate of 5,379 reviews each year, it would take the OFCCP *more than 46 years* to review all contractors even once. Accordingly, contractors do not really have to worry very much about being reviewed.

If the compliance officer and the contractor cannot reach an agreement, there are several levels of appeal available to the contractor. As noted, recalcitrant contractors can ultimately be debarred; that is, they can lose their existing contracts and be declared ineligible to receive future contracts. However, this outcome is extremely rare.

According to the OFCCP, only thirty-two contractors have been debarred since 1972.[2] These companies account for a tiny fraction of the more than half-million companies that have been government contractors since 1972. Twenty-five of the companies were declared ineligible during the 1972–1980 period, which covered the Nixon, Ford, and Carter administrations. Four were declared ineligible during the Reagan years (1981–1988) and three during the Bush years (1989–1992).

The thirty-two companies range in size from the Hesse Envelope Company of Dallas, Texas, which employed 120 people, to major multinational corporations such as Firestone, Uniroyal, and Prudential Insurance. Fourteen of the contractors are in manufacturing, five in construction, three in food production, and two in financial services. The remaining eight are in individual or unknown industries.

What does a government contractor have to do to be debarred? Although detailed information about debarments is hard to come by, I was able to get limited data on twelve of the fourteen contractors that were debarred since January 1979 by reviewing the official debarment decisions that were listed in various issues of *The Federal Register* (Pincus, 1993). Six of the twelve contractors were debarred for flagrantly defying the OFCCP by refusing even to develop affirmative action plans and/or refusing to submit the required statistical information about their employee records. Two other developed inadequate plans and refused to modify them sufficiently to comply with OFCCP guidelines.

The actual hiring policies of these eight contractors are suspect but unknown. Three of the remaining contractors were debarred for failing to make good-faith efforts to meet their hiring goals, and only one contractor—Uniroyal—was debarred for failing to rectify its discriminatory hiring pattern.

The reality is that the federal affirmative action regulations administered by the OFCCP do not put a great deal of pressure on federal contractors to increase their hiring of women and minority workers. If a contractor is willing to be even the least bit flexible, the chances are good that the OFCCP will sign off on the affirmative action plans of that contractor. Even after being debarred, companies can be reinstated if they make the necessary changes. In fact, the median period of debarment for the thirty-two contractors under study was only eight months.

Many public and private employers have learned to live with goals and timetables. The Reagan administration, however, was hostile toward them and unsuccessfully tried to weaken the regulations in 1981 and 1983. First, the administration tried to reduce the number of contractors that were covered by the guidelines. Specifically, it proposed that the contract minimum be raised from $50,000 in total contracts to a single contract of $1 million or more.

Second, the Reagan administration tried to alter the concept of underutilization. Rather than saying that any underutilization required goals and timetables, it proposed that anything below 80 percent utilization would result in goals and timetables. Only a fierce public outcry prevented the Reagan plan from being implemented.

There is some evidence to suggest that these affirmative action policies had the intended effect of increasing the economic well-being of minority and female workers. Looking at national employment data since the 1960s, we find a modest increase in the percentage of women and minorities in a variety of occupations that previously had been the near-exclusive domains of white males.

Natalie Sokoloff (1992), for example, examined changes in the race/gender composition of fifty male-dominated professions between 1960 and 1980. The percentage of black males in these professions increased from 1.5 percent in 1960 to 2.7 percent in 1980. During the same period, the number of black females in the male-dominated professions increased from 0.2 percent to 1.4 percent, and that of white females increased from 6.2 percent to 18.1 percent. Yet in spite of this progress, race and gender gaps are still substantial. White males still accounted for 77.8 percent of those employed in male-dominated professions in 1980.

The key question, of course, is whether aforementioned employment gains are due to affirmative action or to other factors. One possible explanation is that the numerous federal programs intended to prevent employment discrimination (e.g., the Civil Rights Act of 1964) may have increased minority hiring. Certain structural changes in the labor force may also account for these gains. For example, since professional, managerial, and technical jobs have been expanding at faster rates than other job categories, there is increased availability for women and minorities who wish to occupy those jobs. In addition, the increased educational attainment of women and minority workers has enabled more of them to qualify for these high-level jobs than in the past. Although affirmative action has likely had some positive impact, it is impossible to separate out the effects of these other factors.

Another way to address the question is to compare the race and sex employment distributions in firms that are covered by affirmative action regulations with those of comparable firms that are not covered. Presumably, if the employment of minorities and women in "covered" firms is growing faster than in "non-covered" firms, one can attribute much of the growth to affirmative action.

The results of the studies that have addressed this question on a national level are reasonably consistent: Blacks, both male and female, have shown faster rates of employment growth in covered firms than in noncovered firms. This is especially true in firms that have undergone compliance reviews (Donohue and Heckman, 1991). The rate of employment of white women has also increased faster in covered than in noncovered firms, although compliance reviews do not have positive effects on the employment growth of these women (Leonard, 1986; Smith and Welch, 1984). Firms with the biggest goals show the largest growth in minority employment. These findings, of course, are consistent with the view that affirmative action promotes minority and female employment.

However, other evidence regarding the effects of affirmative action is inconclusive. For example, the available studies do not show consistent declines in black/white and male/female wage gaps in covered firms compared with noncovered firms. Similarly, there is no consistent evidence that blacks and women in covered firms have higher-status jobs than those in noncovered firms.

Critics (e.g., Beller, 1978) have responded that it is not enough to show growth of minority employment in covered firms since employment may have dropped in noncovered firms. If minority employment increased in covered firms but decreased in noncovered firms, the overall effect of affirmative action could be zero. Thus far, however, there are no data to support this assertion. Dave and June O'Neill (1992) argue that since most of the gains discussed above occurred prior to the time that the OFCCP began enforcing affirmative action, the gains may not be due to affirmative action. Clearly, more research is needed to disentangle all of the variables involved. At best, the available data suggest that affirmative action may have a modest but positive effect on increasing minority employment.

QUOTAS IN HIRING AND PROMOTION

The most controversial of all affirmative action policies are "quotas"—that is, programs that reserve certain positions for qualified minority or female candidates. Quotas specify a hiring or promotion *floor,* the lowest number of women or minorities who must be hired or promoted. (This is different from the historical use of anti-Semitic quotas as a *ceiling,* whereby no more than a certain number of Jews may be hired.)

Quotas are highly unpopular among white Americans, many of whom refer to them as a form of "reverse discrimination." In 1991, for example, more than half the whites in a survey sample opposed laws that would require businesses to hire black and other minority workers in the same proportion as exists in the local community (Hugick, 1991). Only 8 percent of the whites said that women and minorities should be given preferential treatment in hiring and college admission, whereas 84 percent said that only test scores should be used (Gallup and Newport, 1991).

Black attitudes toward affirmative action are more positive than white attitudes but are highly dependent on how the question is phrased. In the survey cited above, more than three-quarters of the blacks *favored* the proportional hiring of black and other minority workers. On the other hand, when given the choice between preferential treatment and test scores, 24 percent of the blacks chose the former and 60 percent chose the latter. The term *preferential treatment* has a negative connotation for blacks; the term *proportional hiring* does not.

Whatever one's view of quotas, however, this point is clear: *Quotas and goals are not the same.* Especially in the context of court-imposed quotas, the employer or school must hire a minority or female for the position in question, under penalty of law. If no qualified minority or woman is found, either the position must remain empty or the employer must seek special permission to hire a white male. In the case of goals, on the other hand, the employer must merely make a good-faith effort to hire a qualified minority or woman; if none is found, no legal consequences ensue and a white or male may be hired.

Moreover, in a quota situation a white male with superior work experience or credentials could be passed over in favor of a *qualified* but less experienced minority or female applicant. In the case of goals, however, a more-qualified white male must be hired over a less-qualified minority or female applicant since the final hiring must be meritocratic.

Before a quota can be imposed by a court, a group of minority or female employees must sue an employer for discrimination. For private employers, the suit is generally handled by the Equal Employment Opportunities Commission. For public agencies, the suit is handled by the Civil Rights Division of the Justice Department. A disproportionate number of cases pertaining to public employers involve police and fire departments.

The government and the employer may enter into a consent decree, which entails a legal agreement, approved by a judge, that contains a quota system of hiring and/or promotion. At least fifty-one consent decrees involving public employers were in effect during the early 1980s. Such a quota system might, for instance, require the hiring of one black for every white until the percentage of black employees reaches a certain point, which generally corresponds to the availability pool.

Even under this quota system, employers are not forced to hire unqualified people. Most employers specify criteria by which prospective employees can be deemed "qualified": an educational credential, a minimum score on a test, a minimum level of experience, and so on. Employees who do not meet these criteria cannot be considered for the position. Conversely, however, all those who *do* meet the criteria are seen as being able to carry out the duties of the position.

According to this quota system, qualified whites are ranked from "most qualified" to "least qualified" in terms of the criteria. The same is done for qualified minorities. If only ten people can be hired or promoted and there is a fifty-fifty quota, the top five whites and the top five minorities are chosen. Even if all of the selected minorities are qualified, it is possible that some of them may be less qualified than some of the whites who were not chosen. If there were only four qualified blacks on the list, the remaining position would either remain unfilled or go to the sixth white candidate.

There is a widespread belief, especially among whites, that quotas are abundant across the country and that any minority male and almost any female can get a job, as long as they are breathing. White males, on the other hand, are seen to be at a disadvantage, no matter how qualified they are. Government statistics suggest, however, that whites still have the employment advantage, even among the small select group of young college-educated minorities. In 1991, the unemployment rate for 16- to 24-year-old whites with four years of college was 6.4 percent; the rate for comparable blacks was 11.3 percent, and for comparable Hispanics it was 9.2 percent (*Employment and Earnings*, 1992).

In fact, court-imposed quotas are few and far between. It is generally illegal for an employer to voluntarily adopt a quota hiring system without getting court approval. Courts impose quotas only when there is a long history of explicit discrimination and when the employer fails to take corrective action. In short, quotas are generally seen as policies of last resort.

Hiring and promotion quotas were declared constitutional by the U.S. Supreme Court in 1987, despite the fierce opposition of the Reagan administration. Clarence Thomas, now a Justice on the U.S. Supreme Court, joined the administration's opposition to affirmative action while he was serving as the head of the Equal Employment Opportunity Commission during the late 1980s.

In the landmark 1987 *U.S.* v. *Paradise* decision, which involved the Alabama state police, the court outlined the criteria that must be present for a quota to be deemed constitutional.

1. The attempt to remedy explicit past discrimination provides a compelling government interest.
2. Some form of quota system is the only way to achieve the goal of ending discrimination.
3. The quota system is narrowly tailored in terms of specific jobs in specific agencies.
4. The quota system is sufficiently flexible that, for example, whites could be hired if there were no qualified minorities.
5. The quota system is temporary; it will exist for a certain period of time or until a certain percentage of employees are minority.
6. The quota system is fair to whites who will not be totally excluded from a position but whose chances will simply be reduced.

The Supreme Court has also ruled that employers may voluntarily decide to consider race or gender as one of many factors in hiring (see *Regents of the University of California* v. *Bakke* [1978] and *Johnson* v. *Transportation Agency Santa Clara County* [1987]). This "one of many factors" policy is not considered to be a quota since the positions in question are not reserved for women or minorities. In other words, race or gender can be considered *one* factor along with education, test scores, work experience, and so on.

Seniority presents another controversial issue, inasmuch as promotions are often awarded on that basis. Since minorities tend to be the last hired, they often have less seniority than whites. Some consent decrees have suggested separate seniority lists for blacks and whites. In this case, it is possible that all blacks selected for promotion because they are at the top of the black seniority list will have lower seniority than a white candidate who was not selected. Is this an equitable policy?

On the one hand, separate lists could be seen as unfair to white workers because such lists violate the seniority principle that is part of many contracts, both union and nonunion. However, if an employer has a history of discrimination against blacks, the principle of seniority itself would hurt black workers since they would tend to have less seniority than whites and would be less likely to be promoted in the indefinite future, even if there was no continuing discrimination. A separate black seniority list may be the only way to overcome the effects of past discrimination and give black workers a fair chance of being promoted. The Supreme Court has ruled that separate seniority lists for promotions are constitutional in consent decrees.

Seniority presents another dilemma when it comes to layoffs. In many contracts, layoffs are decided on a "last hired, first fired" basis. In this case, the effects of a quota consent decree in hiring can be reversed through seniority-based firings. One recommendation has been to implement a quota system in layoffs to protect recently hired blacks, but the U.S. Supreme Court has declared this arrangement unconstitutional (*Firefighters Local Union No. 1794* v. *Stotts* [1984]); quotas can be used only in hiring and promotions.

Quotas do serve the purpose of increasing minority and female employment in specific firms. A study of police departments around the country, for example, supports the view that quotas help women (Warner and Steel, 1989). Departments with no affirmative action plans or with voluntary plans were more likely to show a below-average utilization of women than were departments with court-ordered plans or consent decrees.

MINORITY SCHOLARSHIP PROGRAMS

The underrepresentation of blacks, Hispanics, and Native Americans in higher education has been a major national issue for the past thirty years. In the 1960s and 1970s, the federal government expanded its programs to provide financial aid for students who could not afford college. Although many of these programs disproportionately helped minority students, students of all races benefited.

Some states and many individual colleges, both public and private, also established scholarships for minority students only; in such cases, whites could not even apply. The number of these scholarships is relatively small—between 35,000 and 45,000. According to the American Council on Education, fewer than 3 percent of minority students receive scholarships especially designated for minorities. These scholarships account for 2 percent of all aid to college students (DeWitt, 1991). Clearly, they are a significant help to the small number of students who get them.

In 1990, Assistant Secretary of Education Michael L. Williams suddenly announced that these scholarships were generally illegal because they discriminated against whites. A tremendous public uproar ensued, after which the Department of Education backtracked and said it was studying the matter.

One year later, Secretary of Education Lamar Alexander announced a new set of rules that would ban most minority scholarships that used public funds. Such scholarships could continue to be given only if they specified race as one of many criteria considered for the scholarship award. In June 1992, the Education Department agreed to postpone implementing these rules until Congress had studied the matter. And in 1993, the new secretary of education, Richard W. Riley, announced that the Clinton administration considered minority scholarships to be legal and would no longer pursue the matter.

Elimination of these scholarships would be harmful because it would reduce the financial support desperately needed by minority students. Equally significant would be the message implied: that the federal government is no longer concerned with minority college students.

SUPPORT AFFIRMATIVE ACTION

Affirmative action is an essential tool in the struggle for racial and gender equality in the United States. Given this country's history of racism and its current economic structure, minorities and women must receive special consideration if they are ever to achieve the income and occupational status available to white males.

Although racial discrimination is less of a problem now than it was fifty years ago, it clearly still exists. Meritocratic decisionmaking by employers is far from being a reality. Nevertheless, the goals and timetables administered by the Office of Federal Contract Compliance Programs are of significant help when it comes to setting realistic hiring goals and establishing criteria to monitor their progress. Employers who wish to hire on the basis of meritocratic criteria now find it easier to do so, whereas those who prefer to discriminate find it more difficult.

Recalcitrant employers who insist upon discriminating can be punished by the federal government. As noted, the OFCCP can debar contractors who refuse to comply with affirmative action guidelines. The Justice Department and the Equal Employment Opportunity Commission (EEOC) can ask the courts to impose hiring and/or promotion quotas on employers who continue to discriminate. And the federal government can set aside a percentage of contracts and subcontracts for minority-owned businesses.

The U.S. Supreme Court has ruled affirmative action programs to be legal within certain guidelines. Empirical studies have shown that these programs offer at least modest benefits for minorities in terms of providing more jobs and expanding their business opportunities. Indeed, they are instrumental in mitigating the effects of continuing, intentional racial discrimination.

Even in the absence of *intentional* racial discrimination, however, some kind of affirmative action would be needed to overcome the effects of past discrimination. Minority populations are disproportionately poor and, therefore, less likely than whites to have the educational credentials and job training to qualify for many jobs. Given the history of past discrimination, minorities also tend to have less seniority than whites. Thus hiring or promoting on the basis of the apparently neutral criteria of meritocracy and seniority leaves minorities at a disadvantage.

In fact, meritocratic criteria are not neutral at all. Rather, they are intensely political. As Paul Lauter (1991) has pointed out, "'standards' do not fall from the sky. ... What was not seen when such meritocratic standards were erected was that they incorporated then existing assumptions of what was meritorious ... and that they thus institutionalized existing relations of power" (pp. 214–216).

The LSAT, for example, predicts success in law schools that were built by whites during a period when blacks were not permitted to attend. During the past decade, however, an intense debate has been waged over both the type of pedagogy that should exist in law schools and the importance of racial diversity. Gary Peller (1991) offers the following analysis:

> There is no neutral way to define "merit" or "qualifications" for legal study beyond a bare minimum of literacy skills. ... The question of how to distribute the benefits of education, whether by limiting admission to those with a particular standardized test score or by practicing affirmative action, inevitably is political. The two possibilities simply would produce two different sets of lawyers and presumably two different professional cultures. But the choice between these alternatives cannot be predicated on the existing concepts of merit or qualification. (p. B2)

Simply ending discrimination is not enough to create genuine equal opportunity. As discussed, affirmative action programs are one way to deal with intentional discrimination, past and present, at both the institutional and individual levels. Yet many of the problems faced by minority communities have nothing to do with intentional racial discrimination and thus cannot be solved by affirmative action. In fact, many of these problems are shared by the white working class.

Working people face the loss of jobs as employers move their plants in search of cheaper labor, lower taxes, and less stringent environmental controls. Unions have come under attack from employers and the federal government and are increasingly less able to protect the jobs and living standards of their members. Government cutbacks have reduced both the quality and quantity of education, health care, welfare, housing, and other social services. And small businesses, regardless of the owners' race, experience high failure rates because they have trouble competing with large multinational corporations, most of which are owned and controlled by wealthy white males.

With each advancing year, then, the rich get richer, the poor get poorer, and the majority of working people—male and female, white and minority—get squeezed. Affirmative action cannot really help. Only a multiracial working people's social movement, committed to race and gender equality, has the potential to turn the tide.

COMMENTS ON CRITICS

Although criticisms of affirmative action come from a variety of political perspectives, most come from conservatives. One of their main objections is that racial discrimination has been reduced so significantly as to no longer be a major barrier to blacks and other minorities.

Conservatives acknowledge the existence of statistical disparities between the incomes and occupational distributions of blacks and whites, but they argue that these disparities are not necessarily caused by racial discrimination. Rather, they could have been caused by differences in cultural preferences, individual motivation, education, geographical distribution, and a variety of other benign factors.

An overwhelming majority of the white population accepts the viewpoint that discrimination is no longer a problem. In a 1991 poll, for example, 70 percent of whites stated the belief that blacks in their community have as good a chance as whites to get a job for which they are qualified. And 80 percent maintained that blacks in their community can get as good an education as whites (Gallup and Newport, 1991).

If discrimination is no longer deemed a problem, affirmative action can be seen as both unnecessary and unfair. Individual effort determines who succeeds and who fails, so the argument goes; this is the American way. Those who fail simply did not try hard enough (Kluegel and Smith, 1986).

Although statistical disparities do not necessarily constitute evidence of racial discrimination, they are cause for serious suspicion. And, indeed, this book has presented ample evidence that intentional racial discrimination is still a major problem; that white males are still the most privileged group, with the highest incomes and the best jobs; and that, because the cultural behavior of different groups is shaped by a group's economic circumstances, an individual's motivation and self-discipline can be negatively affected if his or her racial group faces severe racial discrimination.

Conservative critics of affirmative action also argue that it is wrong to assume that the *absence* of historical discrimination would have resulted in a proportional representation of all racial groups in the occupational distribution. Since we cannot know what would have happened in the absence of discrimination, they continue, it is irrational to say that true equality of opportunity will exist only when blacks make up 12 percent of managers or Hispanics make up 6 percent of professionals.

Although it is indeed impossible to determine what the occupational distribution would have been in the absence of discrimination, statistical guidelines are needed to assess the efforts being made to overcome the effects of past and continuing discrimination. Proportional representation, however mechanical it may appear, is not a bad place to start. If all discrimination is genuinely removed and disparities still exist, the guidelines can be reexamined.

Note, too, that the conservative argument against proportional representation does not apply to the concept of "availability pool" in the affirmative action regulations administered by the OFCCP. Readers should recall that the availability pool is an estimate of the minority population that is *presently qualified* to do various jobs in a particular geographical region.

A third criticism of affirmative action has to do with its cost to individual corporations and the economy as a whole. William Beer argues in the following chapter that the private sector has spent more than $3 billion annually to comply with affirmative action regulations. Peter Brimelow and Leslie Spencer (1993) put this figure at $5 to $8 billion a year.[3] Conservatives claim that such expenditures hurt corporate profitability and therefore reduce the competitiveness of U.S. corporations in the world economy.

Although the precise cost of affirmative action is unknown, spending money on *effective* policies to achieve racial equality is certainly worthwhile. Historically, corporations have saved billions from paying black workers lower wages than whites. So individual corporations can afford to spend thousands of dollars each year to ensure that minority and female workers receive the same pay as white males. Perhaps highly paid executives, who are predominantly white males, can voluntarily take a few thousand dollars from their exorbitant salaries to fund their companies' affirmative action programs. Similarly, the federal government might fully fund the OFCCP with money saved by manufacturing fewer high-priced weapons.

Several studies have suggested that many large corporations are not opposed to incorporating goals and timetables into their hiring procedures (Fisher, 1985). And many public employers who were operating under consent decrees did not support attempts by the Reagan administration to roll back those decrees.

Conservative critics have also expressed concern about the cost of affirmative action to white male workers who have lost jobs to minorities and women. Although one-fifth of surveyed whites reported being victims of reverse discrimination (Gallup and Newport, 1991), the real percentage of whites who were denied jobs because of affirmative action is probably much smaller.

This issue is a difficult one because it can easily be argued that most whites have benefited from living in a racist society. Nevertheless, some individual whites who are qualified for jobs and/or promotions will clearly be hurt by affirmative action policies. Gertrude Ezorsky (1991), a *supporter* of affirmative action, has argued that such whites should receive financial compensation from the federal government since they have been forced to make sacrifices for the larger good.

Still another conservative criticism is that affirmative action hurts successful minorities because their skills and qualifications may be in doubt (Carter, 1991). Are they successful because of their own talents or because of affirmative action? This doubt is said to be perceived by both whites and minorities. Unfortunately, no empirical studies of this issue are available. The fact remains that elimination of affirmative action is not the solution to this problem. Much of the aforementioned doubt is due to racial prejudice in any case. Successful minority individuals, especially blacks, have always been viewed with suspicion, even before the implementation of affirmative action.

Equally important, little concern has been raised about the psychological well-being of the recipients, mostly white males, of other forms of preference. The children of alumni who get preference for college admission do not walk under a cloud of doubt. The relatives of bosses and the recipients of political patronage who get preference for certain jobs are not troubled by doubts about their competence, particularly if they can show they're able to do the job. Why, then, should minorities and females be singled out?

Consciousness-raising groups for white employees and support groups for black employees would go a long way toward creating the attitude that a given individual can succeed or fail on the basis of his or her own abilities. But it would be both unwise and unnecessary to eliminate affirmative action programs in order to strengthen the psychological well-being of successful black employees.

Criticisms of affirmative action do not come from conservatives alone. Certain liberal and Marxist critics have argued that race-specific policies like affirmative action are undesirable because they tend to prevent the formation of multiracial political coalitions. What is needed, they argue, are universalistic policies that benefit everybody. Calls for a national public works program to provide more jobs for everyone, they continue, would be preferable to demanding that blacks get preference for the existing jobs.

Of even greater necessity, in my judgment, is a combination of universalistic programs and affirmative action. Universalistic policies, alone, would still leave minorities at a disadvantage, relative to whites. On the other hand, white support for affirmative action would send a signal to minorities that whites are genuinely interested in racial equality. This interest, in turn, would encourage minorities to join multiracial coalitions and fight for universalistic programs.

As long as race continues to be a dominant factor in American life, affirmative action will be a necessary tool in the struggle for racial equality.

NOTES

1. The following discussion is based on a review of federal affirmative action guidelines and on discussions with several OFCCP officials in 1992.

2. The following discussion of affirmative action violators is based on a list entitled "Companies Ineligible for Federal Contracts Under the Regulations of the Office of Federal Contract Compliance Programs" (no date) that was sent to me by an OFCCP official early in 1993. See Pincus (1993) for further details.

3. Brimelow and Spencer argue that quotas cost the economy more than $300 billion per year in direct, indirect, and opportunity costs, accounting for 4 percent of the total 1991 GNP. Although this contention is absurd, no affirmative action supporter has taken up their challenge to provide alternative estimates.

REFERENCES

Beller, Andrea H. 1978. "The Economics of Enforcement of an Antidiscrimination Law: Title VII of the Civil Rights Act of 1964." *Journal of Law and Economics* 21, no. 2 (October): 359–380.

Brimelow, Peter, and Leslie Spencer. 1993. "When Quotas Replace Merit, Everybody Suffers." *Forbes* (February 15):80–102.

Carter, Steven L. 1991. *Reflections of an Affirmative Action Baby.* New York: Basic Books.

DeWitt, Karen. 1991. "Limits Proposed for Race-Based Scholarships." *New York Times* (December 5):A26.

Donohue, John J. III, and James Heckman. 1991. "Continuous Versus Episodic Change: The Impact of Civil Rights Policy on the Economic Status of Blacks." *Journal of Economic Literature* 29 (December):1603–1643.

Employment and Earnings. 1992. U.S. Department of Labor (January).

Ezorsky, Gertrude. 1991. *Racism and Justice: The Case for Affirmative Action.* Ithaca, N.Y.: Cornell University Press.

Fisher, Anne B. 1985. "Businessmen Like to Hire by the Numbers." *Fortune* (September 16).

Gallup, George, Jr., and Newport, Frank. 1991. "Blacks and Whites Differ on Civil Rights Progress." *Gallup Poll Monthly* (August):54–59.

Hugick, Larry. 1991. "The 'Quotas' Issue: Advantage Bush." *Gallup Poll Monthly* (June):32–35.

Kluegel, James R., and Smith, Eliot R. 1986. *Beliefs About Inequality: Americans' Views of What Is and What Ought to Be.* New York: Aldine De Gruyer.

Lauter, Paul. 1991. *Canons and Contexts.* New York: Oxford University Press.

Leonard, Jonathan S. 1986. "What Was Affirmative Action?" *American Economic Review* 76, no. 2 (May):359–363.

Lloyd, Mark, 1990. "Affirmative Action Victory." *Focus* (July):3–4.

O'Neill, Dave M., and June O'Neill. 1992. "Affirmative Action in the Labor Market." *Annals of the American Academy of Political and Social Science* 523 (September):88–103.

Peller, Gary. 1991. "Espousing a Positive Vision of Affirmative Action Policies." *Chronicle of Higher Education* (December 18):B1–B2.

Pincus, Fred L. 1993. "Enforcing Federal Affirmative Action Guidelines: Compliance Reviews and Debarment." *Journal of Intergroup Relations* 20 (Summer).

Smith, James P., and Finis Welch. 1984. "Affirmative Action and Labor Markets." *Journal of Labor Economics* 2, no. 2 (April):269–301.

Sokoloff, Natalie J. 1992. *Black Women and White Women in the Professions.* New York: Routledge, Chapman and Hall.

Warner, Rebecca L., and Brent S. Steel. 1989. "Affirmative Action in Times of Fiscal Stress and Changing Value Priorities: The Case of Women in Policing." *Public Personnel Management* 3 (Fall):291–309.

35

Resolute Ignorance: Social Science and Affirmative Action

WILLIAM R. BEER

In the debate over the effects of reverse discrimination, preferential hiring, and quotas, one surprising fact emerges: social scientists have been almost entirely mute. Twenty years after the enactment of the Civil Rights Act of 1964 and the promulgation of Executive Order 112246 in 1965, there has been no systematic inquiry into the effects of affirmative action on American society, neither its costs to the nation's economy nor its impact on our country's morale. In an age of program evaluation, when most other social experiments are studied almost to death, our profession has shown a resolute ignorance about an extraordinarily controversial policy that has been in place for over two decades. It is as if affirmative action has assumed the status of a religious article of faith, and professionals choose to avoid studying its effects for fear of what they might find.

Any review of the literature on these topics reveals that virtually all of the discussion falls into three categories: polemical generalizations by journalists and editors, legalistic discussions that are only indirectly concerned with social reality, and manpower studies that try to estimate the extent to which racial, sexual, and ethnic quotas in hiring have increased the representation of such groups. If we are to be faithful to the aims of social science, it is high time that systematic study of the effects of affirmative action be taken out of the hands of polemicists, jurists, and bureaucrats.

First, we must, on scientific grounds, dispense with some of the underlying fallacies in which managerial and legalistic discussions of affirmative action and preferential treatment are ensnared. The next area in which these policies' effects must be assessed is in that of public morale. Has it decreased or increased the confidence of people who allegedly benefit from it? Has it demoralized those not protected? Third is the actual effect of affirmative action on the efficiency of our economy. What have the costs of such government regulations been, and to what extent has the implementation of affirmative action been burdensome to American industry? The last avenue I suggest should be an attempt to study the effects of preferential treatment policies as they have been imposed in other societies.

I dispose of one differentiation at the outset, between the idea of "affirmative action" and "preferential treatment." Affirmative action, in its original formulation, referred to good-faith efforts to recruit qualified members of designated groups into universities, professions, and other respected and well-paid positions in American society. In the ensuing twenty years, affirmative action, in practice, has come to mean something quite different. In a series of bureaucratic and legal decisions largely unseen or unnoticed by the American public, affirmative action has been translated into a series of quotas (sometimes euphemistically referred to as "goals" and "timetables") that benefit certain groups at the cost of others. (Thomas G. Gee provides a dissection of the false legal dichotomy between quotas and goals in the winter 1986 issue of the *Harvard Journal of Law and Public Policy.*)

The Civil Rights Act explicitly states, "Nothing contained in this Title shall be interpreted to require any employer ... to grant preferential treatment to any individual or any group because of race, color, religion, sex or national status of any such individual on account of any imbalance which may exist with respect to the total or percentage of persons of any race employed by any employer." Hubert Humphrey, in his impassioned defense of the bill, said that the act "does not require an employer to achieve any kind of racial balance in his work force by giving any kind of preferential treatment to any individual or group." In July of 1986, however, the Supreme Court declared that preferenmtial treatment was constitutional, even when those who benefit have not themselves suffered from discrimination in the past, and when those who are hurt have not themselves been responsible for past discrimination. In March of 1987, the Court added that preference may be shown for less qualified women and minorities over white males. The success of this undemocratic and semiclandestine metamorphosis was symbolized by Supreme Court Justice Powell saying, in the spring of 1986, "In order to remedy the effects of prior discrimination, it may be necessary to take race into account. As part of the nation's dedication to eradicating racial discrimination, innocent persons may be called upon to bear some of the burden of the remedy." This is an echo of Thurgood Marshall's frank statement several years before, "You guys have been practicing discrimination for years. Now it's our turn." Joseph Rauh, the former chairman of Americans for Democratic Action candidly admitted, "You have to have preference for blacks if you really want affirmative action." Although Humphrey promised that affirmative action would never penalize the innocent, it has not only turned out that the policy does so, but that its more candid partisans say that it should. Affirmative action has come to require preferential treatment. Reverse racial and sexual discrimination have come out of the closet.

FALLACY OF INFERRED DISCRIMINATION

There are numerous studies of the "effectiveness" of affirmative action. Most of them simply measure the extent to which "underrepresentation" of blacks or women or select ethnic groups have been "remedied" as a result of governmental pressure. Affirmative action is deemed effective to the extent that firms or institutions have been coerced into narrowing the gap between the real and a theoretically desirable level of employment or enrollment for designated groups. This line of reasoning is subject to what I call the fallacy of inferred discrimination: the assumption that the extent to which a group is or has been subject to discrimination can be measured by the disparity between its percentage in the population and its percentage in the professions or other prestigious occupations. If a group has relatively few members in elite positions in American society, this is taken as evidence that it was excluded because of systematic past and/or present discrimination. If a group has large numbers in America's prestigious positions, it is presumed not to have suffered seriously debilitating discrimination.

The fallacy derives from a patently false reading of American ethnic history. There is no simple relationship between a group's upward social mobility and the amount of discrimination it suffered in the past. Discrimination can cause low rates of upward mobility, but it does not automatically lead to poor achievement; nor does a lack of discrimination necessarily mean a group will do well. For instance, Jewish Americans suffered pervasive discrimination, but have generally done well, particularly in the professions. The same is true of Japanese Americans and Chinese Americans, whose incomes are better than whites: the median income of Asian Americans in 1980 was $22,713, compared to $19,917 for whites. Conversely, Christopher Jencks, in the July/August 1985 issue of *American Behavioral Scientist,* points out that Irish Protestants, who blended easily into the population of Anglo-Saxons, now have markedly lower incomes than Irish Catholics, who suffered comparatively more discrimination. Nicholas Capaldi trenchantly states, in his *Affirmative Action and the Crisis of Doctrinaire Liberalism,* "It has never been shown that discrimination is the sole cause of statistical disparity; it has never been shown that statistical disparity is an acceptable criterion for defining the problem [of discrimination.]"

The influence of the fallacy of inferred discrimination is particularly strong among jurists, with some bizarre intellectual consequences. For instance, Robert Fullinwider, in his book *The Reverse Discrimination Controversy: A Moral and Legal Analysis,* provides an erudite discussion of the legal implications of affirmative action and preferential treatment. Nevertheless, in a chapter describing his justification for the second policy, he leaves the realm of juridical discussion and enters a world of sociological fantasy. His argument in favor of reverse discrimination is this:

> What is the role of hiring goals and timetables in this process of affirmative action? They serve as automatic monitors. An employer is supposed to evaluate his recruitment and selection procedures and to appraise the labor pool from which he recruits. His aim is to be nondiscriminatory. What would his selection profile look like assuming nondiscrimination? It is this question that should underlie the establishment of hiring goals. The employer should set his goals at that figure one would expect to be realized under nondiscrimination.

Any honest sociologist could have told Fullinwider that it is impossible to tell what the occupational distributions of ethnic groups in American society would have been if there had been no discrimination. The cultural and educational backgrounds of immigrant groups, and the differing stages of American social development at which the different groups arrived, are so widely dissimilar that trying to imagine what American society might have looked like if it had not been for discrimination is a sterile intellectual exercise. It is equally impossible to tell what levels of ethnic representation would be like in the future if there were no discrimination. Even a superficial understanding of the past and present processes of racial and ethnic relations in the United States makes it clear that it is impossible to assert that if there had been—or were in the future to be—no discrimination, the distribution of these groups in the professions and other occupations would have been what their percentages are in the larger population.

The fallacy of inferred discrimination holds that if there is a disparity between a group's overall percentage in the population and its percentage in a profession, then this is the result of discrimination. It leads to the false inference that if there were no discrimination, then the group would be evenly represented throughout America's occupational hierarchy. The latter is a theoretical assertion we might expect from a legal mind, but a position entirely false to a social scientist. The fallacy has thus far been left unchallenged because this intellectual arena has been abandoned by social scientists and take over by legal philosophers.

PREFERENTIAL TREATMENT AND PUBLIC OPINION

One often repeated warning about preferential treatment is that it is likely to damage the morale of those persons who suffer its consequences. At the same time, it is suggested that the beneficiaries of reverse discrimination may come to question their self-worth, to wonder if they really made it on their qualifications, or whether sex, color, or ethnicity explains their success. Both are valid questions. Surely enough time has elapsed since preferential treatment programs have been implemented to allow us to answer these questions. It is nothing short of appalling, then, to realize that there has been no large-scale study of the perceptions of reverse discrimination by white and/or male Americans or of its psychological consequences for its alleged beneficiaries.

One study claims to study white attitudes, but upon closer inspection it does not bear out its promise. Kluegel and Smith, in the March 1983 issue of *Social Forces,* claim to measure "racial affect" among whites, and find that it is an important contributing factor in determining whether whites will be opposed to affirmative action programs. But the measurement they use is a composite of two scales, one of which assesses a respondent's opinion about whether blacks are trying to change things "too fast" and another that asks the respondent's opinions about specific civil rights groups. This is a highly questionable measurement of racial attitudes, since it is possible for a respondent to disapprove of militancy and militant groups but be kindly disposed toward blacks. If Kluegel and Smith's research had used a better measurement of white attitudes toward blacks, this article would have been a good step in the direction I am suggesting.

Kluegel and Smith also dismiss as "naive" whites who question whether discrimination plays an important role in deterring black upward mobility. As I have argued recently in *The New Republic* and *The Wall Street Journal,* the tremendous success of black West Indians, in the face of the same degree of racial discrimination as that to which black Americans are subject, raises doubts about racial discrimination as an explanatory variable. A majority of black Americans, according to a recent study discussed by Linda Lichter in the August/September 1985 issue of *Public Opinion,* say that they have never suffered job-related racial discrimination. Confounded by the fallacy of inferred discrimination, Kluegel and Smith have ignored the possibility that discrimination may not explain poor upward mobility for American blacks. It is not only unfair to dismiss these assertions as "naive," it is arrogant.

There has been no attempt to assess whether or to what extent women and blacks and favored ethnic groups have suffered from self-doubt as a result of their privileges. This is all the more astonishing in light of the fact that public opinion data indirectly show some strong negative emotions on the issue.

Surveys of opinion, without exception, show that the American people overwhelmingly accept affirmative action in its nondiscriminatory, original sense. A CBS/*New York Times* survey in 1977 asked for responses to the statement, "The government should see to it that people who have been discriminated against in the past get a better break in the future." Agreement was expressed by 68 percent of whites and 85 percent of blacks. In 1979, Gallup asked, "Would you favor or oppose the federal government offering special educational or vocational courses, free of charge, to enable members of minority groups to do better in tests?" Fully 60 percent of national opinion was in favor of such a proposal.

Americans, however, are opposed to reverse discrimination. For example, a 1984 Gallup poll asked the question, "Some people say that to make up for past discrimination, women and members of minority groups should be given preferential treatment in getting jobs and places in college. Others say that ability, as determined by test scores, should be the main consideration. Which point of view comes closer to how you feel on this subject?" Only 10 percent of the American population endorses preferential treatment, while 84 percent asserted that ability should be the main consideration. Opinion regarding preferential treatment is more positive when directly juxtaposed with direct and specific cases of discrimination. A CBS/*New York Times* poll in May-June 1985 asked, "Do you believe that where there has been job discrimination against _____ in the past, preference in hiring or promotion should be given to _____ today?" This question was asked with regard to women and blacks. For women, the responses were 48 percent for and 40 percent against; for blacks, the responses were 42 percent for and 46 percent against.

These surveys only assess people's declarations of principle. I have been able to unearth only two questions, in different surveys, that directly indicate white opinion on the effects of reverse racism. According to Cardell Jacobson, in the December 1983 issue of *Journal of Conflict Resolution,* in 1976 and 1978, a sample of whites were asked, "Do you think blacks are given special consideration and hired before whites for jobs frequently, occasionally, hardly ever or never at all?" In these two years the percentages that responded "frequently" were 41.0 and 35.7 respectively. The author does not indicate what percentage responded "occasionally," but the perception of black privilege by whites is unmistakable, even if not a majority opinion. In 1984, Gordon Black Associates found that out of a sample of white registered voters who were asked the question, "Have you, yourself, ever lost a job opportunity or educational opportunity at least partially as a result of policies and programs aimed at promoting equal opportunity for minorities?" one out of ten replied affirmatively. Not only does a substantial minority of white Americans feel that blacks are privileged by reverse discrimination, but one out of ten feel that they have personally suffered as a result. Such suggestive figures cry out for a deep and systematic study of white attitudes, since they suggest a dangerous level of resentment.

Seldom mentioned in the public debate is the fact that a majority of black Americans is opposed to preferential treatment for blacks. A 1981 CBS/*New York Times* poll asked the question "Because of past discrimination, blacks who need it should/should not get some help from the government that white people in similar economic circumstances don't get." Fifty-four percent of blacks said that they "should not." In the 1984 Gallup poll I cited, only 28 percent of blacks said that preferential treatment was desirable, while 63 percent said that ability should be employers' main consideration. Lichter's study confirmed this, with only 23 percent of black Americans expressing support for preferential treatment for blacks.

Blacks are not the only group opposed to preferential treatment for themselves. The available figures, while out of date, suggest that most American women are opposed to preferential treatment for women. In 1976, the *Washington Post* asked "Which statement do you agree with more: (1) Quotas in job hirings should be used to increase the number of women in good jobs or (2) Job hirings should be based strictly on merit." Of women respondents, 79 percent opted for exclusive merit hiring.

Public opinion polls show that preferential treatment and reverse discrimination are rejected by most Americans, no matter what their race or sex. Many feel directly harmed by these policies. This abundant indirect evidence suggests that the morale of many white, male Americans may be seriously damaged by reverse discrimination. It is also probable that blacks and women have had their doubts as to self-worth increased as a result of quotas in their favor.

Bloch and Walker, in *Discrimination, Affirmative Action and Equal Opportunity*, observe:

> Mounting evidence suggests that a high proportion of affirmative action recipients are more accurately described as "underqualified," or at best marginal. For example, Sherman says, "[University] Deans estimated that 80 percent of their black law students [admitted under affirmative action] would not have been admitted in open competition with whites," and the "black enrollments would drop sharply, perhaps by 50 or 60 percent, in the absence of preference." Adelson, in commenting on the Bakke decision, notes "The minority students admitted to the Davis medical school were at the very bottom of the grade distribution."

If true, these facts cannot but impinge on the self-perception of protected groups. The suggestions regarding reverse discrimination's effect on white male, female, and black morale are hypotheses that must be empirically tested, and to which social science has to date turned a blind eye.

COSTS OF AFFIRMATIVE ACTION

The dearth of information about affirmative action and reverse discrimination's subjective effects is accompanied by a similar lacuna in our knowledge of its costs, both in terms of the expenses related to compliance with government monitoring efforts and in damage to efficiency. While sociologists and psychologists can be blamed for voluntary ignorance about the social and emotional effects of reverse racism and sexism, economists must shoulder the blame for our lack of understanding of the nature and dimensions of the relation between affirmative action and the operation of our economy. As with public opinion, there are enough partial and indirect data to indicate that there is a problem of major proportions crying out to be studied.

According to J.S. Leonard, in the winter 1985 issue of the *Journal of Human Resources,* the Office of Federal Contract Compliance, the main affirmative action watchdog, spends $51 million a year in administrative costs alone. Estimates of the additional direct costs of affirmative action programs are spotty:

> Covering just the direct costs of compliance reviews, a 1981 survey of 42 companies with an average workforce of 50,000 found that 80 percent of the reviewed were requested to submit data in addition to the AAP [Affirmative Action Plan], at an average cost of $3000. A similar survey by Senator Hatch's Labor Committee of 245 contractors with an average workforce of 2584 in 1981 reported that 60 percent were asked to submit additional data beyond the AAP, at an average of $24,000.

Leonard cites other figures in a spring 1984 issue of the *Journal of Human Resources.* According to Business Roundtable, a sample of 40 companies spent $217 million in 1977. "This is .1 percent of sales and 1.3 percent of profits for a group of companies accounting for 5 percent of U.S. nonagricultural employees and 8 percent of U.S. sales." As for overall costs, "The Congressional Research Service guessed that $1.6 billion would pay for the cost of affirmative action for all nonconstruction contractors in 1976." Taking inflation into account, it is likely that the present cost of compliance with affirmative action reviews now stands at more than three billion dollars a year for nonconstruction firms alone.

What of the impact of affirmative action on the construction industry? In California, at least, the cost has been high. A study done for the California Construction Industry tried to measure the increase in costs resulting from minority- or female-owned businesses being favored by the Office of Federal Contract Compliance. One finding was that preferential treatment increased costs to taxpayers for public works programs by $41.9 million; if California represents 10 percent of the construction work for the nation, reverse discrimination costs $420 million annually for public works programs. Other findings are that it costs 14.8 percent more to subcontract work to black- and female-owned businesses than it does for a contractor to do his own work. Delays by subcontractors averaged more than a month for the 78 percent of contractors who reported delays with minority contractors. Most ironic, while 78 percent of prime contractors use union subcontractors under normal circumstances, only 32 percent of minority firms are union firms. In the name of social progress, this federal affirmative action program is directly hostile to organized labor.

These extraordinary costs might be bearable if the impact on our country's efficiency were minimal or nonexistent. Again, the data are sparse, but it seems that the economic effects of affirmative action invite serious and rigorously honest scrutiny. Leonard offers the best effort in this direction in his 1984 article. The study is hampered because of the limited period of time considered, between 1966 and 1977, before much of affirmative action's impact may have been felt. More serious is that Leonard comes to some questionable conclusions in the light of his own data.

He asserts that "There is no significant evidence here to support the contention that this increase in employment equity [that is, the increased percentage of black and female white employees] has had marked efficiency costs." Yet he also states,

> the ratio of black to white male productivity increased from .49 to .62. Over the same period the ratio of female to white male productivity increased from .92 to 1.10. ... The point estimates for 1977 ... indicate that minority males are roughly 60 percent as productive as white males at the margin and that females are 10 percent more productive than white males. Multiplying these relative marginal productivities by the change in minority and female employment share in manufacturing between 1966 and 1977, I find that the ratio of the marginal product of the average worker to the marginal product of a white male worker fell by only .007 due to the changing composition of the work force.

There are several problems with the conclusion, in light of the analysis. First, if white employees (male or female) had been hired instead of black employees during that period, overall productivity would have increased, rather than fallen. It is thus less than honest to say that affirmative action has had no negative effect on productivity. Second, it is ingenuous to lump together white female with black male employees in calculating the overall drop in productivity, since we already know that females tended to be more productive than the white males, and they canceled out much of the negative effect of increased black employment. Also, there is nothing in Leonard's analysis to prove that preferential hiring policies were necessary to bring about the increase in black and female employment. In sum, the outdated nature of the statistics and the fact that the conclusions lack some cogency make it clear that an up-to-date and systematic study is needed.

Leonard's evidence indicates that deliberate increases in female employment have a positive impact in industry. Regarding academia, the situation is not as clear. Koch and Chizmar, in *The Economics of Affirmative Action,* straightforwardly assert that affirmative action for women does not increase quality of performance. "If productivity is defined as publication in the most prestigious scholarly journal outlets, then there is strong evidence that female academics are not as productive as men. ... In every discipline, the percentage of scholarly articles emanating from females is substantially lower than the percentage of females in that discipline." Later on, the authors summarize, "Our empirical evidence leads to the conclusion that affirmative action programs must be considered to be the instruments of equity rather than the instruments of economic efficiency."

It may be that affirmative action and preferential treatment were never intended to increase economic efficiency. It may be that it was always recognized that their effects would be socially disruptive, as we well know them to be from opinion polls. Partisans of these programs at first emphasized that these were temporary solutions that would soon disappear. The Carnegie Council on Policy Studies in Higher Education, for instance, said in a 1982 report, "We hope that the current period of transition will not last longer than until the end of the current century—less than a generation." Like Marxists' bland assurances that the state will wither away after the revolution, such a statement seems absurdly complacent. Not only are racial and sexual quotas well on the way to becoming a permanent part of the political landscape (not unlike preferences for veterans, which were also supposed to be temporary); the examples of affirmative action elsewhere show that the policy has a tendency to become both deeply entrenched and divisive.

LESSONS FROM OTHER COUNTRIES

Anyone who believes that reverse discrimination is a solution to past discrimination, or who believes that these policies are temporary remedies, would do well to pay attention to the lessons of India. One of the most distinctive features of precolonial Indian society was the caste system. This was a rigid system of social stratification based on color and function. The caste system has been aptly called a refined form of apartheid, because castes not only fulfilled specialized roles in society, but were segregated and enjoined not to intermarry or even touch one another. Max Weber's masterly work on the religion of India describes just how intricately interwoven caste is with the Hindu view of the world. It is little wonder that the British struggled as best they could against this system, with only modest success.

One of the important measures the British instituted before granting Indian independence was a system of "positive discrimination," in which quotas for government jobs and places in colleges were established for members of lower castes. This system of preferential treatment for previously excluded groups was continued after independence. It remains an important and deeply disruptive part of the Indian political and social landscape to this day. Almost four decades of reverse discrimination in India have gone by. Not only has the kind of stratification it was supposed to erase not disappeared, but the policy itself remains the source of deep and violent conflicts.

As soon as the system of preferential treatment was instituted, some Indians tried to pass themselves off as members of the lower castes. (This is what has happened in the United States: in December of 1985, a news item in the *New York Times* told of how the Police Department was instituting checks on officers' racial backgrounds because some nonminority officers had claimed minority status.) At the same time, caste has hardened into a basis for political grouping analogous to ethnic groups in the United States. As a September 1986 article in *The Economist* indicated, "Positive discrimination pits the castes against each other: politicians appeal to lower castes by promising them bigger quotas of jobs and college places, and to higher castes by offering to cut quotas." The parallel with the American political scene is clear.

The dynamics of the system are also similar to those in the United States. For so-called Scheduled Castes, there are precise numerical quotas for recruitment into the civil service: 15 percent of public enterprise jobs are reserved for Scheduled Castes. As in the United States, standards are lowered in order to fill the quotas. A brochure published by the government of India regarding preferential hiring states, "In rules and regulations governing direct recruitment either by examination or otherwise, provision for relaxation of standards in favor of Scheduled Castes/Scheduled Tribes should be specifically made." The example of the New York City Police Department's promotion of 200 black officers to sergeant, in spite of their having failed the examination, springs to mind, as does the lowering of physical standards for the New York City Fire Department in order to increase female employment.

The parallels go on. In many ways not only have white women benefited more from affirmative action than blacks, but black West Indians, for whom the policy was not designed, are increasingly taking advantage of color conscious recruitment programs. Ironically, the people who could be said to need affirmative action the most are benefiting from it the least, and vice versa. Consider, in this regard, the picturesque language of these comments by P. Verna in *Caste Reservation in India* on the effects of positive discrimination: "The reality is that the benefits are snatched away by the most vocal among these Backward Castes and thus keeping the weakest among the weak perpetually weak and enabling the fortunate upper layer among them to utilize the bigger toast [*sic*]."

As far back as the early 1930s, John Dollard, in *Caste and Class in a Southern Town,* pointed out how the position of blacks in the southern United States was in many ways analogous to that of a subordinate caste. This situation continued at least until the Supreme Court decision of 1954. In America, affirmative action programs are attempting to undo the history of American racial caste by means of the same policy that has been in existence in India for over forty years. Positive discrimination in India has not only not erased the caste system but has added more complications and new sources of conflict and violence to that sorry land. Anthropologists and historians familiar with Indian society are duty bound to tell the American reader in detail about the consequences of preferential treatment in that country.

India is not the only other country that has implemented affirmative action and preferential treatment. In Canada, since 1962, quotas in civil service hiring have aimed at numerical parity for French speakers, roughly 27 percent. This principle was reaffirmed in the Human Rights Act of 1978, which has established preferential hiring for Francophones, females, and members of native populations. In Canada, as in other instances in which reverse discrimination has been implemented, there is a stark contrast between the democratic principle of equality and the undemocratic one of preference. In the words of one Canadian commentator, "Now, unless one accepts an Alice-in-Wonderland worldview, where something is whatever those in power define it to be, then a glaring contradiction is apparent within the Human Rights Act between its commitment to non-discrimination (Section 2) and to affirmative action ideas (Section 15)." I am quoting from L. Roberts, "Understanding Affirmative Action," in the Bloch and Walker volume I have cited. This is exactly the same contradiction that shows up in the Indian constitution, which, according to P. C. Aggarwal in *Equality through Privilege: A Study of Special Privileges of Scheduled Castes in Haryana,* "stresses the equality of all persons before the law and prohibits discrimination in all social matters ... [but] makes clear provisions for special privilege for the Scheduled Castes and Tribes until such time as their glaring deficiencies are removed." The contrast between democratic principles and reverse discrimination is as clear in Canada and India as it is in the contrast between the egalitarian language of the 1964 Civil Rights Act and the discriminatory interpretations of the act by the United States Supreme Court.

There may be other cases in addition to India and Canada. I am convinced that discussion of these parallels should not be left in the hands of jurists. The sociology of law is a social science in its own right, and adding a comparative, cross-cultural dimension would aid in our understanding of affirmative action in other societies as well as the possible future of the policy's effects in our own.

QUESTIONING THE FAITH

There are many reasons for social scientists' neglect of affirmative action. Paramount is that, in general, they do not want to know what the effects have been. Politically, many social scientists are left of center, and are disinclined to put to empirical scrutiny a policy that has become a sacred cow of American liberalism. It is almost as if asking the questions I have asked are tantamount to heresy.

Some have argued that to inquire into the efficacy of affirmative action and reverse discrimination is itself a sign of racism: several serious-sounding theories have been advanced to suggest that anyone who questions recent "gains" by blacks as a result of affirmative action or preferential treatment is a "modern racist." The only comment I can make on this school of thought is to quote Clarence Thomas of the Equal Employment Opportunity Commission: "the most devastating form of racism is the feeling that blacks are inferior, so let's help them. What we had in Georgia under Jim Crow is not as bad as this. This racism based on sympathy says that because of your race, we will give you excuses for not preparing yourself and not being as good as can be." In fact, affirmative action is endorsed by racists, not opposed by them. Consider the words of Imperial Wizard Bill Wilkinson of the Ku Klux Klan, when he was asked why his group has recently increased its membership rolls: "Affirmative Action programs, and the Weber decision of the Supreme Court, [have] done more to make a race war possible than anything the Klan has done."

Let us have done with ad hominem accusations, and get down to the business of social science. Affirmative action and its stepchild, reverse discrimination, have been on the American scene long enough to warrant intense empirical study as to their effects. All of us—sociologists, psychologists, economists, anthropologists, historians—must study this issue, and let the chips fall where they may. Anything less is a betrayal of the ideals of our profession.

PART EIGHT

Los Angeles, 1992:
Lessons for the Future?

We have chosen to end this book with a discussion of the social explosion that took place in south-central Los Angeles from April 29 through May 2, 1992. The outcome was devastating. As many as 52 people died, 8,000 injuries were reported, more than 12,000 people were arrested and jailed, hundreds were deported, and almost all residents' lives were disrupted. Of the more than 1,000 buildings burned, over half were totally destroyed, and the financial costs from arson, damage, and theft were estimated at $750 to $800 million. This was neither the first nor will it be the last of such upheavals. Our question is, What have we learned from it?

Civil disorders need to be approached as sociologically complex events. The individual motives for involvement are mixed. The Los Angeles disorder was neither a commodity riot nor a political insurrection. It was both, and much more. There were petty thieves and organized thieves; there were people who stole food and people who stole luxuries. There were young adults and older ones who engaged in recreational violence, and others who engaged in racial violence. It is important to understand not only that the motives of participants and bystanders were mixed but also that people do not behave according to a single motive. Then, too, motives change over time and in retrospect.

The 1992 crisis differed from that in 1965 in several important respects. The earlier incident was confined primarily to the Watts area and almost all of the participants were black, whereas the 1992 events spread beyond a single neighborhood and entailed a series of interethnic melees involving blacks, whites, Latinos, Koreans, and other Asian Pacific groups. During the first four days of the latter disorder, 700 more Hispanics than blacks were arrested. Twenty-six blacks were killed, as compared to 18 Hispanics. These figures signify the future of ethnoviolence in America.

Along with the mass media and the general public, social scientists ask the following questions: Why do these large-scale disorders occur? What can be done to prevent them?

The event that triggered the 1992 disorder was the acquittal of five white policemen who were videotaped beating black motorist Rodney King. The widespread perception in both the black and Hispanic communities, and even in the white community, was that the verdict represented a gross miscarriage of justice. Underlying this catalytic event, however, was a multiplicity of causes.

Liberal analysts tend to focus on the lack of adequate economic and social opportunities associated with poverty, racial discrimination, and inferior schools. They also view police misconduct and biases in the criminal justice system as contributing factors. All of these problems can be solved, according to liberals, with appropriate legislation and increased government spending on jobs, job training, and education. Although liberals generally look to government for leadership, they perceive the business sector as playing an important role as well.

Following the explosion in Watts in 1965, the McCone and Kerner Commissions (investigative bodies appointed, respectively, by the governor of California and the president of the United States) issued reports that pointed to many of the conditions underlying that disorder. The listing of conditions, which could be the chapter headings for a social-problems textbook, included poverty, housing segregation, inadequate housing, employment discrimination, poor educational facilities, inadequate financial and consumer services in the community, and police abuse. Yet in the years that followed, little has been accomplished, or even attempted; the same problems remain in Watts, in south-central Los Angeles, and in the city as a whole. If anything, the city's economic situation has worsened. Consider just one example: Between June 1990 and February 1992, 300,000 jobs were lost in the Los Angeles area.

The California Assembly Special Committee on the Los Angeles Crisis concluded, in its report of September 1992, "that the causes of the 1992 unrest were the same as the causes of the unrest of the 1960's, aggravated by a highly visible increasing concentration of wealth at the top of the income scale and a decreasing Federal and State commitment to urban programs serving those at the bottom of the income scale."

Conservative analysts, on the other hand, tend to minimize the importance of inequality of opportunity, arguing either that adequate opportunities currently exist or that the situation is rapidly improving. They point to the *culture* of the black underclass as the main cause of the rioting. Weak family structures, they say, either condone violent, criminal behavior or are unable to combat it. And welfare dependency, they continue, eliminates the desire to get ahead through education and hard, honest work. Conservatives also argue that the criminal justice system is soft on crime and that the Los Angeles police failed to act quickly enough because they did not want to be accused of racist behavior.

The solution, say conservatives, is to transform the underclass culture in such a way that young people will take advantage of the opportunities available to them. The schools, of course, are a major priority. And economically depressed inner-city areas can be rejuvenated as enterprise zones, to which private businesses could be encouraged, by means of tax breaks and other incentives, to locate. In addition, conservatives call on the courts to deliver stiffer sentences to criminals and on various levels of government to put more police on the streets and to build more prisons.

Although liberals and conservatives propose different policies for preventing future urban disorders, they both agree that the existing political and economic system can be *reformed*. In short, they agree that both capitalism and the bureaucratic, two-party political system can be made to work more efficiently to improve the lives of poor inner-city minority people.

Radicals, on the other hand, believe that urban disorders are caused by the structure of the capitalist system itself. The concentration of wealth and power in the hands of the top 1 percent of the U.S. population, they argue, is the main cause underlying the economic deprivation that leads to such disorders. Major businesses seek to increase their profits by lowering labor costs, resulting in a loss of inner-city jobs, an expansion of low-paying jobs, and an increase in poverty overall.

Shrinking economic opportunities, say radicals, cause working-class sectors to see one another as the enemy. White and Hispanic workers compete for jobs; black workers battle with Asian small-business owners. But the wealth and power of white elites are not threatened and often go unnoticed. At the same time, radicals continue, the police and criminal justice systems are structured so as to protect the property interests of the business class. And excessive police force, especially in times of political turmoil, is one way to keep minority populations in check.

Neither legislation nor government spending can prevent disorders, radicals argue, because neither attempts to challenge the power of the political and business elites whose concentrated wealth and power are the basic cause of economic inequality in the first place. The solution, they say, is to replace American capitalism with an economic system that emphasizes cooperative ownership and control of capital rather than private ownership. The political system, in turn, must be made more democratic, more responsive to all.

Here are some of the questions we need to ask about the proposals for rebuilding Los Angeles.

- Will there be an end to the prejudice and institutional forms of discrimination that led to the segregation of the city's minority population?
- Will the ethnoviolence that has intimidated this population be dissipated?
- Will potential new jobs be congruent with the needs of the community and the educational and skill levels of the residents?
- Will new businesses be worker owned and managed, or will ownership come from the outside and management hew to the standard bureaucratic, authoritarian line?
- Will real estate belong to the community in the form of land trusts and other cooperative modes, or will it continue to be the basis for speculation and profit?
- Will most of the money generated by residents remain in the community, or will it continue to be drained away by nonresident landowners, banks, and other profiteers?
- Will the police be subject to community control and review, or will they persist in their role as an occupying army?
- Will the residents be able to effect significant political control over the community?

The two essays that follow present dramatically different views of both the causes of and the solutions to the Los Angeles disorder of 1992. The editors of *The*

New Republic offer a centrist argument ("Race Against Time") that draws from liberal as well as conservative analyses. The main cause of the disorder, they say, is the culture of the inner-city black underclass—a conservative conclusion. And the only way to transform this cultural pathology, they add, is through a massive federally financed jobs program—a classically liberal proposal.

Edna Bonacich ("Thoughts on Urban Unrest"), on the other hand, offers a radical interpretation of the events in Los Angeles. She begins by saying that the disorder "can be seen as a product of the working of capitalism, and its concomitant, racism." She ends by saying that "the wealth of this nation cannot be permitted to remain in the hands of a small, largely white elite" and that future uprisings "need to be organized with a view toward winning the social struggles that are necessary to produce equality in this nation."

Readers have a lot to consider.

36

Race Against Time

EDITORS OF *THE NEW REPUBLIC*

Denial will soon set in. But what we have just witnessed in Los Angeles is a glimpse of a racial and urban crisis in this country that is steadily growing in intensity. Neither Republican neglect nor traditional Democratic liberalism comes close to solving it. It's time to start over.

We should start with a rejection of the crasser simplifications that have been aired over the past few weeks. The Rodney King verdict and the riots in South-Central Los Angeles do not necessarily reflect an utterly polarized country, or a society defined solely by differences of race. In many areas—most particularly in the workplace—American life is far more racially integrated than it was two generations ago. Our public culture is saturated with various racial and ethnic influences in which minority tastes are, if anything, dominant. Our major cities, once divided clearly into black and white, are increasingly a jumble of new ethnic groups in which the black-white divide is a fragment of a more complex immigrant drama. Black Americans constitute a smaller and smaller part of the racial mix in our major cities; and South-Central Los Angeles ... is a case in point: African Americans now make up some 55 percent of the population, compared with 65 percent a decade ago; whites have increased their presence slightly; those identified in the Census as Hispanic have jumped threefold. This social transformation has created ineluctable tensions, misunderstandings, and breakdowns; but these breakdowns have been a function of greater, not lesser, access of one kind of American to another. We are witnessing as much the wages of social nearness as the wages of social distance. And alienation from those nearby is especially combustible.

Moreover, these complexities operate within races as well as among them. The emergence of a large and powerful black middle class, in some ways more horrified than its white counterpart by the pathologies of the inner city, has transformed the sociology of race. Thirty years ago James Brown performed on television to help defuse a race riot; in 1992 Hammer spent the weekend after the L.A. conflagration at the Kentucky Derby. For many blacks, the riots took place in another world. Similarly, what job you have and where you live are far more accurate predictors of racial attitudes among whites than they were thirty years ago.

We do scant justice to the efforts and the experiences of millions of white Americans who have come a long way since the 1960s if we equate them all with the jury of Simi Valley.

The lessons of the Rodney King verdict, furthermore, are not reducible to the race of the jurors: fair and decent verdicts are to be expected even from "racially unbalanced" juries. The verdict was owed, rather, to a cultural and economic divide between the most secluded of suburbs and the inner city. Moving the trial out of its original neighborhood turned the central meaning of the American jury on its head. The original point of the constitutional guarantees of trial by jury in this country was not to protect a defendant's right to be judged by his peers (as in England), but to protect the right of local communities to be represented on popular bodies that could check overreaching by governmental officials. The Sixth Amendment requires a jury "of the district wherein the crime shall have been committed," because many Anti-Federalists wanted an explicit guarantee that juries would be organized around local rather than statewide communities, which they thought would be more alert to abuses by central authorities. The result in the King case confirms this original republican insight: if the community's voice is not represented in the jury box, it will be heard in the streets. We hope the federal civil rights case against the police officers in the Rodney King beating is pursued vigorously, and in the district where the incident occurred, an area with a large black and Latino population.

Many, of course, will seize on the King verdict as a sign that American society must become more race-conscious, not less: that we should have more racially contrived juries and judges, more racially determined electoral boundaries, more "multicultural" political and cultural and educational arrangements. Republicans have a history of cooperating on this front, happy to exploit whiter and whiter ghettos as their permanent political power base, and cynically accepting the permanence of racial prejudice and suspicion. Right now the Supreme Court is deciding a case that will determine whether criminal defendants can strike prospective jurors simply because of their race. In a related case, Justices Rehnquist and Scalia recently argued in a dissent that a defendant has a right to be judged by a jury of his own race but has no right to object to the exclusion of jurors of another race. (In other words, the government can't exclude black jurors from the trial of a black defendant, but it can automatically exclude white jurors.) Scalia and Rehnquist would recognize the "undeniably reality" that all racial groups tend to be sympathetic to members of their own race, and hostile to members of others. The separatist assumption of their logic—that justice is inseparable from race—is, of course, shared by many on the political left. Caught in the pincers of this strange political alliance, the cause of colorblind justice will have a hard time surviving.

We do not mean to argue, of course, that the American criminal justice system is not prone to racial bias, or that in general American society does not display lingering and intense signs of racism. We simply believe that the positive developments of the last thirty years suggest that, with time, these elements are superable; that the complex racial dynamics of our society are not easily summed up by blanket assertions of racism; that immigration is continuing to transform the racial—and social—balance of this country, often for the better; that the answer to the problem of racism, in any case, is not to compound it with more racist assumptions.

Moreover, the notion that a civil rights agenda is always the solution to a race-based problem is profoundly faulty. It wasn't even true in the 1960s, when race riots followed civil rights legislation rather than preceded it. Today the disjunction is even more acute. At the root of much of the disturbance in Los Angeles is not an inherently corrupt criminal justice system, but a phenomenon that underpins much of the discussion of race in this country: the black underclass. We say black underclass, because for all the elaborate statistical arguments that can be made, it is still a predominantly black phenomenon. In 1980 blacks constituted some 58 percent of those living in neighborhoods with extreme social problems, and over 60 percent of those on welfare for a long time. The levels of family breakdown are, moreover, far higher among blacks than whites. Even Andrew Hacker concedes that 56.2 percent of black families are headed by single women, compared with 17.3 percent of white families.

The black underclass perpetuates racial division in this country in several ways. It has helped weaken the American city, speeding up white flight to the suburbs and decreasing the level of black-white geographic contact. Where black-white mixing does occur, the powerful image of the black underclass—underscored by the events of the last week—has served to stigmatize the vast majority of middle-class blacks, and to powerfully perpetuate the racism of whites.

Any analysis of race in this country has to grapple directly with this problem. It did not emerge yesterday; nor is it, as some Democrats would have it, a simple creation of the Reagan-Bush era, although, heaven knows, neither Reagan nor Bush showed much interest in alleviating it. We do not believe that even the proposals we make here will fundamentally change life in South-Central Los Angeles within the next generation. But we are equally convinced that they cannot be postponed any longer.

We should begin by recognizing that even the underclass is not monolithic. Within its ranks there are both the truly disadvantaged and the truly deviant. We have seen plenty of both groups in the last week. The former are quite often—and most typically—the victims of the latter, and no attempt to break underclass culture can ignore the presence of this black-on-black violence. When black civil rights leaders said the lesson of the Rodney King case was that no black man was safe on the streets from white policemen, they revealed just how out of touch they are. The real person the black inner-city inhabitant has to fear is another black inhabitant. The vast majority of inner-city crime is black-on-black, and the scope of it is terrifying. In the District of Columbia, some 42 percent of black males between 18 and 35 are enmeshed in the criminal justice system.

Since the 1960s the progressive response to these thugs has been to develop new alternatives to incarceration (or, as probation and parole are now called by academic faddists, "intermediate sanctions"). Today more than 3 million convicted criminals are serving their sentences on the streets, not behind bars. We've tried this approach every which way (intensive supervision, community service, boot camps), and it simply doesn't work. The data on all such probation and parole programs are now in, and they're damning. Whatever you call it, "community-based corrections" spells higher crime and higher social costs than you get from incarcerating street criminals for all or most of their sentences.

The answer, however, is not to lock up the truly deviant and throw away the key. With 42 percent of the young black male population in the inner city involved in crime, the prisons simply aren't large enough. Rather, the answer is more aggressive community policing. Real community policing means lots of cops on the streets working with community leaders, talking to residents, and living in the neighborhoods they patrol. The federal government should provide the funds and training necessary to increase the manpower of all major big-city police departments by at least 20 percent. All of the additional cops should be deployed in the inner cities, and all should be trained, retained, and promoted according to the precepts of community policing. The cost of such a program, according to John DiIulio of Princeton, would be about $2 billion.

Second, the federal government should promote and pay for first-rate prison-based drug treatment programs. In prison or out, the key to successful drug treatment is staying with the program. All the data show that certain types of prison-based programs work very well, especially when there's an after-care, post-release component. The federal prison system is developing a full menu of drug treatment programs for federal prisoners. The feds should mandate, fund, and provide the technical assistance necessary to implement such programs in every state prison system in the country. Just as important is making drug treatment available for those members of the underclass who have managed to stay out of prison.

A far more powerful governmental weapon in the battle to break underclass culture, however, is already in the hands of the federal government. It's the welfare system. The coup de grace last week in L.A. was the sight of lines forming to receive welfare checks the Friday after the meltdown. This, for many, was the return to normal. We don't believe, as some conservatives do, and as Marlin Fitzwater continues to assert, that welfare created the underclass crisis in these communities. Nor do we believe that family breakdown was created by welfare or that fiddling with monetary incentives could put those families back together. We merely hold, as TNR senior editor Mickey Kaus argues in his forthcoming book, *The End of Equality* (New Republic Books), that at this point welfare is the critical sustaining element in the life of the underclass. If we are to break through this culture of idleness, poverty, illegitimacy, and crime, we have to cut off its lifeline.

This does not mean a perpetuation of Republican neglect. The panaceas of "empowerment"—homeownership, tenant-management schemes, and the like—however beneficial in themselves, fail to address the gravity of the situation. Even Jack Kemp, the only member of this administration who shows the slightest empathy for the inner-city poor, admits that it is hard to pull yourself up by your bootstraps when you don't have any boots. Enterprise zones are illusionary in the best of circumstances, and the inner city is not the best of circumstances. Trickle-down economics has never trickled down this far. The culture of dependency is so great that even times of economic boom, such as the mid-1980s, have left the structures of unemployment and despair largely intact.

Our alternative proposal—and Kaus's—is a radical one: to return to Franklin Delano Roosevelt's commitment to "preserve not only the bodies of the unemployed from destitution but also their self-respect, their self-reliance and courage and determination." We propose replacing all financial payments to the able-bodied poor (including Aid to Families with Dependent Children, "general relief," Food Stamps, and housing subsidies) with a simple offer of a government-provided job. This radical shift from the welfare model is the only proposal with a hope of changing the way the underclass thinks and acts; shifting the paradigm of people's lives; relating actions—such as childbearing—to their immediate costs. It has the benefit of not merely encouraging responsibility, but of making it the only option available.

Such a proposal would cost a great deal of money and be an administrative headache. Kaus's best estimate of the cost is somewhere between $40 billion and $60 billion. That's a sum beyond the imagination of today's Washington establishment, but one that could be raised by a simple hike in the gas tax to levels Europeans would dream about, or a claw-back of middle-class entitlements, or a combination of both. In a sane government, given the events of the last week and the developments of the last two decades, it would be approved with dispatch.

It's no panacea, of course, and it requires greater elaboration than we have space for here. The point of the proposal, however, is extremely simple: that only the experience of work can integrate the underclass poor back into our society; that only government can accomplish this task; that, without this effort, we are not only committing more generations to misery and violence, we are poisoning the rest of our society as well.

Our conviction that something this drastic must be attempted is motivated by a belief that what is at stake in the events in Los Angeles is the entire notion of a common American citizenship that can transcend race and class and connect one civic obligation to another civic need. The liberal welfare state, for all its good intentions, has done much to undermine this notion of citizenship. The liberal obsessions with purely racial paradigms has weakened it still further. Conservative cynicism has compounded its demise. If the flames of Los Angeles do not spur us to recover it, nothing will.

Thoughts on Urban Unrest

EDNA BONACICH

The following is my unexpurgated version of what underlies the recent uprising in Los Angeles. It is based on Marxist theories of race and class, including theories of middleman minorities. I recognize that the language used here is completely unacceptable in the U.S. context, where certain assumptions about the way the system works are not permitted to be challenged. Nevertheless, given the theoretical orientation presented here, the uprising came as no surprise.

1. Urban unrest can be seen as a product of the workings of capitalism, and its concomitant, racism. Capitalism is a system that depends on the private appropriation of socially produced wealth. In other words, while everyone contributes to the society's production, only a small class of people are able to expropriate the surplus that is generated, namely, the owners of private property (who take surplus in the form of profit, rent, and interest), and generally credentialed managers and professionals (who take surplus in the form of bloated salaries). At the heart of capitalist society lies a *theft* that has occurred historically and continues on a daily basis.

2. Colonialism was a product of the development of capitalism in Europe, and it added another layer of theft to the general theft of capitalism. This involved stealing the territory of other peoples, stealing the riches of their lands, and stealing their labor and the products of their labor. In some cases, individuals themselves were bodily stolen, in the form of slavery and indentured servitude, and moved to other territories where their stolen labor could be used. Accompanying this colonial theft was racism, i.e., the denigration of the cultures and biological characteristics of the conquered peoples.

3. Despite emancipation from slavery, and formal legal equality, the class system of capitalism remains in place, as does its accompanying racism. Thus, wealth continues to be drained from the poor to the rich, from workers to owners of capital, and from people of color to whites. The earlier thefts established the character of the owning, ruling elite, and although there can be some social mobility both upward and downward, in general its character has not changed much. Having capital (rooted in theft) gives one a tremendous advantage in increasing one's wealth, while working for low wages is a prohibitive barrier to ever crawling out

of poverty. The result is that we have an increasingly polarized population, with the rich controlling billions and billions of dollars in wealth, while others are ground down in poverty.

The rich, it should be emphasized, are not wealthy because they work harder or are more worthy. They are rich because they own property, and often that ownership was based on some form of theft somewhere down the line.

4. The capitalist-racist social order entails the maintenance of racially segregated communities and super-exploited workers. This is clearly seen in Los Angeles with immigrant Latino workers who are maintained as an extra–low wage working class in manufacturing, construction, and services. Their disadvantage is maintained through a host of institutions, including immigration law, housing policy, schooling, welfare, health care, the legal and penal system, etc. Racially skewed unemployment also serves to maintain a relationship between poverty and race.

The globalization of capitalism is exacerbating these trends, by leading to increased international competition, and the decline in labor standards and unionization in the United States. However, although globalization is making things worse, it is only a manifestation of more fundamental ways in which the system works. In other words, the profit system causes gross inequalities, whether profit-making is local or global. The globalization of capital adds to the problem by increasing competition, and pitting workers in different nations against one another.

The globalization of capitalism also stimulates immigration, helping to account for the increasing cultural and racial diversity of Los Angeles. However, the mobility of labor is much more legally restricted than the mobility of capital, creating a legally disabled immigrant workforce who are subject to "super-exploitation."

The police play a special role in relationship to the racially oppressed communities. They serve as a controlling force, protecting the property of the more affluent, generally white, communities from the potential anger and violence of the oppressed. The police serve as a kind of army of occupation, representing the dominant society as opposed to the residents of inner-city neighborhoods.

5. Korean merchants play a particular role in the system of control and exploitation. They perform the function of a "middleman minority," a phenomenon that has been observed in other colonial situations. Rather than having the colonizer or the colonized play the role of shopkeepers and small-scale employers, that role is handed over to a third party, an outsider group. This kind of role was played by Jews in Eastern Europe, by Chinese in Southeast Asia, and by Indians in East Africa.

Having a middleman group play this role is of use to the oppressors. First, the antagonism of the oppressed gets redirected from the primary target, in this case the white corporate establishment, to the middleman group. In other words, the middleman group serves as a scapegoat for the injustices of the system that they did not create. Second, because the middleman group is an outsider group, they can be easily dispensed with. The oppressors have no particular loyalty to them, and so they can be served up as targets for oppressed anger.

Middleman minorities occupy a middle-level position in a system of oppression. To some extent they are beneficiaries of the system. Some of the surplus stolen from the oppressed is appropriated by them, so that the oppressed have a reason to see the middleman as their enemy. On the other hand, most of the surplus is moved on up from the middleman to the white, corporate elites. This second movement is relatively invisible to the oppressed. However, it does mean that the middlemen are also, to a certain extent, oppressed by the white elite, even as they help to oppress those below them in the hierarchy.

6. The uprising in Los Angeles reflects these dynamics:

- The triggering incident of the acquittal in the police trial over the Rodney King beating reflects the festering problem of police relations in racially oppressed neighborhoods. People who experience police victimization on a daily basis were finally in a position to prove beyond a doubt what actually happens to them, only to find that even seeing it with their own eyes could not convince a jury of the atrocities that are committed.
- So-called looting is an expression of the frustration that people experience when they help to create wealth but are not allowed access to it. Theft seems morally justified in a society based upon *legally sanctioned* theft. Of course, the theft committed by "looters" is completely trivial in the context of the large-scale theft committed by billionaire and millionaire property owners.
- The attack on Korean store owners reflects their middleman status in the system. And the fact that the Korean store owners received little protection from these attacks shows how the dominant elite is willing to sacrifice them, when necessary. This was a rude awakening for the Korean community, who learned the hard way that playing the capitalist game by its rules does not protect one from the racist logic of the system.

7. The kinds of solutions being proposed are grossly inadequate to solving the problems of racial and class oppression in Los Angeles (and the United States, in general). The idea that jobs is what is needed arises within the context of accepting the capitalist economic/political system. Providing jobs for workers does not diminish profits for property owners; indeed the theft of surplus from workers will continue, as owners are given incentives to "invest" in the inner city, and thereby extract more profits from these communities.

What is really needed is a system of redistribution of wealth, whereby communities that have been continually robbed of their wealth-making and wealth-controlling capacity have some of the stolen goods returned to them. Thereafter, investment must be turned over to social agents, and not allowed to be kept in the hands of private property owners, whose sole criteria for investment is profit. In other words, instead of creating enterprise zones and Black- and Latino-owned private business, which contribute to corporate profits and help to create a loyal, profiteering sector in the racially oppressed communities, we need to develop economic forms that serve the interests of everyone. This requires breaking with capitalist "business as usual" since the system has proved itself incapable of solving these problems, as class and race inequality have only gotten worse with time.

8. In conclusion, the wealth of this nation cannot be permitted to remain in the hands of a small, largely white elite. It is clear that they are unwilling to give it up, even in the very modest form of increased taxation to cover such basic social expenditures as education and health care. If we cannot even get them to move this far, how can we expect the kind of redistribution that is really needed to solve the massive problems of racial oppression and inequality?

The only solution, it seems to me, is more uprisings. Except that in the future they need to better organized, with a clearer strategy, and based on well-developed coalitions. They need to be organized with a view toward winning the social struggles that are necessary to produce equality in this nation.

Meanwhile, we can participate in the process of social change by helping to dispel some of the myths that serve to rationalize the current system. The tremendous suffering that occurs at the bottom cannot be denied. It will not disappear through the actions of the "free market" and private investment. We must address directly the social consequences of our system or race and class polarization will only get worse.

About the Book and Editors

This comprehensive book introduces readers to the key debates and principal writings on racial and ethnic conflict, representing conservative, liberal, and radical positions. It is the first anthology to integrate social-psychological literature on prejudice with sociological and historical investigations. Presented in debate format, each section offers a provocative discussion of contemporary problems and issues, allowing students to take part in the controversies from an informed perspective. The editors' introductions provide current data and describe cutting-edge arguments that are reshaping the study of race and ethnicity today.

Fred L. Pincus is associate professor of sociology at the University of Maryland Baltimore County. **Howard J. Ehrlich,** a sociologist and social psychologist, directs the Center for the Applied Study of Ethnoviolence.